Elementary Social Studies

Elementary Social Studies
A Skills Emphasis

RICHARD E. SERVEY
San Diego State University

Allyn and Bacon, Inc.

Boston, London, Sydney, Toronto

Series Editor: Margaret Quinlin

Library of Congress Cataloging in Publication Data

Servey, Richard E
  Elementary Social Studies, a skills emphasis.

  Bibliography: p.
  Includes index.
  1. Social sciences—Study and teaching (Elementary)
I. Title.
LB1584.S448   372.8'3044   80-22213

ISBN 0-205-07213-5

10 9 8 7 6 5 4 3 2 1   85 84 83 82 81

Printed in the United States of America.

Contents

Preface

Social studies has a singular focus and purpose in the elementary curriculum. The focus is on human activities—their purposes and how they contribute and interrelate to foster human life. The purpose is to habituate children in the ways that democratic persons follow as they cope with problems in their interrelated personal, social, and physical environments.

Social-studies educators generally agree on focus and purpose, but they disagree on how to accomplish the purpose. As one visits elementary classrooms, where children learn and teachers teach social studies, and attends class meetings in colleges and universities where the pre-service and in-service instruction of teachers occurs, one observes and hears various responses to the question of how elementary social studies is most effectively taught. The responses, described briefly as instructional strategies, include the following:

- by providing children with activities that facilitate the learning of facts and using them in such endeavors as painting murals, dramatizing, constructing models, and the like
- by providing children with activities in which they acquire facts, use the facts to arrive at generalizations, validate generalizations, and integrate their learning through expressive activities
- by providing children with opportunities to explore processes, systems, relationships, eras, and regions in arranged learning environments
- by providing children with opportunities for values explorations related to their personal, social, and physical environments
- by guiding children in solving problems related to social issues
- by guiding children in proving or disproving generalizations through following a model of informal inquiry
- by providing children with opportunities to learn and use the skills characteristic of each of the social sciences as disciplines
- by providing children with opportunities to make decisions in a variety of imaginary and real situations in which various personal, social, cultural, political, and economic forces prevail
- by involving children in the exploration of future problems of survival to surface probable solutions

The list of strategies is not exhaustive, but it is sufficient to reflect a wide variety. Some of the strategies have been brilliantly expressed and defended; some have been subjected to research; and some reflect practices developed through classroom experience. All are workable, and all are similar in that they require, to be effective in use, that children be able to use skills in thinking, information acquisition and processing, and expressing ideas. Some of the strategies may emphasize, and thus lend greater significance, to one set of skills as compared with the others, but all strategies require some level of exercise with all the skills. At any given moment during study children may be using any of the skills subsumed in any set, but each skill is interrelated in some way with the others in its set as well as with those in the other sets. Learning and achievement in elementary social studies, then, are less a matter of teaching strategy and more a matter of the adequacy of children's skills. This book expands on this point of view.

However, strategies are discussed in the book, but none is presented as the best or the one and only strategy for all children. Some strategies are best suited for young children; others are better for older, brighter, or slower children. In the final analysis, the best teaching strategy is that which the teacher can manage efficiently. If there is any precautionary note in the book, it is that the teacher ensure that the learners have the skills necessary to participate in the chosen strategy. A skills emphasis in social studies thus focuses on the needs of children to learn, improve, and apply skills if the purpose for social studies is to be fulfilled.

The focus on skills offers advantages to children as learning persons. Children in school prize accomplishment. To them, skills are real and tangible, and the person who has them can do many things. As they see their own progress in the skills they are learning and refining to higher levels of utility, they can perceive their accomplishment.

At this point one may wonder whether social studies as an area of study is of any significance. Why not teach just the skills? One reason for not following such a practice is that skills, to be mastered for independent use, must be applied to accomplish purposes associated with a particular matter. Without purpose or matter, application cannot occur. Through its topics, themes, issues, or problems, social studies provides purposes and matters of substance with which children apply

their skills. Another reason is that without the application of skills with social-studies content, children do not meet the purpose for social studies. In short, the learning of skills and meeting the purpose of social studies are mutually supportive.

After the first chapter, which describes social studies in its curriculum setting, the book is designed to serve the following four equally important purposes: (1) to serve as a guide for elementary teachers, both pre-service and in-service, as they assess children's needs for learning and improving skills in social studies (Chapter 2) and assess children's achievement in skills as they study social studies (Chapter 11); (2) to serve as a resource for teachers seeking or trying to develop a strategy commensurate with their perception of themselves as social-studies teachers (Chapters 3 and 4); (3) to offer suggestions of procedures for guiding children in learning and improving information-seeking skills (Chapter 5), information-processing skills (Chapter 6), group-work skills (Chapter 7), and skills in dealing with controversial issues (Chapter 8); and (4) to present organizational models for individualizing instruction in social studies (Chapter 9) and for planning instruction generally (Chapter 10).

Basically, the book is a manual as well as a text in which children's need to learn, teachers' need to teach, and society's need to survive are placed in a realistic perspective.

I owe a debt of gratitude for contributions made by many, particularly the children and the university students I have taught. They suffered my efforts and through their reactions taught me.

Among those who made special contributions are Steven C. Mathews, the editor who encouraged me to write the book; Dr. Huston M. Burnside, my colleague, office partner, and friend who good-naturedly served as a readily accessible sounding board for ideas; and Bette, my wife, who served uncomplainingly as first reader and typist and whose good humor and encouragement sustained me throughout the writing.

1

Social Studies
in Its Curriculum
Setting

The purpose of this chapter is to place you amid some of the controversies of social studies—not to overwhelm you but to alert you to the mind-boggling opportunities that social-studies teachers have for making instructional decisions.

A good way to survive within controversy is to decide what you think about it. The questions below will prompt you to express what you think. Read each carefully, think about it for a minute or two, and jot down your response on a piece of note paper.

- What do you think social studies is (do you think of it as singular, like mathematics or linguistics)?
- Why do you think it is included in the elementary curriculum?
- What do you think children should study in social studies?
- What kinds of learning activities do you think should be provided for children in social studies?

Put your notes aside in some easily remembered place. You will be reviewing them later.

TOWARD A DEFINITION

If we define a problem simply as "a matter affecting our lives which demands a decision," we can see in the sketch below that Johnny Doe, a child born and living in a technologically complex society, is subject to the pressure of many problems.

In many moments in Johnny's life he feels no pressure from problems: he pedals his bicycle furiously wherever he wants to go, eats with relish anything set before him, plays with abandon, sleeps soundly, and completes tasks with dispatch. But then there are moments when problems press him. For example, he has a social-studies report due next Monday and he does not like to write reports. Last year the teacher had tried to teach him how to compose written reports, but then always offered choices such as drawing pictures or diagrams for those who did not care to write. Johnny had always taken one of the alternatives to writing. Last week this year's teacher guided the class in a review of report writing, but Johnny did not pay much attention and this teacher offers no choices. To make matters worse, Johnny has always been a star pupil in social studies. If he does not complete the report, it is likely that he will not get an "A" in social studies. What decision must he make to protect his success in school? Get help from the teacher, his parents, or one of his friends? Ask someone to write the report for him? Try to substitute something for the report? Or what?

And sometimes he thinks he has one problem when he really has another. One day a friend in

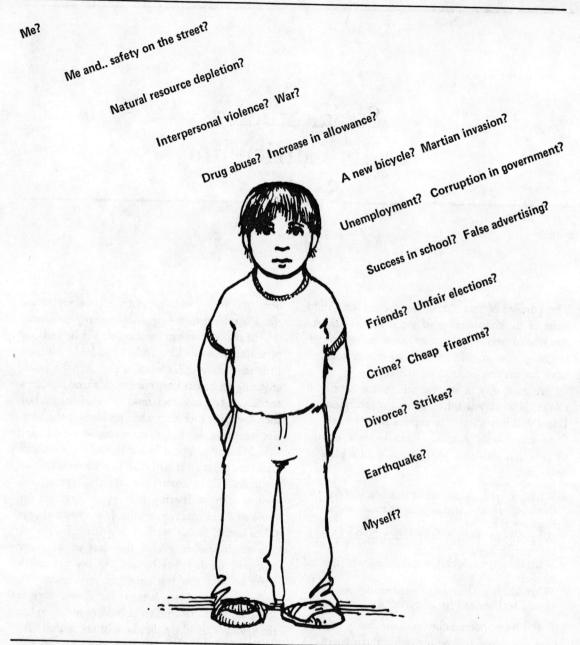

Me?

Me and.. safety on the street?

Natural resource depletion?

Interpersonal violence? War?

Drug abuse? Increase in allowance?

A new bicycle? Martian invasion?

Unemployment? Corruption in government?

Success in school? False advertising?

Friends? Unfair elections?

Crime? Cheap firearms?

Divorce? Strikes?

Earthquake?

Myself?

FIGURE 1–1. *Problems Impinging on Children.*

his gang got a new bicycle capable of incredible speed with little effort. Johnny decided he needed a new bicycle, but when he asked his parents to buy him one, they told him they could not afford it because of inflation—something about the rising cost of living and wages not keeping pace. For a moment he wondered whether his parents still loved him, and then he accepted inflation as a fact.

After all, ice-cream cones he bought a year ago for a quarter now cost thirty-five cents. But how can he get a new bicycle? Earn money for it? By doing what? Ask relatives to give him money instead of presents on his birthday? Try to sell his coin collection? Or what?

Perhaps when he has to reject all the choices he can think of, he will discover his real problem: how to cope with a friend's good fortune.

And so it is with Johnny and his problems. Many are possible in his environment, yet he often appears to live a problem-free life. When a problem impinges on him, he may be able to define it, or he may not. Some problems he may solve, some he may contain, some he may just live with, some he may manage to forget, and some he will grow out of. Whether he is going to define them accurately, and what he is going to do about them, depends in part on his background.

A major element of that background is information consisting of ideas documented in fact. Much of this information is available in the various social-science disciplines—psychology, sociology, anthropology, economics, geography, political science, and history.

Let's analyze the sketch by classifying Johnny's problem areas from Figure 1–1 according to the discipline that focuses on them. The results of the analysis are shown in Table 1–1.

Perhaps you are puzzled by the entries in the table indicating that several disciplines consider a particular problem area as a focus for study. Multiple entries occur because there is an overlap of concerns in the various social-science disciplines.

As we view the table, we can see that Johnny has a rich fund of sources available to him to obtain insights into his problems. Because he lives in a complex, powerful society in which the problem areas are so highly specialized that some people may devote their entire lives to exploring and discovering within an area, he can control his reactions, at least in part, by considering the viewpoints and ideas generated by each of the social sciences.

Each social science is a discipline characterized by (1) a body of knowledge about a broad area of human activity and endeavor, and (2) ways of deepening and extending that body of knowledge. It consists of concepts, or labeled features, that are defined or combined with other concepts into generalizations. These generalizations are statements of broad applicability that are useful in understanding the universe and making decisions about problems met within it.

It is essential for us to recognize that social-science generalizations are the products of experience, study, and research. The process of generalizing is the exercise of inductive thinking—drawing the meaning from experienced facts. This is what we want children to do. For this reason, we shall use social-science generalizations as guides for organizing the content of instruction, not as guides to subject matter to be memorized.

Each discipline requires a library to describe it. However, the following is a brief description of each in terms of theme (label of basic concern), a few sample concepts and generalizations, and method (how scientists work within it).

1. Psychology
   a. Theme: Self and the World
   b. Concepts: behavior, perception, motivation, personality, genetic factors, environmental factors, socialization, etc.
   c. Generalizations:
      • Behavior is what a person thinks, feels, and does as internal and external conditions impinge on him or her.
      • Specific kinds of behavior are produced as a result from the interaction of genetic and environmental factors.
      • How an individual behaves in a group is related to the structure and organization of the group.
   d. Method: Experimenting with subjects, singly or in small groups, observing subjects singly or in small groups as they react to common circumstances, experimenting with animals as subjects, applying deductive logic to produce theories.
2. Sociology
   a. Theme: Social Group
   b. Concepts: community, role, status, family, demography, association, assimilation, competition, cooperation, accommodation, stratification, cohesion, etc.

TABLE 1–1. *Problem Areas.*

Problem Area	Psy-chology	Soci-ology	Anthro-pology	Eco-nomics	Geog-raphy	Political Science	His-tory
Me	x	x	x				
Interpersonal violence	x	x	x			x	x
Natural resource depletion				x	x		x
Safety on the street						x	
Friends	x	x					
Drug abuse	x		x				
Increase in allowance				x			
Myself	x						
A new bicycle				x			
Corruption in government						x	x
Cheap firearms			x				
Inflation				x			
War						x	x
Martian invasion						x	x
Unemployment				x			x
Earthquake					x		x
Success in school	x		x				
Strike				x		x	x
Unfair elections						x	x
Divorce		x					
False advertising				x			
Parents		x				x	

c. Generalizations:
  • Individuals live in communities in which they cooperate and compete with one another in their work, recreation, and government.
  • Assimilation occurs when persons enter a new environment and take on the behaviors of the others living in that environment.
  • Techniques of social control include shunning, ostracism, gossip, praise, and acceptance.
d. Method: Observing groups and individuals within groups, making case studies, making statistical analyses of data, experimental study of subjects, application of deductive logic to produce theories.

3. Anthropology
  a. Theme: Man as Unique and Diverse
  b. Concepts: culture, diffusion, invention, acculturation, adaptation, mores, folkways, myths, clan, tribe, institution, ethnocentrism, ethnic group, etc.
  c. Generalizations:
    • Culture is the ways of living, beliefs, values, attitudes, tools, practices, and behaviors that are developed by a society as a means of survival and transmitted from one generation to another.
    • Diffusion occurs when people from different cultures exchange practices, ideas, materials, and tools.
    • The culture into which individuals are born

and in which they grow up has a strong influence on them throughout their lives.

   d. Method: Observation, assuming the role of participant-observer, interviewing informants, gathering and analyzing artifacts, interpretation through analogy, application of deductive thought to produce theories.

4. Political Science
   a. Theme: Power and Authority
   b. Concepts: law, legislature, monarchy, democracy, politics, special-interest groups, rights, due process, cabinet, political party, judicial branch, internal order, constitution, etc.
   c. Generalizations:
      • The cabinet form of government is centered in the legislature, that is, the legislature elects one of its members to be prime minister, or head of government, and he or she appoints other legislators to serve on the cabinet as advisors and heads of departments.
      • The work of government is to do for the people what they cannot do, or do as well, for themselves.
      • In a democracy the ultimate source of authority resides in the people.
   d. Method: observation, interviewing, conducting polls, questionnaire, statistical analysis of data, application of deductive logic to produce theories.

5. Economics
   a. Theme: Scarcity
   b. Concepts: resources, capital, specialization, supply, price, goods and services, ownership, capitalism, profits, economic welfare, economic system, income.
   c. Generalizations:
      • Because productive resources are limited and human wants are unlimited, people must make careful choices about how to use their resources.
      • The gross national product (GNP) is the total value of all the goods and services produced in one year by a nation.
      • If labor is highly productive, the per-capita income is likely to be high.
   d. Method: observation, statistical analysis of data, application of deductive logic to produce theories.

6. Geography
   a. Theme: Region
   b. Concepts: weather, climate, natural resources, technology, vegetation, topography, landform, population, globe, map, zone, temperate, rainfall, land use, erosion, wind, etc.
   c. Generalizations:
      • The seasons and day and night are related to the movements of the earth as it rotates on its axis and revolves around the sun.
      • The way a people uses an area depends on its location, available natural resources, and the people's level of technology.
      • The earth is divided into climatic regions in accord with the distribution of temperature and rainfall.
   d. Method: observation, mapping, graphing, photographing, census taking, analyzing records, making statistical analyses of data.

7. History
   a. Theme: Change
   b. Concepts: chronology, space and time framework, trend, record, primary source, secondary source, dominant factor, multiple-causation, etc.
   c. Generalizations:
      • What has occurred in the past influences the present.
      • Change may occur toward either progress or decay.
      • Events in human history tend to occur in a similar order, but history does not repeat itself.
   d. Method: analysis of documents, records, and objects, interviewing, observation of selected sites, interpretive reconstruction, use of deductive thought and imagination to interpret history.

Concepts and generalizations are useful in designating the content children are going to experience and the ideas they are going to acquire. However, for curriculum purposes, generalizations are expressed in terms of the study focus. Let us use the following generalization as an example: *What has occurred in the past influences the present.*

For young learners this generalization may be expressed in this way:

We have Thanksgiving Day because long ago the Pilgrims had the first Thanksgiving Day.

Children in fourth grade may be provided learning activities to guide them toward this generalization as a logical conclusion:

Each of the different peoples coming to our state in the past used the land in particular ways, some of which we follow today.

And children in seventh grade may be guided toward this generalization:

English culture was transplanted to the New World, which accounts for our language, some of our religious preferences, many of our laws, and some of our architectural preferences.

As you can see, the meaning of the generalization from history is extended and deepened with each new study, and each focus occurs at a higher level of abstraction.

Concepts and generalizations are the building blocks of social-studies content. Sometimes learning, particularly for young children, is focused on a concept. For example, children in kindergarten may be guided into learning activities that will bring them to the point of generalizing: *A family is some people who live together and care for each other.* The focus is on *family.* The generalization is a definition.

However, children in the eighth grade may be guided toward this generalization: *The nuclear family disintegrates as the children grow up and leave home, or because it cannot cope with cultural, economic, or political forces.* The generalization describes a cause-and-effect relationship. The first element of learning is *nuclear family,* the main concept to be studied until the children can generalize a definition for it to serve as a base for further learning. Each of the other concepts *(disintegrate, cultural forces, economic forces,* and *political forces)* will also have to be defined through study. Then all the concepts will be synthesized to produce the cause-and-effect generalization.

Implicit in all social studies is the learner's concept of him- or herself with relation to the whole world within his or her perception. The methods of social scientists offer learners opportunities to forget bias and concern for self to make objective studies. The results of these studies can then be analyzed for personal meaning.

The methods of social scientists may have a

direct impact on learners in the sense that they open new and interesting vistas and provide a source of personal satisfaction. For example, the child who interviews grandparents and others of their generation to reconstruct the life of a child fifty years ago may discover that historical study is what he or she wants to do as an avocation— ultimately perhaps as a vocation.

Generally, while each has a different viewpoint and concern, the social sciences overlap. History and geography are sciences of synthesis in which concepts from the other sciences, including each other, are explored. Anthropology, sociology, and psychology often deal with similar concepts. Sociology, political science, and economics often appear to touch similar bases.

All the social sciences have the same focal point—humankind, and Johnny's closest tie with humankind is himself. For him, then, the significant area of overlap is himself, as shown in Figure 1–2.

The bodies of knowledge, as well as the methods for deepening and extending them, established by the social scientists are available to Johnny through social studies as a curriculum vehicle. Using what he can acquire from the social sciences, he can bring informed thought to bear on his decision making as he copes with problems. This means that he will be able to surface more possible solutions to his problems, that his solutions will be founded more solidly on facts, and that he will have deeper insights into the possible consequences of each decision.

At this point we can isolate several elements to use in a definition: *children's immediate problems with themselves, others, and the universe around them; curriculum vehicle; informed thought;* and *decision making.* But before we formulate our definition, let's consider Johnny in the light of his future. He will not be a child forever.

As Johnny grows, so will his ability to understand complex ideas and to reason with them to discover ways of coping with problems. However, at any given moment in his development, he cannot predict what degree of complexity or change in magnitude his problems may take. For this

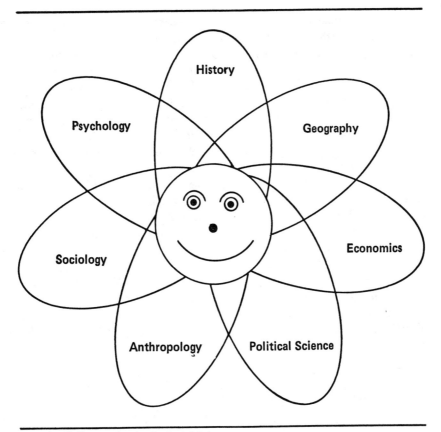

FIGURE 1–2. *Overlap in the Social Sciences.*

reason, his social-studies experience must also take him beyond the problems that impinge immediately on him at any given time.

Including the future as an element, we may derive this definition: *Social studies is a curriculum vehicle through which children learn to cope with their immediate and future problems with themselves, others, and the universe through making decisions based on informed thought.*

This definition is sufficiently comprehensive to permit many approaches to social-studies instruction. The teacher who wishes to guide his or her learners through an inquiry based on scientific method is free to do so. So is the teacher who chooses to guide learners in solving immediate and hypothetical problems. And so is the teacher who is able in guiding learners to generate curiosity or interest to acquire information and then having them discover applications for that information. Also, within the definition teachers are free to follow preferences for administering to classes, groups, or individuals.

However, the definition does impose demands. It requires that if children are in fact involved with social studies, they are digging for facts and learning to dig for facts, organizing information and learning to organize it, interpreting information and learning to interpret it, and applying information and learning to apply it. It is from these *learning to's* that the title of this book has been derived: *Elementary Social Studies: A Skills Emphasis.* Finding, organizing, interpreting, and applying information are the skills basic to learning in social studies.

Why social studies is included in the elementary curriculum is implicit within the definition, but let us look more deeply into this question.

WHY IS SOCIAL STUDIES INCLUDED IN THE ELEMENTARY CURRICULUM?

As an area in the common curriculum of humankind, social studies is a basic subject which predates reading and writing. Human experience over countless years documents that almost every society develops and follows a set of practices in which the young are trained and finally inducted as full-fledged, contributing members of society. These practices fulfill what might be operationally defined as the *social-studies function.*

Let us consider the case of Morning Sun, a child born and living in a preliterate society. Here is how he learns to live in his society:

- *Imitation.* By watching and copying the behaviors of older males, he has learned to handle tools and weapons in basic ways. Much of his play involves imitation hunts and battles.
- *Participation.* Much of what he has learned about language, literature, music, and art is a result of participating in the common rites of celebration, mourning, calling on or appeasing the supernatural, marriage, and so forth.
- *Reward and punishment.* The society has strict rules about men's and women's roles, forbidden activities and foods, and societal property. When Morning Sun shows respect for these rules, he is lavishly praised; when he fails to observe the rules, he is isolated and not given any food for a specified period of time.

By the time that Morning Sun is twelve years old, he has learned much of what he needs to know to be a contributing member of his society. He can solve many problems that he has with himself, others, and the universe lying within a six-mile radius of his village. He has learned through daily, direct contact and interaction with the hundred or so members of his society as they go about the business of surviving and living together. Much

of the social-studies function is the responsibility of the entire society.

When the time comes for Morning Sun to become a full-fledged member of his society, he is taken to a small hut outside the village. There he stays by himself for three weeks, never leaving the hut except for short periods during the night. His mother brings him food and drink, but he is not to talk to her or look at her. Every day he is visited by a tribal elder who instructs him about the finer points of his religion, the gods whom only the men know, and his responsibilities as a man. At the end of his seclusion, his father and a tribal elder take him to a newly made hut just outside the village. He stands with other boys waiting his turn to enter the hut.

Finally, a subchief taps him on the shoulder and motions him toward the doorway of the hut. As soon as he steps through the doorway, the tribal elders, their faces hidden behind grotesque masks, grab him roughly and hold him tight against the ground. Each elder in turn cuts him with a rake-like, scarifying tool. When they finish, he has cuts on his upper arms and thighs. They lift him to his feet. The chief elder gives him a name which he must never reveal to anyone on pain of death. Using his new name, the elders remind him of his new responsibilities and then dismiss him. He scoots out through a small opening in the back of the hut. His father greets and congratulates him. Morning Sun is elated with his new status.

The few weeks of concentrated instruction followed by the rites of passage mark the end of the social-studies function, but note that the instruction and rites are specialized. Only tribal elders are involved. A special period of time is set aside for instruction. Bear these facts in mind as we compare Morning Sun's life with Johnny's.

As can be easily seen in Table 1–2, Johnny's life conditions are much more diverse and complex than Morning Sun's, and for this reason the social-studies function within the institution of education in his society will be extended over a period of years and be much more specialized. Morning Sun's social studies is his entire curricu-

TABLE 1-2. *Life Needs of Morning Sun and Johnny Doe.*

Life Need	Morning Sun	Johnny Doe
Food	Animals, fruits, seeds, herbs, and roots available within the immediate vicinity. The father hunts and the mother gathers food. There is little variety and often a scarcity. Everyone has the same diet.	Meats, dairy products, cereal products, vegetables and fruits, oils, and nuts, most of which are produced and processed far from the immediate vicinity. All are obtained at stores and shops in exchange for money. There is a great variety, and Johnny is aware that some people enjoy better food than he does, while others do not have food as good as his.
Clothing	Grass cloth and animal hides processed by the mother and girls in the family. Each person has one outfit which is replaced when it is worn out.	Synthetic fibers made from petroleum, wood, and coal; natural fibers from cotton, flax, and wool; various kinds of leather. All are produced and processed into garments in various places around the world. All are obtained in stores and shops in exchange for money. Johnny has at least a half-dozen outfits for school and one for special occasions. He is aware that there are differences among people in the variety and quality of their clothing because of differences in income.
Shelter	A hut constructed of posts, poles, and grass obtained in the immediate neighborhood. It is built by his father and uncles. When food becomes permanently scarce in the immediate vicinity, the family moves to another place and a new hut is built.	A house constructed of lumber, steel, copper, lead, zinc, brass, and many synthetic materials. All the materials were transported to the site and assembled by specialists. Johnny's parents have a thirty-year loan to pay for the house. The whole family hopes that the day will come when they can afford a larger, more expensive house. Johnny knows that many people live in houses not as good as his, and some live in houses better than his.
Human Relationships	Morning Sun's closest relationships are with his immediate family, but he also has very close relationships with his uncles, cousins, and grandfather on his father's side of the family. He has a special kinship with all the males in the neighborhood. He is aware that there are other people a few miles away, but they are not to be trusted.	Johnny's closest relationships are with his immediate family. He acknowledges bonds of affection with his grandparents, uncles, aunts, and cousins, but sometimes he feels closer to his neighborhood friends. He feels a sense of belonging to his city, state, and nation. He knows that there are many people far away, some of whom he thinks are enemies.
Sources of Information	All the people around him, but he considers some sources better. His father, his father's brothers, and his father's father are the best sources of information. He believes that the older a person, the better he or she is as a source of information.	All the people around him, but he places greatest reliance on his parents. Generally he considers older people to be better sources. His best-liked friends are also good sources. He is continually bombarded with information from billboards, radio, television, advertisers, newspapers, magazines, and books. He tends to regard what he reads as being reliable information; but he is often not sure. Sometimes he is manipulated by persuasive messages in newspapers and via television, radio, and billboards to persuade his parents to buy things for him.
Concept of His Future	He looks forward to the day when he can be like his father and do the things that he does.	He is occasionally nagged by choices of what he will do as an adult. The available choices are so many and varied and entail so much special training that he is never quite sure.

9

lum, but Johnny's social studies will have to vie for time and attention with other subjects in the curriculum. However, there can be little doubt that social studies has a strong place in the elementary-school curriculum. It could be removed from that curriculum, but only

- If Johnny's life could be locked tightly into an era in which technological, social, economic, and political conditions remain the same.
- If Johnny's cultural, social, economic, and political ties can be restricted to his immediate community.
- If Johnny's concern can be restricted to his own socioeconomic, ethnic, and religious group.
- If Johnny's parents and neighbors would take the time from their busy lives to discuss his problems with him, to guide him into a variety of informational resources in such a way that he develops useful concepts, to teach him the specialized skills necessary to finding and weighing information, and to engage him in the free, rational use of his mind to define problems and to cope with them in satisfactory ways.
- If the television, radio, newspaper, and advertising industries would provide useful sources of information at Johnny's level of understanding and provide him with objective points of view drawn from complete evidence which he could see and interpret.

Nothing short of a tremendous world catastrophe could bring about the first three "if's," and the last two are not likely to be realized in the foreseeable future.

In light of the foregoing, Johnny's need for social studies is readily apparent. The challenge is to provide him with an effective program in social-studies instruction. To provide him with an elementary curriculum bereft of social studies is to deprive him.

WHAT SHOULD CHILDREN STUDY?

As we defined social studies and discussed its place in the elementary curriculum, we already glimpsed what should be studied. Let us consider this issue in historical perspective by seeing what Johnny

would have studied during past eras as well as what he might study today.

The brief historical glimpse of social studies presented in Table 1–3 clarifies why we have several definitions of social studies. Beginning with "Centennial" Johnny, each new emphasis found a place in the social-studies curriculum, and then, although no longer a main emphasis in later periods, remained within the curriculum. History, considered either as social science or humanity, and geography, particularly cultural geography, are synthetic areas of study, one based on chronology and the other on region. Both require social-science concepts and generalizations to be adequately understood, and both provide universes of validation to social-science ideas. For these reasons, history and geography have a place in the social-studies curriculum.

Another idea reflected in the historical perspective is that the social-studies curriculum is strongly influenced by the dominant social forces of the time. "New American" Johnny, for example, studied the Bible because religion was a dominant force in the life of his society, and "Bicentennial" Johnny needs to inquire into and through himself to make decisions to cope with a variety of social forces.

The historical perspective suggests that since the time of "Depression and G. I." Johnny, there has been a growing emphasis on skills learning as opposed to content or factual learning.

What next? Your guess is as good as mine. If the nation should isolate itself from others, there could be a resurgence of emphasis on the nation's history, what the nation is as a geographical entity, and democratic ideals. If ecological concern and control emerge as demanding forces, social studies could become a study of the earth sciences and ways of effectively managing the physical environment. If immediate personal relevance becomes the prime criterion for selecting content, social studies may become a study of consumers' strategies, legal processes, comparative religion, and sociopsychological improvement. Whatever the change, the skills required will remain the same.

TABLE 1–3. *A Historical Glimpse of Social Studies.*

1620–1800 "New American" Johnny	The Bible
1800–1850 "Steam engine" Johnny	Manners and morals
1850–1900 "Centennial" Johnny	Factual history and geography
1900–1925 "New century" Johnny	Factual history and geography (if he had attended some schools, real attempts would have been made for him to discover interests and to become involved with dynamic activities as a way of learning)
1925–1950 "Depression and G. I." Johnny	Factual history and geography (in some schools on the basis of his generated interests in topics and with an emphasis on small-group activity)
1950–1960 "Sputnik" Johnny	Important generalizations from history, geography, sociology, anthropology, psychology, social psychology, economics, and political science (with an emphasis on learning to inquire)
1960–1970 "Space explorer" Johnny	Concepts from history, geography, sociology, anthropology, psychology, social psychology, economics, and political science learned through inquiry
1970– "Bicentennial" Johnny	Inquiry into and through self as related to social-science concepts from history, geography, sociology, anthropology, psychology, social psychology, economics, and political science.

The first set of skills with which we need to concern ourselves as teachers is the interaction skills:

1. Interacting with others.
   a. With teacher guidance in class or small groups.
   b. In spontaneous groups with peer leadership.
   c. In organized small groups with peer leadership.

The next set of skills is basic to inquiry:

2. Defining problems. (Individually and in groups)
   a. Isolating problem forces.
   b. Determining what forces are in conflict.
   c. Selecting dominant forces.
3. Exploring for solutions. (Individually and in groups)
   a. Making hypotheses.
   b. Defending hypotheses.
   c. Selecting hypotheses.
4. Finding information. (Individually and in groups)
   a. Observing at selected sites.
   b. Examining objects.
   c. Listening to resource persons, peers, teachers, and audiotapes.
   d. Viewing pictures, films, and videotapes.
   e. Interviewing resource persons and subjects.
   f. Locating reading sources.
      i) Using the table of contents.
      ii) Using an index.
      iii) Using a card catalog.
      iv) Survey reading.
      v) Skimming.
      vi) Scanning.
   g. Purposeful reading to acquire information.
      i) Verbal text reading.

      ii) Map and globe reading.
    iii) Chart reading.
    iv) Table reading.
     v) Graph reading.
    vi) Diagram reading.
   vii) Interpreting statistical information.
  h. Retaining information.
     i) Note taking.
    ii) Outlining.
   iii) Self-testing.
5. Organizing information.
  a. Making lists.
  b. Writing sentences, paragraphs, and reports.
  c. Summarizing.
  d. Constructing maps, charts, graphs, diagrams, tables, and models.
  e. Making sketches.
  f. Dramatizing.
  g. Giving statistical information.
6. Analyzing information.
  a. Classifying.
  b. Labeling.
  c. Comparing.
  d. Contrasting.
  e. Generalizing or arriving at conclusions.
  f. Drawing implications.
  g. Citing examples.
  h. Comparing conclusions against hypotheses.
  i. Deciding on the tenability of hypotheses.
  j. Validating hypotheses, generalizations, or conclusions in other sources or with further investigation.

The next set of skills brings learners to the point of using factual information and generalizations combined with internalized knowledge from other sources to decide on solutions, generate new knowledge, and make decisions about issues.

7. Using ideas to solve problems.
  a. Recognizing the appropriateness of ideas.
  b. Using ideas in problem-solving activities.
    i) Participating in in-depth discussions.
      • Class and small-group discussions.
      • Debate.
      • Panel discussions.
      • Roundtable discussions.
8. Using ideas to generate knowledge.
  a. Drawing rules and guidelines.
  b. Inventing games.
  c. Composing stories, plays, poems, essays, and songs.

  d. Creating posters, murals, wall banners, and cartoons.
  e. Creating pageants, dances, and assembly programs.
9. Using ideas to make decisions about issues.
  a. Deciding what to do about personal issues.
  b. Deciding what to do about social issues.
  c. Deciding what to do about economic issues.
  d. Deciding what to do about political issues.

This is a formidable array of skills. Many are supported by instruction in other curriculum areas, but additional instruction is often necessary in social studies to help children bridge from acquiring learning skills to using them to learn. Some skills are usually taught as a part of the social-studies curriculum. These include interaction skills, observing at selected sites, listening to resource persons, interviewing, reading and making maps, charts, graphs, diagrams, and tables, reading the globe, role playing, simulation, value clarification, and value analysis. Other skills, most notably the inquiry skills, are taught also in science.

Some instructional programs in social studies emphasize many of the skills while others emphasize only a few. In some instances the skills to be studied are prescribed; in others, the skills are taught as needed by the children as they deal with a particular problem.

The content to be studied also varies. It may be action centered, concept centered, values centered, generalization centered, problem centered, era centered, or region centered. In this book, we shall consider content as being problem centered, because every skill required to work with problem-centered content is useful in some way with all the other modes of content organization.

However organized, content is subject to change. New countries emerge, geographical names change, and boundaries take new shapes. New evidence is discovered about historical eras. Even the meaning supporting useful generalizations changes. For example, the meaning of *exist, adapt,* and *exploit* in this generalization—*To exist, humankind must adapt to and exploit its natural resources*—has changed in the past decade.

Because content is so changeable, we shall focus on the skills needed in social studies. As we guide children in learning and using the skills necessary to effective learning in social studies, we contribute to their breadth and depth of learning and their development as independent decision makers.

In short, there is no dearth of problems or content, but skills always need to be developed to functional levels and improved.

WHAT LEARNING ACTIVITIES SHOULD BE PROVIDED?

The list of skills presented in the previous section indicates also the learning activities into and through which children will be guided.

The learning activities are arranged in sequence to ensure learning. First in the sequence are preparatory activities during which the children have opportunities to express whatever they know related to a central concept or cluster of related concepts and to establish purposes for study. The discussion of knowledge already achieved and the setting of purposes generate interest. Whatever the children do is determined by the teacher's approach to social-studies instruction. (See Illustration 1–1.)

At the beginning of a study requiring at least six or seven daily instructional periods over as many days, there is a likelihood that the first of these periods will be devoted to preparatory activities. These may include any of the following activity clusters:

1. After a multisensory exploration of some objects or viewing a picture related to a person, place, or process, the children discuss their discoveries and what more they would like to know.
2. After viewing and discussing a series of bulletin-board displays and interest centers about a process, region, culture, or era, the children discuss what they already know and what more they would like to know.
3. After viewing a film, a filmstrip, a set of study prints or pictures, a filmloop, or a videotape, or

ILLUSTRATION 1–1. *Young Children Need Assistance to Get Information.*

after listening to a story, poem, or informative article about a process, region, culture, or era, the children discuss what they know and what else they need to know.

4. After a brief discussion of a central concept, the children name different aspects related to it, analyze the aspects as recorded to categorize them into groups and to label each group, generalize to arrive at a definition of the concept, and discuss what more they would like to know about it.
5. After a brief discussion of a central concept, the children discuss an issue related to it, decide where they stand on the issue, and develop questions to answer to validate their stand.
6. After a brief discussion of a school or community problem which they feel, the children suggest solutions, select the one that seems the most reasonable, and then determine what kinds of information they will need to check further on the workability of the solution.
7. After reacting to a contrived situation, role play-

ing a situation, or participating in a simulation based on a system of human relationships, the children will decide on an alternative or set of alternatives to investigate more thoroughly.

In the clusters of preparatory activities above the result is always purpose. The children are involved in determining the purpose, and because of their involvement, the purpose is theirs. As such, it gives meaning and direction for seeking information.

The next cluster of activities in the sequence is comprised of information seeking and expressing activities. (See Illustration 1–2.) Information seeking may occur through listening to audiotapes; listening to and observing the teacher as he or she reads or makes a presentation with illustrative materials such as pictures, flannelgrams, maps, graphs, models, diagrams, or charts; listening to and viewing films, videotapes, filmloops, or television pro-

grams; interviewing resource persons; and reading and recalling orally, taking notes, or outlining. Information-expressing skills may be discussing, summarizing, or reporting (oral or written), charting, graphing, map drawing or completing, dramatizing, making models or diagrams, or deciding in small groups what the important facts are and how they should be expressed.

The activities mentioned above are those which children are often expected to do independently. They require skills developed to a high level of operation. Much of the instructional program devoted to building skills for use in social studies will focus on these skills.

The final cluster of learning activities include those in which children meet their original purposes and are guided in discovering further significance in what they have learned. To see how well they can meet their purposes may involve reviewing their questions and answering them, taking factual tests, and judging an earlier established idea in the light of new information. If they have been studying an immediate problem, they refine their solution and apply it. They may have to validate the idea further to see whether recognized authority accepts it or how true it is in other times, places, or cultures. The activities that facilitate children's discovery of further significance of what they have learned may include in-depth discussions, role playing, simulations, values clarifications, value analyses, recommending procedures, or creating a poem, story, play, mural, or map.

The total sequence of learning activities from preparatory through closure for significance ensures learning through exploring factual knowledge and the application of skills. If the learning activities are to bring desired results, emphasis needs to be given to introducing and improving skills in the social-studies curriculum at all grade levels.

Sometimes the emphasis is achieved through combining skills learning with content factual learning. This may occur at the lesson level during which the teacher guides children in reviewing how to apply a skill, using it as best they can, and evaluating its use. Perhaps an instructional period will have to be used to help children correct their

ILLUSTRATION 1–2.

concept of the skill. Or the skill emphasis may occur as an extended study during which the children listen to the teacher's explanations and experience his or her demonstrations, and then try their skills on practice materials. Ultimately they apply the skill during social studies.

By now you may have concluded that no other curriculum provides as many opportunities as social studies for the learning and application of skills. So strong is the relationship between efficacy of skills and learning in social studies that one may detect whether a classroom, school, or district has really effective instructional programs in reading, oral and written composition, and mathematics by carefully observing, analyzing, and evaluating the learning achieved by children in social studies.

SUMMARY

Social studies may be defined as a curriculum vehicle for informing children about their cultural and national heritage, guiding them in developing social-science concepts, or in providing them with realistic opportunities to exercise basic skills. If one accepts that children feel the impingement of problem forces associated with their relationships with themselves, others, and the universe, one can accept that social studies is the curriculum vehicle for helping children to cope with problems now and in the future. A problems-oriented social-studies program has the potential for stimulating children toward involvement, providing challenges, and laying the foundation for life-long skills in coping with problems.

Social studies has a definite place in the elementary-school curriculum to facilitate the school's role in participating in the social studies function: that is, the practices our society follows to train children to become contributing members and to induct them into full-fledged membership.

Influenced by the social, cultural, political, and economic conditions of an era, past as well as present, the social-studies curriculum provides for children to learn a variety of skills associated with data gathering, organizing, and analysis as it is related to personal, social, cultural, political, and economic problems or topics. The content will vary from program to program, depending on the focus of the program itself.

The learning activities in the social-studies program will involve practicing and learning the skills at whatever level the child can work. Discussion is a central activity.

Children's learning in social studies is effectively approached through guiding them in the gradual mastery of the skills associated with social studies.

The goal of elementary social studies is that children become as active as they can as participants in human affairs as much by interest as by necessity.

The remainder of the book is organized to follow the social-studies teacher's problems in the usual order of their occurrence.

Chapter 2 deals with the first problem, determining what children's needs are in social studies.

Chapter 3 presents ideas about values exploration, a broad instructional endeavor that meets two purposes. The first purpose is to guide children in developing a positive social climate in which learning can occur. Because such a climate is a vital need for both the children and the teacher, this chapter is placed early in the book.

The other purpose met by values exploration is to provide for children to use social-studies content to discover personal meaning. This usually occurs after a comprehensive amount of content has been experienced.

Chapter 4 treats inquiry. It suggests ways of getting started with the formal program in instruction.

Chapters 5 and 6 offer suggestions on improving children's information-seeking and information-processing skills. If these skills are neglected, the program ceases to continue, no matter how exciting or challenging the study opener might have been.

Chapters 7, 8, and 9 focus on some of the special problems met by social-studies teachers as they try to conduct a program. Skills in guiding small-group work, dealing with controversial issues, and individualizing instruction can provide a rich, extra dimension to the social-studies program.

Chapter 10 offers suggestions on how to plan social-studies instruction. By the time the reader reaches this chapter, he or she has been acquainted with all the learning activities used in social studies. This knowledge can ensure a varied, interesting program when the technical aspects of planning are mastered.

Chapter 11 offers suggestions for assessing and evaluating children's growth in social studies. It completes the instructional cycle which begins when children's needs are assessed.

This book may be used in several ways. You may wish to read the last chapter and then, as questions arise in your mind, look in the other chapters for procedures or suggestions that you really want to know about. Or you may wish to read Chapter 10 next. When you see what is involved in effective planning, you may use your discoveries as a base for further reading. Perhaps after reading this first chapter, you are anxious to learn more about certain issues in social-studies instruction. You may list them in the order of your preference and investigate them in that order. Or you may plow straight ahead.

POSTSCRIPT

Take out the notes that you made when you began to read this chapter and review them to see how you defined social studies, why you thought it should be included in the elementary curriculum, what you thought the subject matter should be, and the kinds of learning activities you thought should be provided. What changes, if any, will you now make in what you originally thought?

FOR FURTHER UNDERSTANDING

Cognitive Activities

1. Obtain from the library one of the following social studies textbooks on teaching methodology and scan the first chapter or preface to see how social studies is defined.

- James A. Banks with Ambrose A. Clegg, Jr., *Teaching Strategies for the Social Studies.* Reading, Mass.: Addison-Wesley Publishing Company, 1973.
- Frank J. Estvan, *Social Studies in a Changing World.* New York: Harcourt, Brace, Jovanovich, 1968.
- John R. Lee, *Teaching Social Studies in the Elementary School.* New York: The Free Press, 1974.
- John E. Ord, *Elementary School Social Studies for Today's Children.* New York: Harper & Row Publishers, 1972.
- Elliot Seif, *Teaching Significant Social Studies in the Elementary School.* Chicago: Rand McNally College Publishing Company, 1977.

2. Meet with three or four other class members and decide what you think are the disadvantages suffered by children who have a very weak social-studies program.
3. Start making a glossary of terms that you think will be most helpful to you in understanding what social studies is and in seeking more information about issues in social-studies instruction.
4. If you were developing a school-wide instructional program in social studies and were allowed a choice among the skills used or taught in social studies, which skill or skills would you choose to emphasize? Give reasons for your choice.
5. A common self-therapy for most of us is to think of what might have been. Try to remember what your own experiences in social studies in elementary school were like and how they contributed to your growth as a person. Then imagine that your teachers could have foreseen the cultural, political, social, and economic conditions of today. What do you think they might have taught you to prepare you for life today?
6. Make a diagram showing the role of discussion as a learning activity in social-studies instruction.

Practice Activities

1. Arrange to visit a classroom when social studies is being taught. Observe to see what learning activities the children are doing. Notice also how the classroom environment—bulletin boards, counter and

table displays, special constructions, and the like—reflect social studies. On the basis of what you observe, try to decide which definition of social studies the teacher appears to be following.

If another class member is able to observe with you, pool the results of your observations and try to arrive at an agreement on your conclusion about the teacher's definition of social studies.

2. Arrange to visit a kindergarten or first-grade classroom and a fifth or sixth-grade classroom when social studies is being taught. Observe to see the differences in learning activities as they occur in each classroom. On the basis of what you observe, choose the classroom in which you would prefer to teach social studies. Give some reasons for your choice.

SELECTED REFERENCES

Barr, Robert D., James L. Barth, and S. Samuel Shermis. *Defining the Social Studies.* Arlington, Virginia: National Council for the Social Studies, 1977.

Boyer, Ernest L. "A Global Perspective—The New Imperative." *Today's Education,* 67:68–70 (November–December, 1978).

Dewey, John. "What Is Social Study?" *Progressive Education,* 15:367–69 (May, 1938).

Ellis, Arthur K. *Teaching and Learning Elementary Social Studies.* Boston: Allyn and Bacon, Inc., 1977.

Fenton, Edwin. *The New Social Studies.* New York: Holt, Rinehart and Winston, Inc., 1967.

Gibbons, Maurice. "Walkabout: Searching for the Right Passage from Childhood and School." *Phi Delta Kappan,* 55:596–602 (May, 1974).

Goodman, Yetta M. "Metropolitan Man and the Social Studies." *Social Studies Readings No. 4,* National Council for the Social Studies, edited by Huber M. Walsh. Washington, D.C.: National Council for the Social Studies, 1971, pp. 13–16.

Inlow, Gail M. *The Emergent in Curriculum,* Chapter 9. "Dynamism in the Traditional Subject-Matter Fields: English, Social Studies, Modern Languages, and Fine Arts." New York: John Wiley and Sons, Inc., 1973, pp. 192–222.

Massialis, Byron G., and Joseph B. Hurst. *Social Studies in a New Era.* New York: Longman Inc., 1978.

Muessig, Raymond H., ed. *Social Studies Curriculum Development.* Washington, D.C.: National Council for the Social Studies, 1978.

Shaver, James P., O. L. Davis Jr., and Suzanne W. Helburn. "The Status of Social Studies Education: Impressions from Three NSF Studies." *Social Education,* 43:150–3 (February, 1979).

Wheeler, Ronald, and William F. Losito. "Social Studies: The Child's Point of View." *Social Education,* 42:378–80 (May, 1978).

2

Assessing Children's Needs in Social Studies

In the previous chapter we learned that the purpose of social studies is to guide children in learning how to cope with immediate and future problems with themselves, others, and their physical environment. In this chapter we shall consider the problem of determining the baselines from which to construct our instructional program.

A baseline establishes what children already know how to do. Once we know what it is in a particular skill and plot it on a continuum of the levels of sophistication in the skill, we can determine at what level a learner can operate and toward what level we can guide him or her in developing the skill to higher utility. As we set about trying to establish the baselines, or to baseline the various skills, we have to make certain decisions about procedures.

The first decision is where to start in the scheme of skills. In Chapter 1 the skills were listed in this order:

1. Interacting with others.
2. Defining problems.
3. Exploring for solutions.
4. Finding information.
5. Organizing information.
6. Analyzing information.
7. Using ideas to solve problems.
8. Using ideas to generate knowledge.
9. Using ideas to make decisions.

Which of these would you baseline first? Why?

Which would you baseline second? Why?

Which would you not try to baseline? Why not?

Our second decision is how to get information about the children's skills. We have two choices: we could observe children's performance (and record what we observe), or we could have them respond with pencil and paper. We would then analyze our observation records or the children's paper-and-pencil responses to determine the baselines.

In which of the skills do you think you would use observation more than paper-and-pencil tests? Why do you think so?

Jot down your responses to these questions. Put your notes aside to review after reading the chapter.

Assessing children's needs in social studies is a way of determining what should be taught. Because it is such a broad, sensitive study, subject to change as a result of political, economic, and technological events, needs assessments for social studies may occur at various levels of government and education and within the publishing industry.

Needs assessment may occur at the federal

level. For example, working within the provisions of federal legislation for the improvement of education in the public schools, and after reviewing the latest information about what children are learning in social studies, the social scientists, professional educators, and officers working in the federal Department of Education may decide that greater emphasis should be given to consumer education in grades kindergarten through eight. They circulate bulletins nationally to encourage proposals for projects in which curriculum is developed and tested.

Needs assessment may occur at the state level. For example, a state legislature, responding to the demands of constituents, may enact a law stipulating that at least one third of the instructional time in elementary social studies be devoted to the study of cultural heritage. The professional educators in the state Department of Education develop and distribute a bulletin recommending content and learning activities.

With an eye on the results of federal and state needs assessments in social studies, publishers convene committees of social-studies educators to make recommendations about the social-studies content and skills to include in a projected series of textbooks.

Needs assessment may occur at the local level. For example, on the recommendation of the local historical society irked by increasing vandalism at historical sites, a city board of education may decide that local history with emphasis on site visitations be given more attention in the social-studies curriculum throughout the elementary grades. The curriculum specialists on the superintendent's staff develop and distribute guides for instruction.

Sometimes state, county, or city departments of education make needs assessment in social studies as part of their assigned function to monitor instruction. Such assessments may be "in-house" endeavors in which administrators, specialists, and teachers confer to decide what should be taught, or they may be more broadly based. Representatives from various levels of society, parents, administrators, specialists, teachers, and children capable of participating are convened to decide on

goals to be met through social-studies instruction and to rate their importance. With the rated goals in hand, administrators, specialists, and teachers gather evidence on how well the goals are being met. They arrange for reports on goal-related behaviors as observed throughout the community and for paper-and-pencil tests of various kinds to be completed by a sample of the school population. Analyzing the evidence, they develop a social-studies curriculum for use in the schools.

The results of these assessments of children's needs, whatever the number or nature of these assessments, are strong recommendations often supported with instructional materials and specifications for the content and skills to be taught. They are decisions made by persons outside the classroom (although the teacher and perhaps a child were participants). The ultimate assessment, and the one most vital to children's learning, is that which the teacher must make in the classroom. This needs assessment is focused on the skills which the children in a particular classroom need in order to experience the content of social studies. This assessment is made at the beginning of the school year. Figure 2–1 shows the various levels of needs assessment.

The list of skills given in Chapter 1 is comprehensive. It would be rare for an instructional program at the classroom level to require the use of every skill in the list. The assessment would cover the skills required by the children to learn successfully from the designated program. Precisely what skills are to be assessed is determined by the nature of the learning resources available.

At this point you may be wondering why children's needs for factual background are not assessed. No such assessment is made at the beginning of the school year for these reasons: first, there is no fundamental agreement on what factual knowledge children should have from grade level to grade level (content specifications for social studies vary from state to state, from district to district, from textbook series to textbook series, and often from school to school within the same district); second, needs assessment for factual background is adequately made at the beginning of

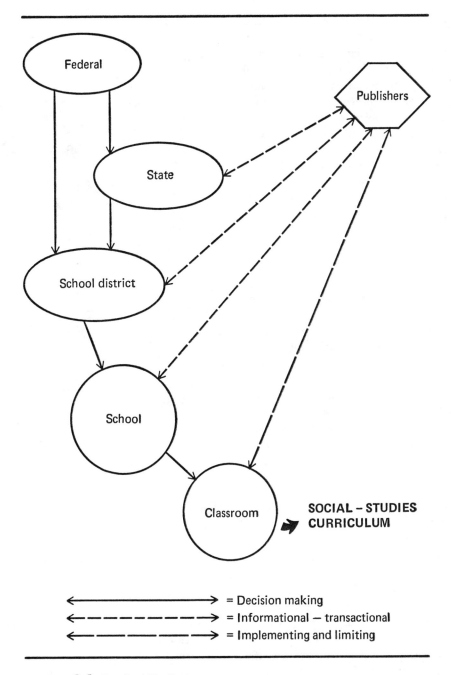

FIGURE 2–1. *Levels of Needs Assessment.*

each new unit of study; and third, the knowledge of content that children can recall at any moment may sometimes be quite large due to frequent television viewing, but their concepts and generalization reflect misinformation and poor organization of thought. Such knowledge is of limited usefulness as a base from which to extend concepts or deepen insights into generalizations, or for use in decision making.

This last reason for not assessing children's needs for knowledge of social-studies content at the beginning of the school year underscores the necessity of teaching social studies with a skills emphasis. Through applying the skills children can learn what is accurate and what is inaccurate about their facts, make the necessary corrections, learn more facts, and organize them into concepts and generalizations to be extended further and used in problem situations.

We also need to recognize that social-studies content, although it is the product of the recorded research, experience, thought, and interpretations of social scientists, social philosophers, and others sensitive to the human condition, is constantly changing. When individuals have mastered the necessary skills, they can independently update their information to be able to make effective decisions.

Now let us consider what we need to bear in mind as we assess children's needs for growth in the skills essential to learning in social studies.

EXPECTANCIES AND SKILLS

As we determine our learners' needs for skill instruction, we are dealing with expectancies and assessments to decide on the learning activities to provide for them.

When we refer to expectancies, we are referring to both the number of skills and the levels at which children may be expected to know how to use them at a particular grade level. For example, we would expect children in the first grade to be able to use observation and listening skills effectively to acquire information, but we would

ILLUSTRATION 2–1. *What Special Needs Do These Children Have for Social Studies?*

not expect them to be able to use reading. Furthermore, we would expect these children to observe and listen during fifteen or twenty-minute lessons when directly assisted by teachers. We would not expect them to use these skills for an hour or so independently.

When we discuss the interaction skills later, the expectancies will be simply described, but when we discuss the other skills, the expectancies will be charted. Described or charted, the expectancies are normative, that is, they reflect what may be expected of most children when the skills are carefully and systematically taught. There are cases in which they are not, and there are differences from one class to another at the same grade level. For these reasons we assess the skills to establish more precisely the expectancies for our learners. We call this a *baseline assessment.*

The baselines resulting from assessments serve

ILLUSTRATION 2–2. *What Social-studies Needs Do These Children Have?*

two purposes. The first is to indicate which learning activities we should provide for initial social-studies instruction. For example, if our baselines indicate that our learners can observe and listen effectively with careful direction, but cannot read the materials provided, we would design the first unit in social-studies instruction to have the children listen and observe under our immediate supervision to acquire information. By doing this, we would be responding to our learners' *immediate study needs* in social studies.

The second purpose served by baselines is that they indicate the points from which skills instruction should proceed. Sometimes the direction is toward greater efficiency. For example, if a baseline indicates that the learners retain what they read well enough to surface the facts, but only when questioned in detail, we would provide learning activities to improve their independent retention skills.

At other times a baseline may indicate a need for children to learn an additional aspect of a skill. For example, the learners may be able to read the conventional symbols on a map, including the direction indicator. They can locate areas when a continent or ocean is given, that is, they can define

ILLUSTRATION 2–3. *And What Social-studies Needs Might These Children Have?*

an area by its contiguity with other areas. They need to be able to locate areas in terms of distance and direction from where they themselves are located or from any other point on the map or globe. We would provide learning activities that would lead toward mastery of the use of scale and direction to locate areas.

As we use baselines as the points from which to plan further learning, we are using them to meet learners' *developmental needs*.

As we provide learning activities in skills, we shall combine them frequently with learning social-studies content. For example, if our area of social-studies learning is the Benelux countries and our learners need to improve in certain map-reading skills, they would be introduced to or practice aspects of the skills by locating the Benelux countries. This is called *correlated instruction*.

Sometimes a baseline indicates a need for our learners to improve in a skill which cannot, for the moment at least, be feasibly combined with content. It may be because of the nature of the skill, a lack of social-studies time, or lack of suitable instructional materials designed for use with the content area. For example, our learners may need to know how to use a variety of pronunciation keys. The learning activities would be experienced during reading instruction. This is called *supportive instruction*. In this way assessing needs to improve in social studies reveals needs to be met during instruction in other subject areas.

Generally, then, established baselines help us decide how to meet children's immediate study needs and developmental needs in learning the skills essential to social studies. Often instruction will be correlated with content. Sometimes it will have to be supported by instruction in other curriculum areas.

At this point, the question is: which skills do we assess? Most assuredly, the interaction skills should be assessed because they are basic to the effective use of all the other skills. We shall also have to assess the information-intake skills necessary for social studies—observing, listening, and general reading, and, from fourth grade on, the special reading skills which include retention,

location, map and globe, and graph skills. The output skills, oral and written composition, will need to be assessed. How well the children use the intake and output skills will influence the effectiveness of inquiry. And, finally, we shall need to assess children's inquiry skills. What we assess specifically will depend on the age of our learners and, in some instances, the quality of past instruction in the skills.

You may wonder why the idea-use skills, the fourth broad category, have been omitted from the initial assessment. They are not assessed at this point because many of the skills, such as those related to art and creative language, are assessed in other curriculum areas. The idea-use skills, requiring personal projection and commitment such as role playing and simulation, require teacher direction, and whether the children are ready to follow this direction is assessed when the interaction skills are assessed.

In our discussion here, we shall start with the interaction skills because they are so vital to learning in social studies. As we assess these skills, we see how well the children interact and what needs to be done to improve the social climate. Often the assessment itself provides for the beginning of growth in a desirable direction.

ASSESSING CHILDREN'S NEEDS TO IMPROVE INTERACTION SKILLS

Much learning in social studies is the result of interaction. Depending on the instructional purpose, children may be interacting: with the teacher on a one-to-one basis, with the teacher and their peers in group or class situations, or among themselves. Productive interaction demands a positive social climate.

The overall characteristic of a positive social climate is the harmonious adjustment of all the members of the class to one another. This adjustment should be so strong that the class can make transitions easily from one activity to another and tolerate disruptions with equanimity. The teacher and the learners know who they are, what is expected of them, and what they can expect from themselves; they know that expectations vary from person to person.

Establishing a positive social climate is a teaching skill basic to effective classroom administration. Developing this climate is much like growing a fragile plant, the positive seed of which is planted on the first day of school, nurtured during the first three or four weeks, and tended carefully thereafter. Teachers vary in the way they raise the plant.

Some teachers approach the problem by asserting firmly to children what is expected in terms of classroom behavior. The children are told how to respond to the teacher and how to conduct themselves both generally and under a few specified conditions. Through monitoring their behavior carefully, noting particularly commendable behaviors and persisting in demands for acceptable behaviors, these teachers establish a positive social climate. However, the teacher is the key figure in this climate. In grades kindergarten through two, this approach works well. In the later grades it works well when the teacher is present, but when he or she is absent, the climate may disintegrate.

Other teachers prefer to have the children participate in determining the appropriate behaviors for learning and living in a classroom. After a discussion to determine what the behaviors should be, they are listed in a prominent place, perhaps on a bulletin board set aside for that purpose; after each lesson or half day of instruction, the teacher guides the children in using the list to evaluate their behaviors. In this way they identify the behaviors needing improvement and make an effort to improve them at the next opportunity. Whenever problems arise, they are fully discussed, and a new behavior may be added to the list. The teacher and the children continue to cooperate in this way until the behaviors become almost second nature to the children. Of course, a few individuals usually have difficulty. Private teacher-child counseling corrects such difficulties.

This latter approach may be effectively used in grades three through eight. Teachers using it in grades four through eight may combine it with assessing interaction skills. Establishing a positive

social climate and assessing interaction can be mutually supportive in those cases when the social climate is neutral at the onset. Such a climate exists when few children know each other well and every child is forebearing as he or she takes stock of the other members. However, when many children bring hostilities to school, the combination of the two procedures rarely works. In this case, a positive social climate has to be established first.

Expectancies in the Interaction Skills

How well children use interaction skills depends largely on their chronological age, the relationship they have with and among whom they are interacting, the nature of the task to be completed through interaction, the number of persons involved, and how they are organized. We shall focus on chronological age as the key factor during the discussion of expectancies.

Children's growth in interaction skills is gradual, but there are three important milestones. At age nine most children are ready *to learn* to complete a given cooperative task in a small group. By age eleven they are usually able to complete such a task in a group. By age thirteen most children can decide on a task and complete it as a small-group enterprise. Here is what we can expect from the various age groups:

• Five-year-old children are largely dependent on the teacher for effective instructional interaction on a one-to-one basis, or while in a group or class situation. To maintain their interaction for longer than a few minutes, they must be given opportunities to participate by speaking, manipulating materials, performing in unison, and pointing to and touching things on pictures or in displays. They tend to be independent in their relationships with other children. In small groups they can play "house" in an area in which dolls and toy furnishings are provided, they can play "cars" in a sandbox, or they can build with blocks, but much of their play is parallel, that is, each person does what he or she wants with no attempt to get others involved. Teacher intervention is required for them to sequence or organize their play to express social-studies ideas.

• Six, seven, and eight-year-old children share similar characteristics. They are still largely dependent on the teacher for instructional interaction. However, from age six to eight, children grow in being able to listen to each other, to add to what another says, and to agree or disagree with another person's ideas. They also grow gradually in how long they can listen to the teacher or a peer without interrupting. Although they interact better when they can move about and manipulate objects or when their attention is arrested by dynamic materials, they grow in their ability to learn without such supports.

• Six and seven-year-old children can do simple tasks in pairs, but both children have to want to do the task and one of the pair is willing to be led by the other. In groups of three or four they can discuss for two or three minutes some matter closely related to their lives, such as what refreshments to have at a classroom party.

• Eight-year-old children can do tasks in groups of four or five if the teacher explains the task in detail and appoints a competent leader. Usually such groups can work together for as long as twenty minutes before group cohesion begins to disintegrate.

• Although still dependent on the teacher for most of their instructional interaction, most nine-year-olds are ready to learn the leadership and followership roles needed for a small group to be able to complete a task which they understand. However, they require the privilege of being able to decide with whom they are going to work in a group. They are more concerned about this than the task to be completed. This marks the emergence of dependency on peers to get things done and at least partial independence from the teacher.

They usually have some difficulty with understanding democratic leadership behaviors and with accepting roles assigned by the leader, a condition which lasts through the tenth year of age.

• Most ten-year-old children reach the stage where they appreciate opportunities to work with their peers in small groups to complete projects,

but they are still dependent on the teacher for interaction as they gather, organize, and interpret information. They require the privilege of deciding with whom they are going to work. They are capable of working together during a succession of daily study periods to complete a task.

• If they have had a consistent and carefully monitored instruction program in interaction skills, most eleven-year-olds welcome a balance between dependency on the teacher and dependency on their peers, as well as occasional independence, in seeking, analyzing, interpreting, and expressing information. Except in isolated cases, there are few difficulties with leadership and followership behaviors.

Although group membership is still a concern, children of this age begin to realize that the task a group is to complete is an important factor in deciding which group to join. The leadership qualities of certain individuals begins to influence choices for membership in groups.

• Twelve-year-olds are much the same as eleven-year-olds, except that they readily adjust to impromptu grouping, that is, teacher assignment of groups for a discussion to be completed within five to ten minutes. Unfortunately, some children need to be carefully monitored in groups to prevent overdependence on their peers for task or study completion.

• Thirteen-year-old children usually like to study in groups either spontaneously formed or according to members' choices. They are very task oriented, and their groups often become competitive in the quality of the tasks they complete.

When the moment arrives to organize and express learnings at the close of a study, these children can decide on their own group task. However, their task selection must be carefully monitored lest they choose an overly grandiose project requiring unavailable materials or too much time.

The above expectancies are based on the assumption that the interaction skills are carefully taught through the grades. When such a program does not exist, it is possible, for example, that a sixth-grade teacher may find that his or her class is at about the same expectancy as a third grade.

Assessing Interaction Skills

To baseline children's interaction skills, we observe for the occurrence of specific behaviors and record them. When observing kindergarten children, the teacher observes them while they are involved with daily learning activities. This occurs also in the later grades, but the teacher may plan assessment trials in which groups of children participate. Children in the later grades may help in the assessment process by completing self-rating sheets.

The kindergarten teacher observes children as they interact with him or her and what they do when with their peers. Here is a list of behaviors that the teacher may use as a basis for observation. The child:

1. Converses with the teacher informally.
2. Listens and watches attentively when the teacher makes instructional presentations.
3. Waits until verbal or other participation is invited.
4. Signals when ready to participate.
5. Participates verbally or in some other way as directed.
6. Follows directions to go from one area to another.
7. Follows directions to work at or complete a task.
8. Accompanies activity verbally, sometimes as a self-induced part of the activity, sometimes to get another's attention for a moment or two.
9. Takes turns.
10. Shares toys, games, materials, and equipment.
11. Shows items brought from home and tells others about them during sharing time.
12. Settles disputes with others without name calling or physical aggression.

The first seven entries on the list are behaviors expected during direct instruction; the last five are expected when the child is with other children. Each interaction behavior is vital to living and learning in the kindergarten classroom.

To use this list as a guide, the teacher reviews it quickly before observing, observes, and then uses it to help him or her recall what was observed. It may be a summary like this:

10/1/8_. As an individual, B. today was able to take care of herself. When involved in activities, she was quiet and had no difficulties with other children. During instruction she was quiet and attentive, but she did not enter into the more active aspects of participation.

Or the record may be an anecdotal record like this:

10/1/8_. During the activity period B. went to the playhouse. When L. told her she was to be the little girl, she nodded, picked up a doll, went to a corner, sat down, and pretended to feed the doll from a dish. Then she began to take the doll's clothes off. When L. told her she wanted the doll, B. gave it to her and got another. This, too, she fed and began to undress. Then L. called her "to dinner." She paid no attention. When L. called more loudly, she went to the table and pretended to eat. When L. left the table, she did, too. She went to the edge of the playhouse area and quietly watched some other children until the activity period was over.

In the above record we can see that the teacher restricted the observation to what the child was doing in an activity area. Probably the teacher has already observed her carefully during instruction.

Instead of observing and composing a record, the teacher may duplicate the list and use it as an observation checklist. Either during the observation or as soon as possible afterward, he or she marks a check after each behavior observed. When the child's name and the date is written on the checklist, it serves as a record. Or the list may be used to make a class record form as shown in Figure 2–2. Here the teacher marks the date after each behavior observed.

Most teachers find the observation checklist or the class record form to be convenient.

Now that the assessment instrument has been introduced, let us consider when and how to use it.

Usually the kindergarten teacher delays baselining children's interaction skills until the beginning of the third or fourth week of school. By this time most of the children have adjusted to going to school and coping with classroom demands. Those children who are still having diffi-

	Mark	Tom	Henry T.	Joey	Lee				
1. Converses with teacher informally	10/3		10/3	10/3	10/3				
2. Listens, watches during instruction	10/3	10/3	10/3		10/3				
3. Waits invitation to participate		10/3	10/3						
4. Signals when ready to participate		10/3	10/3						
5. Participates as directed		10/3	10/3		10/3				
6. Follows traffic directions	10/3		10/3	10/3	10/3				
7. Follows directions for activity	10/3		10/3						
8. Accompanies activity verbally	10/3	10/3	10/3	10/3	10/3				
9. Takes turns		10/3	10/3		10/3				
10. Shares toys, games, materials, equipment	10/3	10/3	10/3		10/3				
11. Shows and tells during sharing	10/3	10/3	10/3		10/3				
12. Settles disputes without aggression		10/3	10/3		10/3				

FIGURE 2–2. *Class Observation Record.*

culties are obvious. How they interact needs to be baselined with care, so they are the first observed. Then each of the other children is observed in turn.

The usual practice is to select from three to five children to observe each day. To observe does not mean to "shadow" or "tail" a child in the manner of a television sleuth; it means paying particular attention to what the child is doing during the day or during certain activities. In most instances it is easier, and just as reliable, to observe the children first and then to record what was observed. Working with children and keeping track of a class record form or several observation checklists at the same time is an almost impossible task. However, it is necessary to record what has been observed as soon as possible. One careful observation of each child is often adequate, but you may want to observe some children at least one more time to verify your findings.

After all the children have been observed, the teacher reviews the records to make interpretations, the procedures for which will be discussed in a later section. However, as a kindergarten teacher, you can already sense the baselines that may emerge.

To observe the interaction skills of children in the rest of the grades, you may institute a variety of assessment trials. When you use an assessment trial, you present the learners with a discussion opportunity and observe for the occurrence of interaction behaviors.

The discussion is initiated with an open question, or a question to which there is no documentable correct answer. Here are a few examples:

• What do you think you would ask for if someone gave you a wish for anything you wanted? Why that?
• If you were allowed to take only one toy or possession with you on a trip, what would you take? Why?
• If you were allowed ten minutes to do anything you like in school, what would you choose?

One way to control the complexity of the interaction situation is through the questions you devise. For example, "What do you think should be done to make street crossings safer for children?" is much more complex than, "If you were given a choice of visiting any country in the world, what country would you choose?" The first question is closer to reality. Deeper reflection is required to respond to it, and your answer could be challenged by others. The second question is about a situation so improbable in most instances that you could make any response. You might even lie a little or surface a fantasy that others might enjoy as much as you.

Another way to control the complexity of the interaction is to vary the ways that groups are formed. These kinds of groupings will serve your purpose:

• Groups of five to eight learners chosen at random to interact with you and each other in the group.
• Groups of five to eight learners chosen at ran-group on the basis that they appear to like being with each other (as they choose where to sit in the classroom or as they enter or leave the classroom), to interact with you and each other in the group.
• Groups of five to eight learners chosen at random to interact while you assume the role of observer.
• Groups of five to eight learners convened as a group on the basis that they like being with each other to interact while you observe.

In the first two groupings your presence is a supportive factor, and because children in grades one through three usually are unable to conduct discussions by themselves, it is advisable that only these groupings be used with them.

In the third and fourth groupings the presence of friends and acquaintances provides support. Such groupings are used in the fourth and later grades. When you convene each grouping, you initiate the discussion with an appropriate open question. As the learners respond, you will be able to observe the effect of the supportive factor.

In most instances each discussion will require little more than five minutes. Because younger learners will tend to ramble or give an extended response when they have a chance to speak, the discussions may be longer than they are for the older learners.

When you are a member of the group, you will need to record your observations immediately after the discussion. You may wish to use a simple checklist similar to that shown in Figure 2–3.

You could also use a checklist similar to this as you observe a discussion conducted by a group. Indicating the type of discussion and the question asked will help you as you make an analysis later.

Immediately after each discussion, have the learners complete a simple self-rating sheet. Figure 2–4 gives an example. This self-rating sheet, which you may have to read to your learners, is designed for use in grades one, two, and three. Older learners may be more comfortable when marking how

---

Discussion: Teacher guided   **Date** _____

Level: Easy   **Grouping:** Random

Question: If you had all the money you wanted, what would be the first thing you think you would buy?

Group Members	Ready to Respond Immediately	Spoke Freely	Listened to Others Patiently	Needed Encouragement	Would Not Speak

FIGURE 2–3. *Interaction Checklist.*

---

they think and feel on a continuum similar to the following:

Place a mark through the line at the point that best shows how you felt or thought about the following:

1. How did you feel   *Relaxed*   *Tense*
   during the discussion? └──────────────────┘

The use of a self-rating sheet offers two advantages. The first is that it offers another kind of information you need to know. In some cases, it may validate what you observed. The second advantage is that it builds your learners' trust in you. You have involved them in an activity and care enough about them and how they feel to ask them about it. Older learners will respond more readily if you do not require them to sign their self-rating.

Let us see how we might set about making these assessments.

1. *Prepare the materials.* Devise observation checklists and self-rating sheets. You make checklists similar to those shown in this section or you may simplify the task by making an observation checklist usable for all situations. Omit the descriptive material, such as the level and kind of discussion, the form of grouping, and the question itself. Devise a code such as an "A B C D E F G H" in the lefthand corner of the checklist. The key of this code is

A = Teacher guided, easy discussion, social grouping.

B = Teacher guided, easy discussion, random grouping.

C = Teacher guided, hard discussion, social grouping.

D = Teacher guided, hard discussion, random grouping.

E = Group conducted, easy discussion, social grouping.

F = Group conducted, easy discussion, random grouping.

Mark an *X* across the face that shows how you felt or thought about each of the following:

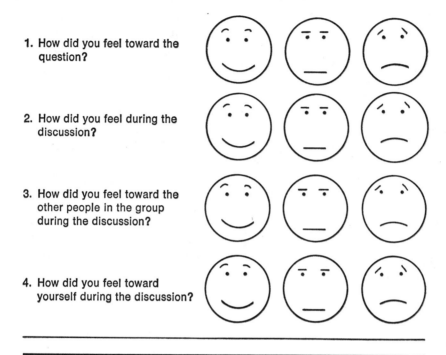

1. How did you feel toward the question?

2. How did you feel during the discussion?

3. How did you feel toward the other people in the group during the discussion?

4. How did you feel toward yourself during the discussion?

FIGURE 2–4. *Interaction Self-rating Sheet.*

G = Group conducted, hard discussion, social grouping.

H = Group conducted, hard discussion, random grouping.

When you use the checklist, circle the letter that stands for the interaction you are going to facilitate. A copy of the key and the questions you are going to ask should be kept in the same folder or box as the checklists.

2. *Compose the questions.* Using the key as a guide, develop a series of questions like this:

a. Suppose that one morning you went out to your backyard and found a baby rabbit nibbling grass there. What do you think you would do? (Suitable for "A" and "E".)

b. Suppose that your mother gave you a dollar to spend in any way you wanted. How do you think you would spend it? (Suitable for "B" and "F".)

c. At the zoo there are signs up all over asking people not to feed the animals. What the visitors feed them sometimes makes them sick. But some people pay no attention to the signs. They feed the animals anyway. What do you think the people at the zoo should do to keep visitors from feeding the animals? (Suitable for "C" and "G".)

d. Sometimes people complain because boys and girls going to and from school run on their grass, step on their plants, and break off their flowers. What do you think should be done to keep boys and girls from doing this? (Suitable for "D" and "H".)

3. *Make provisions for the learners when they are not occupied in a discussion group.* Young learners may be organized to go to learning or play centers, or they may be given several kinds of practice activities to be completed at their desks. Older learners may also be occupied with practice activities to be completed at their desks or in the library. In a departmentalized classroom the learners not occupied will have to be given practice activities. In an open-space classroom, a coteacher may be asked to supervise the learners at practice or study activities in subjects for which he or she is responsible.

4. *Plan the grouping.* Observe the learners as closely as you can for two or three days to determine what associations have been formed. Observing learners on the playground and as they come to or leave school can be helpful. Or you may use a simple sociometric device similar to this in grade three and above:

Make a list of the five persons with whom you would like most to have a classroom discussion. Write the name of the most preferred person first, then the next most preferred, and so on.

This will result in information that will help you form groups in which every learner has at least one preferred person. Random groupings can be made by writing numbers on slips of paper, folding them, and having the learners take them from a box or your cupped hands. They belong to the group whose number is on the paper.

Make a master list of the various groups you plan to work with in each discussion area. Try to change the membership of each group for each ensuing discussion. This may involve a change for one or two persons.

5. *Conduct the assessment trials.*

a. Tell the learners what you are going to have them do and why they are doing it. You might say something like this:

Much of what we do in social studies depends on how we talk and listen to each other. Today I want to find out how well you do these things and how you feel about them.

When I know these things, I will be able to plan lessons to help you to learn.

b. Tell them how the discussions are scheduled and what is expected of them when they are not in a discussion group.

c. Work with as many discussion groups as you can during the period. The learners may complete their self-rating sheets at their desks.

As you can see, each learner could have at least eight different opportunities to react with others to a question. For obvious reasons, it is highly unlikely that you want your learners to suffer so many opportunities. A recommended practice is to plan for three or four.

If your learners are in first, second, or third grades, provide for this sequence:

- Teacher guided, easy discussion, social grouping.
- Teacher guided, easy discussion, random grouping.
- Teacher guided, hard discussion, social grouping.
- Teacher guided, hard discussion, random grouping.

You would not go amiss if you were to omit the last situation for learners in first grade.

If your learners are in grades four and five, provide for this sequence:

- Teacher guided, easy discussion, random grouping.
- Teacher guided, hard discussion, social grouping.
- Group conducted, hard discussion, social grouping.
- Group conducted, hard discussion, random grouping.

If your learners are in grades six, seven, or eight, provide for this sequence:

- Teacher guided, hard discussion, random grouping.
- Group conducted, hard discussion, social grouping.
- Group conducted, hard discussion, random grouping.

These sequences are organized within expectancies. We do not expect learners in grades one, two, and three to cooperate in a discussion without

	Teacher Guided, Easy Discussion, Random Grouping	Teacher Guided, Hard Discussion, Social Grouping	Group Conducted, Hard Discussion, Social Grouping	Group Conducted, Hard Discussion, Random Grouping
Ready to Respond Immediately	‖‖ ‖	‖‖ ‖	‖‖ ‖‖	‖‖ ‖
Spoke Freely	‖‖ ‖‖ ‖‖ ‖‖	‖‖ ‖‖ ‖‖	‖‖ ‖‖ ‖‖ ‖‖ ‖‖ ‖‖	‖‖ ‖‖ ‖‖ ‖‖ ‖‖
Listened to Others Patiently	‖‖ ‖‖ ‖‖ ‖‖ ‖‖ ‖‖	‖‖ ‖‖ ‖‖ ‖‖ ‖‖	‖‖ ‖‖ ‖‖ ‖‖ ‖	‖‖ ‖‖ ‖‖ ‖‖ ‖‖
Needed Encouragement	‖‖ ‖‖	‖‖ ‖‖ ‖		
Would Not Speak	‖‖	‖‖	‖	‖‖ ‖

FIGURE 2–5. *Organized Information about Interaction.*

the support of the teacher. Learners in grades four and five will need support from the teacher from time to time. Learners in grades six, seven, and eight may regard the teacher as a hindrance to their interaction. A teacher-guided discussion is included to provide a get-acquainted experience for both the teacher and the learners.

As you look at the results on the checklists, organize the information as shown in Figure 2–5 (example: fifth grade).

We have used tally marks because they reflect the distribution in a way that is easier to read.

The information on the self-rating sheets should be organized in the same way. We use tally marks after + (relaxed), 0 (neutral) and − (tense). For ease of recording, we could extend the above information sheet as shown in Figure 2–6.

As we analyze the information in Figure 2–5, this is what we discover:

• Readiness to Respond Immediately

This class has six or seven individuals who will respond readily, whatever the kind of discussion.

This may be increased to as many as ten as indicated in the group conducted, hard discussion, social grouping.

• Speaking Freely

More learners tend to speak freely when they are involved in group-conducted discussions.

• Listening to Others Patiently

When the teacher is guiding the group the learners tend to listen more patiently than when they are in group-conducted discussions.

• Needing Encouragement

In group-conducted discussions the learners feel free to participate.

• Not Speaking

There are four or five individuals who do not participate actively. They perform best in the group conducted, hard discussion, social grouping.

This is about what we might expect from a class of learners in fifth grade at the beginning of a school year.

	Teacher Guided, Easy Discussion, Random Grouping	Teacher Guided, Hard Discussion, Social Grouping	Group Conducted, Hard Discussion, Social Grouping	Group Conducted, Hard Discussion, Random Grouping
Feeling about the Question	+ ╫╫ ‖‖ 0 ╫╫ ╫╫ ‖‖ – ╫╫ ‖‖	+ ╫╫ ‖ 0 ╫╫ ╫╫ ╫╫ ‖‖ – ╫╫ ‖	+ ╫╫ ╫╫ ‖‖ 0 ╫╫ ╫╫ ╫╫ ‖ – ‖	+ ╫╫ ‖‖ 0 ╫╫ ╫╫ ╫╫ – ╫╫ ‖‖
Feeling about Discussion	+ ╫╫ ╫╫ ‖ 0 ╫╫ ╫╫ ╫╫ – ╫╫	+ ╫╫ ‖‖ 0 ╫╫ ╫╫ ‖‖‖ – ‖‖‖	+ ╫╫ ╫╫ ‖‖ 0 ╫╫ ╫╫ ╫╫ – ‖‖	+ ╫╫ ‖‖‖ 0 ╫╫ ╫╫ ╫╫ ╫╫ – ╫╫ ‖
Feelings toward Others	+ ╫╫ ‖‖‖ 0 ╫╫ ╫╫ ╫╫ ╫╫ – ╫╫ ‖	+ ╫╫ ‖ 0 ╫╫ ╫╫ ╫╫ – ╫╫ ╫╫	+ ╫╫ ╫╫ ╫╫ ‖ 0 ╫╫ ╫╫ ‖‖ – ‖	+ ╫╫ ‖ 0 ╫╫ ╫╫ ╫╫ ‖ – ╫╫ ‖‖
Feelings toward Self	+ ╫╫ ╫╫ 0 ╫╫ ╫╫ ╫╫ ‖ – ╫╫	+ ╫╫ ‖ 0 ╫╫ ╫╫ ╫╫ ╫╫ – ╫╫	+ ╫╫ ╫╫ 0 ╫╫ ╫╫ ╫╫ ╫╫ – ‖	+ ╫╫ ‖ 0 ╫╫ ╫╫ ╫╫ ╫╫ – ╫╫

FIGURE 2–6. *Information Organized from Self-rating Sheets.*

An analysis of the self-rating sheets (Figure 2–6) reveals the following:

• Feeling about the Question

The nature of the question has its most positive effect when the learners are organized in social groupings and conduct their own discussion. Otherwise it makes little difference.

• Feeling about the Discussion

The learners feel better about discussions when they are group conducted with social groupings.

• Feelings toward Others

The learners feel better toward each other when grouped socially and conducting their own discussion. Teacher guidance or random grouping during hard discussion has a strongly negative effect on feelings toward others.

• Feelings toward Self

The learners generally feel better toward themselves in group-conducted discussions in a social grouping.

This entire procedure, from the planning through the analyses of the results, is thorough. Because students could be adversely affected by closely scheduled discussions, we would schedule assessment trials over a two-week period with a couple of school days intervening between discussions.

If you are a teacher in any grade from four through eight, you may wish to see how your learners interact in a total-class situation, that is, how they interact when grouped at random and during teacher-conducted discussions. Your observation for assessment purposes can occur during the first class meeting. After the learners have introduced themselves or, better yet, conversed in pairs for a minute or two and introduced each other, have them count off to the number of groups desired (in a class of thirty or so learners, they could count off to six to form groups of five). Then you assign a part of the classroom for the learners having the same numbers to meet and have them convene in that area. As soon as they are grouped in their area, present an issue of importance to them in a way similar to this:

I know that the person or persons with whom you sit during class means much to you. I think that it is a good idea for people to sit beside or near those that they particularly like. But all of us know that this sometimes causes problems. For the next five minutes I want you to decide in your groups what you think people sitting with or near their friends will have to remember to prevent problems for themselves and others. I shall tell you when you have a minute left.

The groups begin to discuss the issue. Observe carefully, concentrating on each group for thirty seconds before shifting attention to another group. Look for postures indicating a commitment to the task; you may expect to see a few "loungers" reclining away from the work of a group. You are more concerned with how many of these there are than with who they are. Look also for signs of friction such as shouting, persons standing up to assert dominance, and the like. At the close of the five minutes, regain the learners' immediate attention, have them share their findings and list them on the chalkboard, and guide the class toward closure on those behaviors which they believe will have to prevail in the classroom if people sit with or near those whom they especially like. The learners then choose their seating stations.

If there was no friction, and no more than three or four students refrained from entering the task, you may assume the social climate is already positive. If a couple of incidents of friction did occur, or more than twenty percent of the learners were reluctant to interact with others during a five-minute period, you will need to plan a program to improve social conditions.

The next step in your procedure is to engage the entire class in an open discussion about another issue, perhaps like this:

Now that you are seated where you want to be, let's consider the problem of the new student in the classroom. This usually happens two or three times during the school year, and when it does, what do you think we should do to help that person become a real member of our classroom?

During this discussion, write learners' responses on the chalkboard and continue asking for suggestions until the class begins to repeat itself. Then guide the learners in deciding which of the

items are best. Immediately after the discussion, assign them an independent task such as making a list of the most important incidents that happened to them during vacation. As they do this, make notations on a class roster about which learners respond and which respond most frequently. If at least a third of the learners participate actively, this is as much as can be expected.

If the number of learners who carry most of the discussion is about fifteen percent of the class, the general expectancy for the class is met.

Some teachers use a learner self-rating sheet to help them discover how learners feel involvement with interaction situations. Figure 2–7 presents an example of such a sheet.

The responses to questions 1 and 2 could help you reexamine how you work when conducting a discussion.

The responses to 3, 4, and 5 indicate how learners feel about group-conducted discussions and social grouping.

The responses to question 6 identify learners who like to participate in discussions.

The responses to question 7 indicate roughly how much needs to be done to improve interaction skills as a learning tool.

However you plan to baseline your learners' interaction skills is your choice. The important point is that you do *something*.

Interpreting Your Findings

When you interpret your findings, you follow this line of reasoning: this is the baseline (or where your learners are), and when this baseline is judged against expectancy, their needs are revealed to be this or that. To lead you through this line of reasoning with every piece of data would be a ponderous task. Assuming that it is being followed, we shall focus on needs.

If you are a kindergarten teacher, the results of your observations will identify some children who do not interact to expectancy when you are working with them. This may be because they are not used to taking directions amid so many per-

	Favorable	Unfavorable
1. How do you feel when the teacher begins a discussion with the entire class?	├─────────────────┤	
2. How do you feel yhen you are in a discussion group when the teacher leads it?	├─────────────────┤	
3. How do you feel when you are in a discussion group when a classmate leads it?	├─────────────────┤	
4. How do you feel when you are in a discussion group without any of your friends?	├─────────────────┤	
5. How do you feel when you are in a discussion group with at least one of your friends?	├─────────────────┤	
6. How would you feel (or how do you feel) about being the leader of a group?	├─────────────────┤	
7. How do you feel about discussion generally?	├─────────────────┤	

FIGURE 2–7. *Self-rating Sheet on Discussion Preferences.*

sons, because they are distracted by so many other children around them, or because you appear to be a distant figure on their periphery of consciousness. They need to get to know you. Here are a few strategies to meet that need:

- Greet each child when he or she enters the classroom in the morning. If there is time, talk with them about their appearance, a nice thing they are wearing, something they did well the day before, or whatever, as long as it is positive.
- As often as you can, talk individually with the children during activity periods. Invite them to tell you something about what they are doing. Keep the talk brief to prevent distracting them entirely from the activity.
- Confer individually with them at the end of the school day to discover what they particularly like to do the first thing in the morning in the classroom. This may be a particular activity or it may be a special privilege such as holding the flag during the pledge of allegiance. Promise them an opportunity to do the chosen activity or have the privilege and follow through.
- Bid the children goodbye individually. Make a comment about something they did well during the day.

Children who have much difficulty will need even more of your attention. Perhaps you will have to seat them near you when you are making presentations, or you will need to counsel them individually to set challenges for them. Such a challenge might be as simple as a sketch of a cone on which you draw a scoop of ice cream each time they remember to behave as expected. Keep the sketches in a folder for you and the child to review for progress.

Your observations may identify children who cannot interact to expectancy with their peers. They need to learn the ways of persons who live and work together. Strategies similar to the following help in meeting this need:

- Whenever possible, model expected behaviors, particularly taking turns. Be pointedly courteous, that is, be courteous and give an explanation. Example: "Please excuse me for walking in front of you. I really don't want to make it hard for you to see the picture, but I need to get to the other side to get my pencil."
- Plan an activity in which you tell the children about good interaction behaviors you saw during

the day. Give names as well as what you saw. Encourage the children to do the same.

- Adapting ideas suggested in Chapter 3, encourage the children to role play situations requiring courtesy.
- Present unfinished flannelboard stories about sharing, courtesy, and solving problems with others. Guide the children in discussing what the characters should do.
- Tell simple stories about two sets of characters faced with the same problem. Each set of characters interacts in a different way to solve the problem. Have the children listen to the stories and then decide which set of characters they would rather be and why.

These strategies, with the exception of the first, involve direct instruction. They initiate developmental learning activities requiring careful planning and repetition to be effective. On occasion, similar strategies may be used with children in the later grades.

Let us look now into the interpretation we make in the later grades in which we conduct assessment trials based on discussion.

If you find that during the discussions your learners perform markedly less well or feel much less comfortable when you are leading the discussion than when the discussion is group conducted, or that less than the expected number of learners respond or carry the burden of response when you are leading the discussion, or that self rating sheet items in which teacher guidance is implicit have a less favorable response than those in which the discussion is group conducted, you may want to examine some of your classroom practices more closely.

A good way to do this is to "bug" yourself by turning on an audiotape recorder near your teaching station. Listen to yourself in action. Perhaps you will discover such behaviors as these:

- Overuse of the pernicious "O.K.?" or "Alright?" which means that you have the last word and that you expect the learners to recognize it without question.
- Failure to reinforce or support responses. You accept a correct response as your due and immediately ask another question.
- Throughout the course of a discussion your voice

continues to rise with each question and response you make.

- You sound like a recorded book that can go on for excruciatingly long minutes before you give anyone else a chance to say anything.
- You ask only questions that require short answers.
- You preach and moralize a lot.
- When you try to be humorous it sounds like sarcasm.

In most cases you can improve by deciding which behavior you want to reduce, have it firmly in mind before you start a discussion, remind yourself that no one is perfect, turn on the tape recorder, and conduct the discussion. Listen to it again. Give yourself a reward when you notice improvement.

Something else you might do is put yourself in a good light with your learners. You might want to try some of these:

- Engage each learner in a friendly conversation as soon as you can—in the corridor, on the playground, in the cafeteria, in the classroom after school.
- Ask their advice about bulletin boards and classroom decoration, and then follow it.
- Ask them to help you with worthwhile tasks— putting up a bulletin board, rearranging the books on a shelf, putting up a notice on the chalkboard, etc. Older learners do not mind doing menial tasks if you will join in them. Remember to thank them.

Practices like these can make your learners look forward to being with you and enjoy your presence as you monitor and guide discussions.

Now to the other kind of interpretation in which you consider what you need to include in your instructional program.

If too many learners are unwilling to respond immediately, are unable to speak freely, or need your direct encouragement to become involved in discussions, you will want to provide for them to become deeply involved as frequently as possible in determining their own social-studies purposes and to give heavy emphasis to improving the intake skills. (See the pertinent sections in Chapter 5.) To build their confidence in speaking before others, you may also want to provide for an emphasis in creative dramatics. (See the pertinent section in Chapter 6.)

If learners interrupt each other too frequently, you will provide for role playing explorations of their feelings and behaviors associated with listening attentively, waiting for a speaker to finish before entering or trying to enter the discussion, or coping with an impatient listener. Values clarification related to listening and speaking might also be used. (See the pertinent sections in Chapters 3 and 6.)

If during group-centered discussion the learners tend to ignore the members who need encouragement, you want to provide for opportunities for role playing and may need to include direct instruction in how small groups organize and operate to complete tasks. (See Chapter 7.) The same is true for learners who have difficulty with participating in group-conducted discussions.

If the learners participate poorly in randomly organized groups, provide for role-playing exploration and values clarification about the ways of regarding and acting toward persons with whom one is not well acquainted. (See the pertinent sections in Chapter 3.)

It is in this area of social-studies curriculum planning that we hear the children voice their needs most clearly and urgently. If we make a careful assessment, we hear their voice. Their actions do the speaking.

ASSESSING CHILDREN'S NEEDS TO IMPROVE INFORMATION-INTAKE SKILLS

Secure within a positive social climate, children can direct their efforts toward as full a use of their information-intake skills as their levels of mastery will permit. Their basic intake skills include observing, listening, interviewing, and reading. The younger the learners, the more they will have to rely on observing and listening to acquire information; the older they are, the more will they have to rely on reading.

Because through reading children may independently experience peoples and processes near and far in both space and time, we shall have to scrutinize carefully the extent of their reading skills, particularly those dealing with the special conveyors of social-studies ideas—maps, globes, and graphs—and those which lead toward greater independence in exploration and discovery—the retention and location skills.

We shall consider first the levels of expectancy, or expectancies, throughout the grades, then the modes of assessment, and finally, interpreting our findings.

Expectancies in the Intake Skills

For expository purposes, we shall operationally define expectancies as existing at three levels of mastery: the assisted level, the guided level, and the independent level. (As we discuss expectancies for the information-output skills and the inquiry skills, we shall be using the same levels.)

- *The assisted level.* At this level the learners can perform the skill only when the teacher cues them step by step. They may also need the assistance of their peers to respond to the teacher's verbal cues in the sense that when a child responds, he or she is giving information useful to the entire group. That response may stimulate a response from another child. The group surfaces more ideas than any of the individuals can surface by themselves. The group reacts to all the ideas surfaced to arrive at generalizations.
- *The guided level.* At this level the learners can perform the skill when the teacher identifies or helps them to identify a purpose for using it. The skill may not be applied efficiently. The learners rely on guidance from the teacher to improve their application.
- *The independent level.* When children know skills at this level, they can develop purposes for themselves and meet them through applying the skill with predictable efficiency.

In the charts presented in the text, "A" symbolizes *assisted,* "G" symbolizes *guided,* and "I" symbolizes *independent.*

As you read the charts, you will notice that an

Skills	Grade Levels								
	K	1	2	3	4	5	6	7	8
Observation	A	A	Ⓐ	G	G	G	G	G	I?
Listening	A	Ⓐ	G	G	G	G	G	G	
Interviewing	A	A	Ⓐ	G	G	G	G	G	
Reading		A	A	Ⓐ	G	G	G	G	

FIGURE 2–8. *Levels of Expectancy in General Intake Skills.*

Skills	Grade Levels					
	3	4	5	6	7	8
Note taking	A	Ⓐ	G	G	G	I?
Outlining						
main ideas		A	Ⓐ	G	G	I?
main ideas and facts			A	Ⓐ	G	I?
main ideas and supporting ideas and facts				A	Ⓐ	G	G

FIGURE 2–9. *Levels of Expectancy in Retention Skills.*

expectancy may hold for several successive years. When this occurs, it means that instruction is continuing within that level, but the next level has not yet been met.

Two other symbols are used in the charts. When a symbol is circled, (Ⓐ or Ⓖ), this indicates that during this grade the learners are being helped to make a transition to the next level. Sometimes "I?" is used to indicate that independence may occur for some children but not for all.

Let us consider first the general intake skills: observation, listening, interviewing, and reading. The chart in Figure 2–8 shows the expectancies.

The chart reveals that children in kindergarten are able to acquire information only when the teacher assists in observing (or viewing), listening, and interviewing. The children in grades one are much the same except that they may read with the teacher's assistance (usually only during the last third of the school year). The children in grade two can do guided listening, but they will need assistance with the other intake skills. Children in grades four through eight can perform the basic intake skills by themselves when they have a purpose. Independence in observation skills is not reached until grade eight, if then.

All these expectancies are based on the assumption that articulated, systematic programs have been conducted throughout the grades. When such is not the case, the teacher's assistance may still be needed in the later grades. Carefully conducted programs may bring learners to the independent levels as early as grade eleven. As you can see, growth in these skills is slow and gradual under the best of instructional circumstances.

Specific skills in reading beyond basic word analysis and comprehension skills include the retention and location, or reference, skills.

The retention skills are note taking and outlining as aids to retention. Because they are not taught until children are efficient handwriters and can spell many of the basic English words, we plot the expectancies from grade three on. Because the levels of complexity in outlines are clearcut, we shall use them to indicate expectancies as shown in Figure 2–9. Retention skills do not reach a useful expectancy until grades five and six.

Location skills include using the table of contents and index to locate where to begin reading in a book to find information. Tables of contents occur in first-grade readers. Indexes usually are not provided in textbooks before grade three. Both skills have levels of complexity we can use to indicate expectancies. A table of contents or an index may consist of only primary entries, or a simple list of entries without indentions to accommodate secondary entries. A chapter in a book may be divided into sections. Subentries may occur after a main entry in an index. The expectancies for these skills are shown in Figure 2–10. These useful subskills in reading may be used independently in the later grades.

Other sets of reading skills essential to acquiring social-studies information include globe and map reading and graph reading. Of the two, map and globe skills are the most frequently used. The expectancies are presented in Figure 2–11. We do not expect children to use maps and globes effectively in the classroom until grade six or seven.

Skills	K	1	2	3	4	5	6	7	8
Table of contents:									
chapters only	A	(A)	G	(G)	I	I	I	I	
chapters and sections				A	(A)	G	(G)	I	I
Index									
main entries only				(A)	G	G	(G)	I	I
main entries and subentries					(A)	G	G	(G)	I

FIGURE 2–10. *Levels of Expectancy for Location Skills.*

Children's skill in reading graphs closely follows the development of their mathematics skills. Figure 2–12 presents the usual expectancies.

In graph skills, expectancies occur at all grade levels. Those for younger children reflect readiness expectancies. Useful expectancies at the guided level begin to occur at grade five.

As you can see, expectancies in the intake skills focus largely on reading. In some ways expectancies in listening skills parallel those of reading. However, note-taking skill in listening is generally delayed until after the skills are well established in reading.

Observation and interviewing, as useful as they are in acquiring information, have been so little used that expectancies are difficult to establish. However, because interviewing skill is closely related to a subskill in inquiry, it will be treated when the expectancies for inquiry skills are presented.

The expectancies for the intake skills underscore that young children will need informational resources that they can observe and hear. Older children need guidance from the teacher in the use of many of the skills.

Assessing Intake Skills

As we assess children's intake skills, we shall try to maintain two conditions. The first is that the children sense the purpose of the assessment. Although this condition is less critical for children in grades kindergarten through two, young learners, particularly those in first and second grades, can understand such prologues as these to assessment:

Today I want to see how well you can see and understand things in pictures. It may be a little hard. Just do the best you can. It will help me to know how well you can do it.

Some of you may know a lot about this thing (a globe) that I am holding here. Some of you may know very little. Do not feel bad if you don't. I am just trying to find out what more we need to learn.

Older children, particularly when a paper-and-pencil test is being used, need strong reassurance that the test does not "count" against them but that its purpose is to help the teacher know what to teach.

Skills	K	1	2	3	4	5	6	7	8
Interpreting usual symbols	A	A	A	(A)	G	(G)	I	I	I
Interpreting keyed symbols				A	(A)	G	G	(G)	I
Locating places in contiguity				A	(A)	G	G	(G)	I
Locating places directionally				A	(A)	G	G	(G)	I
Locating places directionally and according to distance					A	(A)	G	G	G
Locating places using latitude and longitude					A	(A)	G	G	G
Computing clock time in distant places						A	(A)	G	G

FIGURE 2–11. *Levels of Expectancy for Map and Globe Skills.*

Skills	K	1	2	3	4	5	6	7	8
Grade Levels									
Picture graphs									
one-to-one correspondence	A	(A)	(G)	I	I	I	I	I	I
one-to-multiples up to 5	A	(A)	G	(G)	I	I	I	I	I
one-to-multiples of 10, 100, and 1000				A	(A)	G	G	(G)	I
one-to-multiples of 10,000, 100,000 and 1,000,000					(A)	G	G	(G)	I
Bar graphs									
one-to-one correspondence	A	(A)	(G)	I	I	I	I	I	I
one-to-multiples of 5 or 10 with interpolation				A	(A)	G	(G)	I	I
one-to-multiples of 100 or 1000					A	(A)	G	G	G
Line graphs									
one-to-one correspondence				A	(A)	(G)	I	I	I
one-to-multiples of 5 or 10					(A)	G	G	(G)	I
one-to-multiples of 100 and 1000						(A)	G	G	G
Circle graphs						(A)	G	G	

FIGURE 2–12. *Levels of Expectancy for Graph-reading Skills.*

The second condition is that the assessment is conducted in such a way that no child feels that he or she knows absolutely nothing. Children feel threatened when they discover that they must start from a learning base of zero. To prevent this, include questions or items to which all the children can respond correctly. Usually these occur during the early part of the assessment.

Assessing Young Children's Intake Skills. The ways that we assess the intake skills of kindergarten children provide a model for procedures to use when assessing the same skills of children in grades one and two.

The first assessment of kindergarteners' intake skills occurs during the first sharing period. You assess the children's tolerance for the activity as well as how well they retain information.

An outstanding characteristic of most kindergarteners is that they like to please, but there are limits to their endurance. As soon as the audience begins to disintegrate—those sitting on the floor will begin to lie down, some will begin to explore their bodies, and a few will begin to visit with their neighbors—note how long the sharing has lasted. The number of minutes transpiring since the beginning of the sharing indicates about how long your learners can stay with most intake activities.

At the close of the period, encourage the children to recall who shared and what they shared. Continue this practice for several periods and call on different children who have not shared to respond. This yields a crude measure of retention as a function of listening and observing.

If you have learners who do not volunteer to respond, do not have the class review the sharing period. Instead, have each of the reluctant respondents whisper in your ear who shared and what they shared.

The next assessment consists of a number of trial lessons directly related to social studies. These are carefully planned lessons based on the usual intake activities and resource materials used with kindergarteners—a selection to be read, a picture to be explored, an object to be examined and discussed, a flannelgram presentation, or a pair of puppets to be listened to as they discuss something. Provide for a series of short lessons, each based on one of the modes of presentation and requiring no less than five minutes but no longer than ten minutes. Plan a good lesson for each. A good lesson consists of a beginning in which children discuss experiences or do some guessing about the topic, and a good lesson communicates a purpose. It provides for a presentation followed by a simple discussion in which the children recall what they experienced through listening and observing.

On successive days teach one of these lessons. Start with those in which children can respond more actively—flannelgrams to be held, discussed, and replaced on the flannelboard, puppets to handle and imitate, or a picture to be approached and pointed to. Save the reading selection for the last.

As you teach each lesson, note how well the children pay attention and willingly enter into the activities associated with it. If the children stayed with the lessons all the way through and responded easily and volubly during discussions, you begin to plan longer lessons.

If the children could stay with some lessons and not with others, note the ones to which they responded most easily. Provide for most of their instruction in social studies to be facilitated by lessons similar to these. At the same time, plan for practice experiences with the skills most needed.

The careful observation of children's use of the intake skills during the sharing period and the conduct of special lessons are also used to assess the skills of children in grades one and two. By the time that they enter these grades, most children are voluble sharers. In many instances when given a few directions, they can conduct the activity themselves. Before the first sharing period conduct a discussion with the children about how they think sharing should be conducted, how they might call on persons to share, and why you would like to hear everyone share at least once. Guide them in discussing the kinds of things that should be shared and develop a schedule for sharing, perhaps five or six children a day, that includes a turn for everyone.

At the close of the sharing period, guide the children in discussing who shared, the sequence of sharers, and what they shared. Note who participates in this activity and the accuracy of their responses. If you wish to make an individual assessment, have the children tell who shared and in what order they shared. Write their names on the chalkboard. Then have each child draw a picture showing what each person shared and circle the picture showing what he or she liked best.

Another way of assessing the quality of listening and observing during sharing is to administer a simple true-or-false test after the last person has shared. Compose the test as you observe the sharing. Immediately after the sharing, provide each child with a yes-or-no answer sheet and administer the test.

When assessing the intake skills of these children, prepare a set of lessons similar to those suggested for kindergarten, but with these differences: plan the lessons to last for fifteen to twenty minutes and include three more different types of lessons. You could use a short film as the informational resource, or a series of study prints, or a filmstrip of twelve to fifteen frames.

As you teach these lessons, observe your learners' reactions in the same way as suggested for observing children in kindergarten.

If you wish, you may assess more precisely how well the children listen and observe. Here is a suggested assessment test to use when assessing observation skills.

---

1. Select a picture filled with detail and activity. A suitable picture found in a magazine is preferable to one obtained at a materials center because it ensures novelty.
2. Prepare a set of four or five questions asking about the actions or functions of things or people in the picture.
3. Compose three titles for the picture. Each should contain a verb, but only one should be accurate.
4. Schedule the children to meet with you on an individual basis.
5. Conduct the assessment in this way:
   a. Without showing the child the picture, engage him or her in a brief, relaxing conversation about the topic of the picture.
   b. Tell the child that you want to find out how well he or she can understand and remember what is seen in a picture. For this reason you are going to let him or her look at a picture about (*the topic of the initial conversation*)

for a little while. Then you will ask some questions about the picture.

c. Allow the child to study the picture for thirty seconds.

d. Turn the picture over and ask the child to name as many things and people as he can remember from the picture. Note the number of items recalled accurately.

e. Ask your prepared questions. Note each correct answer.

f. Tell the child that you have three names for the picture and you want him or her to choose the one that he or she thinks is best.

The results of this test will help you to decide the kind of instructional program you will need to develop. If most of the children can recall less than half of the foreground items and miss half or more of the questions, you know that you will need to give careful assistance when pictures are the main source for information. Do not expect a majority of the children to be able to choose the correct name for the picture. Correct responses to this item will indicate advanced thinking ability.

Assessing listening ability follows a similar procedure. Choose an informational article from a child's encyclopedia (such as *The Golden Encyclopedia*) or from *My Weekly Reader* (from the issue published for use in third grade). The article should be about a hundred words long. Develop at least five factual questions based on the article and a question requiring the child to choose the best title for the article. Introduce the topic of the article in a brief conversation, tell the child your purpose and what is expected of him or her after he or she listens to it, read the article, and ask the questions.

The results of this test will help you to see how well your learners can listen under optimal conditions. If most cannot respond to the questions with better than fifty percent accuracy, you will know that your learners need a program in listening. You will also know that until the program yields results, you will not expect the learners to listen to your reading or audiotaped selections to acquire information.

As you can see, assessing the various skills of children in first and second grade helps you see the kind of assistance you will have to provide to ensure that your learners can acquire and use information.

Assessing the Intake Skills of Children in Third and Fourth Grades. These are the transitional grades in which children are formally introduced to the guided use of skills. This means that soon after a skill is introduced, the teacher will guide the children into using it by giving a purpose and identifying it as the skill to be used. For example, after introducing the rudiments of note taking, the teacher guides the children in reviewing the steps followed in the skill and developing the questions to be answered by note taking. Then the children read and take notes without the immediate assistance of the teacher. Because they are still learning the skill, they share their notes and discuss their accuracy after reading. This is another aspect of teacher's guidance.

When children enter these grades, most of them are fluent in oral language. They can speak in sentences and maintain the point of discourse. However, as a teacher of children in one of these grades, you would assess these skills while you were assessing their interaction skills, as discussed in an earlier section.

At this point, many children can and will read by themselves. You will assess their skills to see how much assistance you will have to give them to help them use the materials available to them. Here is a suggestion for an assessment test.

---

1. Using the textbook provided for your class, open it at a point about a quarter through it. As closely to this point as possible select a factual passage about a hundred words in length. The following is an example.

DEEP-SEA FISHING IN JAPAN

There are many fleets of deep-sea fishing vessels in Japan. They leave the harbors for three-month fishing trips in the Pacific Ocean. Most of the fleets are owned by large companies.

The fleets do not all catch the same kinds of fish. Some catch only salmon. Others catch only tuna, crab, or whales.

The fleets catching salmon or crab include a factory ship. Every day the fishing boats unload their catch at the factory ship. Workers on this ship clean and can it.

About three-fifths of Japan's fish supply is caught by the deep-sea fishing fleets. The rest of the needed fish is caught by smaller fishing boats that stay near the coast.

2. Develop a set of questions about the factual passage. These questions should prompt children to recall facts, make inferences, and define vocabulary. Here is a list of questions developed from the passage given above:

Factual Questions

a. For how long does a fishing trip last for a Japanese deep-sea fishing fleet? (three months)
b. Who owns the fleets? (large companies)
c. What kinds of fish do they catch? (salmon, tuna, and crab, but accept also whales)
d. What is done on a factory ship? (fish are cleaned and canned)

Inference Questions

a. Why are the deep-sea fishing fleets important to the Japanese people? (because they catch three-fifths of the fish needed)
b. Why do you think there are so many deep-sea fishing fleets in Japan? (because they eat a lot of fish)
(*This kind of question is sometimes called an interpretation question because it goes somewhat beyond the facts offered.*)
c. Why do you think salmon and crab are canned very soon after they are caught? (because they spoil quickly)

Vocabulary Questions

a. What is a *vessel?* (a ship or boat)
b. What is a *harbor?* (a place where boats and ships can come to shore, are kept or tied up, etc.)
c. What is a *fleet?* (a group of ships)
d. What does *deep-sea* mean? (out in the ocean where the water is deep)
e. What does the word *coast* mean in what you have just read? (the edge of land along the ocean)

3. Arrange a schedule for meeting with each child individually.
4. When you begin the assessment, inform the children that you are going to have them read something to see how well they can understand and remember what they read.
5. Conduct the assessment.
   a. When each child comes to you, engage him or her in a brief, relaxing conversation about the topic of the reading. (In this case, perhaps about their experiences with fishing, whether they would like to go fishing on the ocean, etc.)
   b. Open the book to the selected passage. Ask the child to read it silently and inform him or her that you are going to ask some questions about it after the reading.
   c. After the child reads, ask the questions and record the accuracy of responses.

The assessment above reveals the following:

1. Whether the children can read silently.
2. Whether they can recall facts.
3. Whether they can infer and interpret what they read.
4. Whether they need assistance with vocabulary.

If many of your learners cannot read silently, you will need to consult an authoritative book on reading methods for ideas on how to organize instruction to meet the need.

If many of your learners cannot respond with at least 65 percent accuracy to the factual and inference questions as a combined list, they will need much assistance when using the book. They may have to be divided into small groups of two or three in which able readers give assistance to less-able peers. You may need to read the book orally as they follow. You may prefer to audiotape portions of the book to which they can listen for information. It will be advisable for you to use as many other informational resources as you can find—series of study prints, filmstrips, resource persons, films, and the like.

As you analyze the results of the assessment focused on vocabulary, you may discover that you will need to develop vocabulary carefully before the children read. If you have many learners who cannot respond with 75 percent accuracy to the vocabulary items, the message is clear.

You may prefer to conduct this assessment with the entire class. If so, duplicate the passage and the questions for class distribution. All the questions, except those asking for interpretational inferences (to which the children will write responses as best they can), should be converted to multiple-choice items (one accurate response from three offered). Give the children the passage to read silently. As they finish, take the reading passages and give them the list of questions to answer.

Most likely this procedure will be frustrating to children in third grade, but those in fourth grade usually can handle it.

Another way of assessing whether children in grade four (and above) can use the basic textbook is to prepare a cloze test from textbook material. This test requires children to supply words deleted from a page of text. Recommendations about how frequently words should be deleted vary. However, for our purposes, the deletion of every fifth word is acceptable. Here is how you prepare the test:

---

1. Select a prose segment of about 300 words in length from somewhere within the first half of the book. Usually the beginning of the first lesson in a chapter serves best.
2. Place a check at the beginning of every fifth word and type the selection, omitting the checked words and replacing each with a blank. All blanks should be the same length and long enough to accommodate handwritten words.
3. Distribute the tests to the children and direct them to write in the blanks the words they think best fit in the blanks. Ask them to spell as well as they can, but assure them that they will not be penalized for misspellings. Inform them that if later in the test they think some of the words they wrote earlier are wrong, they may change them.
4. Score the test by marking through each word that is not the same as the one deleted originally.
5. Count the number of errors, and use the following scale:
   • If the child can fill the blanks with 60 percent (or better) accuracy (36 words or more in a 300-word segment), he or she can read the book independently.
   • If the child can fill the blanks with at least 40 percent accuracy (24 to 35 words in a 300-word segment), he or she will need extra help with social-studies vocabulary and will need well-defined purposes for reading to be able to use this book to acquire information. This is the instructional level.
   • If the child achieves less than 40 percent accuracy (23 or less words in a 300-word segment), the book is too difficult for him or her to use to acquire information. Such a child will need well-defined purposes for listening to a reading of the book to acquire information, or a resource easier to read will have to be provided.

The above test is generally too difficult for children in grade three and lower.

If your learners' skills in reading reveal serious limitations, you may wish to assess their skills in listening and observation as suggested for use with children in grades one and two. Use an excerpt from the basic textbook adopted for use in that grade for assessing listening.

Your learners' map and globe skills will require that you assist them, but you may wish to know what background they have. An easy way to do this is to convene the children in small groups to discuss what a map and globe are, what is represented on them, and what they are used for. What you will be conducting is an *assessment discussion.* This means that you will be asking such questions as "What is this?" "What do you think these lines stand for?" "What does this color mean?" etc. *You will listen to the responses receptively, but you will not be indicating whether responses are right or wrong.* In other words, you will simply facilitate the children's telling you what they know. You will be able to see what their concepts about the globe and maps are.

Generally, as you assess the intake skills of children in grades three and four, you are trying to see how ready they are for the transition from using skills with teacher assistance to using them with teacher guidance.

Assessing the Skills of Children in Grades Five through Eight. In these grades children gradually achieve more independence in the use of the various skills, but with the exception of gifted children, we do not expect them to reach a level of independent mastery where they can select a problem or issue or explore it fully by themselves. And we may discover some children, perhaps as late as eighth grade, who will need a careful reintroduction to certain skills. In short, our assessment will yield a wide range of abilities.

In these grades most information is acquired through reading. Depending on your district or school's textbook-adoption policy, you may have several textbooks to use. You may have a basic textbook for each child, a supplemental textbook for less-able children, and another for children who are better-than-average readers. You will want to ensure that each child has an informational resource that he or she can use.

Teachers have frequently tried to assign these textbooks on the basis of children's reading-grade placement scores. This does not work well for a variety of reasons, the most important being that the skills required for social-studies reading are often measured inadequately in the achievement test. It is strongly suggested here that you use a *reading inventory* developed from the textbooks you have to use.

A reading inventory is a test which reveals the adequacy of a child's skills to cope with the text presented in the book. In the previous subsection, as we dealt with the textbook passage about deep-sea fishing in Japan, you were introduced to the structural aspects of a reading inventory—a passage selected from a textbook from which a list of factual, inference, and vocabulary questions are developed. To prepare your inventory, you will construct a similar test for each textbook. You may administer the tests individually, testing each child with the easiest passage first. If a child has difficulty with this test, you will not subject him or her to the rest of the tests. The same would be true for a child who could barely meet the criteria of accuracy. But, if a child meets the criteria easily, you

would administer the next test, and on to the final test if he or she meets the criteria easily.

As time consuming as it is, this procedure is more humane than administering the tests in written form to the entire class. However, if you wish to administer it in this way, arrange to administer it on three successive days. Correct the test and use the results to determine who should take the next test on the following day.

Another way to assess for children's needs in general-reading skills is to use the cloze test discussed in the previous section. If you have several textbooks available for use, make a cloze test for each and use the results to place children in them.

Be prepared for the disquieting discovery that some of your learners cannot use the easiest book, that most of them can use it, and only a few can use the other two books. Here is what you can do about it:

- If there is another classroom at your grade level in the school, schedule your social-studies period at a time when you can borrow textbooks from that classroom.
- Plan to give more direct assistance to your learners when they are reading to acquire information. This may include more careful development of vocabulary, developing precisely stated purposes for reading, reading aloud, etc.
- Seek other informational resources more suitable to your learners' needs.

We expect children in these grades to be more independent in locating needed information. It is likely that they will have been introduced to these skills in the earlier grades, but we shall need an exact picture of what they can do. Here you have a choice of assessment procedures. You may use either assessment discussions with small groups or a specially devised test.

If you plan to use an assessment discussion, here is a way to conduct it:

1. Form the class into groups of five or six. Convene each group separately while the rest of the class does a paper-and-pencil task of some sort.
2. Have the members of the group bring their basic textbook with them. As soon as they are

seated, inform them that you would like to see how well they can locate information in a book and ask a sample question the answer for which is in the book. Let us imagine that our book is about world cultures. The question: "At what occupation do most of the Turkish people work?"

3. Challenge and build upon responses like this:

Child: You could look in the table of contents.

Teacher: Why would you look there?

Child: Because it has a list of the chapters.

Teacher: Do the rest of you agree with that? Is that what a table of contents lists? You agree? Is that all it lists?

Child: I think that there is a page number after each chapter title.

Teacher: How migh, we check that out?

4. After the children show that they know where a locational aid is in the book and find the answer to the question, give each child a separate question on a card to determine on what page he or she would begin reading to find the answer. Observe each child carefully.

5. After the children finish dealing with one locational aid, ask them whether they know of another. If they do not, chances are that they do not know of it. In this case the other aid is the index. If they know about the index, repeat steps 3 and 4.

As a result of the assessment discussion, which also provides an immediate opportunity for performance, you know who can use locational aids and who cannot. If many of your learners do not know how to use them, you may wish to develop an instructional program in the use of the aids and use the learners who know the skills as teaching assistants.

If you wish to use an assessment test, one that is easy to construct and monitor, it should consist of a dozen questions, each written on a separate card. The questions are based on a textbook which every child in the group has. Convene the children in groups of five or six. Give each a question card, ask them to open their books to the table of contents, and use it to decide on what page they would begin reading to find the answer to the question.

Observe the children carefully as they perform this task. After they finish working with the table of contents, give each of them a new question card, ask them to open their books to the index, and to decide on which page they would begin reading to find the answer. Again observe carefully.

This test will yield results similar to those obtained with the assessment discussion.

Or you may prepare a paper-and-pencil test. Such a test might yield more specific information about your learners' needs. For example, if you were to use a table of contents similar to the following:

CONTENTS

you could ask easy questions like these:

On what page would you start reading to find:
1. What kinds of farming are done in Turkey?
2. What holidays they have in Turkey?
3. How Turkey began?

and hard questions like these:

On what page would you start reading to find:
4. What the Turkish people do during their free time?
5. How many years Turkish children go to school?
6. Where the tallest mountains are in Turkey?

The hard questions require a knowledge of word meanings: that what a people does during *free time* is associated with *sports and recreation,* that *school* is associated with *education,* and that *mountains* is associated with *land.*

When you construct an assessment test, you should base it on the table of contents and index given in the textbook the children are to use. Most likely they will contain main entries and subentries similar to those used in this book that you are now reading.

If you wish, you may construct the assessment test to go beyond indicating the page where one would begin reading to locate information. Your test may require that they find the answer to the question as well. If you devise such a test, observe your learners carefully to see how well they skim through section titles and subheadings to find the best place to read carefully.

How you plan to assess your learners' skills with locational aids is your choice.

The learners in these grades are gradually developing map and globe literacy. To know specifically what they need to learn, you may again choose between the assessment discussion with small groups or the paper-and-pencil test to be administered to the class. To help you know the kind of paper-and-pencil test that you might use, as well as how you might conduct an assessment discussion, see Figure 2–13.

Questions you might ask about the map presented in Figure 2–13 are:

1. Parts of two continents are shown on this map. What are they?
2. What is the capital city of Spain?
3. What four other cities besides Paris are shown in France?
4. What is the name of the island that almost touches Italy?
5. If you flew west from Bern, Switzerland, what country would you cross?
6. If you flew north from Rome, Italy, what other Italian city would you cross?
7. If you wanted to fly from London, the United Kingdom, to Antwerp, Belgium, in what direction would you fly?
8. About how far is it from Paris, France, to Rome, Italy?

9. About how far is it from Dublin, Ireland, to Liverpool, United Kingdom?
10. Write the names of the three countries crossed by the 40° parallel of North Latitude.
11. Write the names of the three European countries crossed by the 5° meridian of East Longitude.
12. What city lies at 46° North Latitude and 13° East Longitude?

The first four items above require an interpretation of the symbols often found on maps. Items 5, 6, and 7 probe into the learners' skills with directions. Items 8 and 9 require the use of the map legend for the meaning of symbols and for the scale in measuring distances. Items 10, 11, and 12 require an understanding of latitude and longitude.

13. If it is 6:00 AM in the United Kingdom, what time is it in Vienna, Austria?
14. If it is 4:00 AM in the United Kingdom, what time is it in Iceland?

These last two items require an understanding of the use of longitude to determine clock time.

This assessment test is a short-answer test. If you preferred, you could use a multiple-choice test based on the same skill and knowledge. If you wished to use an assessment discussion, you would have the children discuss ways of locating places on the map and explaining what the various features on the map meant.

The results of the assessment would indicate the subskills you would need to teach. Of course, the needs would also have to be assessed in terms of the globe and maps available in the classroom and textbooks.

If your learners are scheduled to study economic conditions, it is likely that their textbooks will contain picture graphs. Use an example of each to develop an assessment test or to conduct an assessment discussion. Or, if the textbooks contain mostly picture graphs, you might construct a graph-reading inventory similar to what is presented in Figure 2–14. If a learner can answer all the questions correctly in subtest A, he has a workable idea of what a picture graph is. The rest of

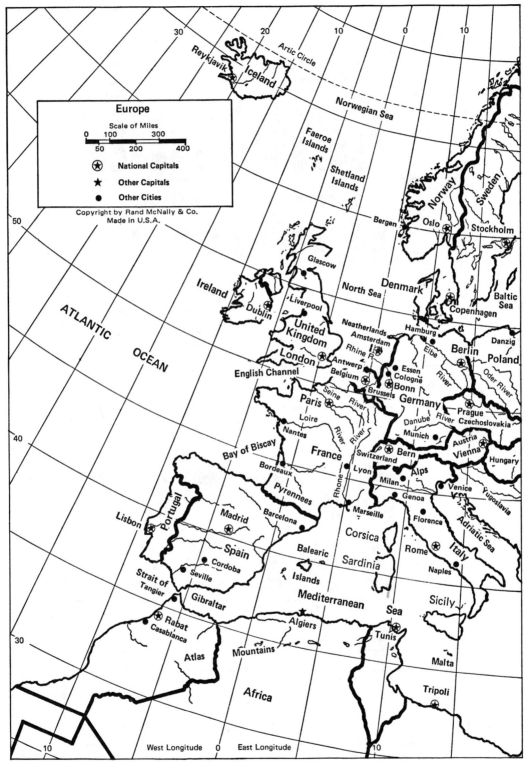

FIGURE 2–13. *Sample Map Test.*[1]

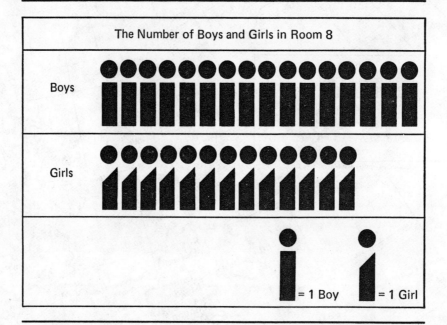

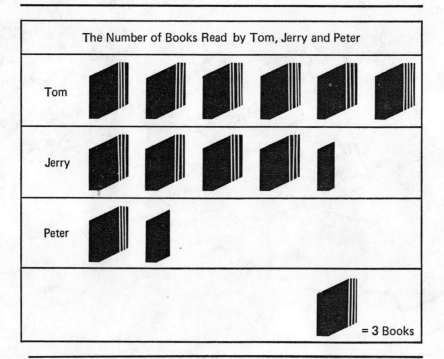

FIGURE 2–14. *Picture Graph-Reading Inventory.*

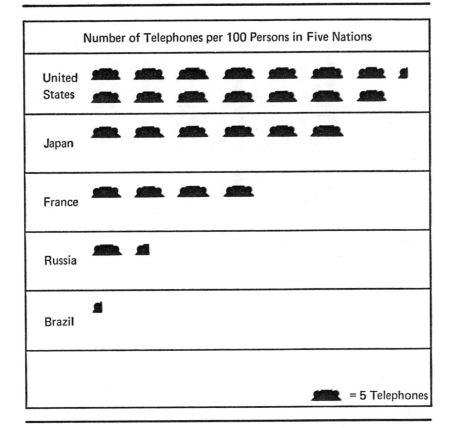

Number of Telephones per 100 Persons in Five Nations

= 5 Telephones

SUBTEST A

1. What does this graph tell about?
2. How many boys are there?
3. How many girls are there?
4. Which of the following sentences says what the graph tells us?
    a. There are more boys than girls in Room 8.
    b. There are more girls than boys in Room 8.
    c. There are both boys and girls in Room 8.

SUBTEST B

1. What does this graph tell about?
2. Who read the least number of books?
3. Who read the most books?
4. How many books did Jerry read?
5. Which of the following sentences says what the graph tells us?
    a. The three boys read a lot of books.
    b. Some boys read faster than others.
    c. Of the three boys, Tom read the most books.

FIGURE 2–14. (*Cont.*)

Number of Persons per Doctor in Five African Countries

Zaire

Kenya

Algeria

South Africa

Egypt

= 1000 Persons

SUBTEST C

1. What is this graph about?
2. Which nation has the most telephones per 100 people?
3. Which nation has the least telephones per 100 people?
4. How many telephones are there per 100 people in Russia?
5. Which of the following sentences tells the idea expressed in the graph?
   a. The people in the five nations have telephones to use.
   b. There are many telephones in use today.
   c. Of the 5 nations, the United States has the most telephones.

SUBTEST D

1. What is this graph about?
2. Which country has the smallest number of persons per doctor?
3. Which country has the largest number of persons per doctor?
4. How many persons per doctor are there in Kenya?
5. Which of the following sentences tells the idea expressed in the graph?
   a. Of the five countries, Egypt has the most doctors.
   b. Of the five countries, Egypt provides the best health care.
   c. Of the five countries, Egypt has the most people per doctor.

FIGURE 2–14. (*Cont.*)

the subtests are based on levels of mathematical skills. The first level at which a learner answers a question incorrectly is his instructional level. You plan instruction to begin at this level.

Because they are useful to facilitate both the intake and output of social-studies ideas, you should assess note-taking and outlining skills in grades five through eight. Again, either an assessment discussion in small groups or an assessment test may be used. If you use an assessment discussion for note taking you will need material similar to that shown in Figure 2–15.

After a brief discussion about department stores and their uses, and informing the children that you want to see what they know about note taking, center their attention on the note card represented on the material and encourage them to tell you how they would use it to take a note to answer the question: "Where did people buy fine things long ago?"

After they have decided how the note card should be completed, have them discuss what an outline is and how the material would be outlined.

As the children deal with note taking, note whether they remember to write the question on the note card, whether they are aware of paraphrasing as opposed to copying entire sentences and paragraphs, and whether they see the need to indicate the source of the information.

As they deal with outlining, note whether they know about the order of an outline and about supporting ideas.

The material given above could very easily be used in constructing a test. Prepare the selection to be read on a separate sheet. Then prepare a response sheet. The top half of the sheet contains these directions above the note card:

The rectangle below is a notecard. Use it to write a note as an answer to this question:

Where did people buy fine things long ago?

You will find the information you need on the reading sheet.

The bottom half of the sheet contains these directions:

Write an outline of the ideas given on the reading sheet. Write on the rest of this sheet. You may use the back if you need it.

The results of this assessment may indicate a need for instructional emphasis for these skills as aids in retaining and understanding what is read, and in gathering information and organizing it for reports.

When preparing your assessment schedule in grades five through eight, your first concern will be to see how well the children can read the material presented in the textbook. Your second concern will be to see how they can use the maps, diagrams, and other graphic materials in the textbook. The assessment of location and retention can be delayed until the children are well into their first instructional unit in social studies.

Interpreting the Results of Intake-skills Assessments

The results of intake-skills assessments indicate the baselines we use to make decisions about the kinds of intake activities to provide for children's immediate study needs as they begin the program in social-studies instruction and their developmental needs to reach higher levels of performance. We must decide also which learning activities are to be correlated with social studies instruction and which are to be taught separately in supportive instruction. Our decisions reflect our interpretations of the assessments.

Here are a few examples of interpretations.

Ms. X has just completed the intake-skills assessments of her kindergarten class. These are the baselines she has discovered: her learners are capable of paying attention and recalling ideas only when they observe, listen, and participate in learning activities in which puppets and flannelgrams are the conveyors of information.

To meet the children's immediate study needs in social studies, she has decided to use these activities for intake purposes during the first unit of instruction, "Families." She searches through her materials for useful puppets and sequences of flannelgrams and finds

TRAVELING DEPARTMENT STORES

A thousand years ago there was no such thing as department stores. Yet people knew about and wanted fine things. To buy them they went to a fair.

A fair in those days was a special traveling market. The merchants, or businessmen, traveled in a train of animal-drawn wagons and pack animals. When they arrived at a town or city, they would unload their wagons and animals and set up their tents. There they displayed what they had to sell. The people in the towns and cities came to buy. So did the people from the countryside for miles around. If there were many people, the fair would stay for as long as a month. If there were only a few people, the fair would stay for only a few days.

Each train of merchants was like a parade. At the front was the flag carrier. The flag was the trademark of the train. With him rode the leader of the train. Soldiers to protect the train walked and rode horses beside the wagons and pack animals. Easily seen as it passed along the roads, word about the train was heard quickly through the countryside.

The people who had money to spend flocked to the fair as soon as it was ready for business. Poor people who just wanted to see fine things also came. The coming of the traveling department store was an important event for the whole community.

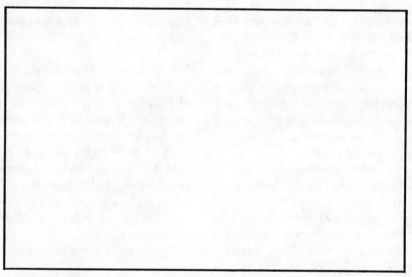

FIGURE 2–15. *Study Model for Note Taking. Book Title:* Buying and Selling Long Ago *(page 37).*

that she will have to construct more of these materials to convey ideas about families.

To meet the children's developmental needs in intake skills, Ms. X plans a program of supportive activities which includes her sharing of interesting pictures at the beginning of each sharing period and a learning center where the children observe a picture and mark the items they see therein on a special practice sheet. Toward the middle of the five-week unit she will correlate skill learning with content learning by using several series of study prints about family life.

Mr. Y, a teacher of third grade, has just finished the intake-skills assessment of his class. As he reviews the results, he discovers these baselines: during his trial lessons with puppets, a filmstrip, and listening to a reading, the class responded so well verbally that every lesson lasted longer than he had intended. When he inventoried their reading skills in the textbook, he found that six children could read it independently, that sixteen children could read it at the instructional level, and that the remaining seven could not read it. When he conducted assessment discussions on location skills with the six able readers, he discovered they knew little about these specialized skills.

Mr. Y has a wide latitude in his choice of learning activities to meet his learners' immediate study needs in intake skills as they study about American Indians. He will have to make some adjustments for the six capable readers and the seven slow readers. For the latter, he audiotapes the necessary portions of the textbook to be heard via a listening post. For the former, he will provide library books about Indians. He intends for the capable readers to validate what is in their textbook by consulting other books.

To meet his learners' developmental needs in intake skills, Mr. Y is planning correlated learning activities with emphasis on staying with the facts discovered during reading and inferring from them. During reading instruction, he will provide supportive instruction dealing with determining the meaning of new words from context clues. He has planned a special program for the capable readers in which they will be introduced to locational skills.

Ms. Z, a social studies teacher in a middle school, is reviewing the baselines for intake skills resulting from a recent assessment of one of her seventh-grade classes. This is what she discovers: all except four of her learners can read the basic textbook at either an instructional or independent level as shown by the results of a reading inventory and a cloze test. During assessment discussions with small groups she discovered that only the very able readers knew how to use a table of contents or an index to locate information. When she gave paper-and-pencil inventories of map and graph-reading skills, she discovered that she had only one learner who could read these accurately at an advanced level.

The first unit of instruction is about "International Economic Organizations in the World," a study which will require advanced levels of skill in map and graph reading. Ms. Z has decided to delay the teaching of this unit for at least two weeks. During this time she will guide the class in supportive instruction in map and graph reading. Later she will provide correlated learning activities as the children are required to read maps and graphs for information. The learner who already knows how to read maps and graphs will be given a choice between being a teaching assistant or doing an independent study requiring the use of his skills.

When she begins the social-studies unit, Ms. Z plans to use as many transparencies, films, and filmstrips as possible, the content of each to be validated whenever possible by reading in the textbook and information sheets. The latter will provide for the needs of the four less-capable readers, but in a special way. The information sheets will be distributed to the entire class with the understanding that they are to be read first. In this way, the less-able readers will be able to use whatever skills they have without being singled out for special treatment. Also, Ms. Z is going to organize the class into reading partnerships to help the less-able readers have access to the textbook. She feels that these strategies will meet the immediate study needs of her learners.

In the meantime, Ms. Z will discuss the special needs of the less-able readers with their English teacher and the reading teacher to whom they report each day for corrective instruction. Perhaps together they will be able to develop a concerted approach to the problems of the poor readers.

In the three examples above we considered three different situations, each reflecting a deep concern about learners' intake skills in social studies. It is predictable that learning will occur in social studies and that intake skills will be improved.

ASSESSING CHILDREN'S NEEDS TO IMPROVE INFORMATION-OUTPUT SKILLS

Children's information-output skills include speaking, writing, and using art media to express what they have retained from information intake. Of these, speaking is the most frequently used, although it is the most fragile of all the skills because its use depends so much on the social climate. A negative social climate discourages or stultifies oral expression. We may establish a positive social climate and still find some learners fearful of saying what they know and think within the hearing of others.

To a certain extent, the exercise of writing and art medial skills is also influenced by the quality of the social climate. Usually, stories, reports, pictures, posters, and the like are shared among learners to validate and reinforce learning. A negative climate discourages the sharing, and ultimately the production, of personal expression.

After ensuring the best social climate we possibly can, we assess children's output skills. Our concern is for children to be able to communicate their ideas accurately and clearly. Inadequate output skills may hinder children from expressing what they really know and understand. Furthermore, many children do not know what they know until they do something with the information they have acquired. They need to compose a picture, poster, model, play, poem, story, speech, or report. They may also need to solve real or academic problems in which their information is vital in seeking solutions, and their previously produced expressions help them to recall the information. In these ways, the output skills are essential to children's learning in social studies.

Just as reading is the most relied upon skill for intake, so is language expression for output. Basic to language expression is the structure of sentences, paragraphs, reports, stories, and poems as conveyors of thought. The ancillary skills of handwriting and spelling are also essential.

During our discussion we shall consider expectancies, modes of assessment, and interpreting the results.

Expectancies in Output Skills

We shall focus primarily on language-output skills. The younger the children, the greater the use of oral language (and art media); the older the children, the greater the use of written language.

The usual expectancies for oral language are shown in the chart presented in Figure 2–16.

Most young children are able to speak in complete sentences when they enter school to attend kindergarten, but they are not sure about when to use them. Frequently they need assistance to generate more than one sentence, and when they use

Skills	Grade Levels								
	K	1	2	3	4	5	6	7	8
Speaking complete sentences	Ⓖ	I	I	I	I	I	I	I	I
Giving multi-sentence responses	Ⓐ	Ⓖ	I	I	I	I	I	I	I
Staying on the point	Ⓐ	G	Ⓖ	I	I	I	I	I	I
Giving a report consisting of one paragraph				Ⓐ	G	Ⓖ	I	I	I
Giving a multi-paragraph report					Ⓐ	Ⓖ	I	I	I

FIGURE 2–16. *Levels of Expectancy for Oral Composition Skills.*

several sentences in a response, they tend to get off the point. Assistance from the teacher is again needed. However, by the time they reach second grade, most can give an oral report consisting of four or five sentences related to the topic, but the sentences may be out of order.

By the time children are halfway through third grade, most can give a simple oral report consisting of several sentences with a topical sentence at the beginning or end when assisted by the teacher. Independence is not reached until grade six.

By the middle of fourth grade, most children can give a multiparagraph oral report when assisted by the teacher. Independence is usually reached at grade six.

As social-studies teachers, we are particularly concerned about what children can be expected to do with expressing themselves in written sentences, paragraphs, and reports. The usual expectancies are presented in the chart in Figure 2–17.

As we view the chart, we can see generally that young children's use of written language output is largely teacher assisted. This means that the teacher will prompt the writing and monitor it carefully, giving much aid in spelling, sometimes reminding children about the formation of letters and spacing between letters and words, and seeing that capitalization, punctuation, and usage rules

Skills	Grade Levels								
	K	1	2	3	4	5	6	7	8
Composing sentences	A	A	(A)	G	(G)	I	I	I	I
Composing paragraphs	A	A	A	A	(A)	G	G	(G)	I
Composing three-part reports				A	(A)	G	G	(G)	I
Composing longer reports						A	(A)	G	G

FIGURE 2–17. *Levels of Expectancy for Written Composition Skills.*

are observed. The second grade is the transitional grade in which children begin to compose sentences on teacher demand. However, they usually need continued help with spelling. Frequently, prior to written composition, the teacher guides the children in preparing a list of needed words recorded on the chalkboard or a chart. This practice often continues until grade five or six.

Grade four, when children's handwriting skills have developed to the point that they can write legibly at a rate almost commensurate with their thinking, and when they can spell most of the basic words of language, is the transitional grade for organizing ideas in paragraphs and paragraphs into reports.

During grades five, six, and seven, children can write paragraphs on demand, but teacher guidance will still be needed to ensure the cohesion and proper sequence of sentences in paragraphs, the use of topical sentences in paragraphs, and the functions of the various paragraphs in the three-paragraph report. Independence in paragraph and short-report writing usually does not occur until grade eight.

The transition into the composition of long reports occurs in sixth grade. The focus is usually on the factual middle of the report in which several aspects of information are covered in two or more paragraphs. Guidance in determining and sequencing subtopics in reports is usually required throughout grades seven and eight.

Social-studies teachers are expected to be competent in language skills themselves, but they are not usually expected to be skilled in construction or the various art skills. Often they provide opportunities for children to explore their use of these special skills. This is particularly true in grades kindergarten through two.

The children in these grades are often willing to try to express their ideas in the same media as they are conveyed to them—through the use of pictures, flannelgrams, and puppets. Their liking for play and construction with boxes, blocks, and miniatures can also be used.

Children in grades three through six are often willing to use their limited skills in drawing pictures, but some are sensitive about their products and would prefer to use oral or written language skills.

Beginning at grade six, children frequently like to construct items which have influence on their lives—posters, signs, billboard displays, wall banners, and bumper stickers.

Personal preference is a significant factor in determining which output skills are to be used. As we consider expectancies, we take this into account while maintaining a strong responsibility for guiding children in improving language skills.

Assessing Output Skills

Assessing Young Children's Output Skills. The same modes of assessment focusing on oral language are used in grades kindergarten through second.

Actually, as you assess your learners' interaction and intake skills, you may also assess their output skills. As you observe children's behaviors during interaction and intake assessments, you also take into account the children's output skills. However, if you find such comprehensive observation difficult to manage, you may arrange for assessment situations in which you focus on the children's output skills.

The first assessment of young children's output skills with oral language may occur during the sharing period. As each child shares or responds to what another child has shared, note particularly the need for children to learn to speak in sentences and to stay on the point.

Observe for the same skills when you conduct assessment trials with lessons built around the use of an object, puppets, a picture, or whatever. Also, at the close of the lesson, encourage the children to tell what they remember from the lesson. This offers them an opportunity to give multisentence responses. Children who are reluctant to respond in a group or class situation may be encouraged to respond in a teacher-pupil conference situation.

Children in grades one and two may be guided in composing an experience story at the close of assessment trials. This means that you write down what they say on a chart or the chalkboard. To prompt responses, use questions such as, "What do you remember from our lesson? . . . What else? . . . Can anyone think of anything else?" After the children have experienced this several times, alert them to your intention to ask some people to tell you what the lesson was about, but only one person at a time will talk about the lesson. If you have an aide, ask this person to record the stories as they are composed orally. Perhaps you can enlist the help of some parent aides to help you make the assessment quickly before the children forget what the lesson was about.

The resulting experience stories will reveal the level of skill each child has at composing sentences and multisentence responses.

After lessons as trial assessment, you may ask the children to draw or paint a picture about the lesson. The result will reveal that they can use simple art media to express ideas. If you wish, you may have the children display and discuss their pictures as another way to help you see how well they can use oral language.

As you can see, there are many opportunities for assessing young children's output skills.

Assessing the Skills of Children in Grades Three and Four. At the beginning of the school year, oral language is still the main output medium for children in grades three and four. Here again, your assessment of children's interaction and informa-

tion-intake skills may provide opportunities for you to assess output skills as well. The sharing or current-affairs program also offers opportunities for assessment as you observe oral language behavior —speaking in complete sentences and giving on-the-point, multisentence responses.

If you wish to make a direct assessment of individual performance, create a situation in which each child is committed to giving an oral presentation about a topic familiar to him or her. An effective way of doing this is to point out to the children that a good way for people to know each other is to have each person tell the others about what he or she likes to do (about a favorite possession, an unforgettable event, a great place to visit, a funny personal experience, or whatever), and lead off by telling the children about the selected topic as related to yourself. Be sure to have an object or two to talk about—your jogging shoes if you are a jogger, your tennis racquet if you are a tennis buff, examples of your watch collection, and the like. Then guide the children in arranging a schedule when each will tell the class about the personal topic. As each child performs, assess for the use of complete sentences, multisentence structures, and the ability to stay on the point.

If you are a teacher of third grade, and you wish to assess the children's written-language skills, guide the children in viewing and discussing an interesting object or picture. Then guide them in making a list of words they believe they would need to know how to spell to write about the picture or object. Record the words on a chart or the chalkboard for ready reference. Finally, have each child write as many sentences as he or she can during a ten or fifteen-minute period. Assess the results for completeness of sentences, the development of ideas if multisentence responses are made, the accuracy of capitalization, punctuation, and usage, and staying on the point whenever more than one sentence is composed.

Children in grade four usually are developing into voluble writers. At the beginning of the school year, most children will have attained sufficient handwriting and spelling skills to say what they want to say. They will need help with spelling words related to specific topics. If you wish to see what skills they have, show them a short informational film, help them develop a vocabulary list to use when writing, and have them write about what they saw to share with someone who had not seen the film. Analyze the results to see how well the children express themselves in complete sentences logically sequenced and on the point of the topic. You may also wish to check for the misspelling of basic words and incorrect use of capital letters, punctuation, and usage rules.

When you make assessments such as these, you discover the children's levels of skills in written language. You will also discover needs for supportive instruction in language composition, spelling, and handwriting.

The children in grades three and four are usually eager to make the transition from teacher-assisted output. They enjoy using newly learned output skills in social studies.

Assessing Children's Output Skills in Grades Five through Eight. In grades five through eight the use of output skills focuses with increasing emphasis on oral reports by groups and written reports by individuals. Whenever oral reports are presented by individuals, they are usually written first and, when the best pedagogical practice is followed, the reporters use notes based on their written copy to guide them as they convey their ideas to others. Because time is limited, rarely is every individual in the class expected to report orally.

Whatever assessment of oral-language skills is necessary is accomplished when the interaction and information intake skills are assessed. The needs surfaced are usually those associated with communicating interpersonally—maintaining eye contact and awareness of the listener or being inhibited in speaking. These are individual problems and are corrected as such.

Because written language is the main output medium used in these grades, an assessment should be made early in the year. To obtain a written composition sample, you may use the same procedure suggested for use in grade four—having the children view a short film and writing a report based on it, but without any teacher assistance in spelling. If you wish, you may permit the children to use dictionaries as a spelling reference if they want to use them.

To assess the compositions, analyze each to see whether it makes a point. Then look for other possible needs such as improving sentence completeness and structure, paragraph development, choice of vocabulary, and the use of punctuation, capitalization, and usage rules.

If you wish to assess children's organization skills preparatory to composing a written or oral report, give a two or three-minute oral report yourself using notes. The report should be about a personal interest. After presenting the report, show the children your notes (a duplicated list in outline form will do). Inform the children that the notes helped you to remember what you wanted to say and the order in which you wanted to say it. Then have them make the notes they would use to report about a personal interest.

When you assess the notes, look for clearly identified main ideas supported by facts, and logically sequenced ideas and facts. Do not be surprised to find that your request for notes has prompted your learners to write a sketchy but almost completely written report.

From the fifth grade on, children may be guided in drawing maps or diagrams, or making graphs and charts, as output. However, the skills are not used frequently enough to be assessed at the beginning of the year. In most instances when they are to be used, a recall of experience with the skills is prompted through an assessment discussion. This establishes an immediate baseline from which you teach whatever is necessary to ensure a satisfactory performance.

As social-studies teachers of children in these grades, we rely heavily on what the children produce during output activities to determine how well and how much they are learning. We have no choice other than to respond dynamically to their needs to improve their output skills.

As the various techniques used for assessing children's output skills were discussed, you perhaps noticed that in several instances the output and intake skills are closely related, and that it is often possible to assess both during the same observation. The nature of the relationship is that the quality of intake skills influences the ideational background to be used in output. The richer the intake, the richer the factual content of output. However, output skills also have their own qualitative aspect related to the selection, organization, and presentation of facts.

The most easily managed output is post-intake interaction. This occurs when the children discuss, either in small groups or as an entire class, the results of intake to generalize and discover what they know. Because interaction can serve the output purpose, the assessment of the more precise, individually used output skills may be delayed until the learners are well into their first instructional unit.

You have probably sensed that instruction in the output skills will often be supportive, that is, conducted in subject areas other than social studies. However, in self-contained classrooms and cooperatively managed lofts, social-studies content may be learned first and then carried over into another instructional program to serve as the factual matter to be used in learning an output skill. For example, during social-studies instruction, a class may learn about changes that have occurred during the past fifty years in the lives of the North Alaskan Eskimo. They interact to surface facts and make a generalization or two. Then, during the language period, they use this content as they are being introduced to how to organize information for a report.

Interpreting the Results of Output Assessments

The baselines established by output-skills assessments are helpful to us in two ways. First, they ensure that we do not commit children to output tasks beyond their skills capability. Second, the baselines alert us to the kind of headstart we must provide in supportive instruction if children are going to integrate, organize, and present information in ways satisfying to themselves and others, and which help them meet the broad objectives of social studies. We interpret the assessment results to decide which output skills our learners already know how to apply, and which skills need to be strengthened.

Here are a few examples of such interpretations.

Upon completing the assessment of the output skills of his learners, Mr. W, a teacher of first grade, has made three lists—one of baseline skills, one of needs for correlated instruction, and one of needs for supportive instruction—to serve as guides to the kinds of learning activities to provide in his social-studies program and to foster growth in the output skills needed in social studies:

Baseline Skills

1. Speaking in complete sentences: the entire class (twenty-six members).
2. Giving multi-sentence responses: eight children.

Needs for Correlated Instruction (to Encourage Multisentence Responses)

1. Having children orally review the previous day's learning (correlated with listening and observing).
2. Guiding children in summarizing ideas and recording them as the children give them (correlated with reading and composition skills).
3. Recording individual multisentence responses and sharing them with the class (correlated with reading and composition skills).

Needs for Supportive Instruction (to Build Output Skills)

1. In art, instruction in various media—collage, clay, and torn paper.
2. In language, learning audience-presence skills, learning to write and spell social-studies words, learning to compose and write sentences.

Mr. W's first instructional unit in social studies will provide activities in which the children rely at first on the baseline skills for expressing output. Gradually he will add the activities in correlated instruction. In the meantime, he is planning learning sequences in art and language to improve children's output skills and provide them with more choices in using these skills.

Ms. V, who works in a loft containing ninety children in fourth grade, is the lead teacher in social studies and mathematics. She has enlisted the aid of the lead teacher in reading and language to help her assess the children's output skills. With the supportive assistance of their aides and the other lead teacher, they have completed the assessment and charted the results.

Baseline Skills

1. All but nine of the children can give multisentence oral responses, every sentence on the topic; thirty children cannot sequence their sentences properly.
2. All but twelve children can write legible multi-sentence responses, but most have problems with sentence structure, capitalization, punctuation, and usage.

Needs for Correlated Instruction (to Foster Growth in Composing Paragraphs)

1. During social studies, composing summary paragraphs from discovered facts as a group activity (correlated with composition skills).
2. During social studies, expanding one-sentence conclusions into paragraphs as a group activity (correlated with composition skills).

Needs for Supportive Instruction (to Extend and Build Skills)

1. Individual or group instruction for the children who are unable to make multisentence responses in spoken or written form.
2. Instruction in sentence and paragraph structure.
3. Instruction in using the dictionary to find the correct spelling of words.

Ms. V intends to substitute interaction activities for the use of output skills during much of the first unit of instruction. She is planning a gradual introduction to correlated learning activities. In the meantime, the lead teacher in language arts has agreed to give the needed supportive instruction. Maintaining close contact, Ms. V and her colleague will know when the students are ready to apply new output skills in social studies.

Mr U teaches a social-studies-language-arts core to children in the eighth grade Here is a chart of the results of the output-skills assessment he has just completed for his class:

Baseline Skills

1. Only one of the thirty children has difficulty with participating in post-intake discussions.
2. Six children can write acceptable one-paragraph responses and three-paragraph reports. The rest of the children have difficulty with organizing their ideas, staying on the point of the paragraph or report, and structuring their sentences and paragraphs to express their ideas clearly.
3. When asked to make notes from a written report to use when giving an oral report, only the six able reporters were able to do it.

Needs for Correlated Instruction (to Improve Composition Skills)

1. Composing one-sentence conclusions, first in groups, then independently, at the close of social-studies lessons.
2. Summarizing social-studies information from a stated sentence of conclusion, first in groups, then independently.
3. Preparing social-studies reports paragraph by paragraph, first in groups, then independently.
4. Preparing outlines of social studies information and using them to give oral reports.

Needs for Supportive Instruction (to Refine Composition)

1. Instruction in sentence and paragraph structure.

Because Mr. U has an extended period for teaching the social-studies-and-language-arts core, he feels that he can conduct correlated instruction in output skills quite easily. As he guides his learners through the first section of his social-studies unit, he plans to use most of the extended period for social studies. He will have the children complete a simple output activity at the close of each lesson. During the last quarter of the period he plans to provide supportive instruction in sentence and paragraph structure. During this time, the six able reporters will be excused to complete independent studies in social studies to terminate in reports.

At certain times during the school year, a third of the extended period will be devoted to social studies and the remainder of the time to language studies of one kind or another.

As you can see, the ways that schools are organized for instruction influences the ways that assessment results are interpreted.

ASSESSING CHILDREN'S NEEDS TO IMPROVE INQUIRY SKILLS

The desire to satisfy curiosity or to follow an interest prompts human inquiry. The skills we use are whatever skills we have to find out about things, and the inquiry ceases whenever our curiosity is satisfied or we have followed our interest as far as we want to go. However, whenever we have an important problem to be solved—a truth or principle to be validated or an important decision to be made—our inquiry requires our following a series of thinking procedures similar to the following:

1. Defining the problem. This helps us sort out factors in conflict. We may discover that we have no problem at all.
2. Hypothesizing or making best guesses about explanations or solutions.
3. Selecting a hypothesis or best guess to try. We select the one that appears most reasonable.
4. Deciding how to check the selected hypothesis. We determine the kinds of information we shall need.
5. Seeking information.
6. Organizing information so that we can interpret it.
7. Concluding from our information.
8. Judging our originally selected hypothesis or best guess against our conclusion.

Using the procedures as a whole is a skill, as is each procedure itself. As social-studies teachers, we often use the above list of procedures as a model of thinking to use as we guide children in learning. We use models as a guide to teaching and learning for two reasons. The first is that the model provides a good way to teach a subject in which the content is constantly changing. The second is that the model helps children to learn to think rationally about problems in their physical and social environment.

Expectancies in Inquiry Skills

As you read the above list of inquiry skills, you may have been impressed about how abstract some of them are. Perhaps you wondered about how far children could go in learning them. The chart in Figure 2–18 presents the expectancies.

As you can see, some of the inquiry skills are not developmental. As far as children in the elementary school are concerned, defining the problems almost always requires the assistance of the teacher. To define the problem is to be able to see the factors in conflict in the problem situation. The teacher presents the problem in such a way that a conflict of factors is apparent. For example, a teacher guiding children in the study of urban change may present the problem in this way: he shows the children a photograph of a shopping area when it is busy and crowded, then he shows a photograph of the area taken five years later

Skills	Grade Levels							
	K	1	2	3	4	5	6	7	8
Defining the problem	A	A	A	A	A	A	A	A	A
Hypothesizing or making "best" guesses about solutions, explanations, etc.	I	I	I	I	I	I	I	I	I
Selecting the most reasonable explanation, solution, etc.	I	I	I	I	I	I	I	I	I
Developing a design for inquiry or composing the investigative questions	A	A	A	A	Ⓐ	G	G	G	G
Acquiring information	A	A	A	Ⓐ	G	G	G	G	G
Organizing information	A	A	A	A	Ⓐ	G	G	G	G
Making inferences from the information	A	A	A	A	Ⓐ	G	G	G	G
Judging the hypothesis in light of the inferences	A	A	A	A	Ⓐ	G	G	G	G

FIGURE 2–18. *Levels of Expectancy for Inquiry Skills.*

when there are few people on the street and some of the stores are boarded up. The children identify what the photographs depict. The teacher informs them that the second photograph was taken five years later. Then he asks, "What is difficult to understand about this shopping area?" The response, "Once it was very busy, later it was not," is the definition of the problem.

The responsibility for presenting the problem in such a way is the teacher's. Without such a presentation, it is not likely that the children will be able to define the problem.

However, once the problem is defined, every child can make best guesses and decide which of several best guesses he or she thinks is the most reasonable. Making and working with hypotheses invites children's involvement.

The rest of the skills are developmental. In grade four, children make the transition from assistance to guidance in developing questions. Composing questions for an interview is also involved in this transition. Acquiring information follows the expectancies presented when intake skills were discussed. The rest of the skills show a transition from assistance to guidance at grade four. Note that independence in these skills is not accomplished by the time the children reach grade eight.

Generally, children in kindergarten through grade three will need assistance in all the inquiry skills except those dealing with hypothesizing. Grade four is the transitional grade. The children in grades four through eight will need teacher guidance in most of the skills.

Assessing Inquiry Skills and Interpreting the Results

Usually inquiry skills are not assessed before grade five. Before children reach this grade, they are either following paths of inquiry stimulated by curiosity or interest or closely assisted or guided by the teacher to follow each procedure. However, as we assess their interaction skills from kindergarten through grade four, we find that they are capable of hypothesizing or making best guesses and sup-

porting their ideas with their own logic (which is often quite different from adults' logic). And they may be able to select, from among several, the one hypothesis that they think is most accurate, again with their own particular logic.

By grade five, many children reach the stage at which they can do some independent reasoning during inquiry. To discover what they can do, we can assess their reasoning skills in an inquiry test similar to the following.

Read the following carefully. You will be asked questions about it.

Zee is a person your age who has about everything you might want—tennis and racquetball lessons, a stereo, a television, wide choices of food and drink at every meal, and a large allowance of spending money every week. During the summer Zee goes to camp or travels to interesting places around the world.

One day a store manager catches Zee stealing a candy bar.

1. What is the hard thing to understand about Zee?
2. Why do you think Zee stole the candy bar? Write as many reasons as you can think of. Use the back of this sheet if you need to.
3. Read your reasons carefully. Choose the one you think is the best and write it here.
4. List the questions you would have to ask to get the information needed for you to know whether your reason was right.

In the above, the first item asks the learner to define the problem, the second invites hypotheses, the third prompts hypothesis selection, and the fourth leads toward the development of questions useful in checking the hypothesis.

Note that this test is about a fictitious person who could be a boy or a girl with a name unlikely to be found in a classroom. This avoids biases that some of the children might have.

As you read your learners' responses, look for good use of reasoning. This will be particularly apparent in the responses to the fourth item. If you find that most of your learners can respond well, you will be able to guide them in studying and learning at a highly abstract level, all other things being equal. Perhaps they will be able to make inquiries independently with occasional guidance from you.

Actually, the baselines possible to establish through an assessment of inquiry skills include the following: (1) the children are capable in inquiry skills; they can do independent, mature reasoning; (2) after defining the problem, the children are incapable of unassisted, mature thought; or (3) the children can define the problem, hypothesize, and select a hypothesis, but they cannot devise the questions leading toward the information needed to check the validity of the hypothesis. Any of the baselines inform us about how much guidance in inquiry we shall have to give.

You have probably noticed that not all the inquiry skills were included in the assessment test. These have been excluded because it would be next to impossible to arrange a realistic situation in which children would acquire information, organize it, make inferences from it, and judge the hypothesis in light of the inferences.

There is no need for us to consider correlated or supportive instruction. Every skill we have discussed in this chapter is in some way correlated with or supportive of inquiry skills.

A GLANCE INTO THE FUTURE

For most of us, guiding children in social studies is an exciting adventure. It is much like being an experienced conductor who delights in sharing the wonders of the world with his or her clients. And like tour conductors, we sometimes have clients who are not prepared for the tour as we have envisioned it, and occasionally we find places not much to our liking on our itinerary. In other words, we may find ourselves with a group of learners who, as our assessment shows, cannot profit from the learning activities we prefer to provide, or we may discover that we are to teach content that we regard as dull, unimportant, or whatever.

We shall consider the content problem first.

Let us assume that as we survey the factual content we are to teach, as it is specified in a course of study, a guide, an instructional manual, a teacher's edition, or catalog of materials, we discover that we are to teach about the Middle East as a world problem area, a topic which we find most distasteful for any variety of reasons. We have at least four options for responding to this state of affairs:

1. We may develop an instructional plan that can be completed within a few instructional periods. The inquiry is brief and shallow, but it serves as evidence that the topic has been treated.
2. We omit this study topic. However, if we intend to do this, we should talk it over with the building administrator.
3. We substitute another topic for this topic. The substitution should be discussed with the building administrator.
4. We may do what we frequently expect children to do without question—make a personal study of the topic. We may read a few periodical articles and books to become better acquainted with it.

The first three options are frequently chosen, but many of us can attest to the validity of the fourth option. Assuming once again the role of learner, we experience the excitement of making discoveries about peoples, regions, processes, and relationships. Besides, the effort often has a payoff in our own development both as persons and social-studies teachers.

And now to the problem of coping with an assessment that our learners need something other than what we would prefer to teach them. Let us assume, for example, that our class in the fifth grade is so deficient in interaction skills that we can barely assess the information and inquiry skills. As we review the results of our assessment of information and inquiry skills, we discover baselines much lower than might be expected normally. With the exception of two or three children, none will be able to use the textbooks, maps, and other classroom materials.

In this case we have only one acceptable option, and that is to build a program focused on interaction skills. The specified content areas can still be experienced, not primarily through reading and writing, but through listening, observing, dramatizing, role playing, simulation, construction, and immediate problem exploration.

The point is this: we assess the skills as objectively as possible and cope with the needs as we find them as best we can. This does not mean a change in teaching style, because all of us tend to give greater emphasis to the learning activities that we can manage most effectively. However, as we work more with less-preferred activities, our teaching style develops an extended, more-effective scope.

Coping positively in the future with problems with content and children's needs promises much for both you and the children to whom you teach social studies.

Assessing children's interaction, information, and inquiry skills at the beginning of the school year helps us establish baselines where instruction begins. The rest of our program building is a matter of developing instructional objectives, lessons, and units of instruction (discussed in Chapter 10), and selecting and sequencing learning activities to ensure growth in skills and reaching the goals of social-studies instruction. Suggested procedures for teaching the skills are discussed in Chapters 3 through 9. As you proceed through these chapters you will discover a variety of learning activities to use as building blocks of instruction.

SUMMARY

Assessments of children's needs for learning in social studies are conducted at the national, state, and local levels of government and professional responsibility. Publishers also conduct needs assessments to prepare instructional materials. The ultimate assessment, and the one most vital to children's learning, is made by the classroom teacher at the beginning of the school year. It focuses on the skills required for learning in social studies.

The overall characteristic of a positive social climate is harmonious adjustment of all persons in the class to one another.

To assess children's needs to establish positive social relationships the teacher organizes assessment trials in which the children interact and he or she observes. Children are also given opportunities to rate themselves on self-rating sheets.

Children's growth in the various intake and output skills is slow and gradual. The levels of mastery occur in this order: the assisted level in which children can perform a skill only when verbally cued; the guided level in which children can perform a skill when given a purpose and are helped to see needs for improvement; and the independent level in which children can identify purposes and use the skills as needed. The skills are assessed with teacher-made tests and analyses of children's products.

Through interpreting the findings resulting from assessments, the teacher determines baselines from which to plan instruction.

When building the instructional program, the teacher first provides for satisfying children's immediate needs to the point that they are ready to begin to meet developmental needs.

POSTSCRIPT

Now review the notes you made at the beginning of the chapter about baselining and observation as a part of the assessment process. How would those notes be changed in light of what you have read?

If you have identified interaction skills as the first to baseline because interaction is basic to learning in social studies and related to thinking skills, the chapter has conveyed a message it was meant to convey.

If you chose the skills related to finding information as the second area to baseline because acquiring information is fundamental to learning in social studies, you received another important message.

In all the skills except finding and organizing information, you will rely more on observation to determine how well your learners can perform.

FOR FURTHER UNDERSTANDING

Cognitive Activities

1. Draw a diagram or a flow chart showing how the elementary social-studies curriculum is developed.

2. Develop a list of rules that you believe teachers should observe when they assume an authoritarian-dominant or democratic-dominant role as they guide children in learning social studies.

3. How do you define *assessment trial, interaction checklist, interaction self-rating sheet, assisted level of mastery, guided level of mastery, independent level of mastery, retention skills, location skills, inquiry skills, intake skills, output skills, assessive discussion?*

4. Suppose that you are a fifth-grade teacher who has just been given enough copies of a new social-studies textbook to use in your class. An instructional manual or teacher's edition accompanies the text. Make a list of the features that you will review in the materials to develop an assessment program to ensure that your learners will be able to use the textbook effectively.

5. Suppose that you are conducting an instructional program in social studies with a strong emphasis on fulfilling your learners' immediate needs. A parent makes an appointment to confer with you about the social-studies program. He is quite concerned that his child is not yet studying a people, region, or process. How do you think you will try to justify your program to him?

Practice Activities

1. Compose two lists of four questions each to use when conducting assessment trials to see how well your learners interact. One list should consist of simple, open-ended questions, the other, of complex, open-ended questions.

2. Choose or develop an appropriate piece of social-studies instructional material and use it to plan a lesson to use in kindergarten or first grade to see how well the children follow an informational lesson.

3. Obtain a picture and develop four or five questions to use to assess kindergarten or first grade children's observation skills.

4. Obtain an information article from a children's

periodical or child's encyclopedia and use it as the basis for five factual questions which you could use to assess young children's listening skills.

5. Obtain a social-studies textbook designed for use in the fourth or a later grade. Excerpt from it a passage of about a hundred words in length. Develop for it a list of questions (factual, inference, and vocabulary) to use to assess learners' ability to use the textbook.

6. Compose the description of a conflict situation which you think that learners in fourth grade and above would understand. Use the description to devise an inquiry test.

7. Arrange to visit a classroom during social-studies instruction. Observe carefully as the teacher works with the children to determine how he or she establishes or maintains a positive social climate. List the behaviors you observed.

Performance Activities

1. In your classroom, conduct an assessment trial to determine how well your learners can interact. Make an interpretation of the trial in terms of what needs to be done in the future.

2. In your classroom, survey the remainder of your social-studies instructional program to see whether a new skill not yet emphasized during this school year will be required. When you identify this skill, plan and conduct an assessment of the skill as a basis for planning instruction in the near future.

SELECTED REFERENCES

Bechtol, William M., and Anthony E. Conte. *Individually Guided Social Studies.* Reading, Mass.: Addison-Wesley, 1976.

Burns, Paul C. *Diagnostic Teaching of the Language Arts.* Itasca, Ill.: F. E. Peacock, 1974.

Carpenter, Helen McCracken, ed. *Skill Development in Social Studies.* National Council for the Social Studies, 33rd Yearbook. Washington, D.C.: National Education Association, 1963.

Ebel, Robert L. *Essentials of Educational Measurement,* 3rd edition. Englewood Cliffs, N.J.: Prentice-Hall, Inc., 1979.

Ekwall, Eldon E. *Ekwall Reading Inventory.* Boston: Allyn and Bacon Inc., 1979.

Fox, Karen F. A. "What Children Bring to School: The Beginnings of Economic Education." *Social Education,* 42:478–81 (October, 1978).

Kurfman, Dana G., ed. *Developing Decision-Making Skills.* National Council for the Social Studies, 47th Yearbook. Washington, D.C.: National Council for the Social Studies, 1977.

Levin, Joel. *Learner Differences: Diagnosis and Prescription.* New York: Holt, Rinehart, and Winston, 1977.

McWilliams, Lana, and Thomas A. Rakes. *Content Inventories: English, Social Studies, Science.* Dubuque, Iowa: Kendall/Hunt Publishing Company, 1979.

Morse, Horace T., and George H. McCune, revised by Lester E. Brown and Ellen Cook. *Selected Items for the Testing of Study Skills and Critical Thinking.* National Council for the Social Studies, No. 15, Fifth Edition. Washington, D.C.: National Council for the Social Studies, 1971.

Nagel, Thomas S., and Paul T. Richman. *Competency-Based Instruction.* Columbus, Ohio: Charles E. Merrill, 1972.

NOTES

1. Map used by permission of Rand McNally and Company. © Rand McNally and Company, R. L. 80-Y-33.

3

Guiding Children
in Exploring
for Values

Here are two polar views about guiding children in studying values:

VIEW 1

The schools should indoctrinate children to love their country and their flag, to cherish democracy and despise communism, and to have an abiding faith in the free enterprise system. Other value-related areas should be taught in the home and church or synagogue.

VIEW 2

The schools should guide children in analyzing their values as a means of knowing themselves better. Activities with values should be the core of the curriculum. Any value about which children are confused is suitable. However, the emphasis is on open-ended exploration, not indoctrination.

Is your view the same as either of these? Or are you somewhere in between? If so, are you closer to one or the other? Or do you see yourself as being precisely in the middle? Jot down with which of these you agree, or, if you agree with neither, write two or three sentences describing your view. Put it aside to review at the end of this chapter.

All that we teach and learn is interrelated in some way, but in our conventional ways of doing

things and because of the structure of knowledge itself, we separate what we teach and learn. At any given moment in social studies, we may be guiding children in their *cognitive* development, *psychomotor* development, or *affective* development.

As we guide children in developing purposes for seeking information, and then guide them in collecting, organizing, analyzing, applying, synthesizing, and evaluating information, we are guiding them through the cognitive domain.

To guide them through the psychomotor domain, we teach them to listen, speak, read, compose, and construct with whatever they have cognitively attained.

And as we guide children in reviewing their cognitive attainments reflected in whatever they have produced during their sojourn in the psychomotor domain to find meaning and relevance for themselves as human beings, we are guiding them through the affective domain.

These domains have been presented here in a usual, logical order. However, they may be viewed as existing in an interrelated structure, as shown in Figure 3–1.

As you can see, when we enter any of these domains and explore within it, we eventually reach an area associated with the others. As a matter of

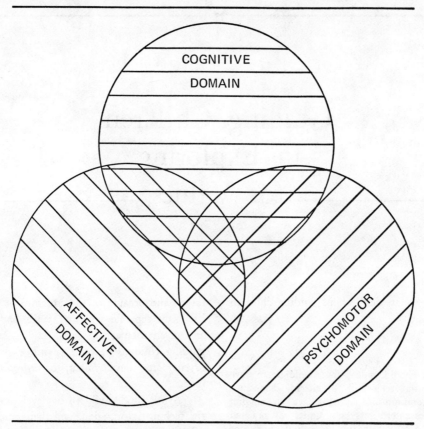

FIGURE 3–1. *Overlapping Domains of Learning.*

choice, we may focus on any domain, but if anything other than the shallowest of teaching and learning are to occur, the focus needs to encompass the overlap of domains as well as the domain of emphasis. For example, a study of conservation may focus on natural resources and ways in which they may be used and abused (cognitive), but the study will yield little if the learners do not actively experience facts (psychomotor) and consider alternative attitudes, values, and actions related to conservation (affective).

The above is a classical sequence for total learning—cognitive, psychomotor, and affective. Other sequences are possible. For example, a study of conservation may begin when learners are angry and upset over the industrial poisoning of a local,

well-used swimming area (affective), continue with listening, observing, reading, and interviewing to become informed (psychomotor), and terminate study with some ideas on which to base actions and attitudes (cognitive). Or children may begin by just reading about conservation (psychomotor), making inferences (cognitive), and deciding what they might do to prevent the abuse of natural resources (affective).

The sequences of instructional activities frequently used in social studies provide for learning in the cognitive and psychomotor domains with an emphasis on one or the other. The less-emphasized domain complements the other. Regardless of which is emphasized, the social-studies concepts and generalizations to be learned are the matter around which instruction is organized. Through the rigorous use of interaction, inquiry, and information-process skills, the children extend a concept or arrive at a generalization. At this point the study terminates. This may be sufficient for social scientists, but it is not for children.

The significance of the social studies facts, concepts, and generalizations that children learn lies in the potential that the subject matter provides for stimulating further thought and personal development. Knowing a fact, concept, or generalization, at least to the extent that one can communicate it to another or talk about it with some authority, serves simply as a base from which learners seek meaning for themselves. Within their own experience and that of their peers, they discover how what they have learned affects them as persons— their values, their attitudes, and their proneness toward certain actions or decisions to act when they meet issues related to the facts, concepts, and generalizations they have discovered.

For example, let us imagine that the children in a sixth grade, when prompted to explore why the Soviet Union is a world power, have garnered enough information to arrive with high confidence at the following generalization: *Since 1931 the Russian government has fostered the development of heavy industry—steel, locomotives, heavy trucks, war planes, warships, etc.—and neglected the development of industry to produce consumer goods.*

With their information obtained and analyzed, they arrive at the generalization. Let us suppose at this moment that a perceptive child remarks in exasperation. "So what? It makes no difference to me that Russia used heavy industry to become a world power!" Such a child makes the point of this chapter. Significance to the learner lies beyond generalizing in terms of discovering:

• Through an in-depth discussion, that the condition described in the generalization has affected and continues to affect international relations to the extent that it touches on every person's feeling of security. How securely people feel influences their willingness to accept higher taxes and prices for defense spending, for whom they vote in a national election, and what they choose to do with their personal lives.

• Through role playing, that a citizen living in the Soviet Union may agree strongly with the policy of maintaining heavy industry because he or she feels that personal security depends on it, that he or she may disagree but has to be careful in expressing disagreement, and that a possible alternative for resolving tension may be to work toward improving communication among peoples everywhere.

• Through simulation, that an emerging nation attempting to generate power through the development of heavy industry has many problems if it lacks resources and if its leaders do not have complete control over the people. An alternative that may be surfaced is that emerging nations should emphasize the production of consumer goods and should rely on the United Nations for protection.

• Through value clarification, that, in spite of the threat to world peace imposed by the Soviet Union government's decision to maintain much of its industry to manufacture arms, Russian literature and music are to be prized, openly praised, and experienced fully.

• Through value analysis, that Russian Communism, as abhorrent as it is to the ideals of democracy and as neglectful as it is of the people's need for consumer goods, has provided a way of life better than they have had in centuries, but that way of life does not compare favorably with what can be achieved through democratic free enterprise.

The discoveries cited above indicate what lies beyond a generalization (or concept). Its significance emerges when it is used as a base from which to think productively. Learning activities which prompt exploration for values give children opportunities to use social-studies facts, concepts, and generalizations discovered through study to discover personal meaning in the form of attitudes, values, and alternative actions. Figure 3–2 offers an illustration of this idea.

The purpose of this chapter is to acquaint you with the learning activities useful in guiding chil-

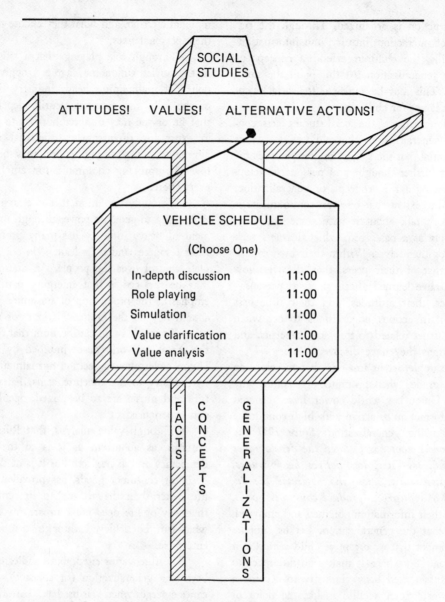

FIGURE 3–2. *Bases, Purposes, and Vehicles for Values Exploration.*

dren in exploring the affective domain as related to learning in social studies. When you read Chapter 2, which dealt with assessing children's immediate needs to be met to ensure their freedom to interact during learning in social studies, you were given a foretaste of what the exploration might entail. Now you will have a more complete sampling.

VALUES AS THE ENTRY INTO THE AFFECTIVE DOMAIN

We have myriads of reactions to things to show their meaning to us. We may rush to an object or race away from it, shout with rage or murmur softly at it, pommel or fondle it, talk about it in glowing or derogatory terms, or plan to obtain or avoid it. Inside us our pulse rate and the flow of vital juices may alter in some way. These may be labeled generally as emotional reactions. When we try to interpret them in others, we sometimes use such words as values, attitudes, and feelings.

Values, Attitudes, and Feelings [1]

Figure 3–3 shows three persons, each making an utterance about doughnuts. The first utterance is saturated with affect. There is no doubt about the meaning that doughnuts have for the speaker. It would be absurd for us to ask this person why he drools because the meaning is so clear, but if we should, he would continue to tell us what he feels as he bites into, chews, and swallows a doughnut. From the moment of his first utterance, he has been communicating his feeling about doughnuts.

The second utterance is a statement of preference. We know that if we were to offer this person a doughnut, she would accept it. There is a chance that she would buy a doughnut if she were hungry, but she also might buy a pretzel. Doughnuts placed on the table in her presence a half-hour before lunch might still be there when lunch begins, or they might not. All we really know is that she has a favorable predisposition toward doughnuts.

If we were to ask her why she liked doughnuts, she might respond in any of the following ways:

"Oh, I don't know. I just like them, I guess."
"I'm a pastry nut."
"They remind me of afternoons I used to spend with my grandmother. She was an excellent doughnut maker."
"Doesn't everyone?"

FIGURE 3–3.

No single response is predictable either in its structure or content. That is the way with attitudes. To say that one likes doughnuts is to express an attitude.

The third utterance is a rating. What the speaker has said is not clear, but it is clarifiable. To the question, "Why do you think so?", the response is a discourse:

"Well, they're not as messy in your hands as a piece of cake and not as crumbly as cookies."
"Is that all that makes them best?"
"Well, they are not as sweet as candy or cake."
"Are they best as a food?"
"They are more filling than popcorn or crackers."

Perhaps the speaker is beginning to be evasive, but he has spoken enough to demonstrate that what he said originally could be analyzed in a rational way. When he said that doughnuts were best, he had stated a value judgment. Because they are more easily treated in a rational way than feelings or attitudes, we shall use values as an entry into the affective domain related to social studies.

(Sometimes value judgments are labeled as personal values. Whenever the term "value" is used here, it refers to either a personal value or a value judgment.)

Let us explore a little further what is meant by values and what is involved when we guide children in exploring them.

Value Objects. In the statement "Doughnuts are best," doughnuts are the value object. A value object is anything which we rate or about which we make a judgment.

In social studies as an objective area of study the value objects include peoples, the ways they live, regions, interrelationships, systems, processes, products, and inferences made from objective facts. Here is a formula to remember:

Value Object + Rating = Value.

Whenever we guide children in activities to help them meet sociopsychological needs, the children themselves are the value objects.

Value Criteria. When our third speaker began telling why he thought doughnuts were best, he was expressing *value criteria*—standards which he thought doughnuts met as a food.

Criterion 1. Doughnuts are best because they are not as messy as cake or cookies.
Criterion 2. Doughnuts are best because they are not as sweet as candy or cake.
Criterion 3. Doughnuts are best because they are more filling than popcorn or crackers.

As we examine the structure of a criterion, this is what we discover: a value object and a rating related to a characteristic of the value object. These three elements will always be involved in a criterion.

To help you remember what a value criterion is, here is a formula:

$$\frac{\text{Characteristic}}{\text{Value Object}} + \text{Rating} = \text{Value Criterion}$$

With further questioning, our speaker would have probably stated more criteria. After he had given all that he could think of, we would have asked him to rank them. This would help him and us to see which he thought were the most important. Let us assume that he did give more, ranked all of them, and discarded some as relatively unimportant. What is left is the above list ranked in his chosen order.

Value Principle. When our speaker has been able to give at least two criteria, we are able to see the emergence of a *value principle* operating in his mind: *Doughnuts are best because they are not as messy as cake or candy, not as sweet as candy or cake, and more filling than popcorn or crackers.*

We wonder how firm he really is in his belief that doughnuts are best. We test his value principle by asking:

"Are you saying that the best desserts are those that aren't too messy, not too sweet, and somewhat filling?"
"No," he replies, "I like very sweet things for dessert and I don't care how messy they are. And there is no question about whether they are filling or not.

I was talking about doughnuts as a snack food, not as a dessert."

"Are you saying then that the best snack foods are those that aren't too messy or too sweet, and that are somewhat filling?"

"Right."

Our speaker has made an accurate value judgment. His point of view was not clear at first.

Point of View. As we have just seen, point of view makes a difference when one is making a value judgment. It could have been that our speaker's utterance was a response to this question: "If you were going to open a convenience store, what do you think would be the best food to sell?"

If this were the case, the characteristics of doughnuts that he might give or list would include the following:

"There is a high markup between the cost of production and the sales price."

"There is a quick turnover, or doughnuts are sold quickly."

"They are easily handled."

"They can be produced at the selling site."

"They are tasty warm or cold."

These are all responses to why doughnuts are best, and as such they are also criteria. However, to make sure that our speaker would go into such a venture with his eyes wide open, we ask him this: "Why might doughnuts be the worst merchandise for a convenience store?" His responses would perhaps include:

"Doughnut-making equipment is expensive."

"Day-old doughnuts are not salable."

"Doughnuts are difficult to display because they attract flies."

"Diet-conscious people won't buy doughnuts."

"Too many doughnuts make some people sick."

As responses to why doughnuts are worse, these are negative criteria. Now our speaker must weigh the negative criteria against the positive criteria to determine the confidence with which he can make his value judgment.

The above point of view was economic. Here are some others to which our speaker might have made the value judgment that doughnuts are best.

Health: "What do you think is the most healthy food for people?"
Political: "What do you think would be the best food for a candidate for office to have served at a block party?"
Cultural: "What do you think would be the best food to represent American food habits?"
Social: "What do you think would be the best food for a wife to serve her husband to maintain positive relationships with him?"
Environmental: "What do you think would be the best food to serve at a picnic to reduce littering?"

Even with the common doughnut as a value object, it is possible for us to explore for values within the areas of concern to social studies. As social sciences, economics, political science, anthropology, sociology, and geography, also are points of view within which we deal with the problems of humankind.

Characteristics of Objects. As you have already seen during the brief discussion about criteria, the characteristics or descriptions of the objective nature of objects are elements within stated in criteria. As our speaker generated criteria, he was also offering the factual evidence necessary to support his value judgment.

The facts were a part of the speaker's background. He had experienced or learned them somewhere. Assuming that he was an honest, well-informed fellow, we never challenged the accuracy of his facts. At any time, however, we might have asked him, "How do you know that?" or "Are you sure about that?" When we are working with children as they deal with values, and they offer a criterion containing facts which do not square with what we know or with the facts that we have helped them to experience during social studies, we shall have to ask them about their informational sources.

An issue arises at this point: should we provide for children to learn many facts before we encourage them to make value judgments, or should we encourage them to make value judgments and then verify the facts they generate to support their judgment? You have to resolve the issue for yourself. Here are a few ideas that may be helpful to you:

- Give serious thought to the value object. If it is very close to the children's lives and something that they are likely to know much about, the judgment first, facts later approach may be better. For example, *family* and *public park* are objects about which most children could make value judgments easily. The reverse would be true of such value objects as *government* or *economic system*.
- Consider the age of your learners. If the value object is abstract for them, they will need many facts before they can make valid value judgments. The facts first, judgment later approach may be better.
- Find out what informational sources are available. If the children can find and use them only with much assistance from you, the facts first, judgment later approach may be better.
- What is your teaching style? If you are the kind of teacher who likes to be able to predict what most of the criteria will be so that you can guide learning activities more efficiently, you will want to use the facts first, judgment later approach. If you are the kind of teacher who likes to get things started in a hurry and to allow emerging needs to indicate the facts that will be needed, you may prefer the judgment first, facts later approach.

Informational learning, then, is vital to guiding children in working with values. The great advantage of guiding children in treating values is that the facts themselves become of value as they are applied in making value judgments.

Values and Decision Making

While you pondered the ideas listed for you to consider as you tried to decide how you felt about values teaching, you were probably struck with the thought that just about every decision a person makes requires making value judgments. Perhaps before you began reading this section, you discovered yourself generating criteria to decide which approach was better for you. If you did, you really sense the relationship between values and decision making.

This brings us to a reason for teaching children how to explore values. That reason is to help them learn rational ways of making decisions either before or after the fact. A decision satisfactorily made is often the result of an accurate value judgment. A decision wrongly made prompts an exploration for new facts and criteria to ensure that the same decision will not be made again.

This section has offered you both an analysis of valuing as a human act and a few broad suggestions about what you might do as you guide children in exploring values. We shall return to aspects of this section again when we discuss *values analysis* as a teaching technique. Before we do, we shall consider some other techniques.

VALUES-EXPLORATION TECHNIQUES

A value may be viewed as having a domain of its own. This domain consists of an area circumscribed by a value object (whatever it may be) and a point of view (whatever it may be). Within the area arranged in concentric circles are value judgment, value criteria, and value principle, as shown in Figure 3–4.

Note also that a value exploration, which may begin at any point around the area, leads entirely through the area and out. This means that a value exploration begins with the learner holding some concept of a value and ends with his or her having a changed concept. We may accept a reaffirmation of the value as a change.

We have five different techniques at our disposal—in-depth discussion, role playing, simulation, values clarification, and values analysis. The one we choose depends on how we interpret the immediate and developmental needs of our learners as well as our skills and ingenuity as a teacher.

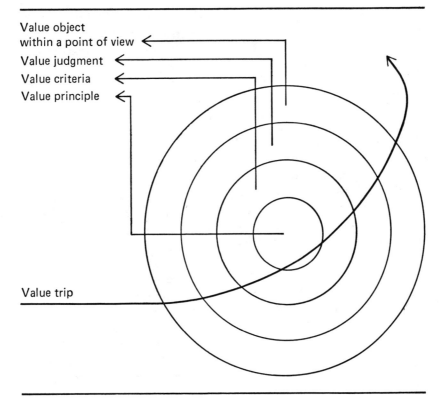

Value object
within a point of view
Value judgment
Value criteria
Value principle

Value trip

FIGURE 3-4. *Value Domain.*

In-depth Discussion

Basically, an in-depth discussion is an extended interaction which you conduct with children. During the interaction, they are free to express opinions and reasons. The discussion may involve the whole class or a group. It works well after your learners have studied and are able to discover a "big idea" or a generalization of broad applicability such as: "Each people coming to America to settle brought with them different ways of living, some of which Americans still follow today." It also works well with learners in the fourth and later grades.

To conduct this discussion you need a *value prompter*. This includes an introduction and a question.

The introduction is a brief review of the facts. The better review is often focused on material which helps the children remember experienced facts. It is accomplished through encouraging the children to express the needed facts as they recall them. Less effective, but often adequate, is a brief review which you give.

The question in the value prompter is based on an important aspect within the generalization. This aspect serves as the value object about which value judgments are to be made. Here are several possibilities for the generalization mentioned earlier:

1. Suppose that the Spaniards had not come to America. How much difference do you think that would have made in our lives today?
2. Of all the peoples who came to settle in America, which do you think made the most important contribution to the ways we live today?
3. What do you think about the diversity or differ-

ences to be found among the many groups of people living in America today?

Each question prompts a value judgment. The answer to the first could be *little* or *much;* to the second, the name of one of the peoples; and to the third, *valuable* or *troublesome.*

The first question leads toward a value judgment of a people implicit in the big idea. So does the second. But the third leads toward the value of a condition which is the theme of the big idea.

All these questions will work, but my preference is for the third. It is more objective and less likely to unearth children's biases toward ethnic groups. However, if I felt that it was necessary for my learners to examine their biases toward ethnic groups, I would use either question 1 or question 2.

Another kind of question we might ask compels learners to make a choice. It may focus on the fact:

Who do you think made the most important contribution to the way we live today—the Indians or the Spaniards?

Or it may focus on the rating:

What do you think about the diversity among the American people today? Do you think it enriches their lives or makes them more miserable?

Some teachers are reluctant to use this kind of question in a values prompter. They think it denies children the latitude of thought they need to make a personal choice. This is particularly true when the question offers two polar ratings, like the one immediately above. This aspect may be softened by saying something like this after the choices are given: "Or do you think something else?" *or* "Or do your thoughts lead you to something between enrichment and misery?"

At any rate, once the value question has been asked, the in-depth discussion is begun in earnest. Your role is to guide it, not to the value judgment which you hold yourself, but to the value judgment or judgments which the members of the class or group can stabilize. This requires you to

be a good listener and facilitator. Here is what you will need to do:

• If a discussant introduces a new fact and no one else challenges it, you should. You can be gentle about it. Say something like this: "Just a minute, Sam, would you please tell us why you think that is true? Did you read it or hear it somewhere?"

• If the discussants appear to be drifting toward verifying a particular value because they are omitting other salient facts which you are certain they know, you may have to intervene to remind them of these facts. You might say: "It seems to me that we are not really using all the facts we know, for example, the different foods and food habits that these different peoples brought with them." Or you might suggest criteria of a rating opposite from the one they appear to be establishing. For example, if your learners were being negative toward diversity, you might say: "I think that because some of our people speak different languages, we might want to learn them ourselves. Knowing another language besides your own makes it possible for a person to communicate with more people and read more books."

• If a discussant introduces a word or idiom into the discussion which might be confusing to the other discussants or might get the discussion off the point, you may ask him or her to define it or to help in surfacing a word or phrase that has the desired meaning.

• If a discussant makes an outrageous statement which none of the other discussants can handle or which takes the discussion off the point, you may intervene to prompt the discussant to consider the implication of what he or she has said. For example, in a discussion about diversity, a discussant says, "I think that once the English had settled on the East Coast, they should have made laws to keep other people out." You might say, "Let's consider for just a moment what might have happened if they really had done that."

The discussion goes on. You will be able to detect whether the class or group is moving toward stabilizing a particular value judgment or developing two opposing value judgments. If they stabilize at a single value judgment, you may encourage them to go one more level in depth by saying, "We appear to be agreed (in this case) that diversity does much to enrich our lives. What might we do to ensure that it continues to enrich our lives?" This brings your learners to the test for the value principle which has provided the basis for their value judgment.

If your learners have established two opposing value judgments, guide them toward suspended judgment. Say something like this: "We simply cannot agree on what we should think. What each one of us thinks is really up to him or her as a private person. But let us be on the lookout for more information before we really make up our minds about what we should think."

An in-depth discussion can be wearing on both you and your learners, particularly if it lasts longer than fifteen or twenty minutes. A good way to prevent this is to vary the discussion activity. You can do this by dividing the class into small, impromptu groups of four or five members to discuss points as they arise, each group discussion to last no longer than five minutes. (See Illustration 3–1.) For example, after you have asked the values

question and the class has responded with a variety of ratings or facts, convene the groups to discuss these further to generate reasons for the responses. After they have discussed, have them share and talk about their findings.

The in-depth discussion is suitable when the value object is abstract and distant from the learners' consciousness. In this case, *diversity* is a good example. But if there were a strike in your community and many of your learners' parents were involved, the value object *strike* would be difficult to treat in an in-depth discussion. Your role might change from facilitator to referee.

Role Playing

Sometimes role playing is confused with dramatization and creative dramatics. A dramatization is usually a group interpretation in play form of a story, incident, or poem that has just been experienced. Creative dramatics is composing a characterization or a play through exploring possible ways of moving, gesturing, and speaking. The children's product is less important than the process

ILLUSTRATION 3–1. *Divided into Impromptu Groups, Older Children Interact to Decide What They Think about an Issue.*

they experience. Role playing is the use of dramatic form to explore a value inherent in a conflict situation. It encourages the expression of value judgments.

However, dramatization and creative dramatics as classroom activities can contribute to successful role playing. They serve as readiness activities. Children who are successful in dramatizations and creative dramatics are often able to move into role playing with little or no difficulty. There are two reasons for this. The first is that these activities can occur only in a positive social climate, which role playing also requires. The second is that these activities help children to develop stage presence. Without this, they may have problems with role playing.

If you are a teacher in a self-contained classroom or in an open space or loft school in which you teach both social studies and language arts,

you can easily provide opportunities for dramatizations and creative dramatics. If you are a social studies teacher in a departmentalized situation, you may use pantomime as a readiness activity for developing stage presence. Of course, a teacher in any situation may use it as a readiness activity. For this reason, a few details about it will be given here.

Pantomime as Preparation. Pantomime is a mode of communication in which body movements, gestures, and facial expressions are the conveyors of ideas. No words are spoken. There are several ways of introducing it to children. The first step in your introductory procedure is to engage your learners in a brief discussion about pantomime to clarify what it is. Encourage them to tell about any mimes they have seen. If you are lucky, you may discover a child who knows a great deal about it and who requires merely a suggestion to demonstrate what it is. That can serve as an ice-breaker that induces several learners to pantomime before the instructional period ends. The introduction is complete!

Such introductions do not often occur. You may have to tell the children what it is. Then you may do one of the following:

• Inviting the children to guess what you are doing, pantomime brushing your teeth. When they guess what you are doing, invite everyone to do it. Terminate the pantomime, and have the children guess what you are doing as you pretend to comb your hair with exaggerated brush or comb strokes. When they guess what you are doing, invite everyone to do it. Repeat this with washing your hands, licking an ice-cream cone, and walking up a flight of stairs. Ask for a volunteer to pantomime something for the class to guess and then do together. This works well with young children and may be used with children as advanced as fifth grade.

• Inviting the children to guess what you are doing, pantomime wrapping a package. Follow this with preparing and eating scrambled eggs and eating a banana. Then ask for a volunteer to pantomime another way to eat a banana. After several children have pantomimed different ways

ILLUSTRATION 3–2. *Young Children Role Playing to Discover Values Held about Personal Property.*

of eating a banana, ask for a volunteer to pantomime something for the rest of the class to guess. Ask for more volunteers. This works well with children in grades three through eight.

• Introduce a pair or several pairs of children whom you have coached beforehand in pantomiming everyday incidents such as borrowing a sheet of paper, offering to carry extra books, helping someone whose arms are full through a door—anything that a pair of people might be seen doing in school. After the children guess what they are doing, ask for volunteer pairs to meet for a minute or two to plan a pantomime and present to the class. The class guesses what each pair does.

After the introduction, you schedule a series of ten or fifteen-minute pantomime sessions occurring every other day or so. During these sessions you gradually increase the emotional intensity of pantomimes through the provisions that you make for situations to interpret. A good way to do this is through the use of cards on which you write the situations to be pantomimed. (Younger children will need to have the cards read to them.) Here are a few examples of amusing situations:

You are eating a very sour pickle.

You are holding a large piece of ice in your bare hands.

You are walking barefoot across a very hot sidewalk.

You have just come home from the barbershop. Some fine bits of hair have fallen down your back inside your clothes.

The understanding is that the child will pantomime the situation described on the card. As you can see, the situations above have a light emotional intensity. If your introduction did not generate much enthusiasm about pantomiming, you may want to use situations similar to these during the first session or two.

In the following situations the intensity is increased:

Your mother has just told you to get ready to go to the dentist.

You have just received a surprise package. You open it to find something that you have wanted for a long time.

Your best friend has just telephoned to let you know that he or she will be able to come over to visit.

Your father has just told you that the family will have to move.

After you present the first of these situations, the volunteer pantomimist may have, ironically enough, "played it for laughs." That is to be expected. However, it gives you an opportunity to have the children compare this situation with the others they have done. You may point out that some situations are funny, may be either funny or serious, or are serious. The first in this series is one that may be either funny or serious. You may give the volunteer a chance to play it seriously.

Or, before you begin a series in which the intensity has been increased, you may read some examples of situations and have the children decide on how they are different from the others they have experienced.

Here are some examples of situations of high intensity:

You have just walked up to your best friend to say, "Good morning," and he or she just walks away without saying a word.

You are underneath a tree and you have just discovered three dead baby birds who have fallen out of a nest.

Your baseball team has just lost the most important game of the year.

You have just opened your lunch and discovered that someone has taken a bite out of everything.

As you compose situations of high intensity, choose those which are common to most children. You have probably noticed that situations of higher intensity often involve another person. Avoid putting parents, siblings, and teachers in a bad light. This makes the pantomime too personal.

During pantomime sessions you will usually want to provide opportunities for children to present pantomimes which they have created and to have the class guess what they are doing. However, as you guide the children in reacting to situations of higher intensity, begin to read the situations to the children and ask for volunteers to pantomime them. Introduce the new term *pantomime role*— instead of soliciting volunteers by saying, "Who would like to act this out?", say, "Who would like to do this pantomime role?" After children begin to volunteer to do described situations, encourage them to differentiate between funny and serious situations. Also encourage the children to evaluate performances on how well the mime communicated the situation. Reinforce acceptable performances with comments such as these: "You really stayed with your role very well." "That was a difficult role, and you did not break it at any time."

Through following practices similar to the above, you help the children to differentiate among roles and to sense what is required of them when they accept a role.

There is one *DO NOT* to observe when you are guiding children in pantomime. That is: *DO NOT TRY TO FORCE A CHILD TO PANTOMIME.* Keep it on a volunteer basis.

When most of your learners have developed stage presence and are able to differentiate between funny and serious roles, they are ready to explore values through role playing.

Conducting the Role Playing. Role playing is interpreting a situation of conflict in impromptu, dramatic form. There are two kinds of participants—the players who accept or choose a role, and the observers, or the audience. The players express their value judgments in dramatic form, and the audience develops value judgments during the enactment of the situation. During the postenactment discussion, the players tell what they felt (feelings are criteria in role playing) and may offer other criteria when asked why they played the role the way they did. The audience may accept or reject the players' value judgments. If they reject them, they suggest another value judgment (a better way of playing the roles involved), and there

is a reenactment. New players choose roles. The process is repeated.

Logically there is no limit on the number of reenactments. Usually a reenactment simply provides another choice which the children may consider. In some cases, particularly in situations of high conflict, it is preferable to leave the children with two choices in which the ultimate choice is regarded as personal. In other cases, particularly when the role playing is directed toward learning a common interpersonal skill, a value judgment about a role needs to be one which everyone can accept.

The values prompter for a role playing is the description of a situation. The description of the situation is based on a value object inherent in a generalization formulated after the study of facts, characteristic of a vital role, or central to a problem.

Let us assume that we are going to use the same generalization as that used earlier when the in-depth discussion was treated: "Each people coming to America to settle brought with them different ways of living, some of which Americans still follow today." As we know, *diversity,* the theme of this generalization and inherent in it, will serve as a value object. Using it, we may create a situation in which two value judgments are in conflict. Here is an example:

Ellen has invited her friend Jane to come over and visit with her one afternoon after school. During the past summer she and her parents took a long trip around North America, and along the way she has collected postcards showing the places they had visited. She wants to show them to Jane.

The two girls are seated on a sofa. The first set of cards shows Williamsburg, Virginia. Ellen comments on the beauty of the old restored buildings and points out that she saw many buildings of the same design in other cities. Jane looks at each card saying little. The next set of cards shows El Paso, Texas. Ellen remarks on the Spanish influences she noticed. Jane looks at each card quickly and lays it aside. The next set of cards are of the French Quarter in New Orleans. Jane barely glances at each card as Ellen gives it to her. Just after she looks at the last card, she says to Ellen, "Didn't you get any cards showing some things that are really American, like the arch at St. Louis, the beaches of Florida, and the Golden Gate Bridge? I really don't care much for all this foreign stuff. I often wish that all the foreigners would go back to their own countries and stay there."

How do you think Ellen feels? . . . (Don't tell me. Just think about it.) . . . What do you suppose she might say? . . . (Keep it to yourself for the time being.) . . . And if Ellen says what you think she might say, how might Jane answer? . . . Who would like to be Ellen? . . . Who would like to be Jane?

A description such as this projects the players immediately into conflict. Some of us may prefer to have our learners move more gently into valuing. Here is the description that we might create:

During the past summer Ellen and her parents took a long trip around North America. She collected several hundred postcards about the people and places she had seen. She thinks that the many differences she saw among people are very interesting. Now she wants to share her postcards with her best friend, Jane. Jane's main interest is sports. She does not care for anything else. But Ellen wants to try to get her really excited about all the different peoples and their ways in America. She has asked her to come to her house to see the postcards.

Now Ellen is waiting for Jane to appear. She has her box of postcards on the sofa. She hears the doorbell ring.

Now think for a few seconds about what will happen next. Think of what you would do and say if you were Ellen . . . If you were Jane. . . .

Who would like to be Ellen? . . . Jane?

In this situation the conflict is less severe. Many children would find it easier to accept the roles in this situation.

Perhaps by now you are beginning to generate ideas that you could use to create situations to be role played. Here are a few more:

- Ellen could try to persuade Jane to take a similar trip with her to enjoy the differences to be experienced.
- Ellen and Jane could become involved in an argument over the values of diversity in American life.
- Ellen and Jane could interact to design a poster which they think best depicts the values of diversity in American life.

- Ellen and Jane could be taking a walking trip on a street in the French Quarter. Each reacts in her own way to what they observe.

Now let us turn our attention to the situation in which the players focus on a characteristic of a vital role. In this case a vital role is one involved in interviewing, an interpersonal skill. We want to guide the children to explore for the preferred behaviors of an effective interviewer. *Effective interviewer* is the value object. Here is an example of a description that could be used with children:

John's class has been studying about jobs in the community. Several of the boys and girls are interested in managing service stations. They would like to know how much training service-station managers need, where they get their training, how much money the managers make, what their greatest problems are, and why they like to manage service stations. John has agreed to interview a service-station manager. He has decided to interview Mr. Hack, who manages the service station near his home. Mr. Hack has always been helpful when John needed to put air in his bicycle tires.

John is now at the service station. Mr. Hack is busy washing a car window. John is ready to start asking questions. Think about how you think he should go about it. Think for a few seconds about it. . . . Now imagine that you are Mr. Hack. How might you be feeling as you wash the car window and you see another car pulling in beside the pumps? What might you say to John? . . . Who would like to be John? . . . Mr. Hack?

The description above is designed to focus the children's attention on the advisability of making arrangements with an interviewee for a time when he will be available. Additional situations would focus their attention on the need for friendly conversation at the beginning of the interview, asking questions courteously, and thanking the interviewee for his or her time.

Role playing is a very effective way of guiding children toward insights in the use of interpersonal skills in standard situations. It is also effective for improving or maintaining the social climate.

Imagine that you are the teacher of a fifth-grade class that has just been informed that they are going to visit another school across town. They know that the children in this school are from ethnic backgrounds quite different from their own. When you inform them about the visit, they accept the news quietly. They neither make comments nor ask questions.

During the next couple of days you observe your learners on the playground. You discover that they are anticipating their visit to the school in ways that you might not have expected. Several children are calling each other by names characteristic of one of the ethnic groups at the school to be visited. One child amuses the others by imitating the language and gestures of an ethnic group. The others encourage him, and often repeat what he says. You can see that many of the children lack the values to have a worthwhile experience during the visit.

This is an opportunity for role playing. Diversity is again the value object. You create a situation related to diversity, but it is somewhat different from the situation you observed on the playground. Here it is:

Jannie has been in his new school for only a week. He is an immigrant from another country. He can speak the language of his new country, but in a slow, bookish way, and he has difficulty with a few of the sounds. In his former country, whenever children had an answer for a question, they stood beside their desks, spoke the answer in a loud, clear voice, made a bow to the teacher, and sat down. When Jannie did this for the first time, the class laughed. Later in the day he saw several children imitating him. He has not volunteered to answer a question since then.

It is the first day of the new week. "Come, Jannie," his mother says to him that morning, "Time to go to school."

"I will not go to that school," replies Jannie.

Take a few seconds to think why Jannie refuses to go to school. . . . How do you think he feels? . . . What will he say to his mother? . . . How might she feel as she hears what has happened? . . . What advice might she give Jannie? . . . Who wants to be Jannie? . . . His mother?

The purpose of this description is to guide children in developing empathy for children who

are different from themselves. The described situation is similar to the real situation, but it is different enough that the children did not interpret it as an ill-disguised attempt by the teacher to make them moralize against themselves.

In casting this role-playing session, you ordinarily would not accept the skilled imitator described above. This problem is too close to his own. This is one of the *DO NOTs* for role playing of this kind. *THE CHILD WITH THE PROBLEM DOES NOT ROLE PLAY HIMSELF OR HERSELF.* The other *DO NOT: DO NOT FORCE A CHILD TO ROLE PLAY.*

As you can see, some kinds of social-studies learnings cannot be accomplished as well in any other way as role playing. Let us see how the situation description fits into the entire role playing session. Here are the procedures:

1. *Introductory remarks.* These lead toward the situation description. When the situation is based on a social-studies generalization developed by the children studying facts, the introductory remarks develop a review of the facts. When the situation is based on an interpersonal skill, the remarks prompt a general discussion of the skill. When the situation deals with a problem emerging from the social climate, a brief remark leading directly into the situation is given. Example: "Sometimes boys and girls going to a new school have difficulties."

2. *Presenting the situation.* This is primarily a matter of relating the situation to the children. It leads directly into roles.

3. *Role acceptance.* As soon as the children volunteer to accept roles, dismiss them to go to another part of the classroom by themselves to think about their roles. Ordinarily they should do this apart from each other. Sometimes children need mutual support. If you allow them to plan together, they may plan a production which inhibits spontaneous reaction. If they plan together, keep the time short. If you wish to ensure more conflict, you may give each child a brief description of his or her role that goes beyond what is given in the situation description. Examples:

You are Ellen. You tend to become a little upset when people don't seem to like what you are trying to do for them. You sometimes have to struggle to keep from exploding.

You are Jannie. You are a shy boy. You do not like to talk about what is bothering you, not even to your mother.

4. *Audience preparation.* While the role players are thinking about their roles, review the situation quickly. Alert them to observe the players carefully to see whether they would react in the same or different way in the situation.

5. *The enactment.* Call the players to the place of enactment. Invite them to consider any properties that they might need for their role playing. Get them started. A player may be suddenly overwhelmed by the center-stage position. Help this person to get into role by saying something like: "Just think about who you are *(the name of the fictitious character).* How do you feel? Say and do what your feeling tells you to." Perhaps you will need to review the situation. Observe carefully. If the players become so deeply immersed in their roles and a fight is about to ensue, stop the role playing. Otherwise, allow it to continue until enough ideas have been given to support a judgment or to clarify the existence of opposing judgments. If a player has had a particularly stringent role, help that person to remove himself from the role by saying something like this: "It is time for you to be your usual merry self, Elsie."

6. *The postdiscussion.* Review the situation quickly, then have the players tell how they felt, what they were trying to do in their role, and why they reacted in the way they did to others in the role playing. Guide the audience in reacting to what they saw. Because they will be critical, guide them in being supportive of what the players did and encourage them to use the role names in their remarks. Perhaps you will want to write this on the chalkboard: "If I had been playing that role, I would have . . ." Focus the children's attention on it and encourage them to use it as a guide in formulating their remarks.

7. *The reenactment.* The need for reenactment becomes evident when new ideas emerge to be explored by further role playing. The situation is still the same, yet somewhat altered as a result of the first enactment. Roles are accepted, the role playing occurs, and another postdiscussion takes place. When your learners accept the value judgment surfaced by the players and reinforced in the postdiscussion, there is no need for a reenactment, unless a child brings up a "what if? . . ." If two positive judgments emerge, these are identified as alternatives, and a discussion of the feasibility of each may occur. If two opposing value judgments are surfaced, there is likely to be a need for reenactment, preferably of the more positive judgment.

8. *The evaluation.* This may involve a scrutiny of three possible kinds of results. The first relates to the impact of the role-playing experience itself. If the experience was focused on a social-studies generalization, you may involve the children in a creative activity such as poster construction or creative story writing related to the value object. You will look for manifestations of the value judgment in these products.

If the role playing was focused on an interpersonal skill, you will observe for the use of the valued behavior or debrief learners about their experience when they tried the behavior out of your sight.

If the role playing was focused on a value to improve the social climate, you will observe learners who originally had difficulty with the value to see whether there is improvement.

The second aspect to evaluate is how the children felt about role playing as a classroom activity. In this case you conduct individual interviews or have the children complete self-rating sheets dealing with how they felt about themselves, others, and the activity itself.

The third aspect to evaluate is how effectively you guided the role playing. You will review how you developed and used the values prompter, filled roles, guided the enactment, and conducted the postdiscussion.

Role playing, then, is a useful technique to

guide children in exploring values related to social-studies content, skills useful in social-studies tasks, and in establishing and maintaining the social climate necessary to interaction to process social-studies ideas. The unfortunate aspect of it is that it is of limited use with young children. Usually, role playing at the level discussed here is beyond the skills of children in kindergarten through third grade.

To children in these grades, roles, other than their own life roles, are imitations of what people do. For example, if a kindergarten child accepts the role of mother in a family, she imitates *her* mother, and often with embarrassing accuracy. However, you may bring young children close to role playing in at least two situations.

Suppose that you wanted your young learners to use a saw in a safe way as they built their boats for their model of the harbor. First you would demonstrate the proper use of a safety block. Then you would pretend that you are a certain child who was not listening and observing carefully during your demonstration. You would role play this child who would cut his or her finger while using the saw. Next you would role play the child who had paid careful attention. He or she does things

correctly and is safe. The children decide quickly whom they want to be like. A child demonstrates how to saw a board in a safe way. In many instances, you can role play certain skills to the benefit of young children.

Suppose that your young learners have just learned how the Eskimo father at one time hunted for the food for his family. Showing some simple puppets of Eskimos, you may guide the children in thinking about how the members of the family feel when the father is successful. Encourage the children to think how the father feels when he brings home a nice fat seal. Ask for a volunteer to take a puppet to pretend that he is the father. Have him say what he thinks the father would say. Then do the same with the other members of the Eskimo family.

These kinds of activities can help young children develop readiness for role playing in the later grades.

Simulation

This technique accomplishes what was for a long time a teacher's dream—total, active class participa-

ILLUSTRATION 3–3. *Two Groups Engaged in a Simulation Designed to Help Them Discover Positive Alternatives for Interacting with People Who Are Physically Different.*

tion. Sometimes it is confused with role playing because it requires that the players participate in roles. Also, conflict is often involved. Some simulations make provisions for the use of observers, but they do not have the same task as the audience in role playing. There are no audiences in simulation. Everyone participates.

Simulations are sometimes called *simulation games.* Many do have a gaming aspect in which a group of players are winners. This increases the motivation of the players and makes the simulation more intense. There is no agreement as to whether the pressure of winning should be provided. Some people have been concerned about the negative aspects of losing and the possible effect that it might have on learners, particularly those in the elementary school. Seeing how simulation activities help children learn, they simply dropped the game aspect.

In social studies, simulations are usually developed from systems in which conflict is inherent—labor-management, industrialists-environmentalists, political parties or candidates trying to win an election, countries trying to wage and win a war, etc. The values discovered are those often related to the system, or operations within the system in which *cooperation, competition, compromise, mode of persuasion, organization,* etc., serve as the value objects. Or the simulation may focus on a tangible value object.

Simulations help children to meet instructional objectives similar to these:

- The children will be able to describe how it feels to be a union negotiator.
- The children will be able to list the qualities needed by a negotiator in a labor-management dispute.
- The children will be able to describe at least one alternative acceptable to environmentalists.
- The children will be able to decide on the best way to organize ideas in a report.

Such objectives might also be met through reading, watching films, and listening to resource persons. The difference that simulation makes is

this: the child meets these objectives through his or her own participation, and thus meets them with greater depth of conviction and certitude.

Some simulations are designed to provide the learners with information as well as with opportunities to apply it. Such simulations may provide the information by computer or through information sheets given to the learners as they proceed through each phase of the simulation, and they may be designed to continue over a series of instructional periods in social studies, perhaps for as much as the equivalent of ten hours or longer. Most of these have been prepared commercially. They are often expensive or they do not meet our learners' needs or program requirements. Few are developed for use in the elementary school. More are available for use in the seventh and eighth grades than in the lower grades. Some are designed for fifth grade and above. Let us consider how we might go about designing simulations suitable for our learners.

Here is a simulation designed for use with a second grade.

EDITORS!

Objective. The children will be able to decide on the best way to organize ideas in a report about bread production.

Prerequisites. The children will have to be able to read simple sentences about bread production. They will also have to be well acquainted with the facts.

Materials. Eight copies of the following cut into separate sentence strips placed in envelopes:

Wheat is an important seed or grain.
It is used to make the bread we eat.
Farmers grow the wheat on big farms.
They sell the wheat to buyers.
The buyers store it and sell it to flour companies.
The flour companies send it to the mills.
There it is made into flour and put in bags.
The flour companies sell the flour to the bakeries.
The bakeries make it into bread and sell it to the stores.

We buy the bread at a store.
Many hands are needed to make our bread.

Each envelope will contain all the strips necessary for a single copy of the report. Paste and a mounting board will be included with each envelope.

Organization. The children will be divided into eight groups.

Conduct of the Simulation

1. Encourage the children to recall what they know about bread production.
2. Give an explanation similar to this: "Today we are going to play a game called 'Editors.' An editor reads people's stories. Sometimes they find that the ideas are mixed up. They try to put them in good order. That is what you are going to do as editors today. You will work in groups with other people in this class."
3. Divide the children into groups.
4. Explain what is contained in the envelopes and how the group is to decide on the order of the sentences. Recommend that they decide on the order of the sentences before they paste them on the board.
5. Distribute the materials and start the simulation.
6. Observe the groups as they work at the task. Help them read words they cannot recognize. To ensure less disappointment, check to see that the children are deciding on the order of the strips before pasting them on the board. As groups finish early, give them the additional task of deciding on a name for the story and the pictures they might make to illustrate it.
7. When the groups are finished, have them share their products. Be prepared for an order a little different from the original. Accept what the children produce as long as they can give reasons for the order they developed.
8. Encourage the children to tell how they worked together and to generate some rules that might be followed by a group given a similar task.

Because it is developed to build a skill, the above is a low-conflict simulation. Having the children discuss their experiences in the group helps them to see the value of cooperation, listening to what others have to say, and the like. This is simply a foretaste for something they will be able to do much more easily in a couple of years.

As you noticed in the prerequisites, the children already had the factual information and ancillary skills needed to be able to perform in the simulation. Also, provisions were made for the immediate participation of all the children in the class.

Now let us look at a simulation designed for use in a fourth grade or higher.

FOR WORK OR FOR PLAY!

Objective. Through simulation the children will explore an alternative for the use of a piece of city land.

Prerequisites. The children will have to be informed about the uses of city land for industrial or recreational purposes. They will have to be able to compose simple statements and to discuss an issue in a group by themselves.

Materials

1. A scenario describing the situation.

The state owns a piece of land in Midville. It is a large piece of land that has no buildings on it. Mostly covered with weeds and litter that people have thrown on it, it does have a few clear areas where children play. It is surrounded on three sides by homes and an apartment house. One side of it faces that part of Midville where the factories are built.

The state government would like to sell the land. Some factory operators have offered a very good price for it. They will build a large factory on it. This will be good for Midville because there are many men out of work there. The Governor thinks this is a good idea.

A community group has written to the Governor asking him not to allow the land to be sold. It is the Community Planning Council. The members of the Council think the land should be made into a city park to be used by families and children. The Governor has read their letter. He has decided not to allow to have the land sold to the factory operators if the Council can give good reasons for having a city park.

The Governor has appointed a Special Commission. The members of the Commission will study the land and the suggestions made by the Council. Then they will make a recommendation as to whether the land should be sold to the factory operators or given to the city of Midville to be used as a park.

2. Information sheets.
   a. *For the Council:* The children living near the piece of land have no good place to play. The factory that would be built on it dirties the air. That does not bother you as much as the need for a place where children can play.
   b. *For the Commission:* The unemployment problem in Midville is very serious. The Governor plans to use the money from the sale of the land to provide jobs until the factory is built.
3. A resolution form to be used by each group participating as a Council. See Figure 3–5.
4. Environmental rules.
   a. All discussion is to stay within the members of the group. There is to be no visiting among groups.
   b. Each group elects a leader. A person may be

Midville Community Center
21 Pine Street
Midville,_____

Date

The Midville Community Planning Council recommends that the piece of land known as Plot Z now owned by the State be given to the Council to be used as a city park. We recommend this

Because_____

_____

Because_____

_____

Because_____

_____

Because_____

_____

Because_____

_____

Signed_____ (Members of the Council)

_____ _____

_____ _____

FIGURE 3–5.

elected as a recorder if the group feels it needs one.
   c. Groups must stop talking when told that the time for discussion has ended.
   d. If a group is having a serious problem, the leader will ask someone to get the teacher.
5. Simulation rules.
   a. Each Council and Commission will meet for twenty minutes. Each Council will decide why Midville needs a city park on the piece of vacant land. Each Commission will develop a list of questions to ask a Council to find out whether they really think a park is needed and the kind of park they want.
   b. Each Council will meet with a Commission for fifteen minutes to present and discuss its resolution and to answer any questions the Commission may have.
   c. Each Commission will have five minutes to decide whether the land should be sold or given to the Council. Each Council will meet during this period to discuss what points seemed most acceptable to the Commission.

Organization. The class will be asked to number off by six. Persons with the same number will meet in a group. Groups with even numbers will be Councils; those with uneven numbers will be Commissions.

Conduct of the Simulation

1. Encourage the children to recall what they know about the different uses of land in a city.
2. Give an explanation similar to this: "Today we are going to do a simulation called, 'For Work or for Play.' You are going to be trying to solve a problem about the use of a piece of city land. Listen to the description of the situation." Read the scenario. Invite the children to ask questions about anything they do not understand in the scenario.
3. Divide the children into groups and assign them to a meeting place.
4. Read the environmental rules and answer any questions the children have about them.
5. Read the game rules and answer any questions.
6. Distribute the resolution forms to the Councils and start the simulation.
7. Observe the groups and give help as needed. Whenever necessary enforce the environmental rules. Watch the time carefully. At the end of the first twenty minutes, terminate the discussion, describe the task, and assign each Council to meet with a Commission. At the end of fifteen

minutes, separate Councils from Commissions, describe the new task, and have each group meet by itself. At the end of five minutes terminate all group discussion.
8. Conduct the postdiscussion.
   a. Have the Commissions report on their decisions and why they made them.
   b. Have the Councils report on what they thought was particularly effective with the Commissions.
   c. Have the class listen to all the resolutions to discuss which they thought presented the best reasons, and to decide what reasons they as a class would list on a resolution.
   d. Invite the children to comment on how they felt about their roles and the kinds of information they would like to have if they were to play the roles again.
   e. Have them consider whether this is really the way that community groups and state agencies work to make decisions.

In the above simulation, as in the previous one, you can see provisions for total, active participation. The value object was *a piece of land*. However, the *mode of persuasion* related to the operation of a community planning council and a state commission was also a value object.

The simulations most accessible and useful to you are those which you devise yourself to be used *after* the children have been well informed and have developed the skills necessary for active participation. Skills simulations like the first presented in this section may be devised for use in grade two and above. Systems simulations similar to the second presented here are suitable for use in grade four and above.

Here are suggested procedures to follow when devising simulations:

Skills Simulations

1. Decide on an objective. It should relate to a discovery about a skill which requires the co-operation of several children in a group.
2. Create a system of groups in which children can participate.
3. Develop and organize the necessary materials.
4. Create an introductory explanation.

Systems Simulations

1. Decide on an objective related to the work of opposing parts of a system to explore within an alternative or to generate alternatives.
2. Decide on the organization of groups from the pertinent human system. Develop the task that each group is to do by itself and the task it is to perform when conferring with another group. Draw up the environmental rules to govern the behavior of participants during the simulation and the game rules to be followed.
3. Develop and organize the necessary materials.
4. Create an introductory scenario.
5. Develop the questions to be used during the postdiscussion. Provide for all alternative ideas to be discussed and weighed, reactions to roles, and consideration of the real-life aspects of the simulation.

Perhaps you have noticed that simulations distort reality. The greatest distortion is in time—deliberating groups have much more time. Also, sizes of groups are often changed, and the genesis of the problem is telescoped into a few sentences. However, particularly at the end of a systems simulation, we invite the learners to consider these distortions. This rarely mitigates against the richness of the experience they have had or the depth of learning they have enjoyed.

Values Clarification [2]

This technique begins when children express individual purposes, aspirations, attitudes, interests, feelings, beliefs, and worries about just about any value object that exists. Any of these expressions is regarded as a values indicator. As a teacher you facilitate the clarification of them by responding in ways that:

1. Encourage children to make choices, and to make them freely.
2. Help them discover and examine available alternatives when faced with choices.
3. Help children weigh alternatives thoughtfully, reflecting on the consequence of each.
4. Encourage children to consider what it is that they prize and cherish.

ILLUSTRATION 3–4. *During Sharing, the Teacher Helps a Young Child Clarify His Values about His Book.*

5. Give them opportunities to make public affirmations of their choices.
6. Encourage them to act, behave, and live in accordance with their choices.
7. Help them examine repeated behaviors or patterns in their life.

From the above we can abstract the three processes on which values are based:

CHOOSING

1. freely
2. alternatives
3. after thoughtful consideration of the consequences of each alternative

PRIZING

1. cherishing, being happy with the choice
2. willing to affirm the choice publicly

ACTING

1. doing something with the choice
2. repeatedly, in some pattern of life.[3]

If a child, then, declared that she wanted to go to Japan, had made her decisions freely after considering Australia, England, and France, joyfully anticipated differences in language and customs, is making a scrapbook about Japan which she brings to school to share with the class from time to time (each sharing begins with, "When I go to Japan, . . ."), has decided to save her money for the trip, and does so regularly, we would say that she truly *values* a trip to Japan.

The child's declaration of a goal or purpose, that she wanted to go to Japan, might have occurred in one of two situations. One is a teacher-pupil situation in which the teacher stimulates the child to make the declaration, and the other is the pupil-teacher situation in which the child makes the declaration of her own volition in the presence of the teacher. Let us consider the latter first.

One day after school four weeks after the class had finished its study of Japanese life and customs, Joan, the learner, stops by the teacher's desk. Ms. White, her teacher, looks up from the papers she is correcting.

"You know what?" asks Joan.

"What?" responds Ms. White.

"I'm going to take a trip to Japan!" (Free choice)

"You are! I would have supposed that you would choose to go to England, or France, or Australia."

"I thought about those, but Japan is where I want to go." (Choice made from alternatives)

"Japan is such a long way off, and the language is so different. So are the foods."

"But I want to eat their foods and to learn their language and songs." (Consequences considered)

"You really want to go to Japan!"

"Do I! I think about it every day. Hardly a day goes by that I do not look at the scrapbook I am keeping." (Prized choice)

"I'd like to see it."

"Sure. I'll bring it to show you tomorrow." (Public affirmation)

"I'll look forward to that. I do hope that you will be able to get to Japan some day."

"I'll get there. I'm saving for it now." (Acting on the choice)

"Really?"

"I'm saving half my allowance every week."

"When did you start that?"

"Four weeks ago. And I haven't missed one week."
(Repeated action)

"I'm looking forward to seeing your scrapbook. Don't forget to bring it tomorrow."

The example above has been offered to show how a child might discover a value goal as a result of learning in social studies. It is possible that she might have discovered the purpose as a result of watching a television program or leafing through a magazine. The teacher's responses would have been similar. The proponents of values clarification believe that any time a child expresses a personal goal, aspiration, strong conviction, or the like, the teacher should give clarifying responses to help him or her explore the value related to the value object.

However, the teacher does not always have to wait for children to make affective assertions. They may be prompted to do so. A useful prompter is the value questionnaire. Let us suppose that Ms. White gave the following value questionnaire at the close of the class study of Japanese life and customs. (The function of each part is labeled here, but headings would not be included on a value questionnaire used with children.)

PROVISIONS FOR FREE CHOICE: NOTE THAT THE LEARNER MAY WRITE IN HIS OR HER OWN

Write all your answers on another sheet of paper. If, after you answer the first question, you find a question you do not care to answer, do not answer it.

1. If you had a chance to do any of the following, which one would you like best to do? Choose one and write it on your paper. If you do not like any, write one that you like.
   a. Read a book about the Japanese people.
   b. Take a trip to Japan.
   c. Write a letter to a Japanese boy or girl.
   d. Visit a Japanese-American family.
   e. Other: write your own choice.

PROVISIONS FOR CONSIDERING ALTERNATIVES

2. All the choices above were about Japan or the Japanese people. Is there some other country or people you like better? If your answer is *yes,* write the name of the country or the people.

PROVISIONS FOR CONSIDERING CONSEQUENCES

3. Answer each of these questions with a *yes* or *no.*
   a. Do you have enough time to do your choice?
   b. Would you spend your own money to do it?
   c. Can you do it by yourself?
   d. Would your parents like you to do it?

PROVISIONS FOR PRIZING AND AFFIRMATION

4. Think about your choice and answer each of these questions.
   a. Do you really like your choice? How much?
   b. Do you really want to do your choice? How much?
   c. Who are you going to tell about it?
   d. Will you tell everyone in the class about it?

PROVISIONS FOR ACTION

   e. If you are going to do your choice, make a list of the things that you can do about it now.
   f. What are you going to do first?
   g. If you have trouble trying to do your choice, will you keep trying? If *yes,* for how long?
   h. If you start following your choice, please let me know. If there is any way you think I can help, please let me know.

In the pupil-teacher situation, the teacher's clarifying responses may be questions or richly expressed reactions which prompt the child to continue to react in a direction of valuing. When using the value questionnaire, the teacher designs it to ask clarifying questions.

After the children complete the value questionnaires in school or at home, the teacher reads them. He or she simply wants to see whether the children have discovered something that they value. There is no concern for incomplete papers, except perhaps to discover children who may profit more from values clarification on a one-to-one basis with the teacher. For example, a particular boy in Ms. White's class gives a very limited response on the value questionnaire, and he is not one of the children who is eager to talk with her from time to time. However, she observes him carefully through the day and notices that he becomes a dynamo during mathematics learning—eager, attentive, responding to challenges successfully and zestfully. One day she stops at his desk while he is doing some independent work. She says, "Do you like math?"

"Yep," he replies, looking up at her as he completes an example.

"Do you like it better than anything else in school?"

"Yes."

"Better even than physical education?"

"Yes, except when we play baseball."

"What would you think about playing baseball every day but having no math?"

"That would be stupid. Math is more important."

And that is as far as she needs to go. This underscores the fact that the entire process is not necessary for clarifying values. Here is another device that the teacher might have used after the study of Japan:

1. Encourage the children to contribute to a list of possible activities that anyone might do after studying about the life and customs of the Japanese people. To get them started you might suggest *"take a trip to Japan"* and *"read a book about the Japanese people."* List these and their contributions on the chalkboard.
2. When the list is finished, conduct a simple vote on each item. Tell the children that they may vote for or against any item and that they do not have to vote on any item they do not have strong feelings about. Asking for a show of hands, conduct a vote on each item, first the *yes* vote, then the *no*. Encourage the children to look around the classroom to see how many people feel the same way they do.
3. (Optional) After the voting, call on children

who were very positive when giving a *yes* vote to tell why they were so excited about a particular choice.
4. Invite the children to tell you later about any choice that they decide to follow. Tell them that you are available to help them with any choice they accept.

The above device focuses on public affirmation as a vital event in the clarification process. It is as much a sharing as it is a self-assertion.

Actually, values-clarification theory supports the use of any of the events in the process—choosing, prizing, and acting—at any particular time, with no requirement that all the events be completed. Children may be involved at any given moment with just choosing, prizing, or acting. However, whenever prizing or acting are involved, the previous events are in some way implicit. The device described above occurs essentially within prizing, but choosing is also involved. The incident with the young mathematician focused on his favorite activity, basically a product of previous choosing and prizing experiences. Value questionnaires may also focus on one or two of the events. Here is an example:

Read the following carefully and write your answers to the questions following it:

Pierre is a French boy about your age. As a child in his family, he knows that his mother and father will decide what is important for him. They often remind him that he must study hard to be a worthwhile person when he grows up. He is expected to study by himself without help from anyone.

When he is at home and he wants to play, he plays with his younger brother. His parents do not want him to play with other children in the neighborhood. If his younger brother is doing his homework, Pierre reads or finds something else he can do by himself.

Pierre's best friend is Henri. Henri is Pierre's age. His mother and father are Pierre's parents' close friends. Pierre is delighted when the two families visit. For a short while he has a playmate his own age.

1. How is Pierre's life as a member of his family different from yours?
2. How do you think Pierre feels toward his brother? Do you feel the same way toward your brothers and sisters? How do you think they feel toward you? What might you do to improve how you and your brothers and sisters feel toward each other?
3. Do you feel the same way as Pierre towards the children of your parents' friends? Suppose that you felt the same as Pierre. Do you think this would make your life more or less interesting? In what ways?
4. If you decide to do something to improve how you and your brothers and sisters feel toward each other, or how you feel toward the children of your parents' friends, let me know about it. If you want to talk about it, let's get together soon.

This value questionnaire focuses on generating choices and acting on them. Prizing is suggested when feelings toward others are asked for.

As you look at the text on which this value questionnaire is based and consider the directions which the questions cast, you can sense the impact of values clarification on social-studies learning. If the facts about children's place in the French family are of such significance that they need to be remembered, assuredly they will be remembered as a result of completing the value questionnaire. More important, this questionnaire leads learners to seeing what is relevant for their lives in social-studies content.

At this point you may be wondering what happens to the value questionnaires after you look at them. You might just read them and hand them back to the children. Or you might write some pertinent comments on the margins: "You thought of a lot of other choices." "I can see you really like this." Or you may select some of the questionnaires to read to the class without identifying who wrote them. Perhaps you will form the class into small groups to share their questionnaires. You could return the questionnaires to the class and have volunteers share their responses with the rest of the class. However, the discussion is not permitted

to become argumentative. The emphasis is on sharing.

And sharing brings us to what might be done about values clarification with young children. As soon as children can speak intelligible sentences and can listen to what others have to say, can "publicly affirm" what they believe, prefer, find interesting, and the like, they can participate in the process of values clarification related to social-studies content. Let us suppose that our kindergarten class has just completed a short social-studies unit about the school nurse. Using a few simple sketches or stick puppets of the characters involved, we tell a "slice of life" story:

Billie is in kindergarten, and his sister Susan is in first grade. Their father does not live with them. Their mother works at a store. In the morning she takes them to Ms. Green's house. They stay there until it is time to go to school. They return to her house after school.
Late in the afternoon their mother comes to pick them up. Together they return to their own home.
One afternoon she drives the car in front of Ms. Green's house as she always does. Billie and Susan race to the open car door as they always do. They hug and kiss their mother as they always do.
As soon as the car door is closed and the car is out in the street again, their mother says, "Billie and Susan, I have a surprise to tell you."
"We are going to have hotdogs for dinner!" guesses Billie.
"I'm afraid not," says their mother.
"We are going to the park for a picnic!" guesses Susan.
"No, not that," says their mother.
"Then what?" ask the children.
Their mother smiles a big happy smile and says, "I am going to learn to be a school nurse!"

We then conduct an oral value questionnaire. The children respond to these questions:

• How do you think Billie feels about this?
• What do you suppose Susan thinks about it?
• What do you think might happen to them now?
• Suppose your mother told your family that she was going to learn to be a school nurse? How might you feel about that?
• If your mother were going to learn to be a school nurse, she would have to go to school. She might

have to study after dinner every night. How might that change what you are used to doing with her after dinner?

• What might you do to help her? What kinds of things do you think would help her most? What things would you like most to do?

This is quite a few questions for a kindergarten. If they became fidgety after the fourth question, which introduces values clarification, we would terminate the discussion. What is important is that the children have experience with the process and not that they answer all the questions.

Sometimes it is possible to give young children a values questionnaire. For example, after our first-grade class has studied a nearby neighborhood shopping center and learned about the different people who work there, we might give them a questionnaire like Figure 3–6.

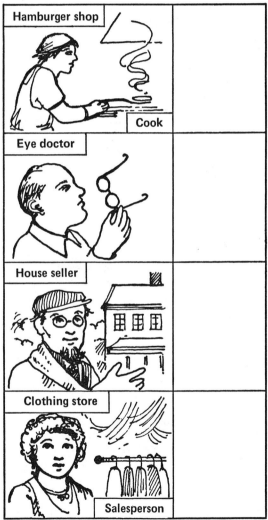

FIGURE 3–6. *Value Questionnaire for a Primary Grade.*

The children would mark an "X" after the illustration of the person that they might like most to be when they grow up. Or they mark "X" after all the persons they would like to be. After the marking, we could have the children raise their hands, illustration by illustration, to indicate which they had marked. They could be encouraged to tell why they would like to be one of the workers.

Frequently values-clarification techniques are used to help young children develop self-concept. In small groups led by the teacher, they might tell why they like certain persons in the group, nice things that they have seen persons in the group do, nice things that they have themselves done, etc. Activities such as these improve the social climate.

And, of course, the pupil-teacher values clarification in the pupil-teacher situation can occur at any grade level.

Values clarification, then, can provide many opportunities for children for values exploration related to social-studies content and to maintain the social climate necessary to positive, productive interaction.

Values Analysis

This technique for values exploration emphasizes the gathering and weighing of information to support a value judgment. A pair of proponents for the technique make this assertion:

In any evaluative decision-making process the following six tasks must be carried out.

1. Identifying and clarifying the value question.
2. Assembling (gathering and organizing) purported facts.
3. Assessing the truth of purported facts.
4. Clarifying the relevance of facts.
5. Arriving at a tentative value decision.
6. Testing the value principle implied in the decision.[4]

This array of tasks, developed and sequenced from a model of logical thought, requires that children be skilled in finding and reading resources and organizing what they find. If materials are available, children in grade six and above may perform the tasks with teacher guidance. Children in grade five and lower will need the teacher's assistance to complete each task.

To enter the array of tasks, the children will need to choose or be given a value object and related issue which they can understand. Let us suppose that your second grade (which is about the lowest grade in which values analysis can be conducted) has just completed a social-studies unit about transportation in the city. They can recognize the various vehicles and how they are used, and they know about the necessity for regulating the flow of traffic through the use of traffic lights, stop and warning signs, and painted lines and curbs. They are well acquainted with the crosswalk, because you know they need to learn to be more careful as they use crosswalks. Crosswalk is the value object. Here is how you might introduce the value object and establish a point of view for it:

Take the children on a walking trip to the crosswalk that they use most frequently to enter and leave school. There is no stoplight and the school patrol members are not there. Guide the children in identifying how they can tell that what they see is indeed a crosswalk—the painted lines crossing the street and the diagonal lines connecting the lines. The curb at either end is painted red. Review what *red* means. Have them discuss why there are crosswalks. Encourage them to tell you about other places where there are crosswalks (at stoplights). Inform them that the kind of crosswalk they are going to be talking about back in the classroom is one just like that in front of the school.

The stage is now set for the value question. The children know the kind of crosswalk they are going to be discussing. When they discussed why crosswalks are needed, they established *personal safety of the pedestrian* as the point of view. When everyone is back in the classroom and ready for the discussion, you communicate the value question:

Encourage the children to help you make the most accurate drawing you can of the crosswalk at the front of the school. Draw it on a large piece of paper. Label the school and streets in the drawing. Then you say "Here is our crosswalk. Do you think it helps you and the other people to be safe? Why?"

The first task is completed at this point. Clarified and identified, the value question has been given. Probably everyone will think that the crosswalk is a safe place. However, if a child or two begins to point out that they are unsafe, encourage them to talk about why they think so. Then inform the class that they will be thinking how crosswalks are both safe and unsafe. Encourage them to choose whether they want to talk about the safety or lack of safety in crosswalks first. Whichever they choose, encourage them to retrieve facts from their experience. (Assuming the children want to discuss the safety of crosswalks first), say something like this: "Many of us think that crosswalks are safe. What is it that makes them safe?"

Possible responses:

Drivers can see them.
Drivers won't drive across them when people are on them.
Drivers are more careful when they see them.

And as each response is given, record it on a chart to the right of the drawing and give a criterion:

Anything that drivers can see to keep them from running into people is good.
Whatever will remind drivers to stop when they see people in the street is good.
Whatever helps drivers to be more careful is good.

If a child should say something like this: "I think it is because they are white," you would respond with: "Right now we want to know what you have seen with your own eyes. What have you seen that shows that a crosswalk is a safe place?"

Then you guide the children in surfacing facts about how crosswalks are unsafe. Record each on a chart to the left of the drawing.

Possible responses:

People sometimes forget that cars cannot stop quickly.
People don't watch the cars.
People play around in the crosswalk.

You give a criterion for each response—forgetting that cars cannot stop quickly can make a crosswalk a dangerous place, etc. If a child gives an opinion, you ask for a fact.

Focus the children's attention on each chart of facts to decide which fact in each list is most important. If they have difficulty with deciding, comment that what seems important to one person is not to another, and terminate the activity.

Because you are working with young children, you combine assembling facts and assessing their truth as they are given. You have determined how the facts should be organized (safe vs. unsafe) and whether a child offers an opinion, you ask for a fact.

Now for the task of helping the children to check the relevance of their facts. Perhaps the best resource is an expert from the city traffic department. Next best would be a police officer because

ILLUSTRATION 3–5. *A Class Contributes to a Statement Chart during Values Analysis.*

his uniform could introduce a bias to whatever he might say. A well-informed member of the school patrol might serve. If none of these is available, you might introduce a puppet as a traffic expert who discusses each of the facts the children have contributed:

Present the puppet: "This is Mr. Green who works in the traffic department downtown. One of the things he does is to decide where crosswalks should be painted across the street. He is here this morning to talk about our facts with us. Good morning, Mr. Green. We are glad you can be with us this morning."

Mr. Green: "Good morning, boys and girls. I am happy to be here this morning. How can I help you?"
Teacher: "We have been talking about safety in crosswalks. Here are our lists of facts. Would you please look at this first one—drivers can see them— and tell us what you think about it?"
Mr. Green: "That is true, even at night. That is why we paint them white."

The discussion proceeds until all the facts have been treated. Mr. Green then takes his leave.

The facts are established as relevant, that is, meet the criteria of safety or danger. The next task is to arrive at a tentative value decision. Here is how you can go about it:

Conduct a review of the contents of the charts, then ask, "What can we say now about the safety of crosswalks? Can we just say, 'Crosswalks are safe,' or 'Crosswalks are unsafe,' or what?"
Be prepared for any of the following responses:

Crosswalks are safe and unsafe.
Crosswalks are sometimes safe.
Crosswalks are sometimes unsafe.

Do not be surprised if your children want to see both the second and the third statements as their value rating.

And now to the final task—testing the acceptability of the value principle. This principle has been operating since the first activity. It might be stated in this way: *When using a crosswalk, we should be careful.* As you work with your second grade, you will be guiding them in testing this principle in some way. Here are some possibilities:

- State the principle, then ask, "Do you think this is a good idea for just boys and girls, or do you think it is good for everybody, children and grown-ups alike?" Guide discussion.
- State the principle, then restate it in a more general form as a question, "Does this also mean that we have to be careful any time we cross a street or a road, whether there is a crosswalk or not?" Guide discussion.
- State the principle, then say, "Let us pretend that everyone remembered to be careful when using a crosswalk. What do you think would happen then?" Guide discussion.
- Conduct a planning session with your learners in which they discuss where a crosswalk might be constructed in the classroom, how it might be made, and what might be made to represent automobiles. Have them complete the constructions they think are necessary. Guide them in using what they have made to explore what being careful in a crosswalk really means. They could do some demonstrative role playing of persons (a) preparing to use a crosswalk and using a crosswalk when they see automobiles near, far away, or stopped, or (b) helping kindergarteners use a crosswalk safely. They might go out to the crosswalk at the front of the school and, as a class, practice what they learned about being careful.

The above activities are choices. My preference would be for the last because it most closely meets the needs of children in second grade.

As you think back over the sequence of activities for second grade presented here, you can see the various ways you have to help them make a values analysis. Your role would be the same with any grade through fourth. It would change if you were teaching children in the later grades.

Let us assume now that you are teaching a sixth grade. Your class has just completed a social-studies unit about diversity of forms of government in the world. They are familiar with such terms as *absolute, limited,* and *constitutional monarchy, constitution, democracy, presidential form of government, cabinet form of government, socialism,* and the like. And they can name a country in which each obtains. However, they have become intrigued with the presidential form of government and cabinet form of government. Sometimes arguments have occurred. The result often is that the children who think that the cabinet form of government is a good alternative are often overwhelmed by the sheer volume of verbiage directed at them. You decide that it would be a good idea for each child to make a values analysis of the form of government they prefer. At this point, the value question has been identified and clarified.

You know that the children's textbooks contain many positive facts but few negative facts. The children will need to have access to more facts of greater recency than those in their textbooks. You decide that recently published almanacs will serve this need. You gather as many of these as you find in the school and materials center. You also prepare a statement sheet with the heading shown in Figure 3–7.

On the right side of the statement sheet the children will write the negative statements expressing facts that are unfavorable to the form of government they are considering. On the left side they will write the favorable statements. However, the statements will be first recorded on note cards or slips of paper, and then ranked. In ranked form they are entered on the statement sheet. You are ready to get the class started with a value analysis. Here are the procedures you might follow:

1. Write on the chalkboard: *Cabinet form of government. Good? Bad? Presidential form of government. Good? Bad?* Have members of the class discuss what they can recall about the two forms of government. Ask the children to indicate which they think is better. List their names after the form they prefer.
2. Showing the almanacs and mentioning their textbooks, tell the students you are going to form them into small groups to read and take notes about the form of government they prefer.

They are to look for facts, not opinions. If necessary, review the difference between facts and opinions. Remind them to record each fact as a statement. Those choosing to make the analysis about the cabinet form should reread the pertinent sections in their textbooks and read the world history sections in the almanacs about the United Kingdom, The Netherlands, and Sweden. Those dealing with the presidential form should use their textbooks also and read in the almanacs about the United States, Ecuador, and Uganda. Form the groups and have them start.
3. After the groups have taken their notes, present the next task. They are to divide their notes into two piles—those which tell about strengths or the positive aspects, and those which express the weaknesses or negative aspects. Then they are to arrange the notes in ranked order, the most important fact first and on down through the notes until the least important occurs at the end. Finally, they are to be copied on the statement sheet. After demonstrating how a statement sheet is to be completed, distribute them and have the groups work at the task. A completed statement sheet might look like the one presented in Figure 3–8.
4. Each group presents the contents of its statement sheet to the class. Different listings and differences in ranking are discussed. Use the results to have two recorders, one for the cabinet form and the other for the presidential form; prepare at the direction of the class a ranked list of negative and positive statements to serve as master lists for the whole class to use.
5. Focus the children's attention on the negative statements in each list. Encourage them to think about possible solutions to improve each system. Form them into their original groups to generate solutions and to develop both positive and negative statements for each in ranked order. A group effort might resemble that shown in Figure 3–9.
6. Each group presents its solutions to the class. Guide the class in accepting each suggested solution as a possible alternative. After the solution, encourage the class to ask questions about points that had arisen in their minds during the value analysis but for which they could find no answers. You answer the questions or, if possible, arrange for an expert to respond to them.
7. Have each child write or record on audiotape his or her own reactions to the value object as a result of the value analysis. Distribute blank paper to the children, have them fold it in half

Form of Government

For	Against
1.	1.
2.	2.

FIGURE 3–7.

Cabinet
Form of Government

For	*Against*
1. The prime minister is a member of the legislature.	1. The prime minister is the head of government only while a majority of legislature has confidence in him or her.
2. He or she is elected by the legislature.	2. When he or she loses their confidence, he or she must resign.
3. He or she can present laws to the legislature and argue for them.	3. Elections may occur often.
4. He or she appoints his or her own cabinet from the legislature.	4. If elections take a long time, the country may have poor government for a while.
5. Members of the cabinet may present laws to the legislature and argue for them.	5. The Netherlands and Sweden have recently had trouble appointing a prime minister.
6. The United Kingdom has had a strong government for many years.	

FIGURE 3–8. *Statement Sheet.*

FIRST SOLUTION

The prime minister should be elected by at least a two-thirds vote of the entire legislature.

Negative	**Positive**
1. This could delay the election of prime minister.	1. A prime minister with two-thirds of the legislature supporting him or her at first would be less likely to lose their confidence.
2. The government would lack needed leadership over a long period.	2. The government would be assured leadership over a longer period.
3. The prime minister would have to make promises to members of the legislature that he or she might find hard to keep later.	

SECOND SOLUTION

Increase the number of times that a legislature has to show its lack of confidence in a prime minister before he or she has to resign.

Negative	**Positive**
1. A prime minister could make too many mistakes before having to resign.	1. This would avoid conducting many costly elections.
2. He or she might begin trying to bribe certain members of the legislature for support.	2. After losing the legislature's confidence once, the prime minister would be more careful.
	3. The prime minister would do more consulting and planning with the legislature.

FIGURE 3–9. *Proposed Solutions.*

horizontally, label the upper half as *Personal Discoveries* and the lower half as *Personal Recommendations*. Inform them that under personal discoveries, they should write any new ideas or personal feelings they discovered as they did the value analysis, and after personal recommendations they should write what they think ought to be done. The children who plan to audiotape their reactions may use the paper as a help in remembering what they want to say.

Because the children in sixth grade can usually read their textbooks and are able to work in small groups, they are able to do the job more independently. After they have done several analyses assisted in ways described above, you may provide for individual value analysis. You do this by developing a direction sheet and recording sheets. An example of a direction sheet is presented in Figure 3–10.

You have already studied about Mainland China. You know how the people live, what they produce, export, and import, and how they are governed. Using this direction sheet, you will find out about *Personal Freedom in Mainland China*. Think about it and make some personal decisions about it. All the materials you will need are at the study center in a green box labeled "PERSONAL FREEDOM IN MAINLAND CHINA." Do all of the tasks listed below. Arrange for conferences with me when you need them and when you complete certain tasks as shown below.

Tasks   **Conference Dates**

1. Get a statement sheet, write your name on it, and write *Personal Freedom in Mainland China* in the blank at the top.
2. Read the materials in envelopes 1, 2, and 3. Take notes as you read. Look for facts favorable or unfavorable to personal freedom in Mainland China.
3. Divide your notes into two piles, one for favorable facts and the other for unfavorable facts.
4. Rank each pile of notes, the most important first.
5. Copy your notes on the statement sheet and arrange to show them to the teacher.   ‾‾‾‾‾‾‾‾‾
                                                                   (Date)
6. Get a solution sheet, write your name on it, and write *Personal Freedom in Mainland China* in the blank at the top.
7. Using negative, or unfavorable, facts on your statement sheet to see what needs to be improved, write at least two solutions.
8. Write on note paper as many negative and positive facts as you can for each solution. Divide the facts into two piles, one for negative and the other for positive facts. Rank each pile of facts, the most important first.
9. Rank your solutions, the most important first, and copy them and the facts that go with them on the solution sheet and arrange to show them to the teacher.   ‾‾‾‾‾‾‾‾‾
                                                                   (Date)
10. Get a reaction sheet, write your name on it, and write *Personal Freedom in Mainland China* in the blank at the top.

FIGURE 3–10. *Values-analysis Sheet.*

Tasks	Conference Dates
11. Reviewing your statement sheet and your solution sheet, write as many statements as you can about your *Personal Discoveries* and as many recommendations as you can under *Personal Recommendations*. Arrange to show your reaction sheet to the teacher.	_____ (Date)

FIGURE 3–10 (*continued*)

This direction sheet lacks provisions for discussing ideas with others in the class and a question and answer session. The conferences with the teacher replace these.

If children have experiences with value analysis in grades two through seven, there is a chance that some of them will be able to do it independently with value objects of their own choosing in grade eight. However, even as an assisted or guided procedure, it helps children discover a rational way of exploring values.

In this section we have reviewed five techniques for guiding children in values exploration. Which is best? That which most closely meets the needs of your children and which you can conduct confidently. If you wish to reach a high level of professional effectiveness in conducting values explorations, master all the techniques and use each as it is most appropriate for each class of children and the learning at hand.

VALUES EXPLORATION IN SOCIAL STUDIES

Some teachers guide children into values exploration when they see a definite need for it. Some think that there should be a daily period for values exploration. Sometimes this becomes the instructional period for social studies. And others think that values exploration is particularly appropriate after the children have learned a comprehensive parcel of social-studies facts. Let us examine briefly each of these points of view.

Exploration as Needed

There are three common situations in which values exploration is needed.

The first of these is characterized by a large number of children in a class who need to gain confidence in themselves and to build trust in others before they can listen, discuss, read, or construct. In this situation values clarification and role playing have been found to be helpful.

The second situation is characterized by a large number of children in a class who must sense the relevance of what they are about to learn before they begin to learn it. Sometimes this occurs with certain subject matter. Here is an example:

Ms. X thought that a study of the United States Constitution would offer a challenge to her gifted fifth-grade class. Her strategy of introduction was to have the children meet in small groups to discuss what good rules they thought might be developed for a classroom. The groups interacted as they usually did— volubly. When the groups were to share their ideas, there was not much to share. They mouthed the usual classroom rules and gave the most vapid of reasons.

X was disturbed. She knew the class would profit from the study. She changed her introductory strategy. She started following it as soon as the children were settled at their seats the next morning.

At the beginning of the school year, the children had decided that their class president would lead the pledge of allegiance and conduct the current-affairs program. This morning, instead of signaling to him that it was time to begin the school day, she led the pledge and current events program herself. The class had decided originally that each of five people would have two minutes to report and use one minute to answer any questions. She allowed four people one minute, would permit no questions, and told the re-maining person that there was no time left for his report.

Usually the class spent five minutes planning their study in social studies. This morning she distributed a long list of questions for each child to answer by reading the text.

Previously the children were able to talk quietly as they worked. This morning she would not permit that. The children were used to sharpening their pencils as they needed to. This morning they could not. An uneasy silence settled over the classroom. Ten minutes before the end of the period, she asked for the written answers to the questions to be handed in. There were some protests. She had said they would have until the end of the period.

Putting the papers down, she faced the class and remarked, "You people are not really yourselves this morning. Is something bothering you?" Now that she was behaving in her usual way, the members of the class were confused. Finally one child said, "We don't feel right because you changed the rules."

"Yes, I did," she said. "I didn't think it would make any difference. You didn't seem to think that rules were important yesterday. I thought that just any old set of rules would do."

This met with cries of, "Unfair!" "You always talk over rules with us."

"Well," she pointed out, "such things do happen when people do not look at their own rules from time to time to see how well they are working."

This led to a decision by the children to make their own constitution using the United States Constitution as a model.

Ms. X contrived a situation which prompted the children to examine what they valued.

In the third situation, a large number of children in a class lack informational background as well as skills in language composition. In this situation, role playing or simulation at the beginning of a social-studies unit may help the children generate interest in the topic and accept their need for more information. Either of the techniques may be used to help them integrate, express, and synthesize the social-studies facts they have acquired. The techniques may be used until the children learn the output skills to a functional level.

When any of these situations is obvious, the teacher gives careful thought to ways of using values-exploration techniques.

Exploration on a Regular Basis

As one reviews the different techniques for values exploration, there emerges the possibility that the instructional program in social studies could be values centered. Such a program might be organized in one of two basic ways.

One way would be to place the greater emphasis on learning activities designed to build self-concept. Such a program would make provisions for many values-clarification and role-playing activities as well as in-depth discussions in both small and large groups. The better program would be based on children's needs as manifested in the classroom.

However, commercial programs such as the *Human Value Series,*[5] *Focus on Self-Development,*[6] *TA* (Transactional Analysis) *for Kids, TA for Tots,*[7] *Developing Understanding of Self and Others,*[8] *Inside/Out,*[9] and others are now available in many school districts. These programs are created on the assumption that all children have the same needs. They have a strong psychologistic flavor. The content and skills of the social sciences are rarely treated.

In some cases these programs are the sole social-studies program. In others, there is a social-studies program, and values education is considered an added, separate subject.

The other basic way of organizing a values-centered social-studies program is to select a cluster of values, such as religious values or cultural-heritage values, on which to base a program, or to sample a variety of values from different social-science points of view—cultural, geographical, economics, political, and the like.

Such a program would make wide use of all the techniques.

If the program were based on a cluster of values developed from a single point of view, such as religion or cultural heritage, the teacher would need to maintain openness for effective values exploration. If it is based on values from a variety of points of view, social-science content and skills objectives would also be met.

Values exploration on a regular basis has a strong appeal. Many of us regard it as a viable alternative for instructional program development in social studies.

Exploration to Extend Developmental Studies

The developmental program in social studies provides children with opportunities to explore many environments from different points of view and to learn the skills that make exploration more fruitful and satisfying. The elements of content or skill are learned in a series of moments designed for those purposes. Each child's self is involved in his or her sense of accomplishment at knowing content and being able to exercise skills in seeking, organizing, interpreting, and using it.

Values exploration, be it at the close of a social-studies unit or during the current-affairs program, provides the child with that needed moment of reflection to decide what particular meaning or relevance this or that discovery has for him or her.

We have discussed three choices here. You will have to make the ultimate choice yourself. My own preference is to use the first choice as a guiding principle—values exploration to satisfy children's immediate needs. If the other choices are open to me, I will use them to organize and conduct a varied program—values-centered units interspersed with developmental units.

SUMMARY

Emotional reactions and expressions of attitudes are indicators of values. Values may be analyzed rationally. The verbal expression of a value often consists of a value object and its rating. A value criterion consists of a value object and a rating related to one of its characteristics. A value principle consists of a value object and two or more characteristics rated at the same value, or two or

more criteria. Point of view makes a difference when one makes a value judgment.

The characteristics of a value object are facts that the valuer knows about it. Children's factual background determines which value objects children will be encouraged to judge.

Making decisions requires making value judgments. Children are taught to explore values to help them make decisions rationally.

A value exploration occurs within a concept of a value object. It includes making judgments, establishing criteria, and applying principles. The exploration results in a clearer perception of the concept, or a changed value.

Children may be guided through values exploration by participating in in-depth discussions, role playing, simulation, values clarification, and values analysis.

In-depth discussion begins with a brief review of the facts about the value object. The exploration is stimulated by a question which encourages children to make judgments and substantiate them.

Role playing requires that children be confident while being observed closely by their peers. Dramatization, creative dramatics, and pantomime experiences help children develop this confidence. The values prompter for role playing is the description of a conflict situation. Volunteers assume the roles in the situation while the rest of the class is the audience. The discussion of the performance surfaces alternative values. The situations role played may be based on classroom problems, problems of people in other times and places, or discovering effective behaviors associated with interaction skills.

Simulations are models of reality in which all the children in a class assume roles. The models require interaction within human systems in which conflict is inherent or within human operations or skills. The learners interact, frequently in a series of phases, and then discuss their experience to surface alternative strategies, feelings, and attitudes. Frequently, meaningful interaction requires factual background.

Values clarification guides children in examining human activities to decide how freely they choose them, how much they prize them, and how willing they are to make them a part of their lives. Clarification occurs in pupil-teacher interactions, completing special value questionnaires, or participating in discussions.

Value analysis emphasizes the gathering and weighing of information to support a value judgment. Young children require teacher assistance, but older children may do much of the analysis independently.

Three strategies are possible for values teaching in social studies: (1) exploration as needed, (2) exploration on a regular basis, and (3) exploration to extend developmental studies.

POSTSCRIPT

At the beginning of this chapter you were asked to take a position on what you felt about values teaching. You made a few notes to describe what you thought. Review those notes now. Have you changed your opinion? If so, in what way? If your opinion is unchanged, what reasons can you give?

FOR FURTHER UNDERSTANDING

Cognitive Activities

1. By yourself or with a discussion partner, develop in your own words a definition for *value object, value rating, value criterion, point of view,* and *value principle.* If you are studying with a partner, reach a consensus on each definition and then validate it by reading the first section of the chapter.

2. Choose a value object, perhaps a food or favored pastime, and make a value diagram showing your analysis of it. If you have a study partner, you may both choose the same value object, make your diagrams independently, and compare the results.

3. Compare role playing and simulation as values-exploration techniques. Determine how they are similar and different.

4. Compare values clarification and values analysis as values-exploration techniques. Determine how they are similar and different.

5. Choose the values-exploration technique that you would prefer to use in social studies. Explain why you choose it over the others and list the problems it might cause you as you try to apply it.

6. How much emphasis do you believe that values exploration should be given in the instructional program in social studies? Give reasons for your opinion.

Practice Activities

(If you are teaching or have a laboratory assignment in a classroom, you may wish to complete the following with the intent of using in your classroom.)

1. Compose a set of rules which you think teachers should follow when conducting in-depth discussions.

2. Prepare two values prompters, one for an in-depth discussion and one for a role-playing session.

3. Invent a simulation to guide children in exploring for values within a situation of conflict or within a skill.

4. Compose a value questionnaire for use at a chosen grade level or cluster of grade levels.

5. Prepare the statement sheet and other materials you would need to guide a class in a value analysis centered on an appropriate value object.

Performance Activities

1. Evaluate the use of the items prepared in response to 2 through 5 above. In your evaluation, respond to these questions:
   a. How effective was it with children? Could they follow your direction and guidance easily? Give examples of evidence of learning.
   b. What is your reaction to your experience? What changes would you make to improve your skill with the technique? Do you want to try the technique again? Give your reasons.

SELECTED REFERENCES

Chesler, Mark, and Robert Fox. *Role-Playing Methods in the Classroom.* Chicago: Science Research Association, 1966.

Fenton, Edwin. "Moral Education: The Research Findings." *Social Education,* 40:188–93 (April, 1976).

Frazier, Alexander. *Values, Curriculum, and the Elementary School.* Boston: Houghton Mifflin Company, 1980.

Furness, Pauline Tymon. "Try Role Playing." *Today's Education,* 66:94–5 (January–February, 1977).

Hersh, Richard H., John P. Miller, and Glen G. Fielding. *Models of Moral Education.* New York: Longman, Inc., 1980.

Metcalf, Lawrence E., ed. *Values Education Rationale, Strategies, and Procedures.* National Council for the Social Studies, 41st Yearbook. Washington, D.C.: National Council for the Social Studies, 1971.

Muir, Sharon Pray. "Simulation Games for Elementary Social Studies." *Social Education,* 44:35–39, 76 (January, 1980).

Pate, Glenn S., and Hugh A. Parker, Jr. *Designing Classroom Simulations.* Belmont, Calif.: Fearon, 1973.

Raths, Louis E., Merrill Harmin, and Sidney B. Simon. *Values and Teaching,* 2nd edition. Columbus, Ohio: Charles E. Merrill, 1978.

Shaftel, Fannie R., and George Shaftel. *Role-Playing for Social Values: Decision-Making in the Social Studies.* Englewood Cliffs, N.J.: Prentice-Hall, 1967.

NOTES

1. This section and the later section on values analysis are based on ideas expressed in *Values Education,* Lawrence E. Metcalf, ed. 41st Yearbook, National Council for the Social Studies, 1971, pp. 1–119. Used with the permission of the National Council for the Social Studies and Lawrence E. Metcalf.

2. The material in this section is based on ideas expressed in *Values and Teaching* by Louis E. Raths, Merrill Harmin, and Sidney B. Simon. Columbus, Ohio: Charles E. Merrill, 1966.

3. Louis E. Raths, Merrill Harmin, and Sidney B. Simon. *Values and Teaching.* Columbus, Ohio: Charles E. Merrill Publishing Company, 1978, p. 28.

4. Jerrold R. Coombs and Melton Mieux. "Teaching Strategies for Value Analysis," in *Values Education,* Lawrence E. Metcalf, ed. 41st Yearbook, National Council for the Social Studies. Washington, D.C.: National Council for the Social Studies, 1971, p. 29.

5. *Human Value Series.* Steck-Vaughn Company, Box 2028, Austin, Texas 78767.

6. *Focus on Self-Development.* Science Research Associates, 259 E. Erie St., Chicago, Ill. 60611.

7. *TA for Kids, TA for Tots.* Jalmar Press, Department M, 391 Munroe St., Sacramento, Calif. 95825.

8. *Developing Understanding of Self and Others.* American Guidance Center, Inc., Publishers' Building, Circle Pines, Minn. 55014.

9. *Inside/Out.* National Instructional Television Center Box A, Bloomington, Ind. 47401.

4

Involving Children in Inquiry

Defined in its simplest terms, inquiry is the act of seeking to find, or find out about, something.

You have already been introduced to some aspects of inquiry—the assessment of inquiry operations in Chapter 2 and the quest for values in Chapter 3. As children inquire into values, they work in a subjective environment—themselves as products of experiences in and out of school. In this chapter we shall deal with how to involve them in quests in an objective environment to discover what it is like, how it is interrelated in function, time, and space, and what is predictable about it.

The following hypothetical problem will help you begin thinking about the place of inquiry in social-studies instruction and in children's learning:

You are the parent of a nine-year-old child who has just moved into a new neighborhood and enrolled your child in the school there. Your child has been in school for a week when you read in the newspaper that the school is continuing its special program emphasizing inquiry in social-studies instruction. The newspaper article reports glowing comments made by the principal and some of the teachers, but offers little explanation about the program.

How do you feel about this information? Do you think that something good is going to happen to your child? Or do you feel somewhat apprehensive? Or will you take a wait-and-see attitude? Give reasons for your feelings.

Write a few notes expressing what you feel, then put them aside for a later review.

INQUIRY AS A WAY OF LEARNING

As a way of learning, inquiry is different from the other ways which children experience in school. Much of what children learn in school occurs as a result of teachers' demands—circle this or underline that, fill these blanks or arrange those items in order, follow these directions as given or solve those equations, or tell me this or draw me a picture of that. These demands reflect the classic teacher-pupil model in which children place unquestioning trust in the teacher and do what they are told, and the teacher takes responsibility for telling them the right things to do. The children have little sense of purpose other than to respond to demands with the least harm to themselves. But inquiry as a way of learning requires that children be involved with establishing a purpose for learning.

Inquiry may be prompted by curiosity. Its purpose is simply to explore to find out about something. Or it may be prompted by interest. The purpose is to follow that interest, perhaps until it is satisfied or for all of one's life. Or it may be prompted by a pressing problem, and the purpose is to relieve the pressure. These prompters of and purposes for inquiry are a part of our life long before we enter the public schools. Of particular significance to us as social-studies teachers is the fact that these prompters and purposes provide models to follow as we guide children in learning about their physical and social environments and how to cope with them.

There is no denying that inquiry prompted by curiosity, interest, or a problem can proceed without recourse to the experience and knowledge of others through reading, listening, and interviewing. There is also no denying that the more exquisite satisfaction of curiosity, the more rewarding satisfaction of interest, or the more effective solution to a problem lies often in the experience and knowledge of others. Certainly, then, there is a place for these forms of inquiry in social studies. The overall goal for their use is to guide children in learning ways to use leisure time, to develop as personalities, and to use their rationality to solve problems.

Another form of inquiry has as its purpose to discover truth in knowledge, albeit tentative truth, and to explore its uses. Referred to as *scientific inquiry,* it, too, can serve as a model for organizing social-studies instruction. Here we guide children through procedures such as these:

1. Defining the problem in terms of the forces in conflict in the universe.
2. Hypothesizing explanations for conflict.
3. Selecting the most reasonable explanation.
4. Deciding how to investigate the explanation.
5. Investigating the explanation.
6. Organizing and summarizing the findings.
7. Judging the hypothesized explanation against the findings to arrive at a conclusion.
8. Recommending uses for the conclusion.

Scientific inquiry requires the rigorous application of logical thinking skills, the skills of information process—gathering, organizing, and expressing—and values-exploration skills. With this form of inquiry, almost all the skills that children learn in school are tested in application.

As children are guided through the procedures listed above, they are prompted to think analytically, synthetically, and evaluatively. Analytical thought leads them toward identifying forces in conflict, selecting the most reasonable hypothesized explanation, deciding how to investigate, selecting pertinent information, organizing and summarizing findings, and arriving at conclusions. Synthetic thought prompts them to pull all they know together to make hypotheses, and evaluative thought has them considering the uses for their discovered truth. This careful use of the thinking process is necessary because truth, tentative though it may be, must be reliable to be widely applicable in making decisions.

Scientific inquiry demands the careful application of information skills. As children experience it, they learn that listening, observing, viewing, interviewing, and reading are necessary for acquiring information; that discussion, in class or small groups, is helpful in clarifying and organizing information, and inferring from it; that oral and written composition skills and graphic skills are helpful in making ideas and structures of ideas emerge more clearly in their minds; and that mathematics is a skill useful in expressing relationships between parts and wholes, time and change, and place and place.

As already stated, the teacher guides children through the procedures of scientific inquiry, but the overall goal is for children to become independent. We do not want children to follow slavishly a formalized series of steps whenever they are faced with an issue they must resolve in order to commit themselves to an action, but we want them to be committed to truth seeking and the exercise of rationality.

As we examine the various forms of inquiry, we can detect common characteristics.

1. Inquiry demands that learners be involved, particularly in establishing and meeting purposes.
2. Inquiry demands the use of thinking skills. Sci-

entific inquiry makes the most stringent demands, but the other forms of inquiry cannot occur without them.

3. Inquiry demands the application of information-process skills, thus providing opportunities for learning to apply them.

4. Inquiry joins thinking skills with information-process skills in a purposeful way. John Dewey, an analytical philosopher who deeply scrutinized human behavior and learning has stated, ". . . Skill obtained apart from thinking is not connected with any sense of the purposes for which it is used." [1]

5. Inquiry is a process in which the significant events are identifying a purpose, acquiring knowledge to meet the purpose, and meeting the purpose. As a procedural way of thinking and extending thought, it is the keystone process in social-studies learning. (See Figure 4–1.)

6. Inquiry is a way of learning to learn how to satisfy curiosity, extend an interest, solve a problem, or seek truth.

At this point, it is almost inconceivable that an instructional program in social studies could be cast within a context other than inquiry, but some programs are. Sometimes the context is that of factual learning. Most of us as students have had so much experience with such programs that there is little need for us to discuss them further. Recently a folkloric context, sometimes labeled *cultural studies,* has been gaining in popularity in schools and districts located in multicultural milieux. In these studies children learn about the folk literature, music, dance, and art of the cultures with which they have personal ties. They find the studies to be enjoyable, and there is no denying that such studies build children's self-esteem and appreciation of the diversity among cultures. Every instructional program in social studies focusing on a culture is enriched with the inclusion of folkloric experiences, but if the total program consists only of such experiences, children's right to learn how to inquire to become informed and to make decisions is violated.

If we were to follow the principles asserted by John Dewey [2] and Jean Piaget,[3] a developmental psychologist whose observations are currently re-ceiving serious attention, we would ensure that each child's inquiry would begin with that child's personally expressed curiosity, interest, problem, or desire for an explanation. Many of us would like to do that, but most of us work with such large numbers of children within such severe limitations of space, time, and resources that we cannot provide for many such inquiries. But what we can do is to provide inquiry-rich learning environments. The characteristics of such environments include opportunities for children to be actively involved in:

• Exploring the known to discover what needs to be known.
• Making hypotheses (whenever appropriate).
• Developing the questions to be answered.
• Using as many resources as possible to acquire information.
• Organizing and interpreting information through personal expression with a self-chosen medium.
• Analyzing information to generate ideas.
• Testing ideas through application.

To these characteristics we might add that an inquiry-rich environment requires a teacher constantly on the alert for the emergence of curiosity, an interest, a problem, or a desire for an explanation as expressed by individual children.

And now let us see how we begin inquiry with children and guide them through it.

INQUIRY MODELS

An inquiry model is a way of initiating an inquiry with children and arranging a sequence of learning activities to facilitate its completion. We shall be considering models based on the forms of inquiry we have already discussed, some variations of these forms, and one new form.

A Model for Curiosity-stimulated Inquiry

The events in curiosity-stimulated inquiry include generating curiosity, extending it, and integrating

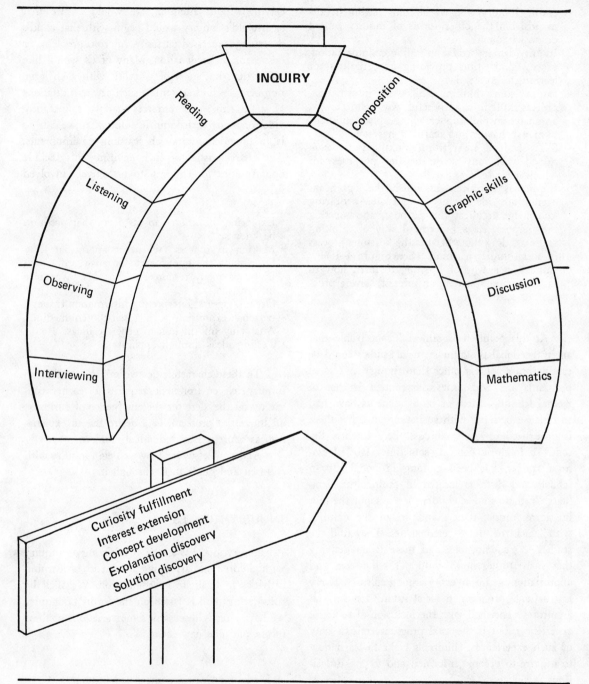

FIGURE 4–1. *Inquiry and the Other Skills Essential to Social Studies.*

it through some form of expression. It is most suitable for children in kindergarten and first grade. We facilitate it by stimulating curiosity, guiding children in building on their discoveries, and providing for integrative activities.

Stimulating Curiosity. We have three possible strategies to use to stimulate children's curiosity.

• Arrange the classroom environment to stimulate and satisfy curiosity. Using social-studies content, provide items such as the following.

View boxes in which miniature settings are displayed. These may be constructed from shoe boxes in which a background and pictures of objects and people cut from magazines are arranged and pasted. For example, young children studying about firemen may view a scene of firemen in action.

An audiotape of the sounds characteristic of the area or process under study. For example, if the study is about transportation, the children may listen to a series of fifteen-second excerpts of sounds taped at a busy street corner.

Touch-and-feel boxes containing real items or items in miniature related to the area of study. For example, if the children are studying the zoo, sev-

eral small stuffed animals or plastic animals could be put in a box entirely closed except for a hole small enough for children to pass their hands through to reach the objects.

Number-to-number or letter-to-letter tracing pictures, which when completed reveal a picture of something studied or to be studied. Simple, disassembled puzzles will also serve. For example, if the next social-studies unit is about safety, the puzzle or tracing picture may reveal a policeman.

In many instances extra visuals are needed to stimulate curiosity. For example, a view box may have a caricature of a person with a long spyglass posted near it, or a pair of binoculars with surprised eyes peering through them.

Curiosity in the above materials is often built and sustained by secrecy. No one is to tell what he or she saw, heard, felt, or discovered until an appointed time. When the moment for building on discoveries arrives, whatever has been used to stimulate curiosity should be brought before the group or class.

• Select or devise colorful materials, preferably those which can be touched or handled by children. Such materials include real objects that can be handled safely, miniature objects such as toy vehi-

ILLUSTRATION 4-1. *A Young Child Inquires through Curiosity.*

cles or dollhouse furniture, small pictures, flannel-grams, and puppets. If the materials are fragile, hold them out before the children and encourage them to identify what they see. Whenever possible allow the children to pass materials among themselves to identify what they are or what they represent. After the children have had an initial, close experience with the materials, enhance curiosity by having them guess what they are going to learn about. Accept all guesses, but if any are correct, do not indicate that they are.

• Present materials in ways that create mystery. For example, if you are going to guide children in viewing a large picture, have it covered or turned over, or have most of it covered with a few clues exposed. Encourage the children to guess what it shows or to build on the exposed clues to make guesses.

Objects may be concealed in paper bags. Only one of a set of pictures, flannelgrams, puppets, or objects may be shown. Curiosity builds as the children guess.

You can probably generate more strategies for stimulating curiosity. Avoid overworking any one strategy.

Extending Curiosity. After curiosity has been aroused, use the materials to help the children validate information they already have as well as to acquire new information. These practices will prove helpful to you:

• Encourage the children to tell what they know about the topic by having them tell about experiences they have had related to it.
• When presenting a set or series of materials, present them in logical sequence and encourage the children to relate ideas together. For example, you are teaching a first-grade class about how lumber is obtained for building houses. You have seven flannelgrams: (1) a tall tree, (2) men falling a tree, (3) a truck hauling logs, (4) stacks of lumber outside a mill, (5) a truck hauling a load of lumber, (6) stacks of lumber at the lumber store, and (7) carpenters erecting a frame for a building. After you have given an explanation for (1), (2), and (3), you may ask what the logs had once been. After telling about

(4) you may ask what has to happen before the lumber is used to build a house, or what will happen next. Children relate the ideas through recall and prediction.
• Provide for as much active participation as possible. Sometimes children may hold materials until you need them. On call, they bring them to you when they are needed. They may hold pictures or take turns holding pictures as you talk about them. They may follow your directions when placing items on the flannelboard.
• At the close of the extending experience have the children review what they have experienced. Encourage them to tell in their own words what they remember, rearrange objects into the correct order, tell what the lesson was about in round-robin fashion—one person telling the first thing, another telling the next, and so on—identifying and telling what they remember about the various objects, and the like.

Finally, the children are guided toward an expressive activity.

Expressing. There must be choices if curiosity is to remain as a stimulator for inquiry. For example, after learning about lumber the children could choose among these activities:

• Telling what they liked about the lumber story into an audiotape.
• Telling what they can remember about the lumber story to the teacher or a teaching aide who records it for them. They then may make their own copy.
• Painting a picture about some part of the lumber story.
• Constructing and "driving" a logging truck made from large blocks or cardboard boxes.
• Making trees, logs, and lumber from modeling clay.
• Making trees from sticks and crepe paper to assemble into a forest.

All this would require six work stations, but they are relatively permanent. The greatest problem is providing for all the children to do what they want to do when they want to do it. Maintaining a roster on which you keep track of who got their first choices each day is helpful.

A diagram of the curiosity-stimulated inquiry model is presented in Figure 4–2.

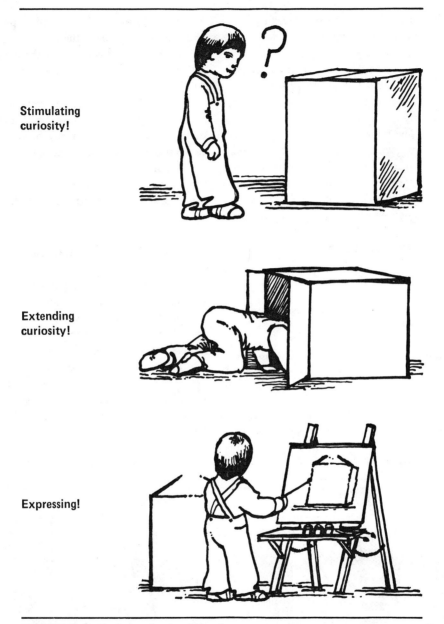

Stimulating curiosity!

Extending curiosity!

Expressing!

FIGURE 4–2. *Curiosity-stimulated Inquiry.*

In some ways curiosity-stimulated inquiry is very appealing. However, it requires much ingenuity in finding and selecting materials and smoothly operating administrative procedures to ensure expression.

We have focused on this form of inquiry as it is used with young children. There are also ways that we can facilitate it with older children. It is not the mainstay of the social-studies program as it is for young children, but it provides a way of personalizing social studies as a supplement to the regular program. It can be facilitated through the use of "curiosity centers."

A simple form of a curiosity center consists of an appealing visual and an informational source situated near it. The visual needs be nothing more than a simple sign easily read from halfway across the classroom. The informational sources may be a newspaper, a magazine, or old textbook clipping mounted on a card, inserted in an envelope, or mounted at the corner of a bulletin board. You may want to provide some informational paragraphs from nonexpendable sources to use in curiosity centers.

Captions like these often work well:

WHAT WOULD YOU DO WITH A NATO? EAT IT? STEP ON IT? OR WHAT?

IF A SALESMAN NAMED OPEC CAME TO YOUR DOOR, WHAT DO YOU SUPPOSE HE WOULD BE SELLING?

WHO INVENTED TELEVISION?

IF YOU THINK LINDBERGH WAS THE FIRST PERSON TO MAKE A NON-STOP FLIGHT ACROSS THE ATLANTIC OCEAN, GUESS AGAIN!

Or you may prefer to make a curiosity box. A shoe box painted or covered with paper will do.

Place an informational source in it, put the lid on, and attach a caption to the lid.

Preferably the contents of the curiosity center are about a topic or issue outside the regular social-studies program.

To sustain curiosity, ask your learners at the end of the period or school day if any have been to the curiosity center. If any have, caution them to keep the contents a secret.

From time to time you may wish to have the members of the class who have visited the curiosity center share what they have learned.

A Model for Interest-stimulated Inquiry

This form of inquiry is particularly suitable for children in grades two through six in self-contained classrooms. Its impact is somewhat blunted in open-space schools and departmentalized situations, but it may still be used effectively.

Implicit in interest is curiosity, purpose, and choice. The inquiry begins with the stimulation of curiosity followed closely by the generation of interests. These are surveyed and choices are made. The choices made then become the purposes to be

ILLUSTRATION 4–2. *Some Children in Fourth Grade Discover Interests in a Bulletin-board Display.*

followed and fulfilled by seeking information. The inquiry ends with an evaluation of interest fulfillment.

The construction of the model follows the above sequence of activities closely.

Stimulating Interest. We can use many kinds of inquiry prompters to stimulate curiosity to lead toward interests. They may be elaborate or simple.

An elaborate inquiry prompter consists of a variety of displays and initial experiences which stimulate curiosity and provide a universe in which children can explore to discover interests. The most elaborate converts the entire classroom into a universe for exploration.

Imagine that you are a fourth-grade teacher constructing such an inquiry prompter in your classroom. Your classroom contains a large bulletin board that runs along one side of the room, and three smaller bulletin boards, one on either of the chalkboard at the front and another at the back of the room. A long counter is situated under the bank of the windows on the other long side of the room. The unit you are to guide your learners through is focused on scarcity. This is how you develop the inquiry prompter:

- On the large bulletin board you post a display which prompts comparison. There are several clusters of pictures, each showing a family portrait, the occupations of the family wage earners, the appliances and machines owned by the family, and the number of dollars available to be spent by the family each week. The clusters depict the economic lives of a southeastern subsistence farmer, a New Mexican craftsman, a middle western farmer, a logger in the Northwest, a factory worker in the Northeast, and a dentist in Chicago. The caption for the bulletin board: THE CHOICES WE HAVE MADE.
- On the bulletin board to the left of the chalkboard: a chart showing how many candy bars a quarter would pay for in 1960 and how many candy bars a quarter pays for today. Caption: WHY SUCH A DIFFERENCE?
- On the bulletin board to the right of the chalkboard: a display of pictures arranged in three columns, the first column pieces of undeveloped land, and the second two showing their possible uses. Example: a piece of forest land—choices, a wildlife refuge or trees harvested for lumber. Caption: WHICH IS BETTER?
- On the bulletin board at the back of the classroom: a display of photographs showing children planning, working on an assembly line making bookends, the bookends being sold at a P.T.A. meeting, and cashing in the stock for a cash reimbursement. Caption: WANT TO GO INTO BUSINESS?
- On the counter three displays: (1) A Monopoly game with ownership cards and play money scattered across it, captioned: WHEN YOU PLAY THIS GAME, WHAT CHOICES DO YOU MAKE? WHICH CHOICES ARE BETTER? (2) A display of a toy bank and a toy cash register, each at the end of a branched arrow, and across the shaft of the arrow this caption: WHICH IS THE BETTER CHOICE? (3) A box containing grab bags, each bag containing a tab on which an amount of money is written—1¢, 5¢, 10¢, 25¢, etc., with no amounts the same—with the caption: TAKE A BAG AND OPEN IT. WHAT CHOICES WOULD YOU MAKE IF YOU RECEIVED THIS MUCH ALLOWANCE FOR THE WEEK? WHAT WOULD YOU DO TO EARN THIS MUCH ALLOWANCE?

Of course, constructing this inquiry prompter requires that you clear all your display space, and to ensure the most desirable effect, you must spend several hours after school putting it up. Your classroom is completely transformed into an exploratory universe.

The next day when your learners come into the classroom for the first time, they are struck by the impact of the change. Their usual behavior is disrupted. Their eyes flit from one display to another. Someone points out something to someone else. They are more quiet than usual. You reduce the usual morning activities to a minimum—the patriotic song and current affairs are forgotten. No one asks why. The moment comes to allow curiosity, already stimulated, to find its way. You say, "I see that you are ready to get a better look at our new displays. Get up and take a good look, and feel free to talk quietly with your friends about what you see."

Some teachers prefer to use less-elaborate inquiry prompters, perhaps transforming two out of four bulletin boards and putting only one display on the counter. Others might choose to use only one of the items included in this universe—one bulletin board or counter display. Or a teacher might use no display and rely on some colorful charts, a film, a filmstrip, an audiotape, or a presentation by a resource person. However, the more restricted the universe presented for initial exploration, the less the curiosity stimulated and the fewer the interests stimulated.

The device you use to present the simple inquiry prompter may add to its effect. The sight of a motion picture projector or videotape projector or a new person in the classroom stimulates curiosity.

Your ingenuity in building mystery can make a difference. For example, to stimulate curiosity about scarcity as a human condition, you might write the following on each of eight cards: "All the members of your group have had their allowance doubled. Decide how this will change your choices in the way you use your new money. Try to decide on the best way for everyone." Place the cards in envelopes. When the class is ready to start with the inquiry, show the envelopes and tell the children you are going to divide them into small groups to discuss the topic described on cards within the envelopes. When they are divided into groups, they are to remove the cards from the envelopes and discuss the topic quietly. They are not to allow any other group to find out what they are talking about.

Or each card could be about some aspect of scarcity in which each group has to assume a different point of view. For example, the use of a piece of undeveloped land could be considered from the point of view of a farmer, a house builder, a nature lover, a city park committee, a miniature-golf course owner, a hunter, an off-the-road motorcycle enthusiast, or a factory owner.

Sometimes a teacher is not that concerned about stimulating curiosity. He or she launches into interest-stimulating activities.

Generating Interests. When an elaborate inquiry prompter is used, the children's exploration of the universe prepared for them stimulates interests. To discover what these are, the teacher circulates among the children as they view and react to the displays. He or she listens to their reactions and takes notes. Here are some possible events:

A boy is standing beside the Monopoly board display, staring at it grimly and shaking his head.

"Do you like to play monopoly, Jim?" asks the teacher.

"Yes, but I never buy that crazy Pennsylvania Avenue. If I land on it early in the game, I just pass it by. I never buy it."

"Why not?"

"It costs too much and you never make any money with it."

"What is a good buy?"

"Vermont, Oriental, and Connecticut. They don't cost much and you can put houses on them right away. You can really make money with them."

The teacher passes by a group of children looking at the large bulletin board. He or she overhears this conversation:

"Did that man with that beat-up old car really choose it?"

"Sure, some people like old cars. It's called nosta—nosta—What's it called?"

"Nostalgia. It's when you like old stuff."

"I don't. If I was going to choose, I'd choose to have two cars, three televisions, seven radios, and four telephones, like that family over there."

Two girls are looking at the bulletin board showing the possible uses of undeveloped land. The teacher approaches them and asks, "Have you made up your minds about the choices?"

"Well, I think I would leave the land the way it is," says one.

"You can't leave all the land the way it is," observes the other.

"Who says?"

"My dad."

As soon as you see that curiosity is beginning to flag, have the children return to their seats. Encourage discussion by asking questions like these: "What did you particularly like among the things that you looked at?" "What do you think was the most interesting thing you looked at?" "If you had a choice among the things to visit again, which would you choose?" Questions such as these invite the expression of general reactions.

The generation of interests occurs as soon as you encourage the children to formulate questions about what they want to know or do not understand. You might use a sequence of questions similar to the following:

What did you see that puzzled you, that made questions form in your mind?
In what way did that puzzle you?
What would you have to find out to solve the puzzle?

Or, you might use your notes taken while the children were exploring. You might introduce your notes in this way:

As I was passing by the big bulletin board over there, I overheard Jody say, "Did that old man with that beat-up old car really choose it?" Did any of the rest of you feel the same way? Why do you think it is so hard for us to understand why people would choose different things?. . . Would any of you like to role play one of these persons to tell why he or she chose certain things? Henry? . . . That was a good try, Henry. Anyone else care to try? . . . No? What do you think we would have to know to be able to role play these people?

As the questions are expressed, record them on the chalkboard or a large chart. Eventually all the displays are brought into the discussion in some way. The result is a list of questions representing the children's interests.

As shown above, some teachers prefer to encourage the children to generate questions directly or use their notes to prompt questions. Others prefer to start immediately with their notes.

Children can often identify what they want to know but have difficulty with formulating questions. For example, many of the children are likely to want to go into business, as suggested by the bulletin-board display. The teacher says,

"You think it would be fun to go into business. What would we have to find out about a business to be able to do that?"
"The cost," volunteers a child.
"The cost of what?"
"The cost of the stuff we use to make something."

"We might express that in this way, 'How much will the materials cost?' I'll write that on our list. Any other questions we need to answer to go into business?"

Let us assume that the teacher has used only the box of grab bags as an inquiry prompter. After the children have reacted to the various allowances that they might have as indicated by the contents of each grab bag, the teacher asks, "Did anyone find that he or she had more allowance than he or she could spend? No one? That shows that no matter how many resources we have, we want more. We always feel that there is *scarcity* and we have to make *choices* about how to use our *resources*.

Scarcity, choices, and *resources* are written on the chalkboard. The teacher continues by encouraging the children to consider their original choices to explore for possible alternatives and to note how limited resources resulted in limited choices. Then the children's attention is focused on *resources*.

"We have been using your allowance as your resource," the teacher points out. "You have it because you are part of a family and your parents think you should have it. Actually, your membership in the family is your resource. Your allowance is just a part of it. What other things does your family provide you?"

After a review of the various items as cited by the children, the teacher asks, "Suppose that you wanted to bargain with your parents to get a larger allowance. How would you go about it?" The ensuing discussion reveals to the children that they have resources—time and skills to do more chores or assume more responsibilities.

At this point, the teacher says, "We now know about the resources of people your age, and we have some ideas about your problems with scarcity. Now let us think about families and countries. Do you think that a family as a whole has problems with scarcity? . . . Do all families have the same problems? . . . To understand these problems, what information would we need?" Later, a country's problems with scarcity would be developed in the same way.

As we can see in the above, the teacher guided the children verbally toward the moment of stimulating interests. He or she implanted the interests as soon as he or she identified *families* and *our country* as areas of further exploration. What one teacher does with displays another does verbally. Interests cannot be generated from a vacuum. The questions stand as indicators of interest. The interests are now to be surveyed.

Surveying Interests. The teacher guides the children in surveying the questions to determine whether there are duplications and to arrange the questions in categories. The children look for questions about the same idea and classify them as such. This often prompts discussions about the precise meaning of the questions. When all the questions have been classified, the teacher copies the questions in their new order on a chart.

The purpose for this procedure is to provide for choices. If the children generate only a few questions, perhaps no more than five or six, this procedure may be omitted.

Selecting Interests to Follow. This is a crucial moment in the interest-stimulated inquiry. The greater the number of interests among which children can choose, the better. The number of choices that can be offered depends on the variety of suitable materials available and the level of the children's information-process skills. Here is a list of possible procedures listed in the order of acceptability, with the best offered first.

• Every child is free to choose any cluster of questions (or a given number of questions if there were too few to survey) to answer. He or she may work independently or with a group interested in the same questions. Once the choice is made, the child may proceed into the inquiry by seeking his or her own materials in the classroom, the school library, or the school materials center, or may follow a direction sheet provided by the teacher. This will indicate the materials to be read, viewed, or listened to.

• Every child is required to answer a certain cluster or combination of clusters of questions (or question or combination of questions), and then is free to choose from any of the others remaining. This is sometimes necessary because certain questions may be foundational to others. The child needs the answers as background to further study. In many cases the required questions are treated as a total-class enterprise—everyone reading the same sources and discussing what they have discovered.

• The teacher guides the class in developing a priority list of questions. The class reviews the questions and decides which cluster or question they most want to answer. Then they decide which should come next, and next, and so on, until the least interesting cluster or question is listed. The class proceeds then as a total group closely assisted or guided by the teacher.

This procedure is followed usually when there are few suitable materials and the learners need assistance with their information-process skills.

The selected interests indicate directions to follow for seeking information.

Following Interests. The above procedures may be completed within a social-studies period or two. Seeking information to follow interests may require anywhere from two or three social-studies periods to as many as thirty such periods. The scope of the unit determines how extended the information seeking will be.

While the class as a total group seeks information together, many instructional periods follow this format:

5–10 MINUTES

The teacher guides the class in reviewing the information they had found the previous day and in deciding specifically the information to be sought during the period at hand. There is also clarification of the resources to be used.

5–20 MINUTES

The children listen, view, read, or interview to acquire information. All the children may be doing the same thing with the same resource, such as viewing a film, or they all may be reading, but in different resources, or some may be reading, some may be viewing a filmstrip, and some may be using a resource under the direct supervision of the teacher or an aide.

10–15 MINUTES

The teacher guides the children in discussing and sharing their findings. Precise answers to definite questions are determined and, if necessary, resources are consulted again. A class record of findings may be made.

As you might guess, a succession of periods such as these without any change in activity could destroy the interest stimulated earlier and make an ironic farce of interest selection. For this reason, as soon as the children have explored completely for an answer to a broad question or for the answers to a cluster of questions, the teacher guides them into learning activities which provide a change and at the same time encourage the children to integrate or apply their information in some way.

Let us assume again that you are the teacher of the fourth grade engaged in the study of scarcity. The children have just completed answering this cluster of questions:

1. What are the resources of a family?
2. Why do some families have few resources and others have many?
3. What kinds of choices have to be made by families who have few resources?
4. How should families make choices?

Here are some of the choices you have for integrative and applicative activities:

- Have the children make facsimile bumper stickers conveying messages about how they think families should make choices about the ways they use their resources.
- Encourage them to draw and share pictures of family members making choices. Cartoon "balloons" are used to show what the person is thinking.
- Guide the children in a simulation in which the members of the family make choices.
- Guide them in role-playing situations in which families are making choices.

- Encourage them to use creative dramatics to develop an incident or series of incidents in which "Snow White and the Seven Dwarfs," "The Three Little Pigs," "Peter, Peter, Pumpkin-Eater," or the characters in "Cinderella" are making choices within their limited resources.
- Encourage them to write and share creative stories about a family or a member of a family having to make a choice within limited resources.
- Form the children into groups which create an imaginary family, construct simple puppets to represent the members of the family, prepare a play and present it to the class. The play shows the family making a choice together.

When children experience activities such as these, the business of stimulating, selecting, and following interests assumes meaning for them.

Other ways to maintain interest at a high level during an extended information seeking include:

- Bring pertinent news items to share and discuss with the children.
- Alert the children to listen to newscasts for pertinent news items to report to the class.
- Use a bulletin board for posting products associated with each phase of the social-studies unit.
- Vary the information-seeking activities as much as possible. Avoid day after day of reading. Intersperse individual activities with group activities.

So far, we have discussed one set of conditions under which children seek information. Now let us assume that the children are going to be following an interest independently. The schedule for the instructional period is something like this:

5–10 MINUTES

The teacher asks whether anyone is having any trouble obtaining resource materials, makes suggestions to those having difficulty, and provides possible solutions for ways of using materials in heavy demand. He or she then reviews the schedule of conferences for the period and reminds the children who need help to sign up for a conference during some open time.

20–30 MINUTES

The children seek information and the teacher conducts individual conferences.

When children are engaged in independent studies, provisions must also be made for them to engage in integrative and applicative activities also. (Suggestions for such activities are given in Chapter 9.)

And when the children are following their interests in small groups, the instructional period follows this schedule:

5–10 MINUTES

The teacher gives the leader of each group an opportunity to report on what his or her group plans to do during the period. The leader also tells what materials will be needed and, if necessary, asks for help in obtaining them.

15–20 MINUTES

The groups seek information. The teacher assists or guides as needed.

15–20 MINUTES

The leaders of each group give progress reports and mention any problems the group had. The problems are discussed. The remainder of the time is devoted to group planning for what is to be done the next day.

Often small-group work is task oriented. This provides often for an integrative or applicative activity. (This is discussed more fully in Chapter 7.)

If interest completely flags before the final question(s) or cluster(s) is answered, information seeking is terminated, or it terminates when all the questions have been answered. But the entire study is not terminated. The final procedure is an evaluation of interests.

Evaluation of Interests. At this point the teacher provides opportunities for children to react to their experience of inquiring into interests. As the teacher, you will want to know what the children liked and disliked about their study, what discovered ideas they think are particularly useful to them, and any ideas they might like to study again in the future. Let us stay with the idea that you are the fourth-grade teacher who has just guided your class through the information-seeking phase in their study. You might use any of the following procedures:

- Prepare an individual rating form similar to Figure 4–3 for each child to complete.
- Conduct a discussion with the total class or small

Name

Date

1. Given below is a list of the things we have studied. Read each thing carefully. If you really liked it, mark an X in the blank after its number. If you really disliked it, mark a 0. If you neither really liked it nor disliked it, make no mark in the blank.
   a. _____ The resources of a family.
   b. _____ The resources of our country.
   c. _____ Making wise choices when buying.
   d. _____ Running a business.
2. Would you like to study any of these things again? If you would, circle the number of the thing above. You may circle more than one.
3. Do you think that any of the things you studied could be useful to you now or some time in the future? Draw a line under any of the things you think could be useful.

FIGURE 4–3. *Individual Rating Form.*

groups to encourage free expression of likes, dislikes, preferences for later related study, and personal discoveries of utility.

- Divide the class into small groups and have them discuss the four points to share and discuss later with the entire class, or to prepare a group report to be given to you.
- Divide the class into evaluative-discussion groups. Each group is to discuss the four points as you observe and take notes about the discussion.

The individual rating form works well in all the grades for which this inquiry is suitable. Frequently the children in grades two, three, and four will need assistance with completing it. The class-wide or group discussion which you conduct is also workable with all the grades. Group-conducted discussions are particularly effective with grades five and six and some fourth-grade classes.

If the interest selection and information seeking has been individualized, you may conduct individual conferences with the children to discuss the four points, or you may invite reactions by having the children react to each of the points in their own words.

The results of the evaluation may indicate whether you should guide the children in extending interests. On rare occasions, the children's reactions are markedly negative. When they are, forget about extending interests and start a new unit as quickly as possible, preferably one very different from the one they just experienced. However, the usual case is that the children are positive toward some aspects, neutral toward others, and negative toward a few. You then proceed with extending interests.

Extending Interests. Interests are extended in two ways. One leads toward an activity or several activities chosen by children to apply what they know. The other leads into values exploration.

You are still working with the fourth grade. Here are some procedures you might use to help the children make choices:

- Conduct a class discussion to encourage the children to surface choices of things they would like

to do or make with what they know about scarcity. Be sure to indicate the time limits (the next two or three social-studies periods, or whatever time you feel that you can allow). Contribute a few ideas yourself. Sometimes children need some "priming" to surface choices. Some of your suggestions might include:

- Preparing a program about scarcity to present at an assembly or to invite other classes to the classroom to see.
- Making murals to show how a person, family, or country makes choices to solve problems of scarcity.
- Composing a magazine containing informative articles, drawings, and cartoons about scarcity.
- Making a videotape or eight-millimeter film telling what is important for everyone to remember about scarcity.
- Composing role-playing situations to role play.

Your suggestions include those things which you know your children can do and which you know you can implement.

- Collect some samples of products which other children have made and present them to the children as possibilities that they might consider as choices of things to do. These samples should be from studies different from what the children have just completed. They might include murals, models, pictures, diagrams, magazines, videotapes, and the like.
- Prepare a chart or direction sheet similar to Figure 4–4; present the chart and go over it with the children, and let them go to work.

Sometimes the children will indicate that they would like to repeat something they have already done during their study, such as making objects on the assembly line, repeating the performance of a play they composed earlier, role playing, or a simulation. If this is what they want to do, let them do it.

If the inquiry has been individualized, offer choices of activities which children can do independently. Provisions for this should be included in the independent study. A direction sheet for such activities may be included with the other direction sheets, or the child may decide during a conference.

You may do any one of the following:

1. Make a poster about scarcity.
2. Write a story about scarcity.
3. Find out how the people of another country work with scarcity and write a report about it, or make up a report to say into the tape recorder.
4. Write a poem about scarcity.
5. Find out how a business works and report about it.
6. Write a play about scarcity.
7. Make a wall hanging about scarcity.

When you decide what you want to do, go to the materials stations at the back of the room to get what you need.

Perhaps you would like to work with some friends on one of the above. You may do that, but let me know.

Perhaps you can think of something else that you would like to do. If you do, come and talk it over with me.

FIGURE 4–4. *Sample Direction Sheet to Provide Choices.*

The children's success with their chosen activity often prepares them for a values exploration. At this point you introduce a suitable values exploration. Here are some possibilities for the fourth graders who have inquired about scarcity:

- An in-depth discussion about the kinds of help that would be best to give to people who have limited resources.
- Complete a value questionnaire on contributing to charities.
- Role play situations in which resources and choices are limited and the need is great.
- Simulate the people of an imaginary country trying to solve their problems with scarcity through deciding on choices.
- Do a values analysis about conservation.

If your learners are younger you would have fewer choices—perhaps only role playing and values clarification.

As we review the interest-stimulated inquiry, we can see that its effectiveness lies in offering as many choices as we can at various times during the inquiry. Much depends on the kind of inquiry prompter that we devise, the number of interests that can be generated, the ways that children can seek information, and the opportunities provided for evaluating and extending interests.

The procedures followed when conducting this form of inquiry are diagrammed in Figure 4–5.

A Model for Scientific Inquiry

Children in grades three through eight may be guided into this form of inquiry. It may be used in any classroom situation, self-contained or otherwise.

If you were going to research social-studies teaching methodology, you would find references to inquiry methods, approaches, techniques, or skills. This is the *inquiry* to which they are referring and which we were discussing in Chapter 2. It closely follows a basic model used for years by physical and social scientists when they make a formal research of and report about a knowledge problem. It follows a series of procedures which include defining the problem, making hypotheses about possible explanations, developing a plan for investigation, investigating to discover information, drawing up findings, judging the hypothesis against the findings, and arriving at a conclusion about how true the original hypothesis is. The purpose of the inquiry is to discover knowledge.

During the 1960's some social-studies educa-

1. Stimulating interests

2. Generating interests

3. Surveying interests

4. Selecting interests

5. Following interests

6. Evaluating interests

And/or

7. Extending interests

FIGURE 4–5. *Interest-stimulated Inquiry.*

ILLUSTRATION 4–3. *As They Contribute Questions to Be Answered, These Children in Grade Five Are Developing a Design for Inquiry.*

tors intuited that children could also discover knowledge if taught the skills of scientific inquiry, particularly as it related to the research methods used by social scientists.[4] A new booth was opened in the marketplace of educational ideas.

Business was brisk. Researches were made. It was discovered that children in the first grade could perform some of the inquiry skills if they were carefully guided by a knowledgeable teacher,[5] that children guided to learn through inquiry retained as much information as children who were not,[6] and that children could learn certain inquiry skills.[7] The case study was established as a suitable inquiry prompter.[8] Several approaches were developed.

The booth is still open, but business is no longer so brisk. Scientific inquiry has become an alternative form of inquiry for social-studies instruction.

Social-studies educators have not been able to develop a universally acceptable model to follow when conducting inquiry in the classroom. Beyer suggests this:

1. Defining a problem or question.
2. Developing tentative answers, solutions, or plans—hypothesizing.
3. Testing hypotheses against relevant data.
4. Drawing a conclusion about the accuracy of the hypotheses.
5. Applying the conclusion and generalizing.[9]

Compare the above with the following suggested by Ryan and Ellis:

- Stating the problem.
- Selecting data sources.
- Gathering data.
- Processing the data.
- Making inferences.[10]

The first emphasizes information seeking until a tentative truth is discovered and validated. The second emphasizes working with information. Both focus on inquiry skills that children can perform with the teacher's assistance or guidance. I find both equally acceptable but prefer an extended model which more narrowly defines each procedural element. It begins, as those above, with orienting children to the problem in some way.

Discovering the Problem. Social scientists involved in research know the limits of their area of knowledge so well that they can decide where they want to extend them. They can decide where they want to discover knowledge and formulate it into a problem. Children cannot do this. To help them, we devise inquiry prompters. These prompters offer a representation of the area of knowledge in which a discovery of a problem is to be made.

Let us suppose that you are a teacher of sixth grade and your class is to be launched into a study of the changes that have occurred in the lives of our people during the past two-hundred years. Listed below are seven examples of inquiry prompters you might use. After the description of each prompter, a series of questions is listed to illustrate how it is used. A hypothesis-inviting question closes each series.

---

1. These two statements written on a chart, or a picture graph expressing the two statements:

    In 1780, 95 of every 100 workers were farmers. In 19 (current date), 5 of every 100 workers are farmers.

    a. How important do you think farming is as an American industry today? . . . You have some good ideas.
    b. Let's take a look at this chart (or graph) to see what it tells us. What does it say?
    c. How might we explain this change?
2. Pictures of three families, one living in 1780, one in 1880, and one in 1980. The pictures may be portraits or scenes of families doing things together.
    a. (Showing the 1980 picture.) This is a picture of a family today. Suppose that we had a Martian visitor and we were using this picture as a basis for describing the usual American family to him. What might we tell him? . . . about the duties and concerns of the mother? . . . of the father? . . . of the children? . . .
    b. Here are two other pictures of families, this one living in 1780 and the other in 1880. What differences do you notice in the pictures of all three families?
    c. Which two of these families do you think are more alike in their duties and concerns and what they have to use every day?
3. Five maps, each showing the territorial limits of the United States at five different dates—1780, 1830, 1880, 1920, and 1980.
    a. Let's describe the United States in terms of where all of it lies on earth. What would be its most northern point? Its most southern point? Its most eastern point? Its most western point? . . . Yes, considering Alaska and Hawaii, it is spread over a large area of the globe.
    b. Here are five maps of the United States, one showing it as it is today, and these others showing it in 1920, 1880, 1930, and 1780. What pattern of change do you notice from 1780 onward?
    c. What do you think brought this change about?
4. An imaginary case to be told to the children:

The other day I overheard two of my friends in an argument about the problems of living. One said, "Today is a terrible time to live! Crowded highways and violence in the streets! Rising prices and not enough jobs! Constant threats of strikes and wars! And the energy crisis! If I could make it come true, I would move my life back to 1880 when a person had a lot of free space to roam in. If you wanted to go downtown, you hopped on a trolley car, and if you wanted to go farther, you would go by railroad. But probably 1780 would be even better. Nothing faster than a running horse and lots of free land on which to make a living! A person could really be natural then."

My other friend replied, "1780! I don't think I'd have cared much for life in those days. When you worked, it was from sunrise to sunset every day except Sunday. If your crops failed, you would nearly starve, and there was scarcely a decent road in the whole country—they were dusty in the summer, and muddy or choked with snow in the winter and spring. And in 1880 things were not much better. Sure, there were trolley cars and railroads, but the roads weren't that good. I'm glad to be living in 1980, and I wish I could live to see what it's like in 2080! It'll be even better than now!"

a. Have you ever heard people talking about "the good old days?" What kinds of things have you heard them say?
b. "Let me tell you what I've heard." Read the case. What did my first friend say about the "good old days?" . . . my second friend?
c. With which of my friends do you agree? Why?
5. A list of dates to be written on the chalkboard: 1780, 1830, 1880, and 1920.
    a. Can you recall any movies or television shows that you have seen about people living in other times? How can you tell that they are living in another time?
    b. What if you had a choice in living at some time other than now in America, and you had a choice among these four dates: 1780, 1830, 1880, and 1920? Which date would you choose? Why?
6. Prepared on a chart, a list of modern appliances used regularly by Americans today: telephones, radios, televisions, calculators, typewriters, automobiles, airliners, motorcycles, power boats, toasters, mixers, can openers, washing machines, dryers, vacuum cleaners, hair dryers, and lawn mowers.

a. Suppose there was a power blackout. No electricity came into your home. What things in and around your home could you still use without electrical power?

b. Here is a list of powered items. Look over the list carefully to see if any that you know about have been omitted. We shall add them. . . .

c. Let's imagine that we are going to climb into a time machine that will take us back to 1880. We are also going to take whatever we think will be useful to us. Which of these things do you think we should leave behind? Why? . . . Now let us suppose we plan another trip to 1780. Which things should we leave behind?

7. A list of modern problem areas: energy sources, unemployment, environmental pollution, international relationships, and crime, etc., to be generated by the class.

a. (To be able to use this inquiry prompter, the children should have been guided for a couple of weeks in a concentrated current affairs program focusing on modern problems.)

Let's quickly review the problems that we have been studying for the past few weeks. . . .

b. Which of these problems do you think is the most serious? Why?

c. Let's take ourselves back a hundred years to 1880. Do you think the people living then had the same or different problems? Why? And let's go back another hundred years to 1780. How about the problems then? Why do you think so?

The last example focuses on a condition essential to the effectiveness of the prompter. That condition is the extent of the children's knowledge background. To ensure that the children had a definitive idea about modern problems, the teacher would guide them in a concentrated, in-depth study about such problems. The other prompters focused on the technological lives of people. A brief discussion before the presentation of the prompter will surface sufficient background for its use.

As you review the questions listed for each prompter, you can see a structure:

• Question "a" surfaces related background.
• Question "b" guides an exploration of the

prompter. This exploration results in a discovery of the problem, either a direction to follow or a conflict to be resolved.

• Question "c" invites hypotheses.

Implicit within the content of the prompter and the hypothesis question is the basic elements of the conclusion that the children are going to reach toward the end of their inquiry. Here are the elements for each prompter:

For Prompter 1

Changes in the occupations of American labor occurred because . . .

For Prompter 2

Families living in 1780 and 1880 are more alike than those living in 1980 because . . .

For Prompter 3

The United States expanded in territory between 1780 and 1980 because . . .

For Prompter 4

It would be better to live in 1780 (or 1880 or 1980) because . . .

For Prompter 5

It would be better to live in 1780 (1830, 1880, or 1920) because . . .

For Prompter 6

As we move back in time, we expect to find these technological changes in daily living: . . .

For Prompter 7

Each era in American history reflects different problems forces at work: in 1880 they were . . . and in 1780 they were . . .

Whatever prompter you use and the way you use it are determined by your teaching style, the availability of suitable materials, the level of abstraction at which your learners can function, and their level of mastery of information skills.

You have used the prompter. You have invited hypotheses. Let us see how you receive them.

Hypothesizing. This is a moment for children to think divergently. They are limited only by the background they have and how they structure it in their minds. Your only concern during this event is that they feel free to make a "best guess," and, hopefully, able to give at least one plausible reason for what they think.

Let us assume that you have just presented prompter 1, which prompts hypotheses about a change in the American labor force since 1780. Working with the entire class you see a half-dozen hands on high. You acknowledge a volunteer: "Jack?"

Jack: Because they have problems.
Teacher: Well, problems can cause changes, but what kind of problems are you thinking about?
Jack: Like strikes and stuff like that.
Teacher: Are you saying that there are fewer farmers in the work force today because they have strikes?
Jack: Yes, and they don't get paid very much.
Teacher: And you think that since 1780 things have gotten worse and worse for farmers?
Jack: Yes.
Teacher: All right, I'll write your explanation on the chart. While I'm writing it, see whether any of you can think of anything else that makes Jack's statement true. . . . Yes, Bob?
Bob: Sometimes farmers have to live in terrible places. I saw that on television the other night.
Teacher: Yes, that could be one of the conditions. Pete?
Pete: That idea doesn't make sense at all. I've seen where farmers live. They live in some pretty nice houses.
Teacher: Just a second, Pete. We are not judging ideas yet. We'll be doing that later. But I can see you are on your toes today.

Let's review what the teacher did. Jack started with a vague response. The teacher helped him clarify it. The result was not an explanation, but a reason. *The teacher helped the child discover his explanation and invited further ideas from the class.* A child begins to attack the idea. *The teacher*

turns the attack aside. And at no time did the teacher reject a respondent. These are teacher behaviors essential to children's divergent thinking. Let us observe for other behaviors.

Teacher: Who else has an explanation for the changes in the American work force since 1780? Hillary?
Hillary: As the years went by I think that farmers learned better ways to raise things. Fewer and fewer farmers were needed.
Teacher: That sounds like a good explanation. Have you any reason for that explanation?
Hillary: Maybe I read it somewhere, but I'm pretty sure about it.
Teacher: You do a lot of reading, so that's quite possible. Does anyone else have any information that supports Hillary's idea? . . . No one? That's not important now. I'll add it to our list. Perhaps someone will think of something later.

A child has given an explanation, but cannot immediately give a reason. *The teacher accepts the explanation and assures the child that it will be considered later.*

Teacher: Yes, Clara?
Clara: In the old days they did not have combinations.
Teacher: I'm not sure I know what you mean by combinations. What is done with combinations?
Clara: Those big machines they use to cut wheat.
Teacher: I see. You mean *combines.*
Clara: That's right.

A child has difficulty with word use. *The teacher asked for information about the word and then supplied it.*

Children often have difficulty formulating hypotheses. If you write the beginning of the hypothesis on the chalkboard, *From 1780 until 1980, the number of farmers in the American work force became less and less because ———,* the children will explore willingly within what they know to complete the statement.

Some children will be able to give hypotheses and explanations without difficulty and others will need help as discussed above. The purpose is to obtain as many hypotheses as possible from the children. Some may be similar to others, but they are accepted and recorded unless the children see a direct duplication. When duplications begin to occur frequently, terminate hypothesizing. The moment has arrived for trying to select the most reasonable hypothesis to investigate.

Selecting a Hypothesis. First, guide the children in deciding whether some explanations mean just about the same thing. Usually the children have little difficulty with this. Occasionally a child suspects that the idea he or she contributed is about to be erased and will argue strenuously to prevent its obliteration in favor of another. The conflict is easily resolved by crediting a particular statement with the names of the children who gave duplicates. If two children begin to argue over whose duplicate idea is better, release them to work quietly together to develop a statement which is acceptable to both.

For clarity of purposes, it is preferable for the children to arrive at a consensus as to which hypothesis in the list is most likely to be true, or most reasonable. They usually have little difficulty with rejecting all but two. When this occurs, either try to guide the class in formulating a new hypothesis from the two or simply accept that they have surfaced more than one hypothesis to investigate. Sometimes having two opposing hypotheses to investigate heightens purposes for investigating.

If you prefer, you may combine the tasks of hypothesizing and selecting a hypothesis by preparing a list of possible hypotheses on a chart or duplicating the list for class distribution. Here is an example of a list of such hypotheses that might be used for a unit on change from 1780 to 1980:

1. The number of farmers in the work force became less because fewer and fewer people wanted to work on farms.
2. The number of farmers in the work force became smaller because fewer and fewer people were needed to produce farm products.
3. The number of farmers in the work force became less because more and more people moved into the cities.

4. The number of farmers in the work force became smaller because the farmers made less money as the years passed by.
5. The number of farmers in the work force became smaller because farming as an occupation became less and less popular among the people.

After the children have read the list, encourage them to contribute any other hypotheses that they can surface. Add their contributions. Then, guiding the class as a total group or forming it into small groups, have the children discuss the hypotheses to decide which they think is most suitable.

Although it reduces the opportunity for divergent thinking, the above practice is helpful to children just beginning with this form of inquiry.

When the hypothesis or hypotheses have been selected, guide the children in deciding the kinds of information they will need.

Developing a Design for Inquiry. When social scientists reach this stage of planning, they develop a research or experimental design. This is often determined by the nature of the statistical analysis they wish to make to determine probabilities.

About as close as we can get children to a research design is to have them develop the questions they will need to answer to have the necessary information against which to judge their hypothesis(es).

During their initial experience with this activity, most children have some difficulty. Here are a few ways to help them:

• After the children decide on the hypothesis(es) to investigate, prepare a list of questions, some of which will be helpful and some of which will not, and have them analyze the questions to decide which they should use. Guide them as a total class or form them into groups to process the questions and share their decisions with the class. Through a comparison of the various decisions the class arrives at a list of questions to use.
• At first encourage the children to identify the areas of information that they think they will have to look for. List these as labels, and then

guide the class in developing questions from the labels.

• Guide the children in analyzing their hypothesis carefully to see whether certain words or phrases serve as clues to needed information. Here is an example: From 1780 to 1980, the number of *farmers* in the work force became smaller because fewer and fewer people were needed *to produce farm products*. Using the italicized words as a focal point, prompt the children to formulate questions, asking, "What might we need to know about how farmers produced farm products in 1780?"

When working with children in fourth grade and above, you may form the children into groups to develop their own design for inquiry. This usually works better after the children have developed designs for inquiry previously in teacher-guided class discussions.

When the design for inquiry is completed, the class has purposes for seeking information.

Seeking Information. What was discussed under *Following Interests* in the interest-stimulated inquiry obtains here as well. Although the children have been actively involved in several ways in developing purposes, a process which has generated interest, they will need learning activities that maintain and heighten interest. These activities also help them understand and conceptualize the ideas they discover.

However, something more may be needed at the beginning of information seeking. It may be considered as the final concern in the design for inquiry or as a beginning concern for information seeking. This additional concern is for the organization of information.

The purpose for organizing information is to make it easier to analyze and interpret. If the children can see initially how it is to be organized, their investigation may be facilitated. Let us assume that our sixth-grade class studying changes in the work force between 1780 and 1980 has developed this set of questions in their design for inquiry:

1. How big were the farms in 1780? In 1880?
2. How big are they now?

3. What kinds of tools and machines did farmers use in 1780? In 1880?
4. What kinds of tools and machines do they use now?
5. How did they get their products to market in 1780? In 1880?
6. How do they get their products to market today?

As soon as these questions have been expressed, you post a six or eight-foot strip of butcher paper over the chalkboard and ask, "How might we use this as a chart for recording the information we find?" You may guide the total class in arriving at a solution, or you may have the children work at a solution in groups, or you may have each experiment for a few minutes with a piece of paper. Remind them to use the questions as points of reference. The solution may look something like Figure 4–6.

Entering their information at the close of each investigational period helps learners to develop a sense of accomplishment.

Not all studies are amenable to this way of organizing information. For example, if the children were studying family relationships or an industrial process, diagrams would be a useful way of organizing information. However, ideas about the form of the diagrams require that the children have the information first. Ideas about the form of the diagrams are generated from the information.

Organizing Information. We already know the purpose of organizing information—to get it in a form that facilitates making conclusions. Let us assume that we did not decide how to do this at the beginning of information seeking. This is what we could do:

• The same as discussed above with the butcher paper. (If the information is not voluminous, the chart might be developed on the chalkboard.)
• Show the children a model of what they might use. Guide them in analyzing it for structure, making whatever adaptations are necessary, and making the necessary entries. In this case, the model would be a chart made by another class using different information. Graphs, charts, ta-

	In 1780	1780–1880	1880–1980
Size of Farms			
Tools and Machines			
Transportation			

FIGURE 4–6. *Sheet for Organizing Information.*

bles, flow charts, time lines, diagrams, and maps are often useful ways to organize information.

- Have the children consult the questions and their notes carefully as you guide them in developing a summary of the main ideas they have discovered.
- If the children have drawn pictures or made paper objects that can be posted on a bulletin board, guide them in arranging these in clusters on a large bulletin board. This is particularly suitable for children in grades three and four.

When this task is accomplished, the stage is set for drawing a conclusion.

Drawing a Conclusion. After children have had experience in drawing conclusions toward the end of several inquiries, you may have them study their information to react to questions such as these:

What conclusion can we now draw about how farmers in America worked from 1780 until now? *Or*

What can we say now generally about how farmers' work changed in America from 1780 until now? *Or*

What is the main idea that all these other ideas tell about? *Or*

Why did American farmers' work change between 1780 and now?

The last question is likely to be more effective with children because it focuses more directly on the conclusion.

Children who have difficulty with drawing conclusions may need a starter such as this: *According to what we learned, American farmers' work changed between 1780 and now because. . . .*

Or, if they have difficulty with formulating verbally expressed ideas, you may give them a list of possible conclusions to choose from.

And again, you have choices in the way the children are to perform the task—individually, in small groups, or as a total class.

As you can see in the above, the children are drawing conclusions from their findings. They are a moment away from discovering how accurate their original hypothesis is.

Judging the Hypothesis. At this moment, you have the children judge their original hypothesis against their conclusion. The two statements may be written on a chart or the chalkboard. Usually the children can see that the conclusion supports the hypothesis, but they will need to discuss the problem for a while before they do.

At this point, the child or children who voiced the original hypothesis and those who agreed with them may act like a baseball team who has just won a game. And a few others may show discontent. Suppose that this happens. You ask one of the discontented, "Do you feel uncomfortable with what we have discovered, that fewer and fewer farmers were needed because new tools and machinery were invented?"

And she responds, "I can see that. But what I don't understand is what happened to all the other workers. Wouldn't the invention of new things make them less needed, too?"

Bless the child. She is asking at least for some kind of validation, and perhaps for a new inquiry. After exploring about farmers and what they used over a period of two centuries, your class may be somewhat jaded. They couldn't care less about what happened to the other workers. Find out by saying something like this: "Donna wonders what happened to the other workers. Could they have become less needed too? What do you suppose happened to them?"

If the rest of the children share Donna's concern, they will hypothesize vigorously. Another inquiry is started. It may be as detailed as the one the children just experienced to this point, or it may be foreshortened to find the answer to the question: "What happened to the other workers from 1780 until now?"

If the rest of the children show little interest in following the suggested inquiry, guide Donna and any others who may be interested in finding the answer to the same question into resources that will be helpful to them. The rest of the class may be guided into a validation of what they now believe.

Validating the New Idea. Two kinds of validation may occur. One leads the children toward finding out what competent authority has to say as a result of having made the same inquiry. Perhaps there is a resource person who is willing to come and make a presentation to the children or is willing to be interviewed by them, either in the classroom or by telephone, or by letter. Perhaps there is a well-made film available. Or perhaps you can find an authoritative book written by an expert from which you can audiotape or read some passages which the children can hear and discuss.

The other kind of validation is a test of universality. To guide the children in making this test, you might conduct a brief study of what has happened with farmers in the work force in Bali or Poland during the past two-hundred years. Or you might make a chart showing the percentages of farmers to other workers in various parts of the world. The children would analyze this chart to see in how many places the same change has taken place, how rapidly it has occurred, and where there has been little or no change. As a result they see how their idea is limited.

Applying the Idea. The procedures to follow at this point are the same as those discussed under *Extending Interests* in the interest-stimulated inquiry. The values-exploration activity might be any of the following:

- An in-depth discussion about imminent changes in technology, how they will affect people's lives, and what might be done to cope with them.
- Completing a value questionnaire on technological change.
- Role playing situations from the past when a new invention threatens a people's means of making a living.
- Simulating a situation in which one group of people are aided by an invention and another group is threatened by it and then exploring for alternatives suitable to both groups.

• Doing a values analysis about technological change.

At this point the inquiry ends. If we had hewed closely to the scientific model, we would have terminated the study after the new idea had been validated, and perhaps with justifiable reasons. The children would have had some social-science experiences, and what they had learned about the ways of the social scientists may have been more vital than the knowledge they acquired. However, in the opinion of the writer, this does not completely meet the *social-studies* requirement that children find a deeply personal meaning in what they study. For this reason, the additional tasks associated with applying ideas are included here. (How to individualize this form of inquiry will be discussed in Chapter 9.)

Figure 4–7 is a diagram of scientific inquiry adapted for use in elementary social studies. Some teachers do not feel comfortable with the scientific-inquiry model. They are not sure about "making it come out right." Others feel that children need a rich background of information before being committed to making hypotheses, which, regarded in one way, may be advertisements of ignorance. They prefer to precede inquiry with expository teaching.

In expository teaching, the teacher regards subject matter in a traditional way: subject matter is what is found in textbooks. The teacher establishes a discipline and the children follow it. Although children's interests are not considered, the skillful expository teacher makes learning as interesting as he or she can. There are many activities which children like to do, and there is usually emphasis on learning facts. The children gauge their accomplishment by how well they do on factual tests.

When the children have learned a comprehensive set of facts, some expository teachers introduce inquiry. They may use inquiry prompters similar to those already discussed. The children hypothesize and defend their hypotheses from an informed position. If there is dispute, the children recheck

their sources. Eventually a single idea emerges as the most reasonable. It is validated and applied in ways similar to those suggested here.

Figure 4–8 depicts the model. Models of inquiry adapted from the scientific model emphasize the development of thinking skills. The ultimate hope is that through their experiences with the model the children will learn how to discover reliable knowledge in rational ways. But the paths of rationality are not restricted to scientific inquiry. They also lead through problem-stimulated inquiry.

A Model for Problem-stimulated Inquiry

This form of inquiry may be used with children in all grades and in any classroom situation.

The line between scientific inquiry and problem-stimulated inquiry is thin. The major difference between the two lies in their purposes. Scientific inquiry is directed toward new knowledge. Problem-stimulated inquiry is directed toward a needed action, and personal value is involved.

A minor difference between the two lies in the role of knowledge background in each. Both require a background of knowledge. In scientific inquiry, it is the broad base in which what is known and what needs to be known is established. In problem-stimulated inquiry, it is in many instances all that needs to be known factually and experientially about the forces in conflict.

This minor difference is of significance to us as elementary social-studies teachers as we guide children in problem-stimulated inquiry. Before guiding children into such an inquiry, we examine the problem carefully to determine whether it is within our learners' knowledge background.

Another minor difference lies in the urgency which impels the two. Usually scientific inquiry is leisurely. If worse comes to worse, it may be delayed, perhaps forgotten. But problem-stimulated inquiry is urgent in a demanding way. It strikes deeply into the emotions.

This aspect of emotionally demanding urgency may be immediate or it may be generated. When

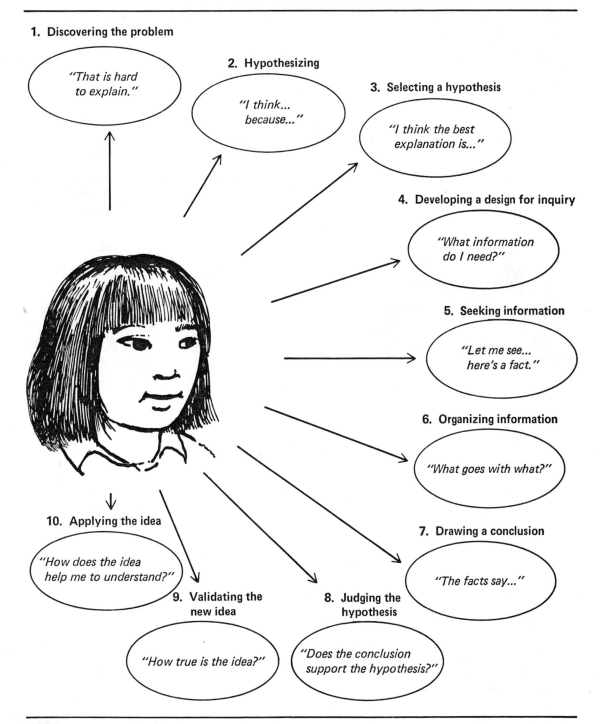

FIGURE 4–7. *Scientific Inquiry in Social Studies.*

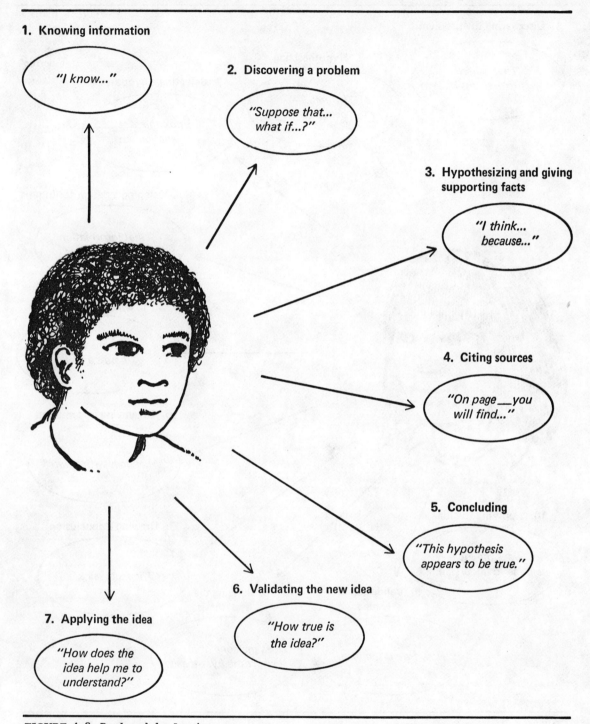

FIGURE 4–8. *Postknowledge Inquiry.*

ILLUSTRATION 4–4. *Applying a Solution to a Common Problem.*

it is immediate, the problem impinges itself on the children in a direct way. For example, when children experience an earthquake or a tornado at school, they are aware of their need to look more deeply into the problem of ensuring their safety.

Let us suppose that the children are earning themselves and their school a questionable reputation because on trash-collection days they are pushing trash cans over as they come to school in the morning. The wind carries much of the trash across the yards, and the community is beginning to look like a dump. In this instance the teacher may introduce a learning activity which generates an emotionally demanding urgency. He or she may have the children: role play a severely handicapped person who has difficulty getting his trash cans out and keeping his yard clean; read a story or newspaper article about rat infestation in a dirty neighborhood and discuss it in depth; or do a simula-

tion on the need for a clean neighborhood. The emotionally demanding urgency is soon generated.

The same urgency may be generated for the many injustices and unresolved issues that permeate life beyond the school and neighborhood.

In its most extended form, a model of problem-stimulated inquiry may include these elements: reviewing knowledge background, receiving the problem, exploring the problem elements, generating solutions, selecting a solution, applying it, and evaluating it.

Let us suppose that you are a first-grade teacher, and the community in which you teach has decided to do what it can to help the victims of a disastrous earthquake in Guatemala. The need for clothing is crucial. A community drive for clothing is being instituted, and the schools are expected to do their share. Here is how you work with your learners.

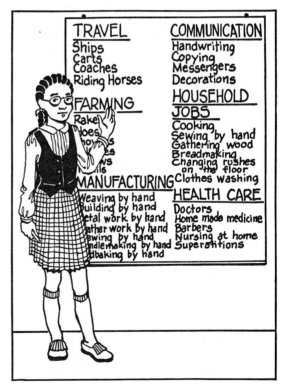

ILLUSTRATION 4–5. *A Child Uses Information to Generalize about Medieval Technology.*

REVIEWING KNOWLEDGE BACKGROUND

You conduct a brief discussion about clothing in which the children talk about clothing they wear and like at different times during the year. The point of the discussion is to help the children think about the place that clothing has in their daily lives.

RECEIVING THE PROBLEM

At this point you introduce the inquiry prompter. It consists of pictures clipped from the newspaper. These show destitute people standing amid and searching through rubble. You also have a news clipping telling about the disaster. You have circled portions of it that you are going to read to the children.

Presenting these items, you communicate the need of the victims. As you talk about each item and encourage children's observations, you can sense a growing awe. Their attentiveness increases. When they speak, it is in hushed, serious tones. They feel the urgency of the need.

EXPLORING THE PROBLEM ELEMENTS

The basic elements for these young children is how clothing is collected and sent to needy people and the kind of clothing needed. To help them explore these elements, you present a flannelgram story. The flannelgrams include the following representations: a large carton of clothing, a truck taking it to the airport, an airplane, Juan and Maria (Guatemalan children), and items of children's clothing some of which are dirty or in poor repair. There is also a heavy coat and cap with earflaps.

Using these items, you tell a story about a carton of clothing collected by the city and taken to a family in Guatemala. Juan and Maria react to the clothing. They are delighted with the items that are clean and in good repair, particularly two pairs of shoes. They are not sure how much use they will get out of the heavy coat and cap because it is so warm. They are saddened by worn-out and dirty clothing.

Guide the children in a brief review of the story.

GENERATING SOLUTIONS

Solutions are generated as soon as you ask the question: "What do you think we might do to help children like Juan and Maria?"

Let us suppose these solutions are generated:

they might collect some money to buy clothing for the children, they might collect children's clothing in their neighborhood, or they might find some clothing at home to send to the children.

As the children are proposing solutions, you accept what they give without asking for explanations or justifications.

SELECTING A SOLUTION

At this point you repeat all the suggested solutions and ask the children to choose the one they think is the best. As you do this, you emphasize what they as *children* can do. Encourage them to give reasons for their choices. Finally the class decides that the best solution is to try to find some clothing at home that they might bring.

APPLYING THE SOLUTION

At this point you guide the children in composing a class letter to their parents informing them about the clothing drive. After the children make their own copies of the letter, you guide them in deciding where the clothing should be put when they bring it into the classroom and how it should be packaged so that no one needs to be embarrassed about what he or she has to bring. You also suggest that if any children are having a problem with finding anything to bring, they may come and talk it over with you.

During the next few days children bring clothing to school in paper bags. The bags are dropped in a large box. Each morning a few comments are made about how full the box is getting. You see to it that the few children who cannot bring things from home have a package to drop in the box (items from your own home or purchased at a thrift store). To help these children maintain their self-respect, you arrange for them to do small tasks for you to "pay" for their contributions.

On the appointed day, the principal comes to the classroom to accept the contributions. He thanks the children on behalf of Guatemalan children, and the custodian takes the box away.

EVALUATING THE SOLUTION

Since the children cannot see the clothing being given to the Guatemalan children or receive their thanks, and since community leaders rarely have the time to write thank-you letters to each class of children who help in such an enterprise, you conduct a discussion about how the solution made them feel. Or you might present the flannelgrams again and encourage the children to create a story about how Juan and Maria react when they get their new, needed clothing. Or the children might pantomime or role play Juan and Maria receiving their clothing. Any of these activities help them to get insights into the value of their solution.

As you can see in the above, guiding young children through problem-stimulated inquiry requires much assistance from the teacher. However, it is possible to omit two of the procedures above. In many instances, the teacher might omit guiding the children in reviewing their knowledge background. The inquiry prompter might be able to surface all the information the children need.

Also, exploring the problem elements might be omitted. Sometimes the urgency built by the prompter is so great that the children want to begin proposing solutions immediately, or the problem may be such that the children did not need more information about the problem elements.

The cited omissions usually occur when the problems are very immediate. This occurs with older children as well as with younger ones.

Let us see what differences occur in the use of the model when it is used with children in fourth grade and beyond.

Older children are capable of working with problems which are more abstract and for which the solutions are controversial. Such solutions may not be applied in an immediate sense. They remain in the minds of children as possibilities. In some instances, children will divide over two opposing solutions. When this occurs, they are encouraged to suspend judgment until some time in the future when more information becomes available.

For example, at the end of an inquiry on labor-management problems, many members of the class may feel that the government should do more to protect the rights and activities of labor unions. Just as many members feel that labor unions should be curbed in what they do. This is an issue, then, which the members of the class should think and

read more about before arriving at a final judgment.

The inquiry prompters for abstract problems may be factually saturated structures or they may reveal only the facts necessary to build urgency. Let us consider the latter first.

Any communication that simply asserts an opinion from a single point of view, or a set of communications expressing at least two opposing opinions, immediately generates urgency. Here are a few examples that could be used with labor-management relationships:

- A cartoon showing labor downtrodden by management, or one showing management downtrodden by labor, or both.
- An editorial citing labor as the major cause of inflation and unemployment, or one citing management as the major cause, or both.
- An overheard conversation which is primarily a strongly stated opinion for labor, or one strongly against labor, or both.
- A quote drawn from a speech made by a political candidate who is strongly for management, or one from a speech made by a candidate who is strongly against management, or both. Quotes from speeches or other works of historical personages may also be used.
- Any mix of the above, such as a pro-labor cartoon and a pro-management editorial.

You can probably predict what will happen when, after the children have discussed briefly what is meant by *labor* and *management,* they experience prompters such as these. They discuss vigorously. Usually the discussion starts and becomes heated more quickly when two opposing opinions are expressed.

Terminate the discussion while it is at a high pitch. The urgency has been developed at this point. Acknowledge the class's strong feelings and point out that as you listen to what they are saying, you are hearing mostly strong feelings, and that perhaps some facts would help them to see more clearly what to think.

Indicate the resources that are immediately available—copies of an article about the life of Eugene Debs, an early union leader: some informational booklets about a labor contract and what both labor and management may do when they cannot agree; and some magazine articles reporting on what management and labor have been able to do with profit sharing and the like.

After the children have read as much as they can about labor and management, conduct a simulation of negotiation between labor and management.

At the close of these activities, conduct an indepth discussion in which the children try to develop a solution for the problems of conflict between labor and management.

As you hear solutions suggested, you make notes of them or begin to list them on the chalkboard. When the children begin repeating themselves or trying to "win" by talking louder and faster, you focus their attention on their solutions to see whether there is one on which they can agree.

Sometimes they appear to be arriving at closure on one particular solution without really considering an alternative solution. If you wish, assume the role of the devil's advocate (the person who argues the other side of the issue for the sake of argument). Inform the children of what you are doing by saying something like this: "Just a minute. I am going to pretend that I am a person who feels that this is what should be done. . . ." Proceed to tell what you think.

When the discussion ends, the children will have arrived at one or more solutions. At this point, you comment positively on the reasonableness of their solution or solutions but suggest that what they think is a good solution now may change. They should think about it from time to time in the future.

As you can see, when children work with an abstract problem, solution, application, and evaluation are limited. The children cannot do much more about the problem than to clarify their thinking by establishing a more rational base. The model followed in their inquiry is similar to the value analysis discussed in Chapter 3.

Let us now consider what happens when we use an inquiry prompter saturated with facts. Here are some descriptions of such prompters:

- Stories, films, videotapes, or excerpts from novels in which persons react as victims of circumstances drawn by adverse social conditions.
- Diaries or excerpts from diaries of observant persons who record details about social conditions.
- Magazine articles or books by observers who report details about social conditions.
- Case studies, excerpts from case studies, or collections of notes taken during a case study as produced by social scientists.

For instructional purposes in social studies, all of the above are labeled as "case studies."

Using a case study such as the above, the teacher follows these procedures:

1. Guides the children in a brief discussion to encourage them to surface what they know about the elements of the problem.
2. Presents the case study. After the children have drawn the important facts from it, they are guided in generalizing. The generalization is a conclusion about the conditions depicted in the case study. The problem forces are identified in the conclusions.
3. Asks the children what might be done to solve such a problem. The children generate possible solutions.
4. Attempts to bring the children to consensus on one solution.
5. Guides the children in suspending judgment about the solution or solutions.

As you can see in the above, no provisions are made for the children to seek any more information than was presented in the case study.

For a more balanced experience with the problem, the teacher provides more case studies written by other observers from other points of view. Then the children compare all the solutions they have generated to try to develop a more comprehensive solution.

So far, then, we have seen the need for information in the problem-stimulated inquiry satisfied in two ways, either as an activity after experiencing the prompter or in the process of analyzing the prompter itself. There remains one more possibility. Seeking information can be delayed until after the children have decided on one or more solutions as best. When this occurs, they are seeking further information to validate what they think.

And there are those problems which are so close to children that there is no need for further information seeking. Figure 4–9 shows information seeking as optional or perhaps needed at certain points in the model. As you can see in the figure, suspended judgment is an alternative to solution application and evaluation.

Generally, problem-stimulated inquiry may take one of several forms, depending on the nature of the problem, teacher preference, the availability of materials, and the children's level of mastery of information-process skills. Young children will need much teacher assistance. Older children will have many opportunities to work in groups as they generate and select solutions.

Each model we have examined has emphasized thinking skills. The next model emphasizes them in a special way.

A Model for Concept-centered Inquiry

Social-studies educators have difficulties with deciding what a "concept" is. Boutwell offers one suitable for our purposes:

A concept is an abstract idea, a "big idea," that organizes specific, real facts. Concepts may range from very simple organizers, such as the concept "dog," to complex abstractions that organize many variables, such as the concept "socialization" or "culture." [11]

By "organizer" Boutwell means the focal point around which we cluster our experiences. To determine the concept a person has about an object (living things, love, generosity, etc., are considered as objects), we would observe a person's behavior (including verbal behavior), as related to the object. For example, if we wanted to know what an eight-month-old child's concept of "dog" is, we would observe his behavior as he catches sight of a dog. As he sees it, he emits loud, happy noises, waves his arms, clasps and unclasps his hands rapidly, and begins to crawl toward it. Freely translated, his concept is something like this: "What a wondrous, exciting thing that moves. I must see what it feels and tastes like!" However, we may hear a friend say, "Irish setter? A very fine dog. I have three very fine puppies for sale in the store. When well-trained, they make excellent pets." Our friend defines his concept of a dog in economic and social terms.

A concept-centered inquiry provides for two basic events: (1) establishing the nature of the concept the children have about an object, and (2) extending the periphery of the concept to greater utility.

Establishing the nature of children's concept of an object follows a series of procedures based on the thinking of Piaget [12] implemented by Taba [13] and her associates. Here is an example of the series as used with a group of children in second grade beginning their study of transportation:

1. *Surfacing the observations made of a concept.* The teacher asks the children in what they ride when they go downtown with their parents. When volunteers express "bus" and "car," list them on the chalkboard. Then ask the children to name all the things they can think of that people ride on or use to haul things. As they name objects, the teacher lists them. The naming ends when the children begin repeating themselves.
2. *Grouping observations.* The teacher asks the children to identify the listed objects which appear to belong together. As the children make selections, the teacher asks them why they think the selection belongs to a particular group. The teacher accepts the reasons, sometimes helping the children to clarify what they mean. A chart is made listing each item in groups.
3. *Labeling groups of observations.* The teacher asks the children to decide on a name for each group. Sometimes several words are used in a name, but as long as the child who suggests it can justify it, it is accepted. The label is written above the group.
4. *Looking for interrelationships among observations.* The teacher asks whether any of the items listed in a group could be also listed in any of the other groups. As a child identifies such an item, he or she is encouraged to tell why it could fit into another identified group.

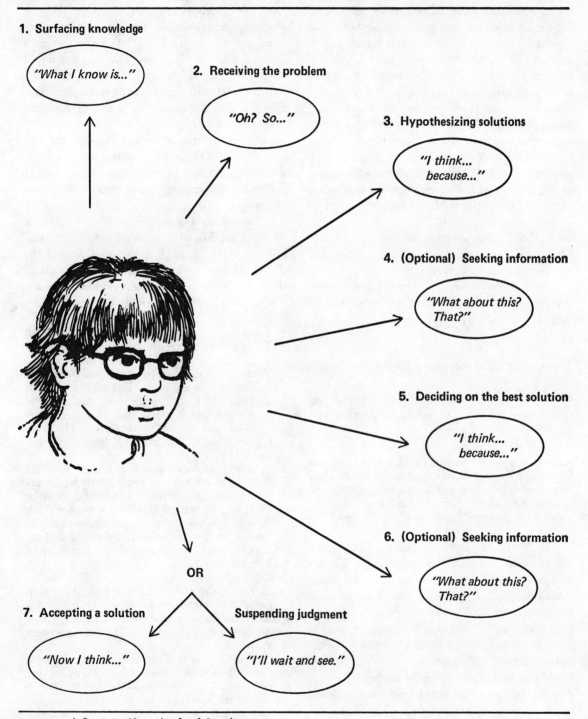

FIGURE 4–9. *A Problem-stimulated Inquiry.*

5. *Generalizing from information organized in labeled groups.* The teacher guides the children in arriving at a generalization based on their organized information. (Any of the aids discussed previously in this chapter may be used.)

As shown in the above, establishing the nature of the children's concept is a matter of guiding children in cataloging what they already know about a concept, analyzing what they know to organize it, and generalizing from their information. *It is an inquiry into what the children already have learned about the concept in or out of school.* The result is a clear picture of what the children know.

From this point onward the children's learning activities carry them into extending what they know about transportation. And the remainder of the learning procedures may be similar to those used in the other models of inquiry discussed in this chapter as shown in Figure 4–10.

It should be noted, however, that teachers who use the concept-centered model of inquiry tend to provide as many activities as possible in which the children compare and contrast facts and sets of facts. Let us assume that the children in a second grade have arrived at these generalizations: *People use many different things to go where they want to go. They use many different things to take stuff everywhere.* (When young children generalize, they often have to use more than one sentence to express an idea which older children can state in a single sentence.) The teacher provides activities such as the following to guide them in extending their concept of transportation as a process:

The children view these pictures: an ocean freighter, a jetliner, a farm tractor, a channel dredge, a tethered balloon used for advertising, and a gravel truck. They discuss the pictures and match them into the following pairs: an ocean freighter and a channel dredge, a jetliner and a tethered balloon used for advertising, and a farm tractor and a gravel truck. (They may decide on another grouping based on their own reasoning. If they do, the teacher permits it.) Then they listen to a description of the work of a channel dredge, a

farm tractor, and a tethered balloon. The children discover the difference between the work of machines—those used for transportation and those used for other kinds of work. They rearrange the pictures to reflect their discovery. The teacher focuses their attention on transportation as a process.

The children follow the teacher's flannelgram presentations showing how a banana and an apple reach the home fruit bowl from the place where they are produced. The globe is used to illustrate the routes followed. By comparing the two routes, the children discover that different physical barriers demand different vehicles for transportation purposes.

The children view two sets of pictures of goods, those frequently transported by freight, and those transported usually by rail or truck. They discuss the different goods and how they are used. The teacher identifies which group of goods is frequently transported by air and which is often transported by rail or truck, and has the children decide why such transportation is used. Comparing the two groups of goods, the children discover that perishable and emergency goods are often shipped by air and that bulky goods not subject to quick spoilage are often shipped by rail or truck.

The children view two short films, one about the Lapps and the other about the people in England to see how the two peoples use transportation. They discover differences and see relationships between transportation and the life circumstances of a people—their culture and geographical location.

In addition to these activities, the teacher provides individualized learning centers in which the children compare and contrast items related to transportation. These activities reinforce what the class has studied as a total group.

Older children are guided into studies in which they compare cultures, regions, eras, economic systems, political systems, and the like.

As you can see, concept-centered inquiry focuses children's inquiry on diversity. As they explore within diversity and the causes for it, they are involved in analytical activities which ensure a solid base for generating ideas.

Concept-centered inquiry may be used in grade one and beyond. However, the children must be

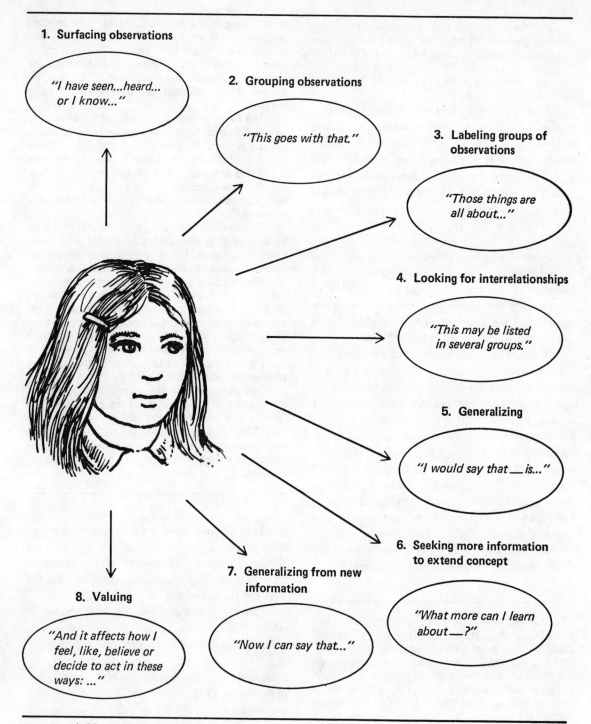

1. **Surfacing observations**

"I have seen...heard... or I know..."

2. **Grouping observations**

"This goes with that."

3. **Labeling groups of observations**

"Those things are all about..."

4. **Looking for interrelationships**

"This may be listed in several groups."

5. **Generalizing**

"I would say that ___ is..."

6. **Seeking more information to extend concept**

"What more can I learn about ___?"

7. **Generalizing from new information**

"Now I can say that..."

8. **Valuing**

"And it affects how I feel, like, believe or decide to act in these ways: ..."

FIGURE 4–10. *Concept-centered Inquiry.*[14]

able to read well enough to recognize words and phrases recorded on a chart or the chalkboard.

Looking back over the several models of inquiry presented in this chapter, you can see that you have several choices of models to use. Some models may be more useful at certain grade levels than others. Some may be more suitable to your teaching style.

The worst thing that can happen is to settle on one model and to repeat it constantly without variation. As soon as the children can begin to predict the procedures, they lose interest. The better practice is to vary your use of the models.

The purpose for presenting five models here is to ensure that you have ways of guiding children in social studies in which they can participate in directing their own learning. Inquiry is a teacher-and-learner enterprise, not a teacher-to-learner demand.

THE ULTIMATE IN INQUIRY

As you read further about inquiry, you will most likely learn about the issue of free-versus-controlled inquiry. Everything discussed in this chapter has been controlled. This means that at the beginning of a unit of instruction or a lesson using the inquiry procedures suggested here, the teacher could predict what the outcome would be—not always precisely, but usually within the realm of possibility.

In free inquiry, the children do not know what the outcome will be. Furthermore, the teacher couldn't care less. This does not mean that he or she does not confer with the children about what they have learned. Whatever they have learned is a plus. More important is how they feel about what they have learned and the process that involved them in it.

Free inquiry is implemented through providing children with many choices. They have many choices among task cards, learning centers, or individualized packages of instruction. They may have choices as to whether they have to finish anything they choose, do a part of it, or do none of it

if it really has no appeal to them. The teacher determines these choices, and thus controls the inquiry.

For my part, free inquiry occurs when a child comes to me with a freely chosen interest, problem, issue, or burning desire to know about something. That is a great beginning. I am humble and privileged to be able to assist.

And the ultimate in inquiry occurs when a child brings me a model or a communication which he or she developed alone. It may deal with the satisfaction of curiosity, interest, or concern within the domain of social studies. It is what all of us hope for but rarely experience.

SUMMARY

Inquiry is the act of seeking to find or find out about something. An inquiry-directed instructional program in social studies actively involves children in purposeful learning, provides practice in the skills of thinking, and offers children opportunities for the realistic application of basic skills.

The model for curiosity-stimulated inquiry includes procedures for stimulating and extending curiosity, and for expressing the results.

The model for interest-stimulating inquiry includes procedures for stimulating interest through heightened curiosity, generating interest, surveying interests, selecting interests to follow, following interests, evaluating interests, and extending interests.

The models for scientific inquiry includes procedures for helping children discover the problem, hypothesize explanations, select a hypothesis, develop a design for inquiry, seek and organize information, find out how conclusions validate ideas, and apply ideas to explore for values.

The model for problem-stimulated inquiry includes procedures for helping children review knowledge background, receive the problem, explore the problem elements, generate solutions, and select, apply, and evaluate solutions.

The model for concept-centered inquiry includes provisions for children to surface, group, and label observations about a concept, to look for interrelationships among observations, to generalize, and to extend the concept through further study.

Each inquiry model requires an inquiry prompter.

Curiosity-stimulated inquiry is suited to the needs of young children. Interest-stimulated inquiry may be used with children in grades two through six. Scientific inquiry is appropriate for grade three and above. Problem-stimulated and concept-centered inquiry may be used at all grade levels except kindergarten.

Inquiry as a way of learning may be free or controlled. Free inquiry as its ultimate begins with the child.

POSTSCRIPT

Now is the time for you to review the notes you wrote at the beginning of the chapter. Read them and decide whether you have changed from the way you felt earlier about your child attending a school which has an emphasis on inquiry in social studies. Have your feelings changed? In what way? Why?

If your feelings remain much the same as they did before, in what way would you extend your reasons?

FOR FURTHER UNDERSTANDING

Cognitive Activities

1. Compose an advertisement or design a poster or a front page of a brochure citing the advantages of inquiry as a way of learning in social studies.

2. Using 3 x 5 cards, make a set of study cards for each inquiry model. On each card write a brief description of a procedure used in the model. Do not number the cards. As you finish each set of cards, try mixing them and placing them in order. Try to recall as much as you can about each procedure. This activity may be used by study partners.

3. Choose the inquiry model that you prefer. Develop a list of reasons for your preference. If you have a study partner who prefers another model, engage him or her in a discussion in which each tries to convince the other to accept his or her preference.

4. Choose the inquiry model you think would give you the most problems. List the problems and then try to develop a possible solution for each problem.

5. Make a values analysis of *inquiry as a way of learning in elementary social studies* as the value object. Share the results with a study partner.

Practice Activities

1. Working by yourself or with a study partner, develop a list of rules which you think every teacher should follow when reacting to children's responses as they are being prompted to begin an inquiry.

2. Devise an inquiry prompter for each of the inquiry models for use at your preferred grade level or cluster of grade levels. If you are teaching or have a laboratory assignment in a classroom, you may wish to make prompters which you can use in your own classroom.

3. Arrange to visit a classroom when social studies is being taught. Observe for evidence of inquiry as a way of learning. If what you see is primarily factual learning with no evidence of inquiry in the display areas of the classroom, try to interview the teacher to see how he or she began the study at hand and intends to terminate it.

Performance Activities

1. Arrange to use at least one of the prompters you devised in response to 2 above. Evaluate your experience by responding to these questions:
   a. What percentage of children were actively involved?
   b. Was the point of the inquiry established? How do you know?
   c. What changes would you make in your prompter or the way you used it to improve prompting inquiry?

2. Audiotape your performance with an inquiry prompter. Listen to the tape to see how you were responding verbally to your learners. List the situations in which you need to improve.

SELECTED REFERENCES

Banks, James A., with Ambrose A. Clegg, Jr. *Teaching Strategies for the Social Studies*. Reading, Mass.: Addison-Wesley, 1973.

Beyer, Barry K. *Teaching Thinking in Social Studies: Using Inquiry in the Classroom,* revised edition. Columbus, Ohio: Charles E. Merrill, 1979.

Boutwell, Clenton E. *Getting It All Together—The New Social Studies*. San Rafael, Calif.: Leswing, 1972.

Brown, Robert. *Explanation in Social Science*. Chicago: Aldine, 1963.

Crowder, William W. *Persistent-Problems Approach to Elementary Social Studies*. Itasca, Ill.: F. E. Peacock, 1973.

Eliason, Claudia Fuhriman, and Loa Thomson Jenkens. *A Practical Guide to Early Childhood Curriculum*. St. Louis: C. V. Mosby, 1977.

Lee, Robert R. *Teaching Social Studies in the Elementary School*. New York: Free Press, 1974.

Mackey, James. "Three Problem-Solving Models for the Elementary Classroom." *Social Education,* 41: 408–10 (May, 1977).

Martorella, Peter H. *Concept Learning in the Social Studies*. Scranton, Pa.: International Textbook, 1971.

Pagano, Alice L., ed. *Social Studies in Early Childhood: An Interactionist Point of View*. Washington, D.C.: National Council for the Social Studies, 1978.

Ryan, Frank L., and Arthur K. Ellis. *Instructional Implications of Inquiry*. Englewood Cliffs, N.J.: Prentice-Hall, 1974.

Shive, R. Jerrald. *Social Studies as Controversy*. Pacific Palisades, Calif.: Goodyear, 1973.

Taba, Hilda, Mary C. Durkin, Jack R. Fraenkel, and Anthony H. McNaughton. *A Teacher's Handbook to Elementary Social Studies, An Inductive Approach,* 2nd ed. Reading, Mass.: Addison-Wesley, 1971.

NOTES

1. John Dewey. *Democracy and Education*. New York: Macmillan, 1916, p. 179.

2. John Dewey. *Interest and Effort in Education*. Boston: Houghton Mifflin, 1913, pp. 65–84.

3. Barry J. Wadsworth. *Piaget for the Classroom Teacher*. New York: Longman, 1978, pp. 48–56.

4. Jerome S. Bruner. "Structures in Learning," *Today's Education,* 52:26–27, March, 1963.

   Jerome S. Bruner, *Toward a Theory of Instruction*. Cambridge, Massachusetts: Harvard University Press, 1966.

   Edwin Fenton. *The New Social Studies*. New York: Holt, Rinehart, and Winston, 1967.

   Bernice Goldmark. " 'Critical Thinking?' Deliberate Method," *Social Education,* 30:329–34, May, 1966.

5. Maxine Dumfee. *Elementary Social Studies, A Guide to Current Research*. Washington, D.C.: National Education Association, 1970, pp. 43–44.

6. *Ibid.,* p. 45.

7. *Ibid.,* pp. 44–46.

8. *Ibid.,* pp. 50–51.

9. Barry K. Beyer. *Teaching Thinking in Social Studies: Using Inquiry in the Classroom,* Rev. edition. Columbus, Ohio: Charles E. Merrill, 1979, p. 39.

10. Frank L. Ryan and Arthur K. Ellis. *Instructional Implications of Inquiry*. Englewood Cliffs, N.J.: Prentice-Hall, 1974, p. 35.

11. Clinton E. Boutwell. *Getting It All Together—the New Social Studies*. San Rafael, Calif.: Leswing Press, 1972, p. 36.

12. Jean Piaget. *The Psychology of Intelligence*. New York: Harcourt, Brace, Jovanovich, 1950.

13. Hilda Taba, Mary C. Durkin, Jack R. Fraenkel, and Anthony H. McNaughton. *A Teacher's Handbook to Elementary Social Studies,* 2nd ed. Reading, Mass.: Addison-Wesley Publishing Company, 1971.

14. The material on concept-centered inquiry is based on the ideas expressed in Chapter 5 of *A Teacher's Handbook to Elementary Social Studies* by Hilda Taba and her associates. Copyright © 1971 Addison-Wesley Publishing Company, Inc., pp. 64–103.

5

Improving Children's Information-seeking Skills

Inquiry in social studies is purposeful, but no matter how skilled you are in guiding children in developing purposes, or how much the children make the purposes their own, frustration is going to occur if the children lack the skills to meet them. This is why so much emphasis was given to the assessment of intake skills in Chapter 2. The purpose of this chapter is to give you suggestions on how to improve children's information-seeking skills.

Listed below is a list of general procedures followed by teachers when teaching skills. Study the list as a social-studies teacher to decide whether the list is complete.

1. *Assessing the skill.* The purpose is to determine what children already know about the skill and what they need to be taught.
2. *Introducing the skill.* During this procedure, the teacher identifies the purposes fulfilled by the skill and gives the children a preview of how the skill works.
3. *Providing activities.* These may have the children making trials with all the subskills in sequential order or with each subskill until it is learned. The elements of each lesson include provisions for children to
   a. *Observe a demonstration.* This acquaints the learners with skills behaviors.

b. *Practice under supervision.* The children try the behaviors under the direct supervision of the teacher who sees that each behavior is correctly practiced.
   c. *Practice independently.* During this procedure the children repeat the behaviors by themselves with practice materials. At the close of each practice the teacher informs the children about behaviors needing improvement. Reteaching or corrective teaching may be needed.
4. *Postassessing the skill.* At this point the teacher uses a test or other assessment device to see at what level the children have mastered the skill with practice materials.

If you think the list is complete, bear your opinion in mind as you read the chapter. If you think it is incomplete, write a note to yourself in which you identify the omitted procedure and give a reason or two for its inclusion in the list. Then put the note aside to review at the end of the chapter.

If children only could

- exchange places with other children living in different circumstances within our society,
- exchange places with other children living in different societies around the world,
- climb into a time machine that would take them

to any moment in the past or the future as it occurred in a particular place, or

• visit the site of any productive endeavor and participate directly and personally in the process,

they could seek information about what they need to know about themselves and others coping with their physical and social environments through experiencing. It is impossible as a total approach, but teachers often provide for such experiencing.

Some young children studying about the dairy still have an opportunity to try to milk a cow or goat and to make butter or ice cream, or, when studying about the bakery, to bake bread or cookies.

Some children studying the changes in America still have opportunities to make candles from tallow, to tan a hide, to heat a branding iron and brand a hide, to make adobe bricks by hand (and foot), to make soap, to dance a minuet or a reel, to dry fruit and vegetables, to splice a rope or make a net, or to ride on an animal-pulled vehicle.

Some children studying about another people still learn the songs and dances characteristic of a people, try their recipes and modes of cooking and eating, and try their crafts.

Such experiences often distort reality through substitutions of materials (most of us would not care to have children brand real cattle), altering the environment from the way it actually was or is, and foreshortening time. Regardless of these shortcomings, these experiences help children discover information by extending through the senses. For example, the meaning of "They rendered the tallow from animal fat" means one thing to a child who discovered the statement in a textbook but another to a child who put the greasy chunks of fat into a pot, who smelled them as they were frying out, who felt the heat of the rendered fat as it was poured into another receptacle, who tasted a fragment of crisp fat soon after it stopped sizzling, who watched the clear grease congeal into a creamy, white mass, and who touched the cooled mass to test its consistency between a thumb and forefinger.

Whenever we can, we shall facilitate such experiences. But it would be futile for us to try to implement all information seeking in this way. We and the children must rely on information

seeking in resources which represent reality in words and other symbols. To help children seek and find information in these resources we guide them in learning the intake skills.

In the previous chapter on inquiry, you discovered the place of the informational-intake skills (observing, listening, reading, and interviewing) in social-studies inquiry. The inquiry, whatever it may be, offers direction toward the kind of information needed, but the quality and abundance of information depends on the effectiveness of children's intake skills.

Information seeking is not always an exciting activity for children. For this reason, as well as to focus more closely on an aspect of critical thinking or on stimulating activities such as role playing or simulation, we may provide the information in the most direct way possible. For example, we may provide our fifth-grade class with a facsimile of an anthropologist's notes consisting of a list of twenty-five entries which the children are to read, analyze, and organize into parcels of related information. Or we provide our eighth-grade class with an information sheet offering the main facts needed to become involved in a simulation. Such practices do reduce the tedium sometimes associated with elementary social studies. But this is just one side of the coin.

The other side of the coin reveals that as social-studies teachers we are also responsible for children's improvement in the life-long skills of observing, listening, reading, and interviewing to acquire information. Our ultimate objective is to bring every child as close as possible to the point of being independent in acquiring information to use in solving problems or making important decisions related to social-studies knowledge.

The instructional program in the intake skills generally reflects children's developing ability to use increasingly refined skills to deal with information at higher and higher levels of abstraction. The skills we teach will depend on the grade level or levels at which we are working.

The children in kindergarten and first grade will have to rely primarily on observing and listening to acquire information. The social-studies textbooks designed for their use convey information through pictures. The verbal text is supplementary. The teacher is expected to guide the children in studying the pictures and to extend their exploration through providing opportunities for them to study other pictures, observe at various sites, view films and filmstrips, follow oral presentations illustrated with flannelgrams or charts, listen to readings, follow presentations made by resource persons, experience puppet performances, and analyze real objects or replicas. The intake activities will have to be carefully guided and characterized by variety and many opportunities for interaction. Interviewing will be limited to factual questions generated in class to be asked of resource persons in the school and neighborhood.

In grades two and three, observing and listening skills are still used frequently for intake purposes, but reliance on these skills is gradually reduced. Social-studies textbooks prepared for grade two will reflect as much reliance on reading as on picture study as a means of acquiring information. The textbooks for grade three provide a transition to a greater reliance on the verbal text. A few simple locational skills with maps will be learned. The children will learn how to use a simple table of contents to locate a chapter to read for information and a simple index to locate a page to read. Interviewing will still be limited largely to class-generated questions to be asked of easily accessible persons. Concepts basic to intake skills will be extended.

During the second and third grades individual differences begin to emerge in the children's ability to get meaning from a verbal text. Some children will still have to rely on observing and listening for informational intake.

In grades four and five the instructional program in intake skills focuses strongly on reading and reading-related skills. Social-studies textbooks designed for these grades reflect the use of verbal text as the major conveyor of information. Pictures and other graphic materials are used to clarify ideas in the text. The children are expected to learn to read political-physical maps (including the use of direction indicators and scale) and picture,

bar, and line graphs, to use tables of contents and indexes to locate where to read for information, and to take notes and outline to retain information for later analysis and interpretation. They are also introduced to the structure and purposes of the interview.

During these grades individual differences in ability to learn and use the intake skills related to reading become markedly pronounced. If all the children are to have an equal opportunity to acquire information, the program for the improvement of intake skills will need to be varied.

In grades six, seven, and eight, the skills taught in the previous grades are maintained and, whenever needed, are corrected to ensure that children are able to use their textbooks and commonly used reference materials—encyclopedias, almanacs, atlases, newspapers, magazines, and library books. Most of the information is acquired from verbal text.

In these grades the intake skills taught in grades four and five are extended and refined. The children learn to read special-feature maps requiring careful attention to map legends or keys—population, production, rainfall, temperature, climatic, and historical maps. Rearranged maps purposely distorted to show political and economic relationships may be introduced. How to use latitude and longitude to locate regions and points on maps and the globe and how to use longitude to determine time around the world are taught. Also, distortions introduced into maps through different methods of projection are explored.

Graph skills are extended to include how to read circle or pie graphs.

Index skills are extended to include how to use the card catalog in the library and the *Readers' Guide to Periodical Literature.*

The reading-retention skills are extended to meet more sophisticated needs. Third (I. A. *1.*) and fourth (I. A. 1. *a.*) level entries are added to outlines. Sophistication is added to note taking through greater attention to bibliographical information, paraphrasing, and selecting quotations.

Interviewing may be extended to emphasis on preparation, greater concern for the interviewer, and listening carefully to ask unplanned but appropriate questions during the interview.

A wide range of differences in intake-skills abilities occurs in these grades. To ensure that children can acquire needed information, the instructional program will have to include corrective measures.

Figure 5–1 provides a quick reference to the grade levels at which certain intake skills are directly taught. The concepts basic to skills and the skill specified at lower levels are regarded as preparatory to the skills at higher levels.

As we explore into the ways of teaching the various intake skills, we shall consider first the basic

Observation	Listening	Reading	Interviewing
Kindergarten and Grade 1			
Skills Observing a process on site and recalling facts during discussion. Viewing pictures, films, etc., and recalling facts during the discussion. Comparing observations and viewings, and discussing the results.	*Skills* Listening to a verbal text and recalling the facts. Listening to two texts and comparing findings. Combining listening with observation or viewing and discussing findings.	*Concepts* Books, newspapers, and magazines as sources of information. A map as a picture of an observed surface area. A symbol as a representation of a real thing. The globe as a symbol of the earth. Directions as constant points of reference.	*Concepts* People as sources of information. *Skills* Composing questions as a group to ask resource persons. Asking a resource person a prepared question.
Grades 2 and 3			
The same as the above.	The same as the above.	*Concepts* An encyclopedia as an alphabetically arranged information source. A graph as a means of showing quantitative relationships. *Skills* Reading a text prepared at the appropriate readability level and recalling the facts during discussion. Comparing what has been read in two or more sources and discussing findings. Comparing what has been read with what has been observed and/or read. Locating points on a community map.	The same as the above.

FIGURE 5–1. *The Instructional Program in Intake Skills.*

Observation	Listening	Reading	Interviewing
		Locating the states on a political map of the United States.	
		Using simple tables of contents and indexes to decide where to begin reading for information	

		Grades 4 and 5	
Skills The same as the above, but more sites are included: historical sites, museums, trade fairs, law courts, etc.	*Skills* The same as the above.	*Skills* Locating points and regions on political-physical maps of states, countries, continents, hemispheres, and the world, and on the globe. Using direction indicators on maps to locate points and regions. Using the scale to compute distances and areas on maps and the globe. Indicating directions from given points in the environment and on maps and globes. Reading picture graphs. Reading bar and line graphs. Using tables of contents and indexes to decide where to read for information. Skimming to find the best place to read. Note taking. Outlining to the second level (I. A.).	*Skills* Composing sets of questions to use during interviews. Conducting interviews individually or in small groups.

		Grades 6, 7, and 8	
Skills The same as the above.	*Skills* The same as the above.	*Concepts* Distortion of maps as a result of projection. Distortion of maps as a way of showing relationships. *Skills* Reading special-feature maps requiring careful interpretation of the legend or key.	*Skills* Planning an interview with the needs of the interviewee in mind. Asking impromptu questions during an interview.

FIGURE 5–1. *(continued)*

Observation	Listening	Reading	Interviewing
		Finding the latitude and longitude of a given point on a map or the globe.	
		Giving the latitudes and longitudes of a given region on a map or the globe.	
		Using longitudes to determine the clock time at various points around the world.	
		Reading circle or pie graphs.	
		Using the card catalog in the library to locate informational books.	
		Paraphrasing during note taking.	
		Deciding to use a quotation in a note.	
		Recording complete bibliographical information on a note.	
		Outlining to the fourth level (I. A. 1. a.).	

FIGURE 5–1. (*continued*)

strategies we may use, and then their application in the various skills.

BASIC STRATEGIES FOR IMPROVING INTAKE SKILLS

Two instructional strategies are available for us to follow as we try to improve children's intake skills. One is the *holistic strategy* and the other is the *stage-by-stage strategy*. Sometimes we have a choice of which to use; at other times we do not. Neither is superior to the other, but one may be better to use with some children.

If the skill we are teaching cannot be reduced into easily identifiable events or subskills, we introduce it and have the children practice it as a whole. We ensure learning by having the children practice the skill first at a level of complexity well within their ability, and then we increase the level gradually. For example, if we wish to improve a child's reading comprehension of social-studies material, we find or develop reading material which he or she can read independently. The shorter the selection and the sentences it contains, and the less the number of different words and long words, the lower its complexity. All factors have to be controlled. We can also lower the complexity of purpose by having the child respond to a few factual questions which can be answered in a word or two. When the child's confidence is established by his success with such material, we increase the level of purpose—more facts to recall, questions demanding recall of how or why, and a question requiring the child to infer. When the child achieves success at this level, we raise the complexity of language by providing selections of greater length containing longer sentences and a greater vocabulary load. The holistic strategy is the only one we can use when teaching this kind of intake skill. Other skills requiring this strategy are observation and listening skills.

However, when a skill can be reduced into easily identifiable subskills, we may use either the holistic or stage-by-stage strategy. If we use the holistic strategy, we introduce the skill as a whole, and the children practice it as a whole. For example, let us suppose we are guiding our third-grade class in learning the skill of using a children's encyclopedia as a source of information. These are the subskills:

1. Clarifying the purpose to find an entry word.
2. Choosing the correct volume.
3. Finding the correct page.
4. Reading the article.
5. Relating the information to the purpose.

To introduce the skill as a whole, we would model how a person finds information in this encyclopedia. Of course, we would slow down the skill to demonstrate and explain each subskill. This would be followed by these learning activities:

1. The children cue the teacher as he or she uses the skill with a purpose similar to that used in the introduction. He or she supplies reminders for what they forget. If they forget too many subskills or the order in which they are applied, the teacher models the skill again. Several repetitions are usually required before the children can cue the teacher accurately.
2. They try the skill as the teacher monitors their efforts. He or she gives assistance whenever necessary. Several monitored trials will be needed before the children can recall all the subskills in the correct order and apply them.
3. They generalize about the subskills and the order in which they occur. The teacher charts the generalizations for future reference.
4. They practice the skill several times independently as an exercise.
5. They evaluate their practice with the teacher's assistance.

If we were to use the stage-by-stage strategy to teach this skill, we would introduce it by modeling how it is used to give our learners a glimpse of what they are going to learn. Then we would provide learning activities in which the children would master each subskill before learning the next. The first stage with the skill described above

would be mastery of how to decide on an entry word; the second stage would be mastery in selecting the correct volume, and so on. However, as a child learns each new subskill after the first, he or she has a repetitive practice with each subskill previously mastered. As the learner proceeds from subskill to subskill, he or she learns the skill accumulatively. The subskills are seen by the learner as sequenced and connected. See Figures 5–2 and 5–3 for graphic representations of the two strategies.

When we have a choice between the two strategies, our purpose contributes to our choice. If we intend to have our learners experience the skill as readiness for later learning to mastery, the holistic strategy will serve our purpose better. The same is true when the need for the skill has suddenly emerged during social-studies instruction (as it often may in the primary grades). In both cases the strategy is modified to include only the first three learning activities: observing as the teacher models the skill, cuing the teacher through a practice, and trying the skill under careful monitoring. If we intend to teach the entire class as an instructional group to master the skill, the holistic strategy works well, but it does require careful monitoring to identify where individuals are having difficulties.

However, if our purpose is to individualize instruction, we may use the stage-by-stage strategy. One unfortunate drawback to the strategy is the scarcity of appropriate learning materials. Often they will have to be specially devised. Finding, devising, duplicating, and organizing such materials demand time and energy. But once the chore has been completed, the materials are available for many classes to come. Examples of useful materials will be given in the next section.

Now let us look into the various skills as behaviors and how learning them might be implemented through activities and materials.

TEACHING SKILLS AS BEHAVIORS

Some of the intake skills are characterized by similar behaviors. For example, in observing, listening, and reading, one must identify details, deter-

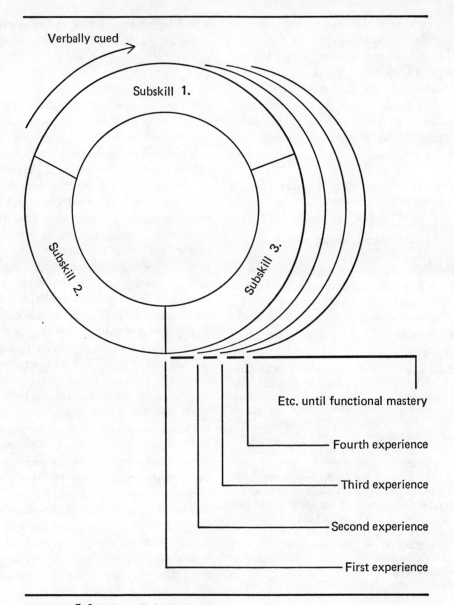

FIGURE 5–2. *The Holistic Strategy.*

mine the functional relationship of details, and generalize from the details and their relationships. Only the intake vehicle is different.

In some skills language is the main medium. This is true of listening and reading. In others, language is a complementary medium, as in observ-ing pictures, filmstrips, films, and videotapes. The main medium is graphic representations of one kind or another. This is particularly true of ob-servation (or viewing) and map, globe, and dia-gram reading.

One of the skills demands social as well as

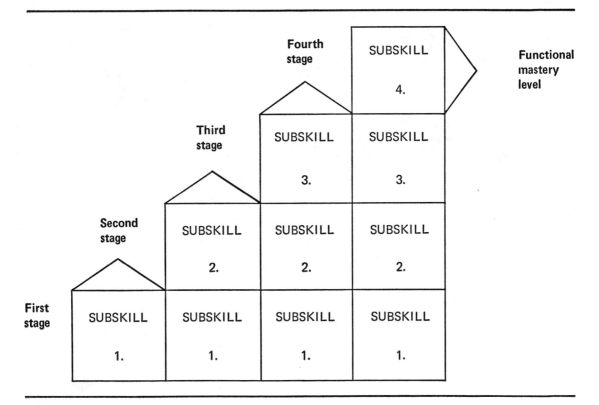

FIGURE 5-3. *The Stage-by-stage Strategy.*

analytical skills. This skill is interviewing, for the interviewer has to be able to respect and be concerned for the interviewee as well as to determine the questions he or she wishes to ask.

Two of the skills, outlining and note taking, are really forms of note taking, but used for different purposes.

And the world of reading is so extensive that it requires special skills just to locate the best place to read for needed information. These are the reading-reference skills—how to use a table of contents, index, or card catalog. And the effective use of these skills depends on the first subskill in the series—how to determine what to look for.

The above is a simple overview of the intake skills which children need to seek and find information. It explains in part why there will be moments when suggestions appear to be repeated.

Most of us separate the skills into these broad categories: observation skills, listening skills, reading skills, interviewing skills, and reading-retention skills. And that is how we shall approach them in this section.

As we treat each of these, we shall consider purposes for their use as well as ways of helping children become more independent in using them.

Observation Skills

Observation is here defined as observing at a site such as a museum, zoo, factory, construction area, etc., and viewing pictures, filmstrips, films, and videotapes.

When the entire class is going to take a field-trip or view a set of pictures, a filmstrip, a film, or

ILLUSTRATION 5–1. *Some Children in First Grade Investigating the Harbor through Observation.*

a videotape, the teacher guides the class in developing purposes as they occur in their inquiry. The purposes may be very specific, as they are in this instance:

A fourth grade class has been studying about Bali for the past couple of days. They know where it is located, that its climate is tropical, and that the main industry of the people is growing rice. Today they are going to view a film, *Daily Life in Bali,* as a resource for information in response to the question, "How do the people in Bali live?" After a brief review of what they learned the previous day about rice growing in Bali, the teacher says, "We are going to view this film to see what we can find out about how the Balinese people live. What kinds of things do you think we should be looking for?" Very quickly these responses are made:

"What they eat."
"What they wear."
"What their houses are like."
"Whether the kids go to school."
"What their schools are like."

The teacher jots these down on the chalkboard as they are given, and then asks, "Do you think that we might look for what the various members of the family do?" The class agrees, and it is added to the list. "Anything else?"

"How the kids and parents feel toward each other." And this is added.

As shown in the above, the children have some definite purposes for viewing the film. They have something to look for. Using the notes on the chalkboard, they will be able to recall and discuss what they observed.

The film may be used in another way. Let us suppose that the class has read in their textbooks about how the Balinese live. The film is going to be used to help them validate their facts. In this case, the teacher says, "Today we are going to look at a film about how the Balinese live. You have already read about it. Let's see where the film and our textbooks agree, and where they disagree."

At this point the teacher might ask the children for ideas about where to be particularly observant, or the teacher may run the film immediately. During the postdiscussion he or she will see how much the children have learned and how well they understand it.

For a change of pace, the teacher might make a general suggestion, "Let's view this film carefully to see what we can learn about how the Balinese live." In many instances, this approach to a film, filmstrip, series of pictures, fieldtrip, or videotape will require a reshowing for the children to get all the desired information.

Whatever informational resource is used, the children have purposes for observing or viewing it before they see it.

When a series of pictures or study prints are used with young children, the teacher assists them in discovering information by using helping questions such as these:

"What do we see in this picture?"

"What things appear to be working together?"

"What does this picture tell us about . . .?"

The ways that a teacher uses with young children when guiding them in viewing pictures provide us with ideas that we might incorporate in helping children generally to become more independently observant. Suggestions to use with young children:

• Take the children on walking trips to see how many different growing things, things used to carry people, buildings, etc., they observe. Permit the children to comment and share ideas as they walk along. When they return to the classroom have them catalog the different things they saw, tear pictures representing what they saw out of magazines, etc.

• Take the children to a particular site such as a busy street corner, a neighborhood shopping center, a construction or razing site, a supermarket, a pet store, or a park. Purposes may be general or specific. When they return to the classroom have them recall what they saw. Guide them in using what they saw to compose an experience story, paint pictures, or do dramatic play.

• Prepare a series of observation lessons based on pictures clipped from magazines or from art prints, or from collections of small objects. Several pictures or objects may be used for each lesson. Inform the children that the purpose of the lesson is to practice looking at things to see how well they can remember them. Display a picture or set of objects and have them look at it for fifteen to twenty seconds. Then, concealing the display, have volun-

teers tell what they saw. Encourage the children to add any object that a volunteer forgets. Show the display again as a check to see whether any items have been missed. Then have the children decide which items seem to belong in a group.

When working with pictures, have the children decide on a name for the picture. Do the same with a set of objects arranged to present a scene.

The children should be divided into groups of five to eight members for lessons. Total class lessons may be presented, but they are not as effective with young children.

• Construct learning centers containing a picture, view box, or collection of familiar objects such as toy vehicles, dishes, furniture, and the like. Have an aide supervise each child's observation. After the observation, limited in time to fifteen or twenty seconds, the child turns his or her back to the display and tells the aide what was observed.

If you have no aide, prepare a picture sheet which contains more items than those in the display. The child goes to the center to observe as long as desired then goes to a study carrel out of view of the display and circles each observed item on the picture sheet.

• Construct an observation game which two or more children may play. Such a game might consist of eight or so magazine pictures mounted on cardboards. Above each picture a number is written indicating the number of things to be observed in the picture. The pictures are stacked face-down in the middle of the playing area. The players take turns at drawing a picture, observing it carefully while the other player (or players) counts slowly aloud, but quietly, to ten, turns the card so all the players can see it, looks away from it, and names the number of objects indicated above the picture. If the number of objects, as validated by the other players, are named, the player keeps the picture. If they are not, the picture is placed on the bottom of the stack. The next player takes his or her turn.

Similar kinds of activities may be planned at a higher intellectual level for older children. For example, here are a few ideas for conducting walking trips:

• Choose an observation site commonly known by the children. Guide the children in trying to recreate that site from memory—perhaps just with notes. Then take them to the site and have them observe. When they return to the classroom, have them make corrections in their notes by deleting mistakes and adding features discovered through observation.

• Divide the class into observation teams to report on what they see at a site. While they are observing, take photographs with an instant picture-development camera. When the children arrive back at the classroom, give each group time to prepare a report on its observations. Showing the photographs on an opaque projector, have each group rate its observations for accuracy and completeness.

• Divide the class into three or six groups. Assign "Eyes," "Ears," or "Nose" roles to the various groups. According to its assigned role, each group is to emphasize observing with that sense. Walk the children to the site and have them observe. Back at the classroom they may exchange notes to use in writing descriptive paragraphs about the visited site.

Using pictures shown on an opaque projector, have the children observe to perform the following tasks after viewing a picture:

• Recall the details, relate them in terms of location and function, and generalize the meaning conveyed by the picture.
• Compose a title for the picture and justify it by giving details and how they are related.
• Take a simple test on the recall of items, how they are related, and the meaning of the picture. The test is immediately corrected.
• Compose a written or oral paragraph in which they give the meaning of the picture and supporting details. The paragraphs are shared and discussed.

The above activities may have the children responding as individuals or in teams. Films run in such a way that the titles are concealed may be used in the same way. To focus on observation skills, run the films without sound.

When constructing learning centers, stock them with several pictures. Prepare directions or task cards similar to these:

---

1. Choose a picture.
2. Study it until you think you know it.
3. Turn it over and write the answers to the following:
    a. Make a list of the important people and objects in the picture.
    b. What are the people doing?
    c. What is a good name for the picture?
4. Get the answer card for the picture and correct your work.
5. Do one of the following:
    a. Draw a picture or write a sentence telling what the people in the picture were doing *before* this picture was taken.
    b. Draw a picture or write a sentence telling what the people in the picture would be doing *after* this picture was taken.

Or

1. Choose a picture and study it until you know what it shows.
2. Put the picture back and take the test for it. The test has the same number as the picture.
3. Get the answer card for the picture and correct your work.

Or

1. Choose a picture.
2. Make a list of the objects and people that you see in the picture.
3. Underline the important people and objects in your list.
4. Write a name for the picture.

Certain procedures such as working with new pictures each time one returns to the learning center and what to do with finished tasks are usually known as a part of the regular routines of the classroom. If you wish to include these details in your directions or task cards, you may.

If you have an activity center for your learners, you might stock it with some task cards similar to these:

OBSERVATION NO. 1

- Doing what you are told on this card will help you learn better how to look at things and help you remember what you see.
  1. Get a picture that you like from the picture file, take it to your seat, and do the following:
     a. Take out a piece of lined paper, write your name and the date on it. On the first line write the label of this card and the number of the picture.
     b. Study the picture until you know what it shows, then turn it over.
     c. Write the answers to these questions:
        (i) What is the picture about?
        (ii) What are the most important things (people are things, too) shown in the picture?
        (iii) Write in a sentence what the picture says.
  2. Put the picture back in the picture file.
  3. Put your paper in the work box on the teacher's desk.

Or

OBSERVATION NO. 2

- This task will help you become a better observer.
  1. Get a friend to work with you.
  2. With your friend, choose a picture from your social-studies book (from a part we haven't studied yet), the encyclopedia, or a *National Geographic Magazine*.
  3. You and your friend are to study the picture until you think you know what it shows.
  4. Turn the picture over.
  5. Working separately, you and your friend write a paragraph about what the picture shows.
  6. When both are finished, read each other's paragraph. If you disagree about anything, turn the picture over to see who is right.
  7. Put your paragraphs in the teacher's in-basket.

In grade four and above, and particularly in grades six through eight, you may wish to encourage the children to develop skits in which actions with specific properties are emphasized.

Conversation is kept to a minimum. For example, such a skit might involve a shopper and a salesperson at a jewelry counter (costume jewelry and whatever jewelry the children happen to be wearing will serve as properties). The jewelry is displayed immediately in front of the salesperson. The shopper asks to see items more closely. The salesperson gives the item to him or her and takes it back before handing over another item. Finally the shopper decides, but just as the salesperson is about to make out the sales slip, the shopper decides on another item. The salesperson returns it to the display, picks up the desired item, and completes the sales transaction, and the shopper leaves. The observers then reconstruct the scene.

When the children are able to observe and retain much of what they have observed, they are ready to learn to use their skill in more critical ways. Exercises similar to the following will be helpful:

- Arrange to take the children twice to the same observation site, but at different times during the day. For example, a shopping area at nine A.M. is quite different at two P.M. Guide children in comparing the results of the two observations. Guide them in generalizing from their observations.

Comparisons may also be made between pictures, sets of pictures, films, and filmstrips showing the same aspect of different cultures, historical change in technology, similar processes in industry, and the like.

- Guide the children in learning from school materials about a process such as construction, canning, operating a convenience restaurant, a trial at court, or banking. Then arrange for them to visit a site where the process occurs to validate what they have learned. Have the children consider the additional dimensions of time, smell, hearing, touch, and perhaps taste as related to the process.

- Encourage the children to observe over a period of a day or several days for examples of good behavior in the classroom, in the cafeteria, on the playground, and, after school, in the neighborhood. Guide them in using the results in deciding how they might conduct themselves to improve relationships with others.

• Guide the children in examining carefully a collection of raw materials used in making a useful article such as a shirt or dress, then have them examine the article closely to see how many different operations were necessary to make the article and in what order they most likely occurred.

• Arrange for the children to observe a process on site or through the medium of film, videotape, filmstrip, or a series of pictures and to discuss the problems that they might encounter if they were immediately involved in the process, what might be done to improve the process or make it safer for the workers, or to decide whether the process is vital to their lives.

As stated earlier in Chapter 2, the improvement of observation skills has not been emphasized in the elementary school. The subskills have not been clearly identified and researched. However, most children need to improve their observation skills. The need for improvement is particularly critical for young children.

As you have probably noticed, the holistic strategy was used in most of the suggestions, for older learners as well as younger. This occurs because the subskills are easily performed, simple operations.

When the children have become proficient in observation skills, less of your time and effort will be required in guiding them to develop detailed purposes.

Listening Skills

Social-studies educators are concerned about children's listening skills for two reasons. First, the spoken commentary accompanying films and which sometimes accompanies filmstrips often is an important informational resource as vital to information seeking as the visual images. And second, through listening to audiotaped information, young children and older children who have difficulty learning to read can assume some independence in acquiring information. Young children do not mind having their contact with informational resources mediated constantly by the teacher, but

ILLUSTRATION 5–2. *These Children in Second Grade Are Using Listening as an Aid to Get Information from a Written Text.*

they do appreciate an occasional opportunity to make the contact by themselves. Older children having difficulty with reading soon recognize their difference as an additional burden. Social-studies teachers do have a responsibility for helping these children improve their skills, but even the most humane and concerned teacher who works enthusiastically with these children cannot completely ease the burden. However, if, from time to time all the children in a classroom can be given a free choice between reading and listening to acquire information, the burden can be eased. If children who can read are also seen listening, being a poor reader is easier to tolerate.

What was discussed about purposes in the section about observation skills also obtains with listening. Children need purposes to be able to listen effectively to acquire information.

Before considering learning activities, we assess children's hearing informally. Here are some basic symptoms indicative of hearing disability:

• Frequently asking for directions to be repeated.
• Straining the head toward the source of sound. When the hearing in one ear is better than in the other, the child may aim the "good" ear toward the sound.
• Frequent colds; frequent runny-nose problems; discharge from the ears easily observable.
• Speaking in a monotone.
• A metallic, high quality in the voice.
• Difficulties with getting along with others.

There are other causes for these symptoms, and not all the symptoms need be present to indicate hearing disability. If you suspect that a child has a hearing loss, see your principal for the necessary referrals and make certain that the child's listening station is near the source of sound.

Let us consider first the learning activities that we can provide for young children. Sometimes children in kindergarten or first grade need to be made aware that information can be gained through listening. To build their awareness, we provide activities such as these:

• Encourage them to listen to environmental sounds. They may sit quietly in the classroom for thirty or forty seconds to see how many sounds they can hear and identify. Other environmental listening experiences may include taking a walk to a busy street corner, a construction or razing site, an open area such as a field or park, or the side of a stream (they cover their eyes while they listen); or listen to audiotapes made at an observation site.
• Have them listen to and identify sounds that you bring into the environment: a bell, a whistle, the crumpling of a piece of paper, the tapping of a shoe on the floor, the opening and closing of a door, and the like. They cover their eyes, listen, and, after you have concealed the noisemaker, they open their eyes and identify the sounds.
• Having them listen to patterns of sounds. Clapping the hands works well. For example, have the children close their eyes and listen for the number of claps you make. After they open their eyes have them clap the same number you did. After you do this several times, introduce hard and soft claps given a number of times. Later, introduce rhythmic patterns characterized by varying intervals between claps.

When the children are aware that they can listen to discover information, start them on a program of listening to short passages of prose about social-studies subject matter. The passages should be no longer than about a hundred words and preferably recorded on audiotape. You could read the passages, but if you use audiotape, the children will listen just as well or better, you will help them become accustomed to listening to the recorder for information, and you will be able to model listening behavior. The first passages heard should be in the form of vignettes like this:

Mr. Fast and his wife have just finished their dinner. Mr. Fast says, "I don't like my job. I don't like loading trucks. The boxes are very heavy, and I get very tired."
"What are you going to do?" asked Mrs. Fast.
"I am going to go to truck-driver's school. I am going to learn to be a truck driver," replies Mr. Fast.
The next day he went to the truck-drivers' school. There he learned about the big trucks. For many days he did not get into a truck. He just learned how they ran and how to take care of them.
Then one day the teacher took Mr. Fast to a truck. He was a little scared, but not for long. Soon he was driving the big truck easily. He could back it up and run it up big hills. Finally his teacher said, "Mr. Fast, you are now a truck driver."

The introduction to the listening experience is a simple statement of purpose, like this: "This tape tells about Mr. Fast. He does not like his job. Let's listen to see what he does about it."

The postlistening activity may be varied: the children may be encouraged to recall the information, answer and discuss questions, listen to a puppet telling what it heard and making corrections, listening to a puppet respond to questions and making necessary additions and corrections, or acting out the vignette in the sequence in which its events occurred.

Gradually increase the length of the vignettes to three or four minutes in duration. At this point you may establish a group-listening center or a learning center equipped with a small recorder.

Purpose setting and directions for a postlistening activity are given on the tape. For example, if you were using the vignette about Mr. Fast, the beginning of the tape would give the statement of purpose similar to that already described. The postlistening activity might be any of the following:

- Return to your seat and draw a picture of Mr. Fast learning his new job.
- When you get back to your seat draw two pictures. One should show Mr. Fast working at his old job, and the other should show him working at his new job.
- Make a flannelgram story to tell about Mr. Fast and what he learned to do.
- Go to the work table and make stick puppets of the people in the story about Mr. Fast.
- Go to the teacher aide and tell him or her the story about Mr. Fast. The aide will write your story for you.

When the children are able to cope with this kind of listening situation, you may begin to develop audiotapes to use in your regular social-studies program. You may use the audiotapes as a means of reinforcing or extending information learned in other ways, or you may use them as basic informational resources for group instruction. For example, you may have a group doing an independent activity at a crafts table, another group working directly with you to study a series of study prints, and another group at the group listening center. During the next social-studies period, the group that worked with you goes to the independent-activity center, the group that listened to the tape works with you, and the group that worked at the independent activity listens to the tape. By the end of the third period, every child has experienced three different learning activities.

When working with children in second grade, you may begin to use audiotapes of five or six minutes' duration and introduce material written in an expository style. Let us assume that your second-grade class is studying about careers and you prepare an audiotape on a day in the life of a supermarket manager. In it you describe how he opens the store in the morning, arranges to get the money for the day's operation, checks each department to see that it is ready, checks to see what new goods need to be ordered and makes out orders, and handles problems with customers.

At the beginning of the tape you might record something like this:

This tape tells about what most supermarket managers do every day in their store. You will be answering some questions about it. Before telling what they do, I am going to be silent for five seconds. During that time, I want you to think whether you would like to be a supermarket manager. Then I shall say, "Write what you decided." I shall wait for another five seconds while you write. Write *"Yes"* if you would like to be a supermarket manager, *"No"* if you would not, and write a question mark if you don't know. Ready?

Do you think now that you would like to be a supermarket manager?

(*Pause* five seconds.)

Write what you decided.

(*Pause* five seconds.)

The supermarket does not open until ten o'clock in the morning. But many people are working there before it opens. The first to arrive is the supermarket manager. . . .

As you see in the above, the beginning of the listening experience is included on the tape itself. The same is true of the postlistening activity:

. . . Late in the afternoon the supermarket manager goes home. The assistant manager will take care of the store until it closes at nine o'clock at night.

(*Pause* a second or two.)

Let us see how well you remember what you heard about the supermarket manager. I am going to say some sentences. I shall say first the number of each sentence. When I say it, write it on your answer paper. Then I shall say the sentence two times. If the sentence is true, write a *"T"* after its number. If it is not true, write an *"N."*

Number 1. (*Pause.*) The supermarket manager opens the supermarket for his workers at seven-thirty. (*Repeat.*)

Number 2. (*Pause.*) The supermarket manager puts things out on the shelves. (*Repeat.*)

Etc.

Do you remember I asked you to decide whether you would like to be a supermarket manager. Look at your answer. Do you still think the same way? If you do, circle your answer. If you do not, cross out your answer and write your new answer. Write a few words to tell why you have that answer. When you finish, put your paper on my desk.

If you wished, you could also provide for self-correction. You could either give the correct answer after each question or present the answers to all the questions after the learners had finished answering them. The question about being a super-market manager would be left open.

Preparing scripts for audiotapes such as these requires much energy and time. Sometimes you can find useful articles in children's newspapers and magazines that are easily adaptable. This reduces the task, but it is usually better to develop your script in the manner presented in this section. Pauses and repeats need to be clearly indicated. The payoff to making audiotapes is that they are often reusable.

From grades three through eight, children may still need instruction in listening as a means of acquiring information. If you plan to have the children use listening regularly, either as a way of helping poor readers or as an additional information-seeking activity, or both, you can prepare the class to use listening through teaching a sequence of lessons based on some carefully scripted audiotapes similar to those discussed. Provide some learning centers for the use of children who need extra help.

If you decide to provide listening opportunities for poor readers, you can make excerpts from both the basic and the supplemental textbooks. Most children can listen to and comprehend material at least two levels beyond their reading level. For example, a child who can read at a third-grade reading level can listen to and comprehend material written at a fifth-grade level.

When you prepare these audiotapes, you may simply read the text into a recorder. However, children's listening will be more effective if you will observe the following practices:

• Keep the time for concentrated listening short. Listening for information is different from listening to a story. Two or three five-minute segments per lesson is enough.
• Compose an introduction for each segment alert-ing the listener to what it tells about. If there is an unusual word in the segment, define it. At the close of the segment, ask a few questions. Pause long enough for the learner to think of a response, then give the correct answer.
• Have the listener use the visual resource to follow what he or she hears. This can help improve reading skill and facilitates the study of illustrations. Whenever a picture, graph, or diagram is presented, direct the listeners' attention to it, read the caption or other explanatory information, and add to the explanation when you think it is necessary.
• If you use a group-listening center, at the end of each segment tell the listeners to stop the recorder to discuss what they have just heard.

If you plan to provide opportunities for listening either to enrich the social-studies program for all learners or to facilitate the use of informational resources which they ordinarily couldn't use, you will find excellent resource material in such magazines as *Time, Newsweek, Reader's Digest, Atlas,* and *National Geographic,* and in the Sunday supplements of many newspapers. A particularly good article could be read into the recorder. You can prepare the children for listening to segments and processing them for information through class discussion. If you wish to use the article for enrichment, prepare it for use in a learning center. Follow the same practices as those recommended above for recording textbook material, but add a terminal activity in which the children compose or construct something based on the article.

Truly independent listening occurs when children do critical listening to discourse designed to influence their behavior as citizens or consumers. This will be discussed in some detail in Chapter 8.

The suggestions for teaching listening skills have generally followed the step-by-step strategy at all grade levels. Selecting and relating details, and generalizing, occur so instantaneously that not much is gained by dividing the skill of listening into subskills. However, there are moments when we may want to do this. When working with children who lack self-confidence or whose ordinary development of listening skills has been retarded for one reason or another, we may develop special lessons in which children are brought first to the point that they can identify and recall details, then to identifying, recalling, and relating, and finally to identifying, recalling, relating, and generalizing.

Reading Skills

As discussed in the previous section, listening may sometimes substitute for reading, and listening and reading comprehension are similar. But the central fact remains that reading skills open a vast world of information which listening cannot approximate. Furthermore, it is a world into which the reader will probe eventually at a faster rate than he or she can listen.

Young children completing third grade may have the concept that reading is doing whatever they do during reading instruction. They think that reading is talking a little bit about something related to the story, doing something with some new words, taking turns reading aloud, learning something about sounds, and completing a practice sheet. Reading as a skill used to acquire information is an alien idea to them.

Or perhaps these children have discovered that reading results in a vicarious experience. Sustained by characterization, plot, and pathos or humor, they can either observe or participate in an experience described in a story. Reading for information is as familiar to them as programming a computer. Thus, our first responsibility as social-studies teachers may be to guide children in developing a concept of reading as a set of human behaviors used in acquiring information.

When this general concept is established, we guide the children as far as they can go in reading special arrangements of facts as shown on globes, maps, graphs, and diagrams. Having discovered that reading also includes decoding and encoding structures other than lines and lines of print, the children are guided into learning the map system for the world of printed information—tables of contents, indexes, and the card catalog. And then, of course, there is the matter of log keeping to help them remember where they have been and what they have read—note taking and outlining.

The skills suggested above exist as strands leading from the basic concept of reading as a means to information. They are treated each year, but none is mastered in any particular year. For example, when a child has a viable basic concept of reading as an informational skill, which may occur as early as second grade, he or she may learn some ideas about the globe and maps, a table of contents, and using sketches to take notes. During the next year, he or she is guided across the strands again, but at a higher level of sophistication.

Let us consider first the ways we might guide children in developing a useful concept of reading as an information-acquisition skill.

Reading for Information. Kindergarten teachers aware of their responsibility of teaching young children the concept of reading for information do the following:

- Teach children to use regularly maintained signs for information about facts used daily: a calendar; a helper chart which indicates who passes out the papers, takes up the papers, leads the pledge of allegiance, straightens up the bookshelf, takes the attendance account to the office, etc.; and reminders about washing hands, hanging up sweaters and coats, bringing in physical-education equipment, etc. The children cannot read these without assistance at first, and they often need picture clues on the charts.
- Guide the children in preparing a newspaper at the end of sharing. This newspaper tells about the important items shared and announces important events. The children reread (idea reading at first—not verbatim reading, just recalling the idea) the newspaper several times a day.
- Use every opportunity to model reading-for-information behaviors—reading newspaper clippings about interesting topics to children, showing how to use a table of contents to find a story in a book, showing how to use an encyclopedia by selecting the proper volume, finding the article to read, and reading it to the children.

The foundation for informational reading can be laid in kindergarten, and much of it with social-studies ideas. The same kinds of activities continue with first and second grades, and these activities are added:

- The teacher introduces books of an "all about" nature and reads excerpts from them to help the children get desired information. He or she also stocks the classroom bookshelf with the simplest "all about it" books for the children to leaf through.
- If the children have a classroom subscription to a weekly newspaper, the teacher guides them through it, emphasizing its informational aspect. Vocabulary is carefully developed, the children are told what the article is about, and they then read it silently to share their discoveries later. The period ends with a discussion focused on questions like this: "What did we find out by reading today?" "What did we read about _____ today?"
- The teacher prepares independent reading activities based on social-studies content. Each activity consists of a text to be read, some questions to be answered, and a suggestion for something to do based on the content. An example is given in Figure 5–4. Activities like this may be used in learning centers or activity centers to which children go as assigned or as a matter of choice after other reading assignments are completed.

When the children particularly like an article in their weekly newspaper, the teacher may use it for an independent activity. The children will enjoy reading it again.

For durability, the activity should be mounted on a card. Each card should be numbered to keep track of what the children do.

The above activities may be basic or supplementary, depending on the nature of the instructional program.

Many publishers of series of social-studies textbooks offer books for use in grades one and two. In the first-grade book, most of the information is conveyed in pictures with the printed text as a supplement. In second-grade books more information is conveyed in the printed text. To emphasize the informational aspect of the printed text, the second-grade teacher follows the same procedures recommended for the use of the children's weekly newspaper. The same practices are followed in grade three where the pictures gradually become supplementary to the printed text.

THE WORK OF A JETLINER

A jetliner is a big airplane.
It carries people.
It flies very fast.
A jetliner flies from airport to airport.
People buy their tickets at the airport.
They get on the jetliner at the airport.
It flies to another airport.
Then the people get off.
Sometimes a jetliner stays at an airport.
It stays for two or three days.
It is cleaned up.
Sometimes it has to be fixed.
Soon it is taking people from airport to airport again.

On your paper write the words that go in the blanks. Use these words to write in the blanks: *tickets, fixed, airplane, people, airport.*
1. A jetliner is a big _____.
2. It carries _____.
3. It flies from an _____.
4. People buy _____ at the airport.
5. Sometimes the jetliner has to be _____.

Draw a picture about a jetliner.

FIGURE 5–4. *Independent Reading Exercise in Social Studies.*

If they have had a carefully developed program in informational reading related to social-studies content, children entering fourth grade have little difficulty making the transition to relying primarily on print for information. Their major problem is dealing with so much print at one time. A third or more of the members of the class may have spent all their primary years at learning word-analysis skills, and just now are beginning to function as readers. Some of these children will need a program of learning activities similar to those discussed for young children. The rest, including the competent readers, will profit from the following:

- Reading material of third-grade difficulty and recalling the facts. The teacher implements this by choosing selections to be read and developing terminal activities based on them. These may include tests consisting of true-false, multiple-choice, fill-in, or matching items, making lists of facts, processing lists of facts to determine which were covered in the reading, developing short reports about the facts, putting the facts in order, and so forth.

The teacher introduces each reading by guiding a brief discussion about its topic, informs the children what they will do after reading the selection and where they will find the materials for doing it, and has the children read silently and complete the terminal activity.

When the children read, they read with the general purpose of trying to remember as much as they can from their reading. When they do the terminal activity, they do it *without* access to the selection read.

Because the children read at different rates, the teacher can correct the terminal activity with some children while the others are finishing.

• After reading a social-studies assignment in their textbooks, the children recall as many facts as possible before any factual questions are treated. As the teacher guides them in a postdiscussion of what they read, he or she encourages them to give as many facts as they can remember, and then has them consider the questions related to the purpose for reading. Occasionally the children may be divided into groups for this activity. Or they may be divided into pairs in which one child is the "teacher" who tells the other, the "learner," what the selection is all about. Later, a pair is chosen at random to perform before the class. The class critiques their performance in a positive way.

• Learning and activity centers used as needed or by learners' choice. These also emphasize reading first, then recalling facts.

The above has been suggested for a fourth grade, but the same situation may prevail at any grade beyond the fourth. Unfortunately, it is still possible that a child may reach grade eight with the concept that reading in social studies is simply a matter of finding the answers to questions, completely disregarding other factual matter contained in the selection. Frequently, answering one question is the signal to go to the next question, but a more complete discussion of the question and its answers may require more facts to be surfaced. The activities suggested here for fourth grade may be needed in higher grades as well.

So far, we have discussed only one stage in learning a viable concept of informational reading—recalling facts. The next stage is drawing conclusions from the material read.

As early as grade two children can choose the correct conclusion from two possibilities, provided, of course, that they know the facts on which it is based. We shall use the idea of helping children learn how to draw conclusions by choosing from two or three given. Provisions for this stage are easily made when the children have developed to the point of being able to reconstruct factually what they have read.

We begin by introducing the concept of conclusion. The formation of the concept begins with exercises similar to those given in Figure 5–5. After completing a series of exercises similar to these and discussing each, the children usually have a basic concept about a conclusion as a statement based on facts. Later, carefully monitoring each child's learning, the teacher incorporates exercises such as these in learning and activity centers. Gradually, more choices of conclusions, higher levels of abstraction, increased emphasis on social-

---

The following sentences tell about Henry:

• Henry goes to the store every day.
• Sometimes he buys candy bars.
• Sometimes he buys suckers.
• Sometimes he buys an ice cream cone.
• He eats what he buys.

Which of the following two sentences tells what is true about Henry?

1. Henry has a store.
2. Henry likes sweet things.

FIGURE 5–5. *Exercise for Drawing Conclusions.*

studies content, and material of greater length are introduced into the series of exercises.

Soon after the concept has been introduced, the teacher introduces the conclusion process as a social-studies activity whenever a reading for information is involved. He or she may do any of the following:

- When the question or cluster of questions the children are investigating demand a conclusion, and after the children have completed the reading, the teacher presents a list of conclusions (two for children in grades two and three, and three for grades four and above) for the children to discuss and arrive at agreement on which is accurate. This may be conducted as a group activity.
- After the children have investigated a cluster of questions resulting in the discovery of details, the teacher forms the class into impromptu groups to discuss the facts and determine the conclusion the facts support. The groups share the results and the class arrives finally at a conclusion. (Children in grade four and above usually can do this.)
- Before the children work with a cluster of questions resulting in the discovery of details, the teacher presents a conclusion to be proved or disproved in the reading. Or the teacher may present two or three conclusions from which the children can choose after they finish reading.
- When the children are involved during several social-studies periods in discovering facts, they are encouraged to arrive at a conclusion or choose one from several given at the close of the first period of investigation. At the close of each subsequent period they consider their conclusion in the light of additional facts.

At grade six, after discovering a cluster of facts, children are often able to respond accurately to such questions as, "What can we conclude from these facts?" "What conclusion can we now make about _____?"

The final stage in the development of the concept of reading as an information-seeking skill is the use of conclusions to generate further thought. Frequently a conclusion made at the end of a social-studies period is little more than a meaningful stopping point in continuing study, but on occasion the conclusion is of sufficient breadth in meaning to stimulate further thought. Let us suppose, for example, that your learners in sixth grade have just concluded that many people of a certain African country think of themselves as members of a tribe rather than as citizens of a country. You might ask questions such as these:

How are these people different from ourselves? *Or*
What if our people decided that they were citizens of the states in which they live and not of the country as a whole? What do you suppose would happen? *Or*
What kinds of problems might the president of such a country have? *Or*
Imagine that the president of such a country was making a speech to his people. What do you think he might say to try to get the people to think of themselves first as citizens of their country? *Or*
Do you think the people of this country should have a stronger feeling for their country? Why do you think so?

Class or group discussions prompted by questions such as these guide children in using conclusions developed from printed facts as springboards to further thought.

Whenever possible, you should encourage such discussions at the close of the social-studies period. If you are using learning or activity centers to improve children's social-studies reading skills, use such questions after reading selections leading children toward broad conclusions. However, most children do not have the skills to respond in written form to such questions until grade five.

To develop a viable concept of informational reading in social studies, a stage-by-stage strategy is recommended for most grades. However, if you are a teacher of grade seven or eight, and your learners are capable readers at grade-level expectancy, but weak at informational reading, you may teach a series of lessons following the holistic strategy, followed by concentrated practice.

Globe and Map Reading. Many children have an early experience with maps as they watch their parents plotting the route of an automobile trip. As they watch the evening newscast they see maps used as a means of locating where events have occurred and seeing how the weather is developing. Map overlays used over photographs of the earth taken by satellite are sometimes shown. Photographs of the earth in the introduction to science-fiction programs convey the idea of the earth as a globe. Some children develop an early consciousness of maps and globes. To other children they have little if any meaning. Helping children learn how to use them has long been an accepted instructional objective in elementary social studies.

Skills in using maps and globes are based on a gradually extended concept of how the surface of the earth can be represented symbolically. Frequently maps and globes are placed in classrooms for children to use as they study about the peoples and countries of the earth. It is not unusual for children to respond with accuracy and enthusiasm to questions or tasks prompting them to use maps and globes, but with the vaguest notion of spatial and directional relationships among the items located. To them, working with maps and globes is a kind of game with form and color clues which anyone with a good memory can master and play. Maps and globes are great fun. They should also be resources for facts that clarify the relationships between nations as well as the learner's relationships with other people. For this reason, a conceptual approach will be developed here.

1. A map is a symbolic picture of a portion of the earth's surface, or its entire surface, very much reduced in size.
2. Directions are points of reference which remain constant and help locate where one is in relation to other people and places as well as where one place or people is in relation to another.
3. The globe is a symbol for the earth.
4. Maps are frequently distorted when the whole earth, its hemispheres, or other large portions are represented.

We shall treat each concept in turn as we consider ways of teaching them.

A Map as a Symbolic Picture. In the instructional program for young children we place heavy emphasis on this concept. The best way of guiding them is through a series of activities which terminates with the children making their own map of an area with which they are familiar. The activities include:

1. Taking the children on a walking trip or a field trip to an area rich in geographical contrasts without too many features added by people. An area with hills and valleys, streams and groves or clumps of trees, fences and a few buildings, and little else, are best. When the class arrives at the site, guide them in observing carefully to discover its various features and where one feature lies in relation to another.
2. When the children return to the classroom, guide them in recalling what they observed. Then take them to a sand table or box to help you construct the site they visited. When the basic topography of hills and valleys has been formed, have the children decide what else is needed and how it might be made. Have the children make representations for the roads, streams, fences, trees, and buildings from construction paper, twigs, cardboard, or whatever is avail-

ILLUSTRATION 5–3. *Children in Sixth Grade Can Use Scale on a Globe to Determine Distances between Given Points.*

able to complete the construction. Guide the class in discussing how their construction is similar to what they had seen originally.

3. Focusing the children's attention on their construction and on a large piece of paper, guide them in discussing how the construction might be shown on a piece of paper. A box of crayons will be helpful. Following their directions, draw lines and figures until the map is made. Emphasize that they have just made a map of the area they visited. Guide them in discussing how the map is similar to and different from the area they had visited earlier. Give particular attention to the lines and other features as symbols.

4. Make a simple map of your bedroom and show it to the children. Encourage them to make a map of their own bedroom. Have them share their maps to discuss the symbols they used for real objects.

This series of activities may be used in a first or second grade. The children usually will obtain a viable concept of what a map and symbols are. Here is another series of activities helpful to young children:

1. Prepare the following: a display of real objects (a pencil, a chalkboard eraser, a small book, a quarter or half-dollar, and a dime, or whatever is easily available in different sizes and shapes) on a drawing board, flannelboard, or large rectangle of cardboard; a three-quarter view of the display, either a photograph or drawn picture; a series of five maps of the display, each reduced in size until the last shows only a very small rectangle from which most of the symbols have disappeared because of the diminished size.

Showing the display, have the children identify the objects. Then show them the three-quarter view of the display, and have them compare the view with the display, with emphasis on the real objects in the display and the symbolic objects shown in the view—the real objects can be taken from the display and used, but the objects in the picture cannot. Emphasize that the pictured objects are *symbols* and that the size of the pictured objects is smaller.

Show the first map, identify it as such, and have the children compare it with the display. Laying the display and the map flat on the floor, have the children stand with their toes touching each in turn to get a bird's eye view of each. Have them discuss the differences and similarities between the two.

Show each of the rest of the maps in turn. Continually emphasize that the objects in the display remain the same size, but in each map they grow smaller because the map is smaller—the symbols become smaller and some disappear.

Guide the children in a discussion in which they decide how they would tell another person what a map and symbol are.

2. Prepare a map of the classroom made with flannelgram symbols or symbols cut from tagboard to be laid on a drawing board or large cardboard rectangle. You will need symbols for the various items of furniture in the classroom.

Place the flannelboard or display board before the class and distribute the various symbols among the children. Inform them that they can use their symbols to make a map of the classroom. Encourage them to discuss and identify the symbols and then to place them on the board. The result is a map of the classroom.

Encourage volunteers to define *map* and *symbol*.

3. Prepare a set of tagboard or construction-paper cut-outs for each child—a square, circle, rectangle, and triangle of varying sizes. If you prefer, you may collect enough small, simply shaped objects for each child to have a set of four or five—spools, blocks, boxes, poker chips, baseball cards, or whatever.

Provide each child with two sheets of 12″ × 18″ newsprint or manila paper. Distribute the cut-outs, or objects. Encourage the children to recall what a map and symbol are. If cut-outs are used, have the children discuss what these might symbolize. If objects are used, have the children decide the kinds of symbols they might use for these on a map. Have the children arrange the objects or cut-outs in any way that they wish on one of the pieces of paper on the floor beside their desk or table and draw a map of it.

When the maps are completed, encourage the children to circulate around the classroom to view their peers' maps and arrangements. Have them discuss what they have learned about symbols and maps.

4. Take the children on a walking trip around the neighborhood to discover the various streets around the school. When they return to the classroom, work with the children to prepare a large map of the neighborhood. Use the school as the central point of reference as they direct you where to draw the lines for the streets and to label them. Then have each child make a symbol for his own home, locate where it belongs on the map, and paste it there.

Activities 1 through 3 are suitable for use with children in first grade, and all the activities may be used with children in grades two and three.

Children in the later grades who appear to have a poorly developed concept of maps and how they symbolize can be helped by doing projects in which they make maps of their bedrooms, homes, the school, and the community.

The activities suggested above emphasize learning a definitive concept of maps through mapping or making maps. These experiences will prove helpful later on when the children draw maps as a way of organizing information or expressing ideas.

Directions. When they enter school, most children have a well-developed sense of direction within the environment in which they live. They can identify useful landmarks to find their way about, which often have special meaning to them—the houses where their friends live, the neighborhood convenience store, the service station their parents often use, the ice-cream store, and the like. Naming these, pointing, and turning their bodies to show change of direction along a route, they can tell another person how to get from one place to another. To extend their concept of direction, we may do the following:

• Have the children discuss the routes they follow to come to school, to go from home or school to their favorite store, to a shopping center, or a park. If a map of the community around the school has been constructed, it can be used to follow or mark routes on.
• Guide the children in studying the directions

marked on a compass and observing how the needle always points in the same direction. Use the cardinal directions as indicated by a compass to post *North, South, East,* and *West* signs in the classroom. Use the signs in a game in which the children use the directions to direct players from one place in the room to another. For example, one child could direct another from his or her seat to the flag in this way: "Stand up, move one step to the West, turn North and walk ten steps, turn East and walk twelve steps." Minor corrections may be made by asking the player to take a few more steps in the desired direction.
• Take the children outside at 12:00 Noon to observe the shadows cast by poles or sticks stuck in the ground. Explain that the shadows point toward North. Have the children indicate the other cardinal directions and to mark them by locating features on the horizon—North may be marked by the crest of a large hill, East by a church spire, South by a water tower, and West by a television relay station. Guide the children in establishing the most common local landmark useful in locating where one is and in what direction one is going. This could be a large body of water such as an ocean, lake, or river; a mountain peak; an expressway; or whatever.

If the children's community map is still posted, guide the children in orienting their map directionally. Mark a compass on it, and have them play a game in which they use directions to direct each other from one place on the map to another.

The above activities are suitable for use in grades one and two. They may also be used with children in the later grades who have a poorly developed concept of direction. The following activities may be used in grades three and above:

• Take down the national or state maps. Lay each one flat on a table or on the floor. Have a group of children orient one directionally as the others observe. Have them use the map as oriented to decide in what direction they would go from where they are to a specific point on the map. Have them point in the direction.

At this time also establish what is meant by *Northeast, Southeast, Southwest,* and *Northwest,* and have the children indicate whether they are pointing in one of the cardinal directions or between them by using the new terms.

- Distribute desk maps or have the children use a map in their textbook or desk atlas. Have the children lay the map flat on their desks and orient it and then help them locate a city in the middle of the map. Using the city as a central location, have the children move their index finger in an indicated direction to name the first city, lake, river, mountain, or other feature they come to. Then have them indicate in which direction they would go to return to the central point. As more places are located, have the children use them to practice using directions from one place to another.
- Assigning the children the same map in their textbook or desk atlas, have them use it to compose directional riddles for states or countries. Example: "I am east of France and north of Italy. Who am I?" (Switzerland.) "To my north lies France, to my east, the Mediterranean Sea, to my south, Morocco, and to my west, Portugal and the Atlantic Ocean. Who am I?" (Spain.)

When the children have developed a reliable sense of direction and can orient a map, the use of distance is helpful to locate points on a map or to describe locations on a map. The scale on the map is the key. Here are a few suggestions for guiding children in learning to use it:

- To introduce the concept of scale, have the children measure the classroom and draw its perimeter to a $\frac{1}{4}''$ to 1' (or 1 cm. to 1 m.) scale. Guide them in discussing other scales that they might use.
- Divide the children into pairs and have them measure each other's height using traditional or metric measurement. Guide them in deciding on a scale they might use to draw their own full-length portraits on a sheet of desk paper. Emphasize how they should use the scale to depict fractional amounts. Have them mark the scale along the margin of the paper, including fractional amounts in the final unit, and draw their own portraits.
- Using whatever wall maps are available, have the children consult the scale on each to obtain information to use when constructing measuring devices. Such a device may be made with string or a strip of paper or tape and resembles a tailor's tape measure, except that each unit of scale is marked in kilometers or miles in accordance with the scale. Only one unit needs to be marked off in fractional amounts. The device should be approximately as long as the map. Encourage the children to choose a point on the map and measure from it the distance to five other points. Have them report on the distances measured.
- Have the children explore the maps in their textbooks, atlases, and almanacs, as well as automobile maps, for scales. Encourage them to use their rulers as measuring devices to help them compute the distance between chosen points.

When the children are efficient in the use of both directions and the scale on a map, they have the means to describe a location with accuracy, particularly as it relates to the point of their own location. Distances may also be interpreted in terms of travel time. Using 650 miles per hour as the average jetliner speed, one may say that New York is about four and a half hours northeast of San Diego. Travel time often has a more personal meaning than a number of miles.

All the suggestions given above are for use with groups or the entire class. To reinforce the learnings in grades three and above, you may construct learning centers and add map activities to your activity center. Figure 5–6 gives examples of task cards that you might use in such centers or incorporate in directions in learning centers.

MAP READING: DIRECTIONS

Get a paper, pencil, and writing board.
Go to the wall map of the United States.
Find the city of Topeka in Kansas. Pretend that you are there. Use the map to write the answers to these questions.

1. If you went north from Topeka, what state border would you cross first?
2. If you went south from Topeka, what state border would you cross first?
3. If you went east from Topeka, how many states would you cross before you came to an ocean?
4. If you went west from Topeka, how many states would you cross before you came to an ocean?

FIGURE 5–6. *Sample Task Cards for Map Skills.*

MAP READING: SCALE

Open your social-studies book, *Our Land,* to page 325. Use the map to write the answers to these questions:

1. How far is it from New York, New York, to Portland, Maine?
2. How far is it from Portland, Maine, to Cleveland, Ohio?
3. How far is it from Cleveland, Ohio, to Miami, Florida?
4. How far is it from Miami, Florida, to Atlanta, Georgia?
5. How far is it from Atlanta, Georgia, to Dallas, Texas?

MAP READING: DIRECTIONS AND SCALE

Open your social-studies book, *Our Continent,* to page 360. Use the map to write the answers to the questions below. Each answer should give a distance and a direction.

1. From Regina, Sask., where is Saskatoon, Sask.?
2. From Saskatoon, Sask., where is Prince Albert, Sask.?
3. From Prince Albert, Sask., where is Moose Jaw, Sask.?
4. From Moose Jaw, Sask., where is Winnipeg, Man.?
5. From Winnipeg, Man., where is Regina, Sask.?

FIGURE 5–6. (*continued*)

You have probably noticed that suggestions for teaching have been restricted to maps. The globe has not been mentioned. The reason for this is that maps represent limited areas of space which are easier for children to grasp. A child can meaningfully map a space with which he or she is familiar and can use the experience to understand more abstract maps and, ultimately, the globe.

The Globe as a Symbol and a Map. Globes are made for use in kindergarten and grades one and two, but they do not have much meaning for children in these grades. Of course, young children can learn to identify a globe and the features on it—but their responses are simple verbalizations that they have learned to make. However, if a

primary globe is available and the teacher is expected to teach children about it, he or she can do no less than help children understand its symbolic nature. Before the globe is introduced, the children should have had the initial mapping experiences and know what a map and symbol are. At this point they can profit from a lesson similar to the following:

OBJECTIVE

The children will be able to identify the globe as a symbol and map of the earth.

MATERIALS

- A map made by the children.
- A real apple.
- A representation of a real apple. (This may be a very small replica of an apple purchased at a variety store or one made from salt, water, and flour and painted to represent the real apple.)
- A globe with a small square area framed with a narrow strip of paper to represent a section from which a map might be made.
- (Optional.) Some pictures of the earth taken from a mechanical satellite or the moon.

LESSON DEVELOPMENT

Introduction

Showing the children the map they made themselves, encourage them to identify what it is and the symbols on it. Inform them that they are going to learn about a new map and symbol.

Exploration

Showing the children the real apple and the "play" apple, have them identify and discuss the differences between the two. (The "play" apple is much smaller than the real apple and it is not good to eat.) Have the children identify which is the symbol.

Showing the children the globe, ask them if they know what it is a symbol of. If any of them do, encourage them to tell what they know. Gently correct any misinformation that they give. If you have any pictures of the earth and the children can recognize them, allow them to discuss what they know about them.

If none of the children know what the globe is,

inform them that it is a symbol of the earth on which we live.

Point out that the globe is many times smaller than the real earth. Show them on the globe where they are located on the earth. Have them consider why there are no symbols on the globe showing boys and girls, the school, or even the streets on which they live. (Their initial experiences with maps should help them to respond that no symbols small enough could be made, or that as the globe was made smaller and smaller, the symbols of small things disappeared.)

Showing the children the framed portion of the globe, tell them that it shows where a map could be made. Have them consider where other maps might be made on the globe.

Point out that the globe is really a map of the whole earth on which they live. Identify the land and water areas.

Termination

Guide the children in reviewing the relationship between the real apple and the "play" apple and the globe and the earth. Encourage them to tell why they can live on the real earth and why they cannot on the globe.

Permit the children to come to the globe to examine it more closely, to touch it, and to make it turn. If there is time, distribute small pieces of clay from which the children fashion their own personal globes or symbols of the earth. Allow the globes to dry for a few days and have the children paint them. This will help them remember about land and water areas.

Sometimes whenever a place name occurs in the news or in the children's reading the teacher uses the globe to illustrate where it is. To help the children understand this better, he or she makes travel-experience references. For example, if your second-grade class in Los Angeles was about to read an Eskimo folk tale, and you have indicated on the globe where Alaska is from Los Angeles, you might extend the meaning of distance and direction like this: "How many of you have ever taken an all-day drive in a car? What did you do all day in the car? How did you feel? Well, you would have to spend seven or eight days like that if you were to take a trip by car to Alaska. It is a long way off."

Children in grades three through eight generally sense that the globe is a map. Their appreciation and understanding of it increase as they explore it through doing direction and distance exercises with it. These activities have already been discussed previously. Their work with both the globe and maps prepares them for understanding the inherent distortions in maps of large sections of the earth's surface.

Distortions in Maps. Because of the curvature of the earth, the smaller the area mapped, the smaller the distortion in the map. When children study the maps of most states and countries, they need not be concerned about the inherent distortions, but when they consult the maps of continents, hemispheres, and the entire earth, they need to be aware of the distortions. Depending on how the map was originally constructed and the specific information desired, the distortions introduce errors in direction, distance, and proportion.

Geographers would like children to be able to identify various kinds of maps in terms of the plotting point used as a base, or the kind of projection used in making the map, but that is more than children need to know. What they need to know is that there are distortions and that they will occasionally need to validate a map against what is depicted on a globe. If the map is too distorted for their purpose, they decide to use the globe.

Social-studies textbooks often contain diagrams and explanations about map projections and the resulting distortions. Guiding children in grades seven and eight in a careful study of these often helps them to understand distortion. Children in grades four through six usually need a less-abstract experience. The following sequence of learning activities is suggested:

1. Using a globe and several pieces of paper long enough to go around its circumference and wide enough to cover it, have the children experiment to see whether there is any way they could use a paper to make an impression of the globe's surface in order to construct a map of it. Have a pair of scissors available for the children to use if

they wish. Guide the class in discussing the possible solutions.

2. Beforehand, get two large, playground balls discarded because of punctures. Cut each of the balls in half. On the outside of each ball draw a square, a triangle, and three dots as shown in Figure 5–7. Using scissors, cut gores in three of the ball halves or hemispheres as shown in Figure 5–8. Show the uncut hemisphere to the children and point out that it represents a half of the globe and that what is drawn on it represents features on the globe. Have them review the difficulties they had had as they tried to fit a piece of paper around the globe and tell them that today they will discover how map makers make a flat map of the globe.

Using the uncut hemispheres as a mold, place hemisphere "B" (in Figure 5–8) over it and show the cuts that have been made in "B." Have them discuss what will happen to the features on "B" when it is laid flat on a surface. Then remove it from the uncut hemisphere and lay it flat on a large piece of paper. Press it as flat as possible and have the children compare its features with those on the uncut hemisphere. To help them

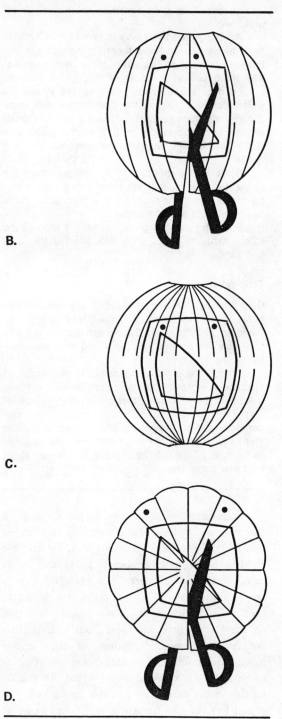

FIGURE 5–8. *Cutting a Distortion Model.*

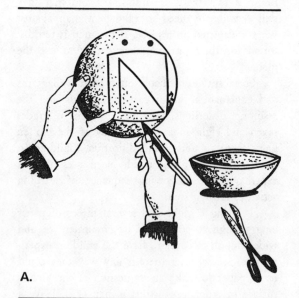

FIGURE 5–7. *Marking a Distortion Model.*

better understand the distortion, join the lines of the features by drawing lines between them on the paper. Have the children compare the distance between the two horizontal dots as shown on "B" and the uncut hemisphere, and the direction from the central dot to the others and the corners of the square.

Repeat the above with hemispheres "C" and "D."

Have the children decide whether the distortions would be greater or less if the cuts in hemispheres "B," "C," and "D" were more numerous.

3. Guide the children in using continental, hemispheric, and world maps to determine the distance and direction between six pairs of points which are also given on the classroom globe. Have them check their answers on the globe.

4. Showing hemisphere "D" as a reminder of what happens when a polar projection is made, guide the children in viewing polar hemispheric maps. Divide them into small groups to determine the directions on a polar-projection map.

Leave the hemispheres on a table to serve as an interest center which the children can visit at their leisure.

Learning and activity centers can provide the necessary learning reinforcement, particularly when the number of maps and globes is limited. Figure 5–9 shows what you might include on a task card or set of directions. The more activities similar to these that you provide for children, the better their concept of the features of the earth and where they are located.

Latitude and Longitude. The most precise way of expressing the location of a point on earth is through its latitude and longitude. This is useful for children to know, but perhaps more important for their use in social studies is how latitudes are labeled and what they mean in terms of seasons and weather, and how longitudes are labeled and how they are used to determine time around the earth.

Latitudes and longitudes are imaginary lines in a grid system which encompasses the earth. Many a schoolboy in grade five and above has

MAP AND GLOBE READING: DISTORTIONS

You will do this work at the map and globe center. To do this work you will need the globe and a world map. Write the answers to the following questions:

1. What is the distance between Quito (Ecuador, in South America) and Lagos (Nigeria, in Africa) as shown on the world map?
2. What is the distance between the above two cities as shown on the globe?
3. What is the distance between Juneau, Alaska, and Helsinki (Finland, in Europe) as shown on the world map?
4. What is the distance between the above two cities as shown on the globe?
5. What is the distance between the Cape of Good Hope (on the southern tip of South America) and Cape Horn (on the southern tip of Africa) as shown on the world map?
6. What is the distance between the two Capes as shown on the globe?

FIGURE 5–9. *Sample Task Card for Map and Globe Reading.*

learned the skill of using a grid to play the game, "Battleship." Let us consider some activities which we might introduce to children in fourth grade to accustom them to using a grid to locate points on a map.

- Construct a simple map of the classroom on a large bulletin board. Using yarn and pins, construct a grid of vertical and horizontal lines to form squares over the map. On the right and left margins of the grid, label each row of squares with capital letters beginning at the bottom row (A, B, C, etc.). At the top and bottom of the map number each column of squares from left to right (1, 2, 3, etc.). Encourage the children to discover a way of using the grid to tell where they usually sit, where the teacher's desk is, where their friends are, and the like.
- Construct an imaginary treasure map on a large bulletin board and place a grid over it. Have the children use the grid to tell the location of objects on the map and to design routes to the treasure that will avoid hazards.

• Guide the children in making their own grid over a blank piece of paper. Divide the children into pairs to play a game. The two children sit at a table facing each other. They stand several large books between them so that neither can see the other's grid. One player fills five squares on his grid by blacking them with a pencil or coloring them with a crayon. These represent places where treasure is buried. The other player tries to guess where the treasure is hidden by calling out grid locations. He marks an "X" through each location that he calls. The game ends when all the treasures are found. The winner is the one who locates all the treasures in the least number of calls.

• Post a large map of the United States, Canada, Mexico, or the World on a bulletin board, cover it with a grid, and have the children use the grid to locate given points.

Activities such as these soon accustom children to how to use a grid to locate points on a map. At grade six, latitude and longitude are introduced. The children have to transfer from using intersecting squares to using intersecting lines. The following activities are suggested.

• Make or have the children make a large map of an imaginary area and post it on the bulletin board. Cover it with a grid in which the squares are two inches wide. Starting with the middle line of the horizontal array and labeling it as "0," number the lines consecutively up and then down. Label the middle line of the vertical array as "0," and number the lines to the right and left of it. When you finish, the grid looks like that in Figure 5–10.

Showing the map to the children, encourage them to see if they can discover a way of using the lines, not the squares, to give the location of items indicated on the map. If they have difficulty, point out that the "0" lines are the key to using the grid, and label the lines above the "0" horizontal line as "North" and those below the line as "South." Label the lines to the left of the "0" vertical line as "West" and those to the right as "East." Locate several points for them demonstrating how one reads a point north or south of "0" and east or west of "0." Give several locations such

as North 2, East 3; South 7, West 1; North 4, West 3; etc. Then have them locate specific points by using the grid.

Explain that the horizontal lines are *latitudes* and the vertical lines are *longitudes*.

Remove lines (and their numbers) 1, 2, 3, 4; 6, 7, 8, 9; 11, 12, 13, 14; etc. from the grid. Now have the children try to interpolate to locate items on the map.

• Have the children make line grids and play a game or two in pairs similar to that already described. If they are provided with graph paper on which to draw their grids, they will not need to draw so many lines and can practice making interpolations as they play. Only lines at five or ten-line intervals would need to be drawn.

• Guide the children in exploring the latitude and longitude markings on the globe and a variety of maps in their textbooks, atlases, and almanacs. Have them practice locating points on the globe and maps.

• Have the children complete a series of exercises in which they follow a line of latitude or longitude around the globe or across a world map to discover what nations and large bodies of water it crosses. Also, have them explore to see what nations and large bodies of water lie between latitudes lying 10°, 20°, or 30° apart, and between meridians of East or West Longitude lying 15°, 30°, or 45° apart.

Map studies with longitude as suggested above are readiness activities for exploring the use of time zones around the world. Two basic ideas to be learned are that the time changes by one hour for every 15° from the "0" meridian of longitude that runs through Greenwich, England, and that the date changes at the 180° meridian. The children should explore for the location of these two meridians on a world map and the globe. After this initial exploration, provide for activities similar to the following:

• Guide the children in using the globe or a world map to construct two time-computation tapes. Both tapes should be twenty-five centimeters or twelve and a half inches long. The first tape should

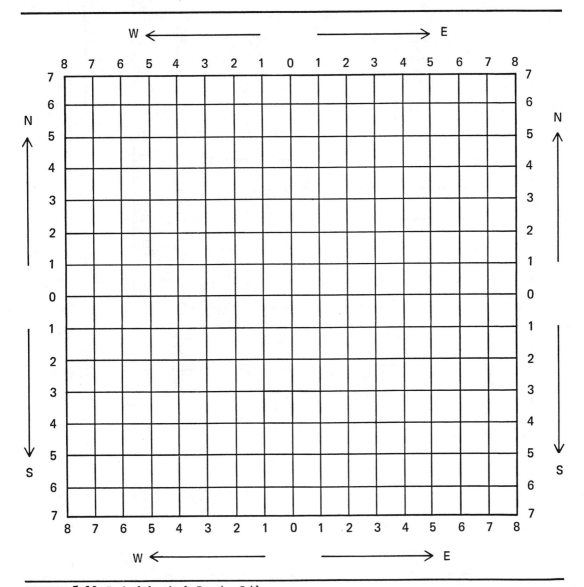

FIGURE 5–10. *Latitude-longitude Practice Grid.*

be about an inch wide, the second, about an inch and a half. Have the children mark off each tape at centimeter or half-inch intervals (depending on the unit of measure being used). On the first tape, they label each interval with a clock time, beginning with 7:00 PM. This is the time tape. On the second tape, they label each interval with a longi- tude, beginning with 105° East Longitude, and a place located on or near (within at least five de- grees) that longitude. This is the place tape. See Figure 5–11 for examples of completed tapes.

When the time tape is aligned with the place tape, the time reading at 0° Longitude (Green- wich, England) is 12:00 Noon. By setting the time

TIME TAPE

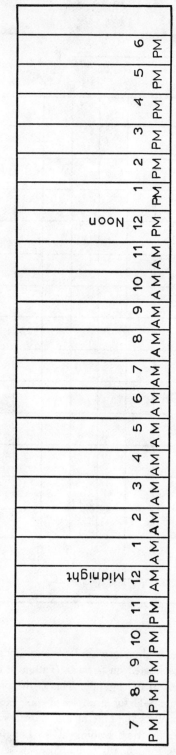

PLACE TAPE

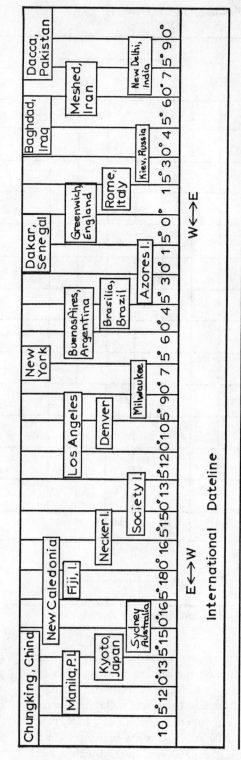

FIGURE 5–11. *Time Computation Tapes.*

178

tape at the current time (to the closest hour) above the city nearest them, the children can determine the time in the other places. If the ends of each tape are fastened together, they may be held on a finger and revolved for a variety of readings.

Explain that the time zones are sometimes altered by an hour to coordinate the activities of people living along the edges of the zones. The children's reading on the tapes are generally accurate within one hour of accuracy.

• Divide the children into groups to discuss how a person situated at the grid North pole would solve his problems of making telephone calls at various times around the world to make sure that we would find people in their offices.

• Divide the children into groups to discuss the advantages of telling time by a twenty-four-hour clock rather than by a twelve-hour clock.

The last two activities help children deepen their understanding about the uses of longitude.

As you have perhaps noticed, the stage-by-stage strategy has been frequently used in guiding map and globe study.

The study of maps and globes, interesting in itself to most children, provides a battery of skills useful in locating places, developing geographical literacy, and for the organization of study about peoples.

Graphs. Young children's introduction to the graph as a device for conveying concise information is similar to what they experience when they learn about maps. Their first experience with a map is constructing one. The same is true with graphs.

By the time that children in first grade can count to one hundred, they are ready to be guided in making their first graph. The first graph they can make is one that shows the number of boys and girls in the classroom. The first experience occurs in two stages:

1. Have each child trace a pattern of a boy or a girl, whichever sex the child is, on paper (a different color for each sex will make the graph more attractive and easier to read) and cut it out. Have the children bring their cut-outs one by one to a chart. Have each girl paste her cut-out along a straight line on the upper part of the chart. Each boy pastes his cut-out in the same way on the lower part of the chart. When the pasting is finished, tell the children they have just made a graph. Have them count the cut-outs in each row and ask them what the graph shows.
2. Have each child trace a pattern of a circle on paper and cut it out. The circles should all be of the same color. Prepare a chart for the children to paste their cut-outs on. To the left in the upper part of the chart write "Boys," in the lower part, "Girls." When the children finish cutting out their circles, guide them in pasting their circles in a row across the chart in the appropriate places. Have them count the cut-outs in each row and ask them what the graph shows.

Have the children compare the two graphs to discover how they are the same and different.

After this initial experience, the teacher guides the children in constructing graphs whenever they are appropriate for the information under study. Sometimes the information is presented with picture symbols. At other times abstract symbols are used. However, the one-to-one correspondence between objects in reality and those shown on the graphs is maintained.

In grades two and three the children's experience with graphs is still focused on graph construction. As the children grow in understanding mathematics, correspondences are gradually increased from one-to-one to one-to-ten. At these grade levels children may also be introduced to constructing simple bar graphs on graph paper. They may be used to maintain a daily record of temperatures, graphing the number of cloudy, rainy, or sunshiny days in a month, graphing the amounts of money contributed by the whole class for charities, graphing the number of private automobiles, taxis, buses, trucks, and bicycles observed on a busy street corner during a five-minute period, and the like. The graphs are posted and read frequently.

From grade four onward, whenever they are studying about economics or historical change, children will be reading graphs. It is generally agreed that bar graphs are introduced in grade four, line graphs in grade five, and circle or pie graphs in grade six. This assumes that children practice during the later grades the skills introduced during the earlier grades.

In most instances the step-by-step strategy is used each time the children meet a graph in their textbooks. The usual way for guiding the children in reading a bar graph comparing amounts unrelated to time follows this order of questions:

1. What does this graph tell about?
2. What is being compared?
3. How much does each square or interval represent?
4. What is the amount given in the first entry on the graph (or for the first country, state, people, or whatever)? The second entry? The third entry? Etc.
5. Which entry shows the greatest amount? The least? Which are about the same?
6. In a single sentence, what does this graph tell us?

In most instances, the children do not need to determine the precise amounts expressed on the graph. However, most children need practice in interpolating fractional amounts. This prepares them for when they graph information themselves.

When guiding children in reading either a bar graph, in which time is a factor, or a line graph, similar questions are asked but with a particular emphasis on time in the first, fifth, and sixth questions in the sequence:

1. What is the graph about? (Responses should focus on change as well as the items compared.)
5. When was the highest point (or peak)? When did the higher points occur? When was the lowest point (or valley)? When were the lower points? What is the pattern of change shown?
6. In a single sentence, what does this graph tell us about the change (or changes) that have occurred in _____?

If children do not understand percentages, they will not be able to read pie graphs. However, the pie graph representing expenditures in which the dollar is the representative symbol may be introduced before the children understand percentages.

For example, children in fourth grade would have little difficulty in understanding the graph in Figure 5–12, showing how a particular sampling of fourth grade children spent their allowance. Such a graph might be used with children in later grades to introduce the concept of a circle graph. What is most difficult for some children to understand is that the circle represents a whole—a whole labor force, a whole income, a whole production, and the like. The precise amount is not given.

To guide children in reading a circle graph, use questions similar to the following:

1. What is the graph about?
2. For what is the largest amount (or percentage) used? What is the next largest amount? The next? The next? Etc.
3. In a sentence, what does this graph tell us?

To help children become independent in graph reading, provide for additional practice in learning

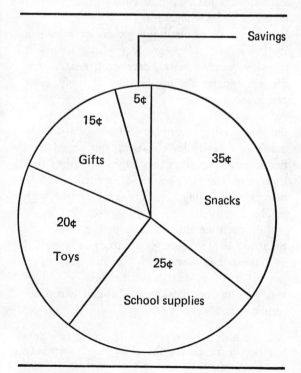

FIGURE 5–12. *How Some Children in Fourth Grade Spend Each Dollar of Their Allowance.*

and activity centers. Use graphs clipped from newspapers, magazines, or discarded textbooks. Task cards or directions for the children will contain questions in sequences similar to those above. Or they contain short true-false or multiple-choice tests based on the graphs.

If children are taught what they can learn about graphs in grades one, two, and three, they develop a useful concept of what graphs are and how they are used. Without these experiences as young children, they may need to be provided with simple graph-making experiences with content interesting to them before they can be expected to read graphs provided in their textbooks.

Diagrams. Children in grades kindergarten through six rarely have opportunities to read diagrams. They are more likely to find them in encyclopedias or in magazine articles. Children in grades seven and eight may find diagrams illustrating economic or political processes as depicted in organization and flow charts in their textbooks. Skill in extracting information from a diagram often depends on its purpose.

A diagram may serve as a basic conveyor of information. This is often the case when the diagram presents a cut-away model of a vehicle, factory, or a section of the earth's surface to show geological formations, or the layout of a building. Such a diagram is labeled or provided with a numbered or lettered key. When it occurs in a textbook, the teacher should focus the children's attention on both the labels or key and the graphic representation to reconstruct in their own minds the information given. The teacher guides them with a sequence of instructions like these:

1. See how the diagram is labeled or keyed.
2. Follow the order of the numbers or letters on the labels or on the key, or the labels themselves, and make notes of what you find.
3. Cover the diagram and use your notes to recall what was shown on the diagram.
4. See how accurate you were by looking at the diagram again.

Sometimes a diagram is a graphic summary of several pages of text. When this occurs, the full meaning of the diagram is impossible without reading the text. This is particularly true of organization and flow charts. Whenever one of these occurs in a textbook, guide the children in using it to recall and organize their own ideas. For example, if they found the diagram in Figure 5–13, showing how a bill becomes a law, you would guide them in studying it in the way presented.

This procedure helps children to learn how to make good use of such diagrams. Again you may wish to have the children generalize from their experience with results similar to this. When reading a flow or organization chart:

1. Determine the beginning and start with the first element.
2. Recall the facts that explain this element, and each thereafter.
3. Cover the chart and see whether you can recall it from memory.

If you wish to help children become independent in reading diagrams and to anticipate their occurrence in resources, you may construct a learning center or provide for practice at an activity center.

Another aspect of learning to read diagrams is using them to organize and express information. For example, as soon as young children have discovered the events in a basic agricultural process (preparing the soil, planting, cultivating, spraying, etc.), they can make a simple flow chart with sketches of the process. Once the children know what is meant by "flow chart," the tasks incorporated in learning or activity centers may have them reading a selection and making a flow chart of the events described.

As you have probably noticed, the step-by-step strategy was used in teaching children how to read diagrams.

Cartoons. Long the bane of the reading teacher, cartoons and comic strips may serve as rich informational sources for children as they study social studies. As media of communication taken in totality, they reflect the common concerns and values of a people as they focus on marriage, childrear-

FIGURE 5–13. *Informational Diagram.*

ing, government, education, law, medicine, commerce, and religion. Very little is sacrosanct from the cartoonist's point of view.

Children like to read comic strips for their humor and suspense, and they enjoy cartoons about everyday family life. With some benefit to their learning and with little damage to their reading habits and preferences, they may be guided occasionally into examining an issue or value presented in a comic strip or cartoon. A view of the roles of parents and children, fantasy heroes, physicians, policemen, kings, or professional athletes may be considered occasionally, and particularly while the children are exploring to know more about human relationships and values. One side of an issue presented in a cartoon or comic strip may prompt an exploration for another side. An insightful discussion may result from asking this question: "Why do you think this comic strip (or cartoon) is so popular?"

The cartoons difficult for children to read are those which make critical comment about international relationships, government, and the economy. One source of difficulty is the symbols that cartoonists use. For example, the use of a pen with a detachable steel point to represent the press or of a bear to represent the United Socialist Soviets of Russia is quite beyond some children. Another source of difficulty is the need for knowledge background to be able to understand the cartoonist's comment. For example, to understand the cartoon presented in Figure 5–14, one has to know these facts:

- That NATO is the acronym for the North Atlantic Treaty Organization, a military alliance formed shortly after World War II to provide for the mutual defense of its members (the United States, Canada, and most of the nations of western Europe) against the incursions of the U.S.S.R.
- That the NATO members are having trouble agreeing on weapons, tanks, and the like, that

"DO YOU GET THE FEELING THE DESIGNERS AREN'T WORKING TOGETHER...?!"

FIGURE 5–14.[1]

would facilitate their operation as a united military force.

If you were guiding a seventh-grade class in studying this cartoon, you would use questions similar to the following:

1. What is the name of the car on display?
2. What does NATO really mean?
3. What is the relationship between NATO and the countries in which the car was made?
4. What is strange about the car?
5. Whom do the people represent?
6. What is the cartoonist saying about NATO?

If the children had been studying about international organizations and had been following the news about NATO, they would probably be able to generalize the message conveyed by the cartoonist and comment about it. If their background were limited and a child had brought the cartoon to school to present to the class during current-affairs study, it could serve as a prompter for the children to consult resources to learn about NATO and its current problems.

To improve children's skill in reading cartoons and comic strips for social-studies purposes, use learning and activity centers.

Note that the holistic strategy has been used here for improving children's skill.

Tables of Contents and Indexes. Children cannot be independently efficient in seeking information unless they know how to use tables of contents and indexes. Using the holistic strategy and often doing most or all of the reading themselves, teachers can introduce the skills to young children.

For example, a kindergarten teacher guiding his or her class in the study of transportation may find a large picture book filled with illustrations of vehicles and organized in chapters. Let us assume that the front cover of the book shows many different vehicles. The teacher's procedure is reflected in his or her verbalizations:

Yesterday we decided that we wanted to know more about trucks. Do you think this book might tell us about them? . . . Yes, I think so too, because we see a truck on the cover.

I don't want to read the whole book just to find out about trucks, so I turn to this page in the front of the book. See, here it is. It will help me to find where to read. (Pointing.) This part of the page lets me know what the book is about. It tells the names of the chapters or parts of the book. I am going to read the names of the chapters to you. When I read the name of the chapter that you think I should read, tell me to stop. Ready? . . . Airplanes, automobiles, boats, buses, ships, trucks . . . You say I should stop with trucks. (Showing the table of contents and pointing.) Do you remember what we call this page? . . . That's right. On this side of the table of contents are some numbers. They tell the numbers of the pages. Can anyone tell me the number across from trucks, right here? . . . Yes, that is number 26 . . I'll turn to that page. (Showing the page.) Is this the right page? . . . How can we tell? . . . Yes, because it has trucks on it. Is there any other way we can tell? . . . Yes, up in this corner of the page is a 26.

Now, let's look at the pages. . . .

As suggested in the section on the holistic strategy, a similar procedure may be used with an encyclopedia. In second and third grade, it may be followed to illustrate the use of an index in an informational book.

Usually in grade four children are ready to be guided toward independence in using the table of contents and index. The stage-by-stage strategy is recommended. The first subskill to be learned is deciding on a word or phrase to use as an entry word or structure in a table of contents or index. The entry word is often found within a question which prompts information seeking.

There are three levels of sophistication: (1) one word or a single phrase in the question will serve for entry purposes; (2) two or more words, one a primary word and the other a secondary word, will serve; and (3) a word will have to be deduced.

Let us begin with the first level. The only material you will need is a set of questions in which only one word is likely to serve, like this:

1. How is cotton grown?
2. Where is gold found?
3. What are services?

ILLUSTRATION 5–4. *Two Children in Fourth Grade Play a Game to Sharpen Their Skill at Choosing the Correct Volume of an Encyclopedia.*

4. How does a person get to be president?
5. Where is Albania?
6. How big is Texas?

Presenting this list to the children, have them study each question to decide which word in each question is most important. Usually, they have little difficulty with this. For the second level, prepare a set of questions similar to the following:

1. How long is the tusk of an elephant?
2. How much coal is mined in Pennsylvania each year?
3. What is the capitol of France?
4. How is milk used in making ice cream?
5. How long does the president of Israel serve?
6. What is the population of New York City?

Guide the children in analyzing each question to decide on the two words that tell what the question is really about and which of the two is more important. Children in grades four and five usually need repeated practices with this subskill. Because of the advanced vocabulary used in their study materials, sixth-grade children will also need repeated practice with series of questions similar to these:

1. What are their main crops?
2. How did they get their goods to market?
3. How much rainfall do they have annually?
4. How did the Indians send messages?
5. What powers does the president of Chile have?
6. What god or gods did the Incas worship?

Depending on the organization and complexity of the index used, one of the entry words will have to be deduced—*farming* or *agriculture* for 1, *transportation* for 2, *weather* or *climate* for 3, *communication* for 4, *government* for 5, and *religion* for 6. As they analyze questions like these, the children are encouraged to think of a more general word which the question is about.

When the children are efficient in this subskill, they have passed the most difficult hurdle in learning how to use a table of contents or an index to locate where to read for information. If they are unable to determine possible entry words independently, they cannot locate information by themselves.

The next subskill we teach depends on the greater need of our learners. In most instances, if their social-studies textbooks contain an index as well as a table of contents, we guide them in learning to use the index because it is more useful. However, if at the moment they are using informational books containing only tables of contents, we continue with the subskills used with a table of contents. Here we shall assume that this is the situation.

The second subskill in using a table of contents is identifying the appropriate chapter and its beginning page. There are two levels of sophistication: (1) using a table of contents with only chapter titles, and (2) using one with chapter titles, section titles, and perhaps side headings. At the second level, the children may have to use both primary and secondary entry words.

The materials needed to introduce the subskill and for practice include a table of contents and a set of questions to be answered in the book. Having the children work with the books they are going to use is preferable to having them work with duplicated tables of contents copied from books or invented for their practice, but this is not totally necessary with this subskill.

Figure 5–15 gives an example of a practice sheet containing both the table of contents and the questions. Two or three practices similar to these are all the children need to learn this subskill. Avoid using tables of contents in which the chapter titles are so cleverly worded that the reader must participate in word games to locate information.

Social-studies textbooks often have an extended table of contents. Here is an example of a single section:

Unit 3. Forms of Government/55
    Chapter I. The Rule of Kings/56
        Kings with Power (Saudi Arabia and Iran)/57
        Kings Who Share Power (Belgium and Bhutan)/60
        Kings without Power (Sweden and Japan)/64
    Chapter II. The Power of Dictators/69
        Some Dictators Take Power/70
        Some Dictators Accept Power/74
        Some Dictators Return Power/80
    Chapter III. Government by Groups/81
        Government in Communist Countries/82
        Government in Some South American Countries/87
        Government by Cabinets/92
    Chapter IV. Presidents in Government/98
        Presidents Who Share Power (the United States and Mexico)/99
        Presidents with Much Power (Gabon and Uganda)/105
        Presidents with Little Power (Israel and France)/110

A table of contents such as this is also useful to children as a preview of what a unit covers. Sometimes the chapter title provides the only useful

Read each of the following questions carefully. Then look in the table of contents in the lower half of the page to decide on what page you would begin reading to find the answer to the question. Write the number on your answer paper.

1. Who invented the ballpoint pen?
2. When was the printing press invented?
3. How does radio send sounds?
4. How can a person really read another person's mind?
5. How did the cavemen communicate?
6. When was the first telephone message sent?
7. What were newspapers like two-hundred years ago?
8. How was a telegraph message sent?
9. How are satellites used in communication?
10. When was the first audiotape recorder invented?

Book title: *Man and Messages*

Chapter	Page
I. Communication among the Cavemen/3	
II. Early Greece and Rome: Runners and Riders/9	
III. The Printing Press/16	
IV. Communication by Fire and by Flag/24	
V. The Postal System: Letters to Everywhere/31	
VI. Pens from Feathers to Ballpoints/39	
VII. Newspapers: Messages to All Who Read/47	
VIII. The Telegraph: Message by Wire/55	
IX. The Telephone: Sound by Wire/63	
X. The Phonograph and Audiotape: New Ways to Record/72	
XI. The Radio: Messages over the Airwaves/80	
XII. The Television: Message by Sight and Sound/88	
XIII. Communication by Satellite: New Routes for Messages/96	
XIV. Mental Telepathy: Who Reads Whose Mind?/105	

FIGURE 5–15. *Practice Sheet for Table of Contents Skills.*

entry. At other times a section title may provide it. Usually practices with an extended table of contents should be conducted with the books themselves.

The next subskill is skimming. When unaware

of this skill, children will often read carefully until they find the desired information, or will become frustrated before they find it. Usually any procedure that saves time and effort is acceptable to them, but at first they are often distrustful of skimming. To introduce the skill and at the same time to make it more acceptable to them, teach an initial lesson similar to this:

Select a chapter from a textbook that is well organized with section and side headings. Using the section and side headings as labels, prepare a diagram similar to the one in Figure 5–16. Duplicate the diagram for class distribution.

INTRODUCTION

Guide the children in discussing their problems when reading to find the answers to specific questions. Inform them that the purpose of the lesson is to help them learn a faster way of locating information.

DEVELOPING THE LESSON

Guide the children in a reading survey of a chapter by having them seek and read the titles of the sections and the side headings.

Have them close their books and distribute the diagram of signposts to them. Guide them in comparing the diagram with what they read in their textbooks.

Asking them each of the following questions, encourage them to indicate which signpost indicates that what follows it is most likely to yield the correct answer. Have them open their textbooks, find the signpost again, and read to find the answer.

1. What form of government do the Australians have?
2. Who were the English explorers of Australia?
3. Who were the first settlers of Australia?
4. What language is spoken by the Australians?
5. What are the important forest products of Australia?

Encourage the children to discuss the answers and where they found them.

GENERALIZING

Have the children define what the signposts are and how they work as aids in locating information.

A lesson such as this helps children develop a concept of skimming as a reading subskill that will also be helpful to them when they are using an index to locate information.

Follow this lesson with at least two more, one in which the children again first preview the signposts and one in which they do not. If they need more practice, provide a learning center or make provisions for practice in an activity center. Figure 5–17 is an example of a task card that you might use in an activity center.

Unfortunately, not all the materials children read for information are organized under section titles and side headings. When the children are able to skim efficiently from signpost to signpost, guide them through a lesson or two in material without the obvious signposts. Have them try reading the first sentence of each paragraph and the last sentence of each long paragraph as well to see how well they can locate specific information. This is a slower form of skimming, but it often works well in carefully written material in which all the paragraphs contain topical sentences.

When the children are adept at skimming, they are ready to apply their table of contents skills to find information. Review the first two stages with them, and conduct some timed practices in which they start with questions, consult a table of contents, and skim to find the answers. Have them discuss how well their table-of-contents skills worked for them as well as the answers they find.

If the children can use a table of contents to find information quickly, they know how to determine an entry word and to skim to find the best place to read for specific information. These two subskills will serve them well as they learn to use the index.

To introduce the index to children is simply a matter of having them turn to an index in the back of a book to become acquainted with its

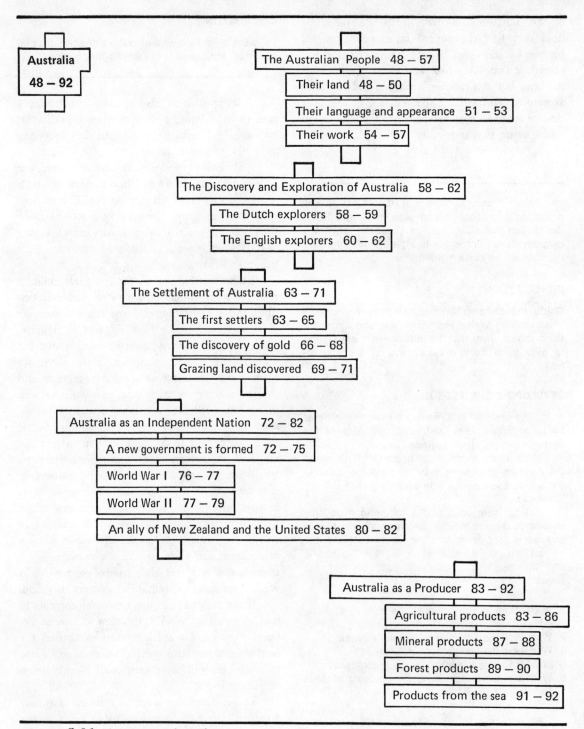

FIGURE 5-16. *Signposts to Information.*

READING: SKIMMING

1. Get a copy of *Our Land Yesterday and Today*.
2. Open it to Unit 4, "Our People Become Many and Produce Much," pages 114–156.
3. Write the clock time on your paper.
4. Skim to find the answers to these questions. Write the answers as briefly as you can:
   a. When was gold discovered in California?
   b. Who was Daniel Boone?
   c. When was the first railroad built?
   d. Who was Cyrus McCormick?
   e. When did Texas become a state?
5. Write the clock time when you finish on your paper. How long did it take you to find the answer to the questions?

FIGURE 5–17. *Task Card for Skill in Skimming.*

organization. If they already know about a table of contents, have them compare the index with it. Its alphabetical structure soon becomes apparent to them. If they know how to locate words in a dictionary, they should have no difficulty finding words in the index. From this point on, the following procedures are suggested:

1. Provide the children with a set of questions, have them analyze them for the entry words, and find the entry words in the index. Be sure to include questions in which there are two entry words. These will help them discover the function of both the primary and secondary entry words. Also include a question or two in which the name of a person, i.e., Clara Barton, Abraham Lincoln, etc., is mentioned. These provide the means for helping them discover that the last name of a person is listed first in an index.

2. To help the children learn how to interpret the locational information listed after the entry words, have them experiment with the information. For example, if the entry word and locational information is "Steel 16, 18, 21–25, 28," have the children read page 16, then page 18, and then pages 21–25 to discover that the cluster of pages in sequence is the better source for information and that the best place at which to begin reading is page 21. (In the occasional instances in

which this is not true, then each of the separate pages must be read.) When no cluster of pages is given, the reader has no choice other than to read each of the separate pages until the desired information is found.

If the children have textbooks in which the index also presents special listings for maps, pictures, and charts or tables, use the index for at least one lesson to focus on these listings. For example, here is a section of an index dealing with Afghanistan:

Afghanistan, 138–163
  area, 138
  farm products, 140, 145, 147–153; *p.* 152–153
  government, 138, 151, 154–157, 148
  history, 154, 156, 160–163
  language, 139, 141
  main cities, 138; *m. 139*
  mineral products, 140, 148
  population, 138
  religion, 139, 141–143; *t.* 142
  transportation, 139, 144–146

Questions such as these may be answered by looking at the special listings:

What is farming like in Afghanistan?
Where are its main cities?
What religions are followed?

3. To guide children in discovering that skimming is sometimes helpful when using an index, guide the children through a lesson or two based on a chapter containing many side headings. Assuming that they are studying about Afghanistan and using the index given above, chances are that they would have to read all of pages 147–153 to find the answer to *How important is farming as an industry in Afghanistan?* However, if they were trying to answer *How important is sheep farming in Afghanistan?*, the specificity of the question would demand the use of skimming to find the answer in the shortest possible time.

When the children can perform these subskills, they are ready to apply them in using the index to locate information.

In this section we have assumed that table-of-

ILLUSTRATION 5–5. *This Student Is Taking Notes to Retain Information to Use When Participating in a Discussion or Writing a Report.*

contents skills have been taught first because this is usually the case. If the index skills were taught first, the children would already be partly prepared to use the table of contents, but learning to skim would need to be given greater emphasis.

After the various subskills for using the index have been introduced and practiced in class or group situations, they may be reinforced in learning and activity centers.

Note Taking. Because it aids the retention of located information, note taking is particularly useful when taught as an adjunct to table-of-contents or index skills. If children have written notes of what they have read, they may use them during discussions, for organizing information, and as recorded facts to be used in composing reports.

Children's handwriting skills are not usually adequate for note taking until they reach grade four. Although emphasis needs to be given to paraphrasing, the holistic strategy is used. To introduce the skill, prepare a large note card as in Figure 5–18 on a chart. Using the chart, teach a lesson similar to the following:

INTRODUCTION

Guide the children in discussing the problems they have with remembering facts and answers to questions during discussions. Ask if any have thought about taking notes as a way of helping them remember.

DEVELOPING THE LESSON

Present the chart showing the note card. Guide the children in discussing the three parts and the reasons for including them on a note. (The written

---

Purpose: What crop is most important to the people of Afghanistan?

Note: Wheat

Source: Peoples and Their Ways, page 147.

FIGURE 5–18. *Note-taking Card.*

purpose helps to identify the note and the bibliographic information after "Source" is helpful in rechecking the accuracy of information.)

Focus the children's attention on the note itself. Explain that because the question plus the note are a complete statement, there is no need to write any more words than are needed to express the answer as a note.

Posting a list of three or four questions and distributing cards or pieces of paper to serve as note cards, have the children fill out the purpose section of each note card and label the sections reserved for the note and the listing of the source. Then have them read to complete the note card.

Guide the children in discussing their completed notes and comparing the different notes that they took.

GENERALIZING

Guide the children in describing a note card and defining its purposes.

Such a lesson is all that most children need to begin note taking during the final stage of learning to use a table of contents or an index.

At a later time when the children are going to be seeking information in composing a report, guide them in considering the different kinds of information they will need to prepare a particular kind of report. For example, let us assume that the children have finished their study of Afghanistan which terminated in writing a class report about the country. Now each child is going to choose another country in Asia to investigate and prepare a report about. Have the children decide on the topics they will have to investigate. The result will be similar to this:

• The geography of the country
• Physical characteristics of the people
• Language and religion of the people
• Main farm products
• Main manufactured products
• Government

Draw a large note card on the chalkboard. Write one of the topics after "Purpose:" on the note card and guide the children in deciding the kinds of notes they would enter on the card if they were again writing about Afghanistan. Have the children prepare note cards according to topics before beginning to investigate to find desired information.

Because the resource materials for children are written at as low a level of readability as possible, it is difficult for them to paraphrase or express their facts in words other than those presented in the text. The only choice they have is to paraphrase at a higher level of sophistication, and this they cannot do. For this reason, emphasize that they use only the words they need to answer the question or to fill out their topic. This prevents reams of copying.

Outlining. Outlining is a form of note taking in which the purpose remains ever the same: to obtain a written digest of ideas from a given section of text. The digest is organized after a traditional pattern of main ideas, supporting ideas, and supporting facts, each entry labeled with a letter or number in a given order:

• Roman Numeral: Main idea
• Capital Letter: Supporting idea
• Arabic Numeral: Supporting fact of the first order
• Lower Case Letter: Supporting fact of the second order

Children in third grade can usually learn to outline for main ideas; children in grades four and five can usually learn to outline for main and supporting ideas; and children in grades six, seven, and eight can usually learn to outline through facts of the first order. Rarely is more than this level needed.

As far as children's social-studies investigations are concerned, the only need they have for outlining material occurs when they must use a resource which they cannot take home, bring to the classroom, or have regular access to. This is usually a resource in the reference section of a public library. It may be a special encyclopedia, almanac, or report which is for use only in the library.

There may be an occasion when a child volunteers to prepare an outline of special material to be shared with the class, or when he or she is not sure of what specific information will be needed and decides that an outline will save time in the long run. Children need to know that such occasions do occur and that outlining skill will help when they do.

If children are going to be successful during their initial attempts at outlining, you as the teacher will have to make sure that the material they are to outline is easily outlinable. Such material contains well-organized paragraphs usually headed by topical sentences. If not headed by topical sentences, they should contain a topical sentence at the end. Without this structure, children become frustrated.

You may follow a holistic strategy when teaching outlining to children in third grade. To help them develop a concept of what an outline is, compose or find a suitable reading selection which they can read easily, outline, and write both the selection and the outline on a large chart or prepare it for class distribution. An example is found in Figure 5–19.

As you can see, paraphrasing is also an essential skill for outlining. The underlined words in the paragraphs help the children see how this is done.

Here is an example of an introductory lesson that a teacher might use to introduce outlining:

INTRODUCTION

Write this sentence on the chalkboard: *We had fun last Halloween.* Encourage the children to compose more sentences orally that tell about the fun they had on Halloween. Add their sentences to make a paragraph. After three or four sentences have been given, tell the children they have just written a paragraph and have them discuss why the first sentence is the main idea of the paragraph and how the other sentences are related to it.

DEVELOPING THE LESSON

Present the story and its accompanying outline. Guide the children in reading both and in deciding how the two are related. When they see that the outline consists of the main idea in each paragraph, help them understand the relationship between the main idea and supporting ideas by having them pretend that the sentence giving the main idea was omitted to see whether the other sentences make sense.

Outline	Story
Eskimo Homes	*Eskimo Homes*
I. Two different Eskimo homes.	Some *Eskimoes* had *two different* homes. One was a winter home. The other was a summer home.
II. A winter home made of driftwood, whalebones, and sod.	The *winter home* was a little house *made of driftwood, whale bones,* and *sod.* The driftwood was pieces of logs that washed up on the shore. The whale bones were left after the whales were eaten. The sod was dug from the ground.
III. A tent for a summer home.	The *summer home* was a *tent.* It was made of animal skins. It was put up in the summer and taken down when winter was coming.

FIGURE 5–19. *Outline Study Model.*

Focus their attention on the labeling of the outline. Have them discuss how additional paragraphs would be labeled.

GENERALIZING

Guide them in composing a paragraph telling what an outline is.

After this introductory lesson, you as the teacher would guide the children in a series of guided practices in which the children would outline sections. To encourage them to read each paragraph completely before outlining, you would provide a guided lesson or two in which the main idea of the paragraph would occur in the last sentence. They may need some practice with sets of three or four mixed sentences from which they select the sentence containing the main idea.

A similar procedure is used when introducing outlining to children in grade four and above. An example of the illustrative model that you might prepare for them is seen in Figure 5–20. Note the change in the order of ideas in the final paragraph and how this is reflected in the outline.

Here is an example of an introductory lesson using the outline model in Figure 5–20:

INTRODUCTION

Guide the children in considering the alternatives that they might follow if there was a very important resource in the public library. It contains information they need, but they cannot check it out to take home or bring to school. The library has no copying machine. How can they obtain the information for future use?

DEVELOPING THE LESSON

Present the text and its accompanying outline as a possible alternative. Guide the children in analyzing the illustrative model to determine how the text and outline are related, and why the entries in the outline are labeled in the way they are. Clarify the relationship between main ideas and supporting

ideas by having them cover the topical sentences in each paragraph and read the supporting sentences to try to recall the main ideas.

Focus their attention on the last part of the outline and the final paragraph in the text to demonstrate that the topical sentence may occur at the end of the paragraph.

To demonstrate the usefulness of the outline, have a volunteer try to reconstruct the text by covering it and using the outline as a guide for an informal talk.

GENERALIZING

Have each group make a list of directions for outlining. When they are finished, have them exchange lists of directions and critique them. Guide the children as an entire class to establish the best set of directions.

After this introductory lesson, provide for two or three lessons in which the children outline independently. Examine the results carefully to determine whether some children will need more supervised practice.

To provide for a realistic application of the skills, prepare a list of selected passages from resources in the public library from which the children may choose to outline, and to use the outline in making a brief oral report to the class. The selected passages should include those of common interest as well as some related to the social-studies unit in progress.

If opportunities for realistic application of outlining skills are not provided, the children may regard it as just another one of those meaningless tasks they are asked to do from time to time.

Here we have followed a holistic strategy. The stage-by-stage strategy may also be used. Each stage is a level of sophistication in outlining: first, outlining main ideas; second, outlining main and supporting ideas; and third, outlining main ideas, supporting ideas, and supporting facts, etc. However, before launching children into such a program, the teacher must give careful thought to the utility of outlining in seeking and retaining information in social studies or any other content subject.

Outline	Text
Brazil as a Producer for the World Market	*Brazil as a Producer for the World Market*
I. Brazil, the largest South American country.	Brazil is the largest of the South American countries. Much of it is grazing land, forests, and jungle. Only a small part of it is useful for farming. But this does not prevent it from being an important agricultural country.
A. Covers half of South America.	
B. Mostly grazing land, forests, and jungle.	
C. A little land useful for farming, but Brazil still important as an agricultural producer.	
II. Important agricultural products: coffee beans, castor beans, cacao, cotton, and sugar.	Brazil's most important agricultural products include coffee beans, castor beans, cacao, cotton, and sugar. It is the leading world producer of coffee beans and castor beans and is second in producing cacao. Cotton and sugar are produced in small amounts for shipment to other countries.
A. Leads the world in producing coffee beans and castor beans.	
B. Second in cacao growing.	
C. Small amounts of cotton and sugar.	
III. Many forests and mineral deposits, but little produced for export.	Although Brazil has rich forests and mineral deposits, it produces little from these for export. Some pine lumber and iron ore are shipped to other countries. Most of the lumber and minerals it produces are used within the country itself.
A. Some pine lumber and iron ore.	
B. Mostly used within Brazil.	
IV. A sleeping giant as a world producer.	Brazil is an important producer for the world today. When its people develop their forest and mining industries, it may become one of the two or three leading producers of many kinds of goods for the world market. As a world producer it is a sleeping giant that will awaken one day to do great things.
A. An important producer for the world today.	
B. Could become a world leader when its forests and mines are developed.	

FIGURE 5–20. *Advanced Outline Model.*

Interviewing

An interview is as much information generating as it is information seeking. Prepared with a few questions which are at best directions of promise to explore, the interviewer approaches the interviewee. A human resource, the interviewee requires a special consideration unnecessary with books, films, and the like. As he or she responds, the interviewer listens, picking up this lead or that, and follows it until it ends or proves unfruitful. The interview ends, the interviewee unperturbed and glad that he has been able to contribute, and the interviewer most likely enriched with a fund of discovered information.

The above describes a concept of the inter-

ILLUSTRATION 5–6. *Interviewing a Resource Person at School.*

topic of the interview, the questions they will be expected to answer, and the approximate time of the interview. Interviewees will also appreciate knowing something about the age and background of the interviewers.

Some school districts encourage children's interviewing to seek information by providing telephone facilities for use in the classroom. These facilities consist of a regular telephone and an amplifier which makes it possible for the teacher and the class to listen as a child interviews a resource person. A list of interviewees is maintained by the district, and procedures are developed for the teachers to add to the list or to procure interviewees. With such provisions, only the last of the precautions listed above needs to be observed.

Young children can be introduced to interviewing by asking questions of their parents. For example, a first-grade class studying about different occupations in the community discover they want to know how a baker learns to do his or her job. Knowing that several of the children's parents are bakers, the teacher suggests that these children might be able to interview their parents to find out for the whole class. If the children are willing, the teacher does the following:

• Guides the children in the class in clarifying the question to be asked and in composing any other questions that might be asked. The children decide on these questions:

How do you learn to be a baker?
What do you like about being a baker?

• Using *the firefighter* as a topic, the teacher, assuming both roles, role plays two situations. In the first situation the child accosts the parent, who is trying to mow the lawn before it rains. The child blurts out that he or she is supposed to find out how the parent learned to be a firefighter and insists on being told right away. The child is so insistent that the parent must stop work. Just as he or she finishes being interviewed, the rain begins to fall. Somewhat crossly, he or she puts the lawnmower away.

view that we want to introduce to and extend with children. The three subskills involved are composing the questions to be asked, listening and reacting to responses, and managing relationships positively with the interviewee. The first of these may be learned as a rational thinking skill, but the remaining two require simulated trials.

Certain precautions need to be taken if children are going to seek information through interviewing:

• The teacher should know the interviewees, or they should be chosen from a list of resource persons maintained by the school district.
• The children's parents should be informed about the interview, its purpose, and with whom it is to be conducted before it occurs. The parents should be given an opportunity to approve the interview and given the option of being present when it occurs.
• The interviewees should be informed about the

In the second situation the child tells the parent that his or her class at school would like to know how he or she became a firefighter. When the parent says that he or she must finish the lawn first, the child asks when would be a good time to ask questions. The parent says that he or she finishes in a few minutes and will be glad to talk then. The child waits and then conducts the interview. Both the parent and the child are happy with the experience. (Puppets or flannelgrams used with the role playing will make these performances more effective.)

• The teacher guides the children in comparing the situations to decide which is better and why. Then they practice briefly in pairs after talking about situations in which parents are busy and using different occupations as topics.

• The teacher sends a brief note home with the interviewers to alert the parents to the interview.

On the following day the children share the results of their interview.

Often young children can interview people who work in the school. Gardeners, custodians, cooks, repairmen, and teacher aides often appreciate serving as interviewees. Every school faculty member is a potential interviewee about various skills and experiences. Each time young children have an opportunity to interview, the introductory experience is reviewed and sometimes repeated.

A similar introductory experience is provided with children in grades four through eight, but more emphasis is given to composing questions, or structuring the interview, before role playing. Let us assume, for example, that your fifth-grade class wants a more realistic view of how the Swedish people feel toward their king. There are people in the community who were formerly Swedish citizens and still maintain close relationships with friends and relatives in Sweden. These people, as well as a Swedish vice-consul, have been interviewed previously, and are willing to be interviewed again. As the teacher, you follow these procedures:

• Guide the children in developing the specific questions they will want to ask about the relationships between the Swedish king and his subjects. Two questions are volunteered:

What are the king's responsibilities toward his people?

When do the people get a chance to see their king?

Divide the children into impromptu groups to try to generate more questions. After five minutes of discussion, convene the children as a class again to discuss what they decided. These questions are added to the list:

Have any polls been taken recently about the king's popularity? If yes, what were the results?

Do the people support the king, or does he support himself?

Does the king pay taxes? If he does, are they the same as everyone else's?

• Guide the children in developing a "status question," a question that recognizes the interviewee as a respected person. Such a question usually asks for an opinion. Provide a few questions for the children to consider, such as:

How do you think that most of the Swedish people feel toward the king?

Do you think that the Swedish people will continue having a king in the foreseeable future? Why do you think so?

Again the children discuss in small groups to see what other questions they can generate. During the ensuing class discussion, they decide on the following question:

What do you think the Swedish people would do if they were given a choice between abolishing the office of king or keeping it? Why?

Because this is an interview surfaced as a class need, we would continue immediately with role playing, as described in a moment, to help the children understand how they should conduct an interview. However, if the situation is a hypothetical one used for class practice, we would provide the children with several more hypothetical situations in which they practice developing questions to use in an interview, including the status question. In this real situation, we would follow these procedures:

- Remind the children that the interviewees have their own daily tasks to do, and that by allowing themselves to be interviewed, they are giving up some of their own time. Have them discuss how they should feel toward the interviewees.
- Describe a situation in which a busy businessman has consented to be interviewed late in the afternoon, but the appointed time has passed, and the interviewer still has not appeared. Have the children role play what he must be thinking and how he must feel.
- Give the children several situations to role play. During the postdiscussions, emphasize what the players did to show courtesy to the interviewees and how they reacted to responses made by those interviewed.

After your learners have had several experiences with interviewing, you may wish to make them aware of asking questions which they have not included on their prepared list, and, at the same time, to maintain the point of the interview. To introduce the skill, follow procedures similar to these.

1. INTRODUCTION

Prepare on a chart or for class distribution sequences similar to these:

Interview topic: Education in Japan.
Interviewee: A Japanese businessman hired by his company to work in the United States.
Question: What is the sixth grade like in Japanese schools?
Answer: It is the most difficult grade in the elementary school. The boys and girls study very hard to be ready for examinations in the spring.
Question: What do the boys and girls study?

Interview topic: Life in the United States sixty years ago.
Interviewee: An elderly person.
Question: How did you travel in those days?
Answer: In town many of us rode on trolley cars. There were also many automobiles, and once in a while you would see a horse and carriage on the streets. Some of the poorer farmers still used them to come to town.
Question: What kinds of appliances did you have in your home?

Interview topic: Chinese history.
Interviewee: A person whose hobby is Chinese history.
Question: When did the Chinese invent their form of handwriting?
Answer: No one knows exactly when. Long ago a group of people called the Shang lived in northern China. These people were more advanced than the other groups of people living in China at the time. The Shang are thought to be the first people to use a form of handwriting similar to modern Chinese writing.
Question: For how long has agriculture been an important industry in China?

Inform the children that each sequence is a part of an interview and that each of the questions is on an interviewer's list. Have them read each sequence, perhaps in small groups, to decide what unplanned questions the interviewer might have asked in each sequence after the answer to make it more complete. (First sequence: Why do boys and girls in the sixth grade have to take examinations in the spring? Second sequence: How did you travel when you wanted to visit another state or country hundreds of miles away? Third sequence: When did the Shang live in China?)

2. PRACTICE

Involve the children in activities similar to the following:

- Inform the children about some topics that you could be interviewed about (a hobby, special interest, or unique experience). Have them choose one and work in small groups to compose the questions for the interview. Have them interview you. Respond to some questions in such a way that further questions are needed. After each interview, have the children decide what other questions might have been asked to get more, pertinent information.
- Give the children a written transcript of an interview or have them listen to an audiotaped interview to determine what other questions might have been asked.

3. APPLICATION

After the results of an interview have been reported to the class, debrief the interviewer or group of interviewers about the questions they asked and those they might have asked to get more detailed information.

Asking impromptu questions to pursue a point or to get more information, a skill which requires attentive listening and quick thinking, is emphasized in the later grades.

To help children grow as interviewers, guide them in evaluating themselves as interviewers after each interview to determine the skills they will need to work on in the future. You may wish to check with the interviewees to see how they felt about their experience.

Interviewing as a way of seeking information has a strong social-science flavor. If there is a large number of interviewees, you may guide the children in approaching the interview as a poll. They may be guided in tabulating the results and drawing conclusions from them with particular attention to the diversity of results. Inadequacy of sampling rules out anything more, unless care has been taken in sampling.

Of particular interest is the use of interviewing as a way of introducing to children an aspect of the work of the historian in the development of oral history. Almost every community has older members who have lived there for their entire lives and who are delighted to tell how things "used to be."

Younger children use the person's physical appearance as a crude estimation of "long ago" and can understand differences related to their everyday lives—what school was like, the games that children played, the work children were expected to do, how people celebrated various holidays, and the like.

Older children may use interviewing as a means of creating a history of the community during a chosen era or to learn how the sweep of significant events such as the World Wars, the Depression, and early space exploration affected the lives of ordinary people. The interviews may be audiotaped for later analysis and comparison. The point of view of the interviewees may be taken into consideration. The children may categorize the information into primary, or that which is based on the interviewee's actual experience; secondary, or information reported to the interviewee

by another; and possibly tertiary, or information which the interviewee received third-hand.

A flurry of interest in oral history in a community may prompt the overuse of some interviewees. Before we guide children into an oral history project, we may need to find out from other teachers which interviewees have been used and the nature of their information.

The use of interviews vitalizes the social-studies program. The precautions to be taken are time consuming, but seeing children actively involved in seeking information makes the time well spent.

As we review the strategies used, the holistic strategy is recommended for young children and the stage-by-stage strategy for older children.

In the previous chapter we saw how inquiry emphases in social studies involve children as active participants in making decisions about what they learn. In this chapter we have reviewed the intake skills essential to acting on many of those decisions. If children lack these skills, their decisions can lead only to confusion and frustration.

The effective program of instruction in social studies, then, reflects as much attention to fostering growth in the intake skills as it does to controlling the complexity and sequence of the ideas to be learned through inquiry.

SUMMARY

There are many true-to-life activities in which children can participate to explore how people live and what they do as workers, but such activities cannot satisfy all the children's needs for information. They need to learn to observe, listen, read, and interview to obtain information to follow their inquiries.

Teachers may use either of two instructional strategies. The holistic strategy requires that the teacher cue the learners verbally to perform each subskill. Repetition of the strategy guides learners toward mastery. The stage-by-stage strategy requires that the teacher guide the learners in mastering each subskill before proceeding to the next. Learning is accumulative.

Teachers select the strategy to use on the basis of children's capacity to learn, the nature of the skill, and personal preference.

Most children need to improve in observation skills. Much of the improvement occurs as a result of carefully guided experiences involving walking and fieldtrips, pictures, films, filmstrips, and dioramas.

Through audiotaping, almost every verbal resource for information can be made available to children. Guided listening to environmental sounds and audiotapes help them improve their listening skills.

To be independent information seekers, children need a variety of reading skills: reading for information which involves factual recall and drawing conclusions, globe and map reading, graph reading, diagram reading, cartoon reading, location skills, and retention skills. The learning activities sometimes require specially devised materials, but most are based on the materials available for children's use in the classroom. Many learning sequences begin with developing concepts about how skills operate.

Interviewing is a special skill requiring as much concern for the interviewee as for the information to be obtained. The learning activities include composing questions, listening and reacting to responses, and role playing.

The effective instructional program requires that provisions be made for both content and skills learning.

POSTSCRIPT

At the beginning of the chapter you were asked to consider whether a list of procedures followed by teachers when teaching skills was complete. Take out the notes you made.

If you decided that the list was complete, you were correct as a teacher of skills. However, as a social-studies teacher, you would be concerned about the provisions for applying the skills in social studies. To be complete, this entry should be added to the procedures:

Providing for application of the skill. The children are provided opportunities to use and evaluate the skill.

FOR FURTHER UNDERSTANDING

Cognitive Activities

1. Make a list of as many true-to-life activities as you can bring to mind about any of the following: farming, building construction, life in Norway.
2. Describe the holistic strategy and the stage-by-stage strategy as each would be used to teach a skill. Decide which strategy you prefer and give reasons for your preference.
3. Discuss briefly the relationship between purpose and the use of an intake skill.
4. Make a columnar chart of the skills and the subskills discussed in this chapter. Write the name of a skill at the head of each column. Under the name list the subskills associated with each skill. Toward the end of each column, note which strategy you would use to teach the skill.
5. What difficulties do you see in trying to ensure that children learn both the intake skills they need and the prescribed facts and generalizations in social studies? How would you try to reduce these difficulties?
6. Suppose that a parent objects to the emphasis you give to social studies. He thinks that the time and effort might be spent in helping children learn the basic subjects. What would you say to this parent?

Practice Activities

1. Obtain the teacher's edition or instructional manual at a selected grade level above second grade for each of the following: a reading textbook, a mathematics textbook, a language textbook, and a social-studies textbook. Survey each briefly to see what instruction they provide in each of the skills discussed in this chapter.

2. Arrange to visit an elementary classroom during social-studies instruction. Observe to see what the teacher does during the lesson to improve the use of an intake skill or two.

3. Find or make a piece of instructional material usable at a selected grade level for teaching an aspect of each of the following skills:
   a. Observing
   b. Listening
   c. Reading for information
   d. Note taking or outlining
   e. Using an index or table of contents
   f. Graph or diagram reading
   g. Map or globe reading
   h. Interviewing

   Describe how you will use each piece of material. If you have your own classroom or have a laboratory assignment in a school, bear the grade level of your learners in mind as you select or make materials.

Performance Activities

1. Use as many as possible of the materials produced as a response to 3 above with a group or class of children. Evaluate the results of each by responding to these questions:
   a. What evidence of learning did you see? Is it what you expected?
   b. If the results were less than expected, how do you account for it? What might you do the next time to get better results?
   c. If the results were what you expected, or better, how would you change the material or your procedures to achieve a better result?

NOTES

1. Used with permission of The San Diego Union, San Diego, California.

SELECTED REFERENCES

Alexander, Mary, and Marilyn Childress. "A Political Cartoon." *Social Education*, 44:138–140 (February, 1980).

Atwood, Beth. *Building a Map Skills Program*. Palo Alto, Calif.: Education Today, Inc., 1976.

Beyer, Barry K. "Teaching Basics in Social Studies," *Social Education*, 41:96–104 (February, 1977).

Danzer, Gerald A. "Textbook Graphics and Maps: Keys to Learning." *Social Education*, 44:101–103 (February, 1980).

Durkin, Dolores. *Teaching Them to Read*, 3rd. ed., Chapter 17. Boston: Allyn and Bacon, Inc., 1978, pp. 497–543.

Hash, Ronald J., and Mollie B. Bailey. "A Classroom Strategy: Improving Social Studies Comprehension." *Social Education*, 42:24–26 (January, 1978).

Kramer, Klass. *Teaching Elementary School Mathematics*, 3rd ed. Boston: Allyn and Bacon, 1975.

Lunstrum, John. "Reading in the Social Studies," *Social Education*, 40:10–18 (January, 1976).

Patterson, Charlotte J. "Teaching Children to Listen." *Today's Education*, 67:52–53 (April-May, 1978).

Rowell, C. Glennon. "Vocabulary Development in the Social Studies Program." *Social Education*, 42:10–14 (January, 1978).

Shorr, Jon. "Basic Skills in TV Viewing." *Today's Education*, 67:72–75 (April-May, 1978).

6

Improving Children's
Information-processing
———————— Skills ————————

Two-thirds of children's time in social studies is devoted to seeking information. Much of the remaining third is devoted to processing the information in a meaningful way. The problems associated with teaching children how to process information will be treated in this chapter.

As you read this chapter you will have to resolve an issue. It is related to certain kinds of activities through which a teacher guides children during and toward the end of a social-studies unit. The following is a list of such activities completed by a fourth grade as they studied about natural resources and their use. As you read the list, try to decide whether you as a teacher can see any benefits to learning accruing from the activities.

1. After learning what the natural resources are, each child chose a common object or food and made a chronological diagram of how various resources contributed to its production.
2. After a study of forests, the children used creative dramatics to depict the use of the forests a hundred years ago and how they are used today.
3. After the study of resources in the sea, the children created a mural showing what the sea has to offer humankind.
4. After the study of soil, the children created a map showing how the space in their community might be used better to ensure the availability of more soil for growing crops.

5. After the study of water, the children composed reports on the use of dams, reservoirs, contour farming, removing salt from sea water, and recycling water as ways of conserving its use.
6. After the study of minerals, the children joined small groups to prepare and give presentations about one of the vital minerals.
7. Toward the close of the unit, the children did the following:
   • Made a chart of the natural resources and their uses.
   • Role played producers and consumers in conflict over the use of natural resources.
   • Wrote creative stories about what life would be like a hundred years from now when there will be more people and less resources.
   • Instituted a class-wide conservation program to make better use of materials and equipment.

As a teacher, what value do you see in these activities, if any? Jot down what you think. Give a reason or two for your opinion. Then put your notes aside until you have finished reading the chapter.

The content of social studies is abstract. Children are exposed to much of it at an abstract level. Be it stimulated by curiosity or interest, or designed after a scientific model, inquiry helps children to meet abstractions at their own level, but inquiry is not enough. Much of their real learning occurs, not as a function of how much they can recall and retain, but as a function of how well they can build what they recall into structures meaningful to themselves and others.

INFORMATION PROCESSING AND LEARNING

Processing information to produce meaningful structures requires skills. In self-contained classrooms, teachers have little difficulty guiding children in learning expressive skills in language and other media to apply in social studies. When necessary, they can convert their classrooms into expression laboratories. Because of the need for the careful coordination of teachers' instructional responsibilities, time, and space in the open-space classroom, and because of the time limitation and expected teacher specialization in the departmentalized classroom, social-studies teachers in these situations may have to rely on other teacher specialists to provide instruction in the skills. Regardless of the administrative arrangements for instruction, social-studies teachers have the responsibility for improving the language skills essential to organizing and expressing ideas.

Whatever children compose or construct has meaning for them regardless of the quality of the products. Young children value anything they create. Sometimes the observer is hard put to understand what they create, but usually they are unabashed about explaining their product. From age nine on, children develop increasing sensitivity toward the quality of their products. For this reason, we make whatever provisions we can to help them improve their expression skills and to offer choices of skills. For example, some children may enjoy writing creative stories, some may prefer to draw comic strips, while others may wish to deal with the same problem through creative dramatics. The more skills the children are taught, the greater the number of choices they can entertain.

The skills used in information processing may be broken down into three broad categories: skills in integrating knowledge, applying knowledge, and generating new knowledge.

Processing to Integrate Knowledge

Integrating knowledge is pulling it together in some way to make it more meaningful. One form of integration is to organize it in such a way that it is more manageable or easier to grasp. The other form is to express it in one's own words or in a different medium. Both forms reflect the information studied.

Organizational Structures. How knowledge is to be organized often depends on the nature of the content and study at hand. The chart in Figure 6–1 offers a listing of general study and content areas and the organizational structures frequently used with each.

Learning to use these structures may require intensive instruction or no more than a few opportunities to develop a structure and use it. The skills needed in the latter category include making tables, lists, charts, and flow charts. The skills of map and graph making require intensive instruction.

As important as knowing how to use a structure is knowing when to use it. Learning this is a function of using the structure at every appropriate opportunity.

Children's grade level determines largely which of the structures they will learn to use. Children in grades kindergarten through two can learn to make descriptive charts on which pictures can be pasted or pinned. At grade three, they can begin to make written entries on charts. Graph and map making are restricted generally to grades four and above.

Through the use of organizational structures children learn that accurate inferring is facilitated when the facts are organized in compact, easily readable form.

Using Different Media to Integrate Knowledge. Whenever we guide children in using an organizational structure, we are saying in effect, "This is the structure. Fill in the blanks." But when we ask them to tell us what they know in their own

Study and Content	Organizational Structure
Processes	Flow charts. Chronological diagrams with elements illustrated or labeled. Diagrams of relationships.
Products	Tables or lists. Maps (for regional production). Bar graphs (for comparison of amounts). Circle graphs (for comparison of parts to whole). Line graphs or bar graphs to show change.
Descriptive aspects of a people	Charts with elements listed under each aspect. Circle graphs for expressing distribution of characteristics among a people (religions, languages, ethnic characteristics, occupations, etc.). Bar or line graphs to show changes in aspects. (For comparison of peoples, any of the above for each people placed next to each other.)
Descriptive aspects of a region	Charts with elements listed under each aspect. Maps showing different geographic characteristics and land-use patterns. Bar and line graphs to show changes in aspects. (For comparison of regions, any of the above for each region placed next to each other.)
Polls	List of aspects with tallies showing numbers of responses.

FIGURE 6–1. *Organizational Structures for Integration.*

words, we are saying, "Give us the facts organized intelligibly." There is a vast difference between filling the blanks in a given structure and expressing information in a structure of one's own choosing.

"Tell me in your own words (or in your own drawing, painting, clay figurine, constructed model, dramatization, oral report, written essay, or whatever)," is a demand for children to use a medium, or set of symbols rendered in a particular way to convey ideas, as well as one of the organizational structures commonly used with it. As children respond, they must not only recall the necessary facts, but also exercise the skill and organization required by the use of the medium.

The most frequent error made by teachers is to restrict the integration of knowledge to the use of one medium—many children in grades kindergarten through three may be always asked to draw; those in the later grades may always be asked to write a summary, report, or essay. Such a practice

penalizes children who cannot draw or write well. Poor ability with a medium inhibits their expressing what they know. Besides, always using the same medium is tedious.

When working with young children, we can offer variety, not so much in medium (much of it is in oral language), but in the supplementary materials used to help convey meaning. For example, after we transmit information to the children through the use of pictures, real objects, replicas, puppets, charts, or flannelgrams, we may encourage them to use the same materials to express what they know. Later they may be encouraged to select or make their own supplementary materials to use when telling what they have learned.

Also, young children can learn to express their knowledge through pantomime, dramatization, and the use of the audiotape recorder. They can become proficient in using building blocks.

When they compose summaries or reports,

they need the teacher to prompt thought and record what they say.

When we consider the media available for older children to use, we discover variety. With their better developed coordination, they can construct models, replicas, and geographical sites. Their better control and understanding of the uses of pencil, pastel crayons, charcoal, and ink can result in series of pictures and sketches that express very well what they have learned. Their appreciation of the audiotape recorder and their love for oral language can encourage the recall and expression of what they know. If we occasionally use flannelgrams and puppets to transmit information to them, they will, too. Many take easily to the illustrated oral or written report.

There is little reason for children at any grade level to be restricted to the use of one medium or one way to use it to integrate knowledge. Because integration of knowledge is an individual matter, children should be offered choices—to draw a picture or to record on the audiotape recorder, to write a report or draw a series of sketches, to make a clay figurine or write a description, and so on.

However, to strike a balance between children's need to be able to integrate what they know and their need to improve in language-composition skills, we arrange moments when only the composition skills are to be used. Furthermore, we devote time and effort to teaching these skills, sometimes during time set aside for social-studies instruction.

The integration of knowledge with different media, as much as possible on individual terms, is essential to learning in social studies. It aids children in knowing what they know and its product is a springboard for further thought and learning in social studies.

Processing as Application. The meaning of a social-studies idea surfaced through integration is transient if it is not applied in some way to solve a problem. Use of the idea through application both validates and broadens its meaning.

In social studies, as in other subjects, problems are usually hypothetical but based on reality. As social-studies teachers we have a rich array of ways to bring children into contact with such problems. Let us assume, for example, that our sixth-grade learners have just completed finding out about economic conditions in Bhutan, a small Asiatic country northeast of India. They have integrated their information and used it to arrive at the following generalization:

The Bhutanese people have discovered ways of using their mountains, water, and limited soil for what they need, but produce little to trade with other countries.

Using this as our ideational base, we may encourage the children to consider it for possible problems by asking questions such as these:

As you consider this idea, can you see any problems that the Bhutanese people might have with making a living now or at some time in the future? What problems might they have? What might they do about them?

Or

If you or I were to go to Bhutan to live as the Bhutanese people do, what problems might we have? What might we do about them to be able to live for the entire year?

Or

If a Bhutanese family were to immigrate to this country, what problems might they have with making a living? What would they have to do to solve their problems?

These are simple problem situations to which our learners react.

Another way of presenting a problem to these children would be to have them read a series of statements made recently to a reporter or observer by the Bhutanese king. The series of quotes would serve as a case study which the children would listen to or read to discover the king's view of his country's problems and possible solutions, and then react to his view in terms of what they know.

A more subtle way of presenting the problem would be for you to present a role-playing situation. The situation would lead toward some children taking the roles of three village elders discussing what they might do because a drought has limited the supply of water for irrigating the terraces on which the rice grows.

Or the children might be immersed in a simulation in which a people similar to the Bhutanese explore for ways of establishing industries to produce goods to be traded with other countries. After the simulation, they consider the generalization about the Bhutanese people in the light of what had occurred during the simulation.

Or the children might be guided into values clarification related to how they might act when meeting a Bhutanese person for the first time, or into a values analysis about whether a people should or should not be satisfied with a subsistence standard of living.

The models for working with hypothetical problems in social studies follow one of two lines of development. The first has the children discovering the problem and proposing solutions to it, as in Figure 6–2. The second model immerses the children in the problem and prompts them to generate solutions for it, as in Figure 6–3.

Either model brings children to the point of applying what they know. When children are studying the natural environment or the immediate environment, the problems they discover may be real and a proposed solution may be put into action and evaluated. Otherwise, proposed solutions are hypothetical. They remain in children's minds to be evaluated repeatedly as related topics are met from time to time.

Processing to Generate New Knowledge

When children examine recently acquired knowledge in the light of their total experience as it has contributed to the development of their own beliefs, attitudes, feelings, and values, a synthesis occurs. As a result, the children generate new knowledge. This process is creativity.

For this to occur in social studies, four conditions have to prevail. First, the children must know a social-studies idea to serve as a focal point for the recall of many facts. Second, the children must have a disciplined, functional mastery of skill with an expressive medium. Third, they must have an opportunity to use the skill to produce a synthesis.

And fourth, they must accept the opportunity. We shall be concerned here with the second condition.

When children have a disciplined, functional mastery of a skill with a medium, they can use the medium at a level commensurate with their level of development. For example, if a girl in fourth grade wrote a creative story about a French child and family, we would expect a simple introduction to the story problem and at least one event in which a conflict is resolved. The characterization would not be much beyond a simple identification of the main character with perhaps a brief physical description. Spelling, the structure of sentences, and paragraphing would be crude. The richness of the product would lie in how well the child stayed within the limitations imposed by the social-studies idea and at the same time managed to make her own insights and sincerity shine through.

If the child were to participate in creative dramatics, paint a picture, make a poster, the facsimile of a bumper sticker, or a diorama in a shoebox, we would expect similar qualities.

In a self-contained classroom, a teacher can foster children's growth in the skills they can use for creative endeavors. Because administrative factors—instructional responsibility, time, and space—must be carefully coordinated in open-space and departmentalized classrooms, teachers in these situations are limited in what they can do. At the very least, they can help the children grow in the skills through use. Encouraging children to complete creative projects at home sometimes gets them to try the skills. To foster children's growth in skills, teachers accept their products, point out the good use of skills, and make a few suggestions about improvement.

If they have an inkling of how to approach the task, most children will try creative endeavors. Regardless of the objective quality of their product, it has meaning for them which no one can measure. However, if what they produce also has meaning to others, its meaning to them is increased manyfold.

This introductory section has given you an overview of the information-processing skills. The part they play in children's learning is to help chil-

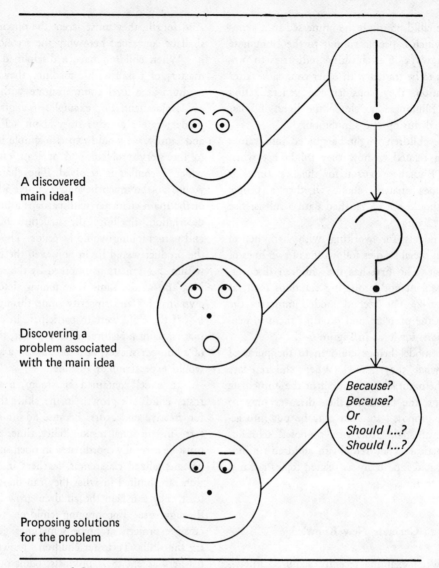

A discovered
main idea!

Discovering a
problem associated
with the main idea

Proposing solutions
for the problem

FIGURE 6–2. *Problem-discovery Model.*

dren learn more about social-studies ideas by arranging or expressing them in meaningful wholes, using them to solve problems, and generating new knowledge from them.

As the various techniques for helping the children learn the skills are discussed, you will notice again the application of the holistic and stage-by-stage strategies introduced in the previous chapter.

TECHNIQUES FOR GUIDING CHILDREN IN INTEGRATING KNOWLEDGE

When we guide children in performing tasks to help them integrate knowledge, we may sometimes be guiding them in developing structures which they think will serve, or we may be teaching them a formal skill consisting of subskills to be applied

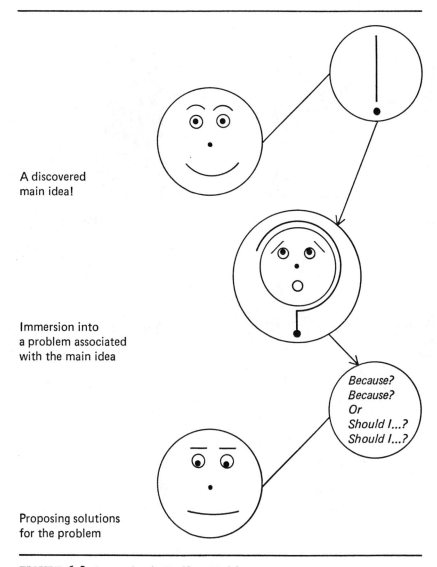

A discovered
main idea!

Immersion into
a problem associated
with the main idea

Because?
Because?
Or
Should I...?
Should I...?

Proposing solutions
for the problem

FIGURE 6–3. *Immersion in Problem Model.*

in sequence. What we do will often depend on: the nature of the content and study at hand or soon to be studied; the product, if any, of a previously exercised skill; and the age of the learners.

Two phases are possible, and both are recommended. First, the children organize the information to facilitate generalization, then they express the generalization in their own terms.

Learning to Organize Information

Tables or lists, charts of aspects, chronological diagrams, diagrams of relationships, flow charts, and polls are organizational structures in which facts are categorized in some way, placed in sequence, or tallied. The structure has to be analyzed for meaning. Graphs as organizational structures present the

ILLUSTRATION 6–1. *Some Young Children Participate in Organizing Information on a Graph.*

ILLUSTRATION 6–2. *Expressing Information in a Precise Way.*

facts and also express a statement. Often they may be read at a glance. As formal structures, graphs are more difficult for children to make. They will need much initial assistance and guidance in using them to express ideas. However, the other structures may often be developed by the children themselves, sometimes with little or no previous experience with using them. For the sake of brevity, we shall refer to these as informal structures.

When an informal structure is appropriate, the teacher often presents it. For example, after a second-grade class has experienced many facts about farming, the teacher prompts them to recall the facts about different kinds of farmers. As the children give these, the teacher lists them on the chalkboard. Later, as the children tell about the different products that each farmer grows or raises, the teacher simply extends the list to the right on the chalkboard by adding the products after each different kind of farmer, like this:

Dairy farmer	butter, milk, cheeses, ice cream
Poultry farmer	eggs, chickens, turkeys, ducks

Or the teacher of a fourth-grade class that has just acquired much information about natural resources and their uses may provide a large chart similar to the one seen in Figure 6–4. The diagram may be prepared on a large piece of paper or drawn crudely on the chalkboard.

Or a seventh-grade teacher whose class has just completed the study of the process of legislation may walk to the chalkboard and say, "Let's make a flow chart of the progress of a bill from the moment a legislator is aware that there is a need for it, until it becomes a law, and finally to the moment that its constitutionality is judged by the Supreme Court. What is the first event?"

For many of us, the practices described in the examples are simple, natural teaching acts. Sometimes with young children they are necessary.

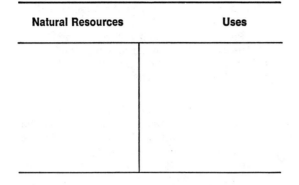

FIGURE 6–4. *Information Organization Chart.*

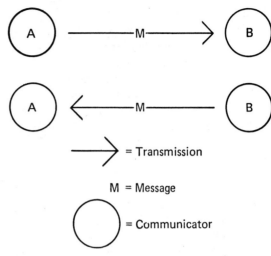

FIGURE 6–5. *Interpersonal-communication Model.*

However, beginning at grade three, the teacher may invite children's participation in deciding how knowledge is to be organized.

For example, the seventh-grade teacher could have invited participation in this way: "We have taken a careful look at how we get our federal laws. Do you have any ideas about a chart or diagram we might construct to show the entire process from beginning to end?"

Or the fourth-grade teacher might have shown a large, blank sheet of paper to the children and said something like this to the class: "Do you have any ideas about how we might list what we know about natural resources on this big sheet of paper?"

Some teachers prefer to give children a start. For example, the seventh-grade teacher might have drawn a caricature of an irate citizen on the chalkboard and said, "This represents Mr. Angry Public. He is upset by all the writing that people do on the alley walls of large stores, and he has managed to find a large number of people who are upset by the same thing. This is the possible beginning for a law. I am going to form you into small groups to finish a chart using sketches like these to show how a law is made and finally tested."

The fourth-grade teacher could have presented the chart with some lines drawn on it to suggest where listings might be made.

Let us suppose that a fifth-grade teacher guiding his children in the study of communication has used the diagram in Figure 6–5 to show what occurs during basic, interpersonal communication.

Drawing the diagram on the chalkboard, he says, "Earlier, when we finished studying about basic communication, I used this diagram to illustrate what occurs. Now we have just completed studying about mass communication. How might we use the same elements in the diagram to illustrate what occurs during mass communication?"

Occasionally young children may be encouraged to decide how information is to be organized. For example, a first grade has acquired a lot of information about different common occupations. At the close of each instructional period, the children drew pictures about an occupation. The teacher has a sample from each period. Pinning these out of order across a large bulletin board, the teacher asks the children, "Can you think of a way for us to arrange these pictures so that those that tell about the same person are all together?" Most likely, the children's organizational structure will be quite different from what the teacher has in mind, but it will have meaning to the first graders.

Informal structures provide opportunities for children to develop what they believe is appropriate and helps them gain a modicum of independence in organizing what they know.

In the previous chapter, it was suggested that children should make graphs to help them learn how to read them. If every opportunity for using graphs to express ideas has been used through the grades to develop mathematics skills, there is little need to spend much time teaching the skills. However, if children have had few opportunities to make and read graphs by the time they reach fifth grade, guide them through activities similar to these:

1. Guide the children in making a simple, one-to-one picture graph of the number of boys and girls in the classroom. Then have them make the same graph with abstract symbols with a one-to-two, or one-to-three correspondence (whichever is needed to ensure that a fraction of a symbol is used), and a bar graph expressing the same information.
2. Select some data that can be expressed on a bar graph. Here is an example:

Four car dealers, Mr. A, Mr. B, Mr. C, and Mr. D, have just reported their new-car sales for the month of April to the company that manufactures the cars they sell. This is what they report:
- Mr. A   60 cars
- Mr. B   43 cars
- Mr. C   29 cars
- Mr. D   11 cars

To encourage the dealers to try to sell more cars, the car company has a graph of their sales made to send them. At a glance, each car dealer will be able to see how well he is doing compared to the others.

Using these data, prepare a graph consisting of a mat and four overlays made of sheets of transparent plastic (felt pens containing carbon-base ink will leave permanent marks on plastic) as presented in Figure 6–6.
Using the graph mat and overlays, demonstrate the steps that a graph maker follows when making a bar graph:
a. Listing the entities to be compared.
b. Determining the value of each interval on the map.
c. Drawing the bars.
Use the fourth overlay, which shows the sales of the other car dealers, to check on the

children's understanding of the interval and its estimated fractions.
Provide the children with a comparable set of data and have them make a bar graph.
3. Select some data that can be expressed in a line graph. Here is an example:

Mr. D., a car dealer, is disappointed to learn that, compared to other car dealers, he has the poorest sales record. To improve sales, he has hired more salesmen and arranged for more advertising. He keeps a record of the sales for the next six months:
May	20 cars
June	19 cars
July	32 cars
August	37 cars
September	40 cars
October	46 cars
He makes a line graph to show his salesmen how well they have done.

Using these data, prepare a line graph consisting of a mat and five overlays, as shown in Figure 6–7.
Using the graph mat and overlays, demonstrate the steps taken to make a line graph:
a. Deciding on the trend to be plotted.
b. Determining the time intervals.
c. Determining the scale of measurement.
d. Determining the points and plotting the points.
e. Drawing the lines between the points.
Have the children compare the data as originally expressed and as expressed in the graph.
Use the last overlay, showing the sales for the next six months, to check on the children's understanding of the time and scale intervals. Have them express the data in prose and compare the results as expressed on the graph.
Provide the children with another set of data to use in constructing a graph.
When teaching the children about the line graph, you may wish to express the same data in a histogram and have them compare it with the line graph to detect similarities.
4. Similar procedures may be used to help children learn how to make circle graphs. Here is an example of a set of data that you could use:

Mary is preparing a report on the occupations of the people in New Zealand. She has these notes.
Workers in New Zealand

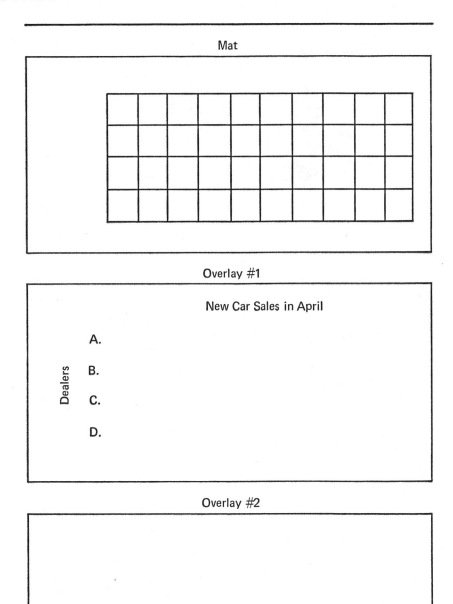

FIGURE 6–6. *Bar-graph Mat and Overlays.*

Overlay #3

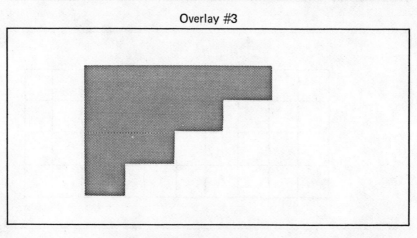

Overlay #4

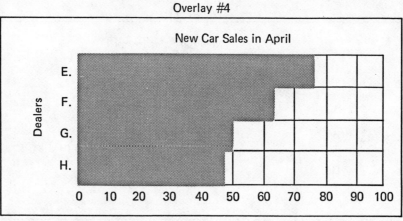

FIGURE 6–6. (*continued*)

Those who provide services (people who work in government, stores, schools, repair shops, etc.)   52%

Those who work in industry (people who work in factories, mines, mills, etc.)   36%

Those who work in agriculture (farmers, cattle and sheep raisers)   12%

To help her class see these facts at a glance, Mary makes a circle, or pie, graph.

See Figure 6–8 for examples of the graph mat and overlays that you would prepare.

The steps followed in making a circle graph include:

a. Drawing the circle and a radius within it to serve as an initial baseline.

b. Multiplying the percent representing the largest segment by 3.6 to determine the number of degrees in the circle that the segment will cover.

c. Using the baseline and a protractor to draw the segment.

d. Repeating steps 1 through 3 with each of the remaining segments, but using the line of the previously drawn segment as a baseline.

e. Providing another circle graph for the children to read.

f. Providing them with new data from which to make a circle graph.

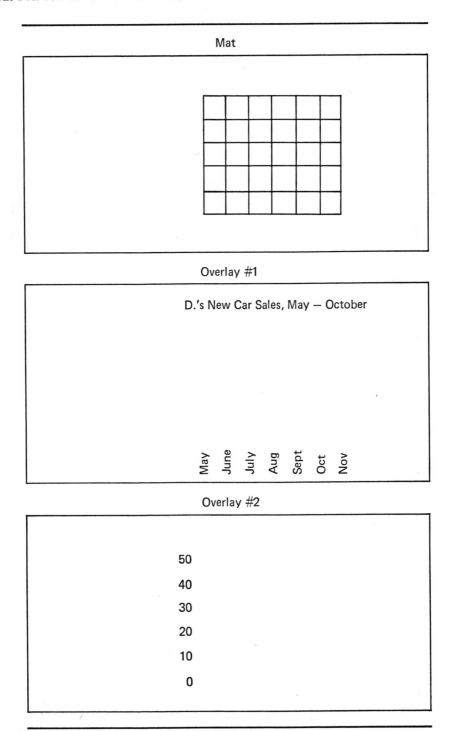

FIGURE 6–7. *Line-graph Mat and Overlays.*

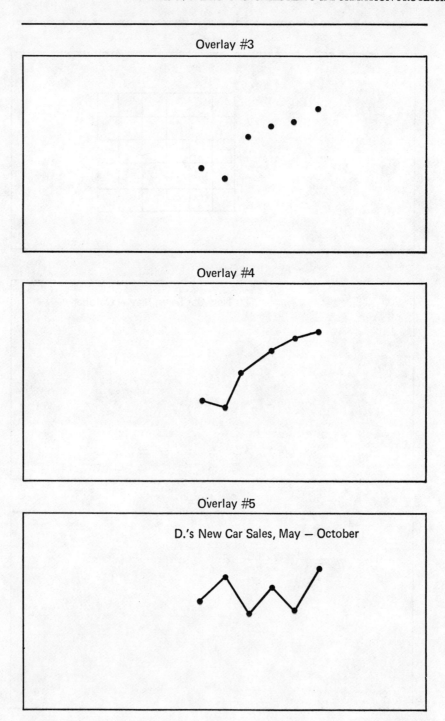

FIGURE 6–7. (*continued*)

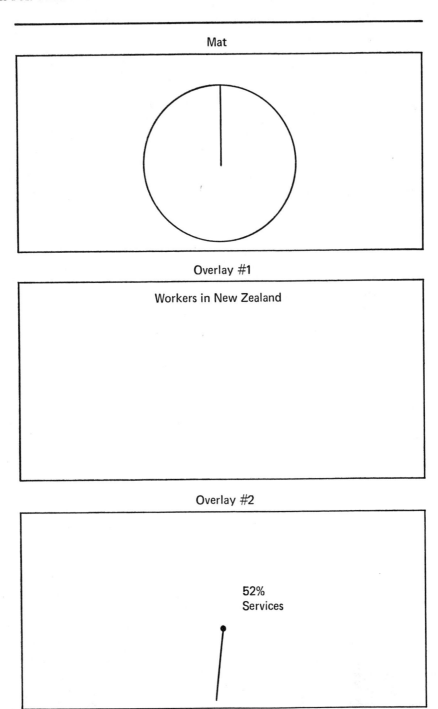

FIGURE 6–8. *Circle-graph Mat and Overlays.*

Overlay #3

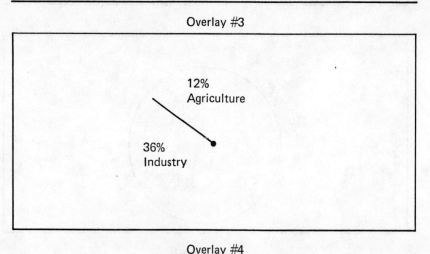

Overlay #4

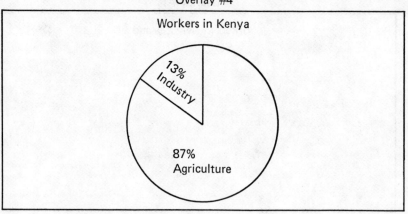

FIGURE 6–8. (*continued*)

In the above, emphasis is given to having children express data first in one way and then in another. This is essential to their learning to organize what they know in graphs.

There will be occasions when the children have categorized some numerical information in a list or on a chart of aspects. Such information may often be graphed.

In the previous chapter we discovered that map making is an initial activity in learning to read maps. However, the map making was re-stricted to mapping the immediate environment. In the later grades, children need additional instruction to draw maps of areas of greater size and of greater distance away.

The need for map drawing will vary from study to study. Often outline maps are provided for desk work. When the children need a large map, they may often make what they need by using a textbook map in an opaque projector to trace the image as shown on a large piece of paper. Occasionally children study areas, such as separate countries or states, for which no outline maps are immediately available. In this instance, you may try either of the following:

- Encourage the children to try to liken the area they wish to map to some common object or shape—Spain and Portugal together are shaped like a square, Italy like a boot or stocking, France like a house, California like a caterpillar making a half-turn down a tree, India like a huge inverted triangle, and so forth.
- Demonstrate how a larger or smaller area can be mapped by covering the map to be copied with a grid of squares (lines may be drawn on a sheet of transparent plastic to make a grid) and then drawing the map on a grid of penciled squares. The children will find that duplicating the line in each grid will result in an accurately drawn map of the proper proportions.

Young children studying about their community can use a large teacher-made map on which to organize their knowledge. Map drawing of states, countries, and continents begins at grade four and continues through the rest of the elementary grades.

Having children make relief maps helps them conceptualize the topography of an area, but with some obvious distortions in the elevation of hills and mountains. These distortions may be reduced by guiding the children in making a large relief map as a class project on as large a piece of plywood as can be accommodated in the classroom (and which can be carried comfortably by a teacher and a custodian). Having children make desk-sized maps on chipboard helps them conceptualize gross features of topography and their approximate location in a region. At any rate, after children have made relief maps, they should be guided in understanding that their representations are distorted, not because of carelessness on their part, but because of the nature of the medium with which they worked.

The procedures for making relief maps include:

1. Making an outline map on the board. Using a grid (not too fine) or an opaque projector works well for making the map on a large board. Desk maps may be traced on small boards.

Sometimes making relief maps leads children to conceptualize regions as islands. For this reason, the outline should also include indications of adjacent areas. These areas do not need to be reliefed, but they should be labeled on the finished product.

2. Covering or reliefing the surface. Flour, table salt, and water mixed in equal proportions produce a workable medium. The flour and salt are mixed first. The water is added gradually until a desirable consistency results. Sometimes, coarse salt is substituted for some of the table salt to make the mixture more stable.

Paper maché also works well as a reliefing medium.

When they are working with the flour and salt mixture encourage the children to place the mountains and hills first, then to cover the other areas by gradually reducing the elevations as they cover the flat areas. When they work with paper maché, they cover the entire area and add material to build elevations.

3. Drying the map. Just leave it in an open space until the features are hard enough to withstand brisk brush strokes.

4. Painting the map. Tempera paint is suitable for all maps regardless of size. Desk maps may be painted with water color. Often the colors used on topographical maps are also used on relief maps.

Usually the making of relief maps begins at fourth grade.

Activities for Making Replicas

Whenever we prompt children to draw a picture, make a model, diorama, puppet or set of puppets, or flannelgrams, or dramatize to recall and organize what they know, we expect a simple replica of what they have experienced during information seeking. Our intent is not to stimulate creativity, but to give the children an opportunity to organize what they know. The discipline of factual demands

ILLUSTRATION 6–3. *Young Children Make a Replica of a Bus with Cartons.*

ILLUSTRATION 6–4. *Using a Diorama to Integrate Information about the Westward Movement.*

limits creativity, but some children will make a creative response within the limitations. For example, a child in sixth grade may respond to the suggestion to make a diorama of the daily life of the Camayura Indians by producing a composition of figures and colors that conveys the mystery of primitive confidence within a foreboding Brazilian jungle. Whoever views it has a singular experience. However, the child's peers also produce dioramas which are factually accurate but mere reflections of what they had studied.

Frequently the skills of making replicas are simply those which most children have and like to use. Young children enter zestfully into activities in which they make things. Often they need little more than the sight of some materials and some stimulation on how they might be used. Here are a few examples:

- Indicating a large packing carton obtained at a furniture or appliance store, the teacher says to a kindergarten class: "How might we use this big box to make a home that we could play in as we learn about the family?"
- Indicating a stack of cartons obtained at a drugstore or supermarket, the teacher says to a kindergarten class: "How might we use this bunch of

boxes to make a tugboat in which some of us might pretend to be the captain and his crew?"

- Indicating a stack of dismantled cartons lying flat, the teacher asks a first-grade class: "How might we use these big pieces of cardboard to make an igloo?"
- Indicating a large dismantled carton lying flat on the floor, a stack of household boxes, and some toy vehicles, the teacher asks a first-grade class: "How might we put all these things together to show the work of the traffic policeman?"
- Indicating a dollhouse, some miniature furniture, and a set of figurines, the teacher asks a kindergarten class: "How might we use these things to show the jobs of the different people in the family?"
- Indicating a toy cash register and a large carton filled with empty cans and food and soap boxes, the teacher asks a first grade: "How might we use these things to show how a supermarket works?"
- Indicating a stack of board ends obtained at a lumber company or building-supply store, a teacher asks a first-grade class: "How might we use these blocks to make a complete community where people live, work, and play?"

As you can see in the above, the replicas that young children can make are simply settings. These the children will use for play activities in which they will apply what they have learned in social studies.

If you are a kindergarten or first-grade teacher working in an older school, you may find under a counter a stack of blocks resembling short pieces of two-by-four-inch lumber of various lengths from six inches to a couple of feet, and a few wooden arches. The blocks are stained and varnished. These are play blocks from which young children can make replicas of harbors, communities, airports, houses, or whatever. To avoid pandemonium, you will have to teach the children how to remove and store the blocks, and how to use them quietly.

Young children like to construct replicas such as trucks, boats, buses, airplanes, and the like. Some of the primary classrooms in older schools are also equipped with toolboxes containing small hammers, saws, and clamps. Unless you have had a course in industrial arts for children, avoid having children try to use the tools.

After young children have made their replicas, they use them as devices for simple recall, or at least so it will appear. The observant teacher will discover them having minor problems during their play and will use these to clarify misunderstandings or to extend study. For example, two children pushing toy vehicles toward each other discover that the street in their community replica is too narrow for them to pass. After a brief argument, one child lifts his automobile to allow the other to pass. The teacher uses this incident for a class discussion after play. The point of the discussion is what community planners must do when planning a city or when they discover they have made a mistake after the community is built.

Older children can construct remarkable models of vehicles, primitive villages, missions, futuristic cities, and the like, but the models are just that. They are past the stage of play with what they construct. Some older children who have difficulty with written composition can participate effectively in organizing knowledge by building models and discussing them orally with the class.

The well-conducted instructional program in art often supports the ways in which children can organize knowledge during social studies. The main characteristic of such a program is that it offers children sufficient repetitive exploration of techniques with a medium until they feel free to express with it.

When both the teacher and older children are at base zero, but they have an example of what would be appropriate for organizing knowledge, such as a set of unfired clay figurines, they may approach the task of making figurines through examining them and deciding how they might go about making them. For example, they might discuss such questions as these:

- How large a piece of clay will be needed?
- Should a figurine be carved or pinched, squeezed, poked, molded and the like, with the fingers? If fingers are not to be the main tools, what kinds of tools will be needed? How might they be obtained?
- Might a figurine need an internal support (armature)? If so, what should it be made from?

- Would a preliminary sketch be helpful? If so, how much detail should it show?
- How might color be applied?
- When should color be applied?

The discussion augmented by investigation in the library produces a workable approach. There may be a few errors, but the products are good enough for the purpose of organizing knowledge.

In most instances, before starting a replica of any kind, children need a readiness discussion to explore possibilities in content and to recall aspects of a technique.

Generally replica production is a favored activity among elementary school children in grades kindergarten through six. Children in grades seven and eight who develop strong interests in the social-studies area under study may wish to make replicas as individual projects.

Activities for Learning to Summarize and Report

Summarization and report composition are the "tell-it-in-your-own-words" organizational structures. Both require the careful exercise of certain language and thinking skills, but most children can be guided in learning and using the skills in social studies. As a matter of fact, social studies offers realistic opportunities for using the skills.

At all grade levels something can be done to help children learn the necessary skills.

Let us consider summarization, the easier of the two, first.

Toward the end of a social-studies period, after information has been acquired and discussed, the teacher may assist children in kindergarten and first grade in summarizing. For example:

After a kindergarten has heard and discussed the duties of the zookeeper, the teacher asks, "Let us think about the really important things that a zookeeper does at the zoo. What was the first thing we learned about?"

"He feeds the animals," responds a volunteer.

"I remember that. Do the rest of you remember? I can see that you do, and you probably want to tell

ILLUSTRATION 6–5. *Making Certain That a Written Report Meets Criteria.*

what he feeds the different animals. But right now we are just talking about the main things he does. Can anyone else think of another?"

"He eats his lunch," responds another volunteer.

"Yes, he does that. That helps us remember he is a person just like us. But what else does he do for the animals?"

"He cleans out their cages," says another volunteer.

"Good! That is important. Is there anything else? . . . Does he sometimes help another worker at the zoo?"

"He sometimes helps the zoo doctor with sick animals."

"Very good. We have learned three important things about the zookeeper's work. We learned first that he feeds the animals. Then we learned that he cleans the animals' cages. And finally we learned that he sometimes helps the zoo doctor with sick animals. All these ideas make a summary of what we learned today."

As exemplified above, summarization in kindergarten and first grade is an oral activity in which the teacher elicits main ideas from the children, repeats them in sequence, and identifies them in total as a summary. Toward the close of successive social-studies periods the teacher will encourage the children to recall the summarization act by

• Asking them whether they remember what they did toward the end of the period on the previous day.
• Asking whether there is anyone who can tell what a summary is.
• Asking them to recall what they usually do during the end of the social-studies period.
• Presenting a summary and encouraging the children to consider how accurate it is.
• Encouraging the children to tell a puppet how to summarize their lesson.

In grades two and three the teacher records the summaries given by the children. They may also process summaries for accuracy or direct a puppet in preparing a summary.

ILLUSTRATION 6–6. *Deciding Which Pictures Represent Ideas Studied Today.*

In grade four, the children are guided in learning how to prepare independent written summaries of lessons and what they have discovered through listening, discussing, or reading. These summaries serve as the children's individual records of what they have experienced. They are useful for review and for organizing information for an entire social-studies unit.

The same useful purposes are served when children learn to summarize independently. Independent summarization is taught at grade four. The summaries serve as children's independent records of what they have experienced.

If the children have had experience with much summarization during the early grades, the transition to the independently written summary is easier. However, the shift to individual responsibility requires additional, direct instruction.

If you find that your fourth-grade learners have had much experience with the teacher recording their summaries in group or class situations, you may guide them in the study of a model similar to that in Figure 6–9. Presenting the model to the children, have them study it to see whether they can see the relationship between the summary and the complete text. If you prefer, you may have them study the model in small, impromptu groups who, after their study, compare their discoveries. Close the lesson by having the children generalize what a summary is, or the steps that one might follow in making a summary.

Another study model that you might use is similar to the above, except that you present three summaries from which the children select the best. For example, the summary given in Figure 6–9 would be labeled "Summary A." Two additional summaries, as seen in Figure 6–10, would also be offered. This model would be used in the same way as the other. It assumes that the children have a limited concept of what a summary is. As they study the model to determine which is the best summary, their concept is strengthened. Only the first summary contains all the main ideas in the text. The others, serving as foils, contain omissions, ideas out of order, and the use of supporting ideas instead of main ideas.

Asia

Summary. Asia is the largest continent in the world. More than half the world's people live there. Because of its size, temperatures are different. It contains many different kinds of land. The people there are very different from each other.

Asia is the largest of the continents. It is as big as North America and South America put together. It is larger than Europe and Africa combined.

More than half the people of the world live in Asia. Most of the people live in very crowded areas. Much of it is open space with very few people living on it.

Asia is so large that it has very different temperatures from place to place. It gets very cold in the north in the winter. In some places it is cool all year long. In the south it gets very hot.

Just about every kind of land that you can think of is found in Asia. Some of the tallest mountains in the world are found there. There are also deserts, jungles, forests, grasslands, and lands where crops can be grown.

The people in Asia are made up of many different groups. Some have light skin and others are dark. Some are tall and others are short. They have many different ways of living.

FIGURE 6–9. *Study Model for Summarizing.*

The models serve as introductions. You may use either the holistic or stage-by-stage strategy. If you use the former, you provide a sequence of activities in which the children write summaries from a selection of texts. Choosing only the main ideas is emphasized. Paraphrasing is also stressed. The practice continues until the children can summarize accurately.

When following the stage-by-stage strategy, provide opportunities for the children to work on various aspects of summarizing to anchor the concept of summarization in their minds before they attempt to summarize independently. All the activities would focus on summaries. Here is a sequence of such activities in which the children are analyzing summaries and the texts on which they are based:

1. The children detect main ideas out of order.
2. They look for omitted main ideas.
3. They detect supporting ideas used as main ideas.
4. They look for poor paraphrases and change them to adequate paraphrases.
5. They rate summaries as good or poor and tell what is wrong with them.

Such a sequence of activities requires an abundance of duplicated summaries and texts, but once the materials are prepared, they may be used repeatedly with future classes.

The use of written material is recommended first because a text is permanent and can be consulted again and again. When the children are able to summarize under such controlled situations, you may guide them in summarizing indepen-

Summary B. More than half the people in the world live in Asia. It is a very large continent. It gets very cold there in some places. There are some very tall mountains there. Some of the people are short and some of them are tall.

Summary C. The largest continent in the world is Asia. Many people live there. The land is very different from place to place. There are tall mountains and deserts. The temperatures are different from place to place. Asia must be a very strange place.

FIGURE 6–10. *Foil Summaries.*

dently class discussions, group discussions, and what they hear and/or view on audiotapes, films, filmstrips, and videotapes.

If you prefer, you may begin concentrated instruction in summarizing by having the children make independent summaries of class discussions. Each trial is discussed in class to help the children see their own growth or needs for improvement.

As you have probably noticed, summarizing is similar to outlining main ideas. When the children have learned one of these skills before the other, instruction in one skill supports the other.

Skill in summarizing takes children a long way toward becoming independent in organizing knowledge for their own purposes in social studies. The strategies suggested for teaching children to summarize may also be used in teaching them how to report.

Reporting has a social function in the sense that the report conveys ideas to others. Often children take the responsibility to investigate a topic or issue to report their findings to others. Thus they perform a service for others. This social function can serve as an emphasis. It involves making an interesting introduction, conveying information, and indicating the significance of the information.

During the sharing or show-and-tell period, young children in kindergarten and first grade can be assisted in making simple reports about things that interest them. The teacher uses verbal cues which help the children organize their thoughts. Figure 6–11 shows examples of verbal cues, their intents, and the likely responses that might be made to them in a situation in which a child has brought a picture of a truck to share with the others.

Repeated verbal cuing brings some children to the point of reporting independently as they share. Others will forget one of the intents and need to be cued.

Children in third grade may be taught to follow visual cues on a chart similar to the one in Figure 6–12. The teacher may introduce the chart to the class by having the children read and discuss its contents. Then, to illustrate how it serves as a guide, the teacher gives several reports, either directly or through the use of a puppet. The children listen to each report and decide whether the reporter was using the guide properly. Or the teacher and the puppet may compete, each giving a report about the same topic. Sometimes both give acceptable reports, or neither one does, or only one does. After the chart has been introduced, the class uses it to evaluate reports during sharing.

At grade four, independent report writing is introduced. If the children have had experiences with oral reporting discussed above, they already have a workable concept of what a report is. If they have been guided systematically in developing handwriting, spelling, and sentence-composition skills, the transition to the written report focuses

Verbal Cues	Intents of Cues	Responses
"What did you bring to share with us this morning, Jan?"	An interesting introduction.	"I brought this picture of a truck."
"And where did you find it?"	An interesting introduction.	"I found it in a magazine I was looking at last night."
"Tell us more about it."	Conveying information.	"Well, it was a big truck and it is going at night. It has two men in it."
"Why do you like the picture?"	Indicating significance.	"I brought it because I like big trucks."

FIGURE 6–11. *Structure for Cuing Reporting.*

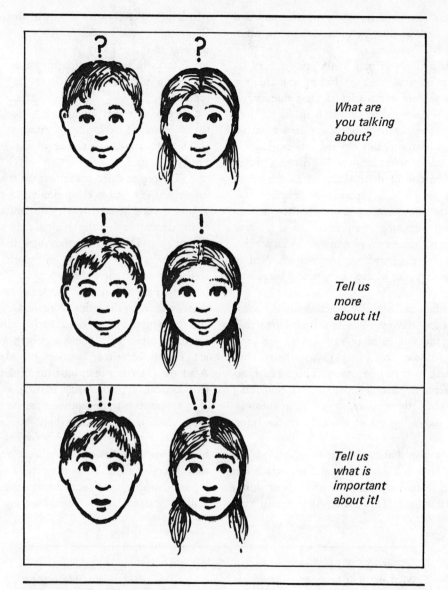

FIGURE 6–12. *Visual Cues for Reporting.*

on learning to write paragraphs. Here is a sequence of suggested procedures:

1. Guide the children in a review of the social functions of a report. A chart similar to the one discussed above will be helpful.
2. Using the content of a unit section, guide the children in responding to the cues on the chart or the generalizations surfaced during the review, and guide the children in composing a single sentence in response to each cue or generalization. Write these on the chalkboard leaving enough space under each sentence to write more.
3. After all the sentences have been composed,

guide the children in extending each sentence with more sentences composed to convey facts about it.

4. Guide the children in analyzing their class product to generalize about how it was composed.
5. Repeat steps 1 and 2 with later sections of social-studies content until the children respond so easily and volubly that they show they no longer need the teacher's assistance.

The above is a holistic strategy that works well in grades four through six.

If the children in a fourth or later grade show that they have a limited concept of what a report is, you may begin with a variation of the strategy described for a third grade:

1. Prepare a chart showing the social functions of a report.
2. Present the chart and have the children read and discuss it.
3. Demonstrate its use by giving two or three brief oral reports based on recently studied social-studies content.
4. Provide for the children to have independent, oral reports based on recently studied social-studies content. They will find it easier to report if they use a map, picture, or set of pictures in their textbook as an aid in conveying information.

When each child has had an opportunity to give an oral report and to have it evaluated by the class, guide the children in learning to compose written reports.

Children in seventh and eighth grades can often profit from a study model similar to the one in Figure 6–13.

Use the model in this way:

1. Duplicate the model for class distribution.
2. Present it and discuss it with the children. Encourage them to generate other beginning paragraphs that would be interesting. Focus their attention on the order in the middle paragraph and how order helps in presenting facts. Have them generate other kinds of final paragraphs that would bring the report to a satisfying close.
3. Guide the children in experimenting with the report by reading it several times and omitting one of the paragraphs each time to see the result.
4. Choosing a topic well-documented with facts during recent study, have the children try their hand at writing a report. When they are fin-

---

The Parts of a Report

The title: tells what the report is about.

The beginning paragraph: introduces the topic of the report in an interesting way.

The middle paragraph: offers facts about the topic of the report.

(A report may have many middle paragraphs.)

The end of the report: tells what is important to remember about the topic.

Balloons

Almost two hundred years ago a way to fly balloons was discovered. Two inventors in France made a huge balloon of linen. They filled it with smoke and hot air. It rose in the air, carrying a passenger load of a rooster, a sheep, and a duck. It stayed in the air for ten minutes, covering a mile and a half.

This first successful balloon encouraged others to find some real uses for it. A way was discovered to make balloons more manageable in the wind. Weights in the basket could be thrown overboard to make it rise. Its gas could be released to make it come down. Finally inventors were able to discover how to make long balloons and to attach engines, propellers, and rudders to them. These new balloons were called dirigibles. During the 1930's, dirigibles carried passengers between Europe and America. Unfortunately, they were filled with easily burning gas. Some terrible accidents brought an end to their use.

Today a few people fly balloons just for the excitement of it. They use the old-fashioned balloons without engines. For most of us the balloon reminds us of an interesting age in the development of aviation.

FIGURE 6–13. *Study Model for Reporting.*

ished, have them share their reports with the class, which evaluates them for completeness and reacts to various aspects of each paragraph.

As each of the next two or three topics are studied in social studies, the children write reports about them and have them evaluated by the class. Basically, this is a holistic strategy.

A stage-by-stage strategy may be used with children in grades four through six. This requires a study model consisting of at least two reports, only one of which is suitable. For example, the one presented in the model above could be used. To serve as a foil against which it is to be compared, another report is written. It lacks a title, begins in a lame, uninteresting way, presents facts out of order, contains extraneous material, and has a dull, nonconclusive ending. As the children compare the two reports to determine which they would have rather written, the foil report brings the qualities of the acceptable report into sharp relief. The comparison of the reports may be conducted as a class-wide activity or as a task for small, impromptuly formed groups.

After the children generalize about their discoveries, they are guided into activities in which they study reports. The tasks they perform include the following:

- Identifying the function of one of a pair of paragraphs.
- Identifying which paragraph is omitted from reports presented as two-paragraph reports.
- Placing the paragraphs of a report in the correct order.
- Identifying extraneous material in reports.
- Rating reports as good or poor.
- Writing beginning paragraphs for reports in which both the middle and final paragraphs are given.
- Writing final paragraphs for reports in which both the beginning and middle paragraphs are given.

In this strategy, children do not write reports independently until they are able to perform all the above tasks successfully.

This strategy requires an abundance of special materials. Preparing them can be facilitated through using reports which children in previous classes have written. Actually, the preparation of such materials is a project for two or three dedicated teachers.

After the children are able to write simple reports about topics and facts studied by the entire class, they are guided toward complete independence in composing reports by gaining a satisfactory mastery of locating information, note taking, and outlining skills. When these skills are combined with those of report composition, the children are ready to investigate and report on their own. The outline also serves a useful purpose as a way of arranging notes for an oral report.

As children are guided in integrating knowledge, they are dealing with it as objective matter, although they are doing it in terms of their own insights and with whatever level of skills they can use. At the close of each social-studies lesson, young children may be involved in two integrating activities—working with the teacher to develop a summary and making a replica. Older children may be organizing information and summarizing. As an important section of a unit or the entire unit is coming to a close, children may be involved in three integrative activities—organizing information, summarizing, and reporting or making replicas. Whatever is important to know of social-studies content emerges during the integrating activities.

GUIDING CHILDREN IN APPLYING SOCIAL-STUDIES KNOWLEDGE

In an earlier chapter we treated the exploration of values. There we discussed the teaching methodology used when guiding children in in-depth discussions, case studies, role playing, and simulation, and asserted that, if total learning is to occur, children need to explore for values within the knowledge they have acquired in social studies. This exploration is an application of knowledge to arrive at a personal meaning.

When we deal with values exploration, we

may consider it broadly as an activity which may be prompted at any time regardless of a knowledge base. Here, however, we shall consider it as proceeding from a knowledge base. The knowledge is of an environment which has its own objective existence. Values exploration accomplishes a fusion between the existing environment and human existence at a personal level.

Here we shall consider only the possibilities for these activities within the different kinds of social-studies content.

Opportunities for In-depth Discussion

Every study in social studies, be it of process, relationship, culture, system, or region, has at least one issue related to it. No process, or whatever, is perfect. All are improvable in some way. And in-depth discussion is a traditional way of applying knowledge from a personal point of view.

The following questions to be used as prompters for in-depth discussions are a brief sampling of the possibilities in the various study areas, which, for the sake of brevity, are listed under systems.

POLITICAL SYSTEM

For Young Children

- If you were a mother or father, what rules do you think you should make for your children?
- How do you think you should act toward a policeman?
- If you see a friend taking something that is not his, what do you think you should do about it?

For Older Children

- How do you think people should decide on the rules they need to be able to live together?
- How do you think people should decide on which candidate for public office they should vote for during an election?
- Do you think that candidates for public office should pay their own campaign costs or that these costs should be supported by public funds? Why?

ECONOMIC SYSTEM

For Young Children

- What do you think boys and girls should do at the supermarket to make sure that the workers there do not have extra work to do?
- What do you think boys and girls should do to help their parents make good use of the things in the home?
- How do you think the workers at the service station should act toward the people who come to buy gasoline and other things?

For Older Children

- How do you think the producer of an item should decide on the price for which the item is to be sold?
- What do you think the members of a union should do to get a fair wage for their work?
- How do you think that goods and services should be advertised?

SOCIAL SYSTEM

For Young Children

- How do you think brothers and sisters should act toward each other in the home?
- What do you think boys and girls should do to help a new person in the classroom?
- What do you think that friends should do to make up after they have had a fight or argument?

For Older Children

- What do you think is a family's biggest problem in maintaining good relationships between the parents and the children? What do you think they should do about it?
- How do you think old people should be treated?
- How do you think criminals should be punished for what they do?

CULTURAL SYSTEM

For Young Children

- How do you think you should act toward another boy or girl whose skin color and way of talking is very different from yours?
- How do you think that boys and girls who go to different churches should act toward each other?
- Everybody is expected to eat nicely. Do you think that everyone should? Why? What do you think

we should do about people who do not eat nicely?

For Older Children

- Almost every nation contains some native tribes whose members are only a very small part of the total population. How do you think the people of a nation should treat their native tribes?
- What do you think we should do about the changes brought about in our lives because of changes in technology?
- What do you think a nation consisting of three or four different peoples whose ways of living are very different should do about these differences?

HISTORICAL SYSTEM

If a study is historical, questions similar to the above are composed within a historical perspective:
- What do you think the people should have done . . . ?
- If you had been alive then, what do you think you should have done . . . ?
- What do you think we should do today to ensure that the same thing does not happen to people in the future . . . ?

REGIONAL SYSTEM

If a study is primarily regional, the questions are composed within a geographical perspective:
- What do you think those people should do about . . . ?
- If you were living in that country, what do you think you should do about . . . ?

An in-depth discussion with young children usually lasts for only a few minutes. It is primarily allowing everyone who wishes to say something to respond. When asked for their reasons for thinking the way they do, they respond in a variety of ways: "That's the way I think." "Because I think so." "That's what my Daddy says." Or they may give a logical response that perhaps does not agree with yours but is undeniably logical.

Older children in fourth grade and above are capable of much greater depth, but often become bored when the in-depth discussion becomes an interaction between the teacher and a few loquacious individuals. However, having the children respond

in impromptu groups and then sharing the group responses generally ensures more active participation, a temporary group cohesiveness which lends urgency to the discussion, and greater depth in the discussion.

To a certain extent, an in-depth discussion is involved in the use of case studies, role playing, and simulations. Each is basically a way of being introduced to a problem, and a discussion always occurs at the point of evaluation.

Opportunities for Case Studies

A case study, be it a short story, a vignette excerpted from a novel, story, or feature article, an editorial, a news article, a letter, or a set of notes, presents a slice of the reality that the children have already explored factually and generalized about. It features an opinion or an action taken or contemplated to which the children react. It may be used at any grade level with any area of study, the only restriction being that it should be expressed in a way that children can understand it.

The authors of social-studies textbooks sometimes create case studies for children to work with. Some teachers do the same. When working with children in grades kindergarten through four, the teacher may seek material in the children's reading textbooks, children's magazines, or books written for children. Suitable material may be found in these resources, but not in abundance. At these grade levels, the teacher has to adapt material or create it. Figure 6–14 is an example of an adaptation of a "letter to the editor" to be used with a fourth-grade class that has been studying urban development.

The children would read or listen to this case study and react through discussion to the opinion and facts expressed. They might agree with the mayor and the council or the letter writer, or they might make recommendations about controlled city growth and how it might be accomplished.

After a first grade has studied about the fireman as a worker for the community, the teacher might prepare a case study similar to the one in

Dear Editor:

I don't think that the mayor and the city council can even think about trying to make our city into a manufacturing city. For a long time they have tried to make our city into a place where people from all over the country and world come to spend their vacations. So many people come that we who live in the city and pay taxes cannot enjoy our own city. We have to wait for hours to play golf or tennis. We even have to wait a long time to get dinner at the good restaurants. The mayor and the council have not helped us who live in the city. Perhaps they have helped the few people who run businesses that make money from visitors.

If our city became a manufacturing city, more people would come here. More buildings would be built. And, before you know it, our city would be just another big city with too many people and ugly buildings, and hidden in smog. Our city is fast becoming that way now.

I think that people who want to come to live in our city should be told the truth. The truth is that we have more people out of work than most cities our size have. If more people come here, they will spoil our city and they won't do themselves any good.

The mayor and the city council should not be encouraging any more people to come here to build and work in factories. The city is almost ruined for those who live and work in it now.

John Doe
The City

FIGURE 6–14. *A Letter Adapted to Serve as a Case Study.*

Figure 6–15 for the children to hear and discuss. The children listen to the story and discuss who was right, Mr. M or the boys, and why.

Children in grades five through eight can often work with case-study materials excerpted from published letters and diaries, newspapers, news magazines, and the like.

Opportunities for Role Playing

At any time that an area of study can be translated into terms of interpersonal conflict, role playing may be used as a device to facilitate children's

Timmie W. and Billie G. are playing in a vacant lot near a store.

"Look at what I have," says Timmie to Billie. He shows Billie a book of matches.

"Where did you get them?" asks Billie.

"At home," replies Timmie, "I thought it would be fun for us to build a fire. We can pretend that we are out camping."

"Let's find a place to build a fire," says Billie. "We'll need some paper and sticks."

There was just such a place beside the store. The boys gathered some paper and sticks and piled them up.

"That will make a good fire," says Billie. "Let me have the matches."

"No," says Timmie, "They are mine. I will light the fire."

"If you can't make the matches work, you will have to let me try," says Billie.

Timmie tore a match out of the book, just the way he had seen his father do it. He tried to make it light. Once, twice, three times he tried, but the match would not light.

"It's my turn," yells Billie.

"No, wait a minute. This match is just no good."

"Let me have them!"

"Maybe you had better let me have those matches," the boys heard a deep voice say. They looked up and saw Mr. M., the fireman who lived on their street.

"They are my father's matches," says Timmie, "I have to take them home to him."

"You had better give them to me," said Mr. M. "You boys should not have matches. I will give them to your father."

Timmie gave Mr. M. the matches.

"I'll see that your father gets these matches," says Mr. M. as he turns and walks away.

"I think Mr. M. is mean," says Timmie.

"So do I," says Billie, "Let's go over to my house and play."

FIGURE 6–15. *Case Study for First Grade.*

application of knowledge. Here is a list of a few possible conflicts that we can associate with various areas of study:

Political System

Parent and child
Citizen and citizen

Policeman and citizen
Legislator and constituent
Legislator and legislator
Governor and legislator
Governor and citizen
Candidate and voter

Economic System

Producer and consumer
Union and management
Boss and worker
Wholesaler and retailer
Governor and producer
Producer and producer
Consumer and consumer
Advertiser and consumer

Social System

Parent and child
Peer and peer
Insider and outsider
Class and class
Superior and subordinate
Old and young
Man and woman
Rich and poor

Cultural System

The culture and the individual
The innovator and the defender of the status quo
Culture and culture

When we convey these conflicts through our descriptions of role-playing situations, we communicate the problem as it may affect human behavior. The children accept the problem and use their persons to discover alternative solutions.

Because of its demands on children's concentration and imagination, we do not usually guide them into role playing before fourth grade. Older children can learn to use it effectively as a tool for applying what they know.

Opportunities for Simulations

Simulations may also be developed from instances of interpersonal conflict. Sometimes children may be divided into pairs or larger groups in which each member has a particular role. For example, three children may simulate the roles of the members of a legislative committee considering a controversial bill. One member has a strongly held view, another holds an opposite view just as strongly, and the third has not made up his mind yet. The purpose is for the children to see how legislators try to get undecided peers to side with them—logical argument, identifying a number of other, powerful legislators who support their view, reminding about a past favor, offering a promise of future support, or whatever. A simulation such as this helps children to apply what they know about political process and provides a deeper insight into the work of the legislator.

Other simulations will have children in groups which oppose each other—labor versus management, rebels against loyalists, immigrants versus aborigines, and the like.

Simulations similar to those discussed above require that the participants have a rich informational background at a high level of abstraction. Usually children are not able to prepare for and participate in such simulations until grade seven.

Simulations may have the children using the skills of social scientists. One of the most popular has been an archeology simulation in which the children make a dig in a specially prepared area containing coins, pottery shards, tools, bones, and the like. The children find the objects, label them, describe where they were found, and make interpretations about the lives of the people who used them. Such a simulation gives children insights into the work of archeologists.

Other simulations may have the children working with sets of data. For example, children may simulate a group of sociologists analyzing the results of a questionnaire. Just as they complete their interpretation, they are informed that there has been a mistake in the sampling. They are given the results of the new questionnaire in which a correct sampling has been involved. The children compare the results of the two questionnaires. The various groups compare their interpretations during the postdiscussion.

These simulations help children develop social-science values. Whenever they read about a dig or the results of a questionnaire, they will bring a special dimension of meaning to any interpretation they make. These kinds of simulations may be suitable for children in grades five through eight.

After studying a culture, the children may simulate a tribe, clan, or family as it responds to a problem characteristic of the culture—coping with a dwindling food supply, a disaster which destroys shelters, trading with another group to obtain desired goods, exploring for ways to maintain peace with another group, etc. Beginning in grade four, children may be able to acquire the necessary knowledge to participate in such simulations.

Young children usually lack the social skills to be involved in simulations of conflict. They may participate in simulations involving dyads or triads, treating simple problems within short periods of interaction. For example, they may simulate small families trying to decide on the five most important items to take on a camping trip in the forest. They must know what the forest provides and the kinds of tools and appliances that people can take on such camping trips. Children in second grade may participate in such a simulation.

Older children usually participate enthusiastically and effectively in simulations of conflict.

Opportunities for Values Clarification

Social studies carries children far into abstractions about peoples, systems, regions, processes, and relationships. Values-clarification techniques may be used to help children see a connection between these abstractions and their immediate lives as persons.

For example, after young children have learned about the trash collector's work in helping the people of the community dispose of waste, they might be guided in responding to a value questionnaire similar to the following:

1. Do you think a trash collector has to be strong?
2. Do you think it is fun to be a trash collector?
3. Do you think that trash collectors like their work?

4. Do you think that trash collectors believe they are helping other people by collecting trash?
5. Do you think people should help trash collectors by putting their trash out in good containers?
6. Do you think that trash collectors are important to you?
7. Do you think that trash collectors like people to say "Hello" to them as they do their work?

The children would respond on simple response sheets. Afterward, they may be guided in sharing their opinions.

In the above, guilt-prompting questions such as, *Would you like to be a trash collector?* or *Would you like your father or mother to be a trash collector?* have been omitted. Granted, such questions would prompt a review of values. They also could serve to surface a bias so strong that other considerations would be obliterated and forgotten.

However, the third question might be suitable for older children who have investigated the hours worked, salaries earned, and benefits enjoyed by trash collectors. The second question could shatter a child whose parent is a trash collector, especially when he or she experienced the responses of classmates.

The choice of trash collector for values clarification here was deliberate. It serves as a reminder of precautions that need to be taken when guiding children in values clarification.

Because people are involved in just about everything studied in social studies, feelings, attitudes, beliefs, and actions toward others can prompt values clarification at the close of the study of most units. In the above example we have touched on values related to community service workers. Workers in other occupations, including those who produce useful services as well as products within the immediate, state, national, and international community are always fit subjects for values clarification. So are historical figures, peoples, and events. In some instances, processes such as manufacturing, mining, conservation, and the like are also suitable subjects.

Generally, values clarification brings children to a fuller appreciation of persons everywhere as well as a deeper concept of interdependence.

Opportunities for Value Analysis

When children in grades six through eight are prompted to do a values analysis of concepts central to their study, they make an exacting application of the facts and generalizations they have learned. Indeed, their use of these is an indication of what they have really learned. For example, the child who completes a values analysis in which the value object is the Constitution (after studying it) must surface both pro's and con's about his value rating of it. If he understands the Constitution, he will be able to do this. If he does not, he can only parrot some of the provisions for government and the safeguarding of individual rights in the pro column.

Issues related to the thematic concepts of change, region, diversity, power, social organization, Self, Other, scarcity, and the like, are suitable subjects for value analysis. Here is a partial list of issue-laden terms related to these concepts:

Unions
Management
"Big business"
Crime
Housing
Capital punishment
Price system
Individual rights
Conservation
Governmental regulations
Sex education
Abortion
Family planning
Public education
Socialism
Career planning
Marriage
Consumers' rights
Affirmative action
Secrecy in government
Foreign aid
Military alliances
Monopoly
International trade agreements
Wage and price control
Welfare
Censorship
Gun control
Income tax

Few studies in which children in the later grades are involved lack an issue-laden term to serve as a focus for values analysis.

As you plan social-studies units, you will need to give careful thought to how you will be guiding your learners to apply the factual knowledge and ideas they have acquired.

A question about another kind of application arises at this point. The question: might we use paper-and-pencil tests in which children solve problems related to social studies? The answer: yes, it is possible. However, children's language and thinking skills are such that in-depth discussions, reacting to case studies, role playing, and participating in simulations, values clarification, and values analysis, are more suitable and effective.

GUIDING CHILDREN IN GENERATING KNOWLEDGE

As we encourage children to use their social-studies knowledge in creative endeavors, they select those aspects of reality which have meaning for them and invent new knowledge. It is the knowledge of what might have been, may be, or perhaps will be. In this sense it is new.

As stated earlier, about all that we can do realistically as social-studies teachers is to foster growth in the skills involved and provide opportunities for the exercise of the skills. The latter presents few problems, but the former can present difficulties, especially when administrative arrangements appear to mitigate against a concern for the creative use of dramatic, literary, and other art skills.

But there is a way to surmount the difficulties. It lies in the point of view that drama, literature, and the other fine arts support the tentative generalizations discovered by social scientists. Our understanding and appreciation of persons, peoples, moments, forces, products, conditions, systems, or whatever, deepens as we experience creative expressions and interpretations. If we have this point of view, we include the products of art as resources for information. We also use them as examples of how some men and women respond to the human condition.

We also recognize children's need for new experience and the ways of seeking it through creativity. No list of prescribed units or textbooks is so vital to children's learning that all must be covered at the neglect of opportunities for children to try to generate new knowledge.

Creative-dramatics Activities

Because social studies focuses so strongly on human activity, the opportunities for creative dramatics are many. As a form of expression it may have children probing deeply within themselves and their experience to create the rhythm and grace of a worker or vehicle, the wonder and force of a moment, or a moving characterization of a historical personage.

As social-studies teachers, we do not teach the skills. We elicit them. Here are a few examples of how we work:

The children in a kindergarten have learned much about the airport. Toward the close of their unit of study, the teacher gathers them on the rug. After a brief discussion in which they recall and describe the various vehicles they have studied, the teacher says, "On our trip to the airport we saw many airplanes landing and taking off. Do you remember that one big jetliner far away on the runway as it took off? Let's close our eyes to see if we can get a picture of it in our minds. I'll tell what I remember as you sit with your eyes closed. Ready? The jetliner has just turned. It is ready to take off. It begins to move . . . slowly . . . slowly . . . now a little faster . . . and faster. . . . Now it is lifting . . . lifting . . . gently it lifts its nose toward the sky . . . up . . . up . . . and it begins to make a slow turn . . . turning . . . turning . . . and now it is gone! Open your eyes. How many of you thought you could really see it? Good!

"Let's have everyone stand. Stretch out your hands and arms to the side and then to the front. If you touch any of your neighbors, move far enough away from them so that you won't touch them. That means we'll have to spread out a lot. That's fine.

"I would like for one of you to come up here to show us with the movement of an arm how the big jetliner moves as it takes off when we see it far away. Jessie, do you want to show us? Hold your arm straight out from your side. Pretend that your hand is the jetliner. Show us how it goes."

ILLUSTRATION 6–7. *Integrating Ideas and Making Discoveries through Creative Dramatics.*

Jessie demonstrates a sweeping movement performed with greater speed than grace. But it is a start.

"That is fine, Jessie. You make me feel that I'm standing quite close to the jetliner. Do it again, Jessie. Let's see whether we can all make the jetliner take off like Jessie does. Let's all follow Jessie. Please do it, Jessie, and all of us will do what you do."

The class follows. Then they move their arms to show three jetliners taking off in succession. The teacher notices one child who is turning completely around gracefully and ending the movement with her hand stretched high in the air as she stands on her tiptoes.

"You may stop now," the teacher asserts. "I just saw Jean doing something different. Jean, will you please show what you were doing?"

Jean demonstrates her movement several times. Some children are already imitating her before she completes her last movement. The teacher smiles and motions for everyone to try the movement.

More individual creations are noticed and tried.

During subsequent periods, the children explore movements for the landing of jetliners, using their whole bodies as jetliners, creating the movements of helicopters and small private planes. Finally the class plans a production during which all the movements of an airport are expressed.

The above has emphasized movement exploration to create in body language. As children grow in the coordination and control of their bodies, they are capable of evoking a moment in such a way that their product approaches expression in ballet.

A fifth-grade class is well-informed about the Westward Movement. The teacher centers their attention on the building of the transcontinental railroad. Pictures of work crews are used to help stimulate thinking.

"In this first picture," the teacher says, "we can see the workers breaking rock for the road bed. Have you ever lifted one of those heavy hammers, or sledges? What is it like? How do you suppose a person carrying one would walk? Would one of you like to show us? . . . You make it really look heavy. How do you suppose a worker would look as he walked along carrying the sledge over his shoulder? . . . Yes, it would weigh heavily on his shoulder, and he probably would hunch his other shoulder up. Does anyone else have an idea of what it would be like? All right, Bob, show us how you think a worker would walk carrying a sledge? Good! Let's see what a crew of workers would be like on their way to work in

the morning. Who would like to be one of the crew? Pete, Anne, Don, Sara, Cal, join Jim and Bob, and go over to the door. All right, crew, you are on your way to the roadbed. You have a long, hard day in the blistering sun ahead of you. . . ."

The crew eventually shows how it swings the sledges, welcomes an occasional drink of water, enjoys a noon break, and comes home.

More crews are considered—those who unload ties and place them in the road bed, the rail carriers, and the spike drivers. By the end of the period, the children have established a series of movements through which they enact the building of the railroad. The close of the period may see a series of crews around the classroom expressing the various stages.

Creativity may stop here, or the children may consider a larger production during which they sing songs, recite choric verse, chant, or perform to music.

Another fifth-grade teacher might encourage the class to explore the dramatic content of the moment of completion of the railroad for a prairie family. A current television program, or reading a few excerpts from Carol Ryrie Brink's *Caddie Woodlawn* or Laura Ingalls Wilder's *Little House on the Prairie* might provide a few clues to possible characterizations.

After a brief discussion about how the completion of a transcontinental railroad would affect the lives of a prairie family, the teacher guides the class in creating a prairie family—the father, mother, and the children, Nat, Millie, Amos, and Betsy. Then the class moves into developing characterizations, starting with the mother.

"Let's think of something that this mother might be saying frequently to her family. What might it be?"

"How about, 'Come to dinner,' " suggests a child.

"That's fine. Who can think of a way of saying, 'Come to dinner,' that tells us something about the mother as a person and how she happens to be feeling? Mary?"

"Come to dinner," Mary calls out in a slow, deliberate way.

"Thanks, Mary. What has Mary told us about her idea of this prairie mother? Yes?"

"The mother is a calm person," points out a child, "And she seems to be sure about the members of her family. She is a strong person."

"Class, do you think that this is the way a successful mother on the prairie would be?"

From this point onward, the class works in much the same way in developing the roles of the various characters. They experiment with characteristic gestures, ways of speaking, and personal mannerisms. The family almost becomes a living presence in the classroom.

Later they develop dramatic action about various incidents in which the family has difficulties because transportation is so poor. The final incident has the family celebrating the completion of the railroad.

This form of creative dramatics is not restricted to historical moments. Other moments might include conducting a close election, the family of a worker on strike, helping a person resistant to change, disagreement in a family over whether it should move or stay where it is, an effort to save an important old building, and the like.

The last form of creative dramatics we shall consider is the monolog in which children develop characterizations of historical persons or representative members of a society. Let us suppose that an eighth-grade class has just completed seeking information and generalizing about the Civil War.

"Let us imagine," the teacher says, "that a time machine has made it possible for Lincoln to be here in this classroom sitting in this chair. We know that he was a very tall, slender man. What do you suppose his posture would be as he sits? Is there anyone who would like to show us how he sits? Frank? You are a tall fellow. I'm glad you volunteered."

Frank sits on the chair and strikes a pose similar to that of the statue of Lincoln in Washington.

"Frank has given us an interpretation of Lincoln. Sitting as you are, Frank, and imagining that you are Lincoln, what do you expect from the people in the class?"

"Some questions, I think."

"Is this the way the rest of you think that Lincoln would sit here at the beginning? All right, I think so, too. But I wonder whether there is another possibility. We've learned that he liked people, he liked to talk with them, and he especially liked to tell funny stories. How might this Lincoln sit in the chair? You want to try, Frank? That's O.K. I see that several others would like to try. Gene?"

Gene sits in the chair and leans forward, his right shoulder high and his right hand cupped loosely on his right knee. His left forearm rests lightly on his left thigh, his left hand dangling loosely just inside the knee. He grins engagingly. He pulls a lock of hair over his forehead. The class laughs.

"Lincoln has just warmed up," someone observes.

"Maybe so," says the teacher, "Perhaps this is the way he would be after he was introduced to the class and had answered a question or two. Thanks, Gene. It is said that Lincoln had a high voice. This means that his voice seemed to echo through his nose a little, but perhaps he did that when he was making speeches to large crowds. I am not sure. Let us see whether we can create a voice for him. Here is a copy of one of his favorite stories. I'll divide you into groups to read and practice with the story. When you finish practicing, choose the person whom you think sounds the most like Lincoln."

The class completes a characterization for Lincoln. Various members take turns being Lincoln while others interview him, asking him what he thinks about the freedoms of people today.

The results of the above are much like a monolog or solo performance. It is particularly useful in the seventh and eighth grades. Once a characterization is developed, it may be used again and again for the expression of different points of view during discussions of issues. Occasionally a child will want to develop the role almost as a private property. Further research and even costume development does make it his or her own.

In each of the examples discussed above, the teacher has elicited the use of natural skills.

Movement exploration is particularly suitable in grades kindergarten through five, dramatization of moments works well in grades three through six, and the development of monologs is good for grades seven and eight.

Creative-writing Activities

Sometimes creative dramatics helps prepare children for creative-writing activities. Successful experiences with creative dramatics acquaints them with the discipline and freedom associated with creative activities. Writing a story about a moment or an imaginary diary entry made by historical persons caught up in the web of living, or writing a poem about a person, people, or environment, is a short step beyond creative dramatics. The differences between the two are basically in vehicle—written language instead of spoken.

The difference in vehicle, of course, demands skills which limit young children. In grades one through three they will need the teacher's assistance in creating poems and stories.

For example, after a first grade has studied about Eskimos, they may be encouraged to name all the things they can remember about the people studied. The teacher writes their responses on a chart. The product might look something like this:

Snow
Ice
Igloos
Sleds
Dogs
Umiaks
Kayaks
Walruses
Whales
Seals
Fish
Parkas and mukluks
Eskimos
In the Far North

As the children hear it, read and repeat it, they may discover a rhythm that they enjoy saying over and over again. This mosaic poem is really theirs.

The mosaic poem is an easy form of poetry which children can compose on their own when their handwriting and spelling skills are sufficiently developed.

Another example occurs in a third grade after the children have learned much about the Plains Indians. The teacher focuses their attention on *tepee* as the topic of a poem and cues them in creating the text:

(The title)	Tepee
(Descriptive words about the title)	Round, pointed
(Action words)	People going in
(Feeling or purpose)	To talk and sleep
(Another word for the title)	Home

The above is a form of cinquain (five-lined poem) arranged in a one-word, two-word, three-word, four-word, and one-word pattern. This, too, is a form of poetry which older children with adequate independent language skills can compose by themselves.

Another example occurs in a second-grade class in which the children have learned much about occupations in the community. First, they listen to and discuss a story containing repetitive incidents until the main character solves a problem. Then the teacher encourages them to invent a character who has a particular occupation and who needs a job. The character they invent is Mrs. Needle, a lady who knows how to sew. Contributing sentences as they think of them, they compose a story that has Mrs. Needle going to different places in the community to find a job. One event is frequently repeated:

"And what can you do?" asks the _____.
"I can sew," says Mrs. Needle.
"We don't need anyone to sew."

Finally she is hired at a clothing store.

This last example underscores the need for children to see how people react to life through creative writing. Beginning in fourth grade, children benefit from listening to or reading and discussing poems and stories to discover how poets and writers react to their physical and social environment. Here are a few examples:

• After studying about urban development, a fifth-grade class reads a few of the poems of James S. Tippett and Carl Sandburg to sense the variety of images, impressions, and feelings that a city can evoke.
• After an environmental study, a sixth-grade class reads nature poems by Elizabeth Madox Roberts, James Stephens, Vachel Lindsay, and suitable Japanese haiku to grasp how poets convey how they feel about nature.
• After their first study about climate, a fourth-grade class reads the poems of Robert Louis Stevenson, Hilda Conkling (a child poet), and Hamlin Garland to discover what poets see in such mundane things as rain and wind.

- After a study of the Revolutionary War, a fifth-grade class listens to excerpts from Esther Forbes' *Johnny Tremain* to discover how the attention to detail and a sense of reality can make an event come alive in the adventures of a fictitious character.
- After a study of the South American rain forests, a sixth grade reads or listens to excerpts from Armstrong Sperry's *Rain Forest* to see how a writer uses the fauna and flora of a region to spin a yarn.
- After a study of ancient Rome, a seventh-grade class reads excerpts from Isabelle Lawrence's *The Gift of the Golden Cup* to discover the possibilities for stories about ancient peoples.
- After a study about socialization, an eighth-grade class reads or listens to excerpts from Ester Wier's *The Loner* to see how a socialization problem serves as a basis for a story.
- After a study of the peoples of western Africa, an eighth-grade class reads *The Cow-Tail Switch and Other West African Stories* by Harold Courlander and George Herzog to taste the humor and irony of folk tales.

After a social-studies period or two devoted to an exploration of literature, the children try their hand at producing literature themselves. The results are often delightful to the observer and satisfying to children.

ILLUSTRATION 6–8. *Experimenting with Folk Art.*

Creative-art Activities

In an earlier section, we discussed guiding children in the use of various media as a way of organizing and expressing knowledge. We also suggested that occasionally a child may produce a creative product. However, because skills with color and form are so refined, there is little that most of us can do to help children develop them to the point that they can truly be creative with them. About all that we can do is provide opportunities for creative effort.

Some of the best opportunities occur when the children are studying about a people who have a characteristic folk art—the Celts, the Northwest Indians, various peoples of Africa and South America, the Arab peoples, the Japanese, the Chinese, the Persians, and many others. The simplicity of design intrigues most children and encourages them to try to create something original.

And there is the expendable art that is popular with the young—the poster and the bumper sticker. These depend on a minimum of words used with effect. Their own ideas about political, economic, social, and cultural conditions may be created and communicated directly through the use of these devices. Often they require a minimum of materials and little time, conditions that social-studies teachers appreciate.

The mural as a class enterprise can be used at every grade level. Frequently a mural is little more than decoration, but if the children discuss the message they want to convey, they will arrive at a more meaningful design as well as ideas about phases in planning. Traditionally, children have been guided in making sketches (that of the best artist is always used) to be drawn (by the best artist), and to be painted by the whole class (the best artists doing the fine work and everyone else painting expanses of sky, sea, or mountains). There are other ways, including having children collect magazine pictures to make a huge collage, or designing a simple background and having everyone paint or color something to be pasted to it.

From grade six onward, children are attracted to personal art with which they can decorate their bedrooms. The mobile and the wall banner have special appeal to them. These may be made from simple materials to express aphorisms about social relationships, personal values, and political, economic, and social ideas.

When guiding children in creating posters, bumper stickers, murals, mobiles, and wall banners, it is often helpful to have examples of these made by other children of about the same grade level of the children who are going to be encouraged to make them. As they examine them, they begin to form ideas about how to create them.

The main guideline to follow when encouraging children to enter into creative-art activities in social studies is to choose those media to which children can relate.

SCHEDULING INSTRUCTION IN THE SKILLS

Many of the skills needed by children to acquire and process information in social studies are included in other subject areas which are taught often by teachers other than the social-studies teacher. As stated previously, as social-studies teachers we are responsible for teaching the information-seeking skills and the language skills necessary for processing information, regardless of what the organization of the school and total curriculum may be. For many of us this is frustrating. However, there are a few practices we may follow to make the responsibility more palatable.

• When teaching or improving a skill, we may use the content of the study at hand to teach or improve it. For example, when committed to teach-ing children a unit about Norway and also improving children's skill in using the index, we use reading material about Norwegian life to introduce and provide practice in using the index. We evaluate both the acquisition of content and the use of the skill.

• We may plan to use the social-studies periods during the first two or three weeks of the semester or term to preassess and teach skills. We supplement the class introduction and supervised practice of skills with special assignments in activity or learning centers for children who need more practice.

• We may plan to alternate skills and content teaching. For example, we may arrange to teach a short unit devoted to a skill or set of related skills immediately before each content unit. The instruction is designed specifically to meet the children's needs in the content unit. For example, if you know that the unit will involve much map reading, the skills unit would be on learning to read maps.

• We may develop social studies units organized to meet both a content and a skill objective. For example, the unit objectives for a fourth grade unit dealing with a study of the state as an economic entity might be expressed in this way:

The children will be able to write three-paragraph reports about industry in the state. (Skill)

They will be able to name and describe, in oral or written language, the three most important industries in the state. (Content)

The learning activities in the unit are arranged in a way to provide for both acquiring information and learning to write reports.

• We may teach the skills in related clusters. For example, outlining, making an outline, and composing reports are closely related in guiding children in independent reporting. They are taught as mutually supportive skills.

Following any of these practices, we can develop a skills program supporting social studies that will help children in three ways. First, they will be able to do study tasks with a sense of accomplishment. Second, they will be able to range more deeply and widely into social-studies content to achieve greater understanding of the physical and social environment in which they live. And, third, they will grow toward independence in the life skills of acquiring and using information for a variety of purposes. In the long run, perhaps the greatest benefit will be the last.

SUMMARY

Much of children's real learning in social studies occurs as a function of how well they can build what they recall into structures meaningful to themselves and others.

Processing information to integrate, apply, and generate knowledge requires special skills in the use of media. Social-studies teachers do what they can to foster growth in these skills but assume responsibility for improving the necessary language skills.

Processing information to integrate knowledge includes organizing it to make it more manageable or easier to understand and expressing it in different media. The organizational structures and the media used vary throughout the grades.

Processing information as application has children solving problems through in-depth discussion, discussing case studies, role playing, simulation, values clarification, or values analysis.

Processing information to generate new knowledge involves children in creative activity. The holistic and stage-by-stage strategies are sometimes applicable in teaching the needed skills.

When learning to organize knowledge to integrate it, children are frequently shown simple, informal ways of organizing it. This practice continues through grade five. In the later grades they are encouraged to decide on organizational structures. Learning to use more formal structures, such as diagrams, graphs, and maps, begins in grade four and continues throughout the higher grades. When guided in making replicas, the children are encouraged to think of ways to use materials. Learning to summarize and report begins in the lower grades as oral language activity cued by the teacher. In grade four and the later grades these are taught as written language skills. Either the holistic or stage-by-stage strategy may be used.

Prompters for in-depth discussions to apply knowledge are open questions about issues related to or inherent in the area of study.

When children are guided into case studies to apply knowledge, they read or listen to a document based on reality and discuss it. The reality is taken from their area of study.

Children can apply what they know about an area of study by role playing conflict situations related to the area.

Simulations provide children with opportunities to explore intrasystem and intersystem conflicts in their areas of study. They may also simulate the roles of social scientists.

Values clarification frequently focuses children's attention on other human beings involved in tasks. Values clarification helps them to appreciate both tasks and persons.

When children make a values analysis related to an area of study, they must apply factual learning rationally.

Through creative-dramatics activities, children generate new knowledge by making dramatic interpretations of processes, events, and conditions related to or inherent in their area of study. The children explore movement, dramatization, and monolog development.

Creative writing as a way to generate knowledge is suitable for all grades. Young children need verbal cuing to write stories and poems. Beginning in fourth grade, the children may experience literature as a way of discovering how creative writers react to their environment.

The teacher provides opportunities for creative art activities. Often folk art, popular art, and murals serve as preferred modes of expression.

Scheduling instruction for information gathering and processing skills presents a problem solvable through combining content and skills instruction and scheduling instruction in different ways. Providing for skills instruction related to social studies helps children grow as students and persons.

POSTSCRIPT

At the beginning of this chapter you were asked to write a few notes about how you felt about a list of activities in which children were integrating, applying, or generating knowledge. Review your notes now. Do you feel the same as you did originally, or do you feel differently? Why?

FOR FURTHER UNDERSTANDING

Cognitive Activities

1. Define: *integrating knowledge, applying knowledge, generating knowledge.*
2. Make a diagram showing the relationship between information processing and learning.
3. Describe what is meant by "in a child's own language."
4. In which of the following is a child *applying* social studies knowledge?
   a. The child draws a map of South America.
   b. The child writes a report about South America.
   c. The child role plays a voting South American.
   Give reasons for your choice.
5. Describe two general approaches to guiding children into problem solving.
6. In which of the following is a child generating knowledge?
   a. The child writes a summary of the contents of an audiotape about Benjamin Franklin.
   b. The child develops a characterization of Benjamin Franklin.
   c. The child participates in a simulation in which he has the role of a diplomat.
   Give reasons for your answer.
7. Assume that you are a teacher who arranges to have information-processing activities as often as you can during social-studies instruction. One day a parent arranges to confer with you. When he enters your classroom, he looks disdainfully at the murals and replicas displayed on the bulletin boards and counters. Eventually he says, "All these things the children have made are nice, but aren't they really a waste of time?"
   What will you say to the parent?
8. Which of the three broad categories of information-processing skills do you prefer as a teacher? Give reasons for your preference.
9. How do you think a social-studies teacher should provide for instruction in the various skills children need in social studies? Give reasons for your opinion.

Practice Activities

1. Develop any of the following materials that you prefer or that you know you will need in your classroom.
   a. Create overlays for teaching children how to make any of the graphs.
   b. Draw a map yourself by using a grid. Take notes on any difficulties you have so that you can alert children to problems they might have.
   c. Make a relief map. Note your problems to use as a basis for guiding children to avoid similar problems.
   d. Make original study models to use when teaching children to summarize and report.
   e. Make a guide chart for young children to use when they share.
   f. Make a puppet to use when guiding young children in summarizing and reporting skills.
   g. Collect a series of newspaper clippings and editorials, or excerpts from a child's book of fiction to use as case studies related to the content of a social-studies unit.
   h. Develop two descriptions of conflict situations that could be used to stimulate children to role play a conflict related to a study area in social studies.
   i. Develop a simulation based on a conflict related to a study area in social studies or the ways that social scientists work.
   j. Collect a series of poems, stories, or excerpts from novels that could be used as models to show how creative writers respond to their environment.

Performance Activities

1. Try any of the materials developed in response to 1 above with a group or class of children. Evaluate the results in terms of evidence of learning and what you might do to improve the material or the way you used it.
2. Try any of the following, as developed for social studies, in your classroom and evaluate the experience in terms of evidence of children's learning and how you would change your procedures to ensure greater success:
   a. Guiding children in the use or development of a chart on which to organize information.

b. Guiding children in the exploration of common materials to make a replica.

c. Conducting an in-depth discussion.

d. Conducting a values-clarification activity or a values analysis.

e. Guiding young children in creative dramatics.

f. Guiding children in developing a creative dramatization or a monolog.

g. Guiding young children in composing a story or poem.

h. Guiding children in using an art medium to create a design, mural, wall banner, poster, or bumper sticker.

SELECTED REFERENCES

Hennings, Dorothy Grant. *Smiles, Nods, and Pauses.* New York: Citation Press, 1974.

Leonhard, Charles, and Robert W. House. *Foundations and Principles of Music Education.* New York: McGraw-Hill, 1972.

McGregor, Ronald N. *Art Plus.* New York: McGraw-Hill, 1978.

Machart, Norman C. "Doing Oral History in the Elementary Grades." *Social Education,* 43:479–480 (October, 1979).

McNamara, Shelley G. "Naive Mural Art as a Vehicle for Teaching Elementary Social Studies." *Social Education,* 43:473–479 (October, 1979).

McSweeney, Maxine. *Creative Children's Theater.* South Brunswick and New York: A. S. Barnes, 1974.

Petty, Walter T., and Julie M. Jensen. *Developing Children's Language.* Boston: Allyn and Bacon, 1980.

Swierkos, Marion L., and Catherine G. Morse. *Industrial Arts for the Elementary Classroom.* Peoria, Ill.: Chas. A. Bennett, 1973.

7

Improving Children's Group-work Skills

As social-studies teachers we may group children in various ways to help them learn. For example, we may group our gifted learners to guide them in making more extensive studies of an issue. This is "ability grouping." When we discover a small number of children who lack map skills, we may form them into a group, teach them, and disband the group. This is "grouping according to need." And there may be occasions when we divide our class into three groups of equal size to make better use of the library or materials center. One group at a time is released to work there while the others remain in the classroom doing other tasks. This is "administrative grouping." These forms of groupings are used in the various school subjects as well as in social studies.

However, social-studies teachers may also use other forms of grouping to facilitate learning. Read the descriptions of the two situations below to discover what they are.

SITUATION A.

After the children in a fourth-grade class have generalized from the information they discovered about their state's physical and human resources, they decide that they want to make some large posters to encourage others to conserve resources. The teacher has each child complete a simple questionnaire to indicate his or her preferences for peers with whom to work to make a poster. The teacher analyzes the completed questionnaires and uses the results to form the children into groups of five or six members each. As soon as it is formed, each group selects a leader who guides the members in deciding what they want to express, how they want to express it, and who is to perform the various tasks. Following its plan, each group works in an assigned space during several instructional periods to produce a poster. During the final period each group displays its poster and suggests how it is to be interpreted.

SITUATION B.

The instructional period of an eighth-grade class begins with a class discussion in which the children review what they have learned so far about Ancient Greece. The teacher points out that evidence of Ancient Greek culture has been found as far east as India, and the children hypothesize explanations about this phenomenon and agree on three reasons as being plausible. Then the teacher divides the children into groups by having every five persons sitting near each other form a group. He gives the groups these tasks: to read about Alexander the Great in their textbooks and, as a group, to summarize their findings and to decide which hypothesis, if any, their summary supports.

Each group arranges their chairs in a small circle and begins to read. Better readers help poorer readers. When the reading is completed they select a member to be their spokesperson. This child asks for informa

243

tion, records it, and guides the group in composing it in a summary and considering the hypotheses.

The teacher reconvenes the class and the spokesperson of each group reports on the group's deliberations. The groups are in agreement on which hypothesis is most plausible. At this point the teacher has the children work again in groups to decide what might have happened to the spread of Ancient Greek culture if Alexander had lived for twenty more years. After the groups discuss this issue for five minutes, they again convene as a class and share their opinions. The bell rings. The period is over.

As you can see, in Situation A the children are formed into groups to work cooperatively to complete a task, and in Situation B, to study. Two instructional objectives, to complete a project and to discuss facts and ideas, are involved. What other kinds of instructional objectives do you see being met as these children work in groups? Jot down your ideas.

How do you think you might proceed to help children learn to work in groups? Make a few notes of your thoughts.

Put your notes aside to review after you have read the chapter.

A RATIONALE FOR GROUP WORK

The learning activity that has just been introduced to you is sometimes called "committee work," or "small-group work." Throughout the chapter we shall refer to it simply as "group work."

As you have already seen, the result of group work is a product, either a performance having definite qualities or a project. Many of us as teachers focus so narrowly on our learners' products as proof of learning that we neglect the kinds of learning resulting from the process involved in making the product. In some areas of learning the neglect is warranted, but rarely is this so with group work. Whenever our learners do group work, we consider also their learning resulting from immersion in the group-work process.

Actually, the learning resulting from experiencing group work is so significant to children's

growth as persons that it provides a rationale for providing them with opportunities to do group work. As children work in groups in which they complete learning-related tasks cooperatively as group enterprises, they learn the following:

- Who they are as persons as they observe their peers' reactions to their suggestions, opinions, requests, and acceptance of responsibilities. Much of what a person knows about the Self lies in what he or she sees in the reaction of Others during interactive situations.
- How Others depend on them to know themselves. Awareness of this helps children to know that when they react to another's behavior, they are reacting to the person as well.
- The behaviors of a democratic leader as one who facilitates the work of the group by helping the members surface their knowledge and apply their skills to complete the task. Knowing these behaviors helps children exercise the role of leader and select leaders.

These learnings alone can serve as a rationale to justify having children do group work. However, we can extend it.

One extension of the rationale is based on children's need of the support of their peers to explore abstract ideas. As soon as a child expresses an idea within a group, the other members react to it. They may agree with it, add to it, ask for a clarification of the idea or a term within it or proceed to clarify it by making personal interpretations, express another idea counter to it and compare the two, or validate it by stating facts. The result is that the child who originally expressed the idea has an understanding of it that would be difficult to acquire in any other way.

When children work with an idea in a group, they pool their background and experience to determine its meaning. When they arrive at a consensus about its meaning and express it in their own terms, it is not an empty verbalization.

If children are denied opportunities to do group work or, at the very least, to discuss ideas among themselves with the guidance of a competent teacher, they are denied opportunities for intellectual growth.

Another extension of the rationale is based on children's need to participate actively and directly in discussion. During a usual class discussion, twenty-five percent or less of the class members participate actively, while the others listen, daydream, or communicate with each other stealthily about matters in no way related to the discussion. Among those who listen are the shy learners. Fearful of what might happen to them if they enter the dynamic exchange of ideas, they sit quietly avoiding eye contact with the discussants. Generally, then, class discussion can generate nonproductive activity for a majority of the children.

If the children can be guided into group work, nonproductive activity is reduced. In a group of five members, a majority will address the discussion task and will continue to urge the remainder of the members to become involved. More than fifty percent of the class is participating directly and actively. If a shy child is going to participate, he or she will most likely do so in a group. He or she feels much less terror when faced with the problem of having to communicate within the confines of the group.

When a class discussion follows small-group work, it is generally more lively. Although the leaders or spokespersons represent their groups in the discussion, they will often ask for support from the other members.

If we wish to increase the amount and quality of participation in class discussions, we may consider group work as a possible strategy.

So far we have been concerned with the psychological aspects of group work as a learning activity. We have been able to develop a rationale with an extended base. Another rationale, based on the cultural aspects of learning, may also be considered.

"Democracy" is a term we frequently use to characterize the core values of our culture. Implicit within this term is reasoning and working together to solve common problems. It is the keystone of the American cultural heritage.

As we trace the development of democratic thought in America, we can document countless instances in which the values related to democratic planning, mutual trust, and cooperation give direction to effective action based on sound decisions. The Mayflower Compact is the first formal document. There are many others, but perhaps the most notable is the first amendment to the Constitution which states that "Congress shall make no law . . . prohibiting the right of the people to assemble, and to petition the Government for a redress of grievances."

The informal documentation of democratic thought is prodigious—the countless houses, barns, churches, and schools erected, fields cleared for cultivation and harvested, provisions made for education, police protection and protection from fire—and much of it at the neighborhood and community level. It continues today with community-planning committees, citizens' advisory committees to schools, and neighborhood groups who plan and organize to get signal lights installed at busy intersections or to protect their children from molestation on the way to and from school.

Group work within the American perspective occurs when a problem is identified by a number of people having a deep concern about it. When the problem is solved or contained within reasonable bounds, the group dissolves. This is the behavior of self-reliant individuals who will exhaust their own resources first or weigh carefully the demands of group effort, as opposed to individual effort, before deciding to join a group.

The cultural aspects of group work serve as a balance against the psychological aspects. Children are guided into group work to perform tasks which they cannot do, or cannot do as well, working by themselves. This prevents group work from encouraging children to become unquestioning conformists.

In a sense, group work in the classroom is an American "basic" subject. When children learn to work in groups, they receive a rich portion of their cultural heritage.

Both the psychological and the cultural rationales may be countered with a negative rationale holding that group work discourages children from developing self-reliance. Those who maintain the rationale point out that group work often presents opportunities for some children to do nothing while the others assume complete responsibility for the group's work. When children seize these opportunities, they are indeed learning how to be dependent on others and, what is worse, how to profit from other people's work. When this condition exists, the rationale is valid.

However, the condition can be prevented. Helping children learn the necessary skills and monitoring group work will eliminate opportunities for children to learn parasitic behavior. Actually, learning to be self-reliant within a group situation is one of the objectives during the instructional program in group work. A true test of self-reliance may occur during participation in a group endeavor when a member must stand up for what he or she believes or knows to be true.

The risk explicit in the negative rationale is amply offset by effective teaching. The positive rationales, the psychological and the cultural, underscore both the need for and benefits of group work in elementary social studies. Although children often group to play, they need careful instruction to be able to do group work. How to teach the required skills is what the rest of this chapter is about.

As we explore the ways of teaching the skills, we shall have to bear in mind that group work is not for all children. Children younger than nine years old usually are unable to profit from instruction in group work. They can work in close proximity to one another, but they are not ready to cooperate in a group enterprise. However, we can provide them with group experiences which will help them to develop readiness for formal instruction later. How we do this will be treated shortly.

Children of nine years and older who carry hostilities with them into the classroom find group work difficult to learn. However, if they are given simple tasks of short duration, they may enjoy success in group work. Such success has two results: first, the children will be able to learn to do group work of greater complexity later on, and second, their feelings about themselves and school will improve. Providing for that initial success is a worthwhile goal.

BUILDING READINESS FOR GROUP WORK

In two instances can we provide readiness activities for group work. One occurs when our learners are nine years or older but who have had few if any opportunities to learn group work, and the other, when our learners are young children.

Several procedures can be followed in both instances. These include:

- Establishing a positive social climate. (See Chapter 2 for recommended procedures.)

ILLUSTRATION 7–1. *By Doing a Simple Task Together, Younger Children Develop Readiness for Group Work.*

- Providing a model for children to follow when they lead discussions. As you guide instruction, use every opportunity to ask children what they think and to make suggestions. Receive their opinions and suggestions positively.
- Involving children as frequently as possible in class discussions dealing with the administration and use of their classroom—color schemes and uses for bulletin boards, ways to make their classroom more attractive, ways to make the best use of space and limited materials, who is to be responsible for clean chalkboard erasers, distributing paper and other materials, and the like.
- Having children participate in "buzz" groups to solve simple problems such as what refreshments to serve at a class party, what to do with the prize earned through the attendance of parents at the P.T.A. meeting, how samples of good work should be displayed, and the like.
- Assigning children in groups of three or four to work together in straightening out the library corner or the shelves where reference books are kept, dismantling a bulletin-board display, preparing materials for an art project, and the like.

The last three activities listed above help children become accustomed to working together. When working with young children, you may provide for activities such as these:

- Assign the children in pairs to work together on construction projects which both children really want to do. For example, after studying about the work of doctors and nurses, two first-grade children make a model of a hospital from a cardboard box and dollhouse furniture.
- Have the children share scissors, paste, staplers, etc., during construction activities.
- Guide the children in simple simulations in which groups of two or three children must cooperate to assemble simple puzzles or follow simple patterns to make designs. During the postdiscussion the children discuss what they learned about working with each other.

Special activities to help older learners get ready for group work include the following:

- Assign children in groups to seek information in sets of varied resources including perhaps an atlas, an almanac, and several different textbooks. Each child has the same list of tasks to perform and the resources have to be shared. One child

may be assigned the additional task of supervising the use of resources.
- Assign children in groups to "brainstorm" an issue or topic to produce as many ideas as they can within a limited period.
- Assign projects in which you form the groups, assign leadership roles, and give specific directions for the completion of specific projects.

The last activity listed above is sometimes regarded as group work, but it is not because the teacher has made all the decisions. The task of the leaders is to serve as pacers of group activity, seeing that each part of the project is completed before the next is started. Leaders follow directions from the teacher.

For young children, the purpose of readiness activities is to give them a foretaste of group work, but for older children, the purpose is to see whether they are ready for instruction in group work. When older children are capable of participating smoothly in the suggested activities, they are ready to learn how to exercise the responsibilities inherent in group work.

ORGANIZING FOR GROUP WORK IN SOCIAL STUDIES

Organizing for group work in social studies requires consideration of three factors: the children's competency in the investigation and production skills needed to complete tasks, how the physical environment can be best arranged to facilitate group work, and how group membership is determined. Failure to take these factors into account impedes children's progress in learning group-work skills. Let us look into group membership first.

How group membership is determined depends on the purposes to be met through group work. When children are grouped to participate in study, the criteria for group membership are less stringent than those used when the children are to work together to produce a project. In the latter case, the demands for cooperation, positive interpersonal relationships, and willing role acceptance are much greater.

Membership in Project Groups

Within a project group, children are expected to organize themselves to complete the project, to develop a design for it, and to accept roles in constructing it. They begin by selecting a leader. He or she elicits their suggestions and opinions and brings them to consensus on each important phase of project development. Because they have so much responsibility and must be able to interact effectively, they need to have a voice in the membership of the group. This need becomes more crucial when they must decide on their own which project they are to complete. Several methods give children an opportunity to exercise their voice.

Some teachers prefer that children have an indirect voice in determining the membership of groups. They implement this practice by observing their learners carefully as they work and play within the school environment. They note which children like to be with each other (as shown by their preferences when they enter or leave the classroom, when they choose seating stations, when they share completed paper work, when they play on the school yard before school, at recess, and during free time at the end of the lunch period, and the like). They look carefully for the children who have leadership qualities. Often they are so interested in discovering leadership potential that they neglect to observe for the constituencies of leadership. To ensure the learning of group-work skills requires that observation be focused on which children support certain leaders and tend to join together during activities or situations. Teachers' observation notes may be no more than simple lists of children observed together with the name of the leader checked or circled, and an indication of the activity or situation. An example is given in Figure 7–1.

Each list is an observed grouping. Sara is identified as a strong leader who probably could guide any of the groupings in which she was observed. Mike and Millie also have leadership potential, but it does not emerge when Sara is in the group. To ensure that they use their potential, they should not be included in a group in which Sara is a member.

When the moment arrives for project groups to be formed, the teacher consults his or her notes to form the groups and informs the children of their group assignments. Teachers who want to make sure that each group has the "right" leader also inform the children which member of the group is designated as leader. This may provide for adequate leadership during the first few group projects, but it may also cause the children to think that the teacher chooses favorites.

Other teachers have the groups select their leaders. The children may not always choose the leader "planted" in the group, but in most instances they select a person they think they can work with. Sometimes such leaders work well. At other times the teacher may have to give special support to the leader.

When the class is to be grouped to work on

ILLUSTRATION 7–2. *Choosing a Group in Which to Work.*

Playground	Library	Activity Center		Classroom Seating	
Jane	Sara	Jane	Peter	Sara	Millie
Sara	Peter	Sara	Mike	Peter	Ellen
Millie	Mike	Anne	Jim	Mike	Bob
Anne	Jane		Millie	Jane	Anne
Sally	Sally		Bob	Sally	Jack
			Ellen		

FIGURE 7–1.

the same project (for example, each group is going to construct a model of something), the teacher may involve the children directly in forming groups. Assuming that each group is going to construct a replica of an Indian village, here is a group procedure to follow:

1. Compose a questionnaire similar to the following to be completed by each child:

   When making an Indian village, I would like to work with

   a. _____.
   b. _____.
   c. _____.
   d. _____.
   e. _____.

2. Explain to the children that you are going to form them into groups to construct Indian villages. Distribute the questionnaires and ask them to complete them to help you know in which groups to assign them. Assure them that you will try to include as many people from their lists as you can in their group. Warn them that there may be instances in which you can assign only one person from their list in their group.
3. Collect the questionnaires, analyze them, and form the groups. The children preferred most frequently by their peers are leaders. The children preferred by no one should be assigned to work with children high on their preferred list, but should not be clustered in a group. Form groups of five to eight members. There is no need to have groups of equal sizes.
4. Inform the children of their group assignments. However, leave the choice of leader up to them.

The above way of forming groups works effectively as long as the children see that you honor their preferences. It is helpful to keep the questionnaires from grouping to grouping to help you remember the children who may have been assigned to a group in which only one of their preferred persons, and a less preferred one at that, was also assigned.

Having the children complete the questionnaire each time they are to be grouped may help you discover the emergence of new leaders.

When a number of projects is possible, you may use the project labels as a way of organizing the groups. Let us suppose that the class has decided that painting a mural, making a product map, making a set of pictures illustrating an industrial process, and dramatizing the daily life of a people are to be the projects. List these projects on the chalkboard and ask the children to raise their hands to indicate on which they would like to work. As they raise their hands, the children will look around to see who else wants to work on that project. That takes care of their personal preferences.

A frequent problem is that more children than eight or nine may choose to work on the same project. The best solution is to tell the children that so many members in a group will make it difficult for them to work together and to encourage them to split into two groups by lottery. If this does not work, encourage the members to choose another group with whom they might enjoy working. If this fails, allow them to remain together. In most instances they will be able to surmount any difficulties they might have as they work to complete their project.

Sometimes less than a desired number of children will want to work on a project. You may ask them if they would like to join another group which can accommodate a new member or two. If they decide against this, make no issue about it. They may need a little more time to complete their project, but they will have little interpersonal difficulty.

When most children are involved in group projects, they are usually more concerned about the persons they are to work with than about the task. For this reason, we do what we can to give them a voice in deciding on group membership, and once they have expressed their preferences, we honor them.

Membership in Study Groups

Because the group task is limited primarily to the use of study skills and discussion, and because the interaction time is so short (anywhere from three or four minutes to twenty minutes), concern for children's preferences about group membership is not so vital. Class cohesiveness is the significant factor. For this reason, a positive social climate must be established before study in groups is begun. Perhaps you will want to start building this cohesiveness by introducing activities similar to these:

• Divide the class into pairs. Have them interact for thirty seconds to exchange names and preferences for free-time activities. Then have each member introduce the other member to the class by giving his or her name and describing the preferred activity. Have the children change partners to exchange names and to tell the state and city in which they were born, and to introduce their partners. You may wish to continue partner introductions and the sharing of information about favorite colors, television programs, foods, and the like. Something special happens when you enter the activities as a class member.
• Have the children take turns standing, giving their name, and telling one important fact about themselves. After each child recites, have the class say the name in unison and the names of all the other children who have identified them-

selves. When all the children have identified themselves, ask for volunteers to try to identify everyone in the class. During subsequent class periods, you may form the children in a circle around the class in an order different from that in which they sit, and ask for volunteers to try to identify all their classmates by name; or encourage the children to sit in a different location each time they enter the classroom and have volunteers identify all of them by name.

Activities such as these help the children become acquainted with each other. When they are at ease with each other, you may begin to group them for study. Here are a few ways to do it:

Locational Grouping

The children are formed in groups with the classmates who are sitting near them. This way of grouping reduces the need for them to have to move to other parts of the classroom. If they have been permitted to select the seating stations they wish, the resulting groups contain members who get along well.

Chance Grouping

The children are assigned to groups in accord with their numbers in a count-off around the classroom or with the numbers they draw in a simple lottery. This form of grouping helps children become acquainted with the others in the classroom. It also provides a test for leadership skills.

Grouping by Classmate Selection

Four, five, or six (whatever number of groups are desired) children are appointed as temporary leaders. They are given a class roster over which they confer to select members for their groups. When they have chosen the members of their groups, they arrange their names in an alphabetical list to conceal whom they chose last. When the groups are convened, the temporary leader conducts an election to determine who is to be the spokesperson or leader.

Grouping by Self-selection

A number of children are appointed as temporary leaders. Their names are listed on a one-sheet ballot. After each name are the number of blanks reflecting the size of each group (for example, if there are to be seven children in each group, there are seven blanks). When the ballot is circulated among the children, they sign their name in any of the open blanks after their chosen temporary leader. When the ballet is completed, the temporary leaders convene their groups and supervise the election of a leader.

Whenever you have your class grouping by chance or by self-selection, make provisions for fairness. Do not always start the count-off with the same person at the same seating station, have the children draw numbers in the same order, or start the circulation of the ballot in the same place. They resent not having a chance to select from a large number of choices.

As you can see, when forming children in study groups, we can group them in a variety of ways. However, as we change the formation, we must be prepared for some expressions of disgruntlement. Children cling to the ties they establish with others and dislike having them disrupted, but this is a time when we stand firm. When children study in the same groups day after day, their relationships stabilize. The same children are always the leaders, always making the important suggestions, and always avoiding their responsibility to the group. The pecking order remains the same. The least-liked person learns about being least liked each day. Considering these conditions, we have to change the membership of groups from time to time.

Sometimes we can soften the harshness inherent in forming new groups by having the children plan with us what basis for new groupings should be used each week. You may start by informing them about the different ways of grouping and the order in which you expect them to try each, and that they will decide each week thereafter which form of grouping they prefer for the week. You will have to set the groundrule that no form may be repeated within a two-week period after it has been used.

Or you might simply express to them that you think they should learn to work with a lot of

different people in the classroom and ask them to suggest different ways that this could be done.

Arranging the Physical Environment

The factors of physical arrangement of concern to us are the classroom furniture and the number of members to include in each group.

The recommended number of members for group work is from five to eight. Smaller groups limit the number of ideas that may be expressed and are subject to being dominated too easily by strong leaders. Larger groups provide more possibilities for the number of different interactions that may take place, but they may be more than most individuals can cope with. Many will assume the roles of spectators or will simply tune out.

ILLUSTRATION 7-3. *A Classroom Arrangement Suitable for the Usual Classroom Activity.*

ILLUSTRATION 7-4. . . . *Changed to Facilitate Group Work.*

The type of furniture that best facilitates group work consists of tables and chairs that can be arranged into group stations to accommodate five or six children. Most suitable are two-station tables, two of which can be pushed together to form a hexagonal table surface around which six children can sit comfortably. Or four of these tables can be pushed together to form an eight-member group station. Figure 7-2 illustrates the versatility of this furniture.

Rectangular tables, either single or double-station, with separate chairs, may also be arranged to form group stations. However, the design of such tables, particularly the form of the legs, does not provide for comfortable seating at the end of the table. If this feature causes a problem, the children may cluster the chairs into group stations.

The main problem is developing an arrangement of furniture that will facilitate both class and group discussions. Some teachers prefer to have the furniture arranged always for group work. However, unless they remember to have the children rearrange their chairs for class discussions, they find themselves in the same situation as the second-rate performer in a supper club. They hold forth mightily while the "patrons" entertain themselves.

A better practice is to have the furniture arranged usually to accommodate class discussions. A large square or circle is the preferred arrangement, or if space does not permit this, a *u*-inside-of-a-*u* arrangement is workable. When group work begins, the children rearrange the furniture to accommodate it. Figure 7-3 shows how this can be done.

When the group work is completed, the children move the furniture back into its arrangement for class discussions. The main disadvantage is the confusion caused by moving furniture. However, its ill effects are counterbalanced by giving children a chance to get up and move around, a need which most have during long class periods.

The most difficult furniture to arrange for group work are the traditional desks fastened in rows to the floor and the single-station units in which the desk and the chair are attached. Possible ways to form group stations include encouraging the children to assemble in any open areas in the classroom, anywhere they can without regard to whether they are sitting on chairs, tabletops, counters, or the floor, or in corridors or patios easily observable from the classroom.

In short, one makes the best arrangement possible with the furniture provided by the school.

Skills Competencies and Group Tasks

When children perform a task as a group, how they feel about themselves as persons and as members of a group, and how they feel about participation in group work, are often affected by how they feel about their performance or end product.

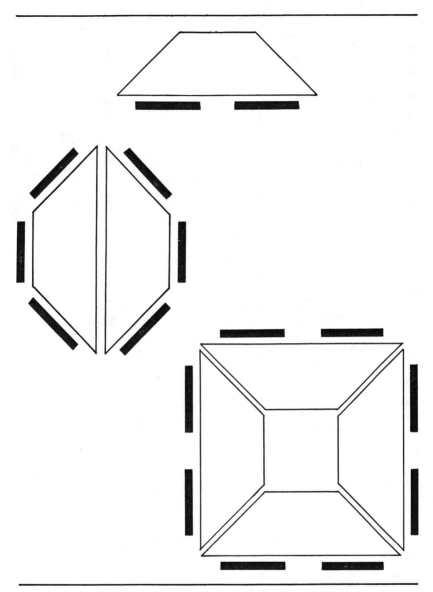

FIGURE 7–2. *Possible Seating Arrangements with Special Tables.*

If they are continually frustrated because of lack of ability in a necessary skill, or are ashamed of their product, they lose confidence in themselves and trust in others, and develop a hearty dislike for group work. To avoid this state of affairs, we need to consider carefully the tasks toward which we guide children in groups.

When the task is to be a project, here is what you can do to ensure successful, satisfactory completion:

• Suggest only projects which you are certain the children have the skills to complete, but assure them that you will be available as a consultant to help them when they have a problem.

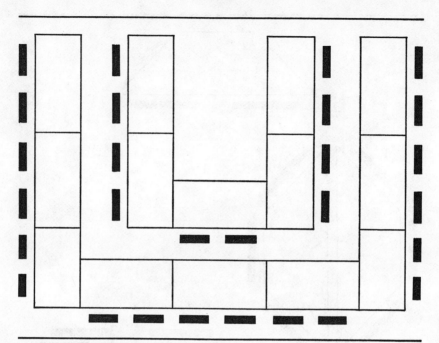

FIGURE 7–3. *Seating Arrangement with Tables or Desks.*

- When all the groups are to produce a similar product, guide the children in making a task analysis to determine the sequence of operations that will be necessary to complete the project.
- When the class is ready to explore for different projects that they might do, alert them to the time and materials available for such projects before they begin to make suggestions. After they have made their suggestions, guide them in making a task analysis of each project and the skills necessary for its completion. These procedures help children avoid grandiose choices that will lead to disappointment and frustration.

When the task is a group study, you will want to be certain that the children have the skills to complete the task that you give. If you plan for them to explore for information together, you will want to be sure that they can read, listen to, or view the resources as well as operate projectors if they are to be used. You will have to provide for slower children. Will they have to rely on other children, or will you provide an access to information that they can use without embarrassment?

Because the children in the fourth and fifth grades are still learning the intake skills, we usually

do not have them explore for information together. Group studies for them are usually group discussions occurring *after* they have gathered information.

If you intend the groups to present their findings in a specific form, you will need to ascertain whether they can produce the form. For example, you will not ask children who do not know how to summarize to prepare a group summary.

Our concerns here underscore the wisdom of determining early in the school year what level of information intake and processing skills the children have.

GUIDING CHILDREN IN PROJECT GROUPS

When we guide children into group work to complete projects, we are helping them meet the learning objectives implicit in the psychological and cultural rationales presented in the first section of this chapter. The social-studies project as a task places a focus on children's reviewing a background of recently acquired facts and ideas, and working cooperatively to integrate and express what they know in a product that communicates to others as well as themselves. The project serves as a vehicle to carry them toward a structure of experience that has an intellectual and personal meaning to them.

Suitable Projects

The projects suitable for group work include those which children cannot do individually within the time available or do not have the perseverance to do. Painting a mural is a good example. A child alone could plan and paint it, but not within the two or three study periods available for it. Even if permitted to use free time, the child would most likely lose interest in the mural before completing it.

Thus group work provides opportunities for children to process information in ways that otherwise would not be available to them. This aspect helps them to accept and anticipate group-work activity as worthwhile.

Projects vary in complexity. Some (such as product, surface feature [showing fauna and flora, for example], and relief maps; sketches illustrating processes or events; relationship, organization, and flow charts; and models of various kinds), reflect only the descriptive organization of the facts and ideas studied. Others (such as creative dramatizations, maps, models, or sketches showing what might be, might have been, or should be, lists of rules or recommendations that might be followed to improve life for everyone, and the like), require deeper thought.

Often the less-complex project, when completed, represents a stage of learning rather than its end. For example, after groups of children have constructed some product maps and presented them to the class, the teacher guides them, either as a class or in groups, to consider the implications for world trade.

The more complex project often serves as a culmination of study. For example, when, after

studying the Constitution, groups of children compose a constitution to use in the conduct of classroom affairs and relationships, the project is the culmination of study.

When working with fourth, fifth, and sixth-grade children, or with slower-learning children in the later grades, it is better to guide them toward less-complex projects, and to follow their completion with more-complex activities. In this instance, the project serves as a constant and immediate point of reference for more difficult activity.

As has been mentioned in the previous section, all the groups may work on similar or different projects. Similar projects often provide for the expression of different points of view and insights about an idea, theme, or topic. Different projects, particularly those serving as parts to a total-class project (such as presenting an assembly program; a complete, detailed model of a system; organizing and operating a special program to prevent littering in the school), help the children build class cohesiveness. They feel that they are part of a greater enterprise.

After the projects have been decided, the groups have been formed, and the work areas have been assigned, the stage is set for group work. How well children do will be determined largely by how well they can use group-work skills.

Establishing Suitable Behaviors

The behaviors which the children will have to learn or improve are those of leaders and followers. From watching television, many children see leadership behaviors as those followed by ranch foremen, police squad leaders, and military officers during critical situations. Good leaders give orders quickly, directly, and often loudly. Television programs have led children to believe that good followers respond meekly, immediately, and without question. Poor followers are those who forget what they are supposed to do, make bad judgments, and botch things up for the leader. Such behaviors may be necessary in dangerous, critical situations, but they are not appropriate for democratic group work. Our task is to help children learn workable concepts that are to prevail during group work.

In group work leaders are facilitators. They ask for and listen to suggestions and opinions, help the members analyze suggestions and opinions to discover better plans and decisions, help members accept tasks, give support to members as they perform tasks, and coordinate the work of the members to bring the project to completion.

In group work the members are participants. They make suggestions, give opinions, listen to and react to those of other members, accept tasks, and cooperate with the leader and other members of the group to complete the project.

Few children have a workable grasp of group-work roles. In Chapters 3 and 4, you were introduced to teaching strategies you can use to guide children in learning the behaviors inherent in group-work roles—in-depth discussion, role playing, simulation, values clarification, values analysis, and problem-centered inquiry.

Using In-depth Discussion

In-depth discussion as a teaching strategy here serves two purposes: to determine the children's background in group-work experience and to surface verbalizations of behaviors to be tried and modified through group work. The strategy follows these procedures:

1. Using a project which a group of children is going to work on, describe a situation similar to this: "Bob, Henry, Ellen, Pam, and Jim are going to build a model of a city. They have met as a group and have decided that Bob should be their leader. Bob is surprised because he did not expect to be the leader. He is not quite sure about what he is supposed to do, but he wants to be a good leader. What suggestions might we give him?" Record the children's responses on a chart or on the chalkboard.

If the children contribute ideas similar to the following, they probably have some experience working in groups:

a. He should give everyone a chance to speak.
b. He should listen to what the others have to say.
c. He should help others decide what to do.
d. He should ask others in a nice way to do things.
e. He should keep the work going.

Responses such as the above indicate that the children are ready for the next procedure.

2. Extend the situation to include the followers in the group in a way similar to this: "Henry, Ellen, Pam, and Jim are not sure about what they should do as group members. What suggestions might we give them?"

Children who have had experience with work groups will give responses similar to the following:

a. They should wait their turn to speak.
b. They should speak quietly.
c. They should give ideas.
d. They should listen to others.
e. They should work with the others and the leader to get the job done.

Responses like these show that the children are prepared to try the next procedure.

3. Focus the children's attention on each of the listed behaviors and encourage them to interpret what each means. Reminding them that these are the "rules" they are going to try to follow as they work together, release the children to begin their group work. Observe each group carefully. If a group is having a problem, join it to help. Be sure to ask the leader first what seems to be the problem. Proceed from that point to get ideas from the others in the group on what needs to be done. When they have a solution that appears workable to them, leave them to continue.

4. At the end of the group work, convene the children as a class to evaluate their performance in work groups. Ask for a review of problems and what was done to solve them. Have each group choose a behavior for the leader and one for the followers to try to improve during the next group-work session. Ask the children whether any of the "rules" should be changed in any way or whether any should be added to the list.

5. At the beginning of the next group session, have the children recall the behaviors that they are going to try to improve before starting to work.

6. Repeat procedures 4 and 5 until the groups work together smoothly.

Now let us consider what we should do if the children could not surface descriptions of behaviors suitable for democratic group work. Suppose that the children had suggested the following during the first procedure:

- The leader shouldn't just make the other people do the work.
- The leader shouldn't holler at the other people.
- The leader shouldn't do all the talking.

Terminate the discussion as gracefully as you can, delay the group work, and plan a set of analyses prompted by your presenting situations similar to the following:

- Mary and Betty are leaders of groups. Each wants to get her group started. Mary says, "Listen, now. We are going to build a little city. I'm going to draw it on the chalkboard so that you will know what kind of city we are going to build. And don't mess around while I'm drawing." Betty says to her group, "Do any of you have any ideas about how we should make our city, or how we should get started?" In whose group would you rather be?
- Benny and Jack are group leaders. Each member of their groups has made a sketch of a model city. Now it is time for each group to consider the sketches. Benny says, "Give me the sketches. . . . Boy, these are terrible, but this is the best one. We'll use it." Jack says to his group, "Let's lay each of the sketches on the table and decide which one we are going to use or how we can combine ideas from them to make a single sketch." In whose group would you rather work?
- Diane and Jill are the leaders of their groups. It is time for them to assign jobs to the other members of their groups. Diane says, "Bill, you cut the chipboard. Manuel and Dick, you start making buildings. And Laura and Stacey, you start making trees." Jill says, "We are ready to make things. Who would like to get the chipboard ready? . . . Who would like to make buildings?" In which of these groups would you like to be a member?

- When Nancy, who is the leader of her group, asks Tom to make trees, he replies, "I don't think I want to make trees." Nancy says, "I don't care what you want. Go ahead and make those trees. Somebody has to make them." When a member of Alice's group tells her that she doesn't want to make trees, Alice says, "I know the trees are not much fun, but if you will make some today, I'll give you your first choice tomorrow." Would you rather work with Alice or Nancy? Why?
- Ned is having trouble making a building. He goes to Nick, his group leader, and says, "I just can't get my building to stand up straight." Nick looks at the building and says, "You're a real dummy. See that piece there? You are supposed to cut it off. Anyone with an ounce of brains could see that. Fix it." In another group, Jason can't get his building to stand up straight either. He says to Lee, his group leader, "My old building won't stand up straight." Lee says, "Let's take a look at it. . . . I think if we cut off this piece, it will stand up." In whose group would you like to work? Why?
- As his group works, George goes from person to person. He says things like this, "That looks nice . . . I see you need some paste. Let me get you some . . . How can I help you?" As his group works, Mike goes over to the library corner and begins to read a book. In whose group would you rather be? Why?

As the children consider each situation, they surface ideas about the behaviors of a leader in a democratic group. A similar set of situations can be developed to help children discover ideas about how a person behaves as a democratic member of a group. The situations might provide for the following kinds of comparisons:

- The child who speaks out of turn as compared to the child who waits his or her turn or responds to the leader's recognition.
- The child who speaks in a quiet voice as compared to the child who shouts.
- The child who gives opinions or suggestions as compared to the child who sits watching or becomes occupied with something else.
- The child who listens and responds seriously to others as compared to the child who reacts hostilely.
- The child who cooperates with others and the leader as compared to the child who refuses to cooperate.

The children might discuss such situations from two points of view, that of a leader or that of another group member.

After the children have surfaced the descriptions of appropriate group-work behaviors, continue with procedures 3 through 6 as given in the list of procedures.

Using Role Playing

Like in-depth discussion, role playing surfaces behaviors. When using it as an introductory strategy, we state the general problem very simply, perhaps like this: "When we work in groups to make something, we have to work closely with each other. Sometimes this is not easy. We are going to role play to try to discover some ways to make our group work go more smoothly."

From this point on, we present simply described conflict situations which the children extend through role playing to discover workable behaviors. Here are a few examples designed to prompt children to explore within certain relationships:

• Ginny and Alma are sharing a small dish of paste as they work on a large poster. It is almost gone. Ginny dips her finger in the dish and removes what remains. She begins to use some of it when Alma reaches her finger into the dish only to find that it is empty. "Oh, Ginny!" she exclaims, "You've taken the last of the paste, and I really need some right now!" How do you think Ginny will reply? (Member-to-member relationships.)
• Frank and Chuck are participating in a work-group discussion with three other children. Donna, the group leader, has just asked her group for suggestions on how they might divide the work in painting the mural. She sees that Frank has an idea and asks him to tell what it is.
"Well," says Frank, "there are five of us. I think we should measure it and divide it into five equal parts. Then each person could be given a part. . . ."
"That is the craziest idea I ever heard!" interrupts Chuck, "Only a stupid jerk would think of such a thing."
How do you think Frank feels? What might he say? What might Donna say? (Member-to-member and leader-to-member relationships.)

• Emory is the leader of a work group that is just finishing the construction of a replica of an Indian agricultural village. Jerry has just finished his task. For fun he begins to tease the other group members who are still working.
"Don't do that, Jerry," asks Emory, "We are almost done. If you want to do something, why don't you start gathering up the scraps of paper and cardboard?"
"What do you think I am?" replies Jerry, "Clean-up man for the group? You can pick it up yourself."
If you were Emory, how would you feel? What might you say? (Leader-to-member relationships.)

Contrary to what is usually recommended for role playing for values, we would list the positive behaviors the children surfaced and use them as standards for judging the appropriateness of the children's own performance during the beginning stages of group work. After the behaviors have been surfaced and verbalized, we have the children try to use them in group work, to determine those needing improvement, and to try to improve them with each group-work session. In this respect the teaching procedures differ little from those following an introduction through in-depth discussion.

If we guide children in exploring for suitable behaviors through role playing as a corrective measure, we present role-playing situations parallel to those needing improvement. However, we leave further learning and self-evaluation completely to the children. Behaviors are not recorded or discussed further.

Using Simulation

The only restriction to using simulation as a strategy to help children discover appropriate group-work behaviors is that it requires children to participate in groups before learning much about how to do it. However, if the simulation is dynamic enough and the interaction is kept short, there should be little difficulty.

It is possible to have children simulate group work in situations similar to those in which they will work in the classroom, but they will participate more actively if the situations are parallel with a touch of the exotic included. Here is an example.

SIMULATION: THIRTY DAYS ON ARIDUS

Environmental Rules

1. The participants will count off by five or six. Number 1 in each group is designated as leader.
2. Each group will meet in a designated classroom area.
3. Each group will work by itself with no communication permitted between groups.
4. After each interaction, the next person in the numbered order becomes the leader. The person who was the leader becomes a follower in the group and takes the number five position. The members of the group renumber themselves.

Simulation Rules

1. *Phase I: Leader-centered interactions.* The leader conducts three interactions as prompted by three action cards 1, 2, and 3. Each interaction is allowed three minutes.
2. *Postdiscussion of Phase I.* The leaders tell about their choices and the crew members tell how they felt about the choices. The class agrees on two or three behaviors that a leader should follow to lead well.
3. *Phase II: Follower-centered interactions.* Crew member No. 2 alerts the crew to a situation and makes a choice about his or her behavior as prompted by interaction cards 4, 5, and 6. Each interaction is allowed three minutes.
4. *Postdiscussion of Phase II:* The crews react to the behavior of Crew Member No. 2. They tell how they feel about it. The class agrees on two or three behaviors that a member of a crew should follow to ensure that whatever needs to be done gets done.
5. *A review of the surfaced behaviors.* The class discusses and decides on how useful these behaviors would be if a group of people were working together on a project.

Conduct of the Simulation

1. Encourage the children to tell what they think the life of a crew on a rocketship might be like. Announce that they will have a chance to be members of a rocket ship.

2. Read the scenario: "You are the members of a crew on a rocket ship from Ploovia, a planet where it rains most of the time. The ship has just developed engine trouble and has had to land on Aridus, a planet where it rarely rains. Number 1, the rocketship captain, has learned by radio that it will take at least a week for a Ploovian rescue ship to come to help them.

"Ordinarily this would have caused no problem. However, the Ploovian crew members must wear water-filled suits to be able to live comfortably, and the water system was damaged when they landed. The water has flowed out and disappeared immediately in the dry soil of Aridus. Each member's suit is now dry.

"Fortunately, they can manage to live if they rub some water into their bodies every two hours. They must start doing this within twenty-four hours.

"Although Aridus is very dry, water is available deep in the ground. The crew knows they can get it by digging. They have two digging tools. But, when not wearing a water-filled suit, a Ploovian can dig for only an hour at a time, and then must rest an hour before digging again. Twelve hours of continuous digging by two men will result in a hole that will fill with enough water to last the crew for twenty-four hours, and a new hole must be dug each day. Because it is so cold at night, members of the crew can dig only during the twelve daytime hours.

"No. 1, the captain, has called the crew together. Ploovian crews use numbers instead of names, and No. 1 is always the captain. No. 1 shows them the tools and explains how they work. Then . . . ."

3. Have the children count off by fives or sixes to form the rocketship crews. Assign them a space for interaction and have them assemble in groups to receive further directions.

4. Explain that the Number 1 person in each group is the leader, and that after each interaction, the Number 2 person becomes No. 1, all members take the next lower number, and the person who was the leader takes the highest number.

Explain that each crew will follow the directions given on three action cards, starting with Action Card No. 1. They will be allowed four minutes to work with each card. Give the crew leaders the action cards and start the simulation.

5. Allow four minutes for an interaction with each action card. At the end of each four-minute interval, stop the interaction, have the children change crew numbers, and begin the next interac-

tion. At the end of the third interaction, guide the children as a class in discussing their experiences prompted by each action card.

ACTION CARD 1. TO BE READ BY THE CREW LEADER.

Read what is written in capital letters to your crew.

WE MUST DECIDE HOW WE ARE GOING TO ORGANIZE TO DIG FOR WATER. JUST TALK AMONG YOURSELVES UNTIL I CAN BE WITH YOU.

Read this to yourself.

You know that if each of four persons digs for six hours a day, there will be enough water for the crew. You must decide to do one of two things:
1. To tell the crew your plan.
2. To ask the crew for ideas about a plan.

Decide what you are going to do and start the discussion.

ACTION CARD 2. TO BE READ BY THE CREW LEADER.

Read what is written in capital letters to your crew.

WE MUST DECIDE ON HOW WE ARE GOING TO WORK. JUST TALK AMONG YOURSELVES UNTIL I CAN BE WITH YOU.

Read this to yourself.

You know that crew members 2 and 3 can work first for an hour, then 4 and 5 can. After 4 and 5 work for an hour, 2 and 3 will work again, and so on during twelve hours. You must decide to do one of two things:
1. To tell the crew your plan about how they will work.
2. To ask the crew for ideas about how they should work.

Decide what you are going to do and join the crew to talk about the problem.

ACTION CARD 3. TO BE READ BY THE CREW LEADER.

Read what is written in capital letters to your crew.

IT IS THE END OF OUR FIRST DAY, AND I CAN SEE THAT YOU ARE VERY TIRED. I HAVE MEASURED THE WATER YOU GOT TODAY, AND THERE IS BARELY ENOUGH FOR OUR NEEDS TOMORROW. WHAT DO YOU THINK ABOUT THAT? JUST TALK IT OVER UNTIL I CAN JOIN YOU.

Read this to yourself.

You must decide to do one of three things:
1. To ask the crew what they think should be done.
2. To praise them for their work and ask them to try a little harder tomorrow.
3. Tell them that they haven't been working hard enough and that they will have to work harder tomorrow.

When you finish reading this card, join your group and do what you think is best.

Focus the discussion on each action card and what the leader decided to do. Have the members of each crew tell how they felt as the leaders followed their decisions.

6. Explain that the next action cards are to be read by the number 2 crew member in each group. After the children have changed their crew numbers, have them begin the second phase. Monitor the interactions as you did during the first phase. At the end of the third interaction, guide the children as a class in discussing their experience prompted by each action card:

ACTION CARD 4. TO BE READ BY CREW MEMBER NO. 2.

Read what is written in capital letters to the team leader and the other members of the crew.

THE CREW HAS WORKED HARD. THEY HAVE ENOUGH WATER TO LAST FOR AN EXTRA DAY. THEY HAVE FOUR MORE DAYS BEFORE BEING RESCUED. NOW THE LEADER MUST GUIDE THE CREW IN DECIDING WHAT THEY MUST DO. HERE ARE SOME CHOICES THEY CAN THINK ABOUT:
1. STOP WORKING FOR A DAY.
2. WORK LESS TIME DURING THE NEXT FOUR DAYS.
3. SAVE THE WATER TO USE IF A TOOL BREAKS OR SOMEONE GETS SICK.
THE CREW, ALL EXCEPT ME, SHOULD BEGIN DISCUSSING NOW.

Read the following to yourself.

When you join the group, you must do one of the following:
1. Agree with everything that people suggest.
2. Disagree with everything they say. You may say things like: "I don't like that." "That is silly." "That's a terrible idea."
3. Listen carefully. Agree with the ideas you like

and disagree with what you don't like, but do it politely.

As soon as you decide what to do, join the group.

ACTION CARD 5. TO BE READ BY CREW MEMBER NO. 2.

Read what is written in capital letters to the team leader and the other members of the crew.

THE CREW IS BORED WITH RESTING WHEN THEY ARE NOT WORKING DURING THE DAY. THEY WOULD LIKE TO PLAY A SIMPLE GAME. BUT THERE ARE NO GAMES LIKE DOMINOES OR MONOPOLY IN THE ROCKETSHIP. WHATEVER GAME THEY DECIDE ON, THEY WILL HAVE TO MAKE IT. THE ONLY MATERIALS THEY HAVE ARE THE SHEETS OF ROCK AND PEBBLES LYING ALL AROUND ON ARIDUS.

THE CREW, ALL EXCEPT ME, SHOULD BEGIN DISCUSSING NOW.

Read the following to yourself.

When you join the crew, you must do one of the following.

1. Suggest *checkers* as a good game and listen carefully to what the others say.
2. Suggest *checkers* as a good game and keep on talking about it until the leader asks you to stop.

As soon as you decide what to do, join the group.

ACTION CARD 6. TO BE READ BY CREW MEMBER NO. 2.

Read what is written in capital letters to the crew leader and the other members of the crew.

TOMORROW THE RESCUE SHIP FROM PLOOVIA WILL ARRIVE. OUR SHIP IS MESSY. THESE JOBS NEED TO BE DONE:

DUSTING
SWEEPING
CHECKING THE WATER SUITS
PUTTING TOOLS AND OTHER THINGS AWAY

THE CREW, ALL EXCEPT ME, BEGINS TO DISCUSS WHICH JOBS ARE MOST IMPORTANT AND WHICH MEMBERS SHOULD DO THEM.

Read the following to yourself.

When you join the group you must do one of the following:

1. Pretend you are taking a nap or reading a book.
2. Volunteer for or accept a job without any argument.
3. When you get a chance, start talking about how

nice it will be to be back in Ploovia again. As soon as you decide what to do, join the crew.

7. Focus the discussion on each action card and what the Number 2 crew member did. Have the crew leaders and the other members react to behaviors of Number 2.

8. Guide the children in developing a list of behaviors that leaders and followers might follow in any work group to ensure that a task is completed and everyone in the group feels good about themselves and the other persons in the group.

As you can see, a simulation is used here to help children discover group-work behaviors. The children will learn the behaviors as they try them in group work and evaluate how well they do.

Using Values Clarification

If you wish to use a strategy which focuses children's attention on the positive aspects of group-work behaviors, you would do well to use a values-clarification strategy. First, you would need to compose three lists of group-work behaviors from which your learners may make choices. One list would be comprised of behaviors similar to the following:

If you were the leader of a group of boys and girls working together to plan and paint a mural, which of the following would you like the people in your group to say?

1. What can I do now?
2. I don't want to do that.
3. That idea is silly.
4. I have an idea.
5. I think that idea will work.
6. I don't like doing this.
7. You expect me to do everything.
8. I would like to do this job.

The above list gives the behaviors that a leader might look for in the other members of the group. Another list would present the behaviors that the followers would expect from the others, like this:

If you were a worker in a group of boys and girls working together to plan and paint a mural, which of the following would you like to hear the other people in your group say?

1. May I borrow your pencil, please?
2. Is there anything I can do to help you?
3. Your idea is no good.
4. Give me back that pencil. Right now!
5. I'd like to offer this idea for people to think about.
6. I don't like that job.
7. I like your idea.
8. Yes, I would like to do that.

And the third list would include what followers might expect from their leaders, like this:

If you were a worker in a group of boys and girls working together to plan and paint a mural, which of the following would you like to hear the leader of your group say?

1. Who has an idea about how to do this?
2. This is the way I've decided for us to do this.
3. Who would like to do this?
4. Do it this way.
5. I am the leader and you will do what I say.
6. Do you need some help?
7. I don't care what you want to do.
8. What you have done is terrible.
9. What do you think we should do now?
10. That is a good job that you have done.

You are now ready to follow these procedures:

1. Encourage the children to tell about the various groups that they form out of school—the groups they may form as they come to school in the morning, as they organize to play or visit after school, and the like.
2. Alert them to your intent to form them into small groups to work together to do social-studies projects, but that before they begin to do such work, they must think about how people work together in groups and how they feel about it.
3. Introduce the first list, either on a chart or duplicated for class distribution, and have the children choose from among the entries about what a leader might prefer the members of his or her group to say. Have them give reasons for their choices. When they finish making choices and giving reasons, conduct a hand vote on the various entries.

(If the discussion has been brisk, you may present the other lists to be treated in the same way. If you wish, you may have the children work with the other lists on successive days.)
4. After all the lists have been treated, guide the children in a review of their preferred choices as indicated by the vote.
5. Form the children into groups and have them work at their projects. If necessary, help them decide who is to be the leader.
6. At the close of each group-work period, conduct an assessment of the group's work. The leaders report on what the groups have accomplished and cite the acceptable behaviors of the members of their groups. The members are encouraged to cite the acceptable behaviors of their peers and the leader.

As was stated at the beginning of this discussion, a values-clarification strategy guides children in learning in positive ways the interrelationship skills needed for effective group work.

If you feel that a value or cluster of values related to group work needs further clarification, you prepare a value questionnaire. For example, if the children are having difficulty in selecting effective behaviors, you might have them react to a value questionnaire similar to the following:

Write your answers on another sheet of paper. If, after you answer the first question, you find a question you do not care to answer, do not answer it.

1. If you had a choice of the following persons for the leader of your group, which is making a cardboard model of a street or village, which one would you choose?
   a. A person who can get others to do what he or she wants.
   b. A person who is your friend.
   c. A person who can help others.
   d. A person who is always saying funny things.
   e. A person who talks a lot.
   f. A person who can make nice things from cardboard.
   Write the description of the person you would choose on your paper. If you do not like any of the descriptions, write one that you like.

2. Read the choices above again. Are you sure you have chosen what you think is really best? If your answer is *no,* write your new choice on your paper.
3. Study the description of the person you would choose as a leader of a group making a cardboard model and answer these questions with a *yes* or *no.*
   a. Do you think this person would ask everyone in the group for their ideas?
   b. Do you think he or she would listen carefully as each group member spoke?
   c. Do you think he or she would boss everyone?
   d. Do you think he or she would be fair to everyone?
   e. Do you think he or she would have to hit or shout to get the group to work?
   f. Do you think he or she would do a share of the work?
   g. Do you think he or she would give the best jobs to his or her friends?
   h. Do you think he or she would care if a person in the group was having trouble doing something?
   i. Do you think he or she would try to be nice to everyone in the group?
   j. Do you think everyone in the group would want to work with this person?
4. If you were in a group as it selected a leader, and a person in the group was like the one you have been thinking about, would you do any of the following? Answer with a *yes* or *no.*
   a. Tell the other people in the group that this person would be a good leader.
   b. Give a hand vote for this person.
   c. Ask a friend to vote for this person.
   d. Try to talk this person into accepting the job of leader.
   e. Vote for this person even if he or she was not a close friend.

After the children do the value questionnaire, have them share their responses in a class discussion. Avoid allowing arguments to develop. Emphasize the importance of just listening to see what others think.

The completion of this questionnaire and the subsequent discussion can have two good effects: first, the children learn about the qualities of leadership and will try to use them when they select leaders, and second, children who are confused because they are not selected as leaders begin to sense why they are not.

The success of this gentle strategy rests on your skills in understanding children and being able to identify specific needs.

Using Values Analysis. If you think that your learners would profit from a careful scrutiny of group work as a human endeavor and you would like to consider its value before trying it, you could use a values-analysis strategy.

To help the children identify and clarify the value question, you provide first a view of group work that helps them recognize at least its most obvious aspects as a human endeavor. A videotape showing children entering each aspect of group work and finally presenting their completed project would be ideal. If you know a teacher who is successful in guiding children in group work and videotaping facilities are available, you might arrange with the teacher to have a videotape made of one of his or her groups at work. A group of children that has already completed a project is usually delighted to act before a camera. A little direction can clarify the aspects to be taped. It should not take long to make such a videotape.

However, if such a videotape is not available or cannot be made, a list of the events that occur will serve the purpose. Here is such a list for a group at work making maps. After the group has been formed, it meets in an assigned area and the following takes place:

1. The group selects a leader.
2. The leader asks the members for ideas about the number of maps to be made, their size, and what they are supposed to look like.
3. The members give ideas, listen to each other's ideas, and give opinions about the ideas they hear. The leader controls the discussion to see that everyone who has anything to say has a chance to say it.
4. The leader has the members review their ideas and decide on the number, size, and design of the maps.
5. The leader asks for ideas on a plan for making the maps.
6. The members give ideas, listen to each other's ideas, and give opinions about the ideas they

hear. The leader controls the discussion to see that anyone who has anything to say has a chance to say it.

7. The leader has the members review their ideas and decide on a plan. The plan is that some members will make the outline maps, some will make lists of items to be put on the maps, all will make items to paste on the maps, and all will work at putting the items on the map.

8. The leader asks for volunteers to make the lists and outline maps. More volunteers than are needed want to make the maps, so the leader asks if any of these would help make the lists. One member accepts this task.

9. During several social-studies periods the group works as they had planned. The leader has had to help the map makers solve a problem about the use of equipment and has had to help the people making the lists. The leader also makes some items to paste on the maps.

10. The leader sees that everyone has a turn at pasting items on the map, and everyone helps in getting the items pasted in the right place.

11. The leader asks for ideas about how to present the maps to the class.

12. The members give ideas, listen to each other's ideas, and give opinions about the ideas they hear. The leader controls the discussion to see that anyone who has anything to say has a chance to say it.

13. The leader has the members review their ideas and decide on how they should present their maps. They decide that each member, including the leader, will tell about a map.

14. Each member plans what he or she will say.

15. The leader guides the group in rehearsing their presentation. The leader and the members give suggestions to each person during the rehearsal.

16. The group presents their maps to the class.

The above list or the videotape will serve the same purpose as you guide children through the following procedures:

1. Engage the children in a brief discussion focused on the differences between a police squad as a group and a P. T. A. membership committee as a group. Encourage them to think about the difference between the leaders of the groups in the ways that they manage the groups' efforts.

2. Alert the children to your intent to have them work in groups in ways similar to those of a committee. Present the videotape or the list of

events occurring when a group completes a project cooperatively.

3. Have the children read the list or view the videotape to detect the important events. Have them decide which events appear to be repeated. Then through discussion, have them surface the behaviors of leaders and followers in groups.

4. Ask the value question: "Do you think that group work might help boys and girls learn in social studies?" As children reply in the affirmative or the negative, ask them to give reasons for their opinion. On the chalkboard or a chart, list their reasons as given under the general label of "yes" or "no." When all who want to express an opinion have expressed it, guide the children in ranking both sets of reasons.

5. Provide for the children to check the relevance of their reasons. You may do this by inviting the group-work specialist from the curriculum office or the teacher in your school who is successful with it to serve as a resource person. This person may come to the classroom to react to the children's ideas and to answer their questions, or he or she may be given the lists of reasons to which to respond on audiotape. A group of children who are skilled in group work can be invited to the classroom to serve as resource persons. The children can judge the relevance of their reasons against what the resource person says.

6. Guide the children in deciding whether group work is helpful or unhelpful to boys and girls to learn social studies. (In most instances children will decide overwhelmingly in the affirmative. If there should be a strong negative response, indicate that everyone will have opportunities to try group work to see whether it is helpful or unhelpful.)

7. Guide the children in testing the value principle. Have them react to these questions:

Do you think this kind of group work might be as useful to police squads as it is to P. T. A. committees? Why do you think so?

Do you think that group work is as helpful to boys and girls learning to read is it is to boys and girls doing social-studies projects? Why do you think that?

Pointing out that they are going to have a chance to see how group work is helpful in learning, list the possible projects or guide the class in developing a list. Form the groups and have them begin working.

8. When the group projects are completed, guide the groups in sharing how they thought group work was helpful or unhelpful.

The weakness of this strategy is that it permits possibilities for considering negative ideas. The strength of it is that it provides for testing both positive and negative ideas.

Issues about group work may arise. Values analysis may be helpful in guiding children to react to them. Here are a few such issues.

• The leader of a group should be elected by the group or appointed by the teacher.
• Leaders should be changed often so that everyone has a chance to be a leader.
• A person should try always to be a member of the same group.

It is possible, then, to use values analysis as a continuing strategy to help children know how to do effective group work.

Using Problem Solving

This strategy requires patience and a deep understanding of children. Learning how to do group work effectively is the major problem, and the children learn to do it by solving problems that arise while trying to work in groups. Here are the procedures to follow:

1. Guide the children in an analysis of the project to determine the necessary subtasks and the order in which they will need to be completed. For example, a group of children developing a creative drama about conditions occurring during the Westward Expansion would find a list of subtasks such as the following to be helpful.
   a. Creating a family as a cast of characters.
   b. Creating a problem or series of problems which the family has to solve.
   c. Deciding who in the group is to play each role.
   d. Creating the dramatic interpretation for each scene, which also surfaces the need for properties.

   e. Making properties.
   f. Deciding on costumes.
   g. Rehearsing with costumes and properties.
   h. Presenting the play.
2. Form the groups and inform the children about the signal you will use to have them stop working and convene as a class. The signal may be turning the light switch on and off several times, ringing a bell, or whatever will get children's attention when embroiled in arguments. Assign the work areas and have the groups get to work.
3. Chances are that the children will have difficulties. Perhaps everyone will want to speak at the same time, or someone will start trying to boss the others, or two or more people begin to play around. The noise level will begin to rise gradually. When it passes that steady buzz of children's voices characteristic of planning groups, signal for the group work to stop and convene the children as a class.
4. Encourage the children to describe without giving names what is going on in their groups. Ask the other children if there were similar conditions in their group and how they tried to solve it. Ask for descriptions of solutions to problems and encourage the children to think of others that might work. Have the children consider which solution or solutions would probably work best. Ask the children to bear the solutions in mind as they return to their work areas and begin to work again. Repeat this procedure until the children learn how to work cooperatively in groups.

You will find it helpful to guide children in considering what they have learned about group work at the end of each instructional period during the learning phase, and then, at the beginning of the next instructional period, having them recall what they had discussed just before starting group work again.

Some teachers regard this strategy as the most realistic of all. The children must recognize the problems before they try to solve them and they must generate and try the solutions.

Using Strategies in Combination. By now it has probably occurred to you that you would not need to rely on one strategy exclusively. For example, you could use an in-depth discussion or simulation as a means of having the children develop the needed behaviors, and then, as corrective measures, guide the children in role playing, values clarification, or values analysis, or some combination of these.

Using one strategy to make an introduction and others for correction offers variety and subtlety to learning.

The strategy you choose to use is your decision.

Evaluating Projects and Group Performance

Whenever we commit children to working as a group to plan and complete a project, we have set them on a course which leads them toward major areas of instructional objectives. One has to do with the integration and restructure of experienced facts and ideas, and the other with learning to interact cooperatively with others in completing a task. We need to evaluate what has occurred in both areas of learning.

Evaluating Projects. Three aspects of the project are of concern to us as we evaluate it. The first is how well the children have applied their production skills in making the project. If we are also responsible for teaching the composition and construction skills in the use of various media, we shall want to see whether the children have used their skills to the level at which they have been taught. What we discover may be of greater importance to us than the children.

For example, let us suppose that our fifth-grade class has worked in groups to prepare imaginary pages of a newspaper published during the five years preceding the Civil War. Each group is to prepare a page. When we look at the finished pages which the groups display so proudly, we are shocked to discover common words misspelled, incomplete sentences, inadequate use of capitalization and punctuation, and poor sequence in the expression of ideas. Such an experience prompts us to review our teaching practices. It is likely

that we shall discover that we have failed to teach these skills to a useful level of transfer.

The second aspect that concerns us is how accurately and imaginatively the project conveys meaning. As we consider accuracy, we have a greater concern for organization of information than for completeness of factual details. However, the project should reflect a careful selection of pertinent facts to express a reasonable organization. The organization should be accurate in sequence, functional relationships, spatial arrangements, and completeness.

For example, if your fourth-grade class worked in groups to make charts of industrial chains showing the collection or production of raw materials, processing them into useful goods, and the distribution process, you would expect each chart to show the complete sequence of events in the right order without omissions or extraneous insertions. If you found errors, you would review the learning activities you had prescribed. Perhaps not enough facts were experienced, or there were too few integrative activities to bring children to the point of arriving at generalizations and expressing them in different ways. However, you may wish to delay your final evaluation until the children have explained their project to the class. Frequently they make the necessary corrections as they discuss their projects.

Often the use of imagination is inhibited or encouraged by the nature of the project. A replica as a project is usually a mirror reflection of knowledge. For example, a model of a Balinese village is a three-dimensional structure of cardboard, paper maché, and paint, which faithfully presents the facts the children have learned from books, pictures, films, and filmstrips. But a model of a community constructed to show how the transportation, energy, and pollution problems might be solved a century from now would offer many opportunities for imaginative thought restricted only by the knowledge of current technology.

Occasionally a group will produce a project which at first seemed to offer little opportunity for imagination, but at its completion, it has a strikingly imaginative quality. Even a project as prosaic as a map may result in a product which reflects an insight so unique that children who had worked in other groups are drawn to it again and again.

The most significant criterion for the quality of a project lies in how the children who made it feel about it. Their feelings are usually obvious when they present and explain it to the class. Usually they are pleased. When they appear reticent and embarrassed, you have a decision to make: either assume that the project result was simply an unfortunate circumstance to be forgotten as soon as possible, or look more deeply into the matter. If you decide the latter, you may confer with each of the members of the groups to learn how each feels about the project. This will give you an opportunity to point out the positive aspects of the project, thus to rebuild the child's confidence in himself or herself and others. Also, the child is helped to anticipate group work in the future with a positive attitude.

Perhaps you will want to see how all the children personally feel about their projects. Figure 7–4 presents an example of a rating sheet developed for use when the project is a map. An abundance of negative responses on the rating sheet often indicates a need for more careful consideration of projects before the children work in groups again. Any of the following will prove helpful:

• Guide the children in making a list of the projects they like and can do. When the group convenes, they decide which project they are going to complete.
• Organize the groups according to project preferences. This involves providing choices.
• Guide the children in making a list of projects they would like to do. Have them rank their choices. Use the results as a basis for planning instruction in the skills necessary for project completion.

Of course, dissatisfaction with a project may be an attitude generalized from an unpleasant group-work experience.

Evaluating Group Work. Some of the procedures suggested in Chapter 2 for assessing children's needs for improvement in interaction skills may be used when evaluating group work. However, because of the well-defined leadership and followership roles involved in group work on projects, evaluation requires that these roles be taken into account.

When observing to see how effective children are in their group-work roles, it is easier to observe the role performances separately. When evaluating leadership, center your attention on leaders. Do the same when evaluating followership.

When observing leaders, you listen for task-supporting utterances which also reflect respect and concern for the other group members. One way to do this is to use specific leadership behaviors as entries on an observation checklist. Figure 7–5 shows such a checklist.

On the line to the right of each question mark an X at a point that best shows how you feel.

	Very Good	Comfortable	Uncomfortable
1. How do you feel about the map you made with your group?	⊢————————————————⊣		
2. If there was a contest for maps, how would you feel about having the map entered in the contest?	⊢————————————————⊣		
3. How would you feel about making another map with a group?	⊢————————————————⊣		

FIGURE 7–4. *Project Rating Sheet.*

Leadership Behaviors	Name ——————— Date ——————— Tallies
Asks for opinions	
Acknowledges opinions	
Asks for suggestions	
Acknowledges suggestions	
Asks for reactions	
Acknowledges reactions	
Asks for volunteers	
Acknowledges volunteers	
Offers help	
Maintains task orientation	

FIGURE 7–5. *Leadership Observation Checklist.*

All the behaviors except the last listed are supportive to group members. The last, "Maintains task orientation," is basically task supportive, but it should be made as person supportive as possible. This is accomplished through the use of indirect imperatives such as, "Let's get back to work," "We had better get busy," or "Let's remember what we are really trying to do."

If you do not wish to use a checklist, bear the behaviors in mind as you observe, and then write an anecdotal record in which you describe the leader's behaviors in a brief paragraph.

Another way of recording a leader's behaviors is to rate and code each utterance as you hear it. Here is a code you might use:

0 = A direct command, a threat, or a sarcastic remark.
/ = A request for information, a task-orienting statement, a summary statement, a positive acceptance of an opinion or suggestion.
+ = An open question.

If you find leaders who "boss" more than guide, you may guide them in improving their facilitation skills by:

- Counselling them individually to try to follow a few simple rules to guide the group toward decisions—
  a. Ask the group for opinions and suggestions.
  b. Give everyone a chance to speak.
  c. Give your own ideas only after everyone else has spoken.
- Convening them as a group to review how groups move toward decisions. Build this list of procedures with them:
  a. The leader asks for ideas.
  b. The members give ideas.
  c. The leader asks which idea is the best.
  d. The members give reasons and react to others' reasons.
  e. The leader asks the members to decide on the best idea.
- Conferring with individual leaders to discuss their problems. Help each to decide on a behavior they want to try as a way of improving their leadership. Then observe to note the occurrence of the improved behavior. Discuss the results with the leader observed.

Following such practices will help your learners develop their leadership potential.

When observing the other members of groups, you observe all members of a group at one time. You will find it easier to use an observation checklist on which you tally the occurrence of each behavior. Figure 7–6 presents an example.

Negative responses include discourteous reactions to what others say, refusal to listen when others speak, insisting stubbornly on one's point of view without giving reasons, being upset when the leader assigns a desired role to another person, and the like.

Sometimes negative responses are prompted by ineffective leadership. For this reason, you should evaluate the effectiveness of leaders first. However, if the leader is performing properly, and a member frequently reacts negatively, the member needs individual counselling. If this person feels animosity toward the leader, assign him or her to another group and observe again. If negative be-

Students' Names	Behaviors					
	Gives opinion	Reacts to opinion positively	Gives suggestion	Reacts to suggestion positively	Volunteers for or accepts task	Negative responses

FIGURE 7–6. *Followership Observation Checklist.*

havior is again evinced, this person is unable to do group work and should be given an individual task.

In most instances, you will detect some children who are reluctant to participate actively. Usually these children are most easily reached through the group leader. Counsel with the leader to suggest an idea or two for him or her to try:

- When asking for ideas, the leader may ask each member to write a brief note expressing an idea. Then the members read their ideas in turn.
- When asking for suggestions, the leader breaks the group into subgroups of two or three members to discuss suggestions to make.
- When guiding the group toward consensus, the leader asks each member by name to indicate agreement or disagreement.
- When guiding the discussion, the leader waits two or three seconds before giving the floor to a member. This gives the slower thinkers time to collect their thoughts and to volunteer a response. By choice, the leader gives the floor to a

late volunteer who does not usually participate actively.
- After group work, the leader makes it a point to go to the reluctant participant to acknowledge especially any active response made during work.

In a sense, the leader is encouraged to become a surrogate teacher. During group work, your role is to observe the groups at work to detect where improvement is needed, and to serve as a consultant when problems with the project occur. When you serve as a consultant, you enter the group as an extra member to make suggestions. You carefully guard the integrity of the leader. When you discover interaction problems, you may need to counsel individually with leaders or followers. This is usually better done when the groups are not at work. Or you may need to stop the group work to convene the class to consider a problem common to most of the groups.

Your careful exercise of your role ensures that

the children meet the many objectives for group work on projects.

GUIDING CHILDREN IN STUDY GROUPS

Often children have had experience working in project groups before they work in study groups, and much of what they have learned about working together transfers to work in study groups. What they have learned about interaction is particularly useful. Their knowledge of group organization may prompt them to select a leader to coordinate their efforts.

As mentioned earlier, frequent work in study groups does not usually begin before sixth grade. It is possible that you may have a sixth-grade class which has never completed projects in groups. This does not mean that the children must do project work as a readiness activity for work in study groups. Their desire to be with their peers and to interact with them is sufficient readiness.

Besides, as you will see, the skills and organization needed to work in study groups are in some ways less stringent than those needed in project groups.

Selecting Appropriate Tasks

The kinds and sequence of study tasks that you select for study groups will reflect the organization of curriculum emphases in your instructional program. If your program is designed to guide children through a formal inquiry process, your learners will frequently be grouped to perform some aspect of it. If your program emphasizes obtaining information before considering issues, your children will be doing tasks devoted to information acquisition, and then tasks in which they treat issues. However, since most of the formal inquiry operations may serve as tasks, we shall consider them first.

All the operations, from defining the problem

to making recommendations based on a conclusion, may be performed by study groups. Deciding the appropriateness of tasks is often a matter of determining how many tasks in an inquiry sequence may be performed by a group before it is called on to share its work with the other groups in the class. At other times it is a matter of deciding how group study should be interspersed with tasks performed by the class as a deliberating body or by individuals working independently.

For example, children in grades four and five who are just learning how to do group study, still striving toward a functional mastery of intake skills, and being introduced to formal inquiry operations, would be guided in a sequence similar to the following:

1. A *class discussion* during which the concept to be investigated is explored and the inquiry prompter is presented.
2. A *group study* in which the children define the problem, hypothesize, and select the most reasonable hypothesis.
3. A *class discussion* in which the groups share the results of their deliberations and come to agreement on the most reasonable hypothesis.
4. A *group study* in which the groups each develop a design for inquiry.
5. A *class discussion* in which each group presents its design, and the class compares designs, ultimately decides on the most adequate design, either one developed by a group or one composed from parts of designs.
6. *Individual study* during which each child seeks information and takes notes.
7. A *group study* in which information is compared, pooled, and organized for expression, and a generalization is drawn.
8. A *class discussion* in which information and generalizations are compared, a generalization agreed on, and the hypothesis judged against it. A conclusion is reached.
9. *Individual study* in which each child seeks information and takes notes to validate the conclusion.
10. A *class discussion* in which validations are compared.
11. A *group study* in which implications are drawn.
12. A *class discussion* in which implications are compared.

This alternation of social organization to complete study tasks lends variety to learning activities. Here is how they might occur during a sequence of instructional periods:

First Period

1. Class discussion
2. Group study
3. Class discussion

Second Period

1. Group study
2. Class discussion

Third and Fourth Periods

1. Individual study

Fifth Period

1. Group study
2. Class discussion

Sixth Period

1. Individual study
2. Class discussion

Seventh Period

1. Group study
2. Class discussion

When working with children in grade six and above, you may prefer to follow a schedule of class activities similar to the above, or you may dispense with sessions when children study independently. In the above, the children study independently whenever they seek information in resources suitable to their level of intake skills. However, if they are capable of using the resources effectively, perhaps with some peer assistance, they may seek information in group studies. The advantage to the above schedule, both as it is and as changed, is that it provides for groups to be changed in membership whenever group study is scheduled.

You may prefer the groups to work independently during a unit or a section of it without changing group membership. At the beginning of study, you would form the groups to discuss the various aspects of the topic or concept to pool their information and share it during a class discussion. During the class discussion, the children would experience the inquiry prompter and define the problem. From this point onward, they would work in groups to perform all the inquiry operations. Each instructional period would begin with a brief class discussion to explore for the solution of problems with materials and maintaining the work of the group. Progress reports on the tasks completed would also be given. When all the operations are completed, the groups convene as a class to compare implications and to decide which groups may need to be reconvened to discuss or revalidate their decisions. Figure 7–7 presents a flow chart showing how study is scheduled.

Perhaps at this point you have sensed that other inquiry operations may also be suitable as study-group tasks. Here are a few examples:

- Analyzing a set of pictures to put them in order and generalize about their meaning.
- Analyzing a single picture to determine how it might have been different fifty years before or after the moment it depicts.
- Deciding on an interest common to all the members of a group to be extended or explored further by the group.
- Analyzing a set of questions to categorize them and arrange them according to logic or interest.
- Making a list of questions expressing what more they would like to know about a people, region, process, system, etc.
- Deciding on solutions to problems impinging directly on their lives—the need for stoplights, crosswalks, a clean, attractive environment, play areas, etc.

If your instructional program emphasizes acquiring information as the basic goal of learning, you may form your learners into groups to seek information. The practice sometimes presents problems when the children use only their textbooks as informational resources. Unvaried tasks with the same resource become tedious. But if you can arrange for a variety of resources besides the text-

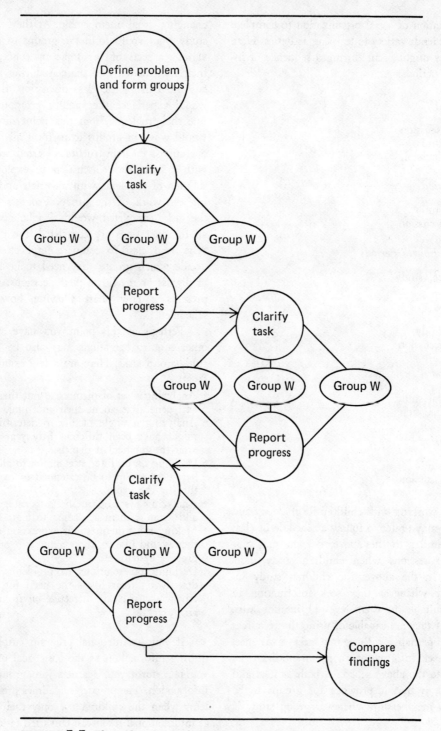

FIGURE 7–7. *Flow Chart for Study When Group Membership Remains the Same.*

book—fact sheets, informational sheets, filmstrips, film loops, maps, audiotapes, pamphlets, periodical articles, and brochures—the children are likely to remain enthusiastic about group study. Particularly effective is having each group work in a different resource about the same topic. Each group depends on the other and class cohesiveness is improved.

Whatever the task, it must be one in which all the children in the group can participate. If reading is involved, all the members of a group should be able to read the resource, or provisions should be made for slower readers. Perhaps you designate one member of the group as the reader. While he or she reads, the others listen. Or you may pair poor readers with able readers. This works well when both understand the arrangement and accept it.

And, finally, there is the matter of study management. Much of this is task centered. One aspect of it is making sure that you describe the task or tasks clearly. Another is stating the time allowed for task completion and whether time may be extended. And often an aspect of it is providing a back-up task for groups who finish earlier than the others. This task should be related as closely as possible to the main task, or it just becomes busy work which children soon see through. Here are a few examples of back-up tasks that may be used when the main task is hypothesizing:

- Have the group reexamine its selected hypothesis to develop a list of reasons to support it.
- Have the group make a list of arguments that other people might use against their hypothesis. This helps them develop a clearer statement.
- Have the group make a list of the resources available in the classroom that they think will contain information about it.

Another aspect of study management is to ensure that the children feel a sense of accomplishment on completing a task. This can be done easily by describing the task again immediately before the groups report and accepting each report in light of the description. Give particular recognition to those reports which meet the description.

If several tasks are to be completed during a group-study session or are to be completed over several periods, you should list the tasks on a chart or the chalkboard to help the groups keep track of where they are in their work.

Selecting appropriate tasks for study groups involves selecting those which best fit your instructional program and which children can do. The appropriateness is also based on how you manage the tasks: how clearly you explain them, provide back-up tasks, acknowledge the results of group study, and help children keep track of what they are doing.

Whatever the tasks, they should be varied. Group study can become just as dull as individual study.

Establishing Group Behaviors

The roles in study groups closely follow the requirements of the assigned tasks and the necessary reporting of task results to the class. All members are contributors to the task. Their activities will always include discussion to arrive at a statement of results. The activities may also include consulting resources to acquire facts and ideas to consider. For example, a group of children in sixth grade may be given an information sheet about the natural and human resources in Angola to perform the dual task of extracting information and using it to decide the potential of the country as a contributor to the world market. And one of the members will have to assume the role of spokesperson.

Because the roles differ little from those that children frequently have in the classroom when they are working directly with the teacher or monitoring themselves at a task, there is usually little need to guide them in exploring the roles in detail to discover suitable behaviors.

The role of the spokesman is somewhat new, but it rarely offers a problem. The children accept that there will be a spokesperson. The role will be assigned in any one of a number of ways. Someone with leadership ability may simply assume it, or he or she may accept it when the other members offer it. The group may conduct an election before getting to the task, or the members may forget about it until the group is asked to report. When asked to report, the members may look from one to another, point, nod, and nudge until someone assumes the role. Or they may look at each other expectantly and finally at the teacher as though expecting him or her to make an appointment. If none is made, one member of the group may find the moment of indecision so unbearable that he or she assumes the role.

However, if the groups have difficulty getting started or staying on the task, or you wish to ensure that the children have insights into what makes study groups work well, you may try any of the following strategies to surface helpful behaviors:

• Coach a group of children to work as a study group in which a task is given and a spokesperson is selected. The spokesperson alternates between being a member of the group and its leader until the task is completed. He or she then reports.

Inform the class that you have coached a group to show how a study group works together, and that the class members are to watch a performance by the group to get ideas about why it works so well. Have the group perform.

Conduct a class discussion focused on the behaviors of the spokesperson and the other members of the group. Identify these behaviors as the criteria that study groups are to try to meet to be able to work effectively.

• The same as the above except an audiotape of an effectively working study group in another classroom is used as an informational resource.

• Have the children role play, in monolog, a situation in which a child is elected as a spokesperson for the first time and thinks about what he or she should do to start the group on a given task. Conduct reenactments until one or two viable alternatives are surfaced.

Continue the role playing with the problems met by the spokesperson, such as keeping the group on task, dealing with members who are impeding the work of the group, keeping the group on task, moving the group from one task aspect to another, and bringing the group to a decision.

Identify the most widely accepted alternatives as criteria to try to meet during group study.

• Develop a simple simulation in which the children are divided into groups to represent small classes arriving at decisions about imaginary situations such as planning a class party, a program for a school assembly, a healthy school menu, and the like. Each situation is a simulation phase. Each group is to select a spokesperson to guide the discussion and report.

After each phase, conduct a class discussion in which the children surface and discuss strategies used by spokespersons and the other members of groups.

Identify the more effective strategies as criteria for effective group study.

• Draw a diagram representing a study group and identify the spokesperson within it. Describe a task this group is to perform. Then elicit from the children the behaviors of the group members and the spokesperson that will help them do their task well. Guide the children in selecting those behaviors which they think are the most important. Have them consider whether the spokesperson is the leader of the group or its agent in reporting its work.

Identify the behaviors as tentative criteria to try during group studies.

Each of the above strategies brings children into contact with criterion behaviors to be met or tried during group studies. To guide them in learning these behaviors you will need to do the following:

1. Remind them of the criterion behaviors before they begin the first group-study sessions and encourage them to monitor themselves.
2. Guide them in evaluating how close they are to meeting criteria and selecting criteria which require greater effort to meet.
3. Conduct discussions before group-study sessions to identify behaviors selected for improvement. Follow up with discussions after sessions to determine whether improvement has occurred.

Which of the strategies you plan to use is your decision. It will be better for both you and your learners if you base your decision on what you discover when you diagnose children's interaction skills as suggested in Chapter 2.

Evaluating Study-group Performance

The evaluation of study-groups' performance centers primarily on the children's interaction skills. The task product does not vary much from group to group, and pride in completing the task is a rarely expressed attitude. Positive spokesperson-member and member-member relationships are necessary to effective study-group performance, but they reflect generally the social organization of the class. Rather than focusing on products or relationships, then, we focus on interaction skills.

Evaluating Interaction Skills. Some of the approaches discussed in Chapter 2 are also applicable here.

A workable way of observing interaction skills is to look for utterances which carry the group to task completion. As these occur, you record them in code after the name of the speaker. Here is a usable code:

/ = Says something
+ = Offers a significant fact, reason, or opinion
* = Offers an opinion and at least one reason
T = Maintains task orientation
∠ = Asks a question or requests a reason
X = Makes a counterproductive remark

If you plan to use this code, arrange to observe the group during a two or three-minute period (the observation time should be the same for all groups), particularly when discussion is active, such as at the beginning or toward the end of the group-work period. List the names of the group members and record their utterances as they occur. An utterance is what a child says before another begins speaking.

As soon as you hear a child begin to speak,

mark a single diagonal line and listen for the rest of the utterance.

If the utterance is little more than a simple agreement or exclamation about what someone has said, and the speaker says no more, the diagonal line signifies that he or she has said something.

However, if the speaker continues, listen carefully. If a pertinent fact, reason, or opinion is given, mark a "plus." Mark a "plus" for each fact or reason. If the speaker gives an opinion and a reason related to it, convert the "plus" into a star or asterisk, and then a "plus" for each additional reason.

If the utterance is counterproductive, such as a sarcastic or otherwise discouraging remark, mark an "X." A counterproductive remark is disruptive. One of the members will often remind the group of the task it has at hand. Mark a "T" after this person's name to indicate a task-oriented utterance.

If a member asks a clarifying question or for more information or a reason, underline the diagonal line.

As you observe, assume an open attitude toward humorous remarks. If the remark relieves the tedium of the group's work, mark it as a "plus." However, if it is an obvious attempt to pull the group off task, mark it as an "X."

As you analyze the results of your observation, you will be able to detect which members are contributing to the discussion and task. The most important utterances are coded as an asterisk or as a "T." Children who have these listed after their name are outstanding contributors. Next in importance are the utterances coded as "plus" or "∠." Children making these utterances are active contributors. Of least importance, but still positive, are utterances coded as a diagonal line. All children will make this kind of utterance, but children who have only these signs after their name are contributing mostly by their physical presence. And "X's" signify detrimental contributions.

Recurring patterns of "X's" and diagonals require correction. In-depth class discussions and role playing may be used to explore the effects of detrimental remarks on persons and discussions, and to surface positive alternatives. Some children may require individual counseling during which self-monitoring plans are developed and put into effect. A self-monitoring plan involves an agreement by the learner that he or she has a problem, a plan for keeping track of self-performance to reduce the undesirable behavior, and validating improvement through the teacher's observations.

Least-effective contributions may be replaced by worthwhile contributions through introducing round-robin practices to group operations. Here is how they work.

Step 1. Every person in the group has a turn at giving an opinion or reason. No reactions to opinions or reasons are given until everyone has had a chance to speak.

Step 2. The members react in turn to the opinions or reasons given by citing a fact or another reason. Each member must have a turn before the topic or issue is open to full discussion.

Step 3. The group continues the discussion in the usual way until they arrive at a conclusion.

Step 4. The members react in turn to the conclusion by citing a fact or reason which they think makes it an acceptable conclusion.

Round-robin practices slow the work down. They should be dropped as soon as the contributions have been improved. Of course, some children may like to use them. Little harm is done if they continue to use them.

Evaluating Roles in Group Study. If your groups tend to organize themselves with selected leaders, you may wish to evaluate their performance of roles. In this case, the roles of leader and spokesperson are usually combined. The evaluation procedures are similar to those discussed for project group work. Because the spokesperson is also a contributing member, you would use criterion behaviors similar to the following when observing spokespersons:

• Asks for task solutions
• Asks for reasons
• Asks for facts
• Asks for reactions

• Offers additional solutions, reasons, facts, or reactions
• Accepts or acknowledges members' contributions
• Asks for consensus
• States personal stand toward consensus
• Maintains task orientation

The following criterion behaviors are useful when observing the performance of study group members:

• Offers task solution
• Offers a reason or reasons
• Gives a fact or facts
• Responds courteously to others' contributions
• Contributes toward consensus

Any necessary correction would follow practices similar to those suggested for correcting project group-work behaviors.

Probably the evaluation of roles is most useful when working with children who have had extensive experience at working in project groups. It provides a mode of communication which they can understand. If it does not have to be used, center evaluation on interaction. As you share with children the results of observing interaction, they become more personally responsible and rely less on rigid organization to help them complete tasks. This is the ultimate that we strive for in study groups.

SUMMARY

The psychological rationale for including group work in social studies is that it helps children know themselves and others as persons, and it provides them with needed support when exploring abstract ideas. The cultural rationale for group work is that it helps children to learn skills of democratic action.

Children usually are not taught group work before age nine or before fourth grade. Younger children are not socially mature enough to learn it.

Readiness is built in part through experiencing a positive social climate, a teacher who conducts discussions democratically, and classroom planning. Learning activities to build readiness consist of arranged experiences in which children share materials or do simple tasks in groups. The tasks are of short duration. Older children may build readiness for group work by working in carefully organized groups which follow the teacher's specific directions.

Organizing children for project group work requires that they be given a direct or indirect voice in determining the membership of groups. Organizing children for study group work requires that they be given opportunities to work with many of their peers. The recommended number of children in each group is from five to eight.

The furniture in the classroom must be arranged to facilitate communication or the children must be free to use it in ways that support communication.

The tasks given to groups should be those for which the children have the skills instrumental to their completion.

Projects as tasks help children integrate and express what they have experienced through investigative activities. Suitable projects are those which children cannot do very well as individuals. The complexity of projects is often determined by when they are to be completed.

In project work groups there are distinct roles to be learned. These include that of the leader as facilitator, and the member or follower as participant. Children may discover the behaviors characteristic of these roles through in-depth discussion, role playing, simulation, values clarification, values analysis, and problem-centered inquiry. They learn the behaviors through trying them and evaluating their success.

When children do project group work, both the project and the interaction process are evaluated. Project evaluation consists of making judgments about how well children have applied production skills, how accurately and imaginatively they have expressed facts, and how the children feel about the project. Evaluating interaction process involves seeing how well the children performed as leaders and followers in their groups.

Study in groups helps children participate more fully in study. The tasks they complete are associated with information acquisition and processing for complex ideas. Group study may be alternated with class and individual study. Operations from both formal and informal inquiry may be used as study tasks. If study groups are to work effectively, the teacher has to define tasks clearly, inform the children about time limits, provide back-up tasks, and help children keep track of what they are doing.

Children usually have little difficulty learning to work in study groups because their roles are similar to those they already have in the classroom. The role of spokesperson is new but not complex. Some children will need special experiences to learn to work in study groups. Observing a coached group or videotape of a working group, role playing, simulation, and in-depth discussions help children surface behaviors to try and evaluate.

Evaluating the performance of study groups involves observing children to see how they are interacting to complete the study task. Roles may also be evaluated through observation.

POSTSCRIPT

At the beginning of this chapter, you were asked to read two descriptions of group work. Each group met an objective related to task completion, either a project or a study. You were asked to interpret the situation to see what other kinds of objectives you could list as also being met in group work.

You were also asked to make a few notes on the procedures you would use to help children learn how to work in groups.

Take out your written interpretation and notes to see whether you still think the same way. If not, what changes would you make? Why?

FOR FURTHER UNDERSTANDING

Cognitive Activities

1. Make a diagram of the psychological and cultural rationales for including group work in the elementary social-studies curriculum.

2. Compare project group work and study group work. Tell what they have in common and how they are different.

3. Which of the six strategies (in-depth discussion, role play, simulation, values clarification, values analysis, or problem-centered inquiry) or which combination do you think you would use to help children discover suitable behaviors for project group work? Why?

4. Suppose that one of your groups produced a mural which at first glance seems a catstrophic mess. How would you go about evaluating it?

5. Describe how the task given to children influences the success of group work.

6. Suppose that one of your colleagues on an elementary-school faculty complains bitterly that his or her learners have difficulties doing study group work. After the learners are grouped, only a few work at the task while the others play around. What recommendations would you make to this colleague?

7. How much emphasis do you think should be given to group work in elementary social studies? Why?

Practice Activities

(If you are teaching or have a laboratory assignment in a classroom, you may wish to complete the following for use in your classroom.)

1. Develop a set of guidelines to use when teaching children how to do project group work.

2. Develop a set of guidelines to use when teaching children how to do study group work.

3. Devise a strategy for assessing children's interpersonal relationships and interaction skills and building readiness for group work.

4. Prepare the following:
   a. a prompter to use in an in-depth discussion to surface the behaviors for project group work.
   b. three prompters to use to focus children's attention on specific behaviors of leaders or followers.
   c. two conflict situations in group work to use to guide children in role playing to discover alternative behaviors.
   d. a simple simulation which helps children discover the alternative behaviors for leaders and followers.
   e. a value questionnaire to prompt children to think about the positive characteristics of effective leaders or followers.

   f. procedures to help children analyze their values about group work.
   g. procedures to guide children into problem solving to discover effective ways of working in groups to complete a project.

5. Devise an assessment strategy to follow when evaluating children's project group work.

6. Devise a strategy for introducing study group work to a class.

7. Devise an assessment strategy to follow when evaluating children's study group work.

Performance Activities

1. Evaluate the use of the items prepared in response to 1 through 7 above. In your evaluation of each set of items, respond to these questions:
   a. What is your reaction to your experience? What changes would you make in the material you devised? How would you change the way you used it?
   b. (For items 3 through 7.) How effective was it with children? What evidence of learning did you see?

SELECTED REFERENCES

Bany, Mary A., and Lois V. Johnson. *Educational Social Psychology.* New York: Macmillan, 1975.

Cooper, Cary L. *Learning from Others in Groups: Experimental Learning Approaches.* Westport, Conn.: Greenwood Press, 1979.

Rose, Sheldon D. *Treating Children in Groups.* San Francisco: Jossey-Bass, 1972.

Schmuck, Richard A., and Patricia A. Schmuck. *Group Processes in the Classroom,* 2nd ed. Dubuque, Ia.: William C. Brown, 1975.

Servey, Richard E. *Teacher Talk: The Knack of Asking Questions.* Belmont, Calif.: Fearon, 1974.

Stanford, Gene, and Albert E. Roark. *Human Interaction in Education.* Boston: Allyn and Bacon, 1974.

Wallen, Carl J., and La Donna Wallen. *Effective Classroom Management,* Abridged Edition. Boston: Allyn and Bacon, 1979.

8

Helping Children Deal
with Controversial
Issues

Social forces may be defined in different ways. Here we shall define them as pressures impinging on all of us. These pressures, emanating from changing conditions in our cultural, economic, and political life, compel us to reexamine our roles as human beings. As we reexamine our roles, we scrutinize our beliefs, values, attitudes, and preferred patterns of action to see whether they are adequate to accommodate the pressures. If they are not, we must decide on a change. Torn between what we are and what we may have to be, we find the decisions difficult to make because no one best, predictably certain change is available.

As we struggle with the decisions, we entertain several possible changes. What is at *issue* is which change to accept and implement. We may define an issue as an unresolved choice among alternatives.

We teachers, as well as parents and other adults concerned about children, may try to shelter children from issues. Ironically, we are not very successful. Issues await children as they turn on a radio or television, leaf through a newspaper or magazine, observe the concerns of parents and teachers, or read a juvenile classic.

As teachers we have an issue to resolve. It deals with our role as mediators between children

and issues. What do you think we should do? A list of practices is given below. Read them carefully. Add any other practices you know about. Then rank all the practices in order of their importance as you see it, the most important first.

1. Seize every opportunity to guide children in exploring issues.
2. Guide children in exploring issues only when they bring the issues to you.
3. Individualize the exploration of issues by working with individual children who obviously have issues needing resolution.
4. Avoid becoming involved with the exploration of issues.
5. Guide children in exploring issues which are troubling them or in which they show a deep interest.
6. Guide children in exploring issues related to topics they have studied.

Put your ranking aside to review after reading the chapter.

At the close of Chapter 1, the goal of elementary social studies was described in this way: that every child become as active a participant as he or she can in human affairs, as much by interest as by necessity. It is within the sphere of controversial issues that children practice as participants in human affairs. Frequently, as they deal with controversial issues, they test the utility of the skills and content they have learned during social-studies instruction.

The extent to which your learners will be using previously learned content and skills when dealing with controversial issues will depend on the instructional strategy you choose to use. If you decide to emphasize your learners' use of inquiry skills, you may use the problem-solving inquiry—having the children define a problem characterized by human or social conflict, hypothesize solutions, select a solution on the basis of its possible consequences and related values, seek and organize information about consequences, and apply the solution or seek a new one.

If you decide to emphasize the use of recently learned content and values-exploration skills, you have two choices. The first is to use the content of a subject-matter unit, and the second is to use the content resulting from the current-affairs program. Using the content to present a conflict situation, you may involve the children in an in-depth discussion, role playing, simulation, values clarification, or value analysis.

If you decide to emphasize values exploration and information skills, you may have the children first clarify a value, role play, simulate, or discuss in-depth, then seek and organize more information about the situation, and finally clarify the value, role play, simulate, or discuss in-depth again as based on the new information.

The strategy you use to guide children in dealing with a particular controversial issue depends on the skills and content they have experienced and what you think is most appropriate for the issue, the children, and yourself. Whatever the strategy, the children will be applying previously learned skills at the level at which they have mastered them.

One reason, then, for guiding children in dealing with controversial issues is to provide them with realistic opportunities to use what they have learned in social studies. They discover the relevancy of social-studies learnings to their own lives.

Another reason is that practice in dealing with controversial issues helps children learn what to do when they have to cope with a controversial issue. Just as important is what children learn about themselves as persons as they deal with controversial issues in classroom situations. Almost every controversial issue presents a conflict in values. As children consider these, they come to know themselves better.

Social-studies educators often offer another reason for having children deal with controversial issues. These educators sometimes underscore that society in general is apathetic toward issues. What is worse, the apathy tends to be increasing. However, if there is any real hope for the future, it lies in helping children become interested in controversial issues and learning how to deal with them.

At this point we may conclude that an instructional program in social studies which does not provide children with opportunities to deal with controversial issues is a less-than-adequate program. It promises little for children and less for society.

In the rest of the chapter we shall be looking more closely at the nature of a controversial issue, the factors to consider when we select issues to be treated, and techniques for guiding children in dealing with controversial issues.

WHAT IS A CONTROVERSIAL ISSUE?

We have already defined an issue as an unresolved choice between or among alternatives. The alternatives are patterns of action which include what we hold as values as well as what we do. Frequently one alternative is what we are doing or have been doing and the other (or others) is something different. An issue arises when the consequence of what we are doing is no longer suitable. Suitability may be a question of efficiency, safety, or morality, or any combination of these. The greater the lack of suitability, the more pressing the issue.

Let us follow the development of an issue from the moment when the consequence of what is being done is discovered to be no longer suitable.

A critical situation emerges. The following list of facts describes a critical situation existing within a nation:

1. The depth of the fertile topsoil is gradually decreasing.
2. The area of fertile topsoil is diminishing as more buildings, highways, and parking lots are built.
3. The water table beneath the soil is diminishing.
4. Petroleum and other nonrestorable mineral resources are being rapidly used up.
5. The population is growing.
6. Each person in the population consumes more than persons have in the past.

A review of the facts reveals the matter of the issue—the use of natural resources. The matter is placed in issue when a concerned individual asks this question of a group of equally concerned associates:

"How should we use our natural resources when we know the resources are diminishing and the demands for their use are increasing?"

Someone responds by saying, "We should conserve our natural resources." (A general alternative suggested.)

(The discussion continues. Here are some of the utterances.)

"What do you mean by conservation? Using only what we need without wasting?" (Request for clarification.)

"Sure. Waste not, want not." (A value statement.)

"Right. Wasting is wrong." (A value statement.)

"And we can do it. During both World Wars our people conserved gasoline, meat, and clothing. Furthermore, we have had a conservation program since the days of Theodore Roosevelt." (Facts supporting the general alternative.)

"And all of us can start conserving." (An action statement.)

"Of course, we can. It will be hard at first learning how to do without." (A consequence statement.)

"And we'll have to eat all the leftovers. Ugh!" (A consequence statement.)

"But think of what we will be doing for future generations!" (A consequence statement.)

"Doing something for our children and their children is very satisfying." (A value statement.)

"Let's prepare a curriculum proposal on instruction in conservation to be instituted in the schools." (An action statement.)

"I'm going to start conserving right now. Instead of taking the bus home, I'm going to walk." (Following the solution.)

"And let's meet again a week from now to see what we have done and to make further plans." (Monitoring the solution.)

As we review the above statements, we can see what happens when an issue emerges from a critical situation. The first reaction to the issue was the suggestion of a general alternative. What followed was a request for clarification, value statements, expressions of facts, action statements, consequence statements, and utterances showing the solution being put into effect. In this case, everyone agreed on everything. The issue never became controversial. Figure 8–1 shows how an issue is resolved without controversy.

Now let us suppose that as soon as the critical situation was described, someone in the group had responded in this way: "That is a very bleak picture you have given us, and I think you have exaggerated the way things are. Conditions are better than they ever were in the past. Most people enjoy a high standard of living. Two-car families are quite common, more than one television in a household is not unusual, and just about everyone over the age of seven has a radio. Many people travel abroad each year. New labor-saving devices are constantly entering the market. The gross national product continues to grow. The only thing that threatens us is government regulation. That, too, grows each year. This is what I see, and not all that business about increasing population and decreasing resources."

Now we have a controversy. The issue as defined emerges like this: which situation better reflects reality, those conditions which threaten continued life or those which threaten continued economic growth and prosperity?

It is predictable that clarification will be requested, values expressed, and facts offered. Particularly strongly stated will be values about the sanctity of life itself and the right to prosper and enjoy the fruits of one's labor. One value is pitted and measured against the other. In effect, values are tested. As the discussion proceeds, some mem-

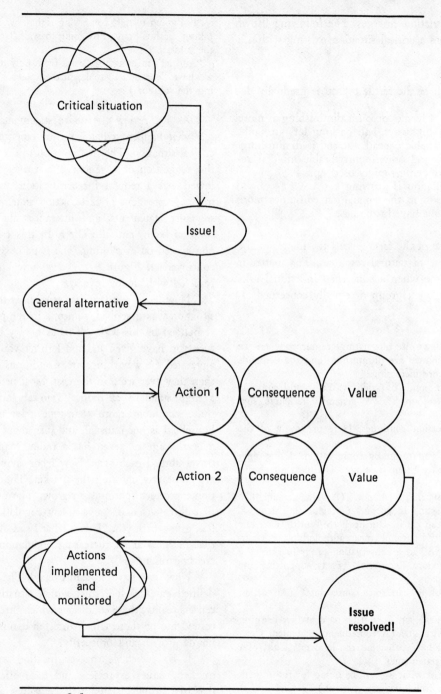

FIGURE 8–1. *An Issue Resolved without Controversy.*

bers of the group feel their values strengthened, some find themselves drifting toward another value, and most begin to qualify their values with statements like these: "Prosperity is O. K., but not when it deprives many people;" "Life is valuable, but only when it has an acceptable quality." However, rational resolution in this case rests on acquiring and processing more information. Possible actions and consequences may be suggested, but they will need to be checked against further information. Or the group may not be able to decide which situation is more critical. In this case, they may decide to suspend judgment, or wait and see what happens, or they may decide that it is best left to individual, personalized judgment in which each person decides privately for him or herself.

This controversial issue over which conditions are more critical we shall label as a "first-level" controversial issue.

At this point we shall assume that discovered information has revealed that increasing population, increasing individual consumption, and dwindling natural resources better reflect today's conditions. The issue is again introduced, "What can (should, might, ought, must) we (people, everyone) do about these conditions?"

We know from a previous example that the issue might be resolved without controversy. But something else may occur. After a brief discussion about conservation as the broad alternative, someone says, "I appreciate what conservation can do, but I think we should get to the heart of the problem—too many people. I think that reducing the growth rate of population is the way to resolve the issue."

This introduces another broad alternative to vie with conservation. The issue is now controversial. Some people who do not care much about conservation begin to make clarifications, state values, give facts, suggest actions, and describe consequences related to reducing the growth rate of the population. Again values are tested against each other. Consequences are compared. Facts are challenged. And, most likely, more information will be needed. If no information is immediately

available, the resolution of the issue may be subject to suspended judgment, that is, further consideration postponed until more information is available. Or, by sheer force of argument or by compromise, one alternative is selected for further consideration. The compromise may hold that both alternatives be applied simultaneously, one after the other, or after the one tried first appears to fail. Or, again, there may be suspended or personalized judgment.

An issue involving controversy between or among broad alternatives will be labeled here as a "second-level" controversial issue.

Let us assume that conservation has been selected as the broad alternative to be explored further. What remains to be done is to consider possible actions and consequences. This question is asked: "What will (might, must, ought, should) people (we, everyone) do to conserve our natural resources?" We already know that no controversy may arise at this point. The group may agree on actions, their consequences, and what to do, and then proceed to do it. However, let us assume that the participant at the first meeting who plans to begin to conserve by walking home is now approaching the door to leave. Suddenly a perplexed look crosses her face. She stops, turns, and calls out to the other participants, "Just a minute. Let's not leave yet. I wonder just how effective this is going to be. If just our group conserves, what good is that going to do for everyone else in the country, or for ourselves, for that matter?"

She has just challenged the consequences of the agreed-upon action. Here are some of the responses to her challenge:

"People will usually follow exemplary behavior." (A value statement.)

"Ha! They will only when it is in their own best interest." (Opposing value statement.)

"I know that _____ wouldn't. She'll just go on driving that gas guzzler of hers two blocks to the store to get a loaf of bread, and she'll go on filling a garbage can every day with wasted food." (Facts given.)

"No matter what _____ does, you have to start

somewhere. From little acorns do big oak trees grow."
(Value statement.)

"Not those eaten by the squirrels. I think we should
do something else, like forming a political-action committee." (Alternative action suggested.)

"What's that?" (Clarification requested.)

"It's a group of people to generate power by writing
and publishing articles, making speeches, participating
on television panels, and getting press releases reporting what people are doing to support a cause or movement. The committee also establishes contact with the
power structure—the city council, the county board
of supervisors, and the state legislature." (Facts given.)

"And how might it work for us? If it is just going
to publicize what we are doing, I think we might form
a public-relations committee." (Clarification requested
and an alternative suggested.)

"Well, to make sure that everyone conserves, a
political-action committee might suggest a program
of rationing, run by the government at the state and
local level." (Facts given and a further implementation of a suggested alternative given.)

"Not rationing! I read an article about that the
other day. It pointed out that rationing causes cheat-
ing. People form black markets and a person can get
anything she wants by paying a big price for it. Scarce
goods are hoarded or stolen. People lie to get more
than their share. I want no rationing!" (Facts given
about consequences of an alternative.)

"Which do you think would be better: most people
getting their share while a few cheat, or some people
using only what they need as a choice while others
may choose to use whatever they want without regard
to wasting or what is their rightful share?" (Consequences compared.)

"Well, I think individuals should have the right to
choose." (Value statement.)

"Even when there is a good chance that their choice
may eventually harm themselves and others?" (Value
challenged.)

"Yes, to a certain extent. I think everyone should
be told about recommended limitations and the most
extreme limitations permitted." (Value qualified.)

"And what might the limitations be?" (Clarification
requested.)

"We would need to look into that." (Need for information indicated.)

"I think we are back to our original idea of each
person conserving and trying together to get an educational program started." (Original alternative asserted.)

"Do we need a political-action committee or a
public-relations committee?" (Alternative implementation.)

"I think a political-action committee would be better
as long as it refrains from trying to get rationing
started. When I think of what political-action committees have done for minority groups and women, I
am convinced that we need one. It could really help
us get our educational program across." (Alternative
implementation and facts given to support an anticipated consequence.)

"Who wants to be on the committee?" (Alternative
implemented.)

"Who wants to find out about recommended limitations and acceptable extreme limitations to use in the
educational program?" (Alternative implemented.)

"When shall we meet again to review how well we
are doing?" (Provisions for monitoring the alternative.)

As we can see in the above, controversy may
arise over the specific alternative chosen. When this
occurs, values are tested (often against consequences), consequences are surfaced and compared, facts are given, needs for further information are identified, and the alternative is confirmed
and implemented.

We shall label an issue involving controversy
over a specific alternative as a "third-level" controversial issue. At this level, suspended or personalized judgment is least likely to occur, but it
may occur. The alternative may be delayed, or a
compromise may be formed from some or all the
alternatives suggested. There is a possibility that
none of the alternatives is suitable or practical at
the moment. If the situation is very critical, the
group members may continue their search for other
alternatives. If it is not, they may drop the issue.
See Figure 8–2 for a diagram of the development
of a controversial issue.

According to the construct we have just discussed and pictured in the diagram, controversy
over an issue may arise at three moments: first, over
the conditions which prompt the issue; second
over the general alternatives for action; and third,
over the specific alternatives for action. This has
implications for us as social-studies teachers as we
make decisions about guiding our learners in dealing with controversial issues.

If our decision is to provide children with
conditions in which they can have the greatest in-

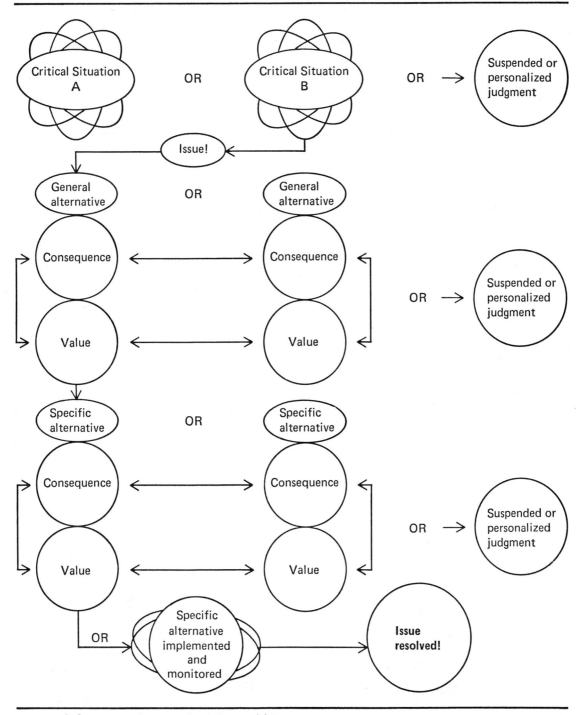

FIGURE 8–2. *The Development of a Controversial Issue.*

volvement and the greatest number of choices, we would arrange for the children to:

1. Experience some mixed facts which they would then classify into categories. Each category would reflect a different set of conditions.
2. Decide which set of conditions was most critical.
3. Acquire more information, if necessary, to decide which set of conditions is most critical.
4. Suggest general alternatives.
5. Decide on a general alternative, suspend judgment, or personalize judgment.
6. Suggest specific alternatives (if a general alternative has been accepted).
7. Decide on a specific alternative, suspend judgment, or personalize judgment.
8. Implement the specific alternative (if a specific alternative has been accepted).

This follows the diagram precisely. The main limitation to this model based on the diagram is that it demands the use of skills which most children are not expected to have until grade six or later.

Another choice available to us is to initiate dealing with a controversial issue at the second level. Most of the practices developed by social-studies educators for dealing with controversial issues begin at this level. It is a particularly attractive level for a number of reasons. First, it is a richly philosophical level which has children exploring and testing values. Second, it is suitable for a wide range of controversial issues, from how to improve traffic conditions at the school crosswalk to what to do about international disarmament. Third, it provides sufficient latitude to permit the suspension of judgment, the personalization of judgment, or to proceed to the third level in which a specific alternative is involved. And fourth, it provides for a logical application of social-studies content. When the children have learned a comprehensive parcel of social-studies content, that parcel serves as an informational base from which a critical situation can be developed.

A criticism of the practice of beginning at this level is that the teacher channels the children's attention to the issue itself, without allowing them to consider in-depth the critical situation from which the issue emerges.

When work on a controversial issue begins at the second level, the teacher provides for the children to:

1. Observe, listen to, or read about a critical situation designed to make the conflict strong and obvious.
2. Suggest general alternatives.
3. Decide on a general alternative, suspend judgment, or personalize judgment.
4. Suggest specific alternatives (if a general alternative has been accepted).
5. Decide on a specific alternative, suspend judgment, or personalize judgment.
6. Implement the specific alternative (if a specific alternative has been accepted).

This practice is suitable for all grades. The complexity of the issue is the governing factor.

The final level available to us is to have children begin the process of dealing with a controversial issue at the third level. This practice is most suitable for issues which children can do something about. When issues about the use of materials, space, and equipment, and about personal safety within the immediate environment reach the point of controversy, the children may be guided in considering the issue at the third level. Suitable for use in all the grades, this level is particularly appropriate for use from kindergarten through grade three.

It should be pointed out that just about every controversial issue is resolvable to a degree through some sort of action. The children themselves may be powerless to instrument an action, but they can contact a power structure to move it toward a direct action. For example, children who think that world disarmament should proceed at a faster pace along a particular line of reasoning, may write a letter to the President, the Secretary of State, or a Senator to express their concern and to make a recommendation. The response may be no more than a form letter signed by an assistant hired to make such responses, but the children will have done what they could.

Young children who cannot write letters independently may be guided in composing a class letter to the mayor, city council, school principal, the traffic commissioner, or whoever is responsible for taking action on specific problems. The response, usually personal, direct, and prompt, helps young children to develop concepts about their role in government.

To initiate the study of an issue at the third level the teacher provides for the children to:

1. Observe, listen to, or read about a critical situation designed to make conflict strong and obvious; or express feelings and concerns about a situation critical to them.
2. Suggest specific alternatives.
3. Select a specific alternative.
4. Implement an alternative.

Note the additional option in the first procedure. It permits the children to initiate the issue themselves as they react to a situation critical to them.

If you wish to use the construct of controversial issues as a guide to help you decide at what level to initiate children's work with issues, you may follow these guidelines:

• If an in-depth treatment appears feasible, initiate work at the first level.
• If an emphasis on values is desirable, initiate work at the second level.
• If immediate action is possible, initiate work at the third level.

The construct also provides for three opportunities for an issue to be resolved through suspended judgment ("Let's wait and see") or personalized judgment ("This is what I think is right and what I'm going to do about it"). The latter is usually involved whenever we guide children into role playing, simulation, values clarification, or values analysis. It leaves the decision completely up to the individual. It is a safe way of dealing with controversial issues. Some teachers feel it is the only way.

However, if we provide only for personalized judgment to close dealing with controversial issues in the classroom, we may be denying children the opportunity to work together to resolve issues related to their general welfare.

The construct is built on the rationale that it is usually the teacher's responsibility to introduce the critical situation and to monitor objectively what occurs thereafter. Within this rationale, if no issue emerges or no controversy occurs as deliberations continue, it is accepted as a natural result. If the children identify no issue or do not reach a point of controversy, that is simply the way it is. The advantage to this is that children do not become uselessly involved with what has little or no meaning to them. The disadvantage is that the children may miss an opportunity to test their values and to consider another point of view.

To correct for the disadvantage, the teacher is free to contribute additional facts to the critical situation to prompt the surfacing of an issue or to suggest an alternative to introduce controversy. However, the additional facts and alternatives must be well within the understanding of the children.

The construct of the development of controversial issues also underscores the significance of behaviors focused on considering values, consequences of actions, and the need for further information. These three elements are closely interrelated—values are tested against consequences, consequences may indicate values, and further information about consequences may affect values. The interrelationship among these elements is such that it undergirds the feasibility of certain techniques for dealing with controversial issues. Role playing and simulation have children immersed in consequences to surface values and needs for further information. Value clarification and value analysis encourage children to identify their values; they may then test against possible consequences and further information. And, in some way, these three elements will have a place in almost every strategy devised for guiding children in dealing with controversial issues.

Issues usually emerge at points of change in our economic, political, cultural, and social lives. The conflict is usually between what we have always done (and which most of us continue to do) and what should be done in the face of changing conditions. These changing conditions compel us to think of alternatives.

Issues about government often have us swinging back and forth between two general alternatives: the government which governs least and that which governs most.

We inherit many issues from being born into our society. They are related to our way of life. Figure 8–3 presents a partial list of these issues and some of the alternatives associated with them.

The issues in the figure include some of those with which we have always had to deal. Others, particularly those concerned with human rights and taxation, could be added to the list.

Other issues have been recently identified. Figure 8–4 offers a partial list of these.

Many other issues, such as the fair treatment of children at home and schools, the fair treatment of spouses, adequate care of the elderly, welfare, maintaining a health-sustaining environment, and the punishment of criminals, could be added to this list.

Some issues, such as the reduction of inflation and unemployment, emerge only during adverse economic conditions. Others, such as euthanasia, the dignification of dying, spelling reform, and an international calendar, are broadly philosophical and of concern only to small groups of people.

Any of these issues might find its way into your social-studies curriculum.

FACTORS TO CONSIDER

Because guiding children in exploring issues is a sensitive area in our work as social-studies teachers, we need to bear in mind constantly the factors that influence what we do. Remembering these, we

Issues	Alternatives
1. Maintaining a democracy	a. Forbid the existence of political parties following ideologies which are antidemocracy. b. Have citizenship education at all grade levels in the public schools. c. Safeguard through law the rights of individuals. d. Form strong political and economic ties with nations maintaining the democratic form of government. e. Allow democracy to find its own way and develop its own forms. f. Participate in all phases of government.
2. Ensuring that politicians are statesmen	a. Limit the terms of office and the number of terms of public executives and legislators. b. Raise the salaries of public officials. c. Maintain a strong two-party system. d. Audit the earnings of public officials. e. Base the length of term in office of public officials on the number of votes cast as a percentage of the total number of votes possible.
3. Maintaining freedom of speech	a. Develop laws supporting freedom of speech as both a right and responsibility. b. Define libel as simple untruth. c. Remove censorship of all kinds. d. Encourage all persons to say what they think in any way they wish.

FIGURE 8–3. *Inherited Issues and Alternatives.*

Issues	Alternatives
1. Using natural resources	a. Use only what is absolutely necessary. b. Allow people to use what they can afford to buy. c. Determine the lowest levels of use needed to support existence and regulate distribution to ensure that each person gets an equal share. d. Avoid the concern or deny that it exists. e. Allow business to solve the problem. f. Regulate business and commerce.
2. Coping with violence on television	a. Censor television programs more rigidly. b. Restrict the times when violence may be shown. c. Document how violence on television distorts children's values. d. Boycott programs which predictably use violence. e. Boycott companies which support shows characterized by violence. f. Provide awards for programs that show no violence but attract large audiences. g. Educate audiences to be critical in what they choose to view.
3. Reducing crime	a. Increase the police force. b. Improve police training. c. Make punishment more harsh and restrictive. d. Improve rehabilitation programs for first-time offenders. e. Base punishment on realistic retribution to victims or society in general. f. Improve the living conditions of poor people. g. Educate children about the consequences of crime. h. Publicize fully all instances of crime.
4. Preventing drug abuse	a. Destroy drug-producing areas around the world (except those necessary to supply medical needs). b. Sell all drugs only on a prescription basis. c. Make limited amounts of drugs available to addicts. d. Punish severely those who traffic in drugs. e. Regulate the sale of drugs to which people may become addicted. f. Educate people to be critical in their use of drugs. g. Inform people about the hazards of drug abuse. h. Educate children to avoid taking anything harmful into their bodies. i. Allow each person the right to determine the drugs and amounts of them he or she wants to use.

FIGURE 8–4. *Recently Identified Issues.*

can guide children effectively in learning about issues and how to deal with them. The factors include the teacher's approach, the community, the school-district policy, and the children's capacities to treat an issue.

The Teacher's Approach to the Responsibility

Guiding children to learn how to deal with issues often forces us to clarify or analyze our own values about academic freedom and responsibility for children. These may be in sharp conflict. At one extreme we may feel strongly that we should be free to choose any issue, including definitely those for which we have deep commitments related to a particular alternative or set of alternatives, and to speak out resolutely for what we believe. At the other extreme, we may be convinced that because children are in their formative years we should exercise utmost caution in dealing with issues in the classroom. Many of us would plot our position somewhere on the continuum stretching between these two extremes.

As we try to place ourselves on the continuum, some of us are concerned about what we as persons present to children as a model of a human being dealing with an issue. Should we be bold-eyed, dauntless warriors ready to do battle or start one with every issue? Or should we be clear-eyed, steady sea captains meeting the issues we must with all the intelligence we can bring to bear? The model you choose, and it is yours to choose, will help you locate yourself on the continuum. Where you place yourself is a prime factor contributing to what degree and how you will react to the other factors.

The Community

The nature of the community influences which issues may be deliberately introduced and thoroughly explored. For example, an attempt to guide chil-dren into an in-depth, objective scrutiny of issues related to the conflict between labor and management in a community of factory workers may result in futility. As far as the children are concerned, there is only one side of the issue. If you were to try to get them to consider another side, they would become upset. If you tried to play the devil's advocate, you would become the devil's advocate in truth as far as the community was concerned.

Of course, if you feel that the children must consider the views of management, the propitious time for it would be during moments of calm. During a strike or threat of strike would be the worst possible time.

Little imagination is required to envisage communities in which issues about welfare, racial interrelationships, pollution, or regulation of farm crops would be sensitive topics. In most cases, such communities can be easily identified, but simple identification is hardly adequate. If you take a position in a new community, you will do well to consult with the principal about sensitive topics.

In most instances, every community has issues about which its members have sharply divided opinions, but these emerge only when certain events occur. For example, the recall of public officials may surface conflicts between particular groups about who should hold the base of power. Who should have it? With what possible consequences? And, of course, the most apparently serene of communities boastfully proud of its religious tolerance can become a monument of outrage and anger over such issues as the selection of social-studies or reading textbooks. In a real sense, then, the state of the community at any moment may surface issues needing to be treated in some way in the schools.

If you work in a large school district, you may tend to regard the confines of the district to be the same as those of the community. This is rarely so. Most districts encompass a plurality of communities which differ widely. If you change positions within the same district, you will still need to study the new community to find out what you can about sensitive topics.

School-district Policy

Most school districts have an unwritten policy about the issues to be treated in classrooms. The expression of this policy is found in its curriculum documents, such as the course of study and instructional suggestions offered in guides and bulletins. The areas to be taught and ways of teaching them are specified. By specifying areas and methods of teaching, the district exemplifies what its expectations are. These serve as restraints in the sense that what is not specified is undesirable in some way, and if any teacher guides children into such an area or goes further than suggested, he or she does so at some risk.

Another expression of the district's unwritten policy lies in the materials provided for instruction. These are restrictive in the same way as curriculum documents. Before adoption, social-studies books are usually carefully analyzed to ensure that undesirable areas of study are not included and that sensitive areas are treated factually. The only materials not carefully examined are weekly periodicals such as *My Weekly Reader* and *Junior Scholastic*. The publishers of these have long enjoyed the trust of school districts, and with good reason. The periodicals are factual, interesting, simply written, somewhat timely, and noncontroversial.

Newspaper and magazine clippings are usually the only materials permitted in the schools without previous, careful scrutiny. Either the expectation that the teacher will conduct a current-affairs program or specification in a social-studies guide ensures that these materials will be brought into classrooms. Whether they are appropriate is left to the teacher's judgment. However, their use is directed more often toward reading for information and learning how to read a newspaper or magazine. Suggestions for using the clippings or articles for exploring issues are either weak or omitted entirely.

When you are not sure about issues which are interesting to children but not supported in curriculum documents or officially provided materials, consult your principal.

Few school districts have written policies for teachers to follow when they are guiding children in coping with issues. If they do, they quite likely will emphasize the teacher's responsibility to children.

Children's Capacities

Innocence is often its own protector. This condition may prevent children from exploring deeply and widely into an issue. However, sometimes an issue emerges unexpectedly during social-studies instruction, and our only reasonable choice is to guide the children quickly into an activity to help them forget the "uninvited" issue because they lack the background and skills to cope with it rationally. Usually we "invite" the issues. To do this, we are on the alert for opportunities to guide children in exploring issues which we are certain impinges on their lives or most certainly will in the future. For example, after our first-grade class has learned about the workers hired by the community to perform vital services for everyone—policemen, firemen, and trash collectors—we may think that they are prepared to consider issues about the fairness of the property tax to pay for the needed services. At this point we must ask ourselves these questions:

1. Are the children really interested in this issue, or can they be guided in developing a genuine interest in it?
2. Is their background of knowledge sufficient to explore the issue, or, if their background is insufficient, are they capable of acquiring the necessary background with a modicum of time and effort?
3. Are authoritative materials available in which they can find information about more than one alternative to the issue?
4. Have they the skills to acquire the information from the materials?

All these questions must be answered in the affirmative before guiding children in exploring the issue. It would be the rare first grade who could deal with the issue about taxes. However, they might deal with an issue about how people should feel and act toward the community helpers. Their interest could be generated through arranging the visit of a policeman or policewoman to the classroom. Their recent study has acquainted them with how police officers work and what their responsibilities are. They can discuss with their parents to discover alternatives. They can ask simple questions. In this case, all the requirements are met.

Most elementary social-studies teachers accept and use the questions listed above as criteria against which to judge any issue they might place before their learners for exploration. For them, the most significant factor is children's capacities to deal with issues.

TECHNIQUES FOR GUIDING CHILDREN

At the beginning of the chapter it was suggested that children's participation in dealing with controversial issues should be motivated as much by interest as by necessity. Some of the techniques, such as role playing and simulation, are interesting to children, but they may not generate interest in dealing with controversial issues. To develop and maintain interest, we may follow guidelines such as the following:

• Arrange for the treatment of controversial issues to be predictable occurrences in your social-studies program. Close each unit of instruction with a guided foray into a controversial issue related to it. If you are working with older children, you may initiate an issue-of-the-week program—introduce the issue on Monday, alert the children to think about it and to look for information pertaining to it throughout the week, and guide them in treating it on Friday.
• Early in the school year in grades four through eight, guide the children in discussing what is meant by a controversial issue and the behaviors required for dealing with it—expressing what one thinks, listening to what others think, and making or suspending judgment. As each con-

troversial issue is introduced, identify it as such and encourage the children to recall what had been discussed during the initial discussion. Close the treatment of each controversial issue with a class evaluation of how well the members listened and responded to others.
• Regard controversial issues humbly. This means accepting that such issues usually cannot be completely resolved in the classroom and that the direction of resolution may not parallel your values.
• Respect children's right to remain aloof when certain issues are being treated, when personal involvement in immediate, future, or hypothetical action to resolve the issue is being discussed, or when personal values are being discussed.
• Guide the children in reconsidering issues which they have treated previously to see whether there is any change in what they know, think, or feel, or whether they have heard or thought of other points of view.
• Prompt opinions about controversial issues as openly and directly as possible: "What do you think people should do about _____?" "What do you think might be done about _____?"
• Master and use as many techniques as you can to avoid routinizing dealing with controversial issues.

As we discuss techniques, you may feel as though you are revisiting Chapter 3. In a sense you are, but in this chapter we are concerned with the application of the values-exploration skills to guide children in dealing with controversial issues.

The technique or techniques that we choose may be determined by the circumstances under which an issue is introduced in the social-studies program, your learners' information skills, or your personal preferences in curriculum development. We shall focus on techniques related to the "uninvited" issue, the current-affairs program, the application of values exploration, and an in-depth exploration of an issue.

The "Uninvited" Issue

Imagine that you have your fourth-grade class settled down and ready to begin learning in social studies. You have already greeted them and you ask, "Who brought an interesting news clipping to share with us this morning?"

Eight or nine hands are raised. Wishing to get off to a good start, you call on a child whom you know to be reliable and capable.

"Yes, Joan," you say with cheerful expectation, "what do you have to tell us about?"

"I have a clipping about how the Norwegians celebrate Christmas," replies Joan, "But before I report on it I want to know something. Who is God?"

This is one example of an uninvited issue. It is a product of a child's curiosity, and such issues may emerge at any time. Here are a few practices you may consider to save both you and the child any embarrassment:

• If the issue is one that can be discussed publicly, such as the one above, explain simply points of view that different people have, how they come to have such a point of view (perhaps from their parents or specialists in the field, or through reading), and underscore that every person decides for himself or herself. If you can, telephone the child's parents to describe the situation and how you managed it.
• If the issue is one that is usually considered taboo for the questioner (and the listeners), tell the child that the question is one that you cannot answer as a teacher. As soon as possible, telephone the child's parents to alert them to what appears to be of concern to the child and leave to them the responsibility for dealing with it. They may appreciate your offer of help.
• Gently request the child to see you privately for a few minutes at recess, at noon, or after school, to see what can be done about finding an answer to the question. If the child forgets to do this, make no issue of it. If the child remembers, explain that you cannot answer the question as a teacher, but perhaps his or her parents will when asked privately. Then, as suggested above, call the child's parents to inform them of the circumstances under which the question was asked.

As you can see, informing the parents by telephone is a part of each practice. During this person-to-person communication you can allay their fears or suspicions about what occurs in school, be a positive advocate for the child, and perhaps give a few suggestions.

In a previous section we discussed briefly another kind of situation when an issue comes uninvited to the classroom. This occurs when an issue over which the community is sensitive or has strongly divided opinions makes itself felt in the classroom. For the moment let us imagine that we are in the community of factory workers and a strike has been called. Our class of sixth graders, usually an active, boisterous group, appears at first to be little affected by it. They study and play much as they always have, perhaps because earlier in the year we had guided them through a brief study of labor-management relations and how negotiations are conducted. They are definitely prolabor, but they also have some understanding of the problems of management.

This morning we are ready to have them begin their study of the diverse cultures of Africa. As they come into the classroom, we perceive a change. Some of the children are glaring at each other angrily. Their attention is drawn to two disheveled boys as they mutter to each other behind their hands. You hear an angry accusing whisper, "Scab!"

Here is another example of an uninvited issue. Conditions in the community have thrust it into the classroom. The following procedure may be helpful:

1. Prepare the children for a discussion of the issue. You might say something like this: "Let's talk this problem out."
2. Establish some ground rules for the discussion. They should include: a) everyone who has something to say will have a chance to say it, b) no references by name to anyone in the classroom or to a parent are to be permitted, and c) attacks on any remark will not be permitted.
3. Set the direction for the discussion to ensure that statements about the different sides are expressed. In this case you might explain to the children that the problem has been caused by differences in opinions about workers' rights. Some workers feel that they have a right to join a union whose leaders will negotiate with management for them. Other workers think that they have the right not to join a union and that each person should negotiate with management. Write these two opinions across the top of the

chalkboard and encourage the children to give reasons for why workers feel the way they do. List their statements under the opinion they support.

4. Review the statements and underscore that regardless of the reasons listed each person must decide where he or she stands and that it is a personal matter.
5. Remind the children that no matter what their opinions are about the issue, it is not theirs to resolve, but they still have to live together in school. Guide them in developing the rules of behaviors they might follow to ensure interpersonal harmony in school.
6. (Optional) If the local newspaper is receptive to letters from children, guide them in composing a class letter to express how the conflict over the issue is affecting their lives and to request the parties in conflict to find better ways to resolve it.

The final step in the procedure helps children to feel that they are not completely the victims of circumstances over which they have no direct control and for which they exercise no responsibility.

Perhaps you have noticed that we have said nothing about guiding young children in dealing with "uninvited" issues. The reason for this is that young children are rarely affected.

Generally, what we do with children when guiding them in dealing with "uninvited" issues focuses primarily on our concern for the children. One of the best ways of preparing children to deal with such issues is an on-going program in which they deal with those invited into the classroom. A lively current-affairs program invites issues and provides opportunities for practice in dealing with them.

Developing and Maintaining a Current-affairs Program

A current-affairs program based on newspaper and magazine articles and radio and television broadcasts is an ideal vehicle for bringing issues into the classroom. The transmissions by the public mass media are commonly received in most homes and are accessible to children. Young children as

well as older children may be provided experiences with issues. And as children become older, they can assume more responsibility for their work with issues as they use mass media as basic resources.

Four basic instructional strategies are available to use, some of which may be used in all grades, and others applicable only in the grades in which children can read independently. These include having the teacher as the reporter, using global coverage, discovering and following trends, and following up recently studied social-studies units.

The Teacher as the Reporter. When working with young children, or with older children who might resist using mass-media resources, the teacher may assume complete responsibility for the program— selecting the article or articles to be presented, presenting them, and guiding discussions about them. A subtle strategy, it has the teacher serving as a model of a person who reads and listens to discover what is going on in the world.

When working with children in kindergarten and grades one through three, the teacher looks for newspaper and magazine articles illustrated with large pictures which serve as the focus for the reports. The pictures should depict some objects which the children can identify. Suitable topics include the first big snow storm in some part of the country, a new road being built, a new animal at the zoo, a story about a boy or girl who has done something out of the ordinary, a recently invented vehicle, a distant forest fire, an oil slick, and the like.

When working with kindergarten and first grade the teacher paraphrases the article and uses the picture to illustrate what he or she says. After the presentation, the teacher invites questions and asks a question which helps the children to project themselves into the topic:

If that big snow had fallen here, what do you think you might be doing after school this afternoon?

How do you think this new road will be helpful to people? Or What do you think is the most fun about building a road?

Do you think you would like to go to the zoo to see this new animal? Why?

Suppose that you were this boy. How do you think you would feel right now?

What do you think it would be like to ride in this big airplane?

When I see that a fire has burned through a forest, I feel very sad. How do you feel? Why?

What do you suppose will happen to birds that get into the oil slick? Or, this oil may wash up on the shore. Would you like to go to the beach then? Why?

The teacher finishes the presentation and discussion by placing the picture on a table or posting it on a bulletin board for the children to look at later. He or she also suggests that children might look in their newspaper at home for pictures to bring to school to tell the others about.

When working with children in the second and third grades, the teacher using this strategy may also read excerpts from the article accompanying the picture, but rarely reads the entire article. When this is done, the children think that sharing a news article is reading it.

In fourth grade and later, the teacher presents articles which may or may not be accompanied by pictures. The content includes important events occurring everywhere in the world and only excerpts are read to emphasize certain points or to quote from a statement made by someone. By doing this, the teacher models how to report on an article.

As each article is introduced, the teacher refers generally to its content and asks whether anyone has heard anything about it over radio or television. Those who have are encouraged to tell what they heard or viewed. Then the content is presented. Questions are invited. The teacher may ask whether anyone is interested in finding out more about some aspect of the article to report to the class. Children who volunteer are helped to find a resource and arrangements are made for them to report their findings to the class.

The teacher closes the presentation by asking a question which encourages the children to pro-

ject themselves into the topic or, if the teacher intends to follow a trend in the news, asks the children to predict what will happen next. The article is posted on a special place on a bulletin board for those who wish to read it for themselves. The final event in the presentation occurs when the teacher encourages children to look for articles to report on.

As further encouragement, some teachers bring their own newspaper to the classroom for children to read to find articles they would like to present to the class.

The purpose of the procedures above is to get children to look for news articles and to report them to the class. As the teacher relinquishes responsibility for reporting, he or she assumes a new role. This role has him or her asking the issue-oriented question after a child reports on an article related to an issue-fraught topic. Here are a few examples:

The child has reported on an article about	The teacher asks
Some land-developers who wish to buy from the city some open land to build homes on; some citizens are objecting.	Do you think the city should sell this land? Why do you think so?
A person who is recalled from public office.	How do you think that people can make sure that their elected officials will do a good job?
A person who refuses to pay his income tax.	Why might a person feel that his tax is unfair?
Farmers withholding crops from market to get a better price for them.	Can you think of any other way for farmers to make sure they receive fair prices? What is it?
Two nations going to war over a small region.	What other ways besides war might these nations use to decide who owns the region?
A recently enacted law protecting a forest from lumbering interests.	What do you think is good about this law? For whom might it be a poor law?

The child has reported on an article about	The teacher asks
A new convention center is planned for the city.	How might this new convention center help the people of the city? How might it be a burden?
A change of climatic conditions in a country with the result that there is poor crop production and starvation for many of the people.	What do you think people in other countries should do to help these people?

The advantages of this strategy are: it is non-coercive; the children observe the teacher serving as a model and emulate him or her when they are ready; they learn what is suitable for reporting in the gentlest of ways; and the strategy may be used in all grades. It is particularly suitable for young children.

The main disadvantage is that the teacher may have to wait for what seems an interminably long time before the children begin to assume responsibility for reporting events in the news. However, as soon as one child volunteers and is well recognized for his or her effort, the others begin to participate.

The next strategy assumes that children are to be guided immediately into assuming their responsibility.

Using Global Coverage. This strategy, suitable for grades three and beyond, is a popular one. It involves getting children to read newspapers and magazines and to listen to radio and television broadcasts to find a wide variety of items to share and discuss with their classmates. Its successful use requires the teacher to guide the children in developing criteria to use when selecting items to report and to develop a management system for the conduct of the program.

The criteria for the selection of items to report are based on children's capacity to deal with them and their suitability for classroom discussion. Items dealing with unfortunate circumstances such as automobile and airplane crashes and with crimi-

nal acts such as murder, rape, and robbery are generally not considered appropriate at any grade level. Children, like most of the rest of us, are awed and fascinated by such events, but they need to know that these events usually prompt little productive thought. This point does not need to be belabored with children. In most instances, if they are carefully guided in learning the criteria of suitability, they will follow them. How to provide this guidance will be treated shortly.

Children in grades three, four, and five cannot be expected to deal with the complex ideas that older children can treat. They are limited in what they can read and understand. Guiding them in learning the criteria for selecting items differs somewhat from what we do with older learners.

Here are a few practices helpful in guiding children in the third, fourth, and fifth grades toward useful criteria:

• After mentioning a few people in the news, such as the President of the United States and farmers, or showing two or three news items focused on people, have the children tell what other people are often in the news. List whatever they say. When they start repeating themselves, guide them in grouping and labeling the different people. Inform them that the labels indicate the kinds of people about whom they are to find items for the current-affairs or news programs. (If the children include such people as murderers or kidnappers, point out that these people do nothing that is helpful to others and that discussing what they do leads nowhere.) If the children forget that boys and girls their age are sometimes in the news because of something special they have done, remind them of this and add *Boys and Girls* to the list of labels.
• Conduct a similar procedure with important events in the news and deal with events unsuitable for extended discussion in the same way.
• Prepare a current-affairs bulletin board divided into sections. Each section is labeled to indicate desired items: *The President and His Family, What is New in Our Community and State?, Science,* and *Sports.* Post an example item or two in each section. Introduce the bulletin board. Encourage the children to suggest the nature of items they would seek. Present some items and have the children decide where they would be posted. Tell the children that these are the kinds

of items they are expected to read and report about during the current-affairs program.

- Bring a newspaper to class for three or four days. During social studies on each day, introduce the children to a section of the newspaper and read the headline for each item and have the children label its content. List the labels on the chalkboard. When the survey of the section is completed, guide the children in analyzing the list and ranking items in order of importance and interest. Guide them in discussing why they ranked the items in the way they did. This usually dispenses with undesirable items. Indicate that the highly ranked labels serve as guides for items the children are to seek.

The practices above focus on both aspects of criteria for children in grades three, four, and five. And you may find any of them useful with children in the later grades. However, because children in grades six, seven, and eight are capable of dealing with more abstract material, you may wish to use one of these practices:

- Using newspapers published over a week, clip from each newspaper as many useful articles as you can (considering that newspaper pages are printed on both sides). Include cartoons of critical comment, editorials, sports events, and feature articles. Put the articles clipped from each newspaper in a separate envelope. During a social-studies period divide the class into seven groups, give each group an envelope of clippings, and have the members process the items in this way: classify the items into groups, rank the items in each group by importance, and rank the groups by importance. Reconvene the children as a class and have each group report its findings. Guide the children in analyzing their findings to determine the kinds of items most suitable to look for and to discuss in class.
- Prepare a bulletin board divided into four sections. Label the first section "International," the second "National," the third "State," and the fourth "Local." Post a sample article in each section. Introduce the bulletin board and encourage the children to discuss the kinds of articles to be posted in each section.
- Do the same as above, except use a bulletin board divided in sections labeled "International relations," "National and state government," "Business," "Community issues," "The arts," and "Sports."

After the criteria for selection have been introduced, inform the children of the management system. At this point you have a decision to make about whether the children are going to participate in the program as a function of interest or of assigned responsibility. There is much to be said for and against both, but we shall consider only the practices you may follow with either choice.

If you wish the children to participate as a function of interest, that is, to bring items to share and discuss because they want to, you may encourage participation by using any of the following practices after inviting the children to bring items:

- Show your appreciation openly and fully every time a child brings in an article and shares it.
- Combine the practice of map skills with reporting. At the beginning of the reports, the children locate the place where the news occurs on a map.
- Using an expendable world map on the current-affairs bulletin board, have the children who report post their article on the bulletin board, attach a strand of yarn between the article and the point on the map where the news occurred, and have the children post small cards bearing names and the date when the article was reported.
- Maintain a "Newshounds" bulletin board on which children's participation may be recorded. The children's names are listed on the board. Place a star or other marker after the name of a child each time he or she makes a report. Levels to meet such as cub reporter, reporter, special-assignments reporter, star reporter, and anchorperson can be marked on the board to make it more stimulating.
- Suggest that the children follow a television newscast format. Usually all that is needed to get them started is a table and a few dummy microphones. You will have to help the volunteers each morning before school to organize their program. Do not be surprised if as late as sixth grade some children will want to make pretend cameras to be manned during each program. A field trip to a television station will give them ideas for making their newscasts more realistic.

All the above provide psychological reinforcement as a means of generating and maintaining children's interest in the news. Similar practices may be used to make assignments more acceptable when you make current-affairs study mandatory.

The following practices are sometimes used when organizing the program:

- Maintain a roster from which you assign so many children each day for the next day's current-affairs reporting.
- Divide the class into five reporting teams and assign each team to a day of the week. Each member of a team is to bring an article to report on the appointed day. If you think that the reporting teams should be smaller, make them smaller and organize them on a schedule by calendar dates. Or you may organize teams, each of which is to assume responsibility for current affairs for a week at a time.
- Post or circulate a sign-up sheet with four or five more sign-up blanks than the number of children in the class. This does not force anyone to accept an only open date. Open dates may be used for volunteer, extra credit reports.

When current affairs is regarded as a study in which all children are expected to participate, parental support is often helpful. Many parents are willing to assist when they are informed about the program, its objectives, how it helps their children (references to improvement in reading and oral language as well as social studies are well accepted), how their child is expected to participate, and what they can do to help him or her. A carefully prepared notice sent home is quite effective.

When the management system and the criteria for selecting items have been established, this strategy works well. In some classrooms the children conduct the program by themselves, but the teacher still has a significant responsibility: to listen carefully to the children's reports and to ask the issue-oriented questions. Such questions do not need to be asked after every report but should be asked after any report about an issue in the forefront of the news.

The main advantages of the global-coverage strategy is that it provides for a wide coverage of the news and it is relatively easy to follow. Its main disadvantages are that children's lack of background often leads toward shallow reporting and that there may be little continuity in following issues.

The next strategy provides for both background and continuity.

Following a Trend. This strategy involves guiding children in discovering a trend in the news, acquiring background, considering related issues, and following the trend toward a point of resolution. It is particularly suitable for children in grades six through eight. The procedures to follow include:

1. *Discovering a trend.* If you intend for the children to use the newspaper as their main resource, guide them in collecting headlines and the titles of reports from the front page of the daily newspaper or newspapers serving the region. The survey should last for two weeks. Clipped from the newspaper, the items are posted daily on a bulletin board under the date of their publication. At the end of the two weeks, guide the children in analyzing the contents of the bulletin board to determine the trends and ultimately to decide on one to follow.

If you intend for the children to use newspapers, news magazines, and television newscasts as resources, organize them in groups to assume responsibility for analyzing a newspaper, a news magazine, or listening to a newscast for the most important news topics. The more resources reviewed, the better. Each day the children report their findings, which you record on a chart. At the close of the two-week survey, guide the children in analyzing their chart to determine a trend to follow.

2. *Acquiring background and tracking.* After a trend has been chosen, invite class members to volunteer or assign them to gathering background information to report to the class. They may be directed to consult almanacs, encyclopedias, back issues of news magazines, or the *Readers' Guide to Periodical Literature.* Schedule their reports as quickly as possible. Encourage children to make commitments to follow the trend daily or weekly in a resource and to report on it. Other children are free to contribute any fact or idea which they discover which was not reported.

According to your preference, children may be

involved at this point as a function of interest or assigned study.

3. *Considering the related issue.* As the children receive background on the trend and follow its development for a few days, an issue emerges or the appropriate moment arrives for it to be considered. To sharpen children's awareness of the issue, you ask issue-oriented questions. You facilitate exploration by asking the children to define the various stands taken on the issue, to express their opinions as to any stand, and to make predictions about eventual resolution.

4. *Approaching the point of resolution or containment.* Some issues are resolved completely or partially and some are simply contained. This point is approaching as items about the topic disappear from front pages into the inner pages and are treated less frequently in newscasts. At this point, the children review their predictions and discuss how the resolution or containment affects their lives. The next step is to determine another trend to follow.

Following trends eventually may become group enterprises with groups forming to follow trends as they occur. A group may form to conduct a continuing survey to report to the class on a weekly basis. As trends are reported, the children are formed into groups to follow them.

A variation of the above has the children following a trend for a week. The teacher introduces the topic and asks issue-oriented questions. Throughout the week, the children acquire background and track the trend. At the end of the week they reconsider the issue-oriented questions and decide where they stand.

This strategy immerses children into the study of current affairs, but it may require more time than you wish to allow for it. It also requires access to many materials. It offers an excellent opportunity for a unit of study for gifted children to extend over a quarter or semester. In short, the current-affairs program may become the social-studies program.

The strategies discussed so far have treated the current-affairs program as a part of the social-studies program not related to other studies. The next strategy will relate it to the ongoing social-studies program.

Social-studies Follow-up. As we guide children through the several social-studies units prescribed for the year, many of us teach each unit in a workmanlike way. Almost with a sigh of relief we guide the children in terminating the unit and begin to generate enthusiasm for the unit to follow. Each unit is begun, fostered to flourish, and, with a final spurt of energetic activity, put to rest. In most instances, however, much of the learning it has engendered can be applied in the current-affairs program. This means that the unit is not put to rest. It remains alive in the current-affairs program.

For example, after children have completed a unit about consumers and producers, they may be encouraged to be on the lookout for newspaper articles dealing with problems in production and consumership.

When study is historical, children may be encouraged to look for items dealing with how people today deal with the same kinds of problems.

If study is geographical, that is, about a modern nation or group of nations, the children may seek items about these areas.

If study is anthropological, the children may be encouraged to search for items about other peoples or how people in their own society react to situations.

Sometimes the teacher sets the stage for the follow-up in the middle of unit study. As soon as the children have learned a useful idea, the teacher encourages them to look for items related to the idea in some way.

The teacher who plans to use this strategy solely waits until the children are partially through a unit or at the end of it before introducing the current-affairs program. As each unit is completed, a new element is added to the current-affairs program.

This strategy has the advantage of offering children an opportunity to use what they are studying in their regular social-studies program to understand better the world in which they live. What has been learned is applied.

The major disadvantage of the strategy is that it confines the children to areas of study which at any given moment may not present vital issues.

The strategies presented here for current-affairs programs have given particular emphasis to the use of the newspaper as the main informational resource. Sometimes you may be working in a neighborhood in which not many people subscribe to newspapers or news magazines. In this case you will most likely have to bring your own to the classroom. Or use the television newscast as the major resource. Or even the radio.

At this point you may be wondering whether you should conduct a current-affairs program. If you fully accept your responsibility as a social-studies teacher, you will want your learners to deal with issues to help them develop as persons and you will want to give them realistic opportunities to use the content and skills you teach them. The current-affairs program affords these opportunities in a way with which few can argue. What is available in newspapers, news magazines, and newscasts is open to children. They should learn to use it.

Whatever strategy or combination of strategies you choose to use is left to you.

Role Playing, Simulation, and Case Studies

Most of us admire people who take strong stands on issues and sturdily defend them against all opposition. We want to encourage children to do this, but we also want them to learn to suspend judgment. This is often difficult to do when issues are fully and openly discussed. For this reason we may wish to use techniques which give children opportunities to explore within their experience and knowledge for alternative responses from different points of view without feeling that they must make a public stand. These techniques include role playing, simulation, and case studies.

Often these techniques are used during the current-affairs program. For example, when our learners are dealing with an item about setting some forest land aside as a national park, we may find them voicing antagonism against lumbering interests and strong agreement with environmentalists. This may be the moment when we should have them role play a logger interacting with an environmentalist who is trying to point out the need for the preservation of wildlife. The problem may be introduced in this way:

Jim Olson drives a logging truck. For years members of his family have worked at logging. His father, now retired, drove a logging truck carrying the logs from the woods to the sawmill. Jim's life is tied up in his family, his truck, and the forest. These mean so much to him that he is ready to do almost anything to prevent what threatens to change them.

One day Jim pulls his truck into a service station to have it refueled. As he climbs down from the cab, he is met by a young man who hands him a paper containing a list of names. The young man wants Jim to add his name to the list. If Jim signs the list, which contains the names of people who want the forest in which Jim works to be changed into a wildlife refuge, it means that no more trees can be cut there.

How do you think Jim feels about being asked to sign the list of names? . . . What do you think he might say to the young man? What reasons might he give for feeling the way he does? . . . How might the young man reply?

Or the children might be invited to role play a logger and his family reacting to the news that some people are trying to stop tree cutting in the forest so that it can be used as a wildlife refuge.

Another option for you to consider is simulation. Because of the time required for preparing it, you would present it a day or two later. You would perhaps create it to deal with a parallel situation similar to this.

SIMULATION: CABBAGES IN COWVILLE
Scenario

Ever since Cowville was settled as a farm community, its people have raised cows and used them to build a thriving trade with other communities. Their beef, milk, butter, cheese, and leather goods are famous throughout the country.

There is plenty of work for everyone and salaries are high. The people of Cowville are the most prosperous people in the whole country.

In the pastures where the cows are grazed grows a special kind of wild cabbage. It sprouts in the early spring, but there are only a few plants. Long ago the people of Cowville discovered that the cabbages are very tasty, but there are very few of them. Often the cows find and eat the cabbages before the people can pick them. So the cabbages are eaten only on the most important summer holiday, and only the richest people can afford them.

One day a group of people form the Cabbage Association. Its purpose is to get the cow raisers to set aside half the land for the growing of wild cabbages. If they do this, everyone will have wild cabbage to eat on the holiday.

The cow raisers think this will cause them great difficulty. Many of them are sure that they will not be able to make a living if half the land is used in any other way. Besides, a lot of people will lose their jobs.

The Cabbage Association is also worried. During the last three years, the cows had found and eaten so many of the cabbages that only the richest people could have a single leaf each.

The cow raisers and the Cabbage Association are now meeting separately. They are going to be meeting together soon to see whether they can arrive at some agreement on what to do about the land.

Phase I

The children, half belonging to Cabbage Association groups and the other half to groups of cow raisers, confer to develop strategies to use when the opposing groups confer with each other.

Phase II

The opposing groups confer, each Cabbage Association group meeting with a cow raisers' group, to try to develop an agreement.

Evaluation

Guide the children in discussing the strategies developed on both sides, how the members of the various groups felt as they tried to reach an agreement, and how their experience was similar to that of the people who work at lumbering and those who want forests to be set aside as wildlife refuges.

Such a simulation helps children discover that an issue on which they see only one side has another side that can be defended just as rationally. They may need to suspend judgment on it until they can obtain more information.

Sometimes a news item contains authoritative pronouncements. In this instance, perhaps it contains the strongly stated pronouncements of an environmentalist. Or it may be an editorial which asserts the lumbering industry's point of view. Perhaps the children agree wholeheartedly with what the environmentalist says or are outraged by the sarcasm in the editorial. Whichever it is, it is used as a case study. It stands as a specific episode or instance within the field of an issue. We guide the children in exploring the case to see how applicable it may be in a larger set of circumstances.

Let us assume that the news item tells what an environmentalist thinks. We would ask the children to react to questions like these:

1. Do you think that Mr. _____ has taken into account all the people who might be affected by changing this large forest into a wildlife refuge? What people has he not mentioned?
2. Suppose that Mr. _____ and his friends succeed in getting the forest declared a wildlife refuge from which trees are no longer to be harvested. How might this affect all of us? What changes might we have to make in how we live, work, and play?
3. What other kinds of problems might Mr. _____ like to have solved in the same way? How are these problems similar to the forest problem? How are they different?

In this brief review you can see how the issue is left to personalized judgment through the use of role playing, simulation, and the case study. Here we have assumed that the issue arrived in the classroom via the current-affairs program. This does not always need to be so.

As stated earlier, we inherit certain issues. (Figure 8–3 presented a brief list of them). As a society we continue to work to solve them. At any time that we are teaching children a social-studies unit, one of these inherited issues is likely to be related to it. We identify it and, in accord with our

preference for technique, guide them in role playing or simulation. If we can find appropriate case-
study material, we may guide them in exploring it.

In-depth Issue Exploration

If you decide that a controversial issue merits a
detailed study, you may create a unit of instruction
consisting of a series of daily lessons to be taught
over a period of a week or two. Such an endeavor
requires a careful marshaling of materials and
other resources, and a meticulous plotting of learning activities. The sequence of activities will follow
closely the construct for the development of a controversial issue introduced earlier in the chapter.
It begins at the second level. The procedures include guiding children in:

1. Developing a background of information from
   which the issue is to emerge.
2. Defining the issue.
3. Surfacing general alternatives for action.
4. Processing alternatives for action to determine
   the one or several offering the greatest possibilities for resolving the issue.
5. Seeking and organizing information to determine the consequences of the selected alternative or alternatives.
6. Considering whether the consequences parallel
   their values. If more than one alternative is involved, the children will compare the consequences and values associated with the alternatives.
7. Considering which consequences they might implement and how they might go about this.
8. Expressing their commitment to implementing
   any, all, or none of the consequences.

And now, using the rights of women and men
as the example area of controversy, here is how we
might implement each of the procedures.

DEVELOPING BACKGROUND

Guide the children in reading or viewing a chronology of events in which women in America have
asserted their rights or have had their rights supported by legislation or other public action—from
1821, when Emma Willard founded the Troy Female
Academy, the first endowed school for girls in
America, to 1976, when the military academies
began admitting women for instruction. (All references to abortion have been omitted because of its
private, personal nature.)

The children are encouraged to guess when
they think each of the rights involved were asserted
for men. Have them consider why it might be difficult to document when men received these rights.

Show the children six pictures, each showing a
healthy man or woman. Three women and three
men are depicted. Some individuals are bigger and
sturdier than others of the same sex. Have the
pictures numbered for easy identification. Ask the
children to rank the individuals in the pictures in
the order in which they would consider admitting
these people into a school for forest firefighters.
Then have them rank the individuals in the order in
which they would admit them to a school for sec-
retaries.

Guide the children in sharing and justifying
their rankings. Expect some children to state that
sex makes no difference in these situations. Expect
some children to take the opposite point of view.

Show the children a list of careers showing
the average annual earnings of each. Have the
children identify those in which women usually
work. Have them generalize about who generally
receives the lower-paying wages.

DEFINING THE ISSUE

Have the children discuss what they have learned
so far about the rights of women and men in
making choices about what they are going to do
with their lives. Ask whether they think that conditions might be improved for both sexes. If some
children openly reject the positive issue, encourage
them to clarify their opinion. Some children may
believe that there is no need for improvement, or
that improvement needs to be made only for
women. When their opinion is clear, suggest that
from this point onward they retain their point of
view and think about it as they discover more facts.

SURFACING THE GENERAL ALTERNATIVE

Ask the children, "What do you think might be
done to improve the personal rights of both women
and men? If you look at the list of events showing
what has been done for the rights of women, you
will get some clues." The results of this analysis
yield that actions by persistent individuals, by persistent groups, and by governmental intervention

were the alternatives used. Ask the children whether they can think of any other possible alternatives. (If a source of alternatives such as the chronology of events were not available, children would be asked for their ideas about possible actions. These would be recorded as given. Then the children could group and label them to surface general alternatives.)

PROCESSING ALTERNATIVES

Ask the children which of the general alternatives for action they believe would be the most effective in bringing about improvement. In this case, it is likely that persistent group action and governmental action will be the alternatives most likely selected. At this point expect statements of values related to the effectiveness of group action and law to bring about change.

INVESTIGATING CONSEQUENCES

Guide the children through the following investigative activities:

FOR GOVERNMENTAL ACTION

- Reading and discussing the Nineteenth Amendment.
- Interviewing persons who were sufficiently grown at the time the amendment was adopted to be able to talk about how men and women felt about it at the time and how women felt when they voted for the first time.
- Reading and discussing the Equal Pay Act, the Equal Opportunity Act, affirmative action stipulations, and the Senate bill (S-2101) on lending and credit practices.
- Interviewing persons who were affected by the policies set in motion by the above.
- Reading and discussing the Equal Rights Amendment.
- Listening to and questioning two resource persons having different opinions about the ERA—concerns for both women and men are discussed.

FOR GROUP ACTION

- Reading and discussing the resolutions (the one about abortion omitted) adopted at the International Women's Year conference in Mexico City in June, 1975.
- Interviewing persons who attended the conference to determine what changes they have experienced due to the conference.

- Reading and discussing observations made and opinions expressed by people around the world about what the conference achieved.

Guide the children in charting their information. If none of the children asks why there are no reports about men's rights, ask the question yourself, perhaps in this way, "Why do you suppose there has been no International Men's Year with a special conference?" When the children state that men have always enjoyed freer conditions and more choices, challenge their statement by asking how many of the boys would consider learning to be a nurse. Then ask the same question of the girls. Encourage the children to discuss their reasons.

Then ask how many of the girls would consider becoming construction workers. Ask the same question of the boys. Have the children discuss their reasons.

To build their awareness of cultural stereotyping, have the children experiment with recasting the roles of females and males to the opposite sex in *Tom Sawyer*, "The Beauty and the Beast," and "Cinderella" or other stories common to them.

Guide the children in generalizing from their experience with recasting roles and then record their conclusions.

Arrange for the children to interview several persons who have selected as a life work a career usually considered to belong to one sex or the other. Have the children chart the results.

EVALUATING THE CONSEQUENCES

Have the children analyze the charted information to decide whether group action or governmental action appears to be the better way to ensure the rights of men and women. They will probably see the relation between the two and decide that both are needed. Encourage them to make recommendations for what both women and men might do and to give reasons for their recommendations.

IMPLEMENTING CONSEQUENCES

Have the children consider what they might do to ensure their rights as males and females now and in the future. List their ideas on the chalkboard.

EXPRESSING COMMITMENT

Have each child write a response to these questions:

1. List two ideas that you learned about the rights of women and men.

2. What do you think you will do to ensure your rights as a male or female?

Have children volunteer to share their responses with the rest of the class. Read privately the responses made by children who do not volunteer.

As you can see in the above, an in-depth exploration of an issue requires careful preparation by the teacher both in researching the issue and in arranging learning activities in such a way that children have freedom of thought.

The above plan is open to question. Why omit considering abortion? It *is* a controversial issue, but in my opinion it is too controversial for consideration in grade six or seven. Why not have more emphasis on stereotyping? I think that it is too narrow a focus which ultimately induces negative attitudes and feelings. Why include men's rights? I think that such an inclusion offers a comprehensive, realistic perspective within which positive choices are provided for all learners regardless of sex.

Questions such as these may be asked about almost every in-depth exploration of an issue. The best that one can do is to respond to them as directly as possible.

Such a detailed study is suitable only for the later grades, perhaps no earlier than grade five. The usual practice is to conduct no more than one or two such studies during each school year.

The outstanding features about an in-depth exploration are that it offers opportunities for applying information skills and it helps children become knowledgeable about an issue. Such knowledge serves as a base from which further learning occurs. The main disadvantages are that it may focus on an issue that is unattractive to many children and that preparing for it places a heavy drain on the teacher's energy and time.

As we guide children in dealing with issues, both the "uninvited" and the purposely introduced, we are helping them learn the skills associated with dealing with issues and testing their values. The generalizations and facts they apply are frequently tentative. The constant is the skills.

SUMMARY

Social forces cause issues, or unresolved choices among alternatives, to emerge.

As they deal with controversial issues, children frequently test the utility of the skills and content they have learned during social-studies instruction. They also discover the relevancy of social studies to their lives and learn about themselves as they deal with conflicts in values. The future of society may depend on children's interest and skills in dealing with controversial issues.

An issue arises when the consequence of what we are doing is no longer suitable. The greater the lack of suitability, the more pressing the issue.

An issue emerges from a critical situation. The persons dealing with it suggest general alternatives, decide on a general alternative, suggest specific alternatives, decide on a specific alternative, and implement it. The issue becomes controversial when there is no agreement on how the critical situation reflects reality and when the consequences of alternatives are in conflict. The issue may be resolved through suspended judgment, personalized judgment, or implementing an alternative.

Each teacher has to decide on the model he or she is to exemplify for children as a person aware of and coping with issues. Each community has its own controversial issues. School-district policy may reflect which issues are to be treated and how they are to be treated. Children vary in the interest they may show or generate in an issue, background, and skills in seeking information if materials are available.

When a child brings an uninvited issue into the classroom, the teacher's first concern is for the child and his or her parents. When an uninvited issue projects itself in the classroom, the teacher works to help children release tensions and to suspend judgment about the issue.

A current-affairs program provides a regularly open channel through which issues enter the classroom. The teacher may use any of four strategies to manage the program.

When working with young children, the teacher serves as the reporter who chooses newspaper items and reports them to the class. The children are encouraged to bring items so they can assume responsibility eventually. This strategy also works with older children.

The global-coverage strategy requires the teacher to guide children in accepting and using the selection of newspaper items. The children may bring items as a function of interest or as assigned.

Following a trend as a strategy requires the teacher to guide the children in establishing trends in the news, seeking background, detecting emerging issues, and treating the issues.

When the strategy of social-studies follow-up is used, the children look for news items related to what they are studying or have studied in social studies.

Articles from news magazines and television and radio newscasts are also resources for the current-affairs program.

Role playing, simulation, and case studies are helpful to children as they treat issues in the current-affairs program. The children can discover various sides to an issue.

An in-depth issue exploration as an extended study provides children with an opportunity to become knowledgeable about an issue.

Opportunities for children to deal with controversial issues are essential to the instructional program in social studies if the program is to prepare children to be participants in human affairs.

POSTSCRIPT

At the beginning of this chapter, you were asked to rank some practices which teachers often follow. Get your ranking now. Look at is carefully. Decide whether you will leave the original ranking or change it. In either case, think about your reasons for your decision. How will your decision affect the current-affairs program you have or will have in your classroom?

FOR FURTHER UNDERSTANDING

Cognitive Activities

1. Choose an issue appropriate for consideration in an elementary classroom and draw a diagram of it showing its development through three levels. Write in the facts describing the critical situation and descriptions of the various alternatives.

2. Draw a simple cartoon illustrating the difference between an "invited" and an "uninvited" issue.

3. Make a chart comparing the various strategies followed in conducting a current-affairs program.

4. Decide on the strategy for conducting a current-affairs program that you think is most compatible with your values and your style of teaching, then make yourself a reminder card on which you state three to five rules you will follow to ensure the effectiveness of your preferred strategy.

5. Suppose that you have a learner in your class who avoids participating in the current-affairs program. He or she never brings a news item, and while the rest of the class is actively involved, this person reads a library book or draws pictures. How might you deal with this problem?

6. Suppose that you are a teacher selected to serve on a committee to make recommendations for a district policy on procedures which teachers should follow when dealing with controversial issues in the classroom. What ideas will you suggest to the committee? What reasons will you offer in defense of your ideas?

Practice Activities

1. Look through a newspaper to find two articles, one suitable for use with a kindergarten, first grade, or second grade and another suitable for fourth grade or above. Decide how you will introduce each article to the class, how you will involve the children in getting the information from the article, and what you will have the children do after experiencing it.

2. Design a bulletin board that you would use to help children learn the criteria for the selection of appropriate newspaper or magazine articles to bring to class. Look through newspapers and magazines to find the articles you will use.

3. Read the main section in a newspaper for three or

four days to discover a trend in the news focused on an international problem. Then, using the most recent almanac available, inform yourself about the important nations involved in the trend.

4. Leaf through a social-studies textbook until you find a chapter or unit that you like. Using the chapter or unit as a reference point, look through a newspaper or two to find articles that would extend and update what is offered in the chapter or unit.

5. Arrange to visit a classroom when the current-affairs program is conducted. Observe to see what role the teacher assumes and how the children participate.

6. Arrange to interview a principal to find how he or she feels about how teachers deal with controversial issues in the classroom. If possible, report your findings to the class.

Performance Activities

1. If you are assigned in a classroom for laboratory experience, negotiate with the supervising teacher to participate in the current-affairs program. If there is no program in the classroom, negotiate to institute one to last at least a week. Evaluate your practice in terms of how well children accepted your participation, what they appeared to be learning, and what you learned from the experience.

2. If you are the regularly assigned teacher in the classroom, try any or all of the devices constructed in item 6 under "Cognitive Activities" and 1 and 2 under "Practice Activities." Evaluate your experience with each to decide how you want to conduct your own current-affairs program.

3. Select whatever materials are necessary for you to conduct a current-affairs program. Using any strategy that you like, organize a program and try it

out with a small group of children. Monitor your program carefully to see how well it is received by children.

SELECTED REFERENCES

Carin, Arthur A., and Robert B. Sund. *Developing Questioning Techniques.* Columbus, Ohio: Charles E. Merrill, 1971.

Cousins, Norman. "Where is the News Taking Us?" *Today's Education,* 66:26–27 (March-April, 1977).

Gregory, George P. "Using the Newspaper in the Mainstreamed Classroom." *Social Education,* 66: 140–143 (February, 1979).

Kurfman, Dana G., ed. *Developing Decision-making Skills.* Washington, D.C.: National Council for the Social Studies, 47th Yearbook, 1977.

Muessig, Raymond H., ed. *Controversial Issues in the Social Studies: A Contemporary Perspective.* Washington D.C.: National Council for the Social Studies, 45th Yearbook, 1975.

Shive, R. Jerrald. *Social Studies as Controversy.* Pacific Palisades, Calif.: Goodyear, 1973.

Silver, James F. "Introduce New Words through the News." *Instructor,* 85:102–3 (February, 1976).

Symposium, Walter Sheehan *et al.* "Need to Know Starts Young." *Instructor,* 83:43–54 (March, 1974).

Whelan, Sallie. " 'Peoria and the World' and '(Your Town) and the World.' " *Social Education,* 41: 20–6 (January, 1977).

9

Individualized Instruction
in Social Studies

Here is an example of what one social-studies teacher in sixth grade does to individualize instruction:

1. He obtains a set of ten pamphlets, five copies of each, to use as the basic medium for information.
2. He prepares the materials for his class's use. This involves:
   - Making an audiotape of the contents of each pamphlet.
   - Composing a single-page study guide for each pamphlet. In this study guide there are five to eight factual questions which the learners are to answer in written form, a bonus "extra-credit" question (optional) requiring creative thinking, a suggestion for a bonus activity (optional) involving drawing or construction, and an individual record for each learner to keep track of what he or she completes satisfactorily.
3. He explains the rules to the class:
   - Social-studies instruction will be individualized for the next three weeks.
   - During the designated period each learner is to complete five study guides designed for pamphlets—any five of his choice—by answering at least the factual questions.
   - Extra credit may be earned by doing the extra-credit activities or completing other study guides at the factual-question level.
4. He explains the pamphlets, has his learners

make choices about the ones they would like to study, and distributes the materials according to their preferences.

What do you think of this example of individualized instruction in social studies? What do you think is commendable? What would you question?

Write your responses to these questions on a piece of note paper and put it in some easily remembered place. At the end of the chapter you will be reminded to review your responses.

VIEWS OF INDIVIDUALIZED INSTRUCTION

Individualized instruction does not mean the same thing to everyone who recommends it as an instructional strategy. To some it means an instruction program designed to enable children to study as individuals at their own pace and rate. Others insist that another condition is necessary—that children must have a voice in planning what they are going to study and how they are going to proceed through it. Still others hold that instructional programs in which individuals study self-chosen and self-organized topics are fine, but only when such studies are the best means available to meet children's individual learning needs. These people also assert that the individualization of instruction is based on teachers' perception of children's individual needs and that children may be assigned to small or large-group activities for learning purposes.

The social-studies teacher who recognizes that the skills essential to learning in social studies are the key aspect of the instructional program in social studies accepts the third view as the most appropriate. Her or his acceptance is based on these reasons:

1. Children develop such skills as map reading, graph reading, note taking, outlining, summarizing, report writing, using an index or table of contents to locate information, and the like, at different rates. For example, some children in a sixth-grade class may be able to use contiguity to locate points or regions on a map or globe, some may be able to use the scale and direction indicator to indicate locations, and a few may be able to use latitude and longitude to locate points and regions but not in precise terms. The teacher will need to individualize instruction to bring all the children to, or as close as possible to, a level of mastery at which they can use the maps and globes available for their use.

2. Most children in a class can be brought to, or close to, a functional level of mastery as they study a particular skill. The next unit may not require use of the skill, but later units will. To ensure that the children maintain the skill until later units, the teacher provides for individualized instruction. For example, half the children in a first grade have reached a functional level of listening to audiotaped information during a study of families. During their next unit, which is about transportation, they will rely primarily on observation for information intake. To maintain the skill of listening as well as to improve it for some children, the teacher provides individualized instruction in listening, a skill they will use frequently in a later unit of instruction about workers in the community.

3. As soon as children have learned to use informational skills independently, they are ready to make choices about issues and topics, and to

explore these as a function of personal interest. The teacher individualizes instruction to encourage the exploration of interests that vary from child to child. For example, during the last quarter of the year after studying five or six units about American history, the children of a gifted fifth-grade class decide they want to write their own history about topics related to the development of sports and the arts in America. Each child chooses a sport or an art form to study independently.

4. The multiplicity of skills and variety of learning situations in the effective social-studies program require the teacher to individualize instruction by making differentiated assignments, assigning children to temporarily formed small groups for special instruction, and providing choices in materials and activities. For example, during a particular social-studies period an eighth-grade teacher does the following:

- Assigns a child who has difficulty working with others to a small group containing members who accept him willingly and whom he likes.
- Provides each group with a variety of materials at different readability levels.
- Suggests that each group decide how to report— through a reporter, as a panel, or by audiotape. This suggestion provides needed opportunities for those who are rarely selected to report.
- Convenes a small group of three children to teach them how to read a circle graph.
- Checks with a gifted learner to see what she plans to do on her independent study during the period.

In general, individualizing instruction in social studies as discussed above meets two basic purposes: to ensure individual growth in the skills and to encourage children to discover and extend interests.

This view of individualized instruction in social studies regards individualization as a broad strategy to use as needed to facilitate children's learning. However, as suggested earlier, this is not the only view giving direction to individualization in social-studies instruction today. A second view regards individualization as a strategy to use when developing the social-studies curriculum. When this view holds sway, social-studies instruction is organized so that every child studies independently.

Certain conditions are central to the effective conduct of such a program. These include:

- The immediate availability of audiovisual equipment and a variety of instructional materials designed to meet both skills and content requirements.
- Painstaking preplanning in sequencing learning activities with frequent provisions for completing exercises and individual projects so that learning can be monitored.
- Differentiated sequences of learning activities to meet the different needs of individuals.
- Suitable vehicles for transmitting directions—by print, audiotape, or directly by voice.
- A management system which ensures accountability and meets the needs of different individuals. Some children need to have direct contact with the teacher more frequently.

An individualized social-studies curriculum which meets all these, or comes anywhere close to meeting them, is a rarity. Joyce has reported such a program.[1] In this program the individual learner begins by being oriented to the use of a data bank equipped with photographic slides, audiotapes, and written descriptions about a community different from his or her own. The learner is encouraged to formulate questions to take to the teacher who helps with finding the appropriate informational materials in the data bank. The learner's first task is to learn all that he or she can about the community to teach what is important about it to another person. When sufficiently saturated with information, the learner prepares an audiotape to use to teach another person.

At this point the teacher organizes the learner with several others who have completed the same task. These children work together at a series of structured tasks: learning about another community, comparing the two to arrive at a generalization, and validating the generalization by studying their own community.

The teacher then guides the learner in using individualized materials to learn some new concepts. When these have been learned, the child works with several other learners to complete more structured tasks. They use the data bank and the community as informational resources.

This program meets all the conditions except one—it lacks differentiated sequences of learning activities to meet the different needs of individuals. The feature that makes it work well is the data bank. Notable also is the use of the immediate community as an area of exploration.

Because it includes provisions for children to study in groups, it would appear that individualization is incomplete. Perhaps so, but having children work in groups is part of the management system.

This is an excellent program. It provides particularly well for the learning of certain inquiry skills such as formulating questions, comparing information, generalizing, and validating generalizations. Most children in fourth grade and above would profit from such a program, particularly if it were part of a total program, that is, used for one or two instructional units during the school year. The recommendation for limiting the use of the program is made for these reasons. First, it fails to provide opportunities to generate purposes and discover interests. Second, it distorts the reality of information process. The children do not learn the skills essential to locating information. Too few opportunities are provided for having children choose ways to organize and integrate ideas. Third, grouping for study tends to be more for the needs of the program than for children's needs. And fourth, provisions are limited for values exploration.

In short, such a program limits opportunities for growth. There is, however, one other possibility for curricular individualization which provides for growth in the application of skills, for the discovery of interests, and for the generation of purposes. In this approach to individualization, the teacher and the learner cooperatively plan an independent study for the learner. In most instances the learner has to be able to use skills at an advanced level to do an independent study. This condition limits the use of such a program to the later grades.

In general, then, individualized instruction in social studies as needed appears to be the better use of individualization. However, this does not entirely reject curricular individualization. This way of individualizing instruction may be appropriate for learning certain skills. The best practice is individualization as needed, including curricular individualization when it best meets the needs of the children.

In the remaining sections of this chapter we shall be dealing with procedures used in both individualization as needed and curricular individualization. We shall need to bear in mind that while we are dealing with both as separate approaches, the two are frequently combined.

INDIVIDUALIZATION AS NEEDED

During social-studies instruction, children's needs sometimes emerge instantaneously, and the teacher responds immediately to such needs. At other times the teacher is aware of children's predictable needs from situation to situation, and he or she responds by arranging the learning environment to accommodate them. We shall examine each of these conditions separately, the first labeled as *individualization as immediate response,* the second, *individualization as environmental accommodation.*

Individualization as Immediate Response

Operating from a concern for each learner and monitoring instruction as it progresses in the classroom, the teacher is alert to those unpredictable moments when a learner known to have a need suddenly makes a positive response to his or her own need. When such a moment occurs, the teacher responds immediately with support. Here are a few examples:

1. A learner always reluctant to enter a discussion suddenly volunteers and makes a statement loosely tangential to the discussion in progress.
    The teacher immediately accepts the statement and guides the learner as well as the

class in building on it, either to bring it in line with the discussion or to extend it toward greater meaning.
2. A learner always reluctant to work in a group asks whether he may work in a particular group after the class has been organized in working groups for some time.
    The teacher immediately takes a "let's-try-it-out" attitude—without exacting any promises of improved behavior from the learner—and arranges for him or her to enter his or her preferred group, observes how well he or she works, and praises his or her every acceptable behavior.
3. A shy learner who has difficulty presenting oral reports asks the teacher whether he might use a puppet as his "spokesman."
    The teacher immediately agrees.
4. A learner is having difficulty finding an entry word in an index.
    The teacher immediately guides him or her in reexamining his or her statement of purpose and looking at a cross reference in the index.
5. Three learners are having difficulty reading a chart.
    The teacher immediately guides them in a systematic approach to reading the chart.
6. When started at an investigative task, the learners begin to talk to each other about it.
    The teacher immediately suggests that the learners form small informal groups to complete the task.

In each of the above, the learner (or learners) has responded to his or her own need by making a special effort or suggesting a solution. Sometimes several learners may be having the same difficulty. Aware and constantly observing, the teacher responds immediately to meet needs.

Individualization as Environmental Accommodation

When teachers know their learners as individuals with particular needs in knowledge background or skills, they individualize instruction by making special provisions in their instructional planning and implementation.

In every classroom there is a wide disparity from individual to individual in the extent of each child's knowledge background. To ensure that every learner has sufficient background to begin a unit of instruction in social studies, the teacher plans an experience to bring all the children to a required level of knowledge. This experience is based on a stimulating, informational activity that is exploratory in nature. It brings the children into contact with concepts basic to studying the new unit. Any of the following will serve as informational activities:

- Taking a field trip.
- Listening to a resource person.
- Listening to the reading of a book.
- Viewing a film, filmloop, filmstrip, or series of slides.
- Listening, observing, and participating in the presentation of a set of flannelgrams or a puppet performance.
- Viewing and studying a series of study prints.
- Reading a magazine article.
- Reading some newspaper articles.

The informational activity is followed by a discussion during which the children retrieve and organize the facts. The teacher encourages the children also to discuss their previous experiences related to the introduced topic, concept, or situation. He or she also guides the children in exploring the meaning of new words.

Immediately after the discussion, the teacher guides the children into an activity in which they integrate the facts they have just experienced. Offering choices so that no child is penalized because of lack of skill, the teacher guides the children into activities similar to the following:

- Making paintings of scenes observed during a field trip that might be used on a guided tour of the site visited.
- Writing group or individual letters to inform parents about the facts experienced.
- Designing and constructing the items needed to make a bulletin-board mural depicting the facts experienced.
- Composing a news item or diary entry telling about the facts experienced.
- Creating impressionistic free verse to communicate the facts experienced.
- Pretending to be a resource person preparing a presentation on the facts experienced.

Carefully observing the children during these activities and analyzing their products, the teacher can detect which children have a sufficient knowledge background. The children who need more background are grouped and more experiences are provided for them.

Another strategy is to guide the learners into activities in which the well-informed individuals share their knowledge with the others. To facilitate this, activities similar to the following might be used after the well-informed persons are identified:

- Conduct a general discussion to elicit the facts. Start by asking and encouraging the learners to do the same. The well-informed learners respond and validate each other's responses.
- Give the well-informed learners a little teacher training, particularly as it relates to the values of illustrative materials such as pictures, diagrams, charts, and realia, and to planning a presentation, and arrange to have them work with small groups.
- Impanel the well-informed learners to present different aspects of knowledge and conduct a question and answer period.
- While the well-informed learners are busy at a task out of earshot, guide the other learners in structuring an interview. Later they interview the well-informed.

At the close of any of the above, the learners need to integrate their newly experienced facts. Usually a class-developed summary or outline will suffice, or any of the communication activities listed previously may be used.

Some practitioners may question the use of this strategy by pointing out that the needs of the well-informed learners are not being met. They are being "used," when they should be guided into the next phase of study. Those who think this way may use the final strategy. However, I am comfortable with the strategy just described because:

1. Sometimes the well-informed learners are not always the same individuals. Most of the learners may have an opportunity at one time or another to serve as a well-informed person.
2. As well-informed learners join the discussion,

they often add a dimension of reality by contributing facts from previous experiences.

3. Well-informed learners often need that extra confidence and recognition generated by sharing what they know with others.

4. It helps the class to develop the attitude that the nice thing about being well-informed is the privilege of sharing it with others.

The third strategy is to do something for or with the learners who are known to have an inadequate knowledge background. A way to do this is to convene them specially and to guide them in any of the activities listed after the first strategy. This would include communication activities as well.

The first strategy is particularly useful in kindergarten through grade three, but it may be used at any grade level. The second strategy is effective with learners in grade four and beyond. The third strategy may be used at any grade level.

Now let us consider the environmental accommodation we might make for learners who vary in the competencies with which they can use skills in gathering, expressing, and processing information.

One strategy is to direct the learners toward materials adequate to their level of skill. For example, a fourth-grade teacher might do the following when her readers are expected to read to find information:

1. Her poor readers are directed to read some *Weekly Reader* articles written at a second-grade level and kept from past issues.
2. Her average readers read in their regular textbook.
3. Her very-able readers are directed to seek information from several *National Geographic* articles.

Another strategy is to provide direct aid as needed. Our fourth-grade teacher might do the following:

1. She helps her very able readers define the kinds of articles that will be useful before sending them to the library to obtain sources to read.

2. She assists her average readers in deciding what part of their textbook will most likely yield useful information.
3. She guides her poor readers in discussing some words important to understanding the topic and which will occur in their reading. Then she guides them in reading selected portions from the regular textbook.

If there are different kinds of informational sources available—series of study prints, films, filmstrips, audiotapes, and the like—her strategy may be to guide her learners toward those in which they use their most proficient skill. In this case we might find the fourth-grade teacher doing the following:

1. She directs the poor readers to listen to an illustrated audiotape.
2. She has her learners who like to use maps but who are dismayed by acres of print consult maps to obtain information.
3. She has another group of learners who are reluctant to read to develop an interview to be used during a conversation with a resource person. They conduct the interview.
4. She guides the learners who read well and who like to read into using a variety of printed materials.

When there is an expressive task to be performed, she may follow the same strategy: some learners write reports, some make illustrative sketches, some prepare oral reports, and some prepare and present a dramatic performance.

And when dealing with a task in information process, she may vary the complexity of the task according to her learners' level of skill: some learners prepare lists of facts on a chart, some make graphs, and some prepare and label maps.

When the moment arrives for her learners to make an inference, she may vary the complexity of the task by having some learners choose an inference from several given, some may validate a given inference or generalization, while others draw an inference from the facts as collected and organized.

Another occasion when environmental accommodations are often needed occurs when the children are going to process information already experienced. They vary in their ability to use different media and the level at which they can perform in any medium. The usual accommodation is to provide for the use of at least two media. The following are a few examples of such accommodations:

- Draw a picture, make a picture from torn paper, or paste on a sheet of paper a collection of pictures clipped from a magazine to show a community helper at work.
- Fold your paper into four parts and on each part draw a picture or write the name of an Indian food.
- Write or audiotape a summary about communication as a process.
- Write a paragraph about each country telling about its products, make a chart showing the products of each country, or sketch the products of each country on a separate sheet of paper.
- Design a bumper sticker or a wall banner, or draw a cartoon that encourages people to conserve gasoline.
- Write a creative story, a short story, or an essay about careers in construction.
- Prepare an oral or written report about Jacques Cartier or Father Marquette. If you prepare an oral report, you may audiotape it or present it directly to the class.

This strategy ensures that children can communicate what they know.

As you review the suggested strategies and the examples given for each as related to different levels of skill, you may wonder why the teacher does not provide specifically for teaching the skills if he or she knows his or her learners need them. This is what he or she may do through curricular individualization (which we shall consider in the next section of this chapter). Or if a majority of the class has the need, and the teacher knows that the skills will be necessary for the successful study of the next topic, issue, problem, or whatever, he or she may teach the skill to the entire class before starting the next unit. However, no matter what he or she does, there will still be differences in skill abilities from learner to learner.

The teacher using environmental accommodation to individual needs is concerned primarily with helping his or her learners to arrive at ideas useful in coping with problems. Through making accommodations, he or she helps them to do this without interrupting inquiry to master this or that skill at a required level. These responses, when interwoven with immediate responses to incidental needs, ensure that his or her learners will discover some useful social-studies ideas during the school year.

CURRICULAR INDIVIDUALIZATION

In recent years curricular individualization has reached a high level of sophistication. The first major thrust occurred when educators became particularly concerned with meeting the needs of gifted children, and it was discovered that providing for individual projects or independent studies was a satisfactory way of meeting these children's needs, particularly in social studies. The second major thrust occurred when publishers began to produce individualized kits of instructional materials. A few kits dealing with skills used in social studies, such as map, diagram, graph, and picture reading, were produced. And the most recent thrust has resulted from a high interest and well-developed techniques in the construction, use, and management of learning and activity centers.

Today a variety of approaches to curricular individualization are used in social studies.

- *Total individualization* through the use of learning and activity centers, study modules, and/or independent studies.
- *Individualization as needed* through the use of instructional kits and learning or activity centers.
- *Individualization as complementary study* through the use of learning and activity centers.

To be able to understand these approaches we need to examine the tools used in them. A few of the many good textbooks on the construction and use of learning centers, activity centers, study modules, and independent studies are listed at the end of the chapter. We shall take just a brief glimpse at each tool.

The Learning Center

The classical structure of the learning center provides for motivation, direction, activity, evaluation, and accountability. It is a classroom station usually designed to accommodate one learner at a time. It may be as simple as a desk placed off to one side, a section of cleared table space or floor space, or as elaborate as a library carrel in which the learner is isolated as much as possible from the sights and sounds of the classroom. See Figure 9–1 for examples.

Teachers who stress the functional aspects of learning centers tend to use the simpler structures which require much less time and energy to prepare and are much easier to set up in limited space and to dismantle and store. Teachers who believe that attractiveness encourages the use of a center will tend to use the more elaborate structure. All the structures are similar in that each provides the materials and directions for a learning activity. (These are often omitted from centers to be used by young learners who cannot read and need orally given directions.) The elaborate structure differs from the others in that it provides also for motivation and purpose, and often guides learners in assessing the activity and participating in their own accountability. Figure 9–2 shows a center designed to teach a map skill. With all three parts provided as shown in the figure, this center could be used in two ways: as an activity to be freely chosen by individual children or as an assigned activity.

This center is largely self-introductory. However, when carefully introduced to a class or group, it provides easily recallable clues about what is to be done in it.

Learning centers may be planned in curricular sequence. For example, a sixth-grade teacher might construct a series of centers dealing with various subskills in map reading as listed below:

I. Finding directions on a map.
II. Identifying symbols on a map.
III. Locating features and places directionally from a given reference point.
IV. Using a map scale to compute distances between points.
V. Locating features and places in terms of distance and direction from a given reference point.
VI. Locating features and places through the use of map coordinates.
VII. Using latitude and longitude to locate given points or express locations of points.

Center I would be presented first to the children. As soon as about a third of them had completed it, Center II would be set up. And then Center III. As soon as all the learners had finished the first center, it would be put away, and another center set up. No more than three centers would be in operation at any one time. Eventually the learners would experience all of them. By checking the tasks completed, the teacher would know how well each learner had done and what he had completed.

Learning centers are useful for both factual and skills learning.

The Activity Center

An activity center may consist of a shelf or set of shelves, a large table, or a cleared section of a table, counter, or floor. It contains task cards (prompters for activities) which have children using their skills to explore for ideas or to apply skills as a matter of choice from several given. The child goes to the center, chooses a task card and picks up any materials that may be included for the activity (or the task card informs him what materials to get), goes to his study area, and works at the activity.

Exploratory activities are usually open ended, that is, they have learners doing something for which there is no one correct answer or solution, but many reasonable answers are possible. Figure 9–3 shows how such an activity might be presented.

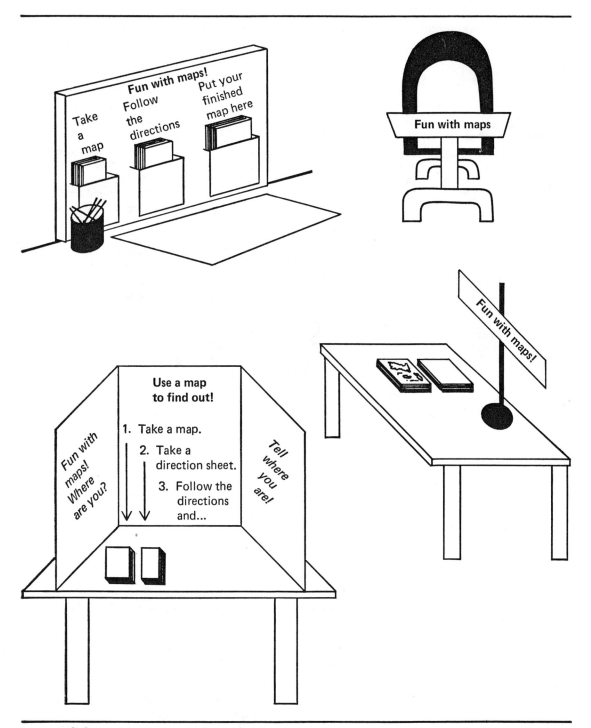

FIGURE 9–1. *Possible Placements of Learning Centers.*

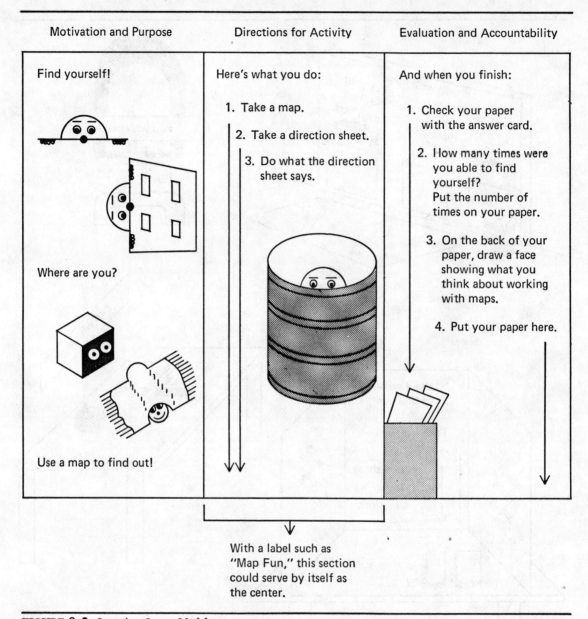

Motivation and Purpose	Directions for Activity	Evaluation and Accountability
Find yourself!	Here's what you do:	And when you finish:

Motivation and Purpose

Find yourself!

Where are you?

Use a map to find out!

Directions for Activity

Here's what you do:

1. Take a map.

2. Take a direction sheet.

3. Do what the direction sheet says.

Evaluation and Accountability

And when you finish:

1. Check your paper with the answer card.

2. How many times were you able to find yourself? Put the number of times on your paper.

3. On the back of your paper, draw a face showing what you think about working with maps.

4. Put your paper here.

With a label such as "Map Fun," this section could serve by itself as the center.

FIGURE 9–2. *Learning Center Model.*

The task card in Figure 9–3 contains these directions:

1. Build your own town at the end of the road on the map by drawing symbols for homes, a factory, a business area, a park, two churches, an elementary school, a high school, and an airport. You may draw them anywhere you wish on the map, but should have some good reasons for drawing them in a particular place.

2. Tell why you drew the things where you did.

BAY

PLAN YOUR OWN CITY!

TASK CARD

1 _____

2 _____

FIGURE 9–3. *Activity Center Model.*

The child applies whatever he knows about community planning. The only requirement is that he have reasons for his plan. The important point is that this is his chosen activity and whatever he does represents his best effort.

Practice activities provide the learner with opportunities to apply skills already treated in class or in a learning center. Figure 9–4 shows what might be offered a child who has mastered the fundamental index skills.

And Figure 9–5 shows what a child who has studied map skills might like to do.

Activity centers contribute to that aspect of individualization which offers the learner choice in activity. Sometimes learners are required on the

TASK CARD NO. 1: HOW WELL CAN YOU USE AN INDEX TO FIND INFORMATION?

1. Get a copy of the *Encyclopedia Almanac.*
2. Make a note paper by writing a., b., c., d., and e. in a column down the left side of a sheet of paper.
3. Use the index in the almanac to help you to find whether the statements below are true or false. Write *true* after its letter if it is true, or *false,* if it is not true. Also write the number of the page where you found the needed information.

FIGURE 9–4. *Task Card for Index Skills.*

a. John Adams was the second president of our country.
b. Gibraltar is an island.
c. A meteor is a unit of measurement.
d. There are more than 50,000 buses in our country.
e. A pulsar is an object found in space.
4. Check your answers with the answer card made for this task card.

FIGURE 9–4. (*continued*)

PLAN A TRIP AROUND THE WORLD!

1. Get a globe and a tape measure.
2. Plan a trip around the world by choosing at least eight (8) cities and measure the distance and direction from city to city until you arrive home.

FIGURE 9–5. *Task Card for Map Skills.*

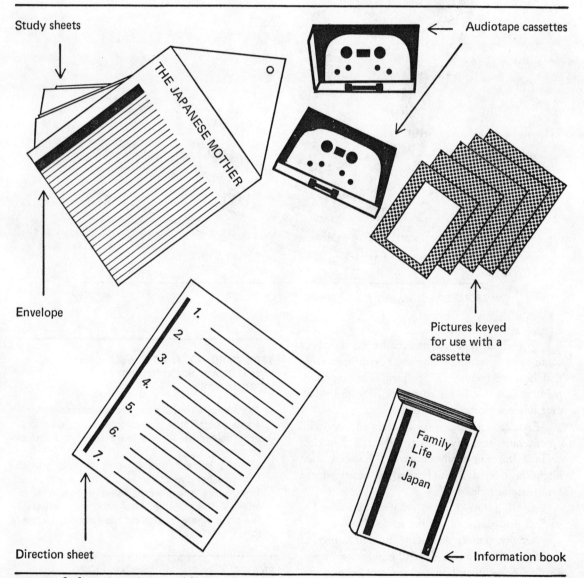

Study sheets

Audiotape cassettes

THE JAPANESE MOTHER

Envelope

Pictures keyed for use with a cassette

Direction sheet

Family Life in Japan

Information book

FIGURE 9–6. *Study Packet Materials.*

basis of need to do a specified number of task cards from a large number available. When this is the case, all the cards will treat the same skill, but the task and content is varied to attract learners' interest.

The Study Module

A study module is an individual packet containing directions which the learner follows at his or her own rate until he or she completes the study. Figure 9–6 shows the materials included in a packet based on the role of the Japanese mother. Figure 9–7 shows what is written on the direction sheet.

The direction sheet reveals the basic structure of the module:

THE JAPANESE MOTHER

_____
Name

Purpose: When you finish this module, you will be able to tell in some way what a Japanese mother does within her family.

As you finish each task, write your initials before its number.

Initials   **Tasks**
_____1. On study sheet No. 1 mark a check after each of the things that you are sure an American mother does within her family.
_____2. Read the following sentences and underline the sentence you think is the most true.
   a. A Japanese mother and an American mother do the same things within their families.
   b. A Japanese mother and an American mother are different in what they do within their families.
   c. A Japanese mother and an American mother are alike in some ways, but different in others, in what they do within their families.
_____3. Make a note sheet. Write at the top of it:

What does a Japanese mother do within her family?
_____4. Do at least ONE of the following. You may do all if you want to.
   a. Read Chapter 3 in the book, _Family Life in Japan,_ and write on your note sheet the facts you discover about the Japanese mother. Or
   b. Listen to the cassette titled _Mrs. Yamamoto,_ and write on your note sheet the facts you discover about the Japanese mother. Or
   c. View the pictures (be sure they are in the right order) and listen to the cassette titled, _The Japanese Mother,_ as you view them. The cassette will guide you as you study the pictures. Write on your note sheet the facts you discover about the Japanese mother.
_____5. Compare what you have on your note sheet with what you checked on study sheet No. 1. Then decide whether the sentence you underlined in 2 above is most true. If it is, write OK here: _____. If it is not true, write the letter of the most true sentence here: _____.
_____6. Do at least ONE of the following. You may do all if you want to.
   a. Using study sheet No. 2, mark a "J" before each task a Japanese mother does with her family. Or
   b. Make a wall picture with sketches or cut-outs showing what a Japanese mother does within her family. Or
   c. Pretend you are a Japanese man who has just lost his wife. You make a poster to advertise for a new wife to be the mother in your family. To be sure you get the right lady, list what you expect her to do on your poster.

Put the cassettes, pictures, and book back in the envelope labeled, "The Japanese Mother," and put it in the box under the sign "Used Modules."

Put your study sheets, note sheet, and direction sheet in your folder.

If you made a wall picture or a poster, be sure your name is on it and post it on one of the bulletin boards.

Sign up for a conference with the teacher to discuss your work in this module.

FIGURE 9–7. _Direction Sheet for Study Packet._

1. *Statement of purpose:* this informs the learner about the instructional objective for the module. If there are several objectives, they are often listed separately under "Objectives" and the purpose is expressed in more general terms.
2. *Provisions for learner accountability:* the learner is to track him or herself through the module by initialing each task as he or she completes it. Sometimes a separate record sheet is used. In long modules, the date of completion for each task is entered.
3. *Preparatory tasks:* these guide the learner in doing the necessary probing into his or her own background and in preparing for new learning. (See 1, 2, and 3 on the direction sheet.)
4. *Tasks leading toward new learning:* these help the learner experience facts and ideas not learned previously, although he or she may have had unorganized exposure to them before. Alternatives are frequently offered. (See 4 on the direction sheet.) Long modules may require a sequence of such tasks or sequenced lists of alternative tasks.
5. *Postassessment tasks:* these prompt the learner to do activities in which he or she shows what has been learned and whether he or she has met the objective. Alternatives are frequently offered. (See 5 and 6 on the direction sheet.)
6. *Management provisions:* these provide for the learner to return materials to the appropriate places and to arrange to confer with the teacher to discuss what he or she has done.

As we review the structure of the study module, we can easily see the provisions made for individualization. These are apparent in the alternatives for new learning and assessment tasks. As an individual, the learner chooses among these as best fits his or her interest or skills.

If all the instruction in an area of study is prepared in modules from which learners choose what they want to study, another dimension of individualization is added. This may occur when the modules are nonsequential, that is, none must be studied before others are attempted.

Some modules may be organized as prerequisites to be completed by all learners, with the rest of the modules offered on a self-selection basis.

If we are using study modules and want to make as many provisions for individualization as possible, we seize every opportunity to offer as many alternatives as the availability of materials and our learners' level of skill will permit.

The Individual Study Packet

In many ways similar to the study module, the individual study packet may provide for the learner to participate in selecting his or her own objectives in accord with the interest generated as he or she progresses through it. This is facilitated by offering choices at points throughout the packet.

The packet is organized in sequences of learning activities having specific purposes:

- *C-Activities,* or activities designed to guide the learner in developing a *concept.*
- *G-Activities,* or activities designed to guide the learner to acquire information and to use it to arrive at a *generalization.*
- *E-Activities,* or activities designed to prompt the learner to *express* what has been learned at one or more levels of abstraction. These may involve the learner in integrating information and presenting it in pictures, reports, diagrams, maps, and the like; or they may have the learner applying generalizations to solve problems, synthesizing the meaning of generalizations through creative products, or using generalizations to make judgments about actions, values, attitudes, or feelings.

The sample study packet offered in Figure 9–8 will give you an idea of how such a packet might be organized.

PACKET NO. 7: JAPAN: WHERE IS IT?

C-Activity 1

Where are you? Another way of asking this question is: What is your location? Your location is where you are. Location sounds like this: loh-KAY-shun.

Suppose that you just met a new friend. Your friend is on the telephone and wants to know your location. What are you going to tell him? Read the

---

FIGURE 9–8. *An Individualized Study Packet.*

sentence below to yourself and put the needed word or words in each blank.

I am in _____ classroom in _____ School in _____ in _____ in _____.

If you spoke this sentence to your friend, he would know where you are. He would have a good idea of your location.

Suppose that you wanted to give your exact location in your classroom. What would you tell him? Read the sentences below to yourself and put the needed word or words in each blank.

I sit near _____.
I sit far from _____.

If you spoke these sentences to your friend, he would have a good idea of your location in the classroom. He would know that you are near someone or something and far from someone or something.

Suppose now you wanted to give your friend an even more exact location. If you will read the sentences below and put the word or words needed in each blank, you will find another way for giving your location.

_____ is right in front of me.
_____ is right in back of me.
_____ is right next to me on my right side.
_____ is right next to me on my left side.

Now your friend has a good idea of your location. You told him the places you were in, something or someone near to you and something or someone far from you, and what or who was all around you.

You are now going to find the location of Japan. Make a list of the questions that you will have to answer to find the location of Japan. When you have your list done, go to G-Activity 1 *or* do the next C-Activity.

C-Activity 2

Another way of telling a friend where you are is to tell him exactly how far you are from him. The figure on page 322 shows a lot of squares in rows. The black square is where you are, and the squares with letters are places where your friend might be.

1. How many squares is A away from the black square?

2. How many squares is B away from the black square?
3. How many squares is C away from the black square?
4. D? E? F? G? H? I? J?

As you can see, a way of measuring can help your friend to decide where you are. Let's work this in another way without any squares.

A very simple map is given on page 323. The big black dot is where you are. The smaller dots with the letters near them are the places where your friends might be. At the lower lefthand corner of the map is a line. This line is equal to a hundred miles. Make a measuring string by taking a piece of string and marking it with black water color, ink, little pieces of cellophane tape, knots (this can be hard), or using any kind of markers you can think of. Make the distance between each pair of markers the same as that of the line at the bottom of the map. Using your measuring string, find the distances between the big black dot and the other dots.

1. How far to A?	6. How far to F?
2. How far to B?	7. How far to G?
3. How far to C?	8. How far to H?
4. How far to D?	9. How far to I?
5. How far to E?	10. How far to J?

Now you know another way of finding the location of something or someone. Take your list of questions that you made at the end of C-Activity 1. Add some new questions to it. Here are the names of some countries for you to use. Choose at least one from each list to make questions like these: How far is Japan from _____?

Canada	Belgium
The United States	Germany
Mexico	Italy
Guatemala	Spain
Panama	Norway
India	Australia
Korea	New Zealand
Turkey	Fiji Islands
Philippine Islands	New Guinea
Cambodia	Borneo
Argentina	Libya
Brazil	Union of South Africa
Chile	Nigeria

FIGURE 9–8. (*continued*)

Paraguay	Kenya
Colombia	Egypt

Now do G-Activity 1, or do C-Activity 3.

C-Activity 3

We have learned that distance also helps to tell where something or someone is. There is another way of locating. It is by directions.

There are several kinds of directions. One depends on how you are facing. The direction your eyes look is *ahead*. The direction just in back of you is *behind*. The direction from the lefthand side of your body is *to the left*, and the direction from the righthand side of your body is *to the right*.

Another kind of direction is toward something. If you point toward the chalkboard, the direction is *toward the chalkboard*. If you look at the play-

ground, the direction is *toward the playground*. The direction may be toward anything you can see.

There are several kinds of directions. One kind has to do with how you are facing. Here is an experiment for you to do to discover directions. Put your pencil on your desk. Have it point straight away from you. What direction is it pointing? Turn it so it points straight toward the left side of your desk. What is the direction? Now make it point straight toward the right side of your desk. What direction is it pointing? Now pick up the pencil and put it on your shoulder so that it points straight away from your back. What direction is it pointing?

You may have given these directions some special names, such as *ahead, to the left, to the right,* and *behind,* or *in back of.* They are very useful directions to use everyday.

FIGURE 9–8. (*continued*)

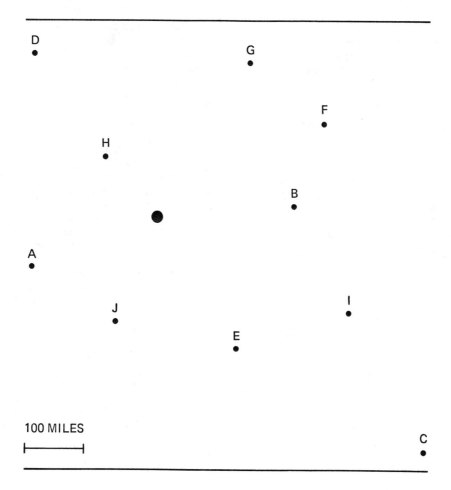

D
●

G
●

F
●

H
●

●

B
●

A
●

J
●

I
●

E
●

100 MILES
├─────────┤

C
●

Here is another experiment for discovering directions. Put your pencil on your desk. Do not worry how it points. It is pointing toward something or someone. What or whom? Toward a classmate or toward the chalkboard? Toward the teacher or toward a door? Toward anything or anyone is really a direction. Move your pencil about and see how many different directions you can find.

Now get the envelope with this label on it: "Japan: Where Is It? C-Activity 4."
Do whatever the sheets in the envelope tell you to do.

C-Activity 4

In this envelope you have found, besides this card, two compasses. The small one has a metal arrow in it. If you place it flat on your desk, the metal arrow points toward N or North. Turn it until the

arrow points to N on the compass. Perhaps it points toward the piano, the teacher's desk, a certain place on the chalkboard, or something in the room that usually stays in the same spot. Whatever this happens to be in your classroom, use it as a marker to help you to remember where North is. It is an important direction.

The big compass is a square card with a large circle cut from the middle of it. Across the circular hole are two rubber bands attached to make a cross over it. One rubber band has an N at one end and an S at the other. This is the North-South line. The other rubber band has an E at one end and a W at the other. This is the East-West line. This compass is useful when you know where the directions really are.

Now place the big compass over the little

FIGURE 9–8. (*continued*)

compass. The little compass should be in the center. Holding the little compass still, turn the big compass until its North line is lined up over the metal arrow in the little compass. Both compasses now point in the same direction.

You already know where North is. South is the opposite direction. Sometimes it is just marked with an *S* on a compass. Look to where South is in your classroom and find a marker. Keep in mind what this marker is.

Now, using the compasses as your guide, face to the North. You may have to move your chair or get out of it. Another important direction lies to your right. If you look on the right side of your compasses, you will see what direction it is. It is *E*, or East. Choose something on that side of the classroom as a marker. The opposite of this direction is to your left. You will see what it is when you look at the compasses. This direction is *W*, or West. Choose something for a marker on that side of the classroom.

Now you know about the four important directions. Read the following and fill in the blanks. You do not have to write. Just say them quietly to yourself. Think about your markers as you fill in the blanks:

• North is toward _____.
• East is toward _____.
• South is toward _____.
• West is toward _____.

Now you know about the four important directions. Other directions can be made from them. These directions have already been marked on the large compass. Look at North on the large compass and let your eyes move down around the compass to the right. Stop at the place where *NE* is marked. What direction is this? Northeast is right. It is between North and East. Now find these directions on the large compass: Southeast, Southwest, Northwest.

Using the large compass with the little compass, find markers in your classroom for these new directions. Then fill in the following blanks by saying quietly to yourself what goes in them:

• Northeast is toward _____.
• Southeast is toward _____.
• Southwest is toward _____.
• Northwest is toward _____.

Now you can put the little compass to one side. There is a map on the next page. It shows a camera and some animals. Take it out and look at it now. Somewhere on it you will see a picture of a compass. Put the big compass over it and line it up so that both compasses are pointing in the same direction. Turn the map so that it is lined up with the North marker in the classroom. Now move the large compass so that the camera on the map is right in the center of the compass. Be sure that the compass is still pointing North.

Pretend that you are going to take pictures of each of these animals. Use the compass to find what direction you will have to point the camera to take a picture of the rabbit. The squirrel. The elephant. The cat. The turkey. The lion. The deer. The skunk. The duck. The rhinocerous. The pigeon. The rat. The bear.

Here is something else you can do. See if you can use the compass to see what direction the rabbit is from the lion. The elephant from the rat? The rhinocerous from the skunk? The camera from the squirrel? The bear from the tiger?

If the cat is going to catch the rat, what direction will it have to go? If the dog is going to catch the cat, what direction will it have to go? If the lion is going to catch the deer, what direction will it have to go?

You know how to use the compass if you can do all of these things. Take out your list of questions. You are ready to write some more questions about finding where Japan is. Here is a sample question to help you get started:

• What country is north of Japan?

Another kind of question is:

• What direction is Japan from the United States?

Now do as many G-Activities as you need to answer your questions.

G-Activities

If you have done C-Activity 1, or C-Activities 1 and 2, and no others, do this G-Activity:

Using the globe and the wall map of the world, answer all your questions about the location of

FIGURE 9–8. (*continued*)

Japan. There is a measuring string at the globe and one at the map.

If you have done all the C-Activities, 1 through 4, do this G-Activity:

Using the globe and the wall map of the world, answer all your questions about the location of Japan. There is a measuring string at the globe and one at the map. The compass made of cardboard and rubber bands will help you answer your questions about directions.

Below are some more things you may do. Do at least one of these. You may do more if you want to.

1. Using a world map, answer all your questions about the location of Japan. If the answers are different from what you found on the globe, try to find out why.
2. Read pages 7–9 in *How People Live in Japan.*
3. Read pages 17–19 in *Japan* (grey book). Make notes about any new things you have learned about Japan.
4. Pretend that a line runs east and west through Japan all the way around the globe. Make a list of the other countries on the globe that this line would cross. Use a globe or a world map to find the answer.
5. Pretend that a line ran from the North Pole to the South Pole through Japan. Make a list of the other countries that this line would cross. Use a globe or a world map to find the answer.

E-Activities

Now you are to make, draw, or write something that shows what you really know about where Japan is. You may make, draw, or write anything you want, or you may choose one of the activities given below. You may do more than one if you want.

If you did C-Activity 1, or C-Activities 1 and 2, and no others, and you can think of nothing to make, draw, or write, do something from the first THREE (1, 2, or 3) activities.

If you did all the C-Activities, 1 through 4, and you can think of nothing to make, draw or write, you may do any of the activities listed below.

1. Plan a lesson in which you are going to teach someone where Japan is.
2. Pretend that you are preparing some questions

for a quiz program. You are going to make up some "Yes" or "No" questions about where Japan is. Make as many questions as you can.
3. Write, or prepare on a tape recorder, a paragraph that would tell a person where Japan is.
4. Make a sign that you can put on your desk. Write or print "JAPAN" on it and point it in the direction where Japan is. If you wish, you may put other information on the sign, such as how many miles away it is, how many hours away it is by airplane, and how many days it is by steamship.
5. Pretend you are in Tokyo, Japan. Make a circle about as wide as your hand is long. Write or print "TOKYO, JAPAN" on it in large letters. Now make a sign for each of the following:
   • San Francisco, the United States
   • Darwin, Australia
   • Magadan, Siberia
   • Peking, China
   Using Tokyo, Japan, as the center, place the signs in the right location from Tokyo on the top of your desk, or paste them in the right place on a large piece of colored paper.
   If you wish, you may put more information on the signs telling how far these cities are from Tokyo, Japan.
6. Ask the teacher for a desk outline map of Asia. Use it to show where Japan is. Put as many different kinds of information about the location of Japan on it as you can.
7. Ask the teacher for a desk-outline map of the world. Use it to show where Japan is. Put as many different kinds of information about the location of Japan as you can.
8. Pretend that you are taking an airplane to Japan from the city of San Francisco. Your airplane can go only two thousand miles on the gasoline it can carry. It must land before it runs out of gasoline and it cannot land on water. Plan your route. Tell the places where you will have to land and the direction from one place to another.
9. Ask your teacher for a desk-outline map of the United States. Using a map of the United States, locate and write in the names of the following cities on your desk map:
   • New York, New York
   • Boston, Massachusetts
   • Seattle, Washington
   • San Diego, California
   • Portland, Oregon

FIGURE 9–8. (*continued*)

- Houston, Texas
- Atlanta, Georgia
- Chicago, Illinois
- Miami, Florida
- Wichita, Kansas

Pretend that an airplane will start from one of these cities and will fly directly *West*. Draw a straight blue line to the west from each city whose airplane will reach Japan. Draw a straight red line from each city whose airplane will miss Japan.

10. Make up a game for a steamship race from San Francisco to Tokyo, Japan. Make sure that the players will have to use a map to play the game.

11. Make a mobile which shows Japan's location.

FIGURE 9–8. (*continued*)

If a learner going through this study packet discovers that he or she knows all he or she wants to know about the location of Japan when finished with C-Activity 1 or 2, he or she is directed to complete a G-Activity and an E-Activity. Any of the E-Activities prompt the learner to meet an acceptable objective. If a learner completes all the C-Activities, he or she has a wider choice among G and E-Activities. If the learner is really charged with interest in Japan's location, he or she may meet as many objectives as he or she wants.

The use of individual study packets demands that the teacher acquaint the learners with the organization of the packets and what their options are.

If a topical study is organized in nonsequential study packets, the learners will be able to individualize their own study through the choice of packets to study and how far they wish to go in each packet.

Although the sample packet does not show this, the choices among generalization and expressive activities could include group enterprises, the only requirement being that several children progress through the same packet at about the same rate.

The advantages of individualizing instruction through the use of study packets are readily ap-

parent. The greatest disadvantage lies in the time, energy, and materials required in their construction.

The Independent Study

All the curricular devices we have discussed so far have had the teacher preparing the banquet table of instruction. The independent study has the teacher and learner planning instruction together.

In the primary grades the teacher offers the learner choices, decides when the study is to be completed, and helps to determine the consequence he or she is to experience if he or she completes the study satisfactorily on time. Figure 9–9 shows an example of an independent study devised for second grade.

The learner's choices in the above contract may be limited by his or her skills. For example,

ILLUSTRATION 9–1. *This Child's Skills Are Sufficiently Developed to Permit Her to Make an Independent Study.*

What kinds of homes do the Eskimo have?		
Choose one:		
Listen to the tape, "Eskimo Homes," and look at the pictures that go with it. ___X___	Look at the pictures in the set, "The Eskimo at Home." _____	Read pages 10, 11, and 12 in the book, *People of The North.* _____
Choose one:		
Make a list of the different Eskimo homes. _____	Tape what you know about Eskimo homes _____	Make a torn paper mosaic showing Eskimo homes. ___X___

March 3, 198-
Date

I will have this work done on *Friday, March 5, 198-*

If I get it done on time, and it is all right, *I can go to the science corner by myself for 10 minutes on March 8, 198-.*

B. Jalle
TEACHER

Billy K.
PUPIL

FIGURE 9–9. *Independent Study for Second Grade.*

he or she may not be able to read the book independently, and making a list of the homes may be impossible. If this is the case, the teacher helps the learner to recognize these limitations during the teacher-learner conference when the study is being planned. During this conference the time for completion and the consequence are also decided. These two aspects are discussed realistically and the ultimate decision rests with the learner.

An independent study is sometimes called a *contract study*. You can see why. Perhaps you can also appreciate the positive consequence—ten minutes extra at the science corner—as truly balancing the contract. The learner does something and receives something in return. Negative consequences such as reducing the grade or mark, or withdrawing privileges, unbalances the contract to the point that it becomes a teacher's enforced decree which the learner has to sign. Besides, what agony it must be for a learner to decide his or her own negative consequence!

The above independent study reflects a concern for the learner's skills as a student and respect for him or her as an individual. When the teacher works with older learners, these attitudes still prevail, but they are followed in a different way.

The genesis of an independent study occurs when the older learner and the teacher first confer to decide what the study is to be. Learners accustomed to making independent studies often are ready to suggest the kind of study they want to make. When this occurs, the teacher's first concern is whether the learner has the skills to complete the study. For example, if a learner said that he wanted to make a set of diagrams with explanatory notes to show the different organizations of government in Massachusetts from its founding to the present, he would need to be proficient in these skills:

- Inquiry skills—how to define the problem and how to develop a list of questions to guide him toward the desired information.
- Reading-reference skills—how to use indexes and the card catalog to locate informational sources.
- Organization skills—how to classify and sequence informational notes.
- Note-taking skills—how to select pertinent information and how to paraphrase it.
- Composition skills—how to compose easily understood explanatory notes.
- Graphic skills—how to design and complete diagrams.

If this was the first independent study at the beginning of the school year and the learner was new to the teacher, the teacher would interview him briefly about any independent studies completed previously and ask him whether he knew how to perform certain skills. The outcome of the interview might be that the learner would complete certain instructional sequences as a part of his independent study. For example, the learner might consult a book or view a film to obtain ideas about how to design a diagram.

The teacher's second concern is that the learner have a basic idea about the central concept involved in the study, in this case, *governmental organization*. The learner's responses to a few questions will establish this. He may need to consult a source to clarify his ideas.

Of course, if the interview with the learner reveals so many special needs that he will probably lose interest in his study before he is prepared to do it, the teacher may suggest that he consider another independent study and may help him decide by offering suggestions about studies more suitable to his skills.

Frequently a learner will have little or no idea about any independent study he or she would like to make. When this occurs, the teacher guides him or her in considering the concept he or she would like to extend or explore. Let us suppose that the general area of study is *government*. The teacher might suggest the following:

1. Local, state, or national government.
2. Different forms of government.
3. Elections.
4. Political parties.
5. The law-making process.
6. Individual rights in a democracy.
7. The work of the president.
8. The work of a senator.
9. The work of a judge.
10. The work of a sheriff.
11. Political polls.
12. Taxation.

When the concept central to the study is identified, the teacher focuses on the learner's skill preferences to determine the terminal project involved in it. Here is a list of possible suggestions:

For Children Having an Interest in Mathematics

- Develop a questionnaire about a student issue within the classroom, distribute it, and make a statistical analysis of the results.
- Represent in a bar graph the results of the last presidential election.

- Represent in an area or circle graph the percentages of state income from its various tax and fee sources.
- Develop a graph projecting national income-tax returns based on population growth and growth in the gross national product for the next year or for several years in the future.

*For Children Having an Interest in
Science*

- Using one hundred as a representative sampling, make an analysis of the characteristics of voters in a selected area in terms of sex, occupation, and political affiliation.
- Poll the classroom on a selected student issue, organize and analyze the results, and make a prediction on how the class would vote on a related issue.
- Make an objective analysis of two constitutions on the basis of their provisions for a check-and-balance control of governmental power.
- Make an analysis of the workings of the British parliamentary form of government for weaknesses and strengths.

*For Children Having an Interest in
Language*

- Write a one-act play which takes place in the campaign headquarters of a candidate for the state legislature.
- Write a poem reflecting the feelings of three voters, each of whom is from a different walk of life, as they enter the polls.
- Prepare an opening statement for a debate on a critical student issue in school.
- Interview a successful lawyer to obtain his opinions about the limitations of the law and report findings in a feature article.

For Children Having an Interest in Art

- Draw a cartoon which expresses one side of a current political issue.
- Develop a series of sketches showing how a city government legislates.
- Develop a series of wall pictures to express this theme: "Man seeks to establish and maintain a public authority."
- Sculpt a figure reflecting man as a political being.

Ultimately a contract is developed, as shown in Figure 9–10.

This contract reveals that Jan needs to do some extra reading and develop some skills as a part of her independent study. The teacher helped her organize her study into tasks. Together they decided on completion and conference dates, and Jan suggested the consequence herself.

The organization of the tasks and the number of scheduled conferences are "tailor-made" in accord with Jan's needs as a learner. Other learners may need a different organization of tasks and more or less conferences.

The independent study has been presented here as it is used under the most professional circumstances to ensure humane individualization of instruction. Of all the devices discussed, it offers the greatest opportunity for instruction based on individual needs and preferences.

The tools or devices for individualizing instruction are impressive. Let us see how they are used when curricular individualization is *total, as needed,* or *complementary.*

Total Curricular Individualization

Total curricular individualization of instruction is most defensible when the learners are gifted and in grades six through eight. By grade six, most gifted learners have either learned or are ready to learn, often with little direct instruction, the study skills necessary for completing independent studies or nonsequential study packets.

If individual study packets are used, the teacher distributes a packet to all the learners, guides them in a survey of its contents, and answers questions about its use. Then he or she distributes a list of the available packets to the learners. Each learner decides which packets he or she wishes to do (a certain number is required) and the one he or she wishes to start with.

As the learners work through the packets, the teacher serves as consultant and confers on a regular basis with learners to see how well they are doing.

If independent studies are used, the teacher surveys the learners' interests and skills. The sur-

Jan Bettle
Name

April 17, 198-
Date

Description of the Study: Set of diagrams and notes to show different organizations of government in Mass. from founding to present.

Tasks	Completion Dates	Conference Dates
1. Read chap. 2 in Heidiger's The Org. of Government	4/18	
2. Complete learning sheets, "How to Use the Card Catalog"	4/19	
3. Make a list of questions to guide research	4/22	4/23
4. Take notes on government in Mass.	4/24	4/25
5. Make rough drawings of diagrams	4/29	
6. Make outline of explanatory notes	4/30	5/1
7. Make final drawings	5/3	
8. Write explanatory notes	5/7	

This study will be completed on May 8, 198- .

If the study is satisfactory and completed on time, Jan will have a morning of free time during the week of May 13.

Jan Bettle
(Pupil's signature)

H. Tomp
(Teacher's signature)

FIGURE 9–10. *A Study Contract.*

vey may be accomplished through a simple questionnaire on which each learner indicates:

1. The topical areas and issues that interest them most within a given social-studies universe. The questionnaire offers a list of areas and issues as well as blanks in which the learners can enter an issue or topic not specifically listed. They might be asked to check or mark the three that interest them most and to rank them in order of preference.
2. The terminal projects that they have completed in independent study. The questionnaire offers a list of possible projects and provides blanks in which the learners can enter other projects. With special markings they indicate those which they really like to do and those which they would like to learn to do.
3. The skills that they consider themselves to be proficient in. The questionnaire offers a list of the skills and blanks the learners can use to enter skills not listed. They may be asked to indicate which skills they would like to learn.

From the data gathered with this survey, the teacher develops a schedule of conferences. The less-competent learners or those who need closer guidance are scheduled first. Because the social-studies period is too short to allow the teacher to confer with more than five or six learners, the teacher has the other learners choosing and completing tasks as facilitated by an activity center. Eventually all the learners are working at independent studies.

From time to time the teacher may convene the learners as a total group to share their experiences and products resulting from their independent studies or study packets. Besides providing a respite from working alone, this procedure also generates interest in other study packets or other kinds of independent studies.

In the foregoing, the most defensible situation for total curricular individualization was discussed. Let us consider now a less defensible situation. This occurs in grades three through eight with learners meeting the usual background and skills expectancies. In this situation the teacher uses learning centers and an activity center.

The activity center provides for learners not occupied at any learning center. It is well-stocked with a variety of task cards and materials designed to help them practice and improve in map reading, using indexes and tables of contents, doing inquiry activities, and using expressive skills to translate ideas or create products from facts learned in the learning centers.

The learning centers provide for the learner's exposure to social-studies facts and ideas. In these centers they read descriptive passages, view filmstrips, filmloops, or series of study prints, analyze maps, charts, or cartoons, or listen to audiotapes. Their purpose may be to gather facts, to infer from facts, or to validate generalizations.

The teacher's responsibilities include routing learners through the learning centers and conferring with individuals on a regular basis to review what they have been doing.

Carefully organized individual study packets may be used in grades four through eight. If organized similarly to the example given earlier in this chapter, the study packets will suffice by themselves. No activity center will be needed. Conferences will still need to be scheduled on a regular basis.

Study packets or learning centers and an activity center—whatever the curriculum organization—there is still a need for learners to be convened as a class to share what they have done. Individualized study can be tedious, and seeing what others have done can be stimulating.

The least defensible, and acceptable only on a better-than-nothing basis, is the situation in which

social studies is a subject area of minor importance in the primary grades. When this situation occurs, one learning center at a time carries the main burden of instruction. Children may be assigned to it, or they may enter it of their own volition. Perhaps a social-studies learning center will be erected only occasionally, perhaps vying with science or health study (also taught through learning centers) for time.

The most acceptable defense for this situation is that children in grades kindergarten through second lack the skills to gather information independently.

In general, then, total curricular individualization in social studies is most feasible with children in grades four and beyond who have the necessary skills to deal independently and meaningfully with gathering and processing information.

Curricular Individualization as Needed

All the devices for curricular individualization may be used to meet the specific needs of individuals while the class is involved with social studies as a class-centered enterprise. The teacher uses these devices to meet needs as they arise. Here are a few ways in which they are used:

- The teacher observes that the fast-learning and gifted learners are bored with social studies. He or she guides them in doing independent studies, the results of which they share with the class.
- The teacher notices that most of the class tends to shirk individual responsibilities for information gathering and processing, participating in discussion, and doing group work. He or she develops a three-week program in which the learners work in study modules or study packets.
- The teacher sees that a third of the class is deficient in map reading. He or she develops a sequence of study modules or learning centers in which these learners work during free time or while the rest of the class studies a special unit.
- During inquiry sessions, all but five learners participate freely. The teacher erects a learning center in which problems are presented via audiotape. The cassette is programmed to prompt the learner to make "best guesses" and to compose

questions to be answered, and then to give examples of good responses.

- After guiding his or her class through a study of how to use an index to obtain information, the teacher observes that eight learners lack confidence in working independently to find information. He or she composes a set of task cards for a section of an activity center. The task cards prompt the learners to seek information through the use of an index. Answer keys are provided to help learners see immediately how accurate they are. The teacher demonstrates the task cards to the learners who need to improve.

In the situations described above, the teacher has used curricular individualization to help either small groups of learners or the entire class to meet an identified need in social-studies learning. Similar procedures may be used with commercially prepared study kits.

Curricular Individualization as Complementary to Class Study

Social studies as a total-class enterprise tends to lock individuals into the teacher's or class's demands. Procedures, tasks, and directions follow the teacher's plan and decisions made by the class or working groups. Curricular individualization can facilitate learners' temporary release from the class enterprise and at the same time help them to grow in social-studies learning. Providing for this individualization is chiefly a matter of offering many choices of activities *after* a skill has been learned, a rich contact has been made with a comprehensive parcel of facts about a topic or issue, or a generalization has been surfaced. Here are a few examples:

1. After learning to read the scale and directions on a map, the learners may go to a learning center to:
   - Play an individual game requiring map skills for participation.
   - Complete a set of practice sheets requiring map skills.
   - Create a map riddle.
   - Create an imaginary pirate's map with directions given for finding the treasure.
   - Plan a trip in which distances and directions are to be determined.
   - Take a test and validate the answers on a map.
   - Build a signpost indicating the directions and distances to the five largest cities in the world.
   - Orient an outline map of the school as to direction and label the symbols on it.

2. The learners may obtain from an activity center a task card which prompts activities such as:
   - Using an automobile map to locate the cities one would pass through when following a single direction to the state border, or to determine how many cities of a given size are located within a hundred-mile radius of a given reference point.
   - Take a simple, self-correcting map test.
   - Draw the compass on a map from given locational clues.
   - Measure the road distance between two points on a map.
   - Determine the compass readings resulting from following a particular road between two points on a map.

3. After learning the facts about Nigerian life, the learners may confer with the teacher to plan an independent study culminating in a creative product to be shared with the class, or obtain from the activity center a task card containing directions for activities such as these:
   - Drawing a picture showing the native homes built in Nigeria.
   - Making a chart showing the different ways of life followed by Nigerian peoples.
   - Writing an imaginary diary entry telling about a visit to the Nigerian capitol.
   - Making a Nigerian garment from paper or a scrap of cloth.
   - Making a replica of a Nigerian artifact from clay or paper.
   - Making a single puppet representing a Nigerian man and preparing a simple speech he might make telling what is best about his country.
   - Making a poster advertising a trip to Nigeria.
   - Taking a self-correcting test on the facts about life in Nigeria.
   - Making a map showing several features of Nigeria.

4. The learners may go to a learning center to:
   - Read a labeled illustration of a Nigerian artifact and a written description of how it is used, and write a paragraph about it.
   - Read and listen (via audiotape) to the description of the life of a Nigerian boy or girl, and list three ways in which the life of a Nigerian

child is like their own, and three ways in which it is different.

- View a chart depicting Nigerian money and the cost of several common items and decide what could be bought with an American dollar.
- View a set of pictures showing the daily life of the Nigerian peoples, and dictate into an audiotape the preferred group to visit and why.

5. After learning that Nigerians and Americans have the same basic life needs, but have developed their own ways to meet those needs, the learners may go to a learning center or use a study module to:

- Validate whether another people has the same basic needs.
- Validate whether Americans living two-hundred years ago had the same basic needs.
- Read or listen (via audiotape) to a conversation between two persons talking from opposite points of view about the Nigerian people and their way of life, decide which person expresses the more acceptable point of view, and tell why in a written paragraph or discourse spoken into an audiotape.

As you can see in the above, curricular individualization as complementary to class and group studies offers opportunities for learners to generate more interest in social studies by offering opportunities for choices in learning activities. The learners are encouraged to make choices freely from among whatever provisions are made. No matter what activities are provided, the learners are never specifically assigned to any.

Three ways of using curricular individualization have been presented. Which of these to use is your decision. All require finding or devising special materials and developing workable management systems.

THE SPECIAL CHILD IN SOCIAL STUDIES

Since the passage of Public Law 94–142 (Education for All Handicapped Children Act of 1975) teachers in the elementary and secondary schools have had to think about the provisions they will make for special children mainstreamed into their class-rooms. These children have learning difficulties for any of a variety of reasons falling within the broad categories of mental retardation, brain damage, emotional disturbance, social maladjustment, physical disability, or educational disability. Mainstreaming is one strategy for providing these children with a nonrestrictive learning environment to ensure an optimum of physical, intellectual, emotional, social, and language development.

Not all special children are to be mainstreamed. Those for whom the least restrictive environment is the special classroom remain there for instruction.

Not all special children are mainstreamed in the same way. For some children, mainstreaming into a regular classroom will be only for instruction in a few subject areas. For others, mainstreaming will mean regular instruction except for subject areas in which their disability limits their performance so seriously that they cannot function within any of the range of activities provided in the classroom. They receive special instruction outside the regular classroom. And some special children will be mainstreamed for all regular instruction.

How much a special child is to be mainstreamed is determined by a group which may consist only of a regular classroom teacher and a resource teacher. The latter is well acquainted with the child's problem, capable of working with the child, and trained in advising others on how to work with the problem. Or, the group may include, besides the resource teacher and the regular teacher, the child's parents, the school principal, a psychologist, a psychiatrist, and a social worker. The nature of the child's problem and how the school district has organized to implement mainstreaming will determine who the members of the group are and how it will operate. It is the responsibility of the group to determine the least restrictive learning environment for the child to be mainstreamed into the classroom, or, put another way, to review the child's individual needs and how best to cope with them in the classroom. This is a facet of individualized instruction.

Because the instructional program in social studies provides a wide variety of learning activities for the participation of groups as well as individuals, and because provisions for social-studies instruction frequently takes into account differences in abilities in informational skills, it is often a subject area into which a special child is mainstreamed. Let us assume that you have been notified that a special child is going to be mainstreamed into your social-studies class.

In the well-administered school or school district, the notification itself is a mark of distinction. When you receive the notification, it indicates that you have been recognized as an effective social-studies teacher capable of being entrusted with a special responsibility. It is likely that the notification will include a date and time when you are to meet with the resource teacher. She or he will be your closest associate in working with the special child.

To prepare for the meeting, you will need to review your practice as a social-studies teacher to be able to respond with as much documentation as possible to these questions:

1. Classroom administration:
   a. When is the social-studies class scheduled? For how long?
   b. What is the seating arrangement in the classroom?
   c. What materials are kept at the children's study stations or personal-materials depositories?
   d. What materials are usually distributed during lessons? How are these distributed?
   e. What centers outside the classroom are children expected to use independently?
   f. How are physical needs taken care of?
2. Classroom discipline:
   a. How are acceptable standards of classroom behavior established and maintained?
   b. What forms of behavior modification or intervention are used to help children who have behavior problems?
3. Instructional delivery:
   a. What is the usual sequence of instructional procedures for each lesson?
   b. How much time is spent generally in class-wide instruction? In individualized instruction? In small-group activity? Is the membership of small groups usually determined impromptuly or through the use of a sociometric device?

c. How often are children expected to use centers outside the classroom?
d. How many instructional periods are usually required to complete a unit of instruction?
e. How many field trips are usually scheduled during the year? How many of these require transportation by bus or automobile? What is usually the ratio between adult supervisors and children on field trips?
f. What paraprofessional aid is provided for the classroom?
g. What is the most frequently used informational resource (textbooks, lectures, illustrated presentations, pictures, films, etc.)?
h. To what extent are other informational resources used?
i. What is the range of readability levels of the reading materials used in social studies?
j. How frequently are children provided with opportunities to choose among informational resources?
k. What activity is most frequently used for integrating and organizing information (written composition, charting, drawing, dramatics, oral reporting, etc.)?
l. What other activities for information process are also used? How often?

4. Assessing children's instructional needs:
   a. Which skills essential to social studies do you normally assess at the beginning of the school year?
   b. How do you assess these skills? What assessment devices do you use? (Samples are useful here.)
   c. To what extent do you share the results of assessment with children?
5. The instructional program:
   a. What content units are generally taught?
   b. What skills units are generally taught?
   c. What specific instructional objectives do you expect the normal child to meet by the end of the school year in the following:
      i. Group interaction skills.
      ii. Inquiry skills.
      iii. Information-intake skills.
      iv. Information-process skills.
      v. Values-exploration skills.
6. Assessing children's achievement:
   a. How do you assess achievement? What assessment devices do you use? (Samples are useful here.)
   b. To what areas of social-studies learning do you give the greatest weight when making evaluations?
   c. What practice do you follow in sharing chil-

dren's achievement with them? With their parents or guardians?

d. What role do you give children in evaluating their achievement? What role do you give parents or guardians in evaluating children's achievement?

The purpose for being able to give so much information is to contribute as much as you can to the development of an instructional program for the special child. The resource teacher will inform you about the child's problem and needs, and advise you on what to expect and what to do as you work with the child. If you cannot describe clearly what you do, and in considerable detail, you will not be able to ask the clarifying questions necessary to understanding the information and advice being offered to you.

More than likely the agreed-on instructional program will include a list of objectives which the child can reasonably be expected to attain in your classroom and a plan for monitoring progress. This may include the resource teacher's observations of the child at work in your classroom and a schedule of meetings at which you and the resource teacher confer over the child's needs and decide, if necessary, new strategies to meet them.

The modifications you may need to make in your program will depend on the nature of the child's disability. If the child is physically disabled, much of what you do will consist of monitoring the adequacy of the physical environment and making changes as necessary—ensuring that the child confined to a wheelchair can get from one study area to another and has the necessary transportation on a field trip, seating the child with a hearing or sight loss near your teaching station, and the like. Some of the other modifications may include:

- Providing children with more choices for informational intake and processing. These choices should be just as available and acceptable to other children as they are to special children.
- Using behavior-modification and individual-counseling techniques more frequently.
- Making more or less provisions for individualized instruction.
- Monitoring more carefully the organization of

small groups to ensure that the special child is placed with peers who can work with him or her.
- Making special provisions for instruction when the child is scheduled for therapy or counseling outside the classroom.
- Modeling the behaviors of a person who gives interested, respectful support to another who has a disability, such as: maintaining eye contact, listening attentively and patiently, and following the stilted language flow of a child who has cerebral palsy.
- Monitoring growth toward instructional objectives more carefully.
- Providing study guides to help children stay on task.
- Emphasizing the learning of social-studies vocabulary through a thorough discussion of each new word, encouraging children to experiment with its use, and maintaining posted vocabulary lists for constant reference.

In most instances, the modifications in practice that you will need to make are a matter of improving the teaching skills you already know. The positive result of having a special child mainstreamed in your class is threefold: first, the special child achieves; second, the instructional opportunities for normal children are improved; and third, you become a more effective social-studies teacher.

At this point we may conclude the following about individualized instruction in elementary social studies:

1. Regardless of the way in which our instructional program is organized, either as a total-class endeavor or as studies made by individual learners, we shall have to make immediate responses and environmental accommodations to meet the different learning needs of children.
2. Making effective immediate responses and environmental accommodations are central to the needs of special children mainstreamed into our classroom.
3. Curricular individualization is particularly effective in helping children reinforce and maintain some of the skills essential to social studies.
4. Total curricular individualization is particularly effective in helping children learn some of the inquiry skills in social studies and in applying a variety of skills at an advanced level.
5. Total curricular individualization is useful as a change-of-pace strategy.

A general principle about the individualization of instruction in elementary social studies may be stated in this way: *individualization of instruction in elementary social studies serves best as a means of meeting individual differences in learning needs to improve skills and to extend interests.*

SUMMARY

When individualizing social-studies instruction the teacher may organize his or her program as needed to cope with individual differences in skills and content or to facilitate learning by having learners study independently.

Individualization as needed in social studies is always feasible. It may be combined with curricular individualization to meet special needs.

The teacher's careful monitoring of learning is essential to effectively individualizing instruction as needed. Individualization as needed includes making immediate adjustments to instruction in process, providing needed factual background, controlling factual-acquisition activities, and providing choices in expressive activities.

Curricular individualization may be used *in toto* for an entire class, as a means of meeting specific needs for a group or class, or as a way of complementing class or group study. The tools used include the learning center, the activity center, the study module, the individual study packet, and the independent study.

Total curricular individualization in social-studies instruction is most suitable for gifted learners in grades six through eight who have the skills and self-discipline to complete independent studies, study modules, or individual study packets. Typical learners in grades three through six may follow an instructional program conducted through learning centers and activity centers. Learners in grades four through eight may profit from a program conducted through individual study packets.

Curricular individualization as needed may be used to meet the needs of gifted children or small groups of learners having specific needs.

Curricular individualization as complementary to the group or class program helps children practice recently learned skills to make them more efficient, to express more freely what they have learned, or to follow a discovered interest.

To meet the needs of special children mainstreamed in the classroom requires close cooperation between the regular teacher and the resource teacher, to develop and maintain the least restrictive learning environment for the children. The cooperation rests in part on the regular teacher's thorough understanding of his or her instructional program.

Because social studies is interactive and social process is centered, the teacher may find that total curricular individualization may not bring his or her learners to all the social-studies objectives.

POSTSCRIPT

At the beginning of this chapter you were invited to assess a teacher's practice related to individualizing instruction. Now is the time for you to review the notes that you made. In what ways was the teacher's practice acceptable when you first assessed them? Do you still feel the same way? What recommendations would you make to him to improve his practice?

FOR FURTHER UNDERSTANDING

Cognitive Activities

1. Think about *individualization as needed* and *curricular individualization* for a minute or two, then define each in your own words. Test your definitions by telling them to a friend to see whether he or she can describe back to you the difference between the two.
2. Describe how each of the following can be used to facilitate the individualization of instruction in social studies: activity center, learning center, individual study module, individual study packet, and independent study.
3. Suppose that a teacher wishes to make a transition from emphasis on group and class instruction in social studies to an emphasis on individualized in-

struction. What problems do you think he or she would have?

4. Try this simulation for two participants with another class member.

THE SITUATION

A parent who believes strongly in curricular individualization is conferring with a teacher who is adept in incidental individualization. The parent wants his or her child's social-studies program to follow curricular individualization. The child is very bright.

PREPARATION

1. Decide between you who is to be the teacher and who is to be the parent.
2. Working separately, spend five minutes deciding how you will try to cope with the other participant—hopefully to win him or her over to your way of thinking.
3. As you plan, remember these rules:
   a. Only respectful, reasonable discussion is permitted.
   b. Citing experiences, stating opinions, and giving reasons for them are permissible; citing expert opinion is not.
   c. The simulation ends automatically when sarcasm or insults occur, or when either participant breaks from the role. In this case both the teacher and the parent lose.
   d. The winner of the simulation is the participant who gets the other to change his or her mind. If this does not occur, the simulation is a draw.
   e. The simulation lasts for twenty minutes.

SIMULATION

Convene and participate.

POSTDISCUSSION

1. Try to determine the winner.
2. Identify the arguments that appeared most effective on either side of the issue.

5. Suppose that you are reading a professional journal when you come upon an article entitled, "Elementary Social Studies Must Be Individualized!" Do

you agree or disagree with this assertion? Give your reasons.

6. Imagine that a close friend of yours who is a teacher confides to you that he or she has been notified about having a child mainstreamed into his or her social-studies class. The person is terrified. How might you counsel this person?

Practice Activities

1. Design a task card that will help fourth, fifth, or sixth-grade children practice using the index to find information. Make or obtain the materials the learner will need to complete the task.
2. Design a learning center in which the learner is prompted to find information from a resource contained within the center. Describe how you will route learners through it and how you will check to see how well each learner has completed his or her study in the center.
3. Design a study module that will guide the learner in validating a generalization in easily available study materials and making a creative product based on the generalization.
4. Make a flow chart for an individual study packet in which the learner has options in how far he chooses to go in learning about a social-studies topic. Choose any topic that you wish. Be sure to include concept, generalization, and expressive activities.
5. Design a checklist of the items you would check to see whether a learner could complete a study in which he or she makes a set of maps to show the production and distribution of a selected world crop.
6. Arrange to visit a classroom in which a teacher uses the tools of instructional individualization (activity centers, learning centers, etc.) in social-studies instruction. Observe to see whether the teacher is using incidental or curricular individualization and the effect it appears to have on learners.
7. Arrange to visit a classroom of special children. Choose a child to observe to see what kinds of immediate responses and environmental accommodations you would have to make if the child was mainstreamed into your classroom.

Performance Activities

1. In your classroom, determine an instructional need in social studies which can be satisfied through an activity center or learning center. Design and construct the center, and organize a plan for routing

learners through it. Introduce it and monitor its effectiveness in terms of what the children learn and how they feel about the center.

2. In your classroom, identify a group of learners who are able to use a study module or study packet, or do an independent study. Following prescribed curriculum requirements for content or a skill, design and construct a study module or packet, or develop a plan for guiding learners in independent studies. Use your materials to guide the selected children in social-studies learning. Monitor your program carefully to determine its effectiveness in terms of both learning and the children's attitudes toward their experience.

SELECTED REFERENCES

Charles, C. M. *Individualizing Instruction,* 2nd edition. St. Louis: The C. V. Mosby Company, 1980.

Fisk, Lori, and Henry Clay Lindgren. *Learning Centers.* Glen Ridge, N.J.: Exceptional Press, 1974.

Herlihy, John G., and Myra T. Herlihy, eds. *Mainstreaming in the Social Studies.* Washington, D.C.: National Council for the Social Studies, 1980.

Howes, Virgil M. *Individualizing Instruction in Reading and Social Studies.* New York: The Macmillan Company, 1970.

Kapfer, Philip G., and Glen F. Ovard. *Preparing and Using Individualized Learning Packages for Ungraded, Continuous Progress Education.* Englewood Cliffs, N.J.: Educational Technology Publications, 1971.

Kaylor, Harriet. "Individualized Instruction in the Social Studies: No!" *Social Education,* 44:322–324 (April, 1980).

Moore, Elaine, and Jerri Greenlee. *Ideas for Learning Centers.* Belmont, Calif.: Fearon Publishers, Inc., 1974.

Morlan, John E., *et al. Classroom Learning Centers.* Belmont, Calif.: Lear Siegler, Inc./Fearon Publishers, 1974.

Reasoner, Charles. *Portfolio of Working Materials for Individualized Instruction.* Englewood Cliffs, N.J.: Prentice-Hall, 1976.

Rogers, Vincent R. "The Individual and the Social Studies," *Social Education,* 31:405–407, 419 (May, 1967).

Searles, John. "Individualized Instruction in the Social Studies: Yes!" *Social Education,* 44:318–321 (April, 1980).

Shea, Thomas M. *Teaching Children and Youth with Behavior Disorders.* Saint Louis: The C. V. Mosby Company, 1978.

Stahl, Dana K. *Individualized Instruction Through Differentiated Learning Programs.* Englewood Cliffs, N.J.: Prentice-Hall, 1976.

NOTES

1. Bruce Joyce. "Social Sciencing—New Concept in Social Studies," *The Instructor* 78:85–92, 1968.

Instructional Planning
in Social Studies

Developing plans for guiding children in learning is a form of instructional engineering. The structural elements are the learning activities and instructional materials. The plans show the specific selection and sequencing of these to guide children toward specific objectives, determined by what society expects them to know, their capacity to learn and know, and where they are at a given moment on a continuum of instruction.

Because learning in social studies requires the use of many skills, instructional planning for the subject is a complex task. Let us begin our exploration of the task by considering an issue related to it. The point at issue is which planning approach to follow. Here are several:

1. Plan from day to day as a way of following children's interest as they emerge during social studies.
2. Using a master plan for social-studies instruction as a guide, plan from day to day in keeping with the children's progress and needs.
3. Make a sequence of daily lesson plans covering an entire topic in social studies.

Other things being equal, which of these approaches do you think will result in the best management of learning and ensure the most learning for children?

Jot down what you think. Also, write your reasons for your choice. Then put your notes aside to review later.

For most of us, the introduction to instructional planning occurs on the day before we are to assume responsibility for the instruction of children for the first time. We are asked to have a lesson plan prepared and approved before we face the children. We submit something that attests to our having thought about the lesson and our good intentions toward children. That is usually enough to ensure our survival.

Later we overhear our supervising teacher talk about his or her social-studies unit about this topic or that. Eventually we get an insight into what a unit is.

In this chapter we shall take a careful look at lesson plans that help both children and ourselves. The unit as an instructional plan will also be explored.

WHY PLAN?

Most social-studies textbooks series have accompanying instructional manuals or teacher's editions which present teaching notes. Often carefully composed, these tell how to conduct lessons and how to introduce and close units of instruction (a unit is an extended plan of instruction covering a broad topic). Frequently the teaching notes seem so complete that there appears to be no need for us to plan instruction. When this is the case, do not be deceived. Further planning is needed for several reasons.

1. Teaching notes frequently reflect a view of typicality not consonant with what one finds in many classrooms at the same grade level. For example, the teaching notes in a fifth-grade textbook may be composed on the assumption that the children in fifth grade know how to use a direction indicator on a map. The children in many fifth-grade classes may be able to identify a direction indicator and use it to determine the cardinal directions as long as North is toward the top of the map. Identifying midpoints and using the indicator when North is to the right or left or to the bottom of the map is beyond the children's ability.
2. Teaching notes can rarely provide workable suggestions for meeting the needs of slow or fast learners. Complete teaching notes will offer suggestions for *additional* activities for such learners, but seldom are suggestions for *substitute* activities given, and when they are, they may recommend materials unavailable to the class.
3. Reliance on teaching notes limits the ways in which the textbook can be used because the notes are designed to be used in sequence from the beginning to the end of the book. They follow a linear, cumulative design for learning. If, because of learners' interest in a topic or issue or a timely event, you attempt to teach a unit toward the end of the textbook before completing those which precede it, you will find the teaching notes to be almost useless. The children will most likely not have the skills or background to meet the expectancy reflected in the notes.
4. The objectives established by the composer of the notes may not be adequate to your learners' needs. The objectives may be difficult or lack challenge.

For the sake of your learners, you should feel free to restate objectives and to reject any or all of the teaching notes and to replace them with notes of your own making. As you make these changes, you are planning.

To organize your plans logically, you should review the textbook unit completely before making any changes. If you change unit objectives, you will have to change lesson and chapter objectives, and if you change the objectives for lessons and chapters, you will also have to change the learning activities. Occasionally you may change learning activities for lessons without changing objectives.

When you finish making changes, either at the unit or lesson level, the results are your own plans. You have used the teaching notes in the instructor's manual or teacher's edition as aids in planning. Effectively done, this kind of planning reflects a high level of creativity in curriculum development.

You may reach a higher level of creativity when, on the basis of your learners' needs, you develop a lesson, a series of lessons, or a unit of instruction in which you compose your own teaching notes for learning activities involving the use of materials which you select or devise. The materials you select may include newspaper and magazine articles, reference books, trade books, brochures, pamphlets, post cards, field trips, and presentations by resource persons as well as films, filmstrips, study prints, and videotapes available at a materials center. The materials you personally produce may include written articles, sketches, cartoons, photographs, films, graphs, audiotapes, flannelgrams, and puppet presentations. When you decide what the instructional objectives are, the sequence of learning activities, and how activities are to be introduced, experienced, and integrated, you make your own teaching notes. Depending on the magnitude of your endeavor, the result is a lesson plan or series of lesson plans, or an instructional unit.

As social-studies teachers, we have many opportunities to supplement textbook offerings with lessons developed around other materials. Unfortunately, we sometimes expect such dynamic, colorful materials as films, videotapes, and filmstrips to carry the full burden of instruction. The use of these materials requires a plan to develop purposes with children and to ensure the integration of learning.

Teachers of young children in kindergarten through second grade often create their own units of instruction in social studies. As they construct a unit, they may include what is offered in the textbook as only a small part of the unit. For example, a kindergarten teacher may find that the textbook unit about families focuses narrowly on the work of the various members of the family. Because many of his or her learners come from broken homes and are part of a transient population, the teacher has added studies about different kinds of family organization, activities that family members can do together, and how family members can help each other.

Teachers of older children may create units to supplement the total program. For example, a sixth-grade teacher whose total instructional program is focused on the diversity of many cultures decides to add a complete unit about the United Nations to help the children see that political interdependency exists within diversity.

Whether you make creative use of teaching notes accompanying the textbook or use other materials and compose original teaching notes as you plan, you will apply certain criteria to ensure the effectiveness of your plans. The remaining sections of this chapter will treat the criteria used in developing lesson plans and units of instruction.

THE DAILY PLAN

The organization of the daily lesson plan serves well as the introduction to any more extended plan. Both contain similar elements arranged in much the same way to achieve ends similar except in scope. Besides, achieving the ends of extended plans depends on the efficacy of daily plans.

A daily plan consists of five parts:

1. Lesson objectives
2. A list of instructional materials
3. Opening activities
4. Developmental activities
5. Closing activities

Let us consider each of these in detail.

Lesson Objectives

Lesson objectives indicate the ends to be met by the learners when they complete the lesson. When we express them, we tell what we expect the children to be able to do as a result of their experience with every activity we have prescribed for them in the lesson.

This can be confusing to some of us because we love such eloquent terms as *understand, know, appreciate, learn,* etc. They are useless in statements of objectives because they lack precision. This imaginary conversation between a principal and a teacher discussing a lesson plan underscores this:

Principal: What is the objective of the lesson?
Teacher: That the children will be able to understand how a cabinet form of government works.
Principal: And how will you know that they understand it?
Teacher: I'll know when I read the paragraph each child will write at the end of the lesson.
Principal: What is the paragraph to express?
Teacher: It is to tell how a cabinet form of government is formed and how it works.
Principal: With what accuracy?
Teacher: With complete accuracy.
Principal: The objective of your lesson is that *each child will be able to write a paragraph expressing accurately how a cabinet form of government is formed and how it works?*
Teacher: That's right. Then I'll know they understand it.

The reason for stating the objective precisely in terms of what the children will be able to do is that, as we hold the objective firmly in mind as we plan, it serves as a guide to help us remember all we need to consider to bring about this end. Here are the questions the above objective compels us to consider:

1. (Skill.) Can the children write paragraphs in acceptable form? Will they need a review? If they do, how will it be accomplished?
2. (Background.) What do the children already know about the legislative and executive branches of government? Will they need a review? If they do, how extensive will it have to be?
3. (Materials.) What informational materials are available? Are any useful for the lesson opener? Will I have to devise anything special? What special equipment will be needed? If it is needed, how can I be sure to have it exactly when I need it?
4. (Skill.) Can the children read, listen, or view the materials independently? How much assistance will they need from me? Who especially will need it?
5. (Strategy.) What learning activities are needed? In what order should they be presented?

Our responses to these questions may reveal that the children have the skills to profit from this lesson, that a brief review of background will be necessary, that the materials are suitable and available, and that the strategy can be planned. The objective as expressed by the principal during the conversation is appropriate.

Now let us suppose another condition exists. A teacher has been teaching paragraph composition in language arts, and he or she wishes the children to apply what they have learned about it so far in social studies. To ensure this, he or she has to provide in his or her plan some learning activities that will help the children recall what they know about paragraph composition and applying it. He or she devises a cluster of objectives, like this:

THE LEARNERS WILL BE ABLE TO:

1. Recall from their reading and discuss accurately and completely the information about the cabinet form of government.
2. Describe the structure of a paragraph as prompted by reanalyzing a labeled model of a paragraph.
3. Write a paragraph independently expressing accurately how a cabinet form of government is formed and how it works.

In the above, we see a sequence of objectives, the first dealing with social-studies content, the second dealing with a skill, and the third dealing with processing content through the exercise of a skill.

Now let us suppose that the teacher knows that his or her learners cannot write paragraphs. He or she decides to introduce the skill during the social-studies lesson. This is the cluster of objectives he or she uses when planning it:

THE LEARNERS WILL BE ABLE TO:

1. Recall from their reading and discuss accurately and completely the information about the cabinet form of government.
2. Participate in selecting from three given generalizations the one that best describes the cabinet form of government and how it works.
3. Participate in using the generalization as a topical sentence to compose a paragraph as cued verbally by the teacher and recorded on the chalkboard.
4. Participate in generalizing about the attributes of a paragraph as a verbal structure.

In the above cluster of objectives, the sequence is as follows: the first deals with content, the second, with generalizing from content, the third, with a guided composition experience, and the fourth, with generalizing from the experience as a basis for further learning.

As shown in the above, when a skill emphasis, whatever the skill may be, is included in the lesson, it is reflected in the objectives section of the plan. If no skill emphasis is included, a single objective may serve.

At this point you may be somewhat confused by the fact that social-studies lessons may be taught without any provisions made for learning or improving a skill. However, there are moments during social-studies instruction when the children are expected to apply skills as a response to the learning situation. When these moments occur, you observe the children to see whether they apply the skill automatically. If they do, they have met a high level of independent use of the skill; if they do not, you will need to provide more instruction in the skill during subsequent lessons.

Later, when we deal with unit construction,

you will see that social-studies units may also be planned without provisions for skills instruction.

Instructional Materials

When planning at the lesson level, you usually have some instructional materials immediately at hand. If you are teaching young children, these are the kinds of materials you may have available (presented in approximately the order in which they are usually available):

- Teacher-collected sets of pictures clipped from magazines, brochures, posters, and the like.
- Teacher-made sets of flannelgrams and a flannel-board.
- Puppets used to convey information.
- Objects or replicas.
- Teacher-made sketches.
- Simply written, well-illustrated storybooks.
- Simply written, well-illustrated informational books which the children can listen to and understand.
- A set of simply written, well-illustrated encyclopedia.
- Sets of study prints.
- Filmstrips.
- Audiotapes or transcriptions.
- Films.
- Videotapes.
- Field trips.
- Textbooks. (Usually none are provided for kindergarten. Frequently none are provided for first and second grades. The young child may not see a social-studies textbook until he or she is in third grade.)

When you teach social studies to young children, you rely primarily on materials which you can gather or make or which you can read or mediate to the learners in some way to help them gain information.

If you have a choice among materials to use with young children, choose those which meet these criteria:

1. They should convey the needed information in a clear-cut, direct way.
2. They should be free of distractive elements.

3. They should be accurate and realistic.
4. They should meet the learners' needs in terms of vocabulary, sophistication of language, and attention span.
5. Whenever possible, they should be manipulable —things that children can pick up, feel, and peer at closely, or that can be sorted, arranged, and rearranged.

Frequently a set of flannelgrams presented well to children will be more effective for their learning than a film.

When you are working with older children, these are the materials that you will usually have available:

- Textbooks, perhaps at several levels of readability.
- Reference books (encyclopedias, almanacs, and atlases).
- Teacher-collected sets of pictures, photographs, postcards, newspaper clippings, etc.
- Teacher-made adaptations or rewrites of text material.
- Teacher-made sketches, charts, graphs, diagrams, models, etc.
- Study prints.
- Replicas or real objects.
- Filmstrips.
- Audiotapes or transcriptions.
- Films.
- Videotapes.
- Field trips.

Textbooks and reference books stand at the head of this list because they are the most available. They will be the main resources for information. This means that the way you use these materials is always going to be determined by how well the children can read. You may need to give serious thought to ways of individualizing information-acquiring activities. These ways have already been discussed in Chapter 9.

Your choice of materials to use in a lesson and how you intend to use them should be governed by these criteria:

1. They should convey the needed information in a clear-cut, direct fashion.
2. They should meet the learners' needs in terms of their level of skills in general reading and in

reading maps, globes, diagrams, graphs, charts, and tables; in viewing and listening for specific purposes; and in retaining what they read, view, or hear.

3. They should provide for a reasonable reconstruction of the reality they represent.

In the final analysis, the usefulness of a piece of material for social-studies instruction is determined not by whether it is read, heard, or viewed, but by how purposefully it is used.

So far we have dealt only with the materials needed for content learning. If we are going to teach a skill or some aspect of it, we may need some additional materials.

If we are in the process of teaching a skill in another subject area, or have completed an instructional program in the skill, we may use the materials utilized while teaching the skill to help children recall what they have learned. Charts, models, summaries describing skills, lists of procedures, and the like, from reading, language arts, mathematics, or whatever the subject, may be reintroduced and used in the social-studies lesson.

Often social-studies textbooks are accompanied by skill-learning books (workbooks) containing introductory and exercise materials that may be used in the social-studies lesson. Special exercise materials prepared to provide practice in such skills as map and globe skills, index skills, and the like, may also be used.

However, if you want the best possible combination of skill and content materials, that is, skill materials dealing directly with the content of the lesson, you will have to devise them yourself. You may use skill-learning books or copies of special materials as guides to helping you devise what is needed.

When you have selected your materials, you are ready to begin to think about how you will open the lesson.

The Opener

The opener in a lesson plan prepares the learners for new learning. At the very least, it has them recalling what they can remember from previous experiences. In most instances, the most recent pertinent learning occurred in the previous lesson. When this is the case, the most direct way we have for opening the lesson is to ask a question like these: "What did we learn yesterday about ————?" or "Who remembers what we learned about ———— yesterday?"

Better openers are those that generate learners' interest. Here are a few procedures that may be used with young children:

• If the previous lesson closed with making a picture or object, focus the children's attention on a few samples of these to invite recall of what they had learned.
• Use a puppet to relate what was learned previously—a puppet who cannot remember (the children help it to recall), or who makes a few mistakes when telling children what it remembers (the children make corrections).
• Use a grab bag of items related to the previous day's lesson. Have the children reach into it, select an item through touch, and then tell about it.
• Tell riddles about things previously studied. To make correct guesses the children must recall what they have learned.

Older children generate greater interest in study when procedures similar to the following are used:

• Divide the class into "buzz" groups to interact for two or three minutes on what are the most important things to remember from the previous lesson. Reports from the groups soon indicate what is important to remember.
• Have a pair of volunteers role play an interviewer and an interviewee interacting over the previous day's learning. If other members of the class disagree, they may reenact the interview.
• Prompt a class discussion with a "what if?" question demanding recall of the previous day's learning for reasonable responses.
• Give a three-to-five-item short-answer test or crossword puzzle based on the previous day's learning. The test or puzzle is corrected and discussed immediately in class.
• Invite a group to charade, pantomime, or perform an impromptu dramatization to convey the

previous day's learning. The other children participate by guessing or by watching and reacting to accuracy.

The beginning lesson in a sequence sometimes offers no opportunity for review, but children usually have some background related to the study topic. In most instances, the beginning of a study is concept-centered. Using this initial concept, you may use procedures similar to the following to encourage young children to tell what they know. (Transportation is the initial concept here.)

· Have the children tell all the different ways they know to go places or to haul things from one place to another. Use their ideas to introduce the verbal term for the concept, "transportation."
· Have the children imagine that they are standing on a street corner looking to see what is carrying people and things, or take the children on a walking trip to a street corner to observe carriers. Return to the classroom to discuss their findings. Use their ideas to introduce the verbal term for the concept.
· Show a collection of pictures or sketches of vehicles and have the children identify them. Introduce the verbal term for the concept to them as a way of referring to all the vehicles.
· Encourage the children to use classroom furniture as props to show what they know about riding a bus, taxi, airplane, train, helicopter, etc. Then introduce the verbal term for the concept and invite the children to give other examples.
· Pantomime riding in an automobile (getting in, sitting, pulling away from the curb, waving to friends and neighbors, turning your head to hold an object in sight as long as possible, stopping, and getting out). Invite the children to guess what you are riding in. When they guess correctly, invite them to pantomime riding in other vehicles. The class guesses. Introduce the verbal term for the concept and ask for more examples.
· Using flannelgrams, tell a simple story about a family that moves over a very long distance using many vehicles. After the story, have the children identify the vehicles, name any others they can think of, and introduce the verbal term for the concept.

If older children were studying transportation, we might use any of the following procedures to generate their interest in the lesson:

· Ask the children to give the best definition of transportation that they can formulate.
· Have each child list all the vehicles he or she has ridden in. Pool all the lists to make a chart on the chalkboard of the vehicles experienced by the members of the class. Mark a tally for the mention of each vehicle. Introduce "transportation" as the label for the concept the learners have been considering. Invite further discussion to define it more precisely.
· Invite the children to decide how they would define "transportation" to an imaginary creature who traveled only by telepathic transfer.
· Tell the children that their next study topic will deal with a process vital to everyone's life in the modern world. Encourage them to guess what it is by asking you questions which you can answer with "yes" or "no." Have a child keep track of how many questions are asked until someone guesses what it is. When it is finally guessed, have the class formulate a definition for "transportation."

Often the success of a lesson depends on the quality of the opener. A good opener helps children start thinking about the topic and anticipating new learning.

The Developmental Section

The developmental section of a lesson plan prescribes the learning activities for acquiring and/or processing information and, if necessary, for skill learning. Except for a review of a skill or some aspect of it, the section provides for new learning.

The developmental section has two or more parts, depending on whether the lesson includes skill learning or not. If no skill learning is included, the parts include:

1. Establishing a content purpose.
2. Providing for the purpose to be met.

Establishing a Purpose. Children need definite purposes for seeking information. Usually the more involved the children are in establishing a purpose, the more eager they are to fulfill it. Young children can be helped in establishing a purpose with procedures similar to the following:

• Tell the children that the materials and equipment they can see before them will help them learn more about the topic or something definite about the topic.
• Tell the children that the activity (viewing or listening) will help them know how something is done, what someone does, how something works, etc., and that after the activity they will talk about what they have discovered.
• Alert the children to what they will do with the information they discover. They may be making a picture or a design, retelling what they learned, arranging materials in some way, etc.
• Have the children discuss a simple issue related to the information. For example, before looking at some pictures on road building, they might talk about the different kinds of tools they expect to see. After studying the pictures, they will discuss what they saw to see how accurate they were and whether they had discovered anything new.

Older children may be guided in doing the following:

• Making predictions about what they will find.
• Discussing the meaning and purpose of the questions that will be answered.
• Discussing whether a generalization related to the content they are to learn about is true. After viewing, reading, or listening, they will review what they originally thought.
• Formulating questions related to the topic to see which are answered during the intake activity.
• Using the experienced content to formulate questions to use in a quiz show after the intake activity.
• Discussing the objective of the lesson and what special behaviors they may have apply to be able to reach it.

Such procedures help children anticipate the intake activity.

Providing for the Purpose to Be Met. This part of the plan describes what the children are going to do to learn new information. Our decisions about this are usually made when we select the materials for the lesson. Here is how you express them in your plan:

1. For young children—
• The children will listen to a flannelboard story about _____.
    Or
• The children will listen to a puppet talking about a set of sketches about _____.
    Or
• The children will listen to a resource person telling about _____.
    Or
• The children will listen to the reading of pages _____ in the book _____.
    Or
• The children will be guided in a study of the first four pictures in the series entitled _____.
    Or
• The children will view the film, ——, about _____.
    Or
• The children will guided in reading silently pages _____ in _____ with helping questions to focus their attention on significant facts. The children will read to find answers, will give them in their own words, and will prove their answers by reading the sentence or paragraph containing the answer.
• The helping questions:
    a. _____ .
    b. _____ .
    c. _____ .
    d. _____ .
    e. _____ .
    f. _____ .
2. For older children—
(The last four notes listed after "For young children" may also be used in a lesson plan designed for use with older children.)
• The children will read independently pages _____ in _____.
    Or
• Mel's group will read independently pages _____ in _____.
• Jane's group will read independently pages _____ in _____.
• Bob's group will be guided in reading a rewrite about life in ancient Rome. (Questions added for guided reading.)
    Or
• Divided into small groups the children will read and discuss pages _____ and prepare a summary of what they found.
    Or

- Tim's group will compare what is given on pages _____ in _____ with pertinent articles in the encyclopedias.
- Nan's group will read independently pages _____ in _____.
- Jim's group will be guided in studying a series of study prints about _____.

When no skills are being specifically taught in the lesson, only the provisions for setting the content purpose and fulfilling it need be made. However, if a skill is also to be taught during the lesson, more provisions for learning must be made: introducing or reviewing the skill as it is to be used with the content and, if a new element of the skill is to be taught, provisions for the children to learn it.

Let us suppose that we are teaching a second-grade class how to listen for specific facts as given on an audiotape. They have already had several lessons in this skill during social-studies instruction and they are improving in it. This is what the entries in the development section of our lesson might look like:

The Children Will:

1. Discuss whether the various American Indian tribes traded with each other for things they needed.
2. Review the rules for good listening by telling the listening puppet what he must do to be a good listener:
   - Know what you are trying to find out about.
   - Listen as carefully as you can while sitting still.
3. Listen to the audiotape about trade among the American Indians.

As you can see, provisions for reviewing the skill follow those for setting the content purpose.

Now let us suppose that we are going to introduce note taking to a fourth-grade class. We know that they have not learned this skill yet. This is what the entries in the development section of our plan might look like:

The Children Will:

1. Discuss what they think about how important Kansas' wheat is to the rest of the world and arrive at suspended judgment.
2. Discuss their problems with remembering what they read.
3. View a large representation of a note to discover what its parts are and how it might be helpful to them in retaining what they read.
4. Make a note card with the question, "How important is Kansas' wheat to the rest of the world?" written on it.
5. Begin a supervised reading in which two notes are discovered and discussed to ensure accuracy and understanding.
6. Complete the reading by taking notes.

As shown in the above, provisions for a "mini-lesson" are inserted after provisions for setting a purpose (1). Entries 2–5 introduce the skill and provide for its limited but supervised practice with social-studies material. Entry 6 has the children trying the skill to fulfill a purpose. Later this is perhaps what we would see in a developing section of a lesson plan to be used with these children:

The Children Will:

1. Formulate questions about what is produced in Texas for world export.
2. Examine notes they have taken in the past to discuss what notes are and the purpose they serve.
3. Consider whether they might use several note cards instead of just one.
4. Make note cards for each of the questions formulated in 1.
5. Inform the teacher when they have finished making their note cards to show that they have made them properly.
6. Complete the reading by taking notes.

In the above, entry 2 provides for review, entries 3 and 4 provide for the introduction of a new element of the skill, and entry 5 provides for supervised practice.

As you can see, whenever a skill or a new element of it is introduced, there should also be provisions for supervised practice of the skill or element before the children are to use the skill by themselves.

The developmental section of the lesson is designed to provide for children's new experience in learning. In the closing section, you find out whether the objectives have been met.

The Closing Section

The closing section of the lesson plan mirrors the objectives listed in the objectives section. When the objectives are written as a cluster of chronological activities, that list may be entered in the closing section. To save time, the planner may simply enter a note: "See objectives above." However, when there is a single objective, the planner must show an approach to the objective. For example, let us assume that a planner has used this objective:

The children will be able to write an ending to a story in which an imaginary person on a wagon train solves a problem in a way that persons of the period usually would.

And here is how the approach is organized:

The Learners Will Be Able to:

1. Summarize the hardships characteristic of travel in a wagon train.
2. Generalize about the traits and motives required of the people who would be able to survive wagon-train travel.
3. Write an ending to a story in which an imaginary person on a wagon train solves a problem in a way that persons of that period usually would.

Ensuring that the children will have an opportunity to meet the objective is not the only concern of the planner. He or she is also concerned that the children be aware that they have learned. A good way to help children sense accomplishment is to give them an opportunity to share and discuss their work with others. Our planner would add this:

4. Share and discuss the endings they have written for accuracy and originality.

Of course the planner may intend to help children sense their accomplishment in some other way at a later time—perhaps by posting the story endings for everyone to read or by conducting an individual conference with each writer.

When teachers plan daily lessons carefully, they do it to ensure that children have the best opportunity to learn, to be confident as they work with children, and to monitor their own effectiveness as teachers. The final part of the lesson plan is an open space labeled "Evaluation." In it the planner responds to these questions:

1. How well did the children meet the objective? As shown by what?
2. If all the children did not meet the objective, why not? What can be done in subsequent lessons to ensure greater success? In what way can opening procedures be improved? Developmental procedures? Closing procedures?
3. If all the children met the objective, was there any part of the lesson that could be improved to provide better transitions from one part of the lesson to the other? To provide more challenge?

So far we have treated the kind of lesson plan with which you will most often be involved in social studies. This is the lesson in which the children acquire information and do something with it to show that they have learned. Another kind of lesson is that in which the entire social-studies period is devoted to an expressive activity. This activity usually occurs after the children have acquired a comprehensive parcel of information which needs to be tied together. Perhaps five or six regular lessons have been taught. At this point you design a lesson like this:

OBJECTIVE

The children will be able to compose watercolor pictures showing ways of conserving forests as a natural resource.

MATERIALS

Three watercolor paintings from a recent art lesson, watercolor paper, individual sets of watercolor paints, brushes, newspapers, water, and water containers.

OPENING SECTION

The children will

1. Assist in preparing for painting—spreading newspaper over the desks and obtaining paper and water and receiving clean-up assignments.
2. Discuss what they have learned so far about forest conservation.

DEVELOPMENTAL SECTION

The children will:

1. Discuss possible scenes about forest conservation to depict.
2. View three paintings to refresh what they know about brush techniques and picture composition.
3. Paint pictures.

CLOSING SECTION

The children will:

1. Share and discuss their paintings with the class on a volunteer basis to determine accuracy and commendable use of art skills.
2. Decide on a display schedule for all the pictures.

EVALUATION

The above plan, suitable for a fourth grade or above, shows provisions for the distribution of special materials managed first in the Opening Section. This builds anticipation for the activity as well as ensuring a direct flow of the lesson. Next, provisions are made for the children to recall information to use in their expressive task.

The Developmental Section provides for an approach to the expressive task. Provisions are made first for the exploration of possible ideas, then for a review of skills already learned, and finally for the painting itself.

The Closing Section provides for the children to integrate what they know as they consider accuracy and the commendable use of skills. Finally,

provisions are made for them to develop a sense of accomplishment.

Another kind of plan you will be using involves such activities as role playing, simulation, value analysis, or value clarification. Usually these activities prompt children to explore for alternatives related to attitudes and behaviors in situations of conflict. In the lesson plan below you will note that the objective ensures only that the children will have an exploratory experience.

OBJECTIVE

The children will explore through role playing for alternatives in attitudes and behaviors toward policemen.

MATERIALS

A role-playing prompter: "Johnny is at the street corner waiting for the 'Do Not Walk' sign to change to 'Walk.' How he wishes it would change soon. It seems to him that he has been there for a very long time. Suddenly he notices that there are no cars in the street, but still the sign has not changed. It looks safe. So Johnny runs across the street as fast as he can.

"Johnny takes a few steps along the walk when he hears a man's voice say, 'Just a minute, young man, I'd like to talk with you.'

"Johnny turns to see a policeman getting out of his patrol car. He had not seen that it was parked across the street just beyond the crosswalk. Johnny starts walking toward the policeman as he stands beside the patrol car."

Two puppets: One a policeman and the other a schoolboy.

OPENING SECTION

The children will:

1. Tell what they can remember about a policeman's work.

DEVELOPMENTAL SECTION

The children will:

1. Discuss what they should do when they are at a crosswalk where there are signals for pedestrians as well as vehicles.
2. Listen to the role-playing prompter.

3. Assume roles as volunteers or prepare to observe the role playing.
4. Role play with the puppets or observe the role playing.

CLOSING SECTION

The children will:
1. Report how they felt as role players or listen to what the role players say.
2. Discuss what the role players did, possibly contribute another way of reacting to a policeman, and participate in its reenactment.
3. Draw pictures of people and policemen interacting.

EVALUATION

As you can see, this lesson plan reflects no concern for factual accuracy or quality of skill performance.

The question is frequently asked, "Do teachers make lesson plans like these?" Student teachers do as an aid in learning how to organize instruction and to bear in mind their responsibilities to children. Teachers in the field usually do not. However, teachers who are deeply concerned about what they have children do will make detailed lesson plans when they are mastering a new technique and as a means of self-diagnosis to discover needs for improvement.

Lesson plans are most efficiently made between lessons, that is, between the lesson just taught and the lesson to be taught. Loose ends or faulty procedures in the first lesson can often be remedied in the second. For this reason, it is often wasteful of time and energy to plan lessons for a period of days in sequence. Loose ends, ineffective procedures, and interruptions during the early part of the sequence may render useless the plans in the later part.

The *daily* in daily lesson plan has two meanings. It denotes a lesson plan to be used on a particular day. It also means day-to-day planning. The teacher who wishes to monitor learning effectively will plan from day-to-day as guided by learners' progress along a path of learning which he or she has plotted. This requires an extensive plan.

WHY AN EXTENSIVE PLAN?

Traditionally, elementary social-studies instruction has followed an extensive plan which has come to be known as a "unit." Frequently, professional educators have referred to social-studies instruction as unit teaching, or teaching according to a big plan related to a broad topic. Following the plan was a matter of weeks or months. The tradition is still with us.

The long life of the tradition is attributable mainly to two advantages. The first of these is that the topic of a unit could be as broad as the planner wanted to interpret it. This meant that many interesting learning activities could be included and that the instructional objectives could be stated eloquently. Such objectives may touch the heart and liven the spirit. They remind the planners of the great enteprise in which they are involved.

The second advantage is that a unit facilitates the management of learning. Teachers following units can frequently arrange to order films, filmstrips, and other special materials from district depositories to arrive when they will be needed. When units organized under broad topics are required to be taught in a school district, expensive instructional materials such as films can be bought with assurance that they will be used. And, because sequences of learning activities are given in the unit, lesson planning is simplified.

As we weigh these advantages, we can see that they appear to be more in favor of the needs of teachers than those of children. True, broadly stated, eloquent objectives do foster the use of many exciting, interesting learning activities during instruction, but exciting and interesting to whom? Not necessarily to elementary children, because when they are given opportunities to rank their school subjects in order of preference, they rank social studies low!

Studies of children's preferences for school subjects show that mathematics and spelling rank high. There is a reasonable explanation for this. When children take weekly spelling tests, they are eager to know the results. Soon after the test they know. They feel that they have accomplished something. Completion of every mathematics exercise frequently has an immediate payoff. They soon know how well they did. Again they have a sense of accomplishment. Unfortunately, such incidents may not occur frequently in elementary social studies when planning is simply topical.

This sense of accomplishment may be falsely based in terms of true learning. Children who get high scores on spelling tests frequently misspell in their written work the very words they correctly spelled on a weekly spelling test. High scorers in daily mathematics exercises may do poorly in mixed practices or when examples are presented in different forms.

To update the traditional use of instructional units in social studies, we need to focus our efforts on planning (and conducting) instruction in such a way that children can frequently sense accomplishment solidly based on true learning. This means that our unit objectives will frequently be specific, monitorable, and documentable. As we monitor instruction, we can communicate to children our concern for their learning and make the corrections necessary to successful learning. As we document learning, we can communicate to children that they have learned. Doing these things is the main reason for us to plan instructional units in social studies.

This does not mean that we shall forget about children's needs for exciting, interesting learning activities and materials. We shall simply add another criterion—purposefulness. As we select materials and activities to use, we shall consider purpose first, and then from those that meet this criterion, we shall select those that are most attractive to children.

And, of course, we shall enjoy the traditional advantage of being able to manage learning more easily and efficiently.

THE UNIT AS A STRUCTURE

As an organizational structure, a unit is similar to a lesson plan in many ways. Objectives give direction to its organization and sequence. In its planning, similar concerns are shown for the appropriateness of materials. It also has three sections with similar purposes: an opener to explore children's background and to generate their interests, a developmental section to provide for new learning, and a closer which brings children to the point of meeting objectives. And, like a lesson plan, it may or may not make provisions for skills learning.

A unit is also different from a lesson plan because it is so much more extensive. Its objectives have a wider scope both singly and taken as a whole. For example, a unit may be headed by these objectives:

The Children Will Be Able to:

1. Complete with 75 percent accuracy a 33-item short-answer test on facts and generalizations about the economy of emergent nations in Africa.
2. Make a guide for the efficient use of an index to locate information in textbooks and reference books.
3. Work in small groups to create murals reflecting insight into the economic problems of emergent African nations.
4. Explore through simulation for alternative attitudes and behaviors toward the peoples of emergent African nations.

With the possible exception of the fourth objective, each of the objectives above will require several social-studies periods of learning activities before the children can meet it. Perhaps fifteen or more periods will be required before the first can be met. And, it is quite likely that part of each of those periods will be devoted to learning how to use an index. The completion of the murals, all the way from initial planning to completion, may require as many as five days. The simulation specified in the fourth objective may require one to three days.

A lesson plan may have children working with one or two pieces of material, but a unit will require many more.

The unit opener may require as many as two or three social-studies periods. For example, children beginning their study of the economy of emergent African nations will need to make an extensive map and globe exploration to discover where Africa and the emergent nations are located in terms of contiguous proximity, distance from the equator, distance and direction from the United States, and the predominant topological and climatic features of the countries. Having this background, they are ready to begin to speculate about the economic conditions within these nations. After arriving at consensus on a few ideas, they develop a list of questions which they know they will have to answer to validate their ideas.

If the unit requires more than a week to complete, its developmental section will most likely consist of several miniunits, each with its own objective(s), opener, developmental section, and closer.

Miniunits, which will be treated in greater detail later in the chapter, are divisions within the developmental section of the unit. Units requiring several weeks to complete frequently should have developmental sections divided into miniunits to facilitate the management of learning. Each miniunit as a division provides for an increment of learning. As it closes, the children are involved in some way to pull together what they know. This helps them know what they know as well as relate their recently acquired knowledge to what they had learned previously. As the teacher, you can see whether the children have established a knowledge base sufficient to further learning. If you find the knowledge base inadequate, you can make further provisions for instruction to ensure that the children are ready for the next miniunit.

A miniunit usually consists of provisions for several lessons. It is called a miniunit because it has the structural characteristics of a unit but is a part of a regular unit.

The closer of the unit will bring the entire unit to a close with the meeting of content objectives related to facts and generalizations—retention, interpretation at a higher level of thinking, and exploration for values related to the content. If a skill objective has been included in the unit,

provisions will be made for assessing and evaluating growth in the skill.

By way of comparison, a lesson plan may be viewed as a plank in the floor of a bridge, a miniunit as a middle span, and the unit as the entire bridge. Just as the strength of each plank and span in a bridge contribute toward its utility and safety, so does the strength of each lesson plan and miniunit contribute toward the effectiveness of the unit. See Figure 10–1 for a structural comparison of the lesson, the miniunit, and the unit.

Because it is such an extensive plan, a unit guides children in discovering ideas of broad applicability. To help children discover these ideas and apply them, we construct the units from two kinds of elements—objectives as ends and objectives as means.

OBJECTIVES AS ENDS

By now you are acquainted with instructional objectives as ends. They describe what the children are to be able to do at the close of a sequence of learning activities. In units, what the children are to be able to do may include passing a test on content or a skill with at least a specified level of accuracy, performing a skill at a specified level of accuracy and proficiency, making a product exhibiting specific qualities, or exploring for values. In short, the objectives are more comprehensive than those used in lesson plans.

Because of the miniunits in the development section, we must consider two kinds of objectives as ends: the *concluding objectives* which are to be met at the end of the unit, and the *supporting objectives* which are to be met at the ends of miniunits and which contribute toward the meeting of concluding objectives.

Concluding Objectives

When we plan social-studies units we shall always be concerned first with social-studies content. The

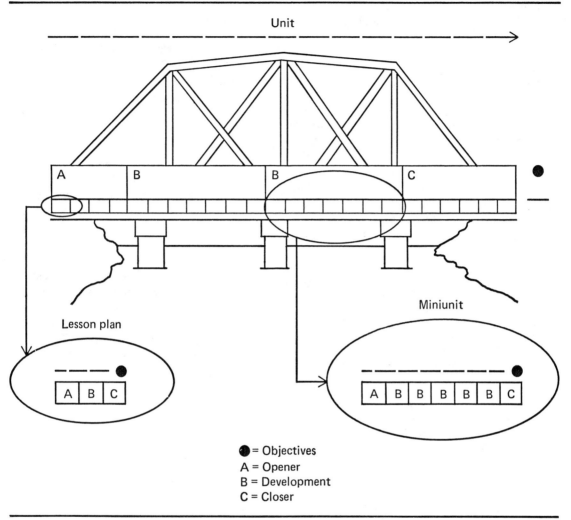

FIGURE 10–1. *A Structural Comparison of the Lesson Plan, Unit, and Miniunit.*

most cogent expression of that content is a generalization. Example:

Many of the emergent African nations have unused natural resources which could serve as the base for a sound economy.

You may find this generalization listed in a course of study, instructional guide, or textbook, or you may have to compose it yourself. With it at hand, you will be able to compose content objectives. As you compose these, you must bear in mind the skills the children have and frequently the skill you plan to teach in the unit.

Since this unit is being constructed for a sixth-grade class in which most of the children can read at the fourth-grade level of expectancy (which we discovered as we assessed the children's needs early in the school year), we may consider a concluding objective which holds the children responsible for retaining content and using it to select generalizations. We compose this concluding objective:

The children will be able to complete with 75 percent accuracy a paper and pencil, short-answer, 33-item test on facts and generalizations about the economy of emerging nations in Africa.

When we include an objective like this we have committed ourselves to providing opportunities for children to be involved in activities which help them retain and integrate information.

Our next concern is for another concluding objective which has the children applying their information at a higher level of thinking. We have many choices, all somewhat limited by the skills the children have. Here are a few:

• *The children will be able independently to draw large maps of Africa showing the products that each nation could produce for export and, through color keying, show the relative need for help by each nation.* (This objective has the children translating or reexpressing what they know in a medium comfortable to them. Most can draw maps easily.)
• *The children will be able independently to write a three-paragraph essay describing the economic problems faced by many emergent African nations and what they might do to solve them.* (This concluding objective has the children applying what they know about the economic problems of emergent African countries. This is a higher level of thinking than translating. Either the children know how to write three-paragraph essays or they will have reached an acceptable level of proficiency by the time the unit is brought to a close, perhaps learned while working with content in this unit.)
• *The children will be able to work in small groups to create murals reflecting insight into the economic problems of emergent African nations.* (This concluding objective has the children applying what they know to create an original product which conveys a message. They have learned how to work in small groups during the previous unit and have sufficient art skills to create a mural.)
• *The children will be able to participate in a panel discussion about how fully developed nations should help emergent African nations.* (This concluding objective has children applying what they know to make judgments. Their oral language skills are generally adequate, but they will need some additional instruction in how to prepare for and conduct a panel discussion.)

As you can see, these concluding objectives have children using their information in ways that help them discover extended meanings of the initial generalization. Perhaps you are wondering whether you might include all these concluding objectives. The choice is yours, but chances are that most children would be so tired of Africa when they completed the last objective listed above that they would never want to hear about Africa or emergent nations again. One, or perhaps two objectives like these, is enough. But there should be at least one.

The last concluding objective to consider is that dealing with values exploration to help children discover a personal meaning in what they have studied. After any of the concluding objectives we have considered so far, every child has the privilege of asking, "So what?" "Who cares?" or "What difference does all this make to me?" We as social-studies teachers have no right to tell him or her what personal significance it should have. But we do have the responsibility to help the child find out for him or herself. To do this, we provide for a concluding objective that brings children to explore values related to the content studied. Here are some choices as to objectives:

• *The children will be able to explore through participation in in-depth discussion for alternative attitudes and behaviors toward foreign aid to emergent African nations from the United States.*
• *The children will be able to explore through role playing for alternative attitudes and behaviors toward the leaders and peoples of emergent African nations as they try to find ways to work together to make better use of their natural resources.*
• *The children will be able to explore through value clarification for alternative attitudes and behaviors about going to an emergent African nation to live for a year.*
• *The children will be able to explore through value analysis for alternative attitudes and behaviors toward tribal diversity in the emergent nations of Africa.*
• *The children will be able to explore through problem solving for alternative attitudes and behaviors*

related to helping a child or as many children as possible in drought-stricken Africa.

With the exception of the first and last of these, children will need direct instruction in how to use specialized skills and procedures if they have never used them previously.

So much for the concluding objectives related to social-studies content at the end of a unit. Once composed for a unit, the objectives represent your commitment to children and their learning. In a sense they are your guarantee of what children will learn.

The following are recommended specifications for concluding objectives for a unit:

1. One concluding objective should deal with the retention of content. (This may be omitted if a succeeding objective will yield a performance or product in which much content is expressed.)
2. One concluding objective should have the children dealing with content at a level of thinking higher than verbal recall.
3. One concluding objective should provide for the children to explore for values related to the content.

Depending on the children's needs for improvement in skills and how the instructional program is organized in your classroom and school, you may be combining skill and content instruction always, frequently, or rarely. There may be times when you introduce and teach a skill in another subject area and transfer it to social studies at an appropriate moment. Sometimes you may introduce a skill during instruction in another subject area and teach it during social studies. Occasionally you may be introducing a skill and teaching it during social studies. Skills dealing with maps and globes, group work, inquiry, and values exploration are usually taught during social-studies instruction. The intake and output skills are more frequently taught during reading, language, and art instruction.

Depending on your situation, you may have no concluding skill objective, you may have one, the provisions for which run throughout the unit

or a part of it, or you may be providing for the learning of several in the unit. If several skills are to be treated in the unit, they may be closely related, as shown in the following:

The Children Will Be Able to:

1. Use an index efficiently to locate information in textbooks and reference books.
2. Use a card catalog to locate informational books in the library.

Or the skills may be quite different:

The Children Will Be Able to:

1. Select a conclusion accurately based on what they have heard on an audiotape about firemen's work.
2. Do a value clarification about firemen's work in the community.

All that can be said at this point is that concluding objectives are based on the children's needs you have discovered.

Supporting Objectives

Like all the other content objectives we have discussed, supporting objectives are related to the content generalization which we considered initially. To decide what the supporting objectives should be, we analyze the generalization in terms of the social-science or knowledge area from which it is drawn. The generalization we have been using as an example is from economic geography, a branch of cultural geography. This means that we can break the generalization down into a series of subgeneralizations each related to a specific region:

1. The nations of northeast Africa await improvement in their agricultural technology.
2. The nations of northwest Africa have mineral resources to be developed.
3. The nations of equatorial and southern Africa have unused minerals and timber in great abundance.

And for each of these subgeneralizations we shall compose at least one objective to serve as a supporting objective to the concluding content objectives of the unit. Again we are concerned about the children's skills. Here are examples of supporting objectives based on the subgeneralizations listed above:

1. The children will be able independently to make an accurate chart of the agricultural resources of the northeastern African nations and the ways in which they may be improved.
2. The children will be able independently to draw a map of the northwestern African nations showing the resources of each country and indicating those for which use can be improved.
3. The children will be able independently to compose written reports about a nation or cluster of nations in equatorial or southern Africa in which the resources used fully and those remaining to be developed are described accurately.

As you can see, the supporting objectives are of the translation type in which the children recall, integrate, and express what they know in a medium which they know how to use.

At this point we must ask ourselves this question: will these supporting objectives adequately prepare the children to meet the concluding objectives for content at the end of the unit? If our learners have well-developed retention skills, perhaps the above are all that is needed. But if they lack such skills, we may need to provide more supportive objectives, such as a supporting objective which provides for an information-recall test based on each subgeneralization. Taking such tests and correcting them in class can help children improve their retention skills.

Or we may provide supporting objectives in which the children apply what they know at a higher level of thinking as related to each subobjective. For example:

1. The children will be able to write creative stories about a northeastern African family which is successful in improving production on their small farm.

2. The children will be able to work in small groups to isolate a problem characteristic of a northwestern African businessman trying to improve mineral production and to suggest a solution for it.
3. The children will be able to work in small groups to develop recommendations to the peoples of equatorial and southern Africa on what they should do to develop their unused resources.

And again we must deal with the question, if one objective is necessary as well as good, would not more be better? And again we must point out, more is not necessarily better. Two or three supporting objectives per subgeneralization is about all that children can be expected to tolerate.

Usually supporting objectives are not desirable for the concluding objective of the unit which deals with a skill. Some skills are amenable to organization into supporting objectives for the organization of learning. For example, when teaching children report writing, we might use the following as supporting objectives:

The Children Will Be Able to:

1. Describe in writing what an acceptable report is and the function of each of its parts.
2. Compose acceptable introductory report paragraphs.
3. Compose acceptable middle paragraphs in reports.
4. Compose acceptable ending paragraphs to reports.

If we did this, we would try to calibrate these supporting objectives with those designed for content. In the end, we would lose track of what we are trying to teach.

The teaching of a skill may be introduced at any point in a unit. Because so much depends on repeated activities and extending skills gradually, we shall be content to see that the necessary repetitious extensions are made within the unit.

Figure 10–2 presents a diagram of the concluding and supporting objectives and some of the options we have as we construct a unit.

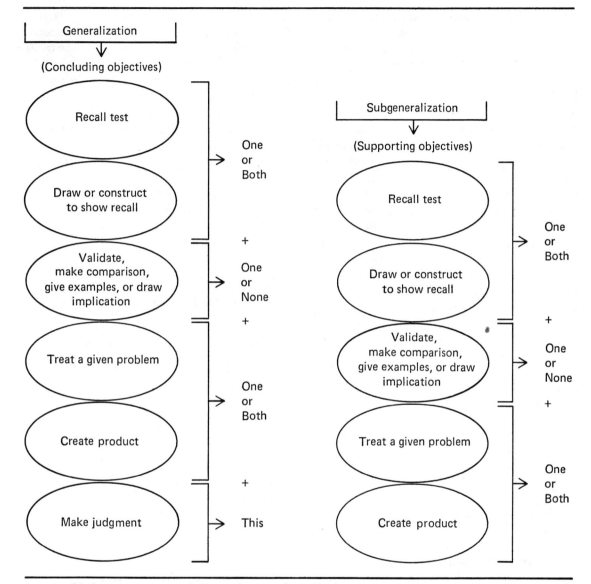

FIGURE 10–2. *Options for Concluding and Supporting Objectives.*

Generalizations and Patterns of Subgeneralizations

We discovered in the previous section that generalizations and related subgeneralizations are useful in determining the content objectives in social studies. If we use appropriate instructional strategies, children will be able to arrive at the generalizations and subgeneralizations as conclusions stated in their own terms. It behooves us to take care in analyzing generalizations for possible subgeneralizations.

How well we make this analysis rests on what we have internalized from social studies in high school and the social-science courses we have taken at the university level and our skill in thinking analytically. Our biggest problem is recall of facts and ideas. For this reason, we develop one of the skills of a successful attorney—the skill of becoming an instant expert on any topic with which we must deal. Before you try to construct a unit, become informed about its subject matter. Review any textbooks you have kept or that you can obtain at a library. Perusing them will help you recall what you once experienced and provide ideas for organizing content.

In this section we shall look at a few examples of generalizations and subgeneralizations as a way of helping you develop the analytical skill necessary to organizing content for social-studies instruction. You will discover that generalizations differ in structure and that the structure gives clues as to what the subgeneralizations might be.

Generalizations are statements which convey something about a concept. Some are definitions. Here is an example:

A geographical region is an area in which certain characteristics exist.

In this generalization, the concept is *region* and *an area in which certain characteristics exist* is its definition. As we scrutinize *certain characteristics,* we can see that the subgeneralizations will have to be related to them in some way.

Now let us consider our learners. In this case they are children in fifth grade. What characteristics will they be able to understand and able to investigate with the instructional materials at hand? *Climate* appears to offer some possibilities. The subgeneralizations will be about *climatic regions.* Here they are:

1. Tropical regions are frost-free throughout the year and have varied rainfall.
2. Polar regions have continued cold temperature and receive little rainfall.

We could add other subgeneralizations about dry, warm temperate and cold temperate climates. If we do, the children will be able to generalize

with greater confidence. However with only two, they may still be expected to generalize accurately.

Let us think for a moment again about the generalization. We might have chosen to focus the children's attention on other characteristics such as landforms, vegetation, land-use patterns, and animal resources. If we had chosen any of these, the subgeneralizations would have been about the one we had chosen.

Now let us suppose that we are planning a unit for kindergarten. We can treat the concept of *region* as an area where kindergarteners do certain things. The generalization does not change, but the subgeneralizations stated in kindergarten language are:

1. At home we eat, sleep, play, and live with our parents.
2. At school we learn and play with other boys and girls.

For kindergarten children, the characteristics of an area include what they do and with whom they do it.

Using a generalization related to our original, we could guide first, second, or third graders toward a concept of region:

Generalization

1. A community is an area in which people live, work and play.

Subgeneralizations

1. In our community there are many houses and streets.
2. In our community there are places where people can go to have fun.
3. The people who live in the community also work in its factories, stores, and shops.

In this case the definitive generalization indicated the subgeneralizations to use. They would have to be about *live, work,* and *play.*

As we review the three examples developed from a definitive generalization, we can surface a guiding principle to use when developing subgeneralizations from such a generalization:

Each subgeneralization after a definitive generalization deals with some part or aspect of the concept it defines.

This same principle is followed whenever we are planning from descriptive generalizations. Here are a few examples of such generalizations:

- Oceans are rich in natural resources.
- Policemen are responsible for the safety of the members of the community.
- Many African peoples are tribal in their point of view.

The subgeneralizations for the first generalization should be about different natural resources. For the second, they would be about the different ways the policemen are responsible. For the third, they would be about different tribes and how their members felt about them.

Now let us consider another kind of generalization. Here are a few examples:

- Factors of climate influence the ways that people live.
- The greater the efficiency of factors of production, the less the cost of goods and services.
- The ways that a person considers self and others are determined in part by the culture in which the person is born.
- The greatest responsibility of democratic government is to protect the rights of the individual.

These generalizations reflect a cause-and-effect relationship. The first subgeneralization for each of these is usually a definition of the concept which learners know less or least about in the statement:

- The factors of climate include temperature, rainfall, and growing seasons.
- The factors of production are natural resources, technology, labor, and management.
- A culture consists of the skills, behaviors, beliefs, and attitudes that a people has found to be workable.
- A democratic government is one in which the people delegate responsibility for government to elected officials.

The rest of the subgeneralizations are about the relationship between the defined concept and that which is better or best known by the learners. These are listed after the first subgeneralization:

1. Factors of climate
   a. Factors of climate determine in part the kinds of shelter people build and the kinds of clothing they wear.
   b. Factors of climate determine in part the kinds of crops that are grown and what people eat.
   c. Factors of climate determine in part what people do for fun.
2. Factors of production
   a. Efficient use of natural resources requires the use of only what is needed and providing for restoration wherever possible.
   b. An efficient technology improves to meet increasing demands and requires careful maintenance.
   c. Labor is efficient to the extent that it is trained and satisfied as to the meaning of its work.
   d. Efficient management coordinates the operation of the other factors without waste or conflict.
   e. If all the factors work well, the cost of an item tends to decrease.
3. Culture
   a. A culture offers choices of roles to a person.
   b. A culture indicates to a person what is right and what is wrong.
   c. A culture indicates to a person what is expected from everyone.
4. Democratic government
   a. To ensure individual rights, a democratic government encourages all qualified voters to participate in elections.
   b. To ensure individual rights, a democratic government makes and enforces laws to prevent people from being exploited by others.
   c. To ensure individual rights, a democratic government maintains a system of courts in which conflicts between individuals and between an individual and the government itself are resolved.
   d. To ensure individual rights, a democratic government invites citizens to hearings where they express what they think about proposed laws.

When planning units for generalizations expressing a cause-and-effect relationship, we use this guiding principle:

The first subgeneralization defines the less or least known concept in the generalization, and the rest of the subgeneralizations relate the defined concept to the better or best known concept in the generalization.

As you can see, there is no specified number of subgeneralizations to be included in a unit. The general criterion is that there be enough to ensure that the children can be expected to arrive at the generalization logically after acquiring the essential facts and supporting ideas.

OBJECTIVES AS MEANS

In a way, objectives as means seem to be contradictory to objectives as ends. They are not. Objectives as ends indicate what children will be able to do after completing a series of learning activities. Objectives as means are the learning activities which enable learning. Each one successfully completed brings learners a step closer to an objective as an end. Here is an example of an objective as a means:

LEARNING ACTIVITY

The children will observe and listen to a flannelboard story about the people who work in the supermarket, and

RESULT

will be able to identify each flannelgram as a person who works in the supermarket and tell what he or she does.

As you can see, the objective as a means describes the learning activity and what it is to accomplish as far as learning is concerned. From this point on, we shall refer to such an objective as a "means objective."

Some curriculum developers prefer to refer to means objectives as "enabling objectives" or "enablers" because they enable children to learn through commitment to an activity. This places the planning emphasis on the selection of learning activities and belief in the efficacy of activity in learning. For this reason, when they compose enabling objectives or enablers, they simply describe the learning activities without any indication of expected results.

Other curriculum developers believe so strongly in the efficacy of activity as an enabler of learning that they see little need for the use of such labels as means objectives, enabling objectives, or enablers. They are content to refer to such things simply as learning activities and, when they describe them, they omit any mention of expected results.

At this point you may wish to follow the practice of either of these groups of curriculum developers as you plan. It is certainly much easier and less time-consuming to specify learning activities under whatever label you wish and to omit specifying expected results. However, before you make a definite decision, consider the advantages accruing to you and your learners from composing means objectives (or whatever you prefer to label them) in which both the activity and its result are specified:

1. The practice saves time. You will not include learning activities, no matter how attractive they may be, for which you cannot specify a result. Your learners will be committed only to those activities which extend a necessary knowledge or skill or ensure the discovery of a pertinent value.
2. The practice improves the management of learning. When you observe an activity not moving toward the necessary result, you may terminate it or make immediate changes to ensure the desired result. This requires discipline and good judgment on your part to avoid doing what may force a result rather than letting it develop logically.
3. The practice may prevent frustration and boredom. Having the result of the activity clearly in mind, you terminate it as soon as the result is achieved. If you terminate before this, the children may not have the necessary background for the next activity, and thus be frustrated. If you allow the activity to continue after its result is achieved, the children will become bored.
4. The practice aids planning. The result of an activity is often the preparation for the next activity. Frequently, when a series of activities is being planned and the result of each activity is known, a logical sequence is ensured.

The choice of what you do is yours. Regardless of what that choice may be, we shall continue the discussion using the means objective as a basic, two-part element in planning social-studies units.

Means objectives may have any one of three purposes, depending on where they occur in the unit. Some, which we shall call "preparation objectives," have the purpose of preparing children for new learning. Preparation involves having the children recall whatever background they have about the central topic and generate interest in further study.

Another kind of means objective has the purpose of involving children in new learning. These we shall call "developmental objectives." The first example of a means objective about the workers in the supermarket is a developmental objective. Usually there will be more of these than any other kind in a social-studies unit.

The third kind of means objective has the purpose of bringing children to closure on ends objectives. We shall call them "closure objectives."

As we construct a unit, we may regard the concluding objectives and supporting objectives as the sturdy skeleton of the unit. We flesh out this skeleton with means objectives.

Means Objectives in the Unit Opener

Usually all the means objectives in openers are preparation objectives. When you begin to plan them, you must decide on the inquiry strategy you intend to follow as you guide children in meeting the content objectives of the unit. The kinds of preparation objectives you plan depend on this decision.

To illustrate how to develop means objectives for the unit opener (and other parts of the unit as well), we shall be using a unit on Japanese culture as a flexible working example amenable to different grade levels and teaching strategies. The generalizations and subgeneralizations are inferrable from the concluding and supporting objectives.

Here are the concluding and supporting objectives for content learning that we shall be using for a unit to be used in first grade:

Concluding Objectives—The Children Will Be Able to:

1. Circle with at least 75 percent accuracy the items on an individually completed picture test about what the Japanese people use in different life situations.
2. Participate in making an accurate wall picture of Japanese life by deciding on the items needed, drawing, and coloring them, and directing where they should be pasted.
3. Dramatize creatively events common to the life of a Japanese family.
4. Participate in expressing with puppets what they might do to make a Japanese child visitor more comfortable in their homes.

Supporting Objectives—The Children Will Be Able to:

- (for subgeneralization No. 1)
  1. Identify accurately items of traditional Japanese dress by coloring them as specified in oral directions during an individual test.
  2. Make individually potato-print designs on a cut-out representing a traditional Japanese garment.
- (for subgeneralization No. 2)
  1. Participate in dramatizing accurately the eating of a meal as a member of a Japanese family.
  2. Draw accurate, individual pictures of foods eaten and utensils used at a Japanese meal.
- (for subgeneralization No. 3)
  1. Participate in using puppets to describe activity in the living room and going to bed in the Japanese home.
  2. Participate in making a miniature representation of a Japanese bedroom or living room from small blocks of styrofoam and pieces of quilted fabric.

Using the above as a base, let us see what preparation objectives we might plan. If we are going to use a curiosity-stimulated inquiry, this is what the preparation objectives might look like:

1. Discussing some of the things they use every day in their homes, the children can have clearly in mind what is meant by things used in the home.

2. Guessing what is in a large package supposedly sent to them from some boys and girls in a faraway land to use in their homes, they can anticipate what is in the package.
3. Examining a pair of chopsticks, a rice bowl, and a kimono, they can discuss the possible uses of the items.
4. Viewing a picture of some Japanese boys and girls who might have sent the box, they can discuss whether the children in the picture live differently and anticipate learning more about them.

The first preparation objective has the children surfacing a simple background. The rest stimulate curiosity. As you read the objectives, you can see how one objective leads into another. To get an idea of how vital this relationship is, cover an objective or two with a strip of paper and note what happens in the progression of learning.

Let us see what might happen if we plan to use a concept-centered inquiry strategy:

1. Identifying the items used in the house as depicted on a chart pasted with advertisement pictures of common items not all of which are useful in the house, the children can have clearly in mind what is meant by things used in the house.
2. Looking for items used in the house as depicted in discarded magazines, they can find pictures of items, cut them out, and paste them on separate sheets of thick paper.
3. Arranging pictures of the items in related groups, they can decide on labels for the groups.
4. Analyzing the labeled groups, they can generalize about the needs for certain items in the home.
5. Viewing a picture of some Japanese boys and girls on their way to school, they can note how the children are the same and different from themselves.
6. Being alerted to future study about the boys and girls to see whether they have the same things to use in their homes, they can anticipate future study.

In these preparation objectives we again see the close relationship from one objective to another and how the solid conceptual base is formed for future study. The last objective prepares them for further learning.

Now let us suppose that we are going to use a strategy related to postknowledge inquiry. The teacher's purpose is basically to focus the children's attention on the new area of study. Here are the preparation objectives:

1. Using puppets to dramatize how they greet each other in the morning on the way to school, the children can have in mind how they interact when they meet their friends in the morning.
2. Examining two Japanese dolls in traditional dress, they can discuss what they find interesting in the dolls' dress and appearance generally.
3. Observing how the Japanese people greet as demonstrated by the teacher, they can discover an interesting difference.
4. Being alerted to the study of the people whom the dolls represent, they can anticipate future study.

Again we find the first preparation objective designed to facilitate children's recall of background. The rest focus attention to the extent of generating some interest. The interest is vague, but it is there.

Now let us see what kinds of unit openers we might devise for older children. First the concluding objectives for content:

Concluding Objectives—The Children Will Be Able to:

1. Take an individually completed 30-item short-answer test with 75 percent accuracy on facts and generalizations about Japanese culture.
2. Work in small groups to prepare accurate comparison charts about Japanese and American daily life.
3. Write creative stories independently about Japanese daily life.
4. Role play situations in which Japanese and American children try to teach their ways to each other.

And we shall also consider this concluding objective for a skill:

5. Take notes while reading and use them to review studied content to participate in class dis-

cussions and small-group work and to prepare for the unit test.

And here are the supporting objectives:

The Children Will Be Able to:

- (for subgeneralization No. 1)
  1. Take independently a 15-item, short answer test with 80 percent accuracy on a generalization and facts about Japanese dress, foods, and homes.
  2. Work in small groups to make accurate dioramas showing Japanese home life.
  3. Write a paragraph independently telling what features of Japanese home life Americans might think about using to make their homes more comfortable.
- (for subgeneralization No. 2)
  1. Take independently a 15-item, short-answer test with 80 percent accuracy on a generalization and facts about human relationships among the Japanese.
  2. Present as the result of small-group work creative dramatizations about Japanese people interacting with each other.
- (for subgeneralization No. 3)
  1. Take independently a 15-minute item, short-answer test with 80 percent accuracy on a generalization and facts about education in Japan.
  2. Work in small groups to make an organization chart showing the levels of education in Japan.
  3. Write independently a diary entry for a Japanese child preparing for examinations to qualify for entrance into a junior high school.
- (for subgeneralization No. 4)
  1. Take independently a 15-item, short-answer test with 80 percent accuracy on a generalization and facts about religions in Japan.
  2. Explain and share takanomas constructed during small-group work.
- (for subgeneralization No. 5)
  1. Take independently a 15-item, short-answer test with 80 percent accuracy on a generalization and facts about the Japanese language.
  2. Make their own nameplate using the Japanese syllabary.
  3. Write a paragraph independently in which they express opinions and give reasons about the Japanese people continuing their traditional forms of writing vs. adopting the Roman alphabet for writing.
- (for the unit skill objective)

1. Describe the format of a written note.
2. Describe the purposes for taking written notes.
3. Prepare suitable note cards.
4. Skim to find information.
5. Take short-answer notes for specific purposes.
6. Write the location of information on the note card.
7. Use note cards during class discussions.
8. Use note cards to review for tests.
- (for subgeneralization No. 6)
  1. Take independently a 15-item, short-answer test based on a generalization and facts about sports and recreation in Japan.
  2. Work in small groups to design an imaginary sports page for a Japanese newspaper.

We shall consider this unit as being prepared for a sixth grade.

Here are the preparation objectives that we might use if we were following the strategy based on interest-stimulated inquiry:

1. Locating Japan on a world map and a globe, determining the direction to it from where they live, and determining the distance in miles, hours of air travel, and days of ship travel, the children can describe the location of Japan in a variety of precise ways.
2. Circulating through, observing, and conversing quietly about an arranged environment displaying aspects of Japanese culture, they can discuss interests discovered in the arranged environment.
3. Formulating questions to use in following discovered interests, they can organize questions into groups.
4. Deciding which questions to answer first, they can anticipate following interests.

In this beginning sequence of preparation objectives the first objective has the children acquiring background through concentrated map study. The rest are devoted to surfacing and organizing interest to be followed.

Now let us see what preparation objectives are planned by a teacher who decides to use a strategy based on scientific inquiry.

1. Locating Japan on a world map and a globe, determining the direction to it from where they live, and determining the distance in miles, hours of air travel, and days of ship travel, the

children can describe the location of Japan in a variety of precise ways.

2. Discussing generally what they know about how the Japanese live (as learned from television, magazines, and newspapers), they can pool what they know into a general level of knowledge about life in Japan.

3. Analyzing in small groups a list of contrasting statements about Japanese life, they can discuss differences difficult to understand or explain.

4. Offering possible explanations for the differences, they can listen to and discuss a number of possible explanations.

5. Deciding which explanation(s) appears to be the most reasonable, they can have a hypothesis(es) to use for further investigation.

6. Developing in small groups a list of questions to use when investigating the hypothesis(es), they can discuss lists of questions to decide on a class list.

The first two preparation objectives in this unit opener are devoted to establishing children's knowledge background. The rest are devoted to discovering an inquiry problem, hypothesizing, selecting a hypothesis, and developing a design for inquiry into the hypothesis.

And, finally, let us glance at a unit opener planned by a teacher using a problem-stimulated inquiry.

1. Entering their classroom to discover it has been converted into an elementary classroom in Japan, the children can listen to the teacher identify himself or herself with an assumed Japanese name and chide them for not knowing their manners in the classroom.

2. Listening to an explanation that for the next month they are to be treated as children who have come to Japan to live with the people and learn their ways, they can discuss those areas of living in which they think they will have few if any problems.

3. Discussing the areas of living in which they think they will have the most difficulty, they can decide on which problems will be most urgent and rank them in order of urgency.

4. Suggesting some solutions, they can decide on the kinds of information needed to decide on workability of solutions.

Because of the nature of the topic of study, the teacher has had to contrive a problem situation.

To ensure the desired impact of the situation, the teacher has presented it in a direct and unexpected way, as shown in the first preparation objective. In the second and third objectives the children explore their own background in light of the problem situation. The fourth objective has them preparing to check out their solutions.

These examples of unit openers demonstrate how teaching strategies influence planning the beginning of a unit. Each contributes a desirable strength.

As we have seen, preparation objectives have the function of ensuring that learners have an opportunity to survey whatever knowledge they have about the topic at hand and to generate interest in its study. In the next sections we shall see another use for them.

Means Objectives in the Developmental Section of the Unit

Earlier we had pointed out that the developmental section of a unit is often divided into a series of miniunits, each with its own opener, developmental section, and closer. Each miniunit has its own concluding objectives (*supporting* the concluding objectives of the unit), developed from a subgeneralization related to the main generalization.

When planning miniunits, a teacher will stay as close as possible to the strategy used in the unit opener. Evidence of this is usually seen in the preparation objectives planned for the miniunit opener and sometimes in the closer. The developmental section of miniunits tend to remain the same from strategy to strategy. In short, children may use the same investigative activities to acquire information, but the kinds of purposes they will try to accomplish will differ in accord with the instructional strategy. For this reason, we shall consider first the investigative activities (or developmental objectives) in a unit for young children and in one for older children.

Here are the supporting objectives used for the first miniunit in the primary unit:

The Children Will Be Able to:

1. Identify accurately items of traditional Japanese dress by coloring them as specified in oral directions during an individual test.
2. Make individually potato-print designs on a cutout representing a traditional Japanese garment.

And here are the developmental objectives that we might plan for our learners in first grade:

1. Viewing pictures of Japanese children in modern and traditional garb, the children can tell which clothing is like their own and which is different.
2. Cutting out a paper doll of a little Japanese boy and girl and their two costumes and coloring them, they can show the dolls dressed in two different costumes and point out the differences.
3. Viewing and listening to a flannel-board story about a little Japanese girl getting dressed for Children's Day in Japan, they can talk about the distinguishing aspects of the garments and name them as the teacher replaces them on the flannel board.
4. Retelling the story using the flannelgrams, they can accurately recall the items of dress and identify them by name.
5. Listening to a story about three Japanese children getting ready for "seven, five, three" day and studying the illustrations, they can recall any garments they have studied before, talk about the distinguishing aspects of the newly introduced garments, and select illustrations of garments they find most interesting.
6. Pantomiming Japanese children walking in their special clothes on the way to the shrine, they can express how Japanese children feel in special clothing.
7. Viewing pictures of American and Japanese farm workers, they can talk about differences in dress between American and Japanese farm workers.
8. Painting a picture of an American and a Japanese farm worker, they can show a picture and tell about the differences.
9. Participating in composing an experience story about the different clothes Japanese children wear, they can recall facts and generalization, recognize words, and read words and sentences about what they have studied.

As we review these developmental objectives, we can detect an alternating pattern between intake and integrative activities. The children first experience new information and then work with the information in some way. The last activity has them using all their information to compose an experience story as a class endeavor, or if the teacher has enough time or assistance, as an individual task. This signals the end of the developmental activities for the miniunit. The rest of the activities will be expressed as closer objectives.

Let us consider now how these miniunits would be begun using a preparation objective or two in accord with a particular teaching strategy. If the teacher was following the strategy of curiosity-stimulated inquiry, the opening part of the miniunit might look like this:

1. Looking at the chopsticks, rice bowl, and kimono again, the children can talk about what they had discussed during the opener—whether Japanese children live differently.
2. Shaking some boxes containing items of Japanese dress and guessing what the contents might be, they can discover a pair of *tabi,* a pair of *geta,* and a pair of *zori,* and guess how they might be worn.
3. Being informed that they will learn what the Japanese people call these items of dress as well as some others, they can anticipate learning more about Japanese dress.

Here we see preparation objectives developed to stimulate curiosity at the beginning of the miniunit. What occurred during the opening part of the unit is tied into the beginning of the miniunit. This will occur with each miniunit.

Here is another set of preparation objectives developed to open a miniunit. As you read them, try to decide whether they are more suitable for the concept-centered inquiry or for the postknowledge-centered inquiry, or are equally suitable for each.

1. Talking about the items introduced during the unit opener, the children can recall being alerted to further study about the Japanese people.
2. Talking about the items they keep in their clothes closet, they can anticipate whether Japanese boys and girls have the same items in their clothes closets.

These preparation objectives will serve the purposes of either strategy. The children who were started with a concept-centered strategy enter the miniunit with a clearer understanding of what they are going to learn more about than the children who were started with a postknowledge inquiry.

We shall proceed with presenting the structure of the miniunit for older children in the same way we did when dealing with the organization of the miniunit for young children—first the developmental objectives and then the others. As we plan, we shall have to keep in mind the concluding objectives for this miniunit (but remember that they are included among the *supporting* objectives for the unit as a whole) and those which support learning to take notes. They are presented once again below for immediate reference for one subgeneralization only:

For Subgeneralization No. 1 the Children Will Be Able to:

1. Take independently a 15-item, short-answer test with 80 percent accuracy on a generalization and facts about Japanese dress, foods, and homes.
2. Work in small groups to make accurate dioramas showing Japanese home life.
3. Write independently a paragraph telling what features of Japanese life Americans might think about using to make their homes more comfortable.

For the Unit Skill Objective the Children Will Be Able to:

1. Describe the format of a written note.
2. Describe the purposes for taking written notes.
3. Prepare suitable note cards.
4. Take short-answer notes for specific purposes.
5. Write the location of the information on the note card.
6. Use note cards during class discussions.
7. Use note cards to review for tests.

As you remember, two of the unit openers (the interest-stimulated and the scientific inquiry) ended by offering the children some choices about the information they would seek first. There is at least a likelihood that the children in the problem-stimulated inquiry might be given the same opportunity. This means that what we have specified

for subgeneralization No. 1 might be covered later in the unit.

With a skill such as note taking, it is usually a good idea to start instruction in the first content miniunit introduced. You will see this included with the developmental objectives for content learning.

1. Viewing a large representation of a note card, the children can identify its parts.
2. After discussing how note cards might be useful during class and group discussions, they can anticipate learning to take notes as they read.
3. After making a note card by writing a question on it, turning to a specified page, and reading it until the desired information is found, they can write a note to answer it.
4. After reading the note to the class and listening to the notes recorded by others, they can make an accurate judgment as to the accuracy and appropriateness of the note.
5. After analyzing the questions about clothing previously developed by the class, they can decide whether more questions need to be composed, and if so, compose them.
6. Making note cards for each of the questions to be answered, they can read and take notes on pages 77–81, *Modern Japan.*
7. Sharing notes, they can decide on correct answers, validating with rereading wherever necessary.
8. After summarizing their findings as a class, they can generalize about clothing worn by the Japanese people today.
9. By evaluating their use of note taking, they can validate the use of notes as study aids.
10. After observing a classmate volunteer to draw a diagram of a note card on the chalkboard and explain it, they can recheck their own ideas about the correct form of a note and its purposes.
11. After analyzing the questions about foods previously developed by the class, they can consider whether more questions need to be composed, and if so, to compose them.
12. Making note cards for each of the questions to be answered, they can read and take notes on pages 70–75, *Modern Japan.*
13. Sharing notes, they can decide on correct answers, validating with rereading whenever necessary.
14. Using their notes in small groups to compose summaries of their findings, they can listen to

group-made summaries and decide whether they are accurate.

15. Discussing the utility of notes to make class summaries, they can recheck their ideas about the usefulness of note taking as a study aid.

16. Analyzing as an individual task the questions about homes previously developed by the class, they can consider whether more questions need to be composed, and if so, to compose them.

17. Sharing ideas about the questions individually with the teacher, they can see how well they are doing with developing questions.

18. Using their questions to make note cards, they can use the table of contents in *Modern Japan* to find the chapter, read it, and take notes.

19. Sharing notes in small groups, they can check notes against those of others and participate in preparing a group summary.

20. Listening to group-made summaries, they can participate in evaluating summaries for organization and accuracy.

21. Observing and listening to a presentation given by a resource person who has lived in Japan and who shows photographic slides taken of the people in various parts of Japan, their homes, and their restaurants, they can check their findings against the information presented by the resource person.

As you can see in the above, content and skill learning are closely intertwined throughout the developmental section of the miniunit. After the opening of the unit, which we shall discuss shortly, preparation objectives are designed to introduce note taking. These are followed by developmental objectives to acquaint children with how to take a note and a trial which is evaluated. Then the note-taking skill is applied and evaluated repeatedly through the remainder of the developmental section of the miniunit.

The remainder of the miniunits would show a continued use and evaluation of note taking until the children begin to prepare for note taking and take notes automatically. At some time later in the unit they will be using the index to determine where to start reading and will learn the fundamentals of skimming to find specific information.

As you review this list of means objectives you may think that it is too detailed, but you can see the advantages to learning that accrue for children. The opportunities for learning both skills and con-

tent are rich. Varied repetition of skill-learning activities offers an opportunity for maintained interest in content and growth in skill.

Regardless of strategy, any sixth-grade teacher would find this miniunit teachable. Let's look now to how sixth-grade teachers might use different strategies to begin this miniunit. This is what a teacher following the strategy of interest-stimulated inquiry might prepare:

1. Looking again at those parts of the arranged environment which first prompted their interest in Japanese clothing, foods, and homes, the children can recall the aspects that originally stimulated their interest in these aspects of Japanese life.

2. Discussing those aspects which they are particularly interested in learning about, they can anticipate learning something about which they really want to know and make a note of it to review at the end of the miniunit.

The exploration for interests has a rich payoff to contribute to the beginning of each miniunit. However, provisions for ways of anticipating what will be learned will have to be varied from miniunit to miniunit.

Now let us see what the teacher who is following the scientific-inquiry strategy plans for the opener of this miniunit:

1. Analyzing their hypothesis(es) and questions resulting from the unit opener to determine which might pertain most directly to clothing, dress, and homes, the children can compose more questions directed toward specific information.

2. Considering whether the contrast would be most marked in clothing, food, or homes, they can hypothesize where the greatest contrast might occur or that the contrast would be about the same in all areas of scrutiny.

3. Reading a page of the text to see what explanatory clues they might look for, they can surface ideas about special explanatory clues that might appear in the text, such as "long ago . . . today," "then . . . but now," and "because . . . a lot . . . a little."

Here again we see a preparation objective referring back to the unit opener. In keeping with his commitment toward scientific inquiry as a way to learn, the teacher again has the children hypothesize about an aspect of the information they are going to be seeking. He will try to arrange this at the beginning of every miniunit.

Finally, let us glance at the opener for the miniunit that might be devised by a teacher following the strategy of problem-stimulated inquiry:

1. Discussing the problem related to living in a Japanese home—learning to like different foods, wear different garments, and become used to different kinds of furnishings—the children can have a purpose for exploring the three aspects of Japanese home life.
2. Considering what specific information they will need, they can formulate questions to be answered during their investigation.

Again the pattern emerges: a preparation objective related to the unit opener, and another which clarifies a purpose.

So far we have seen how strategies for teaching social studies give direction to the openers of miniunits. We have also seen that developmental objectives will not vary much from strategy to strategy. Now let us see what influence the strategy has on the closer of the miniunits.

You know that the concluding (supporting for the unit) objectives for the miniunit are the same for all strategies. Differences will occur usually in the kinds of integrative activities that lead toward meeting the concluding objectives for the miniunit or perhaps the addition of another concluding objective.

We return to the units designed for young children. Actually the concluding objectives for the miniunit are a part of the closer. Here is how the miniunit constructed to follow the curiosity-stimulated inquiry ends:

1. Placing flannelgrams of garments beside or near flannelgrams of the faces of a Japanese man, woman, boy, or girl and discussing them briefly, the children can review what they have learned about clothing.
2. Identifying items of traditional dress by coloring them on a practice sheet as specified in oral directions, they can demonstrate how well they have retained what they have studied about Japanese clothing.
3. Observing the teacher making a potato-print design on a large, cut-out paper garment, they can make their own design on a paper cut-out.
4. Deciding which of the activities or products during the unit they liked best, they can repeat the preferred activity to enjoy the reward of curiosity.

You can easily identify the concluding objectives, and you can understand why the teacher must demonstrate potato printing. The first closer objective prepares the children for the test. The last offers the children an opportunity to express which aspect of their curiosity was most richly rewarding.

The ending for the miniunit designed to follow the concept-centered inquiry strategy takes this form (using the same two middle closer objectives used in the curiosity-stimulated inquiry):

1. Focusing their attention on the labeled group of clothing which surfaced during the unit opener, the children can tell which ones the Japanese people wear also and which others besides these they have to wear.
2. Listening to two puppets, one a Japanese child and the other an American child, tell about their clothing, they can decide on how Japanese and American clothing habits differ.

Here we see the strong influence of the strategy in the closer of the miniunit. The children end with an understanding of the diversity of clothing that can exist between two cultures.

And finally, the end of the miniunit designed to follow the postknowledge-inquiry strategy, using the same first three closer objectives used in the curiosity-stimulated inquiry closer.

1. Listening to two puppets, a Japanese child and an American child of their age, talking about the clothing they wear and ending with a mild argument about whose way is better, the children can suggest ways that the two puppets can settle their argument.

Again the strategy influences the way the miniunit closes. The final closer objective involves the children in an open inquiry which has them combining what they have learned with what they know about themselves to resolve an issue.

As you might well expect, we shall find that same influence to prevail in the closing sections of the miniunits for older children, as well as in the closing sections for the entire units designed to follow each of the strategies. For this reason, the closing sections for the miniunits will be given below without specific comments made about any of them.

MINIUNIT CLOSER FOR AN UPPER GRADE, INTEREST-STIMULATED INQUIRY STRATEGY

- Reviewing their notes in small groups to compose questions to be used in a quiz game, the children can recall facts and generalizations as they prepare for and play the game.
- Taking the 15-item test on the facts and generalization about Japanese dress, foods, and homes, they can achieve at least 80 percent accuracy or receive corrective assistance to meet the criterion of accuracy.
- Working in small groups to make accurate dioramas showing Japanese home life, they can share and discuss their products with the entire class.
- Writing a paragraph telling what features of Japanese home life Americans might think about adopting to make their homes more comfortable, they can express what they think about positive aspects of Japanese home life.
- Reviewing the note made earlier about what they anticipated would be the most interesting aspect, they can express whether their anticipation was accurate or whether they discovered something else, and what they think they might do to continue the interest.

MINIUNIT CLOSER FOR AN UPPER GRADE, SCIENTIFIC-INQUIRY STRATEGY

- Reviewing their notes in small groups to decide whether Japanese food, dress, or homes present greater contrast than the others, the children can generalize about contrasts in Japanese home life. (The rest of the closer objectives, except the last, are the same as those listed for the interest-

stimulated inquiry strategy above after the first closer objective.)

MINIUNIT CLOSER FOR AN UPPER GRADE, PROBLEM-STIMULATED INQUIRY

- Reviewing their notes in small groups to decide where they would have the greatest difficulty in becoming accustomed to Japanese clothing habits, eating preferences, and homes, the children can arrive at consensus at what would be the greatest problem.
- Deciding in small groups what might be done to solve the problem, they can share solutions and, if conditions are feasible, select one to test (arranging a Japanese food-tasting party, kneeling on cushions to do tasks, etc.)

(The rest of the closer objectives, except the last, are the same as those listed for the interest-stimulated inquiry strategy above after the first closer objective.)

Means Objectives in the Unit Closer

After the explanation and examples of closure means objectives for closing miniunits in the developmental section of a unit, little remains to be discussed about their use in the closer section of the unit. However, as you read the examples of unit closers below, bear in mind that the means objectives will closely reflect the unit objectives and the strategy used in the unit opener.

UNIT CLOSER FOR A LOWER GRADE, CURIOSITY-STIMULATED INQUIRY

- Reviewing the different kinds of things they have made throughout the unit, the children can recall facts and generalizations to be prepared for the test.
- Circling the items on a picture test about what the Japanese people use in different life situations, they can achieve 75 percent accuracy or receive corrective assistance to meet the criterion.
- Viewing the background prepared for a wall picture and discussing what they might make to

paste on it to show how the Japanese live, they can decide which items they want to make.

- Making the items, they can decide where they should be placed and have them pasted on the background.
- Inviting another class to come in to see their wall picture, they can explain it to others.
- Discussing life situations in the Japanese family such as eating, getting ready to go to school in the morning, getting ready for Children's Day, etc., they can dramatize the incidents creatively.
- Viewing four puppets, a Japanese boy and girl and an American boy and girl, and listening to problem situations, they can take turns using the puppets to show what American boys and girls could do to make Japanese boys and girls more comfortable if they came to visit.
- Making their own curiosity bag in which to put something they have made to take home to use as a curiosity activity with members of their family, they can share the fun of curiosity and tell something that they know.

UNIT CLOSER FOR A LOWER GRADE, CONCEPT-CENTERED INQUIRY

- Reviewing the different kinds of things they have made throughout the unit, the children can identify them in relation to the items they had grouped and labeled at the beginning of the unit.

(The rest of the closer objectives, except the last, are the same as those listed for curiosity-stimulated inquiry strategy for a lower grade as given above after the first closer objective.)

- Viewing a picture of some Eskimos, they can discuss some differences they would expect to see in the home life of these people if they ever were to visit them.

UNIT CLOSER FOR A LOWER GRADE, POSTKNOWLEDGE INQUIRY

(The closer objectives for this unit are the same as those listed for the curiosity-stimulated inquiry unit for a lower grade as given above, except the last closer objective is omitted.)

- Talking about whether Japanese people might have a hard or easy time living in their community, the children can arrive at a variety of hypotheses.
- Listening to a Japanese resource person tell about his or her life in the community, they can decide which of their hypotheses is true for this person.

UNIT CLOSER FOR AN UPPER GRADE, INTEREST-STIMULATED INQUIRY

- Reviewing their notes and questions in small groups, the children can recall facts and ideas learned during the unit.
- Using their notes and questions to quiz each other in pairs, they can be prepared to take the test.
- Taking a 30-item, short-answer test on the generalizations and facts studied about Japanese culture, they can achieve 75 percent accuracy or receive corrective assistance to achieve the criterion.
- Using their notes in small groups to prepare comparison charts about Japanese and American family life, they can generalize about diversity among cultures.
- Discussing the utility of note taking as a study aid, they can generalize about the utility of notes.
- Reviewing their notes with the teacher, they can see how much they have learned about note taking.
- Discussing what they think would be the most common problems for Japanese families living together, they can write creative stories about self-chosen problems in the Japanese family.
- Reading their stories on a volunteer basis to the class, they can share their ideas with others.
- Listening to situations in which Japanese boys and girls would try to teach each other their ways, they can role play or observe role playing and react to alternatives.
- Writing a paragraph about what they think the most interesting part of the unit was, what they are thinking about doing about it, and whether they would like some assistance from the teacher, they can follow any discovered interest.

UNIT CLOSER FOR AN UPPER GRADE, SCIENTIFIC INQUIRY

- Reviewing their notes and questions in small groups, the children can summarize the facts and ideas learned during the unit.
- Listening to group-made summaries, they can decide on a summary that expresses what was discovered.
- Judging the hypothesis(es) made at the beginning of the unit against the summary, they can decide on the tenability of their hypothesis(es).

(The closer objectives, except the last, after the first closer objective in the unit closer for interest-stimulated inquiry above, are also used in this unit.)

UNIT CLOSER FOR AN UPPER GRADE, PROBLEM-STIMULATED INQUIRY

- Reviewing their notes, the children can recall facts and ideas learned during the unit.
- Using their notes in small groups to develop questions to use in a class quiz show, they can participate in the quiz show as preparation for the unit test.
- Taking a 30-item, short-answer test on the generalizations and facts studied, they can achieve 75 percent accuracy or receive corrective assistance to achieve the criterion.
- Reviewing the problems they had and the solutions they tried as Americans trying to accommodate to life in Japan, they can identify the problems with which they had the most success and those which need better solutions.
- Analyzing their successes, they can decide on recommendations they would make to others who might try to accommodate to life in Japan.
- Reviewing the problems with which they had the least success, they can decide whether much could be done with problems in thirty days and make recommendations for persons who might have to live for a long time with the Japanese.

(The above closer objectives stand in the place of the first three closer objectives listed in the unit for an upper grade, interest-stimulated inquiry. The remainder of the closer objectives listed in that unit, with the exception of the last, are also included in this unit.)

The units presented in this chapter at two grade levels are incomplete because only one mini-unit in each has been presented. A complete unit would contain several more. Two complete units are presented in the Appendix.

The units were presented in parts to help you see where strategy makes a difference in planning. You can now understand why an observer visiting ten classrooms on a given day might assume that every teacher teaches social studies in the same way. On that particular day perhaps all the children in every classroom were at work with developmental objectives. However, on another day, the observer would note marked differences. This would happen perhaps on a day when the teachers were guiding children in opening or closing a unit.

You have also noted probably that basic skills are essential to social studies. You could see very marked differences between the skills needed in lower grades and upper grades. You could see many skills that had been taught to a functional level and were being used at that level as the children proceeded in their study.

Now that you discovered what units are, you can appreciate how helpful they can be as you plan each lesson in social studies. They help you know where the learners are, where they have been, and where they are going. However, units need to be updated as they are used with each new class of children because needs and abilities vary from class to class. It is also likely that as you teach a social-studies unit you will have to make modifications along the way. Think of your unit as a navigator's flight plan—most likely workable but modifiable to meet unforeseen circumstances.

UNITS IN SOCIAL-STUDIES TEXTBOOKS

Most social-studies textbooks are organized into units, perhaps so many chapters to a unit and so many lessons to a chapter. Each textbook is accompanied by a teacher's edition or an instructional manual that offers suggestions for teaching. It is fair for you to ask why we are making such a fuss about unit construction when textbooks offer units with suggestions for teaching. In response to the question, let us consider some of the inherent limitations in textbooks.

First, textbooks are designed to meet the skill levels of most of the children in a particular grade. For this reason, a textbook may be suitable for many children, but not for all. They may be suitable for many classes, but not for all.

Sometimes a textbook is accompanied by a skills workbook or studybook. It is designed to supplement the skills which the author and consultants believe will need strengthening. But again this material may be suitable for many children and classes, but not for all.

Second, the teaching suggestions may be focused narrowly on the most common strategy, a simple knowledge-centered strategy with now and then a suggestion for generating extra interest, a minor inquiry, concern for a problem, and individual differences. At best, these suggestions help teachers survive during social-studies instruction. If the teachers survive, so will the children. Survival is basic to learning but a weak guarantee that learning will occur.

Or the teaching strategies in the manual or teacher's edition may be focused on a strategy that is incompatible with your teaching skills. It may be so intricate that it confuses you, or so banal that it disgusts you.

However, a good textbook can be the mainstay of your instructional program. If it has these features, you will find it useful:

- A well-written, straightforward, expository text. This means that paragraphs will have topical sentences, that the sentences will not be overly long and complicated, and that new words are explained appositively so that readers can use the context to arrive at their meaning.
- The pictures, maps, and other graphic materials are an integral part of the text illustrating and elucidating what is covered in the text. Textbooks for young children should convey information in simple, but correlated ways from picture to picture.
- The study questions at the ends of lessons, chapters, and units should be guides to thinking. The first two-thirds of a cluster of questions should aid children in recalling the important facts. The rest of the cluster of questions should encourage the children to integrate and apply their information to make products as reflections of what they have studied or as creative syntheses of what they have learned or to engage in discussions during which they consider problems or decisions.

A textbook containing these features offers two advantages. First, it is reliable as a tool for learning and instruction. In most cases, there is one for every child and it is always available. Second, you can use it to develop units to serve the needs of both you and your learners.

SUMMARY

The teaching notes in instructional manuals and teacher's editions for social-studies textbooks are useful as aids in planning lessons and units. Lessons and units based on materials other than those found in textbooks often reflect a high order of creativity.

The daily lesson plan consists of lesson objectives, a list of instructional materials, and provisions for opening, developmental, and closing activities to bring children to the designated objectives.

The daily lesson objectives are formulated first to serve as guides to the rest of the planning. There must be at least one objective. When an aspect of a skill is also being taught, three or more objectives may be needed.

Instructional materials vary with the age level of children for whom the lessons are planned. Teachers of young children often rely on teacher-made and collected materials. Teachers of older children rely on textbooks. Young children often can profit from materials they can manipulate. Older children often need special help in reading their materials. All materials need to be purposeful, direct, and well within the children's level of language sophistication and skill.

The opener of a lesson prepares children for new learning by providing for a review of previous learning or general background and generating interest.

The developmental section of the lesson plan prescribes the learning activities for new knowledge in content and often in a skill. During the development of the lesson, the content purpose is established and met. If an aspect of skill is included, a review, if necessary, is conducted, and the new aspect is introduced, tried under the teacher's supervision, and used with content.

The closing section of the lesson prescribes activities which have the children meeting the objective(s). The final part of the lesson plan, although not really a part of it, is the evaluation in which the teacher judges his or her practice in light of what the children learned.

The organization of a lesson in social studies in which children are using a skill primarily or doing values exploration follows an order similar to that used with content or content and skills lessons.

Lesson plans are made daily.

The unit has been used traditionally in social studies. As used today, it facilitates the management of learning by ensuring the availability of hard-to-obtain materials when they are needed, simplifying lesson planning, and providing for children to sense accomplishment.

Except for scope, a unit is similar in structure to a lesson plan. Objectives as ends and objectives as means are used in constructing a unit.

Objectives as ends include concluding objectives to be met at the end of the unit and supporting objectives at the end of each miniunit in the developmental section of the unit. The concluding objectives are based on a content generalization. Supporting objectives are based on subgeneralizations developed from the content generalizations. Skill objectives as ends may occur at any place within the unit.

Objectives as means enable learning. Each consists of two parts, the description of a learning activity and its result. Means objectives may enable learning through preparing children for new learning, prescribing activities to result in new learning, and bringing children to closure on ends objectives.

The opening of a unit consists of preparation objectives dealing with the entire unit.

The developmental section of a unit consists of miniunits, each of which is constructed of preparation, developmental, and closure objectives as means, all of which bring learners to a supporting objective as an end.

The closure of a unit consists of closure objectives as means to bring the children to the concluding objectives of the unit to include content learning, skill learning (often), and to exploring for values related to the content generalization of the unit.

The planner's inquiry strategy influences how a unit and each miniunit begin and end, but the investigational activities tend to remain the same for all inquiry strategies.

Units frequently need to be modified while they are being used.

Social-studies textbooks are organized into units with accompanying teaching notes in a manual or teacher's edition. These are inadequate for the needs of all children and classes, but can be useful.

POSTSCRIPT

At the beginning of this chapter, three approaches to instructional planning in social studies were suggested to you. You were to choose the one you thought would result in the best management of learning and the most learning for children. Take out the notes you made then and review them in light of what you have read.

Do you think the same as you did at the beginning of the chapter? Why? What other reasons can you give now for your choice?

FOR FURTHER UNDERSTANDING

Cognitive Activities

1. Construct your own lesson-plan guide. Label the parts and their functions. Include on your guide the questions you are going to ask yourself to evaluate the lesson. Group yourself with several of your classmates to compare guides.

2. Define what is meant by a minilesson. Describe where it is found and the purpose it serves.

3. Define each of the following: *content generalization, concluding objective, subgeneralization, supporting objective, preparation objective, developmental objective, closure objective,* and *miniunit.*

4. Consider whether means objectives could be used in constructing daily lesson plans. Would there be any advantages accruing to you as the teacher if you followed this practice? Give reasons for your answer.

5. Construct your own unit planning guide. List the procedures you will follow in chronological order.

Compare your guide with those made by other members of the class.

6. From time to time, social-studies educators have recommended that textbook publishers produce materials without teaching notes or instructional manuals. The textbooks would be simply informational resources. Do you think publishers should follow these recommendations? Why?

Practice Activities

1. Select a lesson section from a child's social-studies textbook, a series of study prints, an article or a section of an article from an encyclopedia, or an article from a newspaper or magazine, or make a set of sketches or flannelgrams to use to convey facts about a topic. Use the material you have selected or devised to construct a lesson plan.

2. Find an idea in a social-science textbook or compose an idea wide in scope. Use this as the content generalization from which to plan a unit. Do the following:
   a. Compose the subgeneralizations which support the generalization.
   b. Compose a concluding objective related to the generalization.
   c. Compose supporting objectives related to the subgeneralizations.

3. The following are some descriptions of learning activities in sequence. Convert them into means objectives by composing the result for each activity: The children will
   a. talk about the pictures they made yesterday about how firemen live at the station house.
   b. discuss the rules to follow to be a good listener.
   c. listen to the teacher's reading about how firemen respond to an alarm.
   d. dramatize how firemen respond to an alarm. As a result, they will be able to. . . .

4. Using your response to 2 above and assuming that any materials you want are available, construct a unit opener, a miniunit, and a unit closer.

Performance Activities

Using the social-studies textbook or other instructional materials immediately available to you in your classroom or assigned laboratory, do the following:

1. Arrange to teach a sequence of daily lessons to the class or a group of children, make the plans, follow them, and evaluate the effectiveness of your planning and teaching in terms of what the children learned and what you discovered about your procedures.

2. Arrange to teach a social-studies unit of at least two weeks in duration to the class or a group of children, construct a unit, use it, evaluate the effectiveness of your unit and teaching in terms of what the children learned and what you discovered about your procedures. Did you have to modify the unit? Why? How helpful was the unit in facilitating the management of learning?

SELECTED REFERENCES

Chapman, Anne. "The Textbook as Primary Source: How to Wring Novel Benefits from Conventional Texts." *Social Education,* 44:87–91 (February, 1980).

Charles, C. M., David K. Gast, Richard E. Servey, and Houston M. Burnside. *Schooling, Teaching and Learning: American Education,* Chapters 15 and 16. St. Louis: C. V. Mosby, 1978, pp. 285–336.

Davies, Ivor K. *Objectives in Curriculum Design.* London: McGraw-Hill, 1976.

Dick, Walter, and Lou Carey. *The Systematic Design of Instruction.* Glenview, Ill.: Scott, Foresman, 1978.

Hannah, Larry S., and John U. Michaelis. *A Comprehensive Framework for Instructional Objectives.* Reading, Mass.: Addison-Wesley, 1977.

Jarolimek, John, and Clifford D. Foster. *Teaching and Learning in the Elementary School.* New York: Macmillan, 1976.

Michaelis, John U., Ruth H. Grossman, and Lloyd Scott. *New Designs for Elementary Curriculum and Instruction.* New York: McGraw-Hill, 1975.

Ryan, Frank L. *The Social Studies Sourcebook: Ideas for Teaching in the Elementary and Middle School.* Boston: Allyn and Bacon, 1980.

11

Assessing and Evaluating
Children's Growth
in Social Studies

Whenever we use the terms "assess growth" or "assessment of growth" in education, we are referring to the process of determining how much growth a learner has made. For example, if, at the beginning of a reporting period we document that John, a child in sixth grade, can use distance and location from a given point on a world map to locate any other point on the map, but knows nothing about the use of latitude and longitude for locational purposes, and at the end of the reporting period we can document that he can use latitude and longitude to locate points on the map, we can say that he has grown in learning to locate points on a world map.

We can describe the growth or give our assessment in one of two ways.

We can say: "As of (date), John could use latitude and longitude accurately to locate points on a world map."

Or we can say: "As of (date), if John was given a base point on a world map, he could use that point to locate any other point accurately on the map in terms of distance and direction. As of (later date), he could also use latitude and longitude accurately to locate points on a world map."

Which statement of assessment do you think is better? Why? Make a note of your opinion and list your reasons for it.

Now let us consider the grade or mark we are going to give John in map reading. The reporting period is nine weeks long. Nine weeks ago, he knew nothing about using latitude and longitude to locate points on a world map. You must evaluate, or make a judgment about, his growth by assigning *Outstanding, Satisfactory,* or *Unsatisfactory* to it.

Do one of the following:

1. Make a note of the grade you will give John and give your reasons for awarding it.
2. Make a note of why you cannot give John a grade and tell why you cannot.

Put your notes aside to review later.

The communication of assessment and evaluation of progress are usually moments of agony for the assessors and evaluators as well as for those whose learning is being assessed and evaluated. However, the point of view of this chapter is that the moment of sharing an assessment should be one of joy, and the moment of evaluation needs not be shattering.

Ensuring that these moments are positive events is easier in social studies than in other study areas because we have so many skills to assess. It is highly unlikely that a child will make no progress in any skill. He or she must make some progress somewhere within social studies. If we plan and conduct a well-balanced instructional program in social studies and keep track of what is going on, we shall be able to document for learners, their parents, and ourselves that growth has occurred.

In a sense, this chapter is a continuation of Chapter 2. In that chapter you were given suggestions on how to assess children's needs as a base from which to develop your instructional program. Some of the tools to which you were introduced included: *interaction checklist, self-rating sheet, questionnaire, paper-and-pencil test, reading inventory, assessment discussion, assessment trial, assessment test,* and *inquiry test.* As presented in Chapter 2, these are the tools of initial assessment. In this chapter they become the tools for postassessment. In short, a tool used to determine a need may also be used later to see how much growth has occurred.

In this chapter we shall look at the kinds of assessment we do while our program continues and at specific moments for documenting growth. More ideas about skill assessment will be considered. And we shall have to give some thought to ways of assessing growth in retaining and using content.

However, our first task is to explore the dimensions of the instructional program to see what we are going to assess.

THE ELEMENTS IN A GROWTH PROFILE

A growth profile contains vertical and horizontal elements. The vertical elements consist of the areas of growth. The following is a list of the labels indicating the areas of growth characteristics of a social-studies program for young children (from kindergarten through grade three):

1. Applies social-studies facts and generalizations.
2. Uses informational skills in social studies.
3. Uses expression skills to integrate social-studies facts and generalizations.

4. Participates in social-studies discussions.
5. Makes individual contributions to the social-studies program.

Such a list of elements may come from any of several sources. They may be found in the opening section of an instructional manual or teacher's edition of a series of textbooks or other materials adopted for use with young children, in a course of study or instructional guide provided by the district, on a parent-conference form or a report card used within the district, or in a program which you have organized yourself. When they are listed on a parent-conference form or a report card provided for district-wide use, the elements represent the areas which you are to teach in your program.

As we examine the areas, we can detect where the greatest emphasis is to be made. It is safe for us to say that of all the areas listed, applying social-studies facts and generalizations is more important than the others, and that making individual contributions to the social-studies program is of least importance.

Let us rearrange the list to see what this tells us:

1. Uses informational skills in social studies.
2. Uses expression skills to integrate social-studies facts and generalizations.
3. Participates in social-studies discussions.
4. Makes individual contributions to the social-studies program.
5. Applies social-studies facts and generalizations.

In this list of vertical elements we see the emphasis changed to the use of the various school skills in social studies.

Let us suppose that we see a list in which some of the labels used above have been omitted:

1. Applies social-studies facts and generalizations.
2. Uses informational skills in social studies.
3. Uses expression skills to integrate social-studies facts and generalizations.

From the above we might assume that what is important in social-studies instruction is focused on information process.

Notice also that each of the entries in the list is expressed as a broad area of behavior. Often they are expressed in this way: social-studies facts and generalizations, informational skills in social studies, expression skills in social studies, and the like. However, when the entries are expressed as broad areas of behavior, they indicate more clearly what the teacher will be prepared to document. For example, to document children's application of social-studies facts and generalizations, we might observe for the following particular events. The child:

- retains facts and generalizations as shown on simple tests.
- recalls facts after listening, viewing, or observing.
- uses facts and generalizations accurately to perform study tasks.
- uses social-studies facts and generalizations to relate one study to another or to explain phenomena.
- uses social-studies facts and generalizations in other subject areas.

All the behaviors above are instances in which a child shows that he or she can apply social-studies facts and generalizations. For the moment, we shall forget about describing the precise behaviors for the other areas. That will be more important later.

At this point, you are probably wondering about what should be the broad areas of behavior in the vertical dimension of a profile of growth for young children. Those given in the first list and in that order represent a preference which many social-studies educators would recommend for a well-balanced social-studies program for these children. Other educators would rearrange the items in the list, omit some items, or add others. However, as far as this writer is concerned, the list as given permits children to grow in social studies as members of a class and as individual persons. What is included in your list represents your best judgment about children and their general needs for social-studies instruction.

Let us consider now the broad areas of behavior we might use in the later grades:

For Children in Grades Four and Five

1. Applies social-studies facts and generalizations.
2. Uses informational skills in social studies.
3. Uses expression skills to integrate social-studies facts and generalizations.
4. Participates in social-studies class discussions.
5. Participates in small groups to complete projects.
6. Makes individual contributions to the social-studies program.

In the above, we have added group-work skills as related to project completion. Where it is listed is a matter of personal preference.

For Children in Grades Six, Seven, and Eight

1. Applies social-studies facts and generalizations.
2. Uses informational skills in social studies.
3. Uses expression skills to integrate social-studies facts and generalizations.
4. Participates in social-studies class discussions.
5. Participates in small groups to complete study tasks.
6. Participates in small groups to complete projects.
7. Makes independent investigations.
8. Makes individual contributions to the social-studies program.

In this final list, we see two more additions, one relating to accomplishment in working with study groups and the other to ability to make independent investigations, or to do individual inquiry.

When we have clearly in mind what the broad areas of behavior are to be, we can begin to consider the horizontal dimension of the growth profile.

The Horizontal Dimension

As we attempt to organize this dimension, we must bear in mind that evidence of growth is a function of opportunity to respond or perform and accuracy of response or performance at each opportunity. To understand better what is meant by opportunity to respond or perform, let us consider the opportunities possible for children in grades four through eight in the broad area of applying social-studies facts and generalizations. The child:

- retains facts and generalizations as shown on tests.
- recalls facts after listening, viewing, observing, reading, interviewing, or discussing.
- uses facts to draw conclusions.
- validates facts and generalizations.
- gives examples based on definitions and value statements.
- makes comparisons.
- draws implications.
- uses facts and generalizations accurately to perform study tasks.
- uses facts and generalizations to solve study problems.
- uses facts and generalizations to make decisions related to study.
- uses social-studies facts and generalizations to relate one study in social studies to another or to explain phenomena.
- uses social-studies facts and generalizations in other subject areas.

This list shows that there are many opportunities in this broad area of behavior for children to respond or perform accurately. The teacher who uses this list of specific behaviors will have to provide a varied program to ensure that all the opportunities occur.

The horizontal dimension will have to be developed in terms of accuracy or appropriateness of response or performance. We usually think in terms of some sort of scale. It might look like Figure 11–1. In accord with what we observe children do or what we see in their products, we can make a mark on this scale.

Never Accurate or Appropriate	Always Accurate or Appropriate

FIGURE 11–1.

Using the ideas discussed so far, we can construct a growth-profile form. Figure 11–2 presents it. We have filled out the form for illustrated purposes. The first profile, dated 9/20, shows the teacher's initial assessment about two weeks after school opened. The second shows the postassessment about eight weeks later. The difference between the two shows the growth that has occurred.

Where we as teachers place marks on the various continua or scales rests on what we have observed and recorded in some way. The more abundant our information, the more precisely we can place our marks. In the next section we shall consider how we gather and record information about children's growth.

DOCUMENTING CHILDREN'S GROWTH

To document is to record and maintain records, and in order to record we must analyze tests, products, and performances. When we are documenting children's growth in social studies, we look for how children recall and use social-studies facts and generalizations in tests, products, and performances.

The results of social-studies tests inform us of how children are developing in the cognitive process of social-studies learning. To a certain extent, this influences the things that they compose and construct and the performances they give. However, the skill used to make a product or give a performance influences the use of facts and generalizations. Children may be skillful in cognitive process, but unskilled in production or performance. When operating at a low level of competency in these skills, they cannot express what they know. For this reason, we assess growth in production and performance skills as well as in cognitive process.

In this section, we shall focus first on documenting growth in cognitive process, and then on documenting it in the production and performance skills.

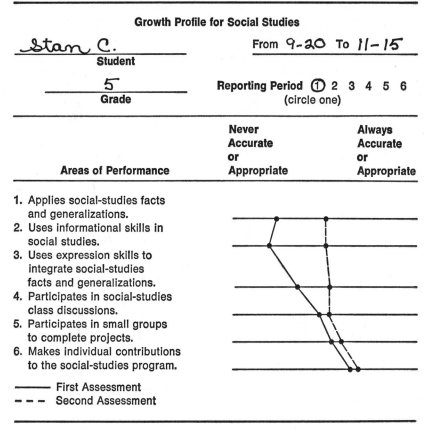

FIGURE 11–2. *Growth-profile Form.*

Documenting Growth in Cognitive Process

As we work to document children's growth in cognitive process, we are trying to see how well children do in recalling facts and generalizations, generalizing, exploring within generalizations to determine their validity, drawing implications, making comparisons, and giving examples, and using generalizations to solve problems, create new ideas, and make decisions requiring judgments. A well-planned unit provides opportunities for children to use all these levels of cognitive process.

The most frequently occurring moment we have for documenting growth in cognitive process is the daily lesson. Most of the lessons we teach

will have children recalling facts and using them for one purpose or another.

The moment next in frequency of occurrence is the close of a miniunit. This has the children dealing with content of a wider scope. The test as a means of assessing growth is used, but that is not all. The children will also be using content to complete tasks of a higher cognitive level.

The big moment occurs at the close of a unit. Testing has a place here. However, the children will again be involved in using social-studies content at higher cognitive levels. Because what they will have learned will be of wide applicability, they are able to perform at more cognitive levels.

The ways that we document growth vary with the ages of our children.

Documenting Young Children's Growth in Cognitive Process.   A good way for us to explore how to document young children's growth in cognitive process is to glance over some documents by a first-grade teacher as he tries to decide how to mark a scale used with cognitive process on a growth profile. The first document is shown in Figure 11–3.

As its label indicates, Figure 11–3 is an anecdotal record written by the teacher toward the end of the social-studies period or as soon as possible after the close of the period. This record indicates what a child did when she had an opportunity to respond after listening to a flannelboard story.

This first-grade teacher makes it a point to observe each child carefully at least once every two weeks. At the close of each reporting period, he has four or five of these records for each child.

The higher the cognitive level at which his learners are working at the end of a unit, the more this teacher tries to get a more precise documentation of what they are doing. He often audiotapes their performances in creative dramatics, role playing, and work with puppets to take notes. His notes often take the form of anecdotal records.

Sometimes the teacher uses a checklist after the children have listened to a story, viewed a film, studied some pictures, or whatever activity is used to acquire information. Figure 11–4 offers an ex-

---

ANECDOTAL RECORD FOR *Joan C.*   10-2
                                              Date

Cognitive Process

After the flannel-board story about a little Japanese girl getting dressed in the morning, Joan generalized, "Japanese girls dress like we do to go to school." Then, using the flannelgrams, she retold the story accurately.

FIGURE 11–3. *Anecdotal Record for a Young Child.*

RECORD OF RESPONSE TO INFORMATION CHECKLIST _____
                                                                                    Date

Students Observed	Volunteered to Respond	Allowed to Respond	Accuracy of Response		
			0	Partial	Total

FIGURE 11–4. *Response to Information Checklist.*

ample. Because this checklist requires only the marking of checks, the teacher can mark it while the children are working with content. At the close of the period he can see at a glance which children are volunteering to respond and the quality of their responses. When he uses it with the entire class, he finds it helpful in seeing to it that all the children who volunteer get a chance to respond.

One of these checklists completed for each week during the reporting period helps the teacher to see who is willing to respond and how accurate they are in their responses. Continuous use of the checklist ensures monitoring progress made by every member of the class. Children who are reluctant to respond or who do not respond well may need some corrective assistance.

From some of his learners, the teacher has some experience stories composed individually after the visit of a resource person:

MRS. YAMASHITA

Mrs. Yamashita came to our room.
She showed some Japanese clothes.
She showed us kimonos.
She had some geta.
I liked the kimono with the birds on it.

Joan C.

THE HAPPI COAT

Mrs. Yamashita showed us a happi coat.
It was blue.
It had a sign on the back.
It is a carpenter's coat.
My dad would like it.

Tommy W.

JAPANESE CLOTHES

Mrs. Yamashita brought her Japanese clothes.
They are pretty.
Some have flowers on them.
Some have birds on them.
They would be nice for dress up.

Sara M.

These stories tell much about what children remember and how they integrate it into meaning.

Whenever the children are expressing themselves by drawing pictures or making simple models or replicas, the products themselves are records. However, because the children like to take them home, the teacher uses a checklist as he analyzes completed products. The checklist is shown in Figure 11–5. Perhaps this product checklist reminds you of the discussion in Chapter 8 about assessing group projects for accuracy in the use of social-study content. The criteria listed in that chapter are also applicable here. Accuracy of detail means that whatever facts the child used are accurate. Completeness of detail refers to the sufficiency of facts to meet the purpose. For example, if a child's picture of a Japanese family on its way to a shrine on a holiday on Seven-Five-Three Day showed the children in ceremonial clothing and the parents in the usual Western garb, it would be complete enough. The shrine does not necessarily need to be pictured.

Originality is frequently an unusual, positive feature not often seen in children's products. For example, if a child takes unusual care in maintaining regularity of design on a drawn kimono, or if the design seems startlingly Japanese, we might view it as an indication of originality. The same would be true if a child, unbidden or not encouraged to do so, drew Mt. Fuji in the background as a part of his or her picture response.

A product checklist for everything that children make or construct during a reporting period often reveals that the children who are reluctant to enter discussions or who do not do well on tests are acquiring information and integrating it into meaningful wholes.

And finally, this first-grade teacher has several tests similar to that shown in Figure 11–6, depicting a true-false test which the teacher administers by reading each item twice. The children respond by making a mark across the square containing the correct answer, in this case, either "yes" or "no." The other kinds of tests include those on which children circle pictures, sometimes circling the correct picture from three given, or circling all the pictures related to a given attribute. Whenever possible, the teacher gives tests in which the

PRODUCT CHECKLIST

Date _____

(Description of Product) _____

Students	Accuracy of Detail			Completeness of Detail	Originality
	O	Partial	Total		
1.					
2.					
3.					
4.					
5.					
6.					
7.					
8.					
9.					
10.					
11.					
12.					
13.					
14.					
15.					
16.					

FIGURE 11–5. *Product Checklist.*

children have to arrange pictures in order or sort them.

As we review all these devices—the anecdotal record, the checklists, the experience stories, and the tests—that the teacher of young children may use to assess their growth in cognitive process, we can see that growth is documentable. The anecdotal records, tests, and experience stories for each child are kept in a folder or large envelope. The checklists are kept in class folders. When a teacher is ready to make the growth profile, he or she consults these sources.

Documenting Older Children's Growth in Cognitive Process. Much of what we have discovered about assessing young children's growth in cognitive process applies as well with older children. Figure 11–7 shows an anecdotal record made by a teacher of sixth grade. Like the anecdotal record made of the young child, this record describes a child's performance. However, this sixth-grade teacher uses anecdotal records in a different way. At the end of each social-studies period, or as nearly thereafter as possible, the teacher writes records about unusual, positive performances. Stan,

---

MINIUNIT TEST

	Name	
1. Japanese boys and girls sometimes wear the same kind of clothes as American boys and girls.	YES	NO
2. Geta are Japanese shoes.	YES	NO
3. Japanese boys and girls wear their school clothes on Children's Day.	YES	NO
4. Japanese people wear kimonos on their feet.	YES	NO
5. A Japanese woman who works on a farm wears special clothes.	YES	NO
6. Tabi are Japanese socks worn with special shoes.	YES	NO
7. The Japanese people have special clothing to wear at special times.	YES	NO
8. A workman sometimes wears a coat that tells what kind of work he does.	YES	NO
9. Japanese boys and girls are different from American boys and girls because they sometimes wear special clothing.	YES	NO

FIGURE 11–6. *Miniunit Test for Young Children.*

ANECDOTAL RECORD FOR _Stan L._ _11-19_
                                        Date

Cognitive Process

This morning when the group spokespersons reported, a single idea emerged: The difference was due to cultural borrowing from Western nations. As the class was about to declare consensus on the idea, Stan began to squirm and frown. He raised his hand and, when recognized, he pointed out "That borrowing started before the Japanese had much to do with the United States and other nations. I think they borrowed from the Chinese centuries before that." He went to the encyclopedia, quickly found the article on China, and used the pictures to show similarities in traditional garb of the Chinese and Japanese. He volunteered to look more deeply into his observation and to report on it tomorrow.

FIGURE 11–7. *Anecdotal Record for an Older Child.*

one of those quiet learners who appears to flow along with instruction, has suddenly given evidence of high involvement. If his behavior is adequately reinforced, he may become more involved. This anecdotal record in his personal folder will serve to remind the teacher of what this learner can do.

Recording unusual performances is a commendable practice, but it categorizes those for whom no records are kept as a colorless lot. A preferable practice is to observe all children in turn for anecdotal records, and to record also any unusual performances.

This sixth-grade teacher also uses checklists to keep track of how the children respond to information and the quality of their products. She also uses tests. Besides the usual multiple-choice, true-false, and matching items on tests, she develops items like these:

1. Suppose a Japanese boy came to stay with you for a month. Check the things below that you would most likely have to do to make him feel the same as he would at home.
   _____ a. Make a bed for him on the floor.
   _____ b. Be more polite to your parents.
   _____ c. Feed him a lot of turkey and hot-dogs.
   _____ d. Take him to church every Sunday.
   _____ e. Make kites with him.
   _____ f. Play basketball with him.
   _____ g. Put your television away.
   _____ h. Have him take off his shoes before entering the house.
   _____ i. Take him to baseball games.
   _____ j. Shorten the legs on the dining room table.

2. The following is a list of the members of a traditional Japanese family. Rearrange them in the order that each member has in the family.
   a. The father
   b. The father's mother
   c. The younger son
   d. The older daughter
   e. The mother
   f. The older son
   g. The father's father
   h. The younger daughter

3. After each of the things listed below write the name of something that Americans have borrowed from the Japanese:
   a. Clothing _____.
   b. Food _____.
   c. Hobby _____.
   d. Design _____.
   e. House furnishing _____.

4. Below are some statements that might be made by both Japanese and American parents, or by either Japanese or American parents, or by neither. Read each statement carefully. If you think Japanese parents would make the statement, write *J* after it. If American parents would say it, write *A* after it. If neither Japanese nor American parents would say it, write *N*.
   a. Little children need to learn how to mind.
   b. When a little child is naughty, you should threaten to leave it.
   c. You should give little children candy to keep them happy.
   d. Little children are fun to be with.
   e. Older children should be examples for younger children.
   f. Children should go to school.
   g. Elementary children should study hard to be able to go to good high schools.
   h. Children should go to the schools in their neighborhood.
   i. Little children should be seen and not heard.
   j. Every child should have a room of his or her own.

Items such as the above have children working with larger groups of facts and generalizations and dealing with interrelationships among facts.

Because the children are able to compose in written form, the teacher frequently adds to each short-answer test at least one item similar to these:

1. Suppose that your family had to move to Japan to live there for at least a year. Write a paragraph telling about the part of school life that you think would be most difficult for you. Tell why you think it would be difficult.

2. Suppose that a Japanese family had to come to America to live for a year. Write a three-paragraph essay telling what you think would be the family's most serious problem and what they might do to solve it.

3. Write a list of at least three rules that you think an American visitor in Japan should follow to keep from upsetting the Japanese people he would meet.

4. Write an imaginary diary entry written by a member of a Japanese family in which he or she tells about something that has pleased or disappointed him very much

5. Write a paragraph telling what you think the American and Japanese people should do to get to know each other better.

6. Sometimes the Japanese people seem ready to discard their traditional ways for ways like ours. Do you think they should do this? Give your reasons.

Questions like the above free children to respond more personally and to use social-studies content in realistic ways.

If the children have poor written-composition skills, some teachers allow them to use an audio-tape recorder to compose their responses to questions similar to the above. Or, they have the children react to the questions in small groups. The group is given the question, a minute or so to think about it, and a signal to begin discussing it. The teacher stations himself or herself near the group, listens, and takes notes on the responses and who makes them. When the teacher is concerned only about content, the notes are taken in a code similar to the following:

+ = a generalization stated.
/ = a fact contributed or a reason given.

But there may also be a skill problem. Children who are uncomfortable in groups or who become nervous when the teacher carefully observes the group may be inhibited from responding.

To ensure that children will have a fair chance to respond accurately, some teachers test less frequently, but when they test, the test is given in two forms—a written form and an oral form.

Sometimes the teachers of older children will give them tests to which they are expected to respond completely in essay form. In most instances, such tests are simply factual-recall tests in which the children are given the additional burden of writing out everything they have to say in complete sentences. The usual case is that children who are deficient in grammar, spelling, and handwriting skills do poorly regardless of what content they know and can use. If tests such as these are used, the least the teacher can do is to ensure that the children have the skills necessary to make accurate, acceptable responses.

Much like the first-grade teacher, the sixth-grade teacher maintains a personal file for each child and folders for class checklists. At the end of the reporting period, he or she uses the materials in the folders to decide where to mark on the cognitive process scale which relates to the applications of facts and generalizations.

The Positive Use of Tests

To help children build positive attitudes toward tests, teachers in all grades follow practices like these:

- Refer to tests as a way to find out what they know or remember about what they have studied. Older children may be guided in maintaining a graph of test scores.
- Inform the children of how well they did as soon as possible after they take the test. Correction in class immediately after the test helps children know immediately what the correct responses were. This also presents an opportunity for the children to ask questions about difficult items, to give interpretations, and to provide proof for their answers. This is a good practice to follow with tests on miniunits.
- Inform the children when a test is going to be given and assist them in reviewing. Young children may discuss some of the things they made as related to their study or they may play a simple game. Often a review discussion is helpful to older learners. Quiz games for review are popular with them.
- Confer with older children about their test success. Some children need this kind of teacher support. It offers an opportunity for discussing study problems and developing a corrective program, or bestowing honest praise.
- Test frequently. Whenever a miniunit is completed, the children are tested for retention and application of content before another miniunit is begun.
- Refrain from threatening reminders such as: "If you don't get busy now, you won't do well on the test." "When you take the test you will find that it does not pay to fool around." "All right. Mess around all you want, but if you don't make a decent grade on the test tomorrow, you will be sorry, believe me."

As you have probably noticed, documenting children's growth in cognitive process is a matter of observing and testing frequently throughout the teaching of each unit, and maintaining records of the results. Sometimes what you have analyzed to document growth in cognitive process may also be used to document growth in needed skills. This is particularly true of product analyses which will be discussed later.

Documenting Growth in Skills

As we document children's growth in cognitive process we are likely to discover needs for improvement in both intake and output skills. As pointed out, deficiencies in these skills influence the quality of children's cognitive learning. The mutually supportive relationship between the skills and cognitive growth is a plus in the elementary curriculum. Faulty applications of the skills in social studies indicate instructional deficiencies which should be corrected in the programs focused on teaching those skills as well as in the social-studies program. The real utility of the skills is discovered in social studies. Every improvement in the skills is marked by an improvement of learning in social studies, and every improvement of learning in social studies sharpens the skills to a finer level of utility. This was a main reason for devoting so much time in Chapter 2 to establishing baselines from which to plan skills instruction.

Each time you teach a skill or an aspect of it during social-studies instruction, you will want to see how much growth has occurred. Page turning can be annoying. However, you will be asked to do it from time to time as we discuss documenting growth in the intake and output skills.

Assessing Growth in the Intake Skills. Effective social-studies teaching usually ensures that children have specific purposes for listening, observing, viewing, reading, and interviewing. The dynamics of the program tend to conceal growth, and most of us are content to consider growth in these skills as assessed sufficiently during our instructional programs in reading and language arts. Furthermore, as long as the children are acquiring content, there seems to be little need for assessing particularly

those aspects of skill necessary to the social-studies program.

However, those of us who are particularly concerned about individual growth in the use of the intake skills may wish to make a more detailed assessment. This requires that we make some tests to administer. One model will illustrate several uses.

The first thing that you will need is an informational resource. Imagine that you have a reading selection, a set of study prints, a filmstrip, an audiotape, or a filmloop which contains information about Eskimo seal hunting. For purposes of illustration we shall present the reading selection:

Years ago the Eskimo of North Alaska depended on seals for much of what he needed. Seals are air-breathing, furry animals that spend much of their time in the water. They live in large numbers in Alaskan waters near the shore. Walruses and whales live in the waters, too, but only at certain times of the year. The seals are always there.

Seals had many uses. The meat and oil from their bodies provided food for the Eskimo. The oil could be burned in lamps. Its skin could be made into clothing and storage bags. Its bones could be used to make household tools.

When the Eskimo hunted seals in the winter, he went out on the ice and looked for a seal's breathing hole. Whenever a seal needed air, it came to this hole. The Eskimo would wait quietly at the hole until the seal came to it. When it did, he stabbed it with his harpoon, a spear with a rope or line attached to it. The rope kept the animal from getting away. The Eskimo used a special harpoon with a line attached to its head. When the Eskimo stabbed the seal, the harpoon head would come off and stay in the seal. Using the line, the Eskimo would pull it up to the ice hole and kill it.

In the spring and summer, the Eskimo used a throwing spear. During these seasons, the seals liked to lay on the ice. The Eskimo would crawl carefully toward a seal. Sometimes he tried to make it think that he was just another seal. At other times he camouflaged himself. He did this by wearing clothing that made him hard to see against the ice and clouds. When he was about twenty-five feet away from the seal, he would stand and throw his harpoon at it. The head of this harpoon did not come off, but the rope on the harpoon kept the seal from getting away.

Seals were so important to the Eskimo that they were often mentioned in his religion.

Using the above as the resource, we develop the test questions—one-half to two-thirds of which are factual, like these:

1. On what did the Eskimo depend for much of what he needed?
2. Why could the Eskimo depend on seals for what he needed?
3. What were two uses for seal oil?
4. Where did the Eskimo find the seal's breathing hole in the winter?
5. Where did the Eskimo find the seal in the spring and summer?
6. How do we know the seal was so important to the Eskimo?

And some questions should deal with vocabulary:

7. What is a *seal?*
8. What is a *harpoon?*
9. What would you do to *camouflage* yourself in a forest?

Plus a question or two at a higher level of thinking:

10. What do you think would be a good title for this article?
11. Why might an Eskimo prefer to hunt a walrus or a whale rather than a seal?

The resource and the questions are basic materials. As they stand, they could be used for an individual test. The child reads the selection silently and responds to the questions orally as they are asked. If the children are capable in written composition, the reading selection could be duplicated for group or class use, and the children could write out the answers to the questions. If the children are not capable in written composition, the questions could be converted into multiple-choice questions.

If we wished to use the reading selection for a listening test, we might read it to a learner or group of learners and have them respond to the questions in written form. Or we might convert the questions to a short-answer form. For that matter, we could audiotape the selection and the questions and provide the learners with a form on which to write their responses.

Now let us suppose that the text resource given above is conveyed via a series of study prints, a filmstrip, or a filmloop or short film. We simply arrange for the children to have contact with the material and administer the test.

When we review the results of a skill test with children, we direct their attention toward the skill aspects. The number of items correctly answered is the focal point. If we give the correct answers to the questions, we limit the utility of the test at a later date.

When we plan to use such tests to assess growth, we usually need alternative forms. When we select text resources, we select them carefully to ensure that they convey information at the same level of sophistication. For example, all the reading selections should be at the same readability level and within the capability of our learners.

Or you may wish to construct a reading or listening inventory which measures comprehension as a function of the difficulty of the material. You can construct an excellent inventory from graded reading selections taken from *My Weekly Reader.* Use the directions given on pages 43–45 and 46 in Chapter 2. However, the inventory, because of the broad levels that it measures, is not useful if given more than twice during a school year.

Interviewing as an intake skill is used so infrequently that we usually have to reteach it every time it is used. However, if it is a skill that you emphasize during a unit, you may test for growth by asking the children to compose a set of interview questions related to a topic similar to one with which they have used interviewing as a way of getting information, or you may have them respond to a test similar to the following:

A person from our class is going to interview Mr. Pierre Durand who is the French consul in our city. This person wants to find out how the schools in France prepare boys and girls for careers. This interviewer has prepared the list of questions below. Draw a circle around the number of each question you think the interviewer should ask.

1. How are you, Mr. Durand?
2. Do you like your job?
3. What are the main public schools in France?
4. What is taught in the elementary schools?
5. What is taught in the high schools?
6. What kind of physical-education program do they have in the elementary schools?
7. What kinds of games do the children in elementary school play during recess?
8. When the children graduate from elementary school, do they go to any junior high school they want to or do they have to take special tests?
9. When does a French child begin to prepare for a career?
10. Will you please tell me how you prepared for your career?
11. How would a person prepare for a career as an auto mechanic in France?
12. Do you think that French schools are as good as American schools? Why do you think so?
13. What changes do you think might be made in the ways French schools prepare boys and girls for careers?
14. Have you enjoyed your stay in America?

The test above assesses for pertinence of questions as well as sensitivity to the feelings of the interviewee.

So far, we have dealt only with assessing for growth in the general-intake skills. In the area of reading, we have a few special skills vital to social-studies learning to assess. These include map and globe skills, the locational skills, graph-reading skills, and the retention skills.

When assessing for growth in map and globe skills, you may use a test similar to that presented on page 48 in Chapter 2.

When assessing for growth in using the table of contents and the use of an index to locate information, you may construct and use a test similar to that discussed on pages 47–48 in Chapter 2.

When assessing growth in graph-reading skills, you may use an inventory similar to the one discussed on pages 48, 50–52 in Chapter 2.

When assessing growth in note taking and outlining skills, you may wish to have the children do a trial task in which they take notes or outline a short passage, or you may use a test as suggested on page 53 in Chapter 2. However, you may find it more convenient to ask the children to review with you a set of notes or an outline made during the course of class work. Or you may ask the children to hand in their notes or outlines to be checked. If you wish to save time, you may use a product checklist as you observe children taking notes or outlining.

Assessing Growth in Output Skills. Usually the application of output skills results in a product or performance. We have already discussed ways of analyzing products for accuracy and originality. Now we are concerned about the efficiency of the skills. We focus primarily on the language skills necessary for oral and written composition.

When children share, participate in the current-affairs program, or give oral reports, their products are primarily performances. To monitor, assess, and record growth we may use anecdotal records. Figure 11–8 offers an example of such a record made when a young child shared an interesting object.

Or the teacher might use an observation checklist on which all the significant behaviors are listed.

ANECDOTAL RECORD FOR _____   **Date**

Oral Reporting

Amy asked me to hold the Japanese doll while she told about it. She told how a cousin had given the doll to the family, identified the garments accurately, and told why she liked the doll. She spoke clearly and distinctly in complete sentences, and maintained eye contact with the class. She answered questions asked by the members of the class quickly and confidently.

FIGURE 11–8. *Anecdotal Record of a Young Child's Report.*

ORAL REPORTING CHECKLIST

Mark an *X* after each
behavior as observed.

NAMES

1. Gave an interesting introduction.							
2. Presented a complete set of facts.							
3. Presented the facts in acceptable order.							
4. Offered a conclusion or summary.							
5. Used complete sentences.							
6. Spoke clearly and distinctly.							
7. Maintained eye contact.							
8. Maintained acceptable posture.							

FIGURE 11–9. *Oral Reporting Checklist.*

Figure 11–9 is an example of such a checklist that might be used when observing older children when they give reports.

As you can see, in both the anecdotal record and the checklist, the teacher has firmly in mind the behaviors to be observed. Similar practices are followed when observing children as they give oral summaries or participate in creative dramatics.

Whenever children write sentences, paragraphs, or reports, their products are tangible and permanent. Samples of these products may be analyzed and filed in the children's personal records. It is a common practice for teachers to write critical or corrective remarks on these products, but learners sometimes feel that these remarks violate the integrity of their products. A product checklist similar to that suggested for the oral report may be used. Entries describing behaviors particular to written language are substituted for those related to oral language. For example, *composes paragraphs correctly, uses punctuation correctly, uses capitalization correctly, spells correctly,* and *writes legibly* replace such entries as *speaks clearly and distinctly, maintains eye contact,* and *maintains acceptable posture.*

Checklists may also be used with such products as maps, charts, and graphs. If you have a strong instructional emphasis in art and crafts in your total program, you may use checklists to record quality of products.

As you consider what has been offered here about assessing children's growth in the use of intake and output skills in social studies, you can sense the mutually supportive relationship between social-studies instruction and that conducted in other areas of the curriculum. In many instances, social studies provides the testing ground for the utility of the skills.

Assessing Growth in the Skills and Behaviors Specific to Social Studies

Participating in social-studies discussion (including those related to role playing and simulation), in small-group activities, in making independent investigations (including involvement in scientific inquiry, values analysis, and values clarification), and in making individual contributions to the social-studies program presents opportunities for children to grow outside of the pale of accuracy and efficiency. Growth in these skills and behaviors is frequently measured on a negative-positive scale. Usually the commitment of person or self to participation, rather than increased mastery of a specific skill, is the factor contributing toward growth. As we assess for growth, we look for positive changes in commitment and, in some instances, changes in skill.

Assessing Growth in Discussions. The suggestions given on pages 28–35 in Chapter 2 are particularly useful here. Of particular utility are the interaction checklist, the self-rating sheet, and the discussion-preference questionnaire. The interaction checklist may be used with the entire class as well as with groups.

When working with young children, you may invite the children to discuss what they liked about the discussion. They may respond in terms of the content treated or in terms of participation. The latter may be expressed in this way, "A lot of people got to talk." "Some people had some good things to say." "More people talked today." You may prompt the discussion by asking them how their discussion might be made better. Do not be surprised if they parrot back what you are continually saying about discussions, but be on the alert for insightful personal observations. Focus the children's attention on such observations.

When working with older children, you may develop a personal-assessment sheet for their use. This includes self-rating as well as an opportunity for the children to tell about personal discoveries. For example, after a role-playing session, you might have the children complete a personal assessment sheet as shown in Figure 11–10. If you prefer, you may have the children consider the last two items on the sheet as optional. They may or may not respond to them.

Personal assessment sheets similar to the one

ROLE PLAYING _____
Name

What Do You Feel?

On the line to the right of each question, mark an X to show how you feel.

	Unsatisfied	Satisfied
1. How do you feel about the role playing we have just had?	├─────────────────┤
2. How do you feel about what you did during the role playing?	├─────────────────┤
3. How do you feel about what the others did?	├─────────────────┤
4. If you knew that we were going to have role playing again tomorrow, how would you feel?	├─────────────────┤

In the space below, write a sentence or two telling how you think we might make role playing better in this classroom.

In the space below, write a sentence or two telling the most important thing you discovered during the role playing today.

FIGURE 11–10. *Personal-assessment Sheet for Role Playing.*

shown in Figure 11–10 may also be used after in-depth discussions and simulations.

Assessing Growth in Group Activities. The suggestions given on pages 266–270 and 275–276 in Chapter 7 are useful in assessing growth in project and study-group skills. See also pages 28–35 in Chapter 2.

Assessing Growth in Making Investigations. An example of an inquiry test that could be used from time to time to assess children's growth in scientific-inquiry skills is given on pages 40–41 in Chapter 2.

When working with young children as they proceed through any inquiry approach, you may make anecdotal records of children's performance either on a whole-class basis or only when children give an extraordinary performance.

Anecdotal records are useful for assessing older children's growth in inquiry skills. Also, on completing a unit, older children may be given a personal-assessment sheet to express how they felt about its content, activities, and any truths or ideas they discovered in it.

After an older child completes an independent investigation, you may include in the terminating conference questions such as these:

1. Now that you have completed your study, how do you feel about it?
2. Would you like to do another study like this? Why?
3. What did you like most about this study?
4. What gave you the most difficulty?
5. What do you think is the most important thing or idea you discovered as a result of doing this study?

Conferences when these questions are asked help children discover that they are not just completing studies as school work. Such studies do have a personal payoff, and the teacher is concerned that learners be aware of it.

In most instances, the results of a value clarification or value analysis has the personal commit-ment as a component. The value sheet or value analysis is itself a sample of the child's thinking and feeling and could be filed in a child's personal-growth folder.

Assessing Individual Contributions. From time to time you will discover that some children are so caught up in social studies that they contribute to the program in special ways. Unbidden, they may bring objects, pictures, brochures, news clippings, and magazine articles to share with the class.

Sometimes contributions may be encouraged. Often the teacher's encouragement helps the child to plan with his or her parents to bring something to school.

There are many opportunities for children to volunteer to make needed contributions—to interview or otherwise investigate and report a topic or issue of interest to the class, to participate in role playing or creative dramatics, or to try an activity for the class's benefit.

Each instance of contribution should be documented in an anecdotal record. Often such a record helps you assess a child in a broader light and may document what you say as you serve as an advocate for the child before his or her parents.

By this time you may wonder when you are going to find time to teach social studies if you are expected to spend so much time documenting children's learning. The first thing to remember is that you will not be teaching and documenting everything covered in this chapter. Your program will be based on your assessment of children's needs at the beginning of the school year and your continued monitoring of needs throughout the year. You will be teaching and documenting only what you emphasize in your program.

The second thing to remember is that you will need to organize an assessment schedule. This means that you will undertake only one or two assessment tasks every day. For example, during the social-studies period you may be observing four or five children to document their growth in discussion skills, and, later in the day, you may be analyzing some paragraphs they have written.

In a moment you will see how all this documenting helps children, their parents, and you.

COMMUNICATING ABOUT GROWTH

Communicating about children's growth involves communicating with children, their parents, and with other professionals, and with oneself. We communicate about it with children because, after all, they are the ones doing the learning, and if they are expected to assume their share of the responsibility for learning, they must have a positive concept of their own growth. We communicate with parents about children's growth to help them see that both we and the children have been responsible and to coordinate all of our efforts, intents, and dreams. Because education is a continuous process, no one teacher can be expected to plan and monitor a child's growth in learning all through the school years. To ensure that children's learning is articulated and accumulative, all professionals must be able to speak a common language to ensure transitions from year to year. And, no matter how hard we try, none of us is able to ensure one-hundred percent success. But we must strive to keep the rate of success high. This requires that we communicate to ourselves about children's growth to assess the efficacy of our every procedure and practice.

Let us look into each of these spheres of communication to see what we might do to ensure that appropriate messages are conveyed.

Communicating with Children about Their Own Growth

Communicating with children about their own growth occurs every day when we react to their responses to our questions and demands. Of course, we want to be positive, but we want also to be honest. The tasks that we provide should be within children's capacity but should still present sufficient challenge to help them sense their own ac-

complishment. However, daily communication is not enough. There must be moments when children can see growth as a function of effort, activity, and time.

At the close of a social-studies unit, and sometimes in the middle of the unit after a couple of miniunits have been completed, we should conduct teacher-learner conferences during which we review children's growth with them individually. At each conference, we share as much of the contents of the child's personal-growth folder as we can. Although our practice is generally the same with both young and older children, there is enough difference for us to discuss the two separately.

Conferring with Young Children. Often it seems that young children in kindergarten and first grade are so filled with wonder at all the new things they are learning that conferences do not seem necessary. However, conferences are recommended at these grade levels to help the children become accustomed to looking for larger increments of learning.

Let us assume that a first-grade teacher is ready to confer with a child about his growth. She has reviewed the contents of his folder. It contains a couple of anecdotal records, two social-studies tests, and a couple of pictures he has drawn. For the time being she is using the round table back in the library corner as the conference site. It seems less formidable and officious than her desk. She calls the child to join her. This is how the conference goes.

Teacher: Sit down beside me, right here, Chad, so we can look at these things in this folder. We are going to talk about what you have learned in social studies. The first things out of the folder are these (takes out the two pictures). Do you remember these?
Chad: Yes, they're pictures I made.
Teacher: And nice pictures they are, too. Do you remember which one you drew first?
Chad: This one.
Teacher: How do you know?
Chad: Because we talked about buses first, and then about airplanes. This is the bus I made.
Teacher: You are right. But I can tell in another

way. Let's look at the two pictures together. Your bus picture shows a bus going along a street. It has many people in it. But look at your airplane picture. You remembered to put more things in it. Do you remember what this is?

Chad: The control tower. And over there is a gasoline truck.

Teacher: Right. It seems to me that you are remembering more things to put in your pictures. When we were studying airplanes, you were learning more. Let's put the pictures back in the folder. Here are two notes that I wrote about you (takes out the anecdotal records). Let's see what they say. (Paraphrasing.) "Chad brought his truck to share with us this morning. He told us where he got it, what other trucks he has seen like it on the streets, and then he stopped. I had to ask him why he thought the truck was important. I also had to keep saying to him, 'Please speak more loudly, Chad.'" My other note says, "Chad brought a picture of an airplane to share with us. He told us why he brought the picture, told about the airplane, and told us why the airplane was important. He spoke loudly and clearly." Can you tell which sharing was better?

Chad: The airplane was.

Teacher: Why do you think so?

Chad: I talked loud.

Teacher: Yes, you did, and you told us what was important about the airplane. You shared better with the airplane than you did with the truck. You are becoming a better sharer. Now let's look at these (takes out the tests). Do you remember them?

Chad: We did this one to see how much we remembered about the bus. And this one was about airplanes.

Teacher: And you remembered quite well. As far as I can see, you did not forget a thing. You can remember what you learn very well. I think you are learning a lot. What do you think?

Chad: I think I learned a lot about airplanes.

Teacher: I think you did too. Some day your mother and father and I are going to talk about the things in your folder. It will be nice to show them how you are learning. You can go back to the listening center now.

Chad has made some interesting discoveries. His teacher keeps track of what he does and then she shares it with him. She must care about what he does. And he is learning something.

You have probably noticed that the teacher underscored the areas of growth with the child and helped him to see them. She also informed the child that the things in his folder would be shared with his parents at a later time. This helps to prepare him for the moment when the teacher and the parents will confer about his progress.

Let us suppose that on the tests the child had remembered much more on the first test than the second:

Teacher: My goodness, look here, you remembered so much more about buses than you did about airplanes. I can't understand that. Do you have any idea about why that happened?

Chad: I got mixed up.

Teacher: I think you must have, but I know that when you don't get mixed up, you can remember very well.

In this instance, the teacher reinforces the child's better performance. You may need to do this with older children as well.

Conferring with Older Children. By the time that most children are seven years old, they can sense their own accomplishment. We can follow the same practice with them and children in third grade as we do with older children.

As a general rule, the older the child, the more persuasive you have to be to convince him or her that growth is occurring. As ironic as it may seem, you have to be the advocate for the child when he or she is both plaintiff and judge. This will be particularly true with children in the later grades who, as a result of past school experiences, are convinced that they cannot learn. You will need to show them as much of your documentation as you can.

Let us assume that a sixth-grade teacher is ready to confer with a child. He has informed the children about his intent to discuss their progress with them. They know that he is doing it for them, because the time for reporting to parents is some weeks away. Independent tasks have been assigned. He has established a conference station in the back of the classroom. Before him he has a child's personal-growth folder. In it are the growth profile used at the last report to parents, some anecdotal records, tests, and some brief summaries made from information on product, group work, and interaction checklists. The teacher calls the child to the conference station.

Teacher: Please sit down, Norma. That is a nice sweater you are wearing. The design on it looks as though it could have been designed by an Aztec weaver.

Norma: That's what I told my mother when I picked it out.

Teacher: You seem to have an eye for design, color, and detail. In my record here (takes out a summary of product analyses), I have noted that everything you draw or paint is unusually good. And you do so well in using the facts and ideas we have studied. That picture you drew of the Aztec temple made me feel as though I was right there.

Norma: I have always liked to do things in art.

Teacher: You use it well to express yourself. How do you feel about expressing yourself in writing?

Norma: I don't care much for that. I'm not sure of my spelling.

Teacher: Maybe you worry so much about your spelling that it interferes with what you are trying to say. My record, see here, shows that all the facts you remember are accurate, but you don't write enough of them. Not like you do when you draw or paint. So I can see that you are learning a lot. But you can see that I have noted here that you appear to be improving. The last paragraph you wrote was the best you had written so far.

Norma: It seemed the same to me.

Teacher: Here, I have the last two paragraphs you wrote. In this first one, you just wrote three facts. But in this other, you started with a strong statement and told about it. You have given five facts. Do you see the difference?

Norma: Yes, the second paragraph is longer.

Teacher: Perhaps each time you write a paragraph, you will want to make a strong statement first and then tell more about it. Just express yourself and we can do something about the spelling later. How do you feel you are doing on the tests?

Norma: I don't care much for those either. Sometimes I do well and sometimes I don't.

Teacher: I have your last three tests here. The first shows an almost perfect score, and the second and third are quite low. That good score tells me what you can do. Can you remember anything special that you did before that test?

Norma: Yes, you had us do a quiz show just before the test.

Teacher: And that helped you remember?

Norma: Sure, the test was easy after that.

Teacher: Do you know that you can have your own quiz show before each test?

Norma: How is that?

Teacher: Just use your note cards. Cover the answer part of each note and see whether you can answer the question. You don't have to answer it in exactly the same words, but you should give the same idea.

Norma: I might try that.

Teacher: If you decide to do it, let me know, and we'll discuss the results afterward. What do you think about working in groups? We've been doing a lot of that lately.

Norma: That's fun, especially when you get to work with your friends.

Teacher: And I see here (shows a summary of Norma's performances as taken from checklists) that you are often a spokesperson for a group and you do very well at it.

Norma: The others always let me be spokesperson. I don't think they care to do it.

Teacher: That's one way to look at it. Another way is to think that the others have confidence in you. They know you'll do a good job.

Norma: Sometimes I don't think so. I get nervous about reporting to the rest of the class.

Teacher: But you do a good job. That convinces me that you are learning a great deal. It balances out how you write and what you do on tests.

Norma: Do you mean that what we do in groups and in art is just as important as what we do on tests, paragraphs, and stuff like that?

Teacher: That is part of it. It also means that when I consider all the things I can, I see evidence of learning. How do you feel about it?

Norma: I do know a lot more about the Aztecs than I did.

Teacher: That is true. Can you think of anything that you would really like to improve?

Norma: I'd like to do better on tests.

Teacher: And we've talked about how you might do that.

Norma: Yes, the quiz game I play with myself just before a test.

Teacher: And if you play the game on the same day that you make the note cards, you will find it easier to beat when you play it just before the test. Do you have any questions?

Norma: I don't think so.

As you can see in the above, the teacher has assumed the role of an advocate helping the learner to see herself in the best possible light. At the same time areas of needed improvement were identified, and suggestions were given on how the improvement might be accomplished. The learner was given an opportunity to express a need, and the conference ended with the learner feeling that improvement, or further growth, was possible.

The way you conduct the conference makes a difference. A favorable comment about the child's appearance or something positive you have seen him or her do is usually a good opener. The teacher in the above was able to lead from the comment into the body of the conference. That is not always possible. Other workable leads include the following:

- Ask the child what he or she thinks is the most interesting thing learned in social studies since the last conference.
- Ask what activities in social studies the child prefers.
- Focusing on a sample of the child's best work, ask him or her to review it with you and to comment on it.

And the best recommendation we can make for closing the conference is to have the child leave the conference with a goal and some ideas about how to reach it. If the teacher in the above conference really wants to underscore his sincerity with the child, he will follow up the goal in some way. He may observe carefully to see whether Norma does review her notes. Or he may ask her whether she has. Or he may go as far as engaging her in trying the review technique in class by asking her to review her note cards for a minute or two and then conducting the quiz himself.

The last conference before the report to parents is particularly critical. During this conference,

ILLUSTRATION 11–1. *A Learner Discovers How Much He Has Learned.*

the child's growth profile should be used as the discussion guide. It should be conducted as a rehearsal or preview for the conference to be held with the parents. How to conduct that conference will be discussed shortly. Suffice to say for the moment that the child should leave the preceding conference with the feeling that he or she has been fully informed about what his teacher and parents are going to discuss, and that the same ideas about his or her progress and goals for the near future are communicated.

Communicating with Parents about Children's Growth

As stated earlier, the child's growth profile serves as the guide during the conference with parents.

The child's personal folder serves as the documentation for the latest profile drawn on the profile form. This folder contains anecdotal records, tests (or summaries of test scores), products (or summaries of information taken from product checklists), individual-performance checklists (or summaries taken from group or class checklists), self-rating sheets, and personal-assessment forms. You will use these items to illustrate what you have to say to parents or to document anything that they question or do not understand. This means that the folder will have to be carefully organized. Items used to document areas on the growth profile should be clipped together and labeled.

And you will most likely need another piece of material—a class-growth record that shows how all the children in the class achieved during the reporting period. You will find this helpful when the parents ask this question or one like it: "How well is our child doing with respect to the rest of the class?" Most of us prefer that the parents focus their attention on the growth of the child and, regardless of what it is, appreciate it. Some can and will; others must know how their child is doing in comparison with others. This has a meaning for them that we cannot deny.

Constructing a class-growth record is time consuming but not difficult. To make it, use a growth-profile form such as Figure 11–2. Instead of the name of a student, write *Class* on it. Then, after you have completed the individual-growth profiles for all your learners, enter the information · from each profile on the class-growth profile. Use a dot for each initial assessment and an *x* for each second assessment (or you could use two colors of dots). See Figure 11–11 for an idea of how the completed class profile looks.

As the parents compare their child's growth profile with that of the class, they can easily see where their child stands with respect to the rest of the class.

At this point you are ready for conferences with parents. They are usually more relaxed if your conference station is at the side of a table long enough to accommodate all of you sitting on one side or arranged at one end of it. If you sit on one side of the table and the parents on the other, an adversary situation is suggested. If there is no table, arrange a semicircle of chairs at which all of you sit as a conversational group. The growth profile and documentation can be conveniently placed at the edge of the desk. Here are a few useful directions:

- When the parents enter, use whatever conversational grace you have to make them feel that they are welcome and that you are interested in them as people. The weather is not a bad topic of conversation.
- Lead into the body of the conference by asking the parents which area of the curriculum or what aspect of social studies (if you teach only social studies) they are most concerned about. Give them the growth profile for their child and explain what it means. Use the contents of the child's personal folder to document both the child's best and worst areas of performance. Focus their attention on the best instances of growth.
- If you have had to label the progress in each area of performance as *A, B, C, D,* or *F,* or *1, 2, 3, 4,* or *5,* or *Outstanding, Satisfactory,* or *Unsatisfactory,* or whatever, use the growth profile for the typical child to explain how you arrived at the label.
- Discuss the new goals that you and the child have agreed upon.
- Ask for the parents' reactions to what they have learned about their child. Be an advocate for the child as necessary.
- Encourage the parents to ask questions.

If the parents ask what they can do to help their child improve in social studies, any of the following suggestions may be appropriate:

- Encourage them to use television as an educational tool. This may involve suggesting that the family view the evening news together and discuss the most interesting event, watch informational programs and discuss them afterward, and plan weekly schedules for viewing to include informational programs.
- Suggest that they give the child the role of navigator when they take automobile trips. If the trip is a long one, allow the child to be the

Growth Profile for Social Studies

Class
Student

From 9-20 To 11-15

5
Grade

Reporting Period ① 2 3 4 5 6
(circle one)

Area of Performance	Never Accurate or Appropriate	Always Accurate or Appropriate

1. Applies social-studies facts and generalizations.
2. Uses informational skills in social studies.
3. Uses expression skills to integrate social-studies facts and generalizations.
4. Participates in social-studies class discussions.
5. Participates in small groups to complete projects.
6. Makes individual contributions to the social-studies program.

——— First Assessment
— — — Second Assessment

FIGURE 11–11. *Growth Profile for a Class.*

keeper of the maps to predict what new place will be seen next. If time permits, stop at parks and historical monuments. Encourage the child to gather materials to make a scrapbook of the trip.

- Suggest that the family buy an almanac which contains maps. They can use it to seek and share information about places in the news.
- Encourage them to use the newspaper as an educational tool. Suggest that the family agree on a particular topic in the news and follow its development for a week and discuss what is happening.
- If the child brings a social-studies textbook home to do some work, suggest that they encourage him or her to discuss the assignment with them and to share content background with them.

Social studies is an area of study in which parents and children can grow together. A con-ference with parents does not need to be just a time when children are judged.

Communicating with Other Professionals about a Child's Growth

You will need to communicate with other professionals about the child's growth on several occasions. When a child is transferred from your classroom to another in the same building or district, or when a child is transferred out of the district, or when the school year ends, you may be communicating with other professionals about how well the child does in social studies. The usual practice is to list on the child's cumulative folder

ILLUSTRATION 11–2. . . . *And His Parents Learn about His Achievement.*

the units he or she has experienced and to send the folder through the appropriate channels when an in-district or in-school transfer occurs, and to communicate nothing when the child transfers out of the district. The practice can be improved.

If the child is transferred to another classroom in the building, the least that we can do is arrange to confer with the other teacher. If we use a district-provided growth profile, we can use it as a guide in discussing the child's growth, strengths, and needs.

If the child is transferred to another school within the district or is leaving the district entirely, a brief summary similar to the following might be prepared on school letterhead stationery:

To _____'s New Teacher
From _____, Room _____.
_____ _____ has been in my fifth-grade class since school opened in September. Since that

time, he has studied these units: The Discoverers and Explorers of America, The Settlement and Colonization of America, and The War for Independence.

As a student in social studies, _____ is a steady, reliable learner. He is attentive and he reads well. He has shown high interest in the globe and maps and uses them well to help him remember important events. He retains well what he learns. He works well with others on projects, but has some difficulty when he does projects by himself.

_____ is an active participant in the current-affairs program. He has been the spark to our program—always bringing in appropriate articles, entering freely into discussions, volunteering for special assignments, and serving on discussion panels.

_____ performs well in social studies. I know that you will enjoy working with him as much as I have.

Of course, if we teach all the subjects in a classroom, the summary would include references to the other subjects. Notice, however, that the summary tells much about what the child can do in the other school subjects.

The summary may be given to the child to give his or her new teacher. At the end of the school year, the summary may be filed with the cumulative record and other transfer documents.

A much more objective communication can be prepared. It would contain a place for listing units and a list of the skills usually taught in the classroom. The teacher might place a check after each skill in which the child performs exceptionally well, an X after each in which the child needs to improve, and nothing after each skill in which the child performs much as most other children do.

And sometimes teachers within the same district simply telephone each other.

Whatever way you choose is your choice. Often you are expected to do little or nothing. It depends on how much you are concerned about the child and his or her growth in social studies.

Communicating with Ourselves about Children's Growth

As we assess children's growth we are also monitoring our own.

We focus first on our successes. What were they? Conducting some really good discussions? Establishing a good social climate? Making good use of a strategy? Teaching a skill particularly well? Making values explorations truly exciting, insightful experiences? Getting children to work well in groups? Or what?

And then we think about what supported the successes. Was it more attention given to planning? Was it a better use made of materials? Was monitoring of learning more painstaking? Were you able to relate more warmly and directly with children? Were you able to get parents more interested in what their children were doing in social studies? Were you able to work more effectively with children who have learning problems?

And finally we try to discover what needs improvement.

And to do something about it.

All for the greater success of children and ourselves.

SUMMARY

A child's growth profile, used as a guide in assessing, evaluating, and reporting a child's growth in social studies, contains vertical elements and horizontal elements.

The vertical elements consist of the areas of growth the instructional program provides for. These areas include content and skill learning as well as skills and behaviors specific to social studies. There are usually more areas for growth included in the profile designed for use with older children than designed for use with young children.

The horizontal elements of the profile consist of the scales for the various areas of growth. These scales are based on accuracy and appropriateness of behaviors ranging from never to always.

Documenting children's growth is recording what they do or how well they do when they take tests, compose or construct products, or participate in activities while involved in the instructional program. Daily performance, as well as integrative

activities occurring at particular moments during the study of a unit or miniunit, is to be documented.

To document children's growth in cognitive process, the teacher uses anecdotal records of performance taken on an assessment schedule or when a child gives a good performance, a response to information checklists, product checklists, the products themselves, and tests. Older children are usually able to respond in writing to test items based on higher cognitive levels, or they respond orally in groups. Personal-growth folders containing documentation are maintained for the children.

Children are to be encouraged to regard tests as experiences which help them discover what they know.

To document children's growth in intake skills, the teacher may devise special tests, some of which are similar to those used for assessing children's needs at the beginning of the school year.

To document children's growth in output skills, the teacher uses anecdotal records and product checklists for skills resulting in no permanent product. Skills resulting in permanent products may be documented by the products themselves or on product checklists.

To document growth in the skills and behaviors specific to social studies, such as discussion, group work, and making investigations, the teacher analyzes children's reactions to participation in the activity as recorded on self-rating and personal-assessment sheets. Discussion and group-work skills may be documented on checklists or anecdotal records.

To ensure documentation of growth, the teacher organizes an assessment schedule.

The teacher communicates with a child about his or her own growth in teacher-learner conferences conducted throughout as well as toward the end of the reporting period. The teacher uses the child's personal-growth folder as a source of documentation of learning to review with the child. Evidence of growth and promise of growth are underscored, and new goals may be set. During the conference just before the teacher-parent conference, the child is informed about what will be shared with parents.

During the teacher-parent conference at the end of the reporting period, the teacher presents the case for a child's growth by using the growth profile and documenting the assessment with the child's personal growth folder. To help parents make an evaluation or to evaluate children's progress with marks or grades, the teacher makes a profile to represent the progress of the typical child in the classroom.

A special checklist or a written summary to accompany the child, or a telephone conference with the child's new teacher, about the child's performance in social studies can be helpful to the transferred child.

The teacher communicates with him or herself about children's growth to ensure greater successes in the future.

POSTSCRIPT

At the beginning of this chapter you were asked to choose between two ways of giving an assessment of growth and to consider a grade or mark you would give a child in map reading. Get the notes you made at that time to see whether you think the same as you did earlier.

Do you still think the same way about how to give an assessment? Why? With what reasons?

Did you decide or refuse to decide on the grade or mark to give to the child? What do you think about that decision now? Why?

FOR FURTHER UNDERSTANDING

Cognitive Activities

1. Define each of the following: *growth profile, area of growth, anecdotal record, response to information checklist, product checklist,* and *personal-assessment sheet.* Give an example for the use of each.

2. Make a chart of the areas of growth, showing under each the device you could use to document a child's growth in social studies.

3. Assume that you are assigned to teach in a classroom just a week before the end of the reporting period. You search the classroom but can find no personal-growth folders for the children. The reporting conferences with parents are scheduled to begin within two weeks. What do you think your problems will be? How might you solve them?

4. Make a set of rules to ensure that you document children's learning in social studies. Compare your rules with those made by other members of the class to develop a better set of rules.

5. A certain pair of parents whose children attend your school have gained some notoriety for their efforts in trying to get the district to deemphasize social studies to provide more time for teaching the three R's. They have been quoted in the newspaper and have appeared on local television to state their views. Now their child is in your classroom. A teacher-parent conference with these parents is scheduled soon. You have never met them. What do you think you should do when you communicate with them about their child's growth in social studies? Share your thoughts with some of your classmates.

Practice Activities

1. Using a child's social-studies textbook and accompanying workbook as reference guides, select a unit and its accompanying materials in the workbook to develop an assessment schedule that you could use.

2. Using the same materials indicated in 1 above, develop a growth profile containing the areas of growth which the materials support.

3. Obtain a report card or parent-conference form from a school or school-district office. Analyze it to discover what areas of growth you are to emphasize in social studies.

4. Obtain a social-studies textbook designed for use with young children and another designed for use with older children. Select a unit from each and use it as a basis from which to construct a short-answer test on social-studies content.

5. Arrange to visit a classroom when social studies is being taught. Select a child whose performance you want to record on an anecdotal record. Observe the child and compose the record. If you can arrange to do this with a classmate, you can compare your

records. This will help both of you improve in taking anecdotal records.

6. Arrange to visit a classroom when social studies is being taught. Use the response to information checklist given in this chapter or the interaction checklist in Chapter 2 to observe some children. If you complete this activity with a classmate, it will be helpful to both of you to compare your observations.

7. Make a test to assess children's growth in an intake skill.

8. Obtain from a classroom paragraphs or reports written by five or six children as individual enterprises. Analyze the products for the variety of facts offered and organization. Then rank the products.

Performance Activities

1. Arrange to document three to five children's growth in social studies over a four or five-week period. If the district provides a growth profile, use it to identify the areas of growth in which documentation will occur. If none is provided, make your own. Then, using whatever devices you think are suitable and whatever the teacher can provide you, document growth and draw the growth profile for each child.

2. Use the growth profile and documentation to role play a teacher-learner conference with a class member.

3. Using the same materials, role play a teacher-parent conference with a class member.

SELECTED REFERENCES

Bloom, Benjamin S., and J. Thomas Hastings. *Handbook on Formative and Summative Evaluation of Student Learning.* New York: McGraw-Hill, 1971.

Cartwright, Carol A., and G. Phillip Cartwright. *Developing Observation Skills.* New York: McGraw-Hill, 1974.

Dominguez, Alyse. "Making Educators Accountable to Parents." *Social Education,* 42:644, 646 (November-December, 1978).

Galbraith, Ronald E. "An Accountability Checklist for Parents and Teachers." *Social Education,* 42:645–647 (November-December, 1978).

Hopkins, Charles D., and Richard L. Antes. *Classroom Testing.* Itasca, Ill.: F. E. Peacock, 1979.

King, Elizabeth C. *Classroom Evaluation Strategies.* St. Louis: C. V. Mosby, 1979.

Morse, Horace T., and George H. McCune. *Selected Items for the Testing of Study Skills and Critical Thinking.* Revised by Lester E. Brown and Ellen Cook. Washington, D.C.: National Council for the Social Studies, Bulletin No. 15, 1971.

Rutherford, Robert B., Jr., and Eugene Edgar. *Teachers and Parents: A Guide to Interaction and Cooperation,* abridged edition. Boston: Allyn and Bacon, 1979.

Appendix

Indians and Pilgrims [1]

This unit has been prepared for use in kindergarten. The skills emphases are on purposeful observation and listening and on the basic aspects of classroom discussion. Note that map reading and reading for information are being developed at conceptual levels—maps show information related to differences and books are resources to be read for information. Developed for a particular class and using nontextbook materials, this unit reflects high creativity in its preparation.

CONTENT GENERALIZATION

American Indians and Pilgrims were able to coexist in the early days of the United States.

VALUE GENERALIZATION

We should respect Indians and Pilgrims for the way they were able to work together in the early years of the United States.

SUBGENERALIZATIONS

1. American Indians were in the United States long before the Pilgrims came.
2. There were many different tribes of Indians here and they lived differently.
3. The Pilgrims came to the United States and had their own way of life and customs.
4. The Pilgrims and Indians came together and shared ideas.
5. The Pilgrims were thankful for plentiful food, warm homes, and friendship in their new land.

SKILLS OBJECTIVES

1. When given purposes, the students will be able to observe and listen to acquire information about the Indians and Pilgrims.
2. The students will be able to integrate and organize information through discussion, drawing, and simple crafts.
3. The students will be able to identify a map as such and a book as something to be read for information.

CONCLUDING OBJECTIVES

1. Working and planning together, the students will be able to have a Thanksgiving Day Feast representing Indians and Pilgrims as they were then.
2. The students will be able to tell why it is important that the Indians and Pilgrims could work together.

SUPPORTING OBJECTIVES

1. The learners will be able to describe accurately what America was like for the Indians before the Pilgrims came.
2. The learners will be able to recognize and describe the characteristics of life of the different tribes of Indians.
3. The learners will be able to describe accurately the way of life and customs the Pilgrims had in the United States.
4. The learners will be able to develop a list of ideas the Indians and Pilgrims shared.
5. The learners will be able to draw pictures of what the Pilgrims were thankful for in their new land.

UNIT OPENER

1. By talking about Thanksgiving Day as a festive occasion, the children can generate interest in Thanksgiving Day generally.
2. After listening to the reading of "The Thanksgiving Story," they can tell what they know about the Indians and Pilgrims.
3. After viewing and discussing pictures of Indians and Pilgrims, they can draw a picture of Indians and Pilgrims.
4. Talking about what more they would like to know about the Indians and Pilgrims, they can contribute in making a list (recorded by the teacher) of things they would like to know more about.

UNIT DEVELOPMENT

Supporting Objective 1

The learners will be able to describe accurately what America was like for the Indians before the Pilgrims came.

1. Discussing whether the Indians or the Pilgrims lived in the U. S. first, the children can tell that the Indians were in the U. S. first.
2. Discussing what the U. S. may have been like, they can tell that there were no big cities and roads—mostly forests, rivers, and open spaces.
3. Discussing and viewing a map of the U. S. showing

where the different Indian tribes were, they can identify where the different tribes were.
4. After listening to and viewing the pictures in a story of Indian life, they can tell some of the basic characteristics of Indian life.
5. Discussing what life was like in the U. S. then, they can make a picture of Indian life.
6. Comparing their pictures, they can discuss the differences.

Supporting Objective 2

The learners will be able to recognize and describe the characteristics of the different tribes of Indians.

1. Viewing pictures of different Indians, the children can see that there were different Indians.
2. Discussing what is necessary for life, they can establish the need for food, shelter, and clothing.
3. Discussing and viewing a map of different Indian tribes, hearing the names of the regions they lived in, they can see where the different tribes were and describe what the regions were basically like.
4. After viewing a filmstrip on "Where Indians Live," they can tell some of the different homes the various regions used.
5. Discussing the various ways of obtaining food used in the five main regions, they can list some of the main ways Indians in the various regions obtained food.
6. Discussing and viewing a chart on symbol writing, they can understand why symbol writing was used.
7. After discussing the clothing worn by the Indians as shown in pictures, they can make a headband and Indian jacket.
8. Discussing the various regions, they can describe what life in general was like in these regions.

Supporting Objective 3

The learners will be able to describe accurately the way of life and customs the Pilgrims had in the U. S.

1. Discussing what the Pilgrims might have had when they came to the U. S., the children can establish that they needed to make or find all that they needed for life.

2. Discussing what is necessary for life, they can establish the need for food, shelter, and clothing.
3. After listening to a reading and viewing pictures of Pilgrim homes, they can tell how the Pilgrims made their homes.
4. After viewing pictures of Pilgrim clothing, they can make Pilgrim collars and hats.
5. After listening to a reading and viewing pictures of the foods the Pilgrims ate, they can tell how the Pilgrims obtained their food.
6. After listening to a reading and viewing pictures of the things the Pilgrims made for their own use, they can help make a teacher-recorded list of things the Pilgrims made.
7. Discussing Pilgrim life, they can describe what, in general, life was like for the Pilgrims and draw a picture of the part they like best.

Supporting Objective 4

The learners will be able to develop a list of ideas the Indians and Pilgrims shared.

1. After listening to a reading about what the Indians and the Pilgrims shared, the children can tell what the Indians and Pilgrims shared.
2. Discussing why the Indians were able to help the Pilgrims, they can conclude that the Indians were here first and had learned to live off the land.
3. Discussing some of the important ideas they shared, they can tell about the ideas shared.
4. Developing as a group a summary of what the Indians and Pilgrims shared, they can make a list of the important ideas the Indians and Pilgrims shared.

Supporting Objective 5

The learners will be able to draw pictures of what the Pilgrims were thankful for in their new land.

1. Discussing how they feel when they have something good to eat when they are very hungry, the children can pantomime and tell how a person feels thankful for food.
2. Discussing how they feel when they walk into a warm house after playing outside in the cold, they can pantomime and tell how a person feels thankful for warmth.
3. After listening as the teacher tells about the hardships of the Pilgrims' first winter, they can work with the teacher to make a summary about the Pilgrims' hardships.
4. After reviewing what the Pilgrims did and learned to do to overcome their hardships, they can draw pictures of what the Pilgrims were thankful for.

UNIT CLOSER

Concluding Objective 1

Working and planning together the students will be able to have a Thanksgiving Day Feast representing Indians and Pilgrims as they were then.

1. Reviewing the list of things about the Indians and Pilgrims they wanted to know more about at the beginning of the unit, the children can tell some of the new things they have learned.
2. Discussing when the Pilgrims had their feast, they can decide on a date for their own feast.
3. Deciding what the Pilgrims and Indians wore, they can plan to use their headbands, jackets, collars, and hats made in class.
4. Deciding what the Pilgrims and Indians ate at their feast, they can plan a menu for their own feast.
5. With the help of their parents, bringing food to cook, they can have a Thanksgiving Day feast.

Concluding Objective 2

The learners will be able to tell why it is important that the Indians and Pilgrims could work together.

1. Observing two puppets, one Pilgrim boy and one Pilgrim girl, talking about Indians, one liking them, and one disliking them, the children can discuss in general why the Indians were good or bad to work with.
2. Taking part as either the boy or girl Pilgrim, they can give reasons why they would like or dislike the Indians.
3. Developing as a group reasons why people should work together, they can understand and appreciate

how special the Pilgrims and Indians were to get
along well.

MATERIALS

Preparation objective to introduce unit: *The Thanks-
giving Story*, Alice Dalgliesh.
Indians of North America—Study Prints 177, #1—
map of Indian tribes in U. S.
Indians—The First Americans, Patricia Miles Martin,
pp. 5–9.
"Where Do Indians Live"—Filmstrip.
Teacher-made chart of symbol writing.
Materials to construct headband and jacket.
The Pilgrims—Brave Settlers of Plymouth, Lynn Groh,
pp. 17–19.
The First Book of the Early Settlers, Louise Dickinson
Rich, pp. 28–29, and pp. 31–32.
Materials to construct collars and hats.
Indians—The First Americans, Patricia Miles Martin,
pp. 60–61.
Concluding Objective 1: Headbands, jackets, collars,
and hats.
Concluding Objective 2: Two Pilgrim puppets, one
boy and one girl.

Brazil [2]

This unit has been prepared for use in fifth grade.
The main skills emphasis in the unit is on the improvement of oral-language composition as used in
discussion panels. Note, however, the application of
such skills as hypothesizing, reading for information,
map and globe reading, map drawing, and formulating questions. In its planning, this unit reflects a high
order of creativity in the development of social-studies
curriculum.

CONTENT GENERALIZATION

Brazil is in the process of exploiting and adapting
hitherto untouched natural resources.

SUBGENERALIZATIONS

1. Brazil is the largest country in South America.
2. The natural resources of Brazil include minerals,

cattle, oil, rubber, and agricultural products such
as coffee, sugar cane, and cotton.
3. Only a small portion of Brazil (in terms of population and land area) contributes economically to the
country.
4. Amazonia, which covers almost half of Brazil, is
only now becoming accessible.

SKILLS OBJECTIVES

The learners will be able to

1. Prepare speeches and serve as panelists about how
Brazilians use their natural resources.
2. Apply the following skills to the teacher's satisfaction:
   a. Hypothesizing.
   b. Formulating questions.
   c. Checking hypotheses against facts.
   d. Reading for information.
   e. Map and globe reading.
   f. Map drawing.
   g. Role playing.

CONCLUDING OBJECTIVES

The learners will be able to

1. Tell on a test with at least 75 percent accuracy
how Brazil is exploiting and adapting hitherto untouched natural resources.
2. Discuss the parallels between the developmental
stages of the United States and Brazil.
3. State their opinion as panelists as to whether they
think Brazil is using its natural resources wisely.

SUPPORTING OBJECTIVES

1. The learners will be able to locate Brazil on a
world map.
2. The learners will be able to list at least three natural
resources of Brazil and prepare a collage which
shows the products made from each of these natural
resources.
3. The learners will be able to participate in a rotating
panel discussion on why only a small portion of

Brazil (in terms of population and land area) contributes economically to the country.

4. The learners will be able to: make a map of Amazonia which shows why, up to now, it has been largely inaccessible; chart on this map the route of the Trans-Amazonia Highway; and explain the significance of this highway.

UNIT OPENER

1. Sharing what they already know about Brazil, the children can establish a background of their existing knowledge.
2. Viewing a series of slides of Brazil, they can show interest in learning more about Brazil.
3. Examining articles which show different aspects of Brazilian life, they can formulate questions about Brazil.
4. Comparing the size of Brazil to that of the continental United States, they can speculate as to why Brazil is not as well-developed as the United States.

UNIT DEVELOPMENT

Supporting Objective 1

The learners will be able to locate Brazil on a blank world map.

1. Discussing where they think Brazil is located, the children can write their best guess on a piece of paper.
2. Studying a world map and/or a globe, they can locate Brazil and list several facts describing its location (i.e., in northeast South America).
3. Checking what they had written earlier about the location of Brazil, they can mark the location of Brazil on an outline map of the world.

Supporting Objective 2

The learners will be able to list at least three natural resources of Brazil, prepare a collage which shows the products made from each of these natural resources, and use the collage to give a speech during a panel discussion.

1. Reviewing how an oral report is prepared and presented, the children can recall the use of notes and illustrations in a report, the parts of a report, the behaviors of the speaker, and audience responsibilities during an oral report.
2. After observing and listening as the teacher shows a sketch of a four-member panel and its chairperson and role plays a couple of panelists and the chairperson, they can compare the panelist's role with that of an oral reporter, and describe the role of the chairperson.
3. Viewing a collage about products made from peanuts, they can discuss how a panelist might use the collage when making a speech about the value of peanuts.
4. Receiving an impromptu assignment to a panel to give speeches about products made from Brazilian natural resources as depicted on collages, they can serve as panelists later.
5. Participating in a class discussion about natural resources, they can define natural resources and list some examples.
6. Examining and discussing a map showing the location of Brazil's natural resources, they can make a list of Brazil's natural resources.
7. Discussing the use of natural resources, they can conclude that natural resources are used to make products.
8. Consulting the list of Brazil's natural resources, they can name several products of each natural resource.
9. Listing at least three natural resources without consulting the list, they can make a collage for each, showing the products made from the natural resource.
10. Preparing panelists' speeches, they can serve as panelists while the teacher serves as the chairperson.
11. Discussing their performance as panelists, they can share how they felt about their performance.

Supporting Objective 3

The learners will be able to participate in a rotating panel discussion on why only a small portion of Brazil (in terms of population and land area) contributes economically to the country.

1. Interacting with the teacher on a discussion of economic conditions in Brazil (in terms of personal

experience), the children can show interest in discovering the reasons behind these conditions.

2. Discussing how people contribute economically to their country, they can suggest the necessary conditions which enable a person to be a contributing part of society.

3. Reviewing what they learned about serving as panelists, they can develop a set of guidelines to follow when serving as panelists.

4. Considering what a panelist would need to know to give a speech about economic conditions in Brazil, they can develop a list of three broad questions to use when reading to get information.

5. After reading the article "The Brazil of the Seventies" (*Manchete,* Rio de Janeiro, 1971), they can discuss the statements made in the article concerning population growth, per capita income, lack of schooling, lack of doctors, etc.

6. Discussing viewpoints that panelists might have, they can develop a list of viewpoints—such as that of a Brazilian businessman, Brazilian factory worker, Brazilian farmer, American businessman, American factory worker, and so forth.

7. Reviewing the outline form of notes, they can prepare independently a panelist's notes from a selected viewpoint.

8. Receiving assignments as panelists, they can serve as panelists and the audience on a rotating basis while the teacher serves as chairperson.

9. Discussing the ideas presented by the panelists, they can conclude that only a small part of Brazil contributes to the national economy.

10. Discussing their experience as panelists and members of the audience, they can identify good areas of performance and those needing improvement.

Supporting Objective 4

The learners will be able to make a map of Amazonia which shows why up to now it has been largely inaccessible, chart on this map the route of the Trans-Amazonia Highway, and explain the significance of this highway.

1. Considering a country which has the following problem: half of its territory is inaccessible due to a thick jungle, the children can discuss the difficulties this could cause such a country and suggest several solutions.

2. Reviewing the map studied in 2 under Supporting Objective 1, and locate the region of Amazonia, they can note the vast mineral wealth which exists there.

3. After reading the article "We Fight Back the Jungle" (*Manchete,* Rio de Janeiro, 1971), they can discuss the solution chosen by the Brazilian for the problem stated in 1.

4. Viewing pictures and a map of the region of Amazonia, they can show interest by asking questions about this area.

5. Participating in a verbal review of all the material presented on Amazonia, they can discuss how the increasing accessibility of Amazonia will affect Brazil's economic future.

6. Referring to maps and information presented earlier, they can, in small groups, make a map of Amazonia which shows why, up to now, it has been largely inaccessible, chart on the map the route of the Trans-Amazonia Highway, and explain the significance of this highway.

UNIT CLOSER

1. Reviewing all products evolved in this unit, the children can discuss Brazil's economic problems and the way in which they are being solved.

2. Discussing their existing knowledge of Brazil and the speculations made at the beginning of the unit, they can compare this with the knowledge they now have and judge how accurate the speculations were.

3. Discussing the parallels between the developmental stages of the United States and Brazil, they can apply their newly acquired knowledge to formulate an opinion as to the possibilities of Brazil becoming a world power.

4. Taking a test on how Brazil is exploiting and adapting hitherto untouched natural resources, they can respond with at least 75 percent accuracy.

5. Stating preferences for persons with whom they would like to serve on a panel and nominating persons for chairpersons, they can receive assignments on panels.

6. Receiving the panel topic, "The Brazilian people are or are not using their natural resources wisely," and discussing viewpoints, they can prepare for panel discussions.

7. Serving on panels, they can state their opinions and respond to questions from the audience.
8. Completing a self-rating sheet on their performance during panel discussions, they can express how they feel about the new skill.
9. Role playing persons reading and reacting to an advertisement asking for contributions to help needy children in Brazil, they can explore for values related to helping others in Brazil.

MATERIALS

Slides procured in Brazil.
Manchete (a special edition of a Brazilian magazine, entitled "The New Brazil," Rio de Janeiro, 1971).
Personal experiences while in Brazil.
Paisagens do Brazil (a book describing Brazilian geography, demography, etc. It contains the maps which will be used).

Bulletin Boards:
One large board, displaying scenic posters of Brazil.
One smaller board, on which will be displayed the learners' work.
Learning Center:
Memorabilia from Brazil: money, magazines, novels, dictionaries, photographs, art objects, slides and slide viewer, etc.

NOTES

1. Used with permission of Carole Landon, Student, San Diego State University, San Diego, California.
2. Used with permission of Mary Hughey, Student, San Diego State University, San Diego, California.

Index

A graduate of the University of California at Los Angeles, Professor Richard E. Servey has taught in the Los Angeles City Schools. Since receiving his PhD at the University of Southern California, he has instructed in elementary teacher preparation programs in the California State College and University System — for the most part at San Diego State University. His publications include *Social Studies Instruction in the Elementary School; Teacher Talk: The Knack of Asking Questions;* and, as coauthor, *Schooling, Teaching and Learning: American Education;* as well as instructional materials for children.